NORWICH SINCE 1550

Norwich since 1550

Edited by

Carole Rawcliffe and Richard Wilson

with Christine Clark

Hambledon and London

London and New York

Hambledon and London

102 Gloucester Avenue,
London NW1 8HX

175 Fifth Avenue
New York, NY 10010
USA

First Published 2004

ISBN 1 85285 450 2

A description of this book is available from the
British Library and from the Library of Congress.

Typeset by Carnegie Publishing, Lancaster,
and printed in Great Britain by Cambridge University Press.

Distributed in the United States and Canada
exclusively by Palgrave Macmillan,
A division of St Martin's Press.

Contents

Illustrations

Text Illustrations

Maps

Tables

Acknowledgements

This brief list of acknowledgements (a fuller version forms the preface to volume one) records our thanks to all those who have assisted us in the past five years. Brevity, however, is no reflection on the warmth of our gratitude.

Generous financial help has come from Thomas Anguish's Educational Foundation, the University of East Anglia and its Centre of East Anglian Studies, Norwich City Council and, above all, Norwich Town Close Estate Charity. Dr Christine Clark has provided valuable research and administrative support throughout the project. The staff of the Norfolk Archive Centre, Clive Wilkins-Jones of the Norfolk Heritage Centre and Norma Watt of the Norfolk Museums Service have been invariably helpful and efficient. In the University of East Anglia we have drawn on the aid of Sheila Davis, Phillip Judge, Laura McGonagle, Judy Sparks and Jenni Tanimoto and the University Library's special collections staff. Successive deans of the School of History, Colin Davis, Edward Acton and John Charmley have encouraged us in our efforts. Peter Martin nobly read and commented upon the manuscripts of all the chapters. We are especially indebted to our contributors, unpaid, generally cheerful and cooperative, and to Alasdair Hawkyard, who compiled the indices to both volumes. Martin Sheppard has been, as increasing numbers of authors find him, constructive, enthusiastic and painstaking at every stage of the two volumes' publication.

Carole Rawcliffe   Richard Wilson

The Contributors

Carole Rawcliffe is Professor of Medieval History in the School of History at UEA, and editor of the medieval and early modern sections of *The History of Norwich*. She is a medical historian, with a particular interest in Norwich and its hospitals.

Richard Wilson is an Emeritus Professor of History at UEA, and editor of the modern section of the *History of Norwich*. His research interests include the history of brewing, textiles and the English country house.

Christine Clark is a Senior Research Associate in the School of History at UEA, and has published on many aspects of the business, economic and social history of East Anglia in the modern period. She has worked as Research Assistant on *The History of Norwich*.

Alan Armstrong has taught at the Universities of Nottingham, Warwick and Kent, where he is now Emeritus Professor of Economic and Social History. His publications are chiefly in the field of rural and demographic history.

Christopher Barringer taught local and regional studies for the Cambridge University Board of Extra-Mural Studies before serving as the first Director of Continuing Education at UEA.

Clyde Binfield is an Emeritus Professor of History at the University of Sheffield. He has published widely on the social and religious history of nineteenth- and twentieth-century England.

Steven Cherry is a Senior Lecturer in the School of History and Director of the Centre of East Anglian Studies at UEA. He has written on medical history in the nineteenth and twentieth centuries, at both a national and local level.

Penelope J. Corfield is Professor of History at Royal Holloway University of London. She began her research by studying the history of Norwich and has published on national as well as East Anglian urban history in the eighteenth century.

Angela Dain is a graduate of Cambridge University who completed a doctoral dissertation at UEA on polite society in Georgian East Anglia.

Barry Doyle is Reader in History at the University of Teesside. His UEA doctoral thesis was on middle class politics in Norwich in the early twentieth century and he has published several articles based on this research.

Paul Griffiths teaches early modern British cultural and social history at Iowa State University. He has written on the young, on crime and order, and on the history of London as well as Norwich.

Andrew Hopper worked on the Virtual Norfolk Project in the School of History at UEA, before moving to the University of Birmingham. He is the author of several articles on regional responses to the English Civil Wars.

Mark Knights is Senior Lecturer in British History in the School of History at UEA. He has produced a book and several articles on the political culture of the later Stuart period.

Roger Munting is Senior Lecturer in Economic and Social History in the School of History at UEA. He is particularly interested in the history of sport, on which he has published articles and reviews.

Stefan Muthesius is an architectural historian who has taught in the School of World Art Studies at UEA since 1968. His many publications on nineteenth- and twentieth-century architecture include work on Norwich.

Margaret Pelling is Reader in the Social History of Medicine at the University of Oxford. She has published widely on health and poverty in Early Modern England, drawing heavily on the Norwich records.

John Pound formerly taught history in the School of English and American Studies at UEA. He has a specialist interest in early modern urban history and the history of poverty.

Roger Ryan studied economic history at UEA, and is currently a Visiting Fellow in the Department of Economics at Lancaster University, specialising in business history. He also teaches history at Edge Hill College of Higher Education.

Michael Sanderson is an Emeritus Professor of Economic and Social History at UEA. A well-known historian of British education, he has recently produced the official history of UEA.

Peter M. Townroe was a member of the Economics Faculty at UEA, then Professor of Urban and Regional Studies at Sheffield Hallam University. Since 1997 he has worked part-time for the Planning Inspectorate and as an independent development consultant.

Abbreviations

Blomefield, *Norfolk*	F. Blomefield, *An Essay Towards a Topographical History of the County of Norfolk* (11 vols, London, 1805–10)
BNP	*Bury and Norwich Post*
CSPD	*Calendar of State Papers Domestic*
CUL	Cambridge University Library
DCN	Dean and Chapter of Norwich (NRO)
DNB	*Dictionary of National Biography*
EAA	East Anglian Archaeology
EconHR	*Economic History Review*
EDP	*Eastern Daily Press*
EEN	*Eastern Evening News*
EHR	*English Historical Review*
HC	Heritage Centre, Norfolk and Norwich Millennium Library
HMC	*Reports of the Royal Commission on Historical Manuscripts*
IJ	Ipswich Journal
NA	*Norfolk Archaeology*
NCC	Norwich Consistory Court (NRO)
NCR	Norwich City Records (NRO)
NC	*Norfolk Chronicle*
NCQS	Norwich Court of Quarter Sessions
NG	*Norwich Gazette*
NHC	Norfolk Heritage Centre
NM	*Norwich Mercury*
Norwich Cathedral	I. Atherton and others, eds, *Norwich Cathedral: Church, City and Diocese* (London, 1996)
NPD	Norwich Private Deeds (NRO)
NRO	Norfolk Record Office
NRS	Norfolk Record Society

Pelling, *Common Lot*   M. Pelling, *The Common Lot: Sickness, Medical Occupations and the Urban Poor in Early Modern England* (London, 1998)

Pound, *Census*   J. F. Pound, ed., *The Norwich Census of the Poor 1570* (NRS, xl, 1971)

PCC   Prorogative Court of Canterbury

PP   *Parliamentary Papers*

PRO   Public Record Office

RCN   W. Hudson and J. C. Tingey, eds, *The Records of the City of Norwich* (2 vols, Norwich, 1906–10)

reg.   register

SRS   Suffolk Record Society

TRHS   *Transactions of the Royal Historical Society*

UEA   University of East Anglia

VCH   *Victoria County History*

Introduction

Richard Wilson

'I should think this city to be another Utopia'[1]

Sir John Harrington on Norwich, 1612

Norwich has always been something of a puzzle to those visitors who jotted down their impressions of it. Even in the late seventeenth and eighteenth centuries, when the prosperity of its great textile industry was at its height, sharp-eyed commentators could not weigh up its impact in an unambiguous fashion. Celia Fiennes, that straight-speaking arch-priestess of modernity, was baffled when she came in 1698. Approving all that was new built and thriving, she found the imprint of the medieval city everywhere. Still bounded by its city walls (a little breached in places, but 'the best in rapaire of any walled city' she knew), and the buildings within them 'all ... of an old form', Norwich was, nevertheless, she concluded, 'a rich thriving industrious place', its prosperity driven by 'very great' markets and fairs, and above all by its textile industry.[2] A few years later, Daniel Defoe recorded a similar puzzlement. During the week Norwich appeared 'a city without inhabitants', yet on Sundays and public holidays there seemed insufficient housing for the crowds that spilled from it, 'the multitude is so great'. Again, an explanation rested with the textile industries. On weekdays the majority of inhabitants were cooped up in their garrets and workshops. Sunday was their day of leisure. Employment in 1723, Defoe was informed, was so full that even children upwards of four or five years 'could everyone earn their own bread'.[3]

Even when the Victorians began to collect a plethora of statistics to chart the workings of economies and societies, Norwich, too, baffled them. None were more bewildered than those members of the House of Lords who were members of its Select Committee on Intemperance in 1877. Attempting to explain and tackle the extraordinary increase in the consumption of alcohol in the previous two decades, they found, when they came to take evidence from Norwich, that it upset almost all their preconceptions and findings. No town in England and Wales possessed more public and beer houses per head of population (incredibly one for every 121 inhabitants including children), and yet no town according to the statistics of prosecutions for drunkenness was more sober. They scratched their heads about the seemingly unreconcilable facts. Were the causes low wages, weak beer or the negligence of the police?[4] Visitors to Norwich always found the contrast of industrial activity cheek by jowl with its castle, cathedral, more than thirty churches and public buildings surprising. A. D. Bayne, the city's Victorian historian, writing in 1872, towards the end of the greatest boom in Britain's nineteenth-century economy, was aware that some aspects were puzzling. He detailed the city's remarkable industrial revival after the collapse of the worsted industry in the thirty years after 1815; he cited the large sums of money which had been expended in widening its streets and in improving its water supply and sanitation. Yet, he continued, 'in traversing portions of old Norwich, we seem to pass through a city of departed greatness'. The city, he believed, occupied more ground than any other town of equal population (80,000) in England, yet the visitor 'feels bewildered when he plunges into its confusion of narrow crooked streets, now discovering half-a-dozen churches within hail of each other'. And in spite of the space to build generously, 'the great number of low mean houses imparts a poverty of aspect'.[5] All in all, a visit to Norwich provided a very different experience from one to the typical Victorian industrial city.

In the inter-war years, there were still features of the city which writers could not easily reconcile. Indeed, in some ways, as the city seemed increasingly marooned in the centre of a large, depressed agricultural region, the contrast of industrial and commercial activity with its wonderful legacy of old buildings, 'crooked' streets and tucked-away courts seemed more marked than ever. H. V. Morton, whose *In Search of England* was the most popular travel book of the period, found the city one of haunting beauty which, in an appropriate metaphor given its famed school of artists, would 'under intelligent treatment ... emerge like a restored oil-painting'. There seemed, however, few tourists to appreciate its charm: 'The most surprising thing about Norwich is that it contains the only Norman Cathedral in England unknown to Americans.'[6]

This volume attempts to explain the features of the city which so puzzled the likes of Defoe and Morton and which set Norwich apart in the four-and-half centuries after 1550. The urbanisation of Britain since the late seventeenth century is perhaps the greatest theme in our island's history. No event so transformed people's lives. A predominantly rural society earning its living from the land was in the course of the two centuries after 1700 changed into one in which four-fifths of the country's

rapidly growing population lived and worked in an urban environment.
No country in the world underwent a more profound transition. Of
course, the routes to urbanisation were very different, whether we consider the growth of London, the great ports of Liverpool, Glasgow, Hull
and Bristol, or the manufacturing centres of Birmingham, Manchester,
Leeds and Sheffield, to name but a handful.[7] Then there were the essentially new towns of nineteenth-century mushroom growth such as Cardiff,
Bradford, Middlesbrough, Swindon and Burton-upon-Trent. Clearly,
Norwich does not fit their patterns of development either. Nor does it
precisely match those which, at first sight, seem comparable communities
sharing similar experiences: the regional centres of York, Exeter, Lincoln
and Shrewsbury. But before I outline the big themes of the nineteen chapters in volume two which detail Norwich's path to urban maturity, I
should, very briefly, comment upon the relationship of the city to its
region.[8] In part, it explains its tendency, in the words of Norfolk's motto,
to 'Do Different'.

Norwich has, since pre-Conquest times, been an important regional capital. It still is, even if the renaissance of Ipswich in the past century and a
half has occupied parts of its southern dominion. Its region, East Anglia in
its historic confines of Norfolk and Suffolk, is well-defined as England's
premier cereal growing province. The relationship between Norwich and
this great arable area is perhaps unique in Britain. The fortunes of both are
inextricably linked. It is not simply that Norwich was the chief market for
East Anglia's corn, malt and livestock, or indeed that some of the city's
industries, especially brewing, leather and, later, the manufacture of agricultural machinery, were so closely identified with the farming enterprises
which surrounded it, but that the city's fortunes mirrored the state of the
region's agriculture. This was especially true after the textile industry with-
ered in the half century after 1815. Problems in the countryside, particularly
in the years from 1815 to 1845, exacerbated by rural overpopulation and the
collapse of hand spinning as a rural by-employment, sharply intensified
difficulties in Norwich itself. Its impact was most evident in the city's reputation as one of the lowest wage centres in urban Britain. Yet, as the textile
industry contracted, Norwich was thrown even more onto its age-old position as the market centre of a vast farming region. When depression hit the
cereal growing area of eastern England with almost unrelenting severity for
sixty years after 1875 (with the brief exception of the First World War and
its immediate aftermath), Norwich's prosperity was as a consequence curtailed. The city did not suffer the extremes of unemployment experienced
in the shipbuilding and mining centres of Britain in the inter-war years,
but neither did it share to any great extent the prosperity of south-eastern

England based upon new consumption industries. The close ties with agriculture, however, were not the sole ones which drew the city and its region
together. There were others.

At an administrative level there were links between region and city, not
only in terms of justice and politics, but also of ecclesiastical government.
The diocese of Norwich, the 'dead see' as it was dubbed in the nineteenth
century, included around 1100 livings in Norfolk, Suffolk and even the
margins of Cambridgeshire. The city as a consequence was the mecca of
ecclesiastical administration, courts and patronage in East Anglia. Even
the clergy of remotest Suffolk were, in turn, summoned to preach in the
cathedral during the summer months when the region's roads stood
the best chance of being passable.[9] After the bishopric of St Edmundsbury
and Ipswich was created in 1914 to ease diocesan management, Norwich's
supremacy in eastern England was barely eroded. As late as 1933,
R. H. Mottram could confidently assert, 'Norwich itself is a good deal more
than the centre of a twenty mile radius, and the capital of East Norfolk. It
is nearly double the size of any town for a hundred miles in any direction.
Between London, Northampton and Grimsby, it has nothing approaching
its size.'[10]

Norwich was always the great shopping centre for the region, the one
town in East Anglia where fashionable metropolitan goods and services
could be purchased. Norwich boasted the earliest provincial newspaper in
the country (1700). Soon there were two, their columns filled with the
advertisements of shopkeepers inviting those who made up the elites of
county and city to view their latest lines from London. The worsted industry itself was martyr to fashion. Indeed, it was a concept deeply etched on
an intensely acquisitive society. Moreover, Norwich in the pre-railway era
was the great cultural magnet of East Anglia. The region's gentry, only too
eager to escape the confines of the countryside, flocked there to enjoy its
assemblies and theatre especially during assize week, at elections or to
attend the great Guild Day dinner in June each year on the installation of
the mayor. When Roger Kerrison, a banker, took office in 1778, 'he outdid
everybody that ever went before', providing 'a most sumptuous entertainment to upwards of 500 people' in St Andrew's Hall. At an incredible cost
of over £500 it was, unsurprisingly, appraised as giving 'universal satisfaction'.[11] Mrs Lybbe Powys visited Norwich during assize week three years
later. Sociable and well travelled, she was impressed with the city's entertainments. She contrasted the great state surrounding the High Sheriff's
attendance on the judges with that of Oxfordshire where her father-in-law
had performed the same duties at a cost of a few pounds. At the assembly
rooms she noted 'numbers of the ladies profuse in jewellery'. When she

visited Jeremiah Ives, the wealthiest worsted manufacturer in Norwich, he provided 'a most superb dinner, eighteen dishes the first course'.[12]

What was unusual was that Norwich could combine a reputation for great sociability with one as a leading manufacturing centre. Here was a link between city and region which was largely non-agricultural. Norwich depended for its supply of finely-spun worsted yarn upon a great network of combers and spinners which stretched across an extended East Anglian region into Cambridgeshire and Bedfordshire. A good deal of the prosperity of this part of eastern England relied upon the fortunes of the Norwich worsted industry in the pre-factory era of textile production. From the transactions between the region's yarn dealers and manufacturers and merchants in Norwich sprang a range of financial connections which were, in part, the origins of Norwich's regional, indeed national, reputation as a leading banking and insurance centre.[13]

When we turn from the numerous links between city and region to focus directly on Norwich itself, it is again economic functions which provide the key to its evolution in the modern period. In the sixteenth century its textile industry underwent many vicissitudes.[14] The central event was the arrival in the 1570s of a flood of Protestant refugees from the war-torn Netherlands. For a while these 'Strangers', as they were known, comprised no fewer than one third of Norwich's population. Having overcome the inevitable problems of integration, they began to exert a formidable influence upon the local economy through a speedy revival of flagging cloth production. Indeed, their contribution to, and absorption into, the economy of the city provides a striking parable for our own times. They also brought a new urgency to the emergent nonconformist culture of the city, which became as notable a feature of life after the Reformation as its exuberant Catholicism had been before. As staunchly Protestant as it had once been fervently Catholic, the city sided with the parliamentary forces in the Civil War, although a vociferous and determined group of royalists made its presence felt during the interregnum. These divisions were to find echoes in the vituperative battles between Whig and Tory, which characterised the political life of Norwich for over two centuries.

The years between the Restoration and the commencement of the French Wars (1793–1815) were the golden age of the worsted industry in Norwich. Along with the West Riding of Yorkshire and the west of England (part of Gloucestershire, Wiltshire and Somerset), Norwich was a principal centre of wool textile manufacture, by far England's greatest industry and source of exports. In comparison with that of the other two regions, the East Anglian industry was increasingly concentrated in Norwich itself. Lord Macaulay reckoned that it was 'the chief seat of the chief manufacture of the realm'; John James, the Victorian historian of the worsted industry writing in the 1850s, compared Norwich at the peak of its prosperity in the mid eighteenth century with Manchester at the height of its fame a century later.[15] As a consequence Norwich continued as England's second city until, in the second quarter of the eighteenth century, it was overtaken by Bristol.[16]

Norwich was famed throughout England as a city which combined the highest manufacturing skills in the pre-industrial era with a reputation for great cultural liveliness and sociability. Clubs of every description flourished; opportunities for leisure were numerous and extending.[17] Like the West of England, however, it also possessed a reputation for difficult labour relations. This was hardly surprising in that its thousands of combers and weavers were, when orders for worsted cloth periodically faltered, thrown out of work for weeks on end. If unemployment coincided with a hike in grain prices or a controversial renegotiation of piece-rates then serious riots, as in 1766, ensued.[18] With the reality of unemployment omnipresent in workers' lives, poor rates in the city were always well above national averages or what the city's rate payers thought was consistent with its long-term prosperity. The city fathers and principal manufacturers, nevertheless, invariably showed a traditional paternalistic concern to relieve the worst effects of poverty.[19] Yet, as in the medieval period, poverty and unemployment bred a worrying unruliness. A visitor in 1741 wrote in his journal: 'The common people are naturally riotous. As they are beneath the laws, they defy them, and keep such a garrison upon some parts of the town, that constables and bailiffs never dare approach their lines.'[20] In the 1790s Norwich possessed the character of the most radical city in Britain. Thirty years later, when unemployment after 1825 reached unprecedented levels for long periods, there were serious Luddite disturbances against manufacturers who attempted to introduce power looms into their workshops.

Prosperity, always subject to fluctuations in the economy, only seriously faltered after 1793. The chief cause of decline was not difficult to uncover. It became increasingly evident that the city's once great worsted industry faltered as that of Bradford carried all before it. The Royal Commission into the State of Large Towns and Populous Districts (1845) stated uncompromisingly:

> Norwich, it is feared, has seen its best days as a place of commerce; and would appear to be in that painful state of transition from a once flourishing manufacturing prosperity to its entire decline, and must 'ere long, revert to its original condition of a capital of an extensive agricultural district ... Neglect

and decay are now conspicuous in the streets and quarters occupied by the working classes, so as to render them places of most dismal aspect.[21]

The three decades after 1815 were ones in which the people of Norwich passed through the wilderness. In his perceptive social survey of the city in 1910, C. B. Hawkins, keenly aware of contemporary issues, wrote that 'the low wages, the low standard of comfort and perhaps some darker things which characterise Norwich may be in some degree the outcome of this long struggle. Thirty years (1815–45) suffering must have profoundly modified the morale and even the physique of Norwich working men.'[22]

But the city did recover. Hawkins and others wondered how. Since Norwich was stranded in the midst of England's prime farming region, it seemed at first sight surprising that industry survived at all. Yet mounting agricultural prosperity in the mid-Victorian period and the railways, the real fillip to the city's recovery, promoted boot and shoe making, engineering and brewing after 1845.[23] Forty years later, and in spite of a downturn in agriculture after 1875, the city was enjoying modest prosperity. White's *Directory* of 1890 made its case in typically robust style:

> By employing an immense capital, exciting industry and remunerating labour they [the manufacturers] have raised the city to its present commercial importance and augmented its population since the year 1811 from 37,313 to upwards of 96,000 souls, and its houses from 8336 to about 25,000.[24]

Norwich had attained a national name for the manufacture of women's and children's shoes; in the sale of fire insurance and the packaging of starch and mustard it was a world leader. Colman's starch was amongst the best known of all British products. The city had attained an enviable equipoise. It was, claimed White, 'a cathedral town without drowsiness, and where noisy factories disturb the ecclesiastical quiet, but have not yet produced the distressing ugliness of the manufacturing towns of Yorkshire and Lancashire'.

Norwich, however, remained unsure of itself in spite of a tendency to self-satisfaction which Dean Wakefield detected at the start of the century. Certainly, it was, he maintained, not very successful at bringing itself 'under the notice of the country generally'.[25] Other commentators, however, were noting, as White had half a century earlier, that its combination of heritage and industry was about right. The new city hall, completed in 1937, was belated municipal testimony to confidence in this amalgam of history and commerce. Arthur Mee, in his popular *The King's England* series, reckoned Norwich might not have solved its traffic problems (what comment would he make now?), but had 'sorted the problem of making a city beautiful and wonderful'.[26] This was on the eve of the Second World War. In the next sixty years, civic leaders together with advocates of tourism and conservation have attempted to achieve compromise in development projects and traffic schemes, as well as in the management of industrial decline and the promotion of new ventures in commerce, education and health care.[27] This has not been an untroubled journey. But most inhabitants – perhaps ignoring Dean Wakefield's strictures – would maintain that it has been, with some reservations, successful. To them Norwich proudly remains 'a fine city'.

The history of Norwich is, then, unusual when compared with standard accounts of the development of Britain's big cities. Not only does it possess a great medieval past, surveyed in volume one, but its pattern of prosperity, decline and revival is different from that of others. Its recent history is also novel in two other significant respects, one financial, the other demographic. After 1800, Norwich sustained an unusually strong interest in banking and insurance, the latter achieving national and international prominence. Its demographic history closely reflects these economic advances and reversals since 1660. After the mid eighteenth century it experienced a curiously fluctuating rate of population growth in comparison with the great industrial towns of the north, which soon overtook it.[28] In some decades of the nineteenth and twentieth centuries growth was stagnant, but in others, as in the 1810s and 1820s, it was, by East Anglian standards at least, rapid. Novel features are once again apparent: infant mortality remained unusually high, as did the strikingly high proportion of native-born inhabitants choosing to stay in Norwich. As in the middle ages, their numbers were bolstered by migration into the city from the region.

In politics, too, highly individual characteristics set it apart. In the eighteenth century, elections to Parliament and to every civic office were exceptionally open. Municipal elections, which outsiders believed had become a running sore and in themselves a prime cause of economic decline by the 1820s, were contested annually. From the 1790s to the 1830s, Norwich possessed a reputation for radicalism as the 'Jacobin city'; in the mid-Victorian period it was notorious throughout Britain for the protracted deployment of traditional bribery practices by both political parties; between the 1930s and 2001 it maintained a remarkable record of Labour rule at first sight difficult to explain.[29] All these factors, both economic and political, together with a degree of isolation – increasingly apparent once a booming national economy emerged in the course of the nineteenth century – have shaped Norwich's singular cultural and social history.

That Norwich continues to offer its historians so many enticing avenues of research is testimony to the wealth of its archives and material remains. Surely its textile industry deserves a history to match those produced for Yorkshire, Lancashire and the West of England.[30] Norwich's path to economic revival after the 1860s and its variable fortunes during the twentieth century have also been curiously neglected. In a sense, therefore, these two volumes are a halfway house which cannot by their nature match the detail of recent urban volumes of the Victoria County History. Our aim is different. It is to convey the richness and vicissitudes of Norwich's history over thirteen centuries and relate it to wider developments, progressively revealed over the last forty years by historians and archaeologists in other English cities. Its two editors, both Yorkshire born and bred, have undertaken this mission with no little trepidation. But they have never doubted either the scale of their task or the allure of the city. J. B. Priestley, another northerner, caught these features with canny perception when he commented on Norwich's long history and civic stature seventy years ago:

> I always find myself happy and at home ... in the cities where I am asked at once, confidently and proudly, what I think of the place. They do it in Bristol and they do it in San Francisco. And of course Norwich is one of these cities ... It may be minute compared with London, Paris, Rome, but nevertheless it lives its life as a city on the same level of dignity.[31]

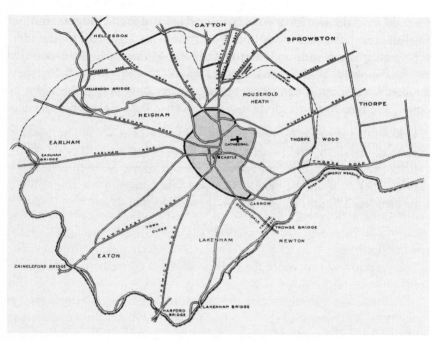

FIGURE 1. Map of the County of the City of Norwich. (*RCN*, i, opposite p. 46).

1

The Changing Face of Norwich

Christopher Barringer

> By the 1590s not only were maps consulted for a host of purposes by
> men of affairs, but they were printed on playing cards, woven into tap-
> estries, engraved on medals and ... Queen Elizabeth I was painted
> standing, symbolically, on a map of England.
>
> Paul Harvey, *Maps in Tudor England*[1]

The charter of 1404 created the city and county of Norwich and that of
1556 confirmed the city boundaries to include the parishes of Carrow,
Lakenham, Eaton, Earlham, Heigham, as well as Mousehold Heath and
Thorpe Wood (Figure 1).[2] This expansion took in the Town Close, between
the Norwich and Ipswich roads and the area that was later to become
Earlham Park and later still the site of the university. These were the areas
into which Norwich was to expand after 1800. The basic plan of the
medieval city was fully established by 1300 and changed little until 1800
when, for the first time since the walls were built, they ceased to define the
built-up area.

The main south to north axis of Conesford Street (King Street) via Fye
bridge and Magdalen Street to its gate remained, as did the main west to
east axis from St Benedict's gate via St Andrew's Street, Princes Street, and
Palace Street to Bishopgate bridge. The south-west quadrant of the city was
formed by the Norman market place and the three Norman parishes of
St Giles, St Peter Mancroft and St Stephen. The castle and the cathedral
with its precinct dominated the earlier Saxon borough, as they still do. The
whole, set within the late thirteenth century walls, has the unusual characteristic for medieval cities of crossing the river to create Norwich
over-the-Water on the north bank. Within the walls the Dissolution of the
Monasteries, friaries and some of the parish churches in the 1530s led to
new uses of the spaces created; however the cathedral in its precinct, Blackfriars and the Great Hospital survive to remind us of something of the
nature of the late medieval city.

New spaces were created: the Hobarts' town house, later to become the

Assembly House, modified and occupied the space of the Chapel-in-the-Fields. The Austin friary like so many other sites went to the dukes of Norfolk and became an open garden with a summer house (the surviving, if ruinous, Howard house). The Greyfriars also went to the Norfolks but then came to the city. The assembly of 8 December 1565 granted leases of the 'late dissolved' Greyfriars for twenty-one years, at the same time as it paid for the 'great house of the Greyfriars to be pulled down'.[3]

Several parish churches held by the dissolved houses also disappeared. For example, St Mary Unbrent lay in the gift of the college of St Mary in the Fields. It went to the dean and chapter of the cathedral who merged its parish with that of St Saviour. The church and its yard was granted to Nicholas Sotherton who demolished it. In 1558 he conveyed to the city a footpath through the north side of the churchyard, now called Golden Dog Lane.[4] This is a detailed illustration of the way in which small scale changes to the topography of the city resulted from the shake out from the Dissolution. Properties such as these once in private occupation could be developed at will; rebuilding on these sites would be mainly in brick.[5]

Just outside the south wall of the city lay the Benedictine nunnery of Carrow. The ten-acre site still remained open in Blomefield's day but, as he noted, 'the church was large though so far demolished, that it was with difficulty I found its site; the parlour and hall are grand rooms and were fitted up by Sir John Shelton Knight at his coming to dwell here, which was not long after the Dissolution'.[6] The ramifications of the Dissolution had a domino effect on the city. Buildings came down and ownership underwent widespread changes. The dukes of Norfolk, the Hobarts and the Sheltons, amongst others, became even greater landowners, and some of the city fathers, such as Nicholas Sotherton, did well.

The evidence for the topographical expression of Norwich comes from a combination of the findings of archaeology, from extensive documentary sources, especially the enrolled deeds of the city, and place and street names. To these, from the sixteenth century onwards, must be added maps. One of the outcomes of the Renaissance was the rediscovery of Greek mathematics and in particular of Euclidean geometry. This led to the possibilities of improved map production. For example, in 1494 the treaty of Tordesillas between Spain and Portugal placed a line on a map 370 leagues west of the Cape Verde Islands, off Brazil, as a line of demarcation with Spanish territories to the west and Portuguese to the east.[7] Surveying and cartography had arrived, allowing a new view of the world to be constructed. Globes became part of the accoutrement of civilized man.[8]

These developments, combined with the increasing fluidity of the land market in England as a result of the Dissolution of the Monasteries, led to the development of increasing interest in the production of surveys and maps for many purposes, ranging from the geopolitical to the mapping of new estates for the generation of landowners who had benefited from Henry VIII's sale of monastic lands. William Cecil, Lord Burghley (1520–98), was a major force behind the development of surveying in England. He wanted to know where defences, such as those at Weybourne in Norfolk, needed strengthening or where reliable and, perhaps more important, unreliable gentry were living. These demands led to the appointment of Christopher Saxton as his surveyor and to Saxton's series of county maps being completed by 1578.

Once the new techniques became available and surveyors began to be trained many landowners, who had themselves studied mathematics, had their newly acquired estates surveyed. Books on surveying such as *The Cosmographical Glasse* (1559) by William Cuningham were published. In it Cuningham illustrated the new art of triangulation by using church towers in Norwich, Wymondham and Swardeston as the corners of a triangle, the sides of which could be calculated by means of the measurement of one baseline and the application of trigonometry to other calculations. Once such a triangle was accurately surveyed, details within it could be relatively accurately fixed. European cities were already advertising their status by employing surveyors. By the end of the fifteenth century superb views, such as that of Florence published by Rosselli in 1482 and of Venice by de Barbari in 1500, were setting examples to other cities wishing to signify their status. Indeed, some historians see this phenomenon as a continued tradition from Roman times and of later maps produced by the crusaders of the cities of the Holy Land.

The first evidence of the new surveying techniques being used in Norwich appears with the production of the Sanctuary map in 1541 (Figure 2). It was rediscovered in 1889 when the Reverend William Hudson reproduced it for the first time.[9] This incomplete map of Norwich was drawn at the request of the government to show all places of sanctuary in the city. Whether it was complete is debatable as it shows only six churches and the cathedral. It does, however, indicate the line of the city walls, the gates, oddly named, and five river bridges. As compared with Cuningham later, it shows the guildhall and the pillory and one or two little groups of houses as, for example, between St Stephen's church and St Peter Mancroft, all of which are marked with chimney-stacks at a time when the survival of many open halls might be expected. No roads are named. Hudson makes the point that the original vellum map in the Public Record Office was much damaged so that the large vacant areas of the city may not

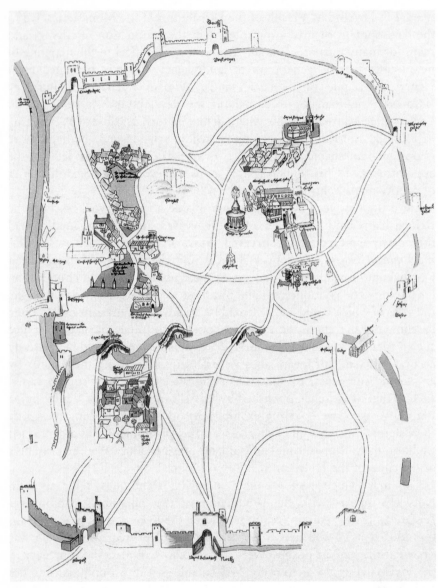

FIGURE 2. The Sanctuary Map 1541. (Kirkpatrick, *Streets and Lanes*, opposite p. 114)

have been shown as such in the original. Blomefield noted a reference in the city chamberlain's account of 1541:

Paid to Thomas Boswell paynter for correcting of a platte that was set up at this term for the establishing of the Seyntwary [sanctuary] within the cyte according to the statute 6s. 8d.[10]

This reference implies that a map had already existed for Boswell to modify and raises the question of when it was drawn and by whom. The proportions of the city north to south and east to west raise the same questions as are posed by Cuningham's view. To what extent was the Sanctuary map based on a measured survey? The generalised road lines and the relationship of New Mills to the guildhall make it doubtful whether any form of triangulation was used. Linear measurements of the south to north access may, however, have been made.

Norwich is fortunate in having a large number of printed maps of the whole city from its first 'view' by William Cuningham, published in 1558, through to the first edition of the Ordnance Survey map in 1838.[11] The best dividing point, however, is 1830, when Millard and Manning's map was published. Before 1830 an impressive list of sixty-one maps and a prospect of the city were produced. Many were in fact reissues of older plates; Cuningham's map was used unaltered many times.[12] The major surveys referred to in this chapter are those of Thomas Cleer 1696, James Corbridge 1727, Francis Blomefield 1746, Samuel King 1766 and Anthony Hochstetter 1789.

The second part of this chapter will discuss Millard and Manning's large-scale map of 1830, Muskett's of 1849, Morant's of 1873, and then the various Ordnance Survey maps, particularly the very large-scale (1:500 or 10.56 feet to a mile) survey of 1885, to illustrate change. The earlier section will focus more on the technique of mapping used in surveys bound by the city walls and the nature of detail they include. The later section, whilst acknowledging the importance of scale, will be more concerned with the sequence of topographical changes that began to affect Norwich outside the walls as well as those, such as the impact of manufacturing industry, within them.

The first attempt to portray Norwich was that produced by William Cuningham in 1558 (Figure 3). As is often the case with early 'platts' or maps, this is aligned west to east, Norwich Over-the-Water being on the left-hand side of the map. This is the earliest surviving printed map of a provincial English town.[13] It is a delightful 'map', and, in that it appears in Cuningham's treatise on surveying – *The Cosmographical Glasse* published in 1559, it was presumably the result of a measured survey. It possibly shows Cuningham's self-portrait in the foreground viewing the city from the west. However, the oblique 'air view' effect of the map means that King

FIGURE 3. William Cuningham's Norwich 1558. (Kirkpatrick, *Streets and Lanes*, opposite p. 117)

Street in South Conesford by the River Wensum has little detail shown as it lies in the 'shadow' of Ber Street.

The layout of the city is beautifully clear. The castle, its mound, access bridge and the shire hall stand out. The city's five bridges, Bishopgate, Whitefriars, Fye bridge, St George's and Coslany, as well as the New Mills are shown. The cathedral and most, but not all, churches are also depicted. St Peter Mancroft, the great market-edge church, is easily identified but what is now known as Bethel Street is shown as reaching the entrance to its tower. King (1766) includes a White Swan Lane along this line, which raises a question as to Cuningham's accuracy.

The line of Pottergate is, however, missing; no guildhall is shown and some churches, for example, St Bartholomew, extant in 1535, in Ber Street, are omitted. Other churches such as St Benedict's appear with a square tower rather than a round one. In St Benedict's (upper Westwick Street) only one church is shown; St Swithin's and St Lawrence's are missing. The clustering of buildings, for example to the west of St Stephen's, appears accurate, however, and buildings are shown conventionally in most cases. The Chapel-in-the-Field (the modern Assembly House) is shown as a more complex building than many others; whether the nave of the church of St Mary-in-the-Field seems to be still standing is debatable.

A theme to be returned to is that of the open spaces within the walls. Most obvious is Chapelfield with its dangerous mixture of cattle and archers; St Catherine's church still stands clear in St Catherine's field, as does a dovecote and cross-wing building. The walls and gates are, not surprisingly, clearly visible as a most striking feature of the city. Outside the walls, Eaton wood, the lazar houses, two windmills and the bishop's palace at Thorpe all stand out. It is a fascinating and in many ways a surprisingly clear attempt to give a 'picture map' of the city.

The layout of the city, set long before any map was made of it, is shown by Cuningham and continued, largely unchanged, for another two hundred years. His 'view' remained the basis for a series of other Norwich views for over a century. Braun and Hogenberg and even John Speed in his map of Norfolk produced in 1611 still used Cuningham with little or no alteration to the actual detail shown within the walls. Peter Eden notes that Norwich paid £20 to a Mr Goodwin in 1572 for 'surveying and measuring out the lands ... as also for drawing and making out diverse plattes'.[14] John Goodwin was admitted as a citizen of Norwich in 1566. He was a surveyor to the city and to its Great Hospital between 1571 and 1600 and special surveyor of lands to Elizabeth I between 1559 and 1595. He was an exact contemporary of Christopher Saxton. No known map of the city attributed to him, however, has survived.

Documentary sources such as the Census of the Poor for 1570 can help to explain why the growth of housing may not have taken place as quickly as might have been expected.[15] Large houses owned by aldermen and common councillors let rooms to the poor; for example, Edward Pye, a councillor in Norwich-over-the-Water, had four houses in Colegate, accommodating thirty poor people, and three houses in Fyebridgegate with fourteen. Thomas Parker, alderman of Ber Street, had four properties in the same area inhabited by thirty-nine people. John Pound estimates that 41 per cent of the population of St Giles's parish were poor. Much subdivision of properties is implied, as is the addition of cheap buildings in the yards behind the main buildings.

Recently a section of a larger manuscript map showing Tombland and the cathedral has come to light; Frank Meeres attributes this to Richard Wright in the late 1630s but Eden has not listed Wright as a known surveyor.[16] Why this flurry of surveyors, even if it was not until 1696 that Norwich was to acquire a scale map of the conventional type for the first time?

Most probably they found employment for their legal talents in the conveyancing of land and the inevitable wrangles which were part and

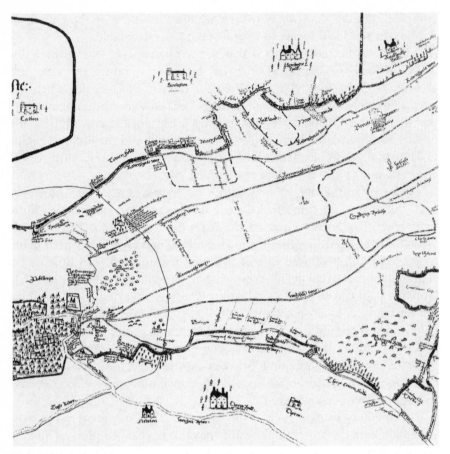

FIGURE 4. Map of parts of Norwich and Mousehold 1585. (Kirkpatrick, *Streets and Lanes*, opposite p. 119)

parcel of the process. For example, a plan of the eastern half of the city and of Mousehold Heath 'as far as Mr Gybson's dole' dated to 1589 was drawn as part of the evidence in a land dispute (Figure 4). The detail inside the city walls is very simplistic and buildings are shown in identical, form, each as a cottage with a chimney. A walled large house called the Lathes appears across the river from the Cow Tower. 'Bishoppsgate' is labelled, as is 'St Michells Chappell' to the east of it across the river. The western boundary of Mr Paston's Thorpe estate, his hall and the remains of Thorpe wood are also distinguished. Many stone pits are marked both within the city boundary and further east into Mousehold. The stone would be flint quarried from both pits and tunnels into the chalk bedrock. Above the chalk are beds of rolled flints and gravels, results of the glaciations. This

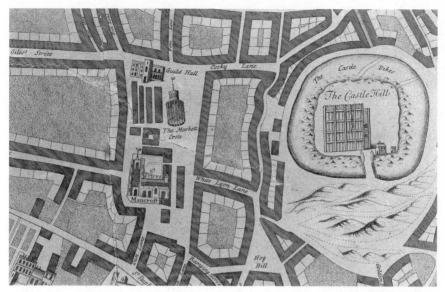

FIGURE 5. Thomas Cleer's Map of Norwich 1696. Detail showing the Market Place. (*Norfolk Heritage Centre*)

flint was an invaluable building material for the ground floors of buildings repaired after Kett's Rebellion of 1549, for upkeep of the city walls, and probably for supplying Yarmouth, which had no surface source of flint.

In 1696 Thomas Cleer produced a map of Norwich (Figure 5). This was the first map of the city within the walls as opposed to Cuningham's bird's eye view or perspective 'platt'. Major buildings were still shown in elevation, for example the castle, the cathedral, all parish churches and the larger private houses. Indeed, the city walls are depicted as if viewed by a bird approaching from the west.

Cleer's map illustrates his technique of indicating a built-up continuous edge to the streets with standardised plots to the rear of the properties and then small open spaces within a continuous enclosure of dwellings. No lanes are shown as running east to west to the east of the market; however, Kirkpatrick, in his detailed examination of the streets and lanes of Norwich, did add (circa 1720) a little lane called Well Yard leading to a common well immediately to the north of White Lion Lane, a feature observed clearly by Blomefield in 1746. Given the nature of property holdings in Norwich and the need for access to yards it is unlikely that several lanes shown by King in 1766 did not exist by 1696.

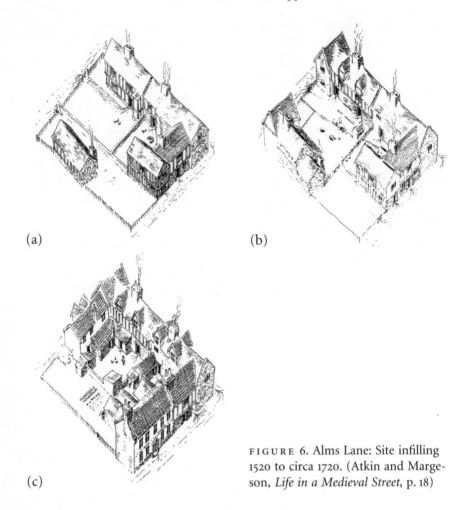

(a)

(b)

(c)

FIGURE 6. Alms Lane: Site infilling 1520 to circa 1720. (Atkin and Margeson, *Life in a Medieval Street*, p. 18)

The detailed work of the Norwich Survey and now of the Norfolk Archaeological Unit has shown that the picture given by Cleer was a diagrammatic one. The Alms Lane excavation (Figure 6) uncovered the amazing amount of infilling that lay between street frontages,[17] as has the more recent work to the east of Dragon Hall where a complex series of buildings extended for at least thirty yards towards the river. Former lanes, as well as important thirteenth-century buildings, have been revealed and these in turn have in some cases provided 'footprints' for a sequence of later buildings. Some areas of garden, such as those to the west of the market place, are included in Cleer's map, probably conventionally, but the main streets are shown with a single line of housing, or at least buildings along them.[18] The detail of street names and to some degree the extent of open spaces within the walls are two other valuable elements of this map. The layout of streets had largely survived into the sixteenth century.

Cleer shows Norwich as bound, to a great extent, by its medieval walls and gates. Details beyond the gates are, however, of great interest, such as Kett's castle on Mousehold, windmills to the north of the city, and the only area of extra-mural settlement outside Heigham gate. The New Mills appear complete with two water wheels. The extent to which areas behind properties bordering the streets were really built up has already been discussed, but larger expanses of grazing, shown by stipple and shading, certainly did exist especially to the north of the river: the gildencroft, for example, and St Margaret's close. 'Chappley Field' was not stippled but was shown as having stock in it.

The map provides an invaluable marker of the extent of the layout of Norwich in 1700. In many ways it has changed little from the city shown more diagrammatically by Cuningham. What cannot be revealed on a map is the extent to which façades along the streets were different from those of the period of Kett's rebellion. In the 1690s Celia Fiennes hinted that Norwich's buildings were, like those of York, rather behind the times.[19] Brick buildings were, however, beginning to replace, or brick skins to conceal, the earlier timber and flint. Colegate has several handsome surviving examples, such as the Old Meeting House (1693), not in fact noted by Cleer or later by Corbridge in 1727.

In 1723 Thomas Kirkpatrick produced a detailed vista of Norwich from the north east in a large drawing (2 x 5 feet). Thomas was the brother of the well-known antiquary John Kirkpatrick, whose *Streets and Lanes of the City of Norwich* was published by the Norfolk and Norwich Archaeological Society in 1889.[20] The view is annotated by a key of numbered and lettered items which include the reminder that the city claimed ownership of the whole river towards Yarmouth as far as Hardley Cross. The viewpoints from which the vista was drawn (Figure 7) were on the hillside to the north of Pockthorpe, almost end-on to the north transept of the cathedral. The detail of the north wall of the city and of the buildings inside it is therefore sharpest. Houses are shown conventionally, almost all of two storeys with dormers in the roof and with chimneys. Immediately in view from the hillside is a large building (not numbered in the key) with a massive external chimney stack.

The foreshortening, stemming from the perspective of an oblique 'air view', displays all the open spaces which lay inside the northern section of the walls. The River Wensum, is however, lost to view. Indeed, the vista suggests a city crammed with housing rather than, as visitors invariably

FIGURE 7. Detail from Thomas Kirkpatrick's View of Norwich from the North East, 1723. (*Norfolk Heritage Centre*)

FIGURE 8. Detail from Buck's Prospect of Norwich from the north east, 1741. (*Norfolk Heritage Centre*)

noted, a city of gardens and orchards. Immediately outside the wall cattle are shown grazing, hay is being cocked, and, immediately below the artist's viewpoint, lime is being burned in a kiln. A large post mill dominates the righthand foreground. Churches are well drawn – St Peter Mancroft (without its turrets) and St Stephen's are both clearly recognisable. Near to the artist, St James's, with the octagonal top to its tower (yet dated 1745 by Pevsner) and St Paul's with its round tower and odd fenestration on its north side, are distinctive.

Buck's prospect of 1741, from the south east, opposite Sandlings (Pull's) Ferry, and another from the north east (Figure 8), from Kirkpatrick's viewpoint, add to our knowledge of the city's topography in the eighteenth century. Buck also numbers churches on his vista and lists them below; otherwise he included far fewer other buildings than Kirkpatrick. The southern section of the city (Conesford) is well drawn, especially the open nature of the hillside between Ber Street and King Street. Tombland appears as a large, clear space. Buildings are less standardised than those of Kirkpatrick. The city, seen from the south east, is one of trees and gardens in comparison with Kirkpatrick's crowded prospect. A wherry is sketched upstream of Bishopgate bridge and one downstream with its mast lowered to negotiate the bridge.

Cleer's map of 1696 may well have provided a base for the next

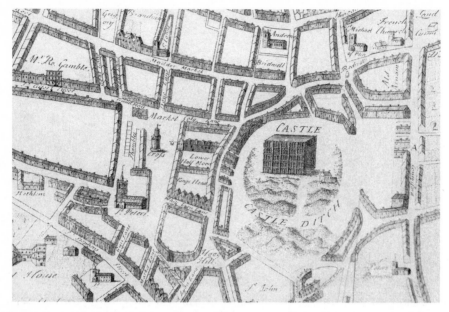

FIGURE 9. Corbridge's Map of Norwich 1727. Detail showing the Market Place. (*Norfolk Heritage Centre*)

topographical marker of the development of the city within the walls. This was a map at a scale of seventeen and a half inches to the mile (1:3400) by James Corbridge which was produced in 1727, on virtually the same scale as Cleer. Two sample areas, the market place and Norwich-over-the-Water, have been selected to illustrate some of the key elements that make this map so valuable (Figures 9 and 10).

There is a part reversion to Cuningham's technique of showing buildings. They are lit with a southern light source and are nearly all depicted conventionally with two or three upper windows, a central groundfloor doorway and a central chimney stack. These can be seen in the Colegate area on Figure 9 and on the river frontage on the north bank. However, occasionally larger houses are marked, for example those of Messrs Hainsworth, Vipont, James Cobb and especially Fremolt. These are distinctive buildings on clearly defined sites (Figure 11). That not one of them now survives makes their location and detail all the more valuable. Of these four men, George Hainsworth became a councillor, Nicholas Vipont was a guardian of the poor in the 1720s, James Cobb a constable, and only Samuel Fremolt attained the office of one of the city's two sheriffs.[21] Did they build these houses or buy and refront them? What they certainly did was to occupy and probably merge former narrower plots into distinctive

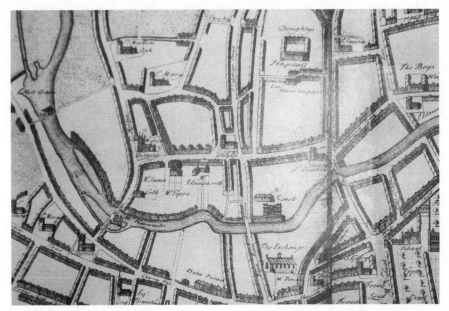

FIGURE 10. Corbridge's Map of Norwich 1727. Detail showing Norwich-over-the-Water. (*Norfolk Heritage Centre*)

properties on sites that were later to be replaced by commercial activities between Colegate and the river.

In the other sample sector, Robert Gamble, described elsewhere as a worsted weaver, occupied the only distinctively drawn house in St Giles's (Figure 10). Sir Thomas Churchman's house, restored in the early 1990s and now the Registry Office, is the only one to have survived from the whole sample chosen. Corbridge's drawing of Churchman House (Figure 11) is, however, very different from the present building, which has been extensively rebuilt and extended in 1751.[22]

The open spaces remain much the same in Corbridge as in Cleer. Both show small detailed areas of gardens at the Greyfriars site due east of the castle, in the cathedral precinct and next to the Assembly House (as it was to become). A single fruit tree is shown per dotted square in these gardens, suggesting that this is conventional mapping. 'My Lord's Garden', the former site of the Austin friary between King Street and the river, has no detail whatsoever on either map.

Corbridge attempted to give some idea of the hilly area between Ber Street and King Street but in a simplistic way. It was not until 1789 that Hochstetter used strong hachuring to give a more accurate impression of the 'quarried cliff' between the two roads. One or two interesting additions

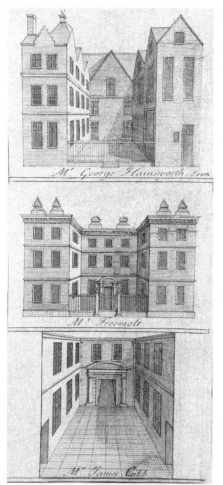

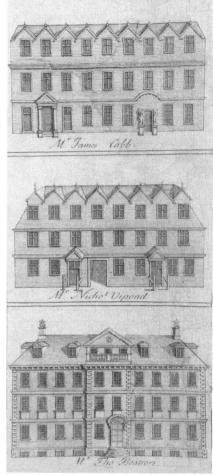

FIGURE 11.
Merchants' houses in
Norwich-over-the-Water,
and left, Thomas Churchman's
in St Giles's from Corbridge's map
of 1727. (*Norfolk Heritage Centre*)

to the face of Norwich and to its range of functions are shown by Corbridge: for example, the Bethel Hospital which was founded in 1712–13 as 'the earliest purpose-built asylum in the country'.[23]

Kirkpatrick's *Streets and Lanes of Norwich* provides a remarkably full account of the many small lanes that cut between the major roads of the city. Corbridge and Cleer both show the pattern of eight lanes that linked Pottergate and St Benedict's between St Andrew's church and St Benedict's gate. Supporting evidence comes from Kirkpatrick, who gives detailed references which follow the evolution of these lanes: for example, Holgate which ran from West Pottergate to cross St Benedict's and then to follow the west side of St Swithin's churchyard. Holgate was first noted in 1288 and is now Ten Bell Lane. The hol (hollow) element refers to the way in which 'before it was paved with stone, [it was] gulled and washed hollow by the water falling in great rains down the hill out of Newport'.[24] This highlights what must have been an increasing problem for the city's streets and lanes as the infilling of yards and open spaces continued. Their paving became an important aspect of the city's administration. In 1559 the assembly ruled that all residents who had houses abutting streets within the walls should 'cawse the same to be reparied and mended ageyne with stone according to the use and custom of the city'.[25]

In 1746 Francis Blomefield produced his plan of Norwich to accompany his two volume account of the city.[26] This is a composite map of inestimable value to the historian of Norwich because it is not only a map of the city of the mid eighteenth century but it also records and locates many former features, for example, the sites of churches that had been demolished by 1746 and of former limekilns. He gives alternative street names such as Over or Upper Westwick or St Bennet's Street. It is drawn to a slightly smaller scale than the reduced version of Cleer's map and that of Corbridge. The extent of built-up street frontage and the recording of some free standing buildings appears to be nearer to that shown by Corbridge, but the inscription notes that Francis Blomefield drew and executed the map himself.[27] Given Blomefield's amazing research skills and energies it is remarkable that he could also be a surveyor-cartographer.[28]

A series of dotted lines appears on this map. These may be intended to show the complex patterns of the parish boundaries within the city but they are not easy to follow and they distinguish too few parishes, as for example within King Street. The additional detail given by Blomefield in the margins of the map is enormous, with a numbered key of 202 items – churches past and present, major residences and ancient features – all testimony to the depth of research undertaken by him.

In 1766 Samuel King produced a new and clear map of the city within

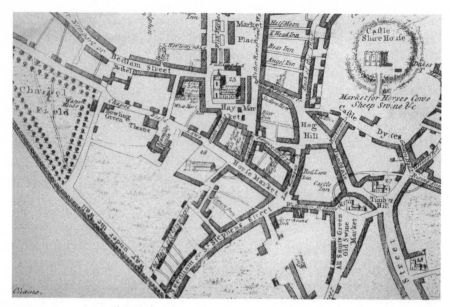

FIGURE 12. Samuel King's Map of Norwich 1766. Detail of the Market Place. (*Norfolk Heritage Centre*)

FIGURE 13. (opposite) King's Map of Norwich 1766: drawings of public buildings shown below the map. (*Norfolk Heritage Centre*)

the walls at a scale of about thirteen-and-a-half inches to the mile (Figure 12). King worked in Norfolk and Suffolk between 1763 and 1768, although his Norwich map appears to be his only piece of urban mapping.[29] The castle bailey was, by this time, functioning as the cattle market, but the outer ditches were still a feature as was that between the castle mound and the bailey. The Assembly House and the long clerestory of St Stephen's church stand out well. The many inns of the city centre and their service lanes, for example those between Gentleman's Walk and Back of the Inns, are well shown. Another series of lanes lay to the west of St Stephen's Street.

Norwich, to quote A. D. Bayne, experienced its 'most prosperous time 1750 to 1780'.[30] The buildings of Thomas Ivory, its busiest Georgian architect, alone give some idea of the way the face of the city was changing between the time of Kirkpatrick's views and King's map.[31]

Methodist Meeting House, Bishopgate	1751–2
House on the west side of entrance court of the Great Hospital	1752–3
The Octagon Chapel	1754–6
The Assembly Rooms	1754
The Theatre	1757–8

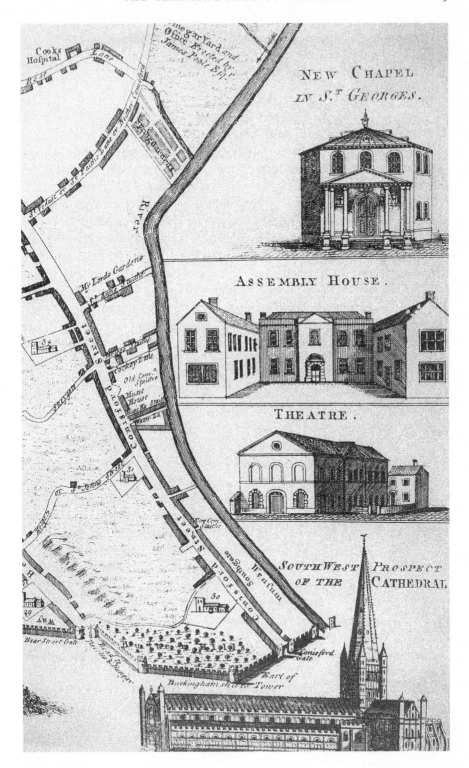

Nos 29 to 35 Surrey Street	1761–2
Nos 25 and 27 Surrey Street	c. 1771
The Artillery Barracks	1771–2
No 31 King Street	c. 1774

King provides drawings of some major buildings below his map (Figure 13). They include the Octagon chapel, Assembly Rooms and the Theatre. These show how the cultural and religious life of the city was flourishing, with the Octagon, built by the Presbyterians, representing an important symbol of the growing importance of the non-conformist communities in the city.

King does, however, show some buildings on the map in elevation. The churches are drawn with and without chancels: St Gregory with a spirelet which it lost later in 1840, and the gildencroft Quaker meeting house is also depicted. Small distributaries, perhaps water extraction points, appear off the River Wensum between New Mills and Coslany bridge. Blackfriars lacks its tower, having lost it in 1712, and its uses as a workhouse, new hall and Dutch church are noted. The near complete ring of open spaces within the walls stands out clearly. Chapel Field, planted with double lines of trees is different from other treeless grazing areas. A water house was set on its eastern side. As a general comment it is still noticeable how much open space, in the form of gardens and orchards, remains between Ber Street and King Street and inside the northern line of the wall between St Margaret's gate and Pockthorpe. The representations of the majority of buildings by King are still conventional. A few public ones such as the Assembly House and the guildhall are shown in plan. The only hint of early industry is a reference to James Poole's vinegar yard and office by the river, downstream of Sandlings ferry. Taverns and inns are named but industrial buildings, such as breweries and weaving and hot-pressing shops, are not.

Hochstetter's map of 1789 marks almost a century of change from the map of the city drawn by Cleer in 1696. It is of a larger scale, twenty inches to one mile (1:3160), and it therefore shows buildings in more detail. The outstanding feature is that the plan of buildings is no longer conventional, as with Cleer, Corbridge and, to a great extent, King. If St Stephen's is taken as an example (Figure 14) the variable plans of buildings running to the back of St Stephen's and along Surrey Street, together with details of individual gardens, all indicate cartographic accuracy.

The depiction of the market place, in some ways less interesting because Hochstetter's mapping techniques are more advanced than those of Cleer with his elevations, retained most of its main elements in 1789 except for the demolished market cross (Figure 15). However, the area between the

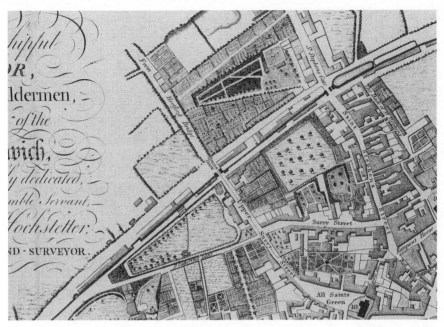

FIGURE 14. Hochstetter's Map of Norwich 1789. Detail of the St Stephen's area. (*Norfolk Heritage Centre*)

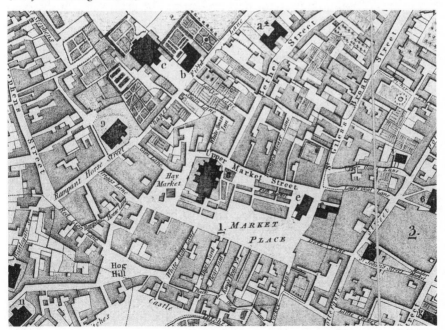

FIGURE 15. Hochstetter's Map of Norwich 1789. Detail of the Market Place. (*Norfolk Heritage Centre*)

market place and the Back of the Inns and castle ditches is mapped in much more detail than by Cleer. London Street was known as Cockey Lane on both maps; Gentlemans Walk was not named as such on either map.

Hochstetter's list of two dozen public buildings gives some idea of the range of religious and cultural activities that had developed in the city by the end of the eighteenth century. The map depicts Norwich a few years after what Arthur Young described as its 'famous era', the great mid century prosperity of England's second city.[32] Old surviving buildings had been developed for new uses: for example, St Andrew's hall, the Bridewell and the Great Hospital. A few buildings had maintained their role, the guildhall, the grammar school and Doughty's Hospital still serving their original purpose. The number of nonconformist churches is also evident. There was even a Romish chapel, but as yet no synagogue. The Norfolk and Norwich Hospital was one of the most recent new developments.

In 1830 the corporation of Norwich instructed W. S. Millard to carry out a survey of the city. This resulted in a fine large-scale map usually referred to as Millard and Manning's map, the latter joining Millard as the second-named surveyor. It is a beautifully drawn map at a scale of 26 inches to a mile. Perhaps the fast-growing population of Norwich from 1811 to 1831 made the corporation aware of new pressures. The great value of the map is that it shows the start of the explosion of Norwich outside the walls. Figure 16, based on Millard and Manning, indicates that the city was beginning to develop to the south west and the north east beyond its medieval boundary. To the north the Pockthorpe area was expanding and the first terraced housing was being built to the south west.

The role of Norwich as a county town, important as it had been for centuries, began to express itself in a new generation of public buildings. The Norfolk and Norwich Hospital had already been established; the new city gaol built in 1826 reflected changing views of the treatment of prisoners; the cavalry barracks emphasised the development of the professional army that was a response to the prolonged wars with France, social discontent expressed in bread and piece-rate riots early in the century, and later, Chartist unrest. At Thorpe St Andrew the asylum, the mental hospital for the county, was founded in 1814.[33]

The map lists thirty-five churches and forty-two public buildings, primarily nonconformist chapels and a variety of schools and hospitals. It is of sufficiently large scale to allow the shapes of buildings to be shown. The nineteenth-century terraces of Peafield, Crook's Place, Grove Place and Union Place, laid out in straight lines and with houses built to standard patterns, contrast sharply with the old irregular yards within the walls.

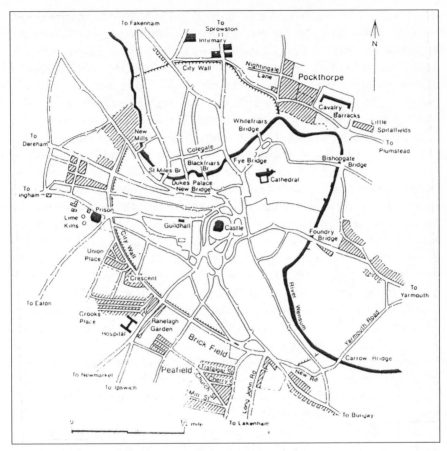

FIGURE 16. Norwich Beyond the Walls, based on Millard and Manning's Map of 1830. (Barringer, *Norwich in the Nineteenth Century*, p. x)

Between 1792 and 1808 the gates of the city were demolished, thus allowing an easier flow of traffic. Although little had changed in the internal layout, the linking of the city to its suburbs was beginning to exert a demand for new bridges. The need to improve the link of industrial Norwich-over-the-Water with the city centre led to Soane's Blackfriars bridge being built in 1784 and Duke Street bridge in 1822. The historic crossing points at Trowse bridge and Bishopgate bridge provided only limited access to the lower Yare Valley and to Yarmouth by road. As early as 1776, a letter to the corporation had expressed support for an act of Parliament for the building of a further bridge to solve the problem. But not until 1810 was Carrow bridge constructed.

A new road, now known as Carrow Hill, was built outside the city wall

down to the new bridge and an extension made across the marsh to link
with the old road to Yarmouth. In 1811 a second bridge, following the
growth of Thorpe, was built by the foundry at the riverside end of St Faith's
Lane. The location of this bridge no doubt influenced the siting in 1844 of
Thorpe Station. A new stretch of road, now known as Rosary Road, was laid
out from Foundry bridge to link with the main Yarmouth road from
Bishopgate. The three bridges, one internal to the city and two linking it to
its eastern hinterland, reflect the start of a period of considerable growth.

In 1849 Charles Muskett published a clearly drawn and annotated map
of the city showing the recent expansion beyond the walls (Figure 17).
Jarrold produced a similar map in 1848 with fewer notes. Given the relatively sharp increase in population from 1821 to 1831, the growth of the city
shown in these maps is surprisingly small. Muskett used Millard and Manning's base map to add a few new streets and buildings, as for example
between West Pottergate and the Dereham Road. Much of St Margaret's
croft and the gildencroft was still open, the growth beyond the northern
section of the city wall had not started, and no infilling between Ber Street
and King Street had yet taken place. The medieval yards and courts were
no doubt taking some of the strain, extra garrets were added to houses, and
further subdivision of some larger ones took place. The famous report by
William Lee (1851) into the sanitary condition of Norwich alerted the city
to the appalling conditions in many of its yards.[34] It was the first step in a
movement which ultimately led to the clearances after the First World War
and the building of new estates.

In 1873 the city engineer, A. W. Morant, produced a large-scale map of
the built-up area of Norwich. This was the result of detailed survey work
to a scale of sixteen inches to a mile and it predated the first Ordnance Survey map of the city at 1:2500 (25 inches to a mile) by twelve years. It
replaced Millard and Manning's map of 1830 in tracing forty-three years of
growth and change. The two sample areas illustrated (Figures 18 and 19)
show further developments in the city centre area, as compared with
Hochstetter's version of nearly a century earlier, and in the Town Close
estate between the Ipswich and Newmarket roads, where development was
well in progress.

Several changes in the internal structure of the city had taken place
between 1830 and 1873. The most obvious one was the construction of
Prince of Wales Road, laid out in 1866. This linked Thorpe Station with the
cattle market. It cut through the site of the Greyfriars' buildings, right
across the foundations of the great church. Large, four-storey buildings
were erected to line the street for much of its length. The city end of this
new road became the focal point for several important new buildings, such

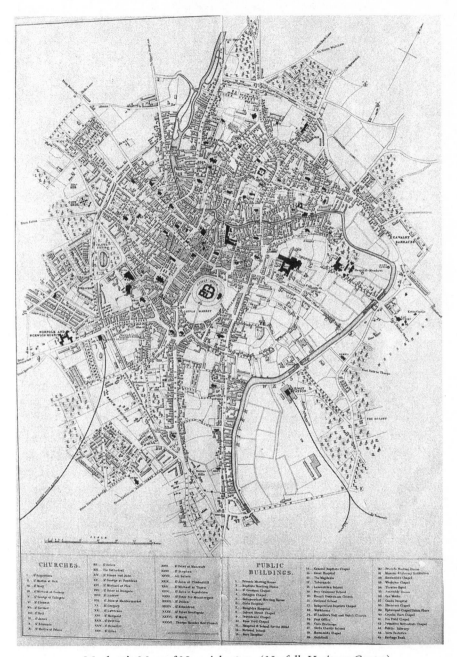

FIGURE 17. Muskett's Map of Norwich 1849. (*Norfolk Heritage Centre*)

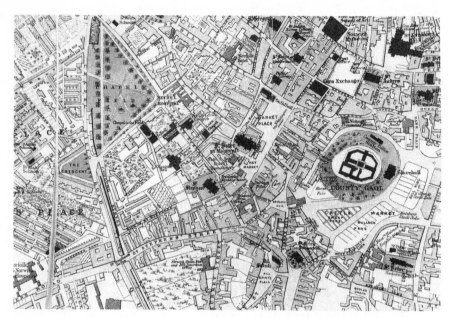

FIGURE 18. Morant's Map of 1873. Details of city centre. (*Norfolk Heritage Centre*)
FIGURE 19. (opposite and overleaf) Morant's Map of 1873. Detail of the Town
Close Estate. (*Norfolk Heritage Centre*)

as the Agricultural Hall (1882), the Royal Hotel (1896–97) and the regional
headquarters of Barclays Bank (1921).

Morant's map was produced at a key moment as the 'explosion' of new
working class housing was just beginning. To the north of Nightingale
Lane lay open country, but by 1907 it was an alley between Silver Street and
Woodhouse Street, an area of typical late nineteenth-century terraces
which rapidly filled the space between Magdalen Road and Silver Road.[35]
To the west of the city Pottergate stretched as far as Alexander Road, and
Heigham had reached Northumberland Street. Caernarvon Road had been
laid out by 1873 but not yet built. Holy Trinity church (1859–61) and Trin-
ity Street then marked the limit of terrace expansion between Newmarket
Road and Unthank Road.

The Ordnance Survey produced maps at the scale of 1:500 (10.56 feet to the
mile) for all towns with a population of more than 4000; by 1894, when the
series finished, Norwich was one of 365 towns in England already mapped.
The map for Norwich was published in 1885. A driving force behind
mapping at this scale was the need for accurate plans for the laying of
sewers and water and gas supplies in response to rapid urban expansion

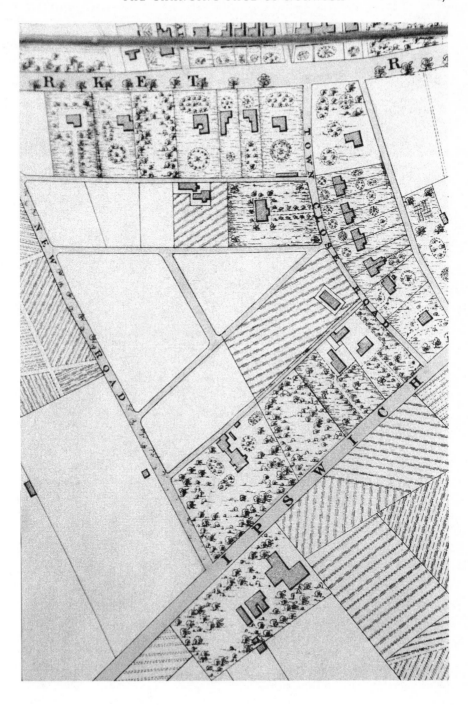

and concerns about public health. The twenty-five sheets of the Norwich series of the 1885 map were reissued in 1971 at a reduced scale of 1:1250 (50.688 inches to the mile).

This map represents the ultimate in urban mapping for the nineteenth century historian. The scale allows the ground plan of all properties to be shown as well as their boundaries. Individual trees were plotted as well as garden layout, and parish and ward boundaries. The information given provides a perfect record of the city in 1883, a wonderful starting point for the study of change in Norwich over the last hundred and twenty years. Three examples have been selected to show the superb detail of the map: first, Crooks Place, Bignold School and The Crescent; secondly, Chapelfield and thirdly, the industrial area which had become established near the New Mills (Figures 20 and 21). The range of industries shown is wide, although, as it happens, no shoe factory to represent Norwich's premier source of employment occurs within the selected area. The contrast between the straight-line, packed terraces of the working classes and the more generous layout of The Crescent is self-evident. The line of the city walls along Chapelfield Road, now revealed to all who drive along the inner-ring road, was then obscured by houses on both sides.

The traditional trade route into Norwich was via the rivers Yare and Wensum. Despite schemes to improve the river from Yarmouth to Norwich in 1682 and from Lowestoft to Norwich in 1827, the river port declined in importance. Even an attempt to facilitate access by building a lock in 1834 came to nothing. Norwich was already the focus of the road system of Norfolk and North East Suffolk, and turnpikes after 1750 improved the roads and increased the flow of goods into the city. Between 1844 and 1885 the building of three railway stations outside the walls led to developments to the south west, west and east of the city and, as we have seen, a new access route within the city from the cattle market to Thorpe Station via Prince of Wales Road.

The provision of gas, electricity, water, sewers, local authority housing and public open spaces have all had an impact on the plans of cities. The relief of a city site especially influences the alignment of sewers and their provision determines lines of further housing and industrial development. Hidden from view, they provided, with their miles of pipes and drains, a sanitary system far more comprehensive than any transport network.[36] These services have, or had, influenced other developments. Derelict gas-work sites, for example, have limited uses because of deep-ground pollution. The present reuse of the riverside site in Norwich imposed major costs of reclamation.

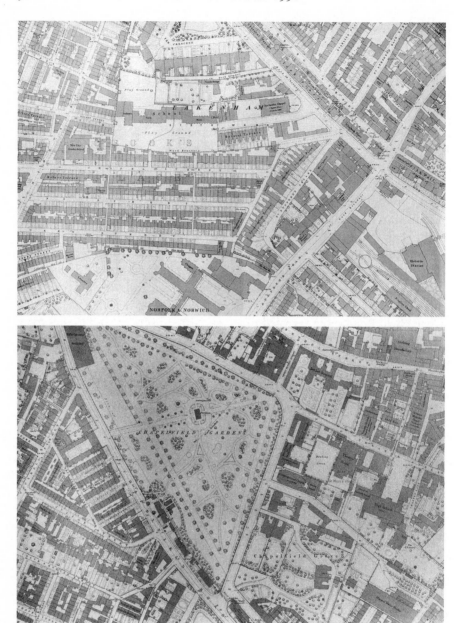

FIGURE 20. Ordnance Survey 1:500 1885. Detail from sheets LXIII 15.2 and LXIII 15.7. Working-class housing between the Norfolk and Norwich Hospital and the Crescent, and (below) Chapelfield Gardens. (*Norfolk Heritage Centre*)

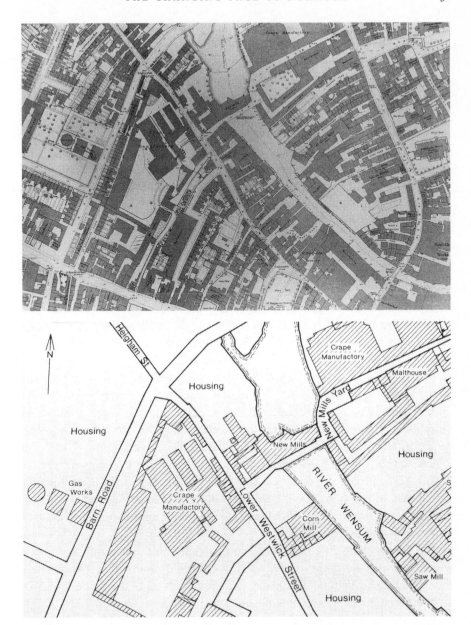

FIGURE 21. Selected Industrial Detail from Ordnance Survey 1.500 1885. The New Mills area, and redrawn as a sketch map. (Barringer, *Norwich in the Nineteenth Century*, p. 148)

William Lee's enquiry in 1851 into the sanitary condition of the city led
to the setting up of the Whitlingham sewage farm.[37] The farm was laid out
three miles to the east of the city, the effluent draining into the River Yare.
Until the late 1860s the River Wensum had been the city's main sewer, but
in 1867 the city sponsored an act of Parliament by which it leased 129 acres
of the Crown Point estate for thirty years. Deep sewers were laid on both
sides of the Wensum, and at Trowse a pumping station was built to lift
sewage to Whitlingham. In this and other ways, the city was spreading well
beyond its boundaries.

William Lee's report also raised concern about the quality of the water
supply. The Wensum, as well as being the city's sewer, was also its principal source of water. New Mills had been used as a pumping station for
water from the river which was circulated by systems of wooden or lead
pipes to the city centre. This lasted until 1794. By 1830 a reservoir had been
built in Chapel Field for storage; finally in 1920 filter beds were laid out in
Heigham on the south side of the river from where water is still pumped
to distribution reservoirs in Lakenham (Figure 22) and Mousehold. The
water in the Wensum is fed by springs from the chalk aquifer beneath the
city so that Norwich, unlike cities such as Manchester, Leeds and Bradford,
has not had to draw its supplies from far afield.

In 1918 Norwich corporation became a housing authority. After 1929
many slums were demolished and their inhabitants moved out to new
estates at Mile Cross, Earlham, Woodrow Pilling and Larkman Lane. Corporation housing became an important element of the city's total housing
stock. After the Second World War the corporation extended the city
boundary to the west in order to lay out a 'new town' at Bowthorpe. A
third, recent phase of growth has been the development of private housing
at Thorpe Marriott to the north west of the city and Dussindale on the
eastern edge. These are in effect satellite villages lying in Broadland district
but intimately linked to Norwich.

Within the walls since 1945 much industry has disappeared or moved to
greenfield sites along the ring road. The city has encouraged civic and private housing to use former industrial sites, such as that on the site of a
former timber yard between Colegate and the river at Friar's Quay.

Outside the walls the largest open spaces are Mousehold Heath, Earlham
Park and the two river flood plains. Mousehold is a remnant of a wide tract
of heathland that reached as far east as Wroxham. The building of the new
corporation housing estates created the need for related public open spaces.
Eaton Park was a classic job creation project of the inter-war years. The
eighty acre site was bought by the city with the help of the Norwich Playing
Fields and Open Spaces Society in 1906. It remained an open grass area

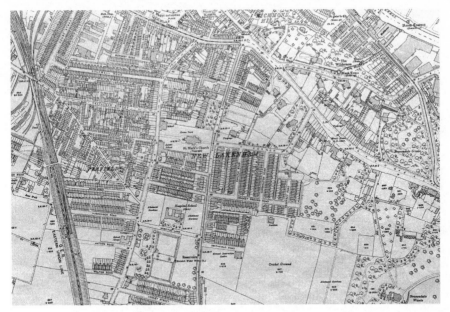

FIGURE 22. Ordnance Survey 1:2500 1914 reduced to 1:4340; Alan Godfrey Maps. The Parish of New Lakenham. (*Norfolk Heritage Centre*)

until the 1920s when Captain Sandys-Winsch, the city parks and gardens superintendent, designed the new park, opened in 1928, and also Waterloo, Wensum and Heigham parks.[38] The four parks have achieved recognition as 'historic landscapes' and have recently received a major Heritage Lottery Fund grant in order to restore them.

Before the reorganisation of local government in 1974 there was much discussion as to whether a Greater Norwich might make administrative sense in recognition of the central role played by the then county borough. This centralist view begged the question of how a county that had lost its core might be organised. In 1974 Norwich suffered, with Great Yarmouth, the indignity of losing its status as a county borough to become a 'mere' district within the county of Norfolk.

From 1500 until the present day Norwich has played a premier role as a market centre for Norfolk and much of north-east Suffolk. It has had an ecclesiastical, legal and administrative function as the seat of a bishop, the location of the county court and of the shire hall. It has now acquired additional roles as an important educational and research centre and as a national business centre for the food, banking and insurance industries. The spatial response in Norwich to these developments, given the relatively

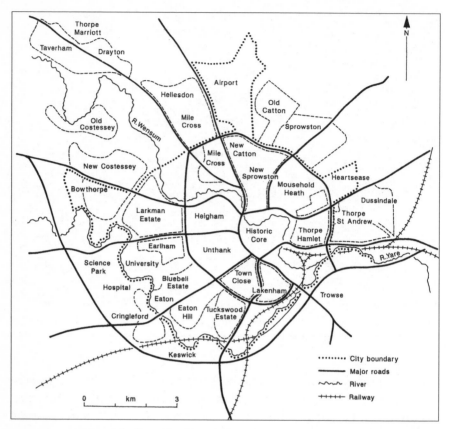

FIGURE 23. Norwich Growth Map. (*City of Norwich Plan* 1945 p. 82, plan by Phillip Judge)

gentle relief of central Norfolk, has been to march along, and spread between, its spine roads. It has already absorbed its first ring of neighbouring parishes in Lakenham, New Catton, Sprowston and Thorpe. A green belt at present divides it from an outer ring of semi-urban parishes which are intimately linked with the city, a link recently recognised by the development of a series of park and ride bus stations which tie the city to Costessey, Taverham and Drayton, Hethersett, outer Catton and Thorpe. The increasing role of the airport has influenced the growth of the city northwards. The final map of the environmental areas of greater Norwich emphasises the extent to which the urban area of Norwich has radiated outwards (Figure 23). The city has become an ever-expanding conurbation around a medieval hub.

2

Government to 1660

John Pound

By reason that the comodities of woorsted makynge is greatlye decayed, by the whiche manye Cittyzens, bothe merchauntes and artizans, that before that tyme hadd ... their wheale lyvinges, and great nombre of poore of the Cyttye were sette on worke ... after manye consultations and devices what trades might be practized to redresse this poore state [the mayor] was given intelligence that dyverse strangers of the Lowe countryes were now come to London and Sandwiche and had gotte lyscens of the Quenis majestye to exercize the makynge of Flaunders comodityes made of woolle, which straungers came over for refuge ageynste the persecution then raysed agaynst them by the power of the Duke Alva principall for the Kynge of Spayne.

Royal Letters Patent of 1564[1]

With the notable exception of the disappearance of its monastic houses – the magnificent Blackfriars apart – the physical appearance of Norwich altered remarkably little during the sixteenth and seventeenth centuries. An exceptionally detailed map of 1558 shows the city with wide swathes of open land. Some of this undoubtedly reflected the disastrous fires of 1507, which had destroyed over 700 dwellings in the northern and central parts of the city, or perhaps 40 per cent of the housing stock.[2] The features most often commented upon remained the walls, the cathedral and the profusion of churches. Only Celia Fiennes in 1698 went beyond that trilogy of tourist attractions to note the width and excellence of the paving. She also observed that to the north of the city, at least, some large brick buildings had sprung up, in contrast to the majority of timber-framed houses which gave Norwich such an antique appearance. It had been left to Thomas Baskerville some twenty years earlier to describe the market in detail, while the medieval guildhall merited no mention whatsoever (Plate 1).[3]

The city so cursorily depicted contained up to 11,000 people in 1520, a figure which altered hardly at all until Norwich had to absorb between five and six thousand Dutch and Walloon refugees in the 1560s and 1570s, following the duke of Alva's invasion of the Netherlands. Any likelihood of a subsequent population explosion was almost immediately nullified in 1579 by the worst outbreak of plague to afflict an English provincial town in the sixteenth and seventeenth centuries. More than a third of the population perished in this epidemic alone, which was followed by recurrent outbreaks of a less virulent nature in the succeeding twenty years or so, and another devastating pestilence in 1603. Statistics for births and deaths had been regularly collected by the mayor's court from 1582 onwards, as a direct result of the plague, and were to be produced until 1646, when the uncertainties of the Civil War period ended the practice. These figures indicated a steady, if variable, rise in the city's population, which had reached some 20,000 by the 1620s and which, on the evidence of both the Hearth Tax returns and the Compton Census, had altered little by the 1670s. Thereafter, there was another steady rise and, according to the statistician Gregory King, Norwich's population had reached almost 30,000 by the 1690s.[4] In the process, there was considerable overcrowding in some areas, notably in the Wymer and Ultra Aquam wards of the city, where the Dutch and Walloons predominated, but also by the later seventeenth century in parishes such as St Peter's Southgate on the southern margins. There more than 90 per cent of all households were poor, containing but a single hearth, while at least three-quarters of the inhabitants of St Julian's, St Peter's Mountergate and All Saints fell into this lowly category.[5] Tudor and Stuart Norwich contained a complex urban society, characterised by extremes of wealth and deprivation.

Throughout the sixteenth and seventeenth centuries, Norwich's system of government followed a pattern established in the middle ages.[6] It altered only marginally when Charles II, and then his brother James II, insisted on intervening in the selection of key officials and having the right to chose certain of the common councillors. The city had an 'upper house' of twenty-four aldermen, who enjoyed life tenure, two of whom were elected from the common council to represent each of the city's twelve petty wards. The aldermen provided the mayor and, until the seventeenth century, one of the two sheriffs, after which date it became a prerequisite to have served as sheriff before election to the aldermanry. The 'lower house', meanwhile, comprised sixty common councilmen, twenty being elected for Wymer, sixteen for Mancroft and twelve each for the wards of Conesford and Ultra Aquam. As in the medieval period, sufficient wealth and the practice of a socially acceptable trade were considered of paramount importance for civic rule; the common councillors were usually drawn from some twenty-four of the city's one hundred or so occupations, yet barely a dozen trades seemed prestigious enough for those of aldermanic rank.[7]

Norwich's common councillors were elected each year by the freemen of the wards they hoped to represent. The city fathers constantly referred to those of the 'first', 'second' and 'third sorts' – effectively a distinction of wealth and status reflecting the aspirations of all concerned. A majority of the common councillors fulfilled their civic duty by serving for a single year. Others, richer and with more time to spare from business, were returned more frequently. A few were regularly re-elected, while others were chosen two, three, four or five times, with a gap of some years between elections. In the process, several served the city for a number of years without ever aspiring to, or attaining, the position of alderman. Striking changes in the pattern of representation are clearly revealed by comparing the number of individuals elected in succeeding twenty-five year periods with the numbers admitted to the freedom of Norwich in the same years. Between 1525 and 1550, for example, 186 or fully 23 per cent of the 811 freemen were called upon to serve, most of them just once. Thereafter, the proportion of freemen elected as common councillors fell quite dramatically, even though the total number of freemen rose. The eighty-seven men elected between 1601 and 1625, out of a total of 1452 potential candidates, constituted no more than 6 per cent of the whole. There was a slight increase in the Civil War years, when the proportion hovered between 7 and 8 per cent; but there was no return to the high level of participation evident during the early Tudor period. As the number of freemen who were willing and elected to serve declined, so too did the range of occupations from which they were drawn. In the reigns of Henry VIII and his son, common councillors had pursued no fewer than forty-two different trades, with the distributive and textile element predominating. Under the early Stuarts, the number had fallen by one-third, only recovering somewhat in the 1640s and 1650s, when the religious criteria imposed during the Civil Wars slightly modified the traditional requirements of wealth and occupation.[8] Many councillors and aldermen were then elected who would not ordinarily have been successful, their religious practices and political views being deemed more important than wealth or social acceptability. In terms of status, prospective alderman were designated by the honorary title of Master, a notable mark of respect. Once elected, they appeared at the very top of any list of ward councillors, immediately after their older and more experienced peers already ensconced on the aldermanic bench. In contrast, lesser men simply jostled together at the end of the list.

The relative wealth of Norwich's individual citizens is apparent from the subsidy returns of the 1520s which – initially at least – provide historians with a reasonably accurate impression of the value of each taxpayer's goods, although not his or her lands. Since the crown's demand for subsidies reached down to humble wage-earners paid no more than 20s a year, it is possible to determine how incomes were distributed. Not surprisingly, wealth was concentrated in a few hands. The rich – those worth the substantial sum of £40 and above – were expected to make their contributions in advance; and the ninety-nine citizens in this category, including all of the aldermen, accounted for some 70 per cent of the city's first payment of the subsidy in 1524. The total collected was £749, which was far in excess of sums raised from other provincial towns, although well below that of London.

Norwich boasted some of the wealthiest citizens in the country. Robert Jannys's assessment of £55, based on £1100 worth of goods, bore comparison with that for the entire city of Rochester, while Thomas Aldrich, John Terry and Edward Rede, assessed on £700, £550 and £500 respectively, had few rivals elsewhere. By 1525, however, when the second instalment of the subsidy was levied, Norwich's recorded wealth had apparently decreased by some 10 per cent. Some of the decline undoubtedly reflected the impact of taxation, the fall in value of Jannys's goods matching exactly the 13 per cent or so of his assets that he was expected to pay. By 1525, however, and again in 1527 when the wealthy were taxed for the third time, it became abundantly clear that they, and some of the not so rich, too, were growing deliberately evasive. The value of Jannys's goods had ostensibly fallen to £600 by 1527, despite the fact that in his will, only three years later, he was able to dispose of over £2700 in cash alone. Other aldermen shared his reticence. Thomas Aldrich declared himself worth no more than £400 in 1527, while Edward Rede claimed to have lost almost half of his fortune. Of the ninety-six people who were taxed in both 1524 and 1525, fifty-six secured lower assessments, thirty-six remained the same and only four were asked for more.[9] Twenty-four of these tax-payers had their assessments reduced yet again in 1527.

This situation was not peculiar to Norwich. In the county of Norfolk, for example, the immensely rich Henry Fermor, who had admitted to being worth £1333 at the time of the Military Survey in 1522, was taxed on only half of this sum four years later. Collectively, the number of individuals worth £40 and above in Great Yarmouth and other hundreds (administrative districts) for which information survives, fell from 170 to 102 and their apparent wealth from £13,131 to £8039.[10] Babergh hundred in Suffolk saw a similar decline, as did places as far apart as Gloucestershire and Yorkshire. Having been ambushed once by the demands of the Tudor monarchy, the rich had no intention of being caught again.[11]

The subsidy return of 1525 survives in its entirety for Norwich and reflects the great disparity of wealth to be found in the early Tudor city. Some 6 per cent of those taxed owned 60 per cent of the property. At the other end of the scale, the 570 wage-earners, comprising 40 per cent of all taxpayers, commanded less than 4 per cent of the city's resources. There were others below even this level. In Great Yarmouth, a full 31 per cent of potential taxpayers were recorded as being of no substance in 1522, while many residents were almost certainly omitted altogether because of their poverty.[12] A similar gulf between rich and poor is apparent in most of the larger English towns, if not the smaller ones. Some caution, however, is needed here, at least with regard to wage-earners. The Military Survey for Great Yarmouth recorded that a healthy 29 per cent of those valued at no more than 20s. actually owned land or other real estate as well, thus providing an important buffer between men and women assessed on wages alone and their wealthier neighbours.[13] The situation was almost certainly similar in Norwich, and should be taken into account when we attempt to estimate the extent of poverty in the early Tudor city.

A majority of the richer citizens lived in the wards of St Peter Mancroft and Middle Wymer, the latter providing almost a quarter of the city's wealth in 1525. The wards of West Wymer, Coslany and Colegate also contained a number of wealthy men. In contrast, the poor tended to congregate in and around Conesford and St Giles's (to the west of Norwich), and continued to do so throughout the Tudor and Stuart period.[14] In the sixteenth century, as in the middle ages, wealth clung to the hands of merchants involved in the distributive trades, notably grocers and mercers, and of those who made or sold other luxury goods. Such men continued to prosper, even as the city's old established textile industry entered a period of decline. The statistics are telling. Already by 1561, Norwich was exporting no more than thirty-eight worsteds from its outport of Great Yarmouth, in contrast to the yearly average of between 1000 and 3000 recorded before 1535. Evidence from the freemen admissions suggests that the industry reached its nadir in the last quarter of the sixteenth century. At that point, barely 14 per cent of new entrants fell into the 'textile' category, which had accounted for almost half of all admissions at the start of the century. This trend is confirmed by two occupational censuses: the first was based on the 1569 muster, when the freemen's lists reveal the presence of 264 textile workers; the second, taken twenty years later, shows that their number had fallen to 113.[15] Both sources significantly appeared *after* the advent of the Dutch and Walloons, and reflect the initial antipathy between the immigrants and the native workforce, which did not immediately appreciate the innovations brought to the city by the refugees.

Norwich merchants, like many others, had long experience of trading with the Dutch, a number of them being members of either the Old or New Hanse, that is the Company of Merchant Adventurers. Since the middle ages, it had been a common requirement of the apprentices of grocers and mercers, in particular, that they spend time abroad learning a language.[16] Many commercial links centred further south on Antwerp, but the Dutch contacts made, not least on this personal level, were to prove extremely useful. There were already forty-two Dutch and Walloon families in residence when 'alien' immigrants were officially allowed into the 'great and empty city of Norwich' from 1565. This development followed requests from the mayor of Norwich and the duke of Norfolk, both pleading the decline of the old textile industry and the desperate need for new blood. Elizabeth I's privy council authorised the settlement of twenty-four Dutch and six Walloon families, the total number being limited to three hundred. They were expected to introduce 'bayes, arras, sayes, tapesterie, mockades, stamins, kersye and suche other owtelandishe comodityes as hath not bene used to be made within this ower realme of Englaunde'.[17]

The mayor's enthusiasm was not shared by many of his contemporaries. The common council, fearing competition, refused to put its corporate seal to the orders and the mayor was obliged to use his own seal to make the immigrants' presence lawful. Once established, the 'alyens' were allowed to rent 'anye dwellinge housse, messwage, or tenemente' in Norwich, and two aldermen, one a JP, were appointed to hear all matters of controversy between them and their new hosts. Certain restrictions were, however, placed upon the Strangers (as these newcomers were soon known), for, apart from observing the laws and constitutions of the city, they were ordered not to buy or sell any goods whatsoever, except those of their own make, which might only be traded between compatriots.[18] Despite these restrictions, the newcomers' first impressions of Norwich were very favourable. Letters home survive from individuals urging other relatives to emigrate: they stress the friendliness of the people, the fact that 'there is a great trade doing', and that 'it will be easy to make money'. Culture clashes were, none the less, inevitable, not least in the matter of diet. One correspondent urged his wife to buy two little wooden dishes to mould butter, 'for all Netherlanders and Flemings make their own butter, for here it is all pig's fat'.[19] The continuing persecution of Dutch and Walloon Protestants in the Spanish Netherlands encouraged further immigration. The 300 official 'Strangers' had increased to 2866 within a few years, including no fewer than 193 woolcombers as well as Norwich's first documented printer.[20] And their numbers continued to grow, despite privy council prohibitions. An official count in 1571 recorded 3925 Strangers, and by 1576, on the evidence of the subsidy of that year, they had reached almost 5,000.[21]

The presence of these 'aliens' undoubtedly stimulated trade in some quarters. The pieces of woven cloth produced by the company of russell weavers, for example, increased almost immediately in number from 276 to 1048, and had reached 2845 by 1572.[22] Despite this encouraging start, hopes that the Strangers would teach their skills to the citizens proved initially abortive, mainly through the disinclination and inability of the natives to absorb the new techniques. They tended to adhere stubbornly to the old methods already familiar to them, even though the New Draperies (as they were termed) soon recaptured the export market for the city and boosted its flagging economy. The Strangers were seen as rivals by many of the citizens and the authorities were inundated with complaints from the tailors, dyers, worsted shearmen, butchers, smiths, joiners and cordwainers about unfair competition.[23]

The opposition secured official sanction 1567 during the mayoralty of Thomas Whall, a grocer 'havinge no lykinge of the straungers'. He alleged bluntly that they 'had done more hurte than ever they wolde do good, and that they dyd but sucke the lyvenges awaye from the Inglyshe, and that if the Lordes of the [Privy] Counsell dyd knowe of yt, he was glad thereof'.[24] Whall promptly imposed an eight o'clock curfew on the Strangers and stipulated that no newcomers were to be lodged in Norwich for longer than one night without the mayor being informed. It was through his activities that the privy council became increasingly concerned about the numbers entering the city and attempted, without success, to restrict them.[25]

Whall was not the only man of substance to prove hostile towards the newcomers, although in some quarters antagonism was fuelled by religious rather than commercial factors. A far more serious event occurred in 1570, when a band of local malcontents planned not only to remove all 'aliens' from Norwich but also to overthrow Elizabeth's government and to restore Catholicism. The leader, John Appleyard, was himself half-brother to Amy Robsart and was thus linked, after her marriage to Robert Dudley, earl of Leicester, to a powerful faction at court.[26] Ironically, under the circumstances, the plot was betrayed to the authorities by Thomas Kett, one of the conspirators, whose family already seemed tarred with the brush of insurrection. The fact that the plotters hoped to betray Great Yarmouth to Alva and his Spanish *tercios* was sufficient to guarantee the execution of three ringleaders as traitors, while a further three were sentenced to perpetual imprisonment and the loss of goods.[27]

Despite opposition of this kind, the Strangers were soon to be found all over Norwich. The largest number, however, congregated in the two wards of Wymer and Ultra Aquam, which housed a full 77 per cent of the new-comers by 1571. Their presence led to chronic overcrowding; they apparently colonised some empty houses, but other dwellings were of such low quality that their presence has only recently been revealed by archae-ological excavation.[28] This fact emphasises the poverty of many refugees, which is also confirmed by the 1576 subsidy returns. At that date, some 88 per cent were recorded as having goods worth less than 20s. Once Wymer ward became filled to capacity it was replaced by Ultra Aquam as the area housing the largest number of newcomers.[29]

The absorption of at least 5000 aliens into a city containing a native population of barely 11,000 souls was bound to create difficulties. This was compounded by refusal of the Dutch and Walloons to pass on all of their secrets, particularly that of wool-combing, together with the initial unwillingness of the locals to abandon their old practices and a barrage of protests from a variety of established trades. It is therefore hardly sur-prising that the presence of the newcomers initially created more problems than it solved. Complaints and counter-complaints from both Strangers and natives rumbled on throughout the 1570s and 1580s, although from the outset the Dutch and Walloon communities endeavoured both to sup-port and discipline their own members through a series of 'Articled Orders'. Approved by the privy council in April 1571, these rules gave con-siderable powers to the ministers, deacons and governors of the Strangers, who were to 'unyte and styll all stryfe and contention [and] avoyde all uncomelyness'.[30]

Apart from this petty quibbling from both sides, the Norwich authori-ties came to recognise the advantages accruing to the city. A document sent to the privy council around 1575 noted that the presence of the Strangers had provided work not only for residents but also for people living up to a distance of twenty miles away, 'to the grete relief of the porer sorte'. Houses were said to be inhabited which had previously been 'in rewyn', the 'aliens' having repaired them and having agreed to pay good rents. Local merchants were exploiting new markets both at home and abroad. Fur-thermore, the Strangers contributed to local and national taxes, including subsidies, manned the city watches and helped to meet the corporation's wage bill. Best of all, the Norwich workforce had at long last begun to man-ufacture the New Draperies, 'whereby the youthe is set on worke and kepte from idlenes'. The last comment, Walloon products apart, was somewhat optimistic as yet, but the report also stressed that the 'aliens' were culti-vating many acres of waste ground in which to grow flax for linen cloth, again generating employment, and also producing root vegetables, 'which is a grete succor and sustenaunce for the pore both for themselves as for all others of citie and contrie'. The newcomers were, to their credit, said to live entirely upon their own labour without begging, which meant that their poor did not become a charge upon the host community. 'And to conclude', ran the report, '. . . they for the moste parte feare God, and do diligently and loborously attende upon their severall occupations, they obey all magistrates and all good lawes and ordynaunces, they lyve peace-ablie amonge themselves and towarde all men, and we thinke our cittie happie to enjoye them.'[31]

This inflated praise of the Dutch, in particular, may well have encour-aged outside interference, typified by the grant of 'hostage' to some of Queen Elizabeth's courtiers and of alnage rights to other influential public figures. Hostage allowed the person who held the grant to entrust all Strangers to the care of English hosts, with whom they were to lodge, the hosts having supervision of their business affairs, which were to be recorded in books kept specially for the purpose. Its avowed purpose was to ascertain the origin and quality of merchandise belonging to the Strangers, to prevent smuggling and the transportation of bullion and coin to foreign countries, to ensure the purchase of English goods to the full value of any imports and to revive the privileges of London which had fallen into disuse in this respect. Royal letters patent granted national rights of hostage to one William Tipper on 24 June 1576, and, having used his authority in London, he proceeded to make similar demands upon Nor-wich and other towns where Strangers were harboured. The proposals were so draconian that many newcomers left the city and others prepared to fol-low suit. In consequence, fearing the loss of their nascent prosperity, the mayor and aldermen themselves purchased the right of hostage in Norwich for £70 13s. 4d. At the same time, they reassured the anxious 'aliens', that the corporation had no intention of exploiting its newly acquired powers.[32]

There were further difficulties to be overcome. Special customs duties were levied on the transport of the New Draperies; and two courtiers, Sir George Delves and Sir William Fitzwilliam, were appointed alnagers and collectors of the subsidy in 1578, for the next seven years. The potential profits were considerable. In 1579 alone £70 was demanded from the Dutch and almost £8 from the Walloons, both sums being payable in London. The mayor of Norwich petitioned unsuccessfully for the removal of the imposition; his failure prompted the corporation to buy out the remaining five years of the grant, and thus enabled it to make a profit of £616 by farm-ing the alnage directly from the crown. Although the rulers of Norwich subsequently offered 400 marks (£266 13s. 4d.) and an annual payment of

£5 to renew the privilege for a further twelve years, they bid too low, and this lucrative grant may have reverted to the Fitzwilliam family.[33]

The alnage controversy was the last commercial incident of note concerning the Strangers in Elizabeth's reign, and it coincided with the devastating outbreak of plague in 1579. The Dutch and Walloon immigrants were especially hard hit, accounting for 71 per cent of all those buried in Norwich during the last months of the outbreak. This high death rate stemmed from the fact that so many worked with cloth and wool (a natural home for fleas) and lived in run-down and rat-infested houses. Their susceptibility to plague continued throughout the next quarter of a century, culminating in 1603 when the 'alien' death rate was twice as high as that of the native English. Appalling though they were, these repeated attacks curtailed the runaway growth of the immigrant population, thus enabling the city to absorb 'an alien population much larger than that attracted to any other provincial town'.[34] Heavy mortality coincided with trade depression where the Dutch were concerned. During the winter of 1587 many Dutch professed to be unable to support their own 'greatly increacyd' poor, being allowed £10 for this purpose from money derived from sealing their cloths.[35] The decline continued throughout the rest of the Elizabethan period. The profits from the sale of bays (a heavy fabric of plain weave), one of the 'owtelandishe comodityes' they were meant to introduce, fell steadily from the peak of 13,652 cloths reached in 1581–82, until their total disappearance by 1600. A similar, albeit more protracted, story was true of the initially successful says (fine woollen cloth). The numbers searched rose dramatically from twenty-eight in 1581–82 to a peak of 8293 just three years later. The city chamberlains derived a substantial income from this source until 1610–11, when the trade also declined rapidly, its profits ceasing altogether in the 1640s.[36]

Despite these vicissitudes, the Norwich authorities continued to emphasise the economic benefits conferred by the 'aliens', stressing to the privy council in the mid 1580s that they lent money to native citizens without interest; that they rendered £400 yearly to the corporation for dues on goods; that the rents of houses let to them had increased more than sixfold; and that they contributed even further to the city's prosperity through the wages, totalling £500 a year, they paid to workmen.[37] Clearly, the fortunes of individual members of the Dutch community varied enormously. But much of the success attributed indiscriminately by the corporation to the two 'congregacions' must have attached itself to the Walloons. In marked contrast to the Dutch, they maintained a high level of productivity for far longer. From 5382 in 1570–71, the number of their cloths sealed rose to 24,106 in 1587–88, reaching its zenith in 1605–6 with a further increase of almost 30 per cent. Although the English were slow to desert their traditional manufactures, and never really mastered the art of bay making, which declined with the Dutch congregation, they took more easily to the Walloon grograines, mockadoes, vellums, buffins and other 'caungeantry'. The production of these specialist wares was of real national as well as regional importance, rising from about 2000 cloths in 1580–81 to between 6000 and 7000 annually over the next five years.[38] By the end of Elizabeth's reign, traditional worsted weaving was all but extinct, and the scene was set for the tremendous boom in the renovated textile industry which followed in the seventeenth century.[39] As a result, the fortunes of the French-speaking Walloon community went from strength to strength. The particular appeal of the Norwich industry lay in its light, bright stuffs, often made of a mixture of wool and silk, 'which came to be the popular wear of the not-too-affluent squire's lady or the tradesman's wife'.[40] The sheer diversity of these textiles was revealed in a letter written by Thomas Anguish, the mayor of Norwich, in 1611 when he itemised some three dozen different 'cloathes and stuffes' being produced at that time.[41]

Both domestic and foreign markets were captured by the New Draperies; and this success encouraged more and more people to enter the reinvigorated worsted industry. During the reign of James I, there were three separate years when more than a hundred youths were apprenticed as worsted weavers. In all, over 800 are known to have been indentured between 1601 and 1625. Admissions of worsted weavers to the freedom of the city never reached that level, partly because of the costs and responsibilities involved. None the less, more than 260 men were admitted as worsted weavers between 1601 and 1625. They were followed by half as many again over the next twenty-five years, and a further 680 between 1651 and 1675. In the process, the textile industry came to account for a remarkable 40 per cent of the freemen, a much greater proportion than that achieved in the sixteenth century. Gentry, clergy and yeomen – men of status who had eschewed the humble textile trades under Elizabeth – reacted favourably to the changing fortunes of the industry. Thus, by the second quarter of the seventeenth century, sons of the clergy provided more than 10 per cent of apprentices; almost one in five of them boasted gentry origins; and those of yeomen backgrounds made up a striking 30 per cent of the rest. Conversely – and perhaps unsurprisingly, bearing in mind their rising expectations – the sons of textile workers constituted no more then 5 per cent of the 321 youths admitted to the trade between 1626–50.[42]

The revival and success of the textile industry played a crucial part in Norwich's economy. Nevertheless, it would be misleading to discuss the city's industrial development solely in terms of a single product. As in any large town, building, clothing and victualling were of prime importance, as were the leather trades. These remained as prominent in the ward of St Peter Mancroft as they had been throughout the later middle ages.[43] Other established occupations, though of less importance numerically, featured prominently in particular areas of the city. Boatmen and keelmen lived alongside the river in Conesford; and tanning was still undertaken further up the Wensum in Coslany. Tailors, grocers and cordwainers always appeared among the city's leading trades, as did carpenters, busy at work on the large number of timber-framed houses which dominated the urban landscape during this period.

Forty new occupations are recorded in the freemen's lists between 1601 and 1675, although several of these had been practised in the city by non-freemen for some time, or possibly as subsidiary trades by the freemen themselves. Roger Horton had, for example, been described as a furrier as early as 1563, yet no freeman was enrolled as such until 1694. John Porter worked as a clockmaker before 1598, but none appears in the freemen's lists until 1613, when, surprisingly, the individual in question had been indentured to a master who began his career as a grocer. Last-makers, coppersmiths and crossbow-makers were among the other occupations to attract recruits, but no freeman was officially admitted as such. During the 1630s one barber, John Adkin, trained three apprentices in the art and science of music as well as barbering, while basket-makers, locksmiths and tailors took hosier apprentices.[44] It is also worth noting that the first of the city's ironmongers began as grocers. An occupational census of the Dutch and Walloons taken in 1622, while emphasising the continuing importance of textile workers, listed twenty-seven hosiers, eight farmers and gardeners, and a small clutch of schoolmasters, physicians and surgeons.[45]

Even when the textile industry was at its height in the early seventeenth century, six out of every ten freemen were employed in other spheres, and far more had followed alternative occupations during the reign of Elizabeth. Norwich was a regional capital catering for the needs of people far beyond its immediate confines, a fact reflected in the phenomenal growth of the grocers in particular, whose trade increased sixfold between 1525 and 1569. Other prestigious occupations, such as mercers, drapers and goldsmiths also flourished. There was a similar upsurge in the professions, the physicians, in particular, increasing steadily in number as well as in prestige. Opportunities such as these encouraged people with social aspirations, and the upwardly mobile from both inside and outside Norwich apprenticed their sons accordingly.

The distributive trades, particularly those of grocer, mercer and draper, furnished Norwich with its wealthiest citizens. This was especially true in the sixteenth century, when, as we have already seen, Robert Jannys was one of the richest merchants in the entire country. His successors in the Elizabethan period frequently left bequests approaching, and occasionally exceeding, £1000 in cash alone, quite apart from their investments in land and other property. By the later sixteenth century, many of them were investing in estates far beyond the city walls and, whenever possible, marrying into Norfolk gentry families. For example, links were made with the Knyvetts, Gawdys, Bacons, Hobarts, Jernegans, Cokes and Cornwallises, as well as with the Heveninghams and Saltonstalls. Three of the city's aldermen, Sir Thomas Hyrne, Sir John Pettus and Sir Peter Gleane, became sheriffs of the county, having already served the city in this capacity.[46]

In the sixteenth century at least, some of these grandees had quite humble origins. Of several examples, two can be quoted here. The Mingays came from the village of Shotesham, some seven miles south of Norwich. The first member of the family to move to the city was Robert, a cordwainer. He inherited some lands and tenements from his yeoman father but added little to these, leaving a respectable, but hardly remarkable, sum of £26 in cash and two tenements in Norwich at his death in 1545. He bequeathed his houses and £10 in cash to his son, William, who proved to be a sound businessman. He had already moved up the social ladder by being apprenticed as a mercer, and, like many ambitious entrepreneurs of the period, he increased his patrimony by shrewd buying and selling of monastic lands. In due course he became an alderman and attained the mayoralty in 1561. By the time of his death, in 1564, he had enhanced the family fortunes to such a degree that he owned manors in both Norfolk and Suffolk, estates, tenements and a rectory at Shotesham, and other property in Framingham. He was also able to dispose of more than £600 in cash. Significantly, with the exception of his Suffolk investments, all of these acquisitions were in the vicinity of his ancestral home at Shotesham. As was so often the case, none of his three ambitious sons went into trade. Two pursued careers in the law and a third became the squire of Arminghall, in the county of Norfolk.[47]

A second example, Sir Thomas Hyrne, has already been mentioned. His grandfather was a yeoman of Drayton, another village just outside Norwich, who had apprenticed his son, Clement, as a grocer there. Like William Mingay, the boy prospered sufficiently to attain both aldermanic rank and the mayoralty, which he occupied in 1593. When he died, Clement Hyrne was worth no less than £1305 in cash, as well as owning a number of houses, and a manor at Haveringland which Thomas inherited. Thanks to a daunting combination of talent and capital, the latter's rise was meteoric. He took up his freedom as the city's first ironmonger on 16 October 1596, succeeded to his father's place as alderman five days later (one of the few to attain this status without first having been a common councillor), became sheriff within less than a year and embarked on the first of his three terms as mayor seven years later. He eventually became the first man to serve as sheriff of both Norwich and the county of Norfolk. He was also knighted by James I, and represented his native city in parliament.[48]

Such people were, of course, in a small minority. Their comparative rarity is apparent from an analysis of the subsidy returns of the sixteenth century and those of the hearth tax of 1671. The disparity in wealth in early sixteenth-century Norwich has already been noted. On the evidence of the Census of the Poor of 1570 and the subsidy return of 1576, the situation was very similar in the middle years of Elizabeth's reign, when fewer than half of all households possessed sufficient resources to pay anything. Yet a far higher proportion had to shoulder the growing burden of poor relief. Some 70 per cent of all citizens were called upon for contributions, even though the circumstances of some were hardly more fortunate. The social divisions were just as acute a century later. In 1671 only 7 per cent of citizens lived in houses containing six or more hearths. These included the great mansions of the duke of Norfolk and Sir John Hobart, with sixty and fifty hearths respectively, as well as those of some city aldermen which had twenty or more. At the same time, however, almost 60 per cent of the city's householders were exempt from taxation on the grounds of poverty. And there was a significant underclass, possibly as many as five hundred householders, many of them women, who went completely unrecorded.[49] In 1525, the relative proportions of the wealthy and the wage-earners – and possibly the proportion of residents of even lower status – were broadly similar to those in other English towns. In 1671, by contrast, the proportion of people exempted from paying the hearth tax in Norwich was considerably higher than that in other provincial towns. Paradoxically, this was a reflection of the city's wealth rather than its poverty. The unemployed flooded into Norwich, attracted by the expanding textile industry. Some were allowed to stay. Others disappeared, almost literally, overnight, a fact made very clear if we compare the names of those exempted from payment of the hearth tax in succeeding years during the 1670s. Norwich was, by the later seventeenth century, a high growth city, which experienced a constant turnover of population.

For a variety of reasons, the cost of maintaining the poor steadily increased. Poverty is, by its very nature, a relative term. An elastic definition in a period of rampant inflation might incorporate all those with goods worth up to £10 before 1600, and up to £15 in the seventeenth century. Some of the people in this category left wills and a few basic possessions. Typical of such delicately placed individuals was Thomas Gray, 'a pore lame man and almost blind which reseived wekely collection'. At his death in 1618, Gray had just 46s. 8d. to his name. Apart from a few items of apparel valued at 6s. 8d., and the bedding which made up half the total of his domestic effects, his sole possessions were three old kettles, an ancient frying pan, two earthen pots, six dishes and wooden platters, a 'cowl', two old coffers, a little box, an old tub, a little sieve, a spinning wheel, two or three old pieces of board, a pail, a little gridiron, a little pair of forks, a 'towcome' (for combing wool), two little pewter dishes, three saucers and six trenchers. Neither chairs nor table evidently graced his single-roomed house, which was furnished with little apart from his eating and drinking utensils and a bed. He must have eked out a precarious living supported by his wife's activities at the spinning wheel. One Edmund Ransom, who died twenty years later, was poorer still, if the inventory of his goods is any guide. The appraisers recorded his worldly possessions in just twenty-four words: 'An old bedstead, fetherbed nat and cord and an old cubbart and an old table, a forme and the old chayres prised at 25s.'. Ransom must have owned some clothes and, presumably, vessels from which to eat and drink but, like Gray, he was virtually destitute.[50]

Others, although still relatively poor, had more to offer. Sixty per cent of Norvicians whose possessions were recorded in the 950 inventories to survive from the period 1584–1675 lived in houses containing between three and five rooms; and a few owned larger dwellings. No more than a quarter of them inhabited single rooms. A small minority kept animals – cows, pigs, horses and chickens – which provided a cushion against unemployment, but most laid claim to little more than their personal property. Of this, bedding was by far the most valuable item, followed by clothing and books. Every fifth person had a few books, most of them being Bibles, psalm books or collections of sermons, with the occasional copy of Foxe's *Book of Martyrs*. Some among them owned several, which suggests a reasonable level of literacy, as well as religious zeal, among people of 'the middling sort'. A number of the poor lived in property which had been renovated, either by themselves or their landlords, and the inventories do signal the slow improvements taking place in the domestic architecture of Norwich, even at the bottom of the social ladder.[51]

The dual problems of poverty and vagrancy were ever present throughout the Tudor and Stuart periods. In general, Norwich dealt with them as effectively as was then possible.[52] Initially, the city followed government legislation and authorised begging by the old and incapacitated, who were licensed to solicit alms. In 1549, however, it became the first provincial town to initiate compulsory payments to finance a civic scheme of poor relief centred upon the refoundation of St Giles's hospital, following this in 1557 with arrangements for the stockpiling of corn supplies and regulations forbidding the settlement in Norwich of anyone without obvious means of support.[53] This policy of selective help, designed to eliminate the 'sturdy beggar', appears to have been relatively successful during this period, if not later. In 1570, on the eve of its greatest triumph in the sphere of poor relief, Norwich was still supporting some 175 of its less able but most apparently deserving inhabitants. There were, however, no grounds for complacency, and the aldermanic body was jerked into a greater realisation of its responsibilities by the Appleyard conspiracy of 1570. The central government also expressed concern, not least because the plot was hatched in a city which little more than twenty years earlier had seen the wholesale participation of many of its poorer citizens in Kett's Rebellion. It was undoubtedly with this in mind that Lord Burleigh wrote to the mayor, John Aldrich, stressing that 'a great multitude of people of mean and base sort cannot be void of fear' and pressing him to act accordingly. The result was the ground-breaking census, ordered by Aldrich, which sought to establish the greatest possible information about a class which had previously been regarded with contempt born of ignorance.[54]

The Norwich Census of the Poor went far beyond anything attempted previously and was much more than a panic measure adopted in the face of pressure from Westminster. It led to a house-to-house survey of all who might reasonably be deemed paupers, taking in the young and able-bodied as well as the old and infirm. The names and details of 2359 individuals – approximately five hundred men, eight hundred women and the rest children under the age of sixteen – were recorded.[55] Together, they comprised some 28 per cent of the city's English population. Everyone's age and occupation were set down, from the youngest child to the men (20 per cent of all males) and women (25 per cent of all females) who were over sixty. In addition, the census noted whether each individual was gainfully employed. Information was also sought about the type of housing in which the poor lived: whether this was owned or rented (many paupers were the tenants of aldermen and common councillors); if it was ecclesiastical property or accommodation provided by the city; or, in extreme cases, whether the truly destitute were actually using the towers in the city wall as living areas. Those examined were required to state how long they had lived in Norwich and, in many cases, to specify their places of origin. Any alms they were receiving at the time of the census were duly recorded, as was information about their children's education. Many boys and girls under seven years old were being taught to read, while a number of older children had advanced beyond this stage and were learning to write as well.

From the city's point of view, one immediate lesson was that far too few people were receiving assistance. Moreover, while two-thirds of the men and about 80 per cent of the women were in some type of gainful employment at the time of the census, the situation remained extremely volatile. The corporation responded by drawing up a Book of Orders for the Poor and doubling the poor rate.[56] All those not receiving assistance (including twenty families named in the census itself) were called upon to contribute to the support of their less fortunate neighbours. Wealthier parishes, such as those of St Peter Mancroft and St Andrew, provided assistance for the poor of the less affluent parishes to the south and north of the city as well as the modest number of paupers living in their midst. Few escaped the net, a fact brought out clearly in 1576, when almost four hundred more people were paying poor relief than were required to contribute to the sub- sidy of that year. Provision was made for all categories of the deserving poor including, uniquely, the able-bodied who genuinely sought work. Thus, within a comparatively short time, some 950 citizens were called upon to provide support for around four hundred or so 'pensioners'. Approximately £500 was collected each year for this purpose, a larger sum than any received by the chamberlains for routine civic business because payments were compulsory and hard to avoid. Some of the old and incapacitated remained permanent pensioners. Others, in temporary difficulties, received temporary help until they managed to find work.[57]

The apparent success of the Norwich scheme had important conse- quences at national level, not least because of the interest shown in it by Matthew Parker, the reforming archbishop of Canterbury, himself a Norwich man and friend to the Strangers, whose brother, Thomas, had been mayor in 1568. Its instigator, John Aldrich, was twice returned as an MP for the city, and in 1576 sat on a parliamentary committee which dealt with the wider question of poor relief.[58] This led to the introduction of compulsory payments for the support of the poor throughout England from 1572 onwards, and, somewhat more tardily, a recognition in 1576 that practical assistance should be provided for anyone seeking employment. These two major developments formed the basis of the later Elizabethan Poor Law (enacted in 1597–8 and codified four years later), which was undoubtedly influenced by the Norwich experiments. The Norwich scheme itself continued for at least a decade, bolstered at intervals by the charitable bequests of its wealthier citizens, until the appalling plague of 1579–80 dealt, at least temporarily, with the problem of the poor in a much more ruthless way. Individual parishes still maintained a poor rate, the wealthier ones continuing to help their less affluent neighbours. And an additional rate was levied from time to time, particularly during pestilences. Theoretically, begging remained forbidden. But poverty defied legislation, and despite all efforts to contain it begging was again authorised in the 1590s, when inflation was at its height and a potentially explosive situation was further aggravated by ruinous harvests.[59]

Inevitably, this crisis led to a growth in vagrancy and, especially after the influx of the Dutch and Walloon refugees, increased overcrowding. Not even the godly aldermen could resist the temptation to profit from a chronic shortage of accommodation. The Census of the Poor reveals some striking cases of exploitation as early as 1570. One of Thomas Parker's houses in Pockthorpe accommodated twenty people, while John Sotherton owned a tenement in St Mary's Coslany which housed eleven families, comprising no fewer than thirty-four lodgers in all.[60] These examples, however, pale into insignificance compared with the seventeenth-century situation. In August 1631 one Mary Newman was called before the city's leet court for allowing four families into her house, 'all wch ar lykly to be chargaball to the parish', the premises in question 'not bein fit for more than toe dwelers and not having a howse of ofis [privy]'. Six years later, Thomas Stalworthy of St Swithin's parish and his wife were similarly indicted 'for over chargeing and pestering theyr howses wth pore people ... they takeing in severall persons from the lazar house. There are severall famylys, forty-six persons, under one rooff and some of them keep swyne in theyr dwelling howses'. The worst example by far concerned Thomas Harrold of Aylsham, who had converted a property in the parish of St Martin at Palace into sixteen tenements, housing eighteen families and a grand total of over seventy persons. Several of the tenements had no sanitation.[61] The hearth tax evidence of the 1670s confirms that many such houses had been converted in this way for multiple occupancy. It is hardly surprising that problems of poverty, combined with those of vagrancy, haunted Norwich throughout the seventeenth century and beyond.

As in many other Tudor towns, vagrants generally travelled alone. Almost 60 per cent of known vagrants were unattached men, while one in five were women, although from time to time whole families attempted to enter the city. 'Professional' vagabonds, if they can be so described, received short shrift, being invariably whipped and sent back to their place of origin. Others were treated more generously, occasionally being given small sums of money to assist them on their way. But non-natives were never welcomed and young children as well as adults were turned away, either to fend for themselves or go home to their villages, sometimes alone or else accompanied by an adult who had volunteered for the task. Indeed, in 1562 a labourer named Robert Morgan was consigned to prison and threatened with the loss of an ear for harbouring such 'young and ydell vagabondes'.[62] Yet children still trudged into Norwich. One eight-year-old girl had come from as far away as Staffordshire, while an eleven-year-old boy had tramped the hundred miles and more from London. In both cases, they were summarily whipped and returned to their birthplaces, no thought whatever being given to the possible dangers of solitary travel.[63] Not everyone was caught. An entry in the court books for January 1600 noted that:

> the Bedells of the cittie doe this day complayne that rogishes boys and beg-gers escape from them and runn into the liberties of Christes Churche [the cathedral] wher they are harbored and not punished and in the eveninges they goe abroade in the cittie begging.[64]

Children such as these were clearly in the minds of Thomas Anguish and Robert Baron, who made provision for the foundation of the boys' and girls' hospitals in 1621 and 1650 respectively. Anguish, in particular, referred to his 'compassion and great pitty' for the young and poor children, 'borne and brought up in this City ... and specially such as for want lye in the streets ... whereby many of them fall into great and grievous diseases and lamenes, as that they are fitting for no profession ever after'.[65]

Charitable bequests of this kind were as vital as they had been in the medieval period to keep a perceived social problem within reasonable bounds. All classes of society made contributions, but those of the wealthy were of prime importance if only by virtue of their size. In 1619, for example, Henry Fawcett, a Norwich woollen merchant and alderman, donated £1395 for good works, including an outright gift of £94 to the poor of Nor-wich, as well as £40 for the Dutch and Walloon communities to buy coal for their own most disadvantaged members in winter. A further £40 was to be advanced each winter to any local entrepreneur who could provide work for poor unemployed masons in the local 'stone mines'. And £360 went into a loan chest, most of which was earmarked for up to thirty poor worsted weavers, with £30 for distribution among six needy dornix weavers, £20 among shoemakers and £10 among poor smiths.[66] The fact that security was demanded for loans of this sort in virtually every case meant, inevitably, that they were of little use to the destitute. None the less, these arrangements took some of the weight from the shoulders of the city fathers, and thus played a valuable role in the system of poor relief for deserving artisans.

Vagrancy was by no means the only problem to come before the mayor's court. In 1570, for example, the Norwich justices dealt with cases of

adultery, disobedient apprentices, assault, begging, breaches of craft regulations, counterfeit passports, misbehaviour by civic officials, debt,
disturbance of the peace, offences by victuallers and brewers, uttering of
seditious words, scolds, theft and unlawful games. They also arbitrated in
quarrels between citizens.[67] Sixty years later, the authorities proved especially intolerant of drunkenness and swearing but, these offences apart,
they were still preoccupied, in all essentials, with the same problems as
their Elizabethan forebears. Offenders were usually sentenced to be fined
or whipped, ducked or put in the cage for scolding, or paraded around the
market place for immorality.[68] The responsibilities of the mayor and his
fellow justices were not confined to their twice-weekly appearances at the
mayor's court. They were also required to preside at quarter sessions in
October, January, early spring and midsummer, with the assistance of the
recorder, steward, coroner and clerk of the peace. The most prevalent
offence, by far, to be tried in this particular court was felony. Indeed, all
but four of the 312 cases brought before the Norwich sessions in the Elizabethan era fell into that category. It was an offence which covered larceny
in all its many permutations, from stealing a purse with a few shillings in
it to the theft of horses and sheep. From a modern perspective, sentencing
appears inconsistent, although it often reflected the value of the items
involved. One man was hanged for stealing a sword, another for cutting a
purse with 12s. 2d. in it. Others were whipped for pilfering articles as
diverse as a coat, a piece of woollen yarn, brass pots, cloaks, small sums of
money, linen, prunes and raisins (then considerably more exotic than they
are today). In 1580, the theft of a gelding incurred the death penalty, yet at
the same sessions thieves who had made off with ewes and lambs escaped
with a whipping in the market place.[69]

Occasionally, prisoners indicted on a charge of felony refused to answer
the charge and were sentenced to the customary punishment of 'peine forte
et dure', being provided with stale bread and stagnant water on alternate
days while successively heavy weights were placed upon their chests, slowly
crushing them to death. Two examples of this occurred in Norwich, one in
1566, the other during James I's reign. Yet, in one respect at least, society
was more tolerant of violence than might be expected. As had been the case
in the later middle ages, prosecutions for murder were relatively few and
far between in Elizabethan Norwich, three of the four persons so charged
being hanged, the other acquitted. With the exception of the Appleyard
conspiracy, treason was rarer still. A single offender, indicted at the
Norwich sessions on 29 March 1592, was hanged, drawn and quartered on
being found guilty. On balance, the civic authorities were relatively lenient
for the times. One hundred and thirty-eight, or just over 44 per cent, of the

312 cases examined at the quarter sessions during Elizabeth's reign ended in an acquittal. Hangings were comparatively rare: no more than forty-nine, or 16 per cent, of people indicted actually suffered the ultimate penalty – rather fewer in number than the fifty-eight individuals who claimed benefit of clergy and escaped capital punishment because of their cloth.[70]

Although the sessions were primarily a judicial occasion, the justices often seized the opportunity to discharge the wider responsibilities imposed on them by the law.[71] These included fixing wage rates, arranging for the repair of bridges, licensing taverns, indenturing apprentices, enforcing the poor laws and awarding pensions to maimed soldiers. Tippling (that is selling alcohol) was commonplace: the 142 places licensed for the consumption of strong drink in 1651, for example, were owned by members of no fewer than thirty-eight different trades. Keeping an alehouse was a popular by-employment (as, of course, was brewing) and twenty years later the number had risen to 243.

As well as maintaining law and order in the city, the mayor's court, like the quarter sessions, was responsible for the general welfare of the citizens of Norwich. Poor relief, the regulation of prices and food standards, the provision of corn in time of dearth and the implementation of sanitary measures were also vitally important issues and never more so than in time of plague. The Norwich citizens were well acquainted with this phenomenon.[72] From its re-emergence in the middle years of the sixteenth century until its final disappearance in 1666, plague remained a living memory. It had struck in a virulent form in both 1544–45 and 1555–56, being followed on the latter occasion by an influenza epidemic which itself swept away half of the city's ruling body as well as large numbers of its lesser citizens. In every decade from the 1580s onwards, the mayor's court had to make provision for the victims of pestilence. Severe attacks of bubonic plague occurred in 1579–80, 1584–5, 1589–92, 1625–6, 1636–8 and 1665–6, but lesser ones regularly punctuated the intervening periods. That of 1579 was almost as serious for Norwich as the original onslaught of the Black Death in 1349, exterminating more than 5000 people, or possibly as much as 40 per cent of the population. At least 3500 people perished in the subsequent Elizabethan outbreaks, and almost as many again in both 1603–4 and 1625–6. For more than a century, then, scarcely a single decade passed without some recurrence. Indeed, its final disappearance in 1666 was preceded by the deaths of more than 2500 individuals in a single year.[73]

The Norwich authorities could do little to counter the onslaught in 1579, other than curtailing the movement of cloth, forbidding the victims to leave their houses for six weeks and providing them with money for their sustenance. Aldermen were expected to contribute 20s. each, past and

present sheriffs 13s. 4d., and the common councillors lesser sums, according to their status.[74] These rudimentary quarantine measures were of little
use during what was to prove the worst of the sixteenth-century outbreaks,
but the Norwich authorities were at least better prepared for subsequent
attacks. At the first suggestion of plague, the aldermen were required to
acquaint themselves with the parishes and houses affected. Bearers,
gravediggers and searchers were given wages for the duration of the outbreak, and were forbidden to mix with the public without a distinguishing
mark on their clothing or a red wand in their hands. The houses of the
afflicted were nailed up, suitable marks were placed on them, and watch-
men posted outside. The period of quarantine varied. In 1637, the mayor's
court agreed that it should last six weeks, but this could be waived if the
suspect was 'wary not to put himself unnecessarily into company'.[75]

All the measures discussed so far required regular and adequate funds,
which were generally forthcoming, even if, on occasion, the mayor had to
resort to threats of imprisonment in the face of resistance.[76] In contrast to
other English cities of comparable size, Norwich was served by two major
financial bodies, organised by the chamberlains and the clavors respectively. The chamberlains were responsible for normal day-to-day
disbursements, recording receipts as well as expenditure, and paying workmen weekly from a designated budget. The clavors, four of whom were
appointed each year, took charge of surplus revenues and duly accounted
for extraordinary receipts and expenditure.[77] Whereas the chamberlains
almost invariably overspent during the sixteenth century, if not thereafter,
the clavors rarely sustained a loss. They were, indeed, normally in a position to bolster the reserves of their colleagues and, if necessary, the other
semi-official funding bodies operating in Norwich.

From the chamberlains' point of view, the financial history of the city
can be described as one of impecuniousness in the sixteenth century and
of relative prosperity in the seventeenth. Deficits were, however, seldom
large and could usually be met by the clavors, who, in return, received
whatever surplus funds became available. While the actual sums of money
involved inevitably increased during the prolonged price inflation under
the Tudors and early Stuarts, the sources of revenue and the areas of
expenditure remained much the same throughout the whole of our period.
Rents from city property provided much of this income, while salaries and
the cost of repairs accounted for the bulk of expenditure. The New Mills
constructed on the Wensum as it flowed into Norwich from the north
west were especially profitable. Their 'newness' had, in fact, rather worn
off since the fifteenth century; but a hundred years after their original

purchase they were still providing Norwich with the respectable sum of £10 a year. Thereafter, partly in response to galloping inflation, the rental income paid by the miller rose steadily in value. It had quadrupled by 1535, increased by a further 50 per cent five years later, and reached just over £53 by the early 1560s, by which date all the local bakers were obliged to grind their corn there. For the next quarter of a century the rent remained stable. It then jumped to £95 in 1588, and had reached £120 before the beginning of James I's reign, a fourfold increase in a period of some seventy years. Subsequent leases took the rent for the mills to £160 a year in 1615 and to an all-time high of £212 in 1625. Thereafter there was a gradual decline in revenue, the rent finally settling at £170 a year in 1655. Yet water mills proved costly to maintain, and Norwich's were not quite as profitable as they appeared on paper. At an assembly meeting held on 16 November 1562, for example, it was noted that the New Mills and Blackfriars bridge were 'in decay and required moche costes'. Shortly afterwards £116 was spent on the mills alone. Twenty-five years later, when the rent had almost doubled, further repairs cost £169, and smaller sums were expended at regular intervals throughout the period. Nevertheless, despite the outlay on fabric and machinery, revenue from the New Mills greatly exceeded the sums spent on them. The available accounts for Elizabeth's reign alone show that in a period of thirty-five years the city obtained £2412 in rents from this source and spent hardly more than £348 on repairs. This was undoubtedly the greatest single source of civic income.[78]

As is the case today, official salaries accounted for much of the corporation's expenditure, rising from £45 in 1531 to a peak of £399 during the early seventeenth century. The annual wage bill then fell slightly to £385 in 1646, thereafter hovering around £345. In part, this reflected the steady rise in prices; yet there had also been a corresponding increase in the number of people employed. The mayor's salary, for instance, rose from the £20 a year paid during Henry VIII's reign to the £100 allocated under Queen Elizabeth. The swordbearer, who initially earned 10s., was paid £3 6s. 8d. in 1600 and as much as £20 in 1675. The growing number of officials is, perhaps, of greater significance than the salaries, which in some cases barely kept pace with inflation. In 1531, the chamberlain accounted for his own fee and those of the mayor, the sheriffs, the recorder, the common clerk, the swordbearer, the waits, the clerk of the market, two mayor's servants and three men 'learned in the law'. By 1600, the payroll had expanded to thirty and by 1657 to thirty-five. Indeed, by 1675, a combination of rising salaries and expanding bureaucracy had produced a bill which bore comparison with the entire annual civic budget of a century earlier.[79]

Although salaries and fees were obviously a major item of expenditure, the cost of repairs was no less important, frequently accounting for half, and occasionally more than half, of the city's total outgoings. The upkeep of the common hall, the former home of the Blackfriars, consumed more than £70 in 1562, a further £44 three years later, and smaller sums, often between £20 and £30, throughout the entire period. Even so, the steady increase in rents from this property, which had reached £57 by 1660, still made it a worthwhile purchase. Possibly stimulated by the relative failure of the defences during Kett's Rebellion in 1549, the corporation also spent heavily on Norwich's walls and gates. Every year the Elizabethan chamber-lains made some reference to a section of the walls being repaired, often at great expense. In 1558 and 1580, for example, the bill came to £43. In 1585, the gates alone cost Norwich more than £74 to maintain; and in the fol-lowing decade sums in the region of £50 and £67 respectively were set aside for this purpose. It was the responsibility of the mayor to decide when such work was necessary, as he did in 1567, when the walls were said to be in such a ruinous state that £20 had to be spent on them annually for the next seven years.[80] From time to time, additional expenses were sanctioned, mainly reflecting the demands of the moment. The chamberlains invari-ably held office for a number of years, thereby gaining valuable experience, not least in dealing with unexpected crises and calls on the budget. Since most of these men and their colleagues were the product of local school-ing, it is worth examining in greater depth how they set out to train future generations of citizens.

The city's practical commitment to the education of the poor is revealed in the 1589 occupational census, which records the presence of nine school-masters in Norwich, most of whom probably taught at a fairly basic level.[81] The city's clergy also offered tuition to their parishioners. Matthew Ston-ham, the vicar of St Stephen's, regularly sent more pupils to Gonville and Caius College, Cambridge, during the first decades of the seventeenth cen-tury than did Norwich School itself. Stonham, a local man, born in the parish of St Michael Coslany, was himself a graduate of this college, obtain-ing his MA in 1595 and becoming vicar of St Stephen's in 1602.[82] By then, he had begun his career as a schoolmaster, owning what was described as a private school, whence five pupils were despatched to Cambridge during the first ten years of the seventeenth century. In the next three decades, nineteen, thirty-three and twenty-nine pupils respectively followed in their footsteps, making a grand total of eighty-six over a period of thirty-five years.

The corporation of Norwich was mainly concerned with its own grammar school. The old episcopal school had come into the city's hands in 1538, following a petition to Henry VIII for possession of the recently confiscated Blackfriars, where, among other things, the corporation proposed 'to fynd a perpetual free-scole therein for the good erudicion and education of yought in lernyng and vertue'. The school was housed in the former friary during the early 1540s, being merged, in 1547, with the hospital of St Giles, which the city then recovered from the crown. A master and usher were appointed, the former at a handsome salary of £10 and the latter at slightly less. Suitable accommodation was also provided for both tutors. The sack of the hospital by Kett's rebels two years later put paid to any plans for a fully integrated system of education and poor relief in one place, and the school moved shortly afterwards to Bishop Salmon's chantry chapel in the cathedral precinct, which it still occupies.[83] Here the two teachers took charge of a hundred children for forty-eight weeks of the year, during which they worked for between nine and ten hours daily, official holidays being limited to two periods of sixteen and twelve days respectively. According to rules established in the 1550s and 1560s, the headmaster was expected to be a university graduate, unhampered by any other living, and of 'sound religion' with a good knowledge of both Latin and Greek. His responsibilities extended to teaching the three upper forms not only 'good lytterature' but also good manners, which were deemed a fundamental part of any decent sixteenth-century education. The usher, himself an accomplished Latinist, coached the three lower forms, while also performing a number of more menial functions. Whatever hopes the corporation may have had about fostering the education of the poor, the new grammar school was in fact highly selective. Pupils were admitted at the discretion of the headmaster upon payment of a modest registration fee. Their parents had to provide them with pens, ink, paper, books and candles for work during the winter months. Any boy who proved incapable of learning was to be promptly removed, as were absentees who missed much more than a fortnight's schooling in any one year. Discipline was clearly deemed to be a potential problem, and parents had to accept a tough regime of corporal punishment. Particular care was taken to preserve the headmaster's dignity, four of the strongest boys being designated to restrain those whom he singled out for a flogging.[84]

The books to be used by the upper school were recommended by the headmaster, but the city authorities specified what they considered suitable for the juniors. First and second year pupils concentrated upon grammar and extending their vocabulary. By the end of the third year, when they were nine or ten years old, boys were expected to have a good working knowledge of both Greek and Latin. Thus, when they passed to the upper school, a considerable portion of their time could be spent in reading classical authors in accordance with the best tenets of the new humanist learning. Scant information about individual pupils survives for this period, but the names of many of the city's aldermen and their sons do appear in the school's early records. It seems therefore that Norwich School may have played a similar role to Bury St Edmunds grammar school, a boarding establishment which catered across the social spectrum for the sons of affluent tradesman as well as scions of the lesser nobility. It sent many of its wealthier pupils to university, some entering the church, others returning home ready to serve as civic officials.[85] University scholarships were certainly available in Norwich. In 1567, for example, Archbishop Parker, the quintessential local boy made good, offered the city £200 to furnish an annuity of £10 to the master and fellows of Bennett (Corpus Christi) College, Cambridge, if they undertook to receive three scholars nominated by the mayor and aldermen. The scholars were themselves to have 53s. 4d. a year, plus 'chamber wasshing, barbor and bedying freely' from the same generous endowment. Aged between fourteen and twenty, they were expected to spend three years in Cambridge reading for the degree of BA and, if appropriate, another three studying divinity. In 1569, Parker extended his scheme by donating a further £200 to fund four scholars and a 'Norwich fellow', who would be responsible for teaching them.[86] Several of the leading aldermanic families were represented among those chosen, the names of Aldrich, Willan, Davy, Aspinall, Anguish, Stile and Quash, for instance, appearing as scholars, and those of Fletcher, Bate, Willan and Anguish as fellows. Undoubtedly, the most famous of Norwich School's 'old boys' in this period was Edward Coke, recorder of Norwich from 1587 to 1592, MP for the county of Norfolk in 1592 and 1625, and chief justice of the common pleas and King's Bench in the seventeenth century.[87]

Throughout this period, Norwich School prospered as did the teachers. The headmaster's salary had doubled by the end of Elizabeth's reign, reaching almost £27 a year, while that of the usher rose at a similar rate. Long service was not uncommon. The puritan, Stephen Lymbert, remained as headmaster for thirty-five years, dying in 1589 'full of dayes and of comfort in the mulitude and proficiencie of his scholars'. One of the ushers, Myles Moore (d. 1619), stayed for forty-five years, before retiring as an almsman to St Giles's hospital.[88] John Buck, another of the masters, deserves special mention in any history of early modern Norwich, being responsible for the verses which encapsulate so many of the pious sentiments described in this chapter:

> Prouyde for the poore that Impotennte bee
> As Charryte maye moue yow theire nede when ye see.

For who so the hungrie and thirstie shall feede
God will rewarde him, seven follde for his deede.
Cause yoothe to be trayned and seasoned in Tyme
In vertew and Labour from synne vice and Cryme.
But when men be Careles and soffer yowthe stylle
The Cyttie ys plaged in wreke of soche eavelle.[89]

Composed by Buck for the inauguration of the new mayor, Augustine Steward, in 1556, this pageant was performed outside the church of St Peter Hungate, near the school, and almost certainly drew upon the talents of the pupils, who regularly trod the boards on such occasions. The infinitely more daunting task of welcoming Queen Elizabeth, on her state visit to Norwich in 1578, also fell to Stephen Lymbert, who produced an accomplished oration in Latin, with a smattering of Greek. The queen, herself no mean classicist, pronounced it 'the best that euer I heard', and congratulated him warmly on his performance.[90]

Despite intermittent challenges, not least those caused by the unending problems of poverty and vagrancy, by the time of the Restoration commentators were unanimous in their praise of the city's size and appearance. Norwich had become far more cosmopolitan than its early Tudor counterpart. A winter season was well established, with theatres, shows and assemblies which attracted the surrounding gentry, even if few of them continued to maintain a town house there. The summer assizes provided the occasion for similar activities, while for the less wealthy there was the mayor's inauguration (for which Lymbert composed his poem), popular entertainments of various kinds and even the county elections, which brought in droves of people from outside the city with money to spend. Professional services were increasingly available, as was a money market for those who chose to take advantage of its facilities.[91] In sum, Norwich approached the closing years of the seventeenth century as it had begun the sixteenth: it was, quite simply, the largest and wealthiest provincial town in England. From the perspective of the ruling elite, it seemed well governed and well organised. It had weathered crises; it had successfully, if slowly and rather painfully, absorbed a large influx of foreign refugees; and, in terms of poor relief schemes, it had provided urban leadership on a national, even international stage. By 1700, therefore, Norwich had every reason to look forward to a century of continuing prosperity.

3

Inhabitants

Paul Griffiths

A table [is] to be made and sett upp in the bowlynge alley of the names
of such as have ben comitted unto Bridewell for hauntyng that place.

Ruling of the mayor's court, 1617[1]

When things seemed bleak in 1570, as begging 'crewes' camped 'at everie
mans dore', Norwich's rulers started to count and number Norvicians.[2]
The resulting Census of the Poor is a sacred scroll for historians of human
suffering. One by one, it takes us inside shabby dwellings, giving us snap-
shots of afflictions and the little expedients through which the needy tried
to scratch a living. The census is raw data for us over four centuries on,
though it was a working document for its commissioners in the Norwich
guildhall, who now had a stack of information at their fingertips.[3] It
revealed the size and shape of problems previously perceived, and it was a
starting point for the social welfare scheme that followed. The 'booke for
the order of the poore' was 'openlye redd' and passed with full 'force and
effecte' by the Assembly in June 1571, and it was 'ratefyed' exactly twelve
months later.[4] As we have just seen Norwich's 'poore booke' was a blueprint for similar schemes across the land, and soon after it was drafted the
city's trained administrators were being headhunted by other corporations
to help them to cope in these testing times.[5]

This was not the first occasion on which Norvicians had been numbered.
Households had been added up as recently as 1563 by the ecclesiastical
authorities.[6] But the Census of the Poor was an arithmetical and investiga-
tive high-water mark. The counting was not simply triggered by panics
about Catholic plotting in the fall-out from the Northern Earls' conspiracy
(1569), as others seem to suspect. This whisper of sedition is not even mentioned in the narrative of complaint in which the civic leaders listed their
reasons for striking back at the unhealthy poverty and clutter that was both
an eyesore and a menace. Heading their concerns were 'strange' begging
'crewes', jobless drones, 'brute' nomads, time-wasters who drained house-
keeping budgets in seedy pubs, 'harlots' who lacked masters or lawful

work, children who were trained up in idleness through grabbing hand-outs, the pox and 'uncurable diseases' that coursed through Norwich in a corrupt flow, crippling need, a resource squeeze (a shortfall in poor rate collections) and administrative blunders and weak spots. The governors were at the end of their tethers. Disorder was 'daylie ... seene' to be 'nowe of late ... growen to the full', they moaned in 1571. This emphasis on a present peak in troubles is striking. It was a call to action and order.[7] And problems had been building up since 1560 when more and more thieves and vagrants were prosecuted.[8]

Just like welfare reform, a census was commonly conducted in troubled times.[9] Now, and later on in this century and the next one, governors claimed that their policy-formation was rooted in current crisis, raw experience and first-hand observation. On the eve of the census, they mingled medical, moral and environmental concerns with alarms about law and order in a sweeping indictment of a city in distress. The messy trail of 'over-gorged' beggars on the streets 'might be followed', they said, 'by the sight' of 'pottage, breade, meate and drinke which they spoiled verie volup-tuously', and the 'verie dunge lefte most fylthelye' that 'declared their filthie disposicion'. A recurring rant against excess linked begging and bingeing with icy indifference ('theis brute people excessivelye gyven to feedinge' squandered God's 'good gyftes' by 'ther excessyve disorder'). Making mock of civic and civil standards, these beggars did not care about work, conduct, clothes, cold, cleanliness, cures, or that 'their fleshe was eaten with vermyne', pox and 'other corrupt diseases' which spread like wildfire. An inevitable sequence of cause and effect linked poverty, idleness, sickness and crime in a single perception; like toppling dominoes, one followed another, 'to the great perill both of their bodies and soules'. Worse still, a generational cycle of contamination suggested a grey future; children were 'altogether brought upp in ydlenesse', and would most certainly end in trouble or even on the gallows.[10]

These concerns were real enough, and they were for the most part a con-tinuation of ones already current in the years leading up to the census. A clutch of by-laws was passed in 1570 reflecting similar perceptions and anx-ieties to those that loomed large in the civic texts explaining Norwich's landmark social policies after the census. 'An Acte for Reformacon of Great Hose' grouped 'monsterous fasshions', theft, idleness and excess in a sin-gle analysis of 'greate dysorder', while 'An Acte for Makyng Cleane the Stretes' was aimed at the dirt, dust, dunghills and noisome drains that lit-tered the landscape. Nor were feelings of vulnerability and a dwindling sense of civic prestige soothed by 'the greate number of reded and thacked houses' or a recent spate of 'casualties and mischaunces by fyer'. With this in mind, 'An Acte ageynste the Reding of Howses' was then tabulated to boost fire-fighting measures and resources. Warmth, safety, dress and disgusting dirt were points of tension in the busy months of policy-making in the next year, as were drinking, late walking at night and 'maydens' who lived in suspicious solitude the subjects of orders around this time.[11] The impact of plots mattered most with regard to the flocks of foreigners who had settled in the city. Privy watches were instructed to put a stop to trouble-causers and rumour-mills; steps were taken to smooth relations between citizens and 'strangers'; while 'the names and faculties' of these 'strangers' were listed in a book, and rushed to the queen's ministers.[12] This was a scare about shady foreigners rather than the poor (though a decade earlier Nicholas Colman told the mayor's court about one of his dreams in which fire-raising 'strangers' dressed in 'beggars clokes' set the city alight).[13] Consequently, while this panic might have been a catalyst for the census, it cannot possibly explain the many-sided, intricate format of 'the order of the poore'. Bit by bit the policy think-tanks put together a scheme that was based on the diagnosis of particular problems stretching back to at least the mid 1550s, when a batch of 'Orders to be hadde for the Poore' had been drawn up.[14] Policies and perceptions were therefore the outcome of a couple of decades of hands-on experience and observation.

The census revealed a hodge-podge of circumstances in which the poor struggled to keep their heads above water. Assembled by house-to-house visits and doorstep interviews, the bulky files informed policy makers about the causes, conditions and consequences of poverty and sickness, recorded by ward and parish.[15] This working archive of the daily ordeals of the feckless, luckless and rootless poor was quickly put to use. It was a register of need and deficiency; of people who lacked work, spouses, parents, limbs, sight, speech, hearing and the few pennies that could make a difference between sinking or swimming. The 'syklye', 'veri syk', 'sore', 'croked', 'lame' and 'lunatick' crammed into the poorer parishes on the city's edges. Here, too, work was hard to come by. As we move out from the plusher centre, we come across more split and 'unorthodox' families where mothers or children were breadwinners, and whole families turned to begging. Paupers whose bond was common need shared rooms and costs, and men spent long and lazy days with little to do. On top of this, it was plain that work was not always enough to keep people on the right side of the law. Rose Fidemund (aged twenty-nine), who had trekked to the city four years ago from the 'west contre' to live with her brother ('nott in worke') and his wife (a working spinner), was said to be 'a gressemayde that spyn webbynge' and a 'harlott'. A carpenter's maid (aged thirty) was likewise 'suspected of evell rule', known to 'have bene a pycker' (thief), and to be hindered by 'a dyseas in hyr legg'. The census showed the shortcomings of existing policies, and that hospitals did not always do a good job; once they were discharged, some people fell back into the quicksand of poverty or chronic ill health. These revelations called for fresh thinking, especially when they cast light on topsy-turvy households in which women and children put bread on the table. From the standpoint of the city's patriarchy, another flaw was the large number of apparently 'idle' young layabouts who stayed at home (ages were supplied), out of service and, by implication, control. Yet another was the series of disclosures of the extent and circumstances of female offending. The counting turned up an uncomfortable number of 'harlotes', sinning singlewomen, 'grasse wenches' pregnant with 'base' children, and women who drifted to the city like the the widow 'Alyce Lyve By Love' (aged forty), a lace weaver, who had just made the trip from Diss. Along with other seemingly self-sufficient women, 'Lyve By Love' let loose fears about the appropriate allocation of scarce work and the 'inevitably' shallow morals of women who lived without a father, husband or master.[16] This was not the first time that such concerns troubled the peace, the difference being that they were now caught on paper on a brand-new scale; moreover, some impression was actually given of individual circumstances through short biographies that were rarely more than a couple of sentences long.

What followed next was nothing less than a wholesale redrafting of social policy after the revelations of the census. Some old measures were fine-tuned and some new ones were put to the test. The city summed up the chief aims of the 'booke of orders' as being 'the better provision of the poore, punishmente of vacabonds, setting at worke the ydle and loyterers and expulcinge of stought and strange beggers, maintayning the indigent and nedye, and trayninge youth in work and learnynge to utterly prohibite open beggynge'.[17] The plan would not even get off the ground unless it had a sound financial base. To this end, weekly collections for the poor were doubled to fill the city's poverty chest. The haphazard flow of money to needy Norvicians had to cease. Laws against begging were quickly passed, as well as warnings to caring householders who were moved by 'foolysh pittie' to give a few pennies to any beggar who came knocking at their doors. From now on, the collection and distribution of charity would be tightly regulated by a central committee of four aldermen, each of whom had responsibility for a particular patch of the city. These 'commissioners for the viewe of the state of the poore' picked officers for the wards and the new Bridewell, established on the site of what had been St Paul's hospital. They also kept an eye on the budgets of each ward so that costs could be met. A 'working place' was opened up 'at the house called the Normans [Bridewell]' to put the shiftless poor to work. Two 'mete men' were chosen to be its 'wardens', and keep the books to make sure that they balanced but, just in case, all their accounts were also audited by the city. They worked closely with the Bridewell 'balie' (a resident governor), who took 'charge' of the day-to-day running of the 'howse'. Rooms were also set aside in the Great Hospital to keep 'twelve poore yonge children' from the street life of the slums that had dragged countless juveniles into a deep pit of immorality. They would be taught 'letters and other exercises', and the points of sound religion.

Back in each of the city's wards, 'two civill and experte men' were selected as deacons 'for the oversight of the poore'. They were key points of contact between the guildhall and the front-lines in the poorer parts of the city. Their tasks included keeping records of inhabitants, rootless vagrants and other trouble-makers, and a 'continuall eye' on any new-comers slipping into the city; passing on the names and numbers of the struggling poor, the workshy, parents lacking the means to cope with small children, 'bygge wenches or boyes' ready for service, and 'disordered per-sons to be ponisshed weeklye'; and ensuring that nobody was without work, unless they had a good excuse. Monthly searches kept the deacons on top of the situation. They were helped by a Bridewell 'survayer', who also made daily laps of the city to pick up any 'apte for Brydewell', and gather information on 'howe the workers in everie warde are ordered and occupied'. Teams of 'selecte women' were handpicked in each ward to tackle two pressing problems revealed by the census: wayward women and children. One of their jobs was to give lessons in 'letters' to pauper chil-dren. Another was to take in 'disordered' women to make sure that they were 'dryven to worke and lerne' until 'their handes be browght into such use and their bodies to such paynes' that 'labore and learning' would seem as natural to them as their former sluggish way of life. The new orders were pinned up in busy spots across the city where people gathered, and 'pub-lyshed' from the pulpits. Stiff penalties and warnings gave them added force: stubborn beggars would get 'sixe stripes with a whippe', select women could 'laye sharpe correccion' on their unruly charges, and steep fines were dished out to lax officers, including a whopping forty shillings penalty for slack deacons.[18]

This 'booke for the order of the poore' must have tightened links between the guildhall and even the furthest-flung suburb by establishing much better pipelines of communication that smoothed the flow of infor-mation in both directions. The guildhall and its committees worked with the wards through their agents on the spot (the aldermen), and by setting up tiers of accountability. The Bridewell was also more exactly positioned in this cross-city grid: the committal process from the wards was spelt out in clear terms, and a chain of command with the mayor at the top bound it securely to the city. As a result of this administrative spring-cleaning, Norwich now had better surveillance and data-gathering techniques to work with, and a sharper sense of its own social layout. Mental maps that pinpointed problems were redrawn after the census.

This civic arithmetic was put to use straight away. To some extent its value and that of the book of orders was judged on balance-sheets, for each was a cost-cutting exercise. The city's economic forecast looked gloomy in 1571, as the poor drained money like a drip-feed. The turnaround was quicker than anyone could have hoped. The new policy was judged to be an overnight success. The city reckoned that it saved the huge sum of £3118 and one farthing in its first year by the canny redirection of charity and schemes for employment. Not everybody was so sure that this approach was in the best interests of the poor. Uncertain about the new measures for gathering and spending the rates in summer 1571, Edmund Prycke was heard to say 'that they that are now collectors for the poor ... do not distribute the money they collect', and was dumped in prison.[19] But for the civic leaders the sparkling results were plain to see. 'Daylie' beggars with nothing but time to spare were now contributing to household budgets. 'Great comendacion' was lavished on the city from outside, and all at once the future seemed rosy. Better still, the disciplinary directives in the wards were already producing results. Bridewell is first mentioned in the mayor's court records in July 1571 when Joan Gedding was packed off there after being carted through the crowded market for 'mysrule'.[20] Very soon, ward-lists of 'those to go' or 'apte for brydewell' were made ready, and runaways, sex-offenders and other pests were locked up there. Payments for caring for the 'prisoners' were jotted down in the first Bridewell ledgers (1571–72). In the wards, checks were made on rowdy houses 'of evell rule' where 'harlots' roomed or 'light huswyfes' danced the night away with servants.

The select women were also getting on with their jobs. A steady stream of such 'harlots' and other dubious characters were put to work with them, including Cicely Brise, 'a grassewoman yt was with the duchman in the churchyarde'; Joan Ledbroke, 'a prestes wyfe', who was picked up for 'incontinenci'; and the 'triple harlott', Elizabeth Gray. These early reports (based on ward returns to update the files of city officials) also listed charity cases, and disclose a drive to push the young into service. The ages of the stay-at-home loafers were written down to authenticate the 'problems' raised by delinquent juveniles. More than ever before, the 'problem' of Norwich youth was highly visible and documented. A clear majority of those out of service proved to be young women, and this flagged a menace that would fox the authorities for many decades to come: single women who were perceived to stray outside the formal lines of authority. There is no doubt that the newly established powers of deacons and select women were tailor-made to deal with issues like these that were vividly revealed by the census. This was also true of the officers who policed street-life, such as the 'master' or 'warden of ye beggers', or the Bridewell 'balie,' who pocketed a few shillings for nabbing beggars 'yt went abegging in the assyses [assize] time'.[21]

A new system was up and running in Norwich, but these early bright hopes would not last for long. The Book of Orders did not offer a quick fix to problems that were already lodged deeply in the crust of the city. Just a few years after its unveiling, new precepts (1573–74) and orders for the poor (1576) were passed to firm up procedures for dealing with parish collections, weekly searches, straggling 'loiterers', the workshy, 'newcomers (being pore)', 'maydens (not in servis)', spendthrift tipplers, beggars who still tramped from door to door, the pox (before it got out of hand), and Bridewell's finances and house rules. A previous 'charge' to parish overseers bolstered the potential for surveillance and keeping track of problems: they were asked to supply regular information about the jobless and lazy, 'poore people' who sneaked out 'at unseasonable tymes in the night', noisy and sleazy alehouses, and the general availability, as well as theft, of fuel. It was also up to them to check that the poor were provided with work and the necessary materials. Police tactics were given a boost by a reward system for rounding up beggars who moved in and out of the city and labourers who pinched 'hedgestuff, pales, gates or other things whatsoever'. Those who tipped off the authorities got their bounty from the suspect's allocation of poor relief, which was automatically stopped for a week, or, if no such funds were at hand, the overseers had to pay informers a few pence out of 'extraordinary gifts or reliefe'.[22]

Such steps were ahead of their time. But Norwich, like all other cities, was a hostage to its fast-changing economic and environmental predicaments. A terrible plague struck the city in 1579, disrupting administrative systems, if only for a while. We are not even sure that the Book of Orders survived intact until the end of the decade. It was clear that entrenched problems would not conveniently disappear. 'Daylie compleynt' of round-the-clock tippling and of pub-landlords who smuggled suspicious stragglers into 'secret corners' were sharp reminders that all was not well in 1586. 'Dayly experyence' showed that begging at doorsteps was still a survival strategy for the poor in the following year.[23] The pace of change speeded up after 1600. Norwich's population more than doubled in the half-century after the census.[24] The Book of Orders had been designed before this boom and no prior plan, however pathbreaking, could cope with such high pressure. The cry in 1602 was that the 'number of the poore people' is 'greatly increased'. Two decades later, trade laws seemed old hat and lagging behind 'the change and alteracon of tymes'.[25] That said, only a few elements of the 1570s scheme were scrapped; the deacons and select women were victims of mounting unease about the legality of the committal process to Bridewell in 1588.[26] Other measures became part and parcel of civic and central government policies, even if they were modified over time. These enduring projects included local rates and collections, medical care, employment schemes, pauper service and Bridewell, though the costs were steep.[27]

Population surges resulted from the continual flow of migrants, and this restless motion, along with recurring hazards such as trade slumps, plague and grain shortages that could cripple the city, makes it hard to think of Norwich as a stable place. Sizeable cities are not trouble free; they always have growing pains. Norwich was a bustling place, not without danger. Its size and shape were swiftly changing, and the civic leaders knew this too; 'ii mappes of this citie' were hung in the 'counsell chamber' in 1584.[28] Making sense of this untidy sprawl and its various causes and consequences was a crunch issue in the new century. More counts took place, new maps were drawn and a modest library of records piled up in the guildhall.[29] There was little new about any of these tactics in either 1570 or 1620. But the scale and diversity of these seventeenth-century data-flows lift them to new levels. The stack of crime files, poor law papers, mortality bills, tax rolls, parish registers and trade logbooks ballooned. The mess and muddle of the city's startling growth were itemised in lists, registers and books. More numerate and statistical ways of managing the city developed over the century. The extent of this surveillance must not be exaggerated, but without doubt far more was known about people, places and problems than ever before. Much of this data-collection was simply routine, concentrating upon the regular recording of births, marriages and deaths in parish registers or, in a more urban mould, the bills of mortality that added up the weekly totals of plague fatalities. The size of the reserve army of able-bodied men was also noted in muster lists.[30] With such rough demographic measurements close at hand, the civic authorities were able to develop impressions of the scale of population growth and loss, perceptions of the urban mass that were also picked up through counts of strangers or recently arrived lodgers (known as 'inmates') who crammed into the dingy parts of the city.

Not for the first time, of course, information was jotted down in neat tables and columns in books that were kept for particular purposes. Books listing taxpayers, newly enrolled apprentices and freemen categorised by occupation were indispensable databases for the organisation of tax collections and trades, as well as being a handy profile of residence, wealth and work across the city. Lists of rules governing particular trades and occupations were also conveniently collected in the 'Tradesmens bookes of orders', just as the laws of the land, city and Dutch congregation were printed in books or in shortened versions hung in the guildhall.[31] The biggest bookkeeping task, however, was the regular levying, gathering and distribution of the poor rate, no minor administrative matter in England's second largest city, where poverty cut deeper after 1600. The regular updating of assessment books, collection books and 'books of the poor' made sure that there was just enough money in the coffers to run the 'poor law machine'. Tickets and tokens were used to show entitlement to civic goodwill, in a manner not unlike the visual displays of dependent status in the badges that were pinned to paupers' sleeves and shirts as a 'conysaunce' or stigma to put them in their place.[32] Quite clearly, the day-to-day working of the poor law was police business too. The poor law authorities collected money and information about background, character and environment. After all, doles were dished out to worthy paupers who behaved themselves well and had lived in Norwich for a certain amount of time (except when one-off payments were made to vagrants to put them on the road back home).

In other ways, too, information gathering was a highly useful law and order measure. The very acts of counting, classifying and describing nagging problems, like penny-pinching 'inmates', on paper can make them seem suddenly more manageable. A list is a start, and from it impressions of offenders and the circumstances of their offending might follow, and policy-making could be adjusted in the light of any new revelations. Up-to-date lists of licensed tipplers and innkeepers, for instance, helped to spot both licit and rowdy alehouses.[33] Along with other vital information for policing, these registers supplied handy insights into trouble spots with clusters of disorderly drinking dens. The spread of this rough trade and drunken socialising was yet another troubling feature of the bigger city. The rapid pace of these changes, the reiterated claim that they were happening right 'now' in front of the authorities' own 'eyes', made it necessary to understand their character and extent in order to soothe concerns about their suddenness and strangeness.

Information was also put in books so that the past history of suspects who ended up before the magistrates could be investigated. This may have been one use of 'the booke of bastardy' started in 1618, though naming fathers and establishing responsibility for child support would have been the top priorities.[34] But keeping track of criminals did lead to the decision in 1624 to begin a multi-volume A-Z listing of the prisoners charged at the city quarter sessions.[35] These long lists of names stretched to seven 'search-books' towards the close of the century. They were arranged with an index for easy use, and we can imagine clerks flicking through them during the trial of a remembered face in the dock. On occasion, we can even see the authorities working with different classes of records, moving between them, checking snippets of information, and even scribbling in the dates of previous court appearances if they came across them.[36] This sort of cross-referencing was entirely possible with the more systematic lists and finding aids of the seventeenth century. It might also explain why large numbers of recidivists were singled out in the records with tags like 'common' or 'old' offender. Such records were, moreover, used to keep an eye on the actions of officials, as well as offenders, and to smooth the legal process. 'Schedules and lists' of sessions business were compiled in 1643 to monitor crooked officers who stuffed their pockets with bribes; a 'noate of [sessions] indictments and presentments' was drafted in 1679, so that the justices could check on the outcome of earlier trials; and, in 1681, the constables were asked to hand a 'fairely written' up-to-date list of their ward presentments to one of the justices at least a week before the start of each sessions to speed up courtroom business.[37] Policing by records and numbers is a less noticed aspect of crime control in the sixteenth and seventeenth centuries. It was not yet a science, but good record-keeping and statistical spadework were valued for their contribution to a developing knowledge of crime and its environments. These records were not initially preserved for us to piece together the past, but as a working archive to help uneasy contemporaries cope with changes as and when they unsettled the city five centuries ago.

   The city was the sum of its parts, and one good way to get to know it better was to pick up information about social pressures or anything else on a ward by ward or parish by parish basis. To this end, the civic authorities commonly instigated 'searches' in these districts to assess the local impact of city-wide troubles, such as plague or the growing scourge of binge drinking. With this information under their belts, the topographies of poverty, sickness or crime, for example, were a little more distinct, and resources could be channelled to where the need was greatest. These searches sometimes targeted specific concerns, at other times they called for more general 'round-ups' of troublemakers. Several were special one-off inquiries; others followed a weekly or monthly timetable, usually until a further order decreed otherwise. Whatever its pattern, this foraging and detecting became essential to the steady growth of an information system and culture of surveillance in early modern Norwich. The number of such investigations picked up in the seventeenth century, a sure sign that the authorities were increasingly troubled by the challenges of swift growth as time passed. Weekly searches were ordered in Norwich parishes in 1600 to take stock of a string of disorders by characters who troubled both the peace and purse: most notably 'inmates or borders' with less than a full year's settled residence; 'maids or singlewomen' younger than forty who 'goe to thir owne hands' keeping 'chambers by themselves'; pregnant 'naughty packs' seeking 'to laye their bellies in this cytie'; workshy paupers wasting their time in bowling alleys and pubs; unlicensed tipplers letting 'lewd' loiterers drink at all hours of the day; landlords lodging 'ydle vagrant people' for a few pennies each week; and workmasters putting 'country journeymen' to work at sweatshop rates. Patience was running thin, judging by the size of the mammoth twenty shilling fine imposed for sheltering illicit 'inmates', and threats of whipping or a stay in Bridewell were used to tackle these messy situations. Questions were also asked about each one of these pests: 'How many naughty packs' were at large? 'What they be' that rented cheap rooms to passing strangers? Answers, written down in 'certificates', were dropped off at the guildhall to be processed. Names were collected and suspects were summoned to appear before the mayor's court as soon as possible. Not a moment was to be lost, and officers were warned that they risked fines of ten shillings for sloppy searching.[38]

Other large-scale round-ups and head-counts followed over the seventeenth century. Troubles did not go away, however, and just a few years after the start of these weekly searches the constables, with other parish officers, were told to file further reports on alehouses, 'newecomers', grubby lodging-houses, lazy children and the ubiquitous self-sufficient single women who should have been in service. A batch of orders about work, rest and play on the sabbath day was also to be implemented.[39] These same concerns and strategies were much in evidence right up until the end of the century. Information was requested about unlicensed pubs, shifty landlords, parasitic 'inmates', and young people out of service in 1679; and regular updates on parishes 'dayly fild with poore' were called for in 1687.[40] At other points in the century data was collected about drunks, forbidden games, breaches of the sabbath and skulking Catholics, amongst other nuisances, and counts of the poor continued as the city kept on getting bigger.[41] With the possible exception of vagrancy, nothing seems to have caused the authorities so much difficulty over the seventeenth century as single women living alone in rented rooms, out of sight and regulation, it seemed.[42] Like other ones, this particular 'problem' was associated with growth, sprawl, clutter, change and loose movement.

Perceptions of crime were modified in fast-growing cities such as Norwich at the turn of the seventeenth century. Like the misery of poverty, the

root causes of rising crime were located in the physical environment as well
as in the frailties of human character. Growth was very visible and could
to some extent be computed in the tallies of paupers, strangers, single
women and others. The scale of the problems facing the city, then, was
partly grasped through counting and numbering. The same documents
that we can now use as the basis of our own calculations and interpretations were used in exactly these ways by the authorities in early modern
Norwich. They tell us that corporate actions were based on first-hand
observation, sight, experience and thumbing through records. Information
moulded perceptions, policies and procedures, and gave rise to a better
understanding of topography, poverty and work cultures, for instance.
What else could these stacks of papers have done? Why else keep them in
better calendared sequences as time passed? Access to them may have been
limited four centuries ago, when only a chosen few were allowed to read
them, but they shaped the way the rulers of Norwich understood the civic
environment and dealt with issues of law and order. Otherwise, their sense
of the city might have been lost in its growth, or they might have been less
able to adapt to the changes going on around them at full steam.

Numbering was not new in sixteenth-century Norwich, but the city did
participate in a more general increase of surveillance, registration and the
alphabetical ordering of records evident across early modern Europe.[43] In
England, this resulted in part from the growing reach of the state and its
wider scope of activity, made explicit in bulging poor law files, orders to
keep up to date parish registers, and the 'statute bookes' that lined the
shelves of Norwich guildhall.[44] The amount of surveillance and catalogu-
ing (along with soaring litigation and heavier workloads for urban
authorities, especially after the 1601 Poor Law) raised concern for the care
and safety of records.[45] These sensitive files were locked up in 'great' chests
that were put in the guildhall treasury for safekeeping. Fees were paid for
cleaning and updating records, and checks were made to stay on top of this
growing pile of information. In 1609, for example, 'all the bookes and
recordes' in 'the clossett in the Guildhall' were listed 'in an inventory'.[46]
Secrecy went hand in hand with this enclosure of information. In 1568, on
the edge of the great flood of data that would begin in a couple of years, it
was ordered that meetings of the ruling elite in the 'councell chamber' were
'all wayes' to be 'done there in moste secret manner', with only the 'comon
clerke' in the room with them to take notes.[47] When doors closed and
everybody else had left the chamber, the civic leaders could get down to
the tough business of running the city. Only they saw the more sensitive
and delicate documents. The information that streamed into the guildhall
in growing bulk was processed and prepared for further action. The public

disclosure of information was highly selective and managed carefully through by-laws or set-pieces, such as the pronouncement of policy decisions in crowded market places. This protection and selective release of information was part and parcel of routine civic government. Norwich's rulers handled more numbers, lists and locks, with the result that they were necessarily more numerate in their approaches to conundrums of law and order. Helpful, too, were the different types of institutions and the uses to which they were put to sort and categorise the swiftly rising population of (mainly) poor people. They were yet another aspect of the information culture that was spreading more thickly across the city. They were places to extract, save and store information, as well as being main planks in the clutch of policies that encouraged counting and data-gathering on such a large scale.

In a margin of the City Assembly Book, next to an entry for 1571 telling us that 'a booke redye drawne for the order of the poore' was to be put in 'force' as soon as possible, the clerk has written 'The Boke for Brydewell'. It may be a slip-up, but it almost seems as if this single institution was being elevated in status to equal the grand plan for poverty itself. 'Brydewell' and 'the order of the poore' appear conflated or even interchangeable. 'Bridewell' is also written in large letters in one of the margins of the Mayor's Booke of the Poore, right next to the first list of its house rules.[48] It cannot be missed, even by somebody rushing through the book at top speed. 'Bridewell' sits prominently in the margins because it was a brand-new institution, and because its rules could be easily spotted on the page and acted on. It was, of course, never synonymous with the full-blown poverty scheme, but the clerk's little lapse (if that's what it was) nicely illustrates the greater role (or diversity) of institutions after the numbering of the poor in 1570. The city already had a very long history of institutional care for the sick,[49] but it seems to me that the scope of its institutions was getting bigger all the time, and that Bridewell was another response to the problems of urban growth. Poverty, sickness and crime were on the rise, and a range of institutional solutions was proposed to tackle these issues over time. Bridewell, a prison workhouse and cornerstone of social policy for several centuries to come, first opened its doors in 1571. Some modest accommodation for the insane followed shortly after, along with special hospitals for children (boys 1621 and girls 1650). As well as these newer additions to the city's institutional stock, the Great Hospital remained the centrepiece of care for the elderly in particular, while the lazar houses at the gates still catered for a variety of medical and moral conditions long after they stopped receiving lepers.[50]

This sounds like the making of a decent-sized framework of care and control. But its scale has been questioned.[51] Certainly, we need to be reminded of the limits of institutionalisation in this city and others up and down the land. We could count all Norwich's early modern hospitals on the fingers of two hands. A bed count would reveal provision in the order of one single bed for between 200 and 250 townspeople by the middle of the seventeenth century, while an inmate count in Bridewell would turn up equally dismal disparities. The number of Great Hospital patients in the seventeenth century ranged from a low of fifty-four (at its start) to ninety-five in 1665–66. The highest number of residents in the first half-century of the Boys' Hospital was nineteen in 1651–52, though this slumped to a steady dozen in the 1660s. Just a handful of girls (two or three) were looked after in the Girls' Hospital in its first few years.[52] Institutional space seems to have been sparse and in short supply. Yet, in matter of fact, this 'numbers-game' with its rigid ratios is just one part of the story, and a restrictive one for all that.

The impact of institutions went far beyond the sum total of beds. In the first place, they were usefully adapted to meet some of the needs and concerns of the growing city: what to do with children hanging about the streets, or women without fathers or husbands, for example, or how to engender the discipline of work and sound religion, and, of course, collect information. Bridewell and the hospitals were further sources of data for the civic authorities. They looked after their own in-house affairs, and also took part in searching, badging, licensing, counting and keeping records. Suspects picked up in searches were often dragged to Bridewell for at least an overnight stay before close questioning in the morning. Hospital and Bridewell staff sometimes passed on their specialist knowledge to the civic authorities when acting as witnesses, consulting others or getting involved in committee work. There were inevitable overlaps of personnel, resources and strategies not only with the civic authorities, but also between the various institutions dotted around the city, and this was an advantage when it came to pooling information.

These institutions worked hand in hand with parishes, communities and families. Skilled craftsmen needed labour and shopped around for raw materials at low prices; patients or prisoners were sent in by neighbours or families who sometimes settled their fees; healers with homes in the city took in patients at a price; while from time to time the costs of running institutions were eased by parish collections, charity baskets and individual gifts. The hospitals and Bridewell did not operate in isolation, and if anything their ties with the city and parishes tightened after 1600. We should see outdoor (parish-based) and indoor solutions to sickness, socialisation and soaring crime working side by side as part of the same plan, especially if we follow the most flexible definitions of institutions to cover apprenticeship, domestic service and the Poor Law.[53] Sick or pauper children and orphans, for example, did not always stay in one place, but were shuttled back and forth between hospitals as their illnesses took a different course or turn for the worse. At landmark stages in the life cycle some people could expect to move between hospitals and households. The last years of a few worthy pensioners were spent in the comfort and shelter of the Great Hospital or one of the almshouses. The age of fourteen or fifteen was a turning-point for pauper youths raised up in the Childrens' Hospital, when they were then put to service with citizen-craftsmen; many more made this major move from Bridewell. In such ways, the criss-crossing territories of the parish, household, hospital and mayor's court made up an institutional grid that stretched to all corners of the city. Even if most of them never stepped inside an institution, Norvicians grew up and old in a culture where the threat of Bridewell or the more comforting prospect of a hospital bed were ever present possibilities.

This last point brings to mind the cultural and mental impacts of Bridewell and the hospitals on townspeople, even though these responses were hardly ever described on paper. True enough, there were a few flashpoints, as when Francis Barton stormed into Bridewell and 'cut the work' of his wife, leaving nobody in any doubt about what he thought of her being locked up there. There were also a few careless quips, such as the one in 1613 when the bellman 'publiquely shouted' that 'yf any' were 'desirous to have their neckes broke yf they cam to Bridewell yt should be done'. He lost his job and bell for this rash prank, though he reminds us that bridewells could seem chilling and gloomy places.[54] This popular assumption was exploited in calculated ways when the courts warned trouble-makers that they would be slung in Bridewell unless they got back on the right track. 'Mere fear' of rough handling and back-breaking work in there was a coercive pressure commonly used, though impossible to quantify.[55] The civic elite were certain that 'the feare and terror of the house of Bridewell' alone caused the number of 'whoremasters, whores and vacabondes' to fall by nine-tenths not long after it first opened.[56] This was a psychological matter, and brand-new prisons or hospitals (even ones in existing buildings) altered both physical and mental landscapes for better or for worse, depending on personal viewpoints. For some, such as Francis Barton, Bridewell represented a most unwelcome trespass on touchy private and domestic matters. Apart from the inevitable grumbling of those whose lives were shaken by a spell there, some legal sharp shooters wondered whether its committal process was above board until changes were made in the late 1580s.[57] But the Bridewell was also a symbol of civic values and activism in testing times when solid lines of defence were necessary. Institutions spawned identities, as well as information. The possession of hospitals and bridewells sent signals that this was a city where authority, charity and pity were deeply rooted. In this sense they were small comforts and reassurances to be valued, and not just by the little ring of magistrates who ran the city, but by anybody else who felt uneasy about the harmful side-effects of the city's rapid growth. Civic-minded Norvicians liked to be associated with the glitter of Bridewell and the hospitals. They felt lucky to have them nearby working for the good of the city, and so they gave money, materials, time and other help quite freely.

The cultural glow or (from a different perspective) smack of institutions was felt in other ways too. Completely in keeping with civic ethics, paternal and domestic vocabularies provided the script for authority to function within the walls. The Great Hospital was known as 'Gods Howse' or 'the howse of the pore people'; the lazarhouse just outside St Augustine's gates was called 'the house of the pore'; and even Bridewell was described as a 'house'.[58] This domestic 'spin' on relations between staff, inmates and patients was meant to signify the possession of pastoral and pedagogic qualities. Just like a householder, it was hoped that Bridewell would turn its charges into sound and sober citizens, using a stick when necessary (the mayor was given the title of Bridewell's 'headmaster').[59] Not only this, one of Bridewell's heaviest case loads was cooling domestic disputes and patching up broken households, as when Martha Thornton refused point-blank 'to live with her husband' and threatened 'to leave her child in the street', or when Bryant Youngman left his family on the brink of 'perishing' in 1646.[60] The household, the linchpin of the social order (and the defining unit of place or residence for the census), was a natural rhetorical resource.[61]

The structuring language of the outside world was put to other uses too. It was the fond wish of the founder of the Girls' Hospital that it would be 'of great benefit to the cittie and comfort to the poore'.[62] The paternal dialogue between rich and poor was repeated in descriptions of patients and prisoners as 'the poor' or 'the poore people', most revealingly in guidelines about top-up relief payments to 'extraordinary poore people', as well as in others concerning health care and the distribution of clothes and bread rations.[63] This was much more than mere allusion to status, because it accommodated both differentiation and identification. Like the ruling rich, the staff had institutional authority on their side, with the head of house at the summit. Yet it was always intended that they would treat inmates fairly and with care, so long as they kept to the rules. And, as with society's high-ranking governors, there were marked limits to their powers, and a recognised route to follow if an inmate had good cause to complain about harsh treatment. Good practice counted for much and institutions were not left alone to run themselves.

Bridewell was called a 'house' or 'hospital', but was also dubbed a 'prison' (though mostly it was just plain Bridewell). This jumble of words should not mask its penal purpose. It gave a bed or straw to its inmates and put food on their table (at a cost), but it also punished them; and in fact we are less likely to see them being called 'the poor', though it did happen. More commonly, they were known as 'prisoners' who were locked up in a 'prison'.[64] Nor was this mere window-dressing. The idea of imprisonment as a tough corrective existed at this time. And, apart from fines, no other penalty was used so much to correct small-time offenders. No regular run of prisoner admission and discharge books survives today. So, with only patchy evidence to work from (mostly committal or release orders from the city's courts), we will never have a full picture of traffic in and out of Bridewell. For what it is worth, however, 1085 offenders are recorded as being sent there from the mayor's court in the seventy-five years after one Mrs Gedding became the first to make this trip in 1571. Movement was slow in the first three decades or so, but it soon speeded up. As few as sixty-four such sentences were recorded before 1600. This number leaped more than tenfold in the first four decades of the new century, and peaked between 1620 and 1640 when 640 petty offenders were locked up (59 per cent of the total tally). In some respects, imprisonment meant what it means today: confinement behind high walls, limits on communications with the outside world, lack of liberty and even use of restraint when necessary. The metal gadgets to restrict movement or aggravate punishment listed in Bridewell's inventories included 'blockes with shackles', 'pothookes', 'cheans for prysoners', 'manicles' and 'handcuffes', while iron bars blocked the windows.[65] Bridewell was not the only lock-up in Norwich. Scattered through the sources are references to 'the free pryson', 'the gaole of the citty', 'th'aldermans prison', the 'comon gaole in the markett place', the 'gaolehouse', the 'prison in' or 'under the Guildehall', 'the men's prison', 'the woman's pryson at the Guildehall' and, in 1588, the new 'cittie prysone' or 'comon gayle' in the east wing of the guildhall.[66] Elsewhere, physical restraint or loss of liberty kept the sick and others in locked spaces. Pesthouses were called 'the prison for infected persons', and payments were made for 'irons for the sicke howses' in the mid 1630s. Poor 'lazars' were banned from begging in the streets as late as 1633 and, as with the hospitals, runaways from the lazarhouses received a sharp dressing down from the magistrates. Nor was Bridewell the only institution to have a hand in policing the city. The Boys' Hospital, for example, paid a shilling towards a watchman's salary.[67]

Bridewell's inmates were mostly poor, more or less evenly split between the sexes (though exact ratios see-sawed over time), and likely to be misfits, unruly servants, rootless vagrants or anybody else whose antisocial acts fell within pliable categories such as idle, lewd or loose. In other cases, a hushed-up illegitimate birth or beer-guzzling householder upset the integrity and viability of the family, departing from the ideal domestic model. In such ways, Bridewell was called on when other institutions, such as the household, could not cope with their wayward outcasts. It was the last port of call in a domestic storm. Quite typical was Grace Newton's son, who was stuck in Bridewell after abusing his mother 'and leavinge his master's worke'; the 'very disordered' widow Alice Tuggs, who was locked up after all else failed because she could 'not be brought to live under government'; and Richard Wells, who 'often' ran away from his master, and 'as yet contineweth running'.[68] Bridewell was frequently filled up with such domestic pests. Even though it only opened its doors to petty offenders at first, the number of thieves sent in from quarter sessions after being branded 'convict', acquitted or simply suspected of felony, or who were found guilty of the lesser charge of petty theft, edged upwards after 1660, as it did in other places. Most were sentenced to one month of grinding hard labour, though longer stretches were not uncommon, as when John Gidding and Edward Bunn were 'acquited of felony' in 1635 but still sent to Bridewell for a year.[69] The lack of admission and discharge files means that another murky area is the length of time inmates spent there. What evidence we can pick up suggests that they were not just shunted in and out, one after another. Sentences varied, doubtless depending on the character of the suspect or the offence. Henry Gigges was locked up from sunrise to sunset for just one day in 1614, whereas perpetual recidivist, Margaret Utting, was put in a cell in 1598 'to dwell and remayne for ever'. Some inmates were only kept overnight, to shake them up a little. Others stayed for several weeks or months, or longer. A tearaway servant, Jeremy Beck, was given a six-month dose of hard work in 1646. Some mothers of illegitimate children were sentenced to one year terms, though nearly all of them were let out early.[70]

Nor were the other city prisons just holding places, keeping suspects safe behind bars until their day in court. Stacks of crimes were punished through custodial sentences in a place called 'prison', and they ranged from uttering spiteful libels to marrying off a daughter to an apprentice, or from leading a 'suspicious life' to making wisecracks at the expense of civic officials. Just as wide was the range of sentences: Nicholas Salter was locked up for three months in 1664 'for destroyinge a swanns egg', while Margaret Needham was put in prison 'for the rest of her natural life' for sticking steadfastly to her Catholicism and her 'hallowed' beads.[71] Some other sentences might seem on the short side to us, however, and the 'faint' impact of bridewells on their 'short-stay' inmates has indeed been assumed because of the limited amount of time people spent there.[72] Yet we should not make this calculation by today's standards when long sentences are so common as to pass almost unremarked, unless they seem unfair. One month or more of hard labour might have been a daunting prospect, enough to crush some offenders. Maybe these months seemed to stretch out into the dim and distant future. It is worth remembering that this was a culture not yet used to stiff (or soft) custodial sentences.

The other common title for Bridewell over this century or so was 'house of correction', a name that hints at heavy-handed discipline.[73] Whipping was called 'ye custome of ye house in such cases', as Robert Burton, a runaway apprentice with light fingers, dicovered to his cost. The number of lashes varied on a case by case basis, though 'six stripes' were most often ordered. To make sure that prisoners toed the line, Bridewell also had its own stocks, whipping posts and a 'chaire for unruly persons'; its 1660 inventory listed 'a whipping post with handstocks'.[74] Yet even if it was first and foremost a disciplinary structure, the wish that people would change there for the better was real enough. The sharpest legal mind of the early seventeenth century remarked that 'few are committed to the house of correction or working house, but they come out better', while the leading justices' handbook of the day recommended that the workshy should be despatched to such places, so that 'by labour and punishment of their bodies, their froward natures may be bridled, their evil minds bettered, and others by their example terrified'.[75] Backbreaking work and punishments were seen as mental corrections in this culture, not least because pain was a matter of the mind (turning thoughts with its spasms) as well as the body.[76] Work was a moral tonic. So, prisoners spent most of the day doing character-building work at Bridewell's own mills and looms, and maybe picked up a few extra pennies for cleaning out the vaults or some such dogsbody task. They were paid for their work, if only in kind (food and board), though it was hoped that the chief recompense would be calculated in clean thoughts or even in saved souls. The Bridewell authorities never lost this care for character. The language of personal reformation flowed freely there throughout the seventeenth century.[77] On top of work, a weekly round of preaching, visiting and catechising by a minister picked from a city parish was supposed to lift thoughts to higher planes of piety and self-scrutiny. Preachers pocketed four pounds a year for 'readynge prayers' and

testing catchumens in the early seventeenth century. The first set of
Bridewell accounts lists the purchase of a Bible 'to read to ye prisoners' and
'a boke of servyce'. Later ones record fees for 'a booke of Comon Prayers'.
The dreary tedium of a fifteen hour working day in summer (it was shorter
in winter) was lightened by meal breaks (thirty minutes) and a fifteen
minute pause for prayer. This, at least, was the blueprint for a brighter
future, one in which identities and moralities would be constructed in
better ways by solid work, sound religion and sharp correction.[78]

The lines dividing Bridewell and the hospitals were hazy. All of them
were disciplinary institutions of a sort. Work and religion, with their
potential to mould minds, were high priorities in the hospitals' timetables
too. Preachers were paid decent salaries for 'catechisinge', 'servinge and
ministeringe to the poore folkes in Gods Howse [the Great Hospital]' and
one of them did so for over two decades. As in the middle ages, this hospital also settled the salary of the 'visitor [chaplain] of the prysoners in the
Guildhall' (over five shillings was spent on a 'service booke for the prisoners' and 13s. 4d. on 'a great Bible'). The minister of St Edmund's parish
doubled up as the Childrens' Hospital preacher and was paid ten shillings
for a six-month stint, though longer connections were eventually built up
– Parson Ireland served in the post for nearly three decades, doing pastoral
duties. The turnover of teachers was similarly slow: John Browne taught
reading for two decades in the Boys' Hospital. The woman who ran spinning and knitting classes in the Girls' Hospital was supposed to be 'aged,
discreet [and] religious'.[79] We might expect that work would have a different part to play in a rest-home for the elderly, such as the Great Hospital,
where the ages of the old folks ranged from between sixty-one and eighty-
one.[80] But, as at Bridewell, in the Boys' and Girls' Hospitals it was
character-modelling with political overtones. In these places young people
were put into service to continue their socialisation and subordination
under the thumb of a master or mistress. The youngest child taken in by a
hospital was six, the oldest was thirteen. But, as we have seen, fifteen
marked a milestone, when one by one the 'children' were placed in work,
though a few of them were simply sent back to the parish 'from whence
they came', and a small group of 'poore' children were shipped across the
ocean to make a fresh start in 'Newe England'.[81]

All in all, there were few major commotions in the hospitals, just some
spats, and occasional smashed objects. A handful of boys were thrown out
for 'nastines', including John Baylie, who had clearly drained the magistrates' patience: 'he cannot be reclaimed', they moaned. They also
grumbled about the poor turn-out of boys in church on Sundays, and told
the keeper to pay for 'a man to take care' of them. Some of the Great

Hospital's widows crossed swords with the nurses, passing snide remarks or blocking their way, and there were rules to check verbal and physical violence and excessive drinking. But whirlwinds were few and far between.[82] It was a different state of affairs in Bridewell and the other prisons, and this should be no surprise. There were escape bids, some of them successful. One father snatched his son out of Bridewell. On another occasion it cost nearly three shillings to fix a wall knocked down by some prisoners. A pair of prisoners plotted to beat up the keeper and start a 'mutiny' in 1617. Others were caught helping themselves to hemp, or overheard muttering that they would set the prison on fire. Squabbles, threats and fist fights were not uncommon in the workshops and cells. Nor was it unknown for men and women to slip into bed together, though work on a new 'woman's chamber' was in full swing in 1619 to put a stop to such mingling, just as the Great Hospital had a 'womens chamber' or 'roome' at the opposite end of the building from the men's. Inmates, however, were not the only ones to rock the boat. Every now and then one of the staff got into trouble for fiddling fees, shirking or, less often, for harming somebody under his or her care.[83]

It is misleading to pin down the character of these institutions with a single description, such as 'therapeutic', 'rest care', or 'disciplinary'. Indeed, 'hospital' seems a strange title for the Bridewell or even, for that matter, a clutch of places that seem more like retirement homes for the needy elderly, or else training camps for children whose families lacked money to look after them. In part, this was the inevitable outcome of the overlaps between medical and moral cause and effect in policies and perceptions. These descriptive and explanatory categories were very fuzzy. So much so, that healing had moral dimensions, just as the root cause of sickness might be an impure thought or act. Nowhere is this better noticed than in the five lazar houses that ringed the city at its principal gates. Leper hospitals in their first colours, they were turned into places for the sick and disorderly poor of all ages over the sixteenth century.[84] We know next to nothing about how many people were bundled into them. But we do know that sick and crippled beggars were locked up there before the watershed census, and that their numbers continued to climb afterwards as the civic authorities took steps to tightly position the lazarhouses in their social programme. In this way, the once virtually independent lazarhouses became as much a civic institution as the Bridewell. As time passed, the city extended its grip, placing them under the authority of the mayor's court, spending more money on their upkeep, obtaining their titles to property, making keepers answerable to civic leaders through rules and rents, and applying civic perceptions of law and order to the criteria for admission.

Finally, in 1633, a quarter sessions ruling stripped keepers of the power to receive inmates without the prior consent of the mayor or aldermen, and took away once and for all the seals through which they claimed authority to do so. This swoop on the lazarhouses was largely the result of dwindling revenues and of a few keepers turning them into little fiefdoms or tippling houses on the side. By now, the civic authorities were sick and tired of pumping good money after bad; and watching some of the inmates begging up and down the streets was the final straw. The 'lazarhowse at St Stephens gates' was shut down in 1634 and, one by one, the rest were put to other uses or brought even more tightly within the civic fold and purse-strings.[85] As late as 1697, the mayor's court ordered the 'keeper of the lazar house' to let officers quartered in the city send sick soldiers there, 'for the convenience of curinge them'.[86]

Even though the lazarhouses drained money, they were a valuable and flexible resource. The grey area between medicine and morality was never better revealed than when paupers (mostly women) racked with pox were carried off to one of them for care. The pox was a moral and medical matter: evidence of smutty acts as well as a body-wrecking sickness. This association was backed up each time a 'harlot' was found 'with a spyce of ye pocks on hyr body'.[87] In matter of fact, pox patients were outnumbered by victims of 'dropsey', 'falling syknes', leg injuries and similar sicknesses. One woman was called 'lyperouse' in 1572. Others were simply diagnosed in general terms, such as 'deseased', 'fowle' or 'syck'. Both short-stay and long-stay patients were given bed and board in the lazarhouses. In 1617, Thomas Anguish left money in his will to put the 'distressed' with 'diseases thought incurable' in them, and they might have been a last resort for such chronic cases. The keepers were certainly obliged to provide long-term care for patients whose illnesses would not go away.[88] More frequent in the city cashbooks are payments to lodge poor 'wenches', widows, children and the helpless elderly, such as 'ould Clarke'. Many just stayed for a few days or weeks until something else could be done for them. Quite clearly, lazarhouses were used as temporary staging-posts for sick vagrants on their way home, resident paupers *en route* to another place of care and travelling soldiers down on their luck. A tiny child 'left in the town closse' in 1626 was also looked after in St Benet's lazarhouse at a cost of over five pounds.[89]

The versatility of the lazarhouses was one of their strengths. They were leading lights in both police work and health care, giving attention to bad behaviour and illness alike. In the case of the former, 'ii rogishe gyrles' were sent to St Benet's gates in 1600, and 'Besse of St George' followed them in the next year. The unlucky victims of crime were also cared for. A young girl who had been 'ravished' by a servant was comforted at one of 'the gates'.

If account books are a rough guide, peak use was made of the lazarhouses by the civic rulers in the decades around 1600. St Bennet's was most used, and the keeper was picking up weekly fees of 2s. 6d. for some patients.[90] As decades passed, however, the sort of cases assigned previously to the care of the lazarhouses were sent elsewhere. Pauper children were far more likely to end up in the Girls' or Boys' Hospital. It even seems that pesthouses took charge of some of these stragglers, lonely elderly and others in poor health. Nobody could then be sure that they would never be used again for plague victims, but right at the end of the century a young girl 'in a noysom condicon' was put in a pesthouse, along with 'a poor man' who was given one of the 'little houses at the pesthouse without St Augustines gate', and a poor widow who was 'sent to the poore house at St Benet Gate' ('pesthouse' is scribbled in the margin), so long as her parish would pay her costs.[91]

The lines dividing sickness and disorder were also wafer thin in the treatment of the insane. Payments appear in the Bridewell account books for work on a 'hows wherein the madd people bee putt' in 1586. That this small accommodation was made for the insane at such an early point, planned and paid for by the city, is worth our serious study. This 'hows' was in the Bridewell compound and the keeper had charge of it – another sign of the overlap between different disorders. We do not know how big it was or how long its 'distracted' inmates stayed there, though the city did provide bed and board for a 'lunetyke' minister for a handful of years. Apart from this small morsel, however, we have little else to go on, beside occasional references to the condition of the patients as they appeared to magistrates sitting in the mayor's court at the point of committal. They seemed 'crazy', 'very distracted', 'crased' or 'lunnaticke' to the city bigwigs. The 'disorderly' went one way to Bridewell; the 'distracted' took another path to the little 'hous' in the yard. But the distinguishing marks of each case are not clear. The magistrates 'thought [it] fitt' to 'secure' 'distracted' Thomas Cotterel in Bridewell, looking on as tears streamed down his son's face, so frightened was he that his father 'should fyre his house'. Disorder? Damage? Distraction? All three are present in one form or another.[92] Nor do we know in what state of mind its 'distracted' inmates left this tiny civic asylum, for that is what it was. The magistrates put their hands to the committal order, and sometimes reached into the city purse to pay lodging fees. More often, however, costs were settled by parishes, parents or other relatives of the hapless 'madde'. A 'paynter of St Symond's' was, for instance, given eight shillings to care for a 'dumbe women in her lunacye' in 1601.[93] When a 'madd' vagrant drifted aimlessly through the city, a civic officer would get a couple of shillings for taking her (it was nearly always her) back to her home in another place.[94] As in so many other cases, arrangements for tending the sick blended civic and communal resources, mixed indoor and outdoor solutions, and worked between as well as within the different institutions.

Margaret Pelling nicely emphasises the flexibility of these institutions, and produces examples of inmates being moved back and forth between different ones according to their needs.[95] Some rowdy patients were removed to Bridewell from the hospitals, while prisoners who fell sick might have gone in the other direction. More frequently, unruly young people were pushed into service in the hope that they would change for the better. On occasion, institutions pooled resources, settled the fees of an inmate packed off to another place, or even (in the case of the Great Hospital) made loans at cheap rates. The hospital also spent large sums of money sending its sick to the lazarhouses, including Richard Garrett who was comforted with 'physicke and surgerie' in St Bennet's at a cost of thirty shillings. The magistrates also dipped into Bridewell's funds to send 'diseased' prisoners there.[96] All in all, there was a moderate flow of traffic between Bridewell, the hospitals and the lazar houses. In such ways, there evolved a system of public health care in Norwich, one that worked in tandem with the parish community and that was extended over time. It did not necessarily regard institutional or community (family) care as separate. Quite the reverse, the city purse met the costs of much of the healing across this comprehensive medical grid: giving hand outs to the sick to help them to find a cure, paying fees or wages to surgeons, bone setters and home helpers and funding surgeons' pensions.[97]

Even though the authorities sometimes sent sick inmates to practitioners' homes for treatment, medical care was also provided inside institutions. As well as supplying warmth, water, washing, clothes, bedding, a decent diet and even Christmas cakes for the Boys' Hospital, Norwich's magistrates ensured that inmates and patients were entrusted to the care of physicians, surgeons, apothecaries and midwives. Bridewell's inmates were treated for leg sores, hand injuries, smallpox and other nasty ailments. Midwives looked after pregnant women, while apothecaries arrived armed with medicine.[98] The Great Hospital hired a barber, bonesetter and surgeon to care for its 'poore'. The surgeons there were kept busy by a couple of outbreaks of 'skurvye' in the first decade of the seventeenth century. An empiric named Elizabeth Willis was given forty shillings from the Boys' Hospital for tending to 'five boys' with 'scald heads'.[99] Many such payments are jotted down in the city records, not to mention others for tending the vagrant walking wounded.

Institutions in early modern Norwich were multi-purpose facilities, flexible and adaptable. Their numbers may not have been large, but their impact was far greater than we might initially suppose. They were part of a chain of care and order stretching from their doorsteps to the guildhall and the parishes. Being well known and highly visible, they were able to offer some sort of reassurance that the city was actively dealing with its disorders. And through close attention to discipline, labelling and diagnosis, they played a key role in the construction of civic identity and morality.

Institutions were not just pillars of civic prestige, worthy and valuable to the city's cause. Along with numbering people, places and problems, they supplied a means through which identities were continuously constructed. With a census the civic authorities could count and classify. The 1570 census (like later ones) located people in a parish and usually in a household, sometimes supplied ages, and nearly always mentioned an occupation or the lack of one. Not infrequently, a note of censure was added to place a character in another dimension of disorder. John Fyn was called 'an evell husbond'; the widow, Joan Hawne, was rounded on as a 'rank beger'; while another widow, Margaret Fen, seemed 'unruly,' and was shipped off to the hospital. In other cases a more sympathetic character snapshot was given: sixty-year-old Maud House was called 'a desolete thinge'. In still others, sickness was the cause of comment: Thomasin Peck was 'somewhat beside hyrselfe', Margaret Lamas was 'lame', while other sufferers appeared to be 'veri sycke', 'syklye', 'croked', 'diseased', 'dombe', 'half blynde' and 'allmost blynde'.[100] There never would be a census quite like this one again, though others came after it, many of which were designed to pick up facts about particular problems. This acquisition of information on a brand-new scale increased the scope for moulding impressions of areas of the city or of the identities of countless Norvicians. Learning so much might, on the one hand, seem intimidating; there was so much going on that required interventions by the authorities. On the other hand, it also gave a sense of understanding, of knowing about the city and its parts, its people and its problems. With such evidence ready at hand, a more finely-tuned policy or even a solution seemed a little more possible.

To this windfall of information we can add the thousands of occasions in the judicial courts when a suspect's character was verbally branded criminous, with a label, such as 'vagrant' or 'pilferer'. These condemnations were backed up by punishments which, after the opening of the Bridewell, included a much greater element of institutionalisation. The benefit of Bridewell, however, was that through the discipline of work and religious education its tainted inmates might have been turned into something like the civic ideal of the worthy and sober citizen. In the other hospitals, too, a similar process of getting patients to toe the line was a major concern.

Civic ethics were probably even more in evidence in these places because they had been brought more tightly under the control of the corporation. From its inception, the city kept a check on all aspects of Bridewell's daily running. The magistrates also had a large say in appointments, admissions, transfers to and discharges from the hospitals. More than this, they were largely responsible for the type of character-building and definition that was a goal in all institutions, not just the Bridewell. Their thoughts about law and order permeated these places. The Bridewell, for example, gave institutional structure to attitudes towards the poor; only workshy and dangerous paupers were locked up there. The anthropologist, Mary Douglas, writes that 'institutions bestow sameness'.[101] This is certainly what they try to do, though it does not always work out that way. But in Norwich they deliberately set out to confer similar identities on their inmates, and to make them recognisable around the city. This was made explicit in the special suits of blue clothes issued to inmates of the Great Hospital and the Boys' Hospital.[102]

It was not always a smooth road for Norwich's institutions. Most of them limped through the sixteenth and seventeenth centuries, stumbling from one financial fix to another. But what is not in doubt is the momentum for information gathering and for institutional cultures and systems at this time. Much more was known about individual Norvicians than ever before. The city, too, was better observed through maps and data-flows, even though it was growing so quickly, spilling over its walls. This civic arithmetic helped the authorities to come to terms with the mass and mess of Norwich. They reeled off one complaint after another as the number of vagrants zoomed upwards. But by counting and categorizing their concerns they tried to keep on top of the situation year after year. Institutions contributed a great deal to this goal, over and above their small number. When the last pauper was counted in 1570, the case for a bridewell seemed stronger than ever. Over the next century a string of policies to tackle poverty and its effects upon health and order made the Bridewell an absolutely indispensable civic tool, along with the hospitals. We usually think that surveillance societies came later than this, maybe in the eighteenth century, and certainly by the one after.[103] That may be so if we have in mind cross-country communications, national head counts, or snooping detectives. But if we leap back a couple of centuries to 1600 or so, we do not find ourselves in a backwater before information or statistics were taken seriously. Far from it, collecting and counting data were then a matter of routine. This was certainly the case in Norwich, where the data-chase picked up speed from the day in 1570 when a decision was made to number poor Norvicians.

4

The Civil Wars

Andrew Hopper

That yeare I lost Repps, some lost theyre witts, others lost theyre hon-
estie, and which is most strange and remarkeable, the Citye of
Norwich lost the Mayor; certainly the Citye was not well kept, when
the keeper of it, could not keep himselfe.

Thomas Ramsey, parson of Crostwick,
to John Utting, Mayor of Norwich, 17 December 1647[1]

So reflected Thomas Ramsey, the recently evicted minister of Repps, on the
outbreak of civil war, when Norwich's royalist mayor was deposed and a
parliamentarian city government established. Yet Norwich is often dismissed as having been only marginally affected by the wars. It suffered no
sieges as comparable provincial capitals did at York, Bristol and Exeter. Situated deep within parliamentarian territory and defended by the powerful
Eastern Association, Norwich came closest to a significant military engagement during the brief siege of King's Lynn in 1643. Familiar features of
Civil War history are absent: there was no garrison warfare, no punitive
raiding, no widespread plundering, nor movements by clubmen. Yet the
city was far from peaceful. Norwich suffered sixteen executions for mutiny
and rebellion, several severe riots, repeated recruiting and impressment,
heavy taxation and a ransacked cathedral. It received visits from Parliament's generals Fairfax and Cromwell. It endured plague and flood, and a
massive explosion that left Mancroft ward devastated. Furthermore, parliamentarian control of Norwich was threatened in 1643 and 1648, since its
citizens were far from united behind Parliament's cause. Most important,
the civil wars deepened religious and political divisions among Norwich's
inhabitants, strengthening factions that endured well into the eighteenth
century.

The religious divisions in Norwich that were so important in 1642 can be
traced back to the 1620s and became pronounced with Matthew Wren's
appointment as bishop late in 1635. The diocese of Norwich was among the

largest and most troublesome in England, while Wren was a forceful supporter of Charles I and his reactionary archbishop of Canterbury, William Laud. Charles and Laud sought to reinforce a high church tradition that stressed ceremony, clerical dignity and order. They insisted upon ministers wearing surplices, and demanded that communion tables be placed behind altar rails in the east end of churches. They restricted preaching and sermons by their critics. Enforcing use of a new prayer book, they excommunicated and removed objecting ministers from their livings. Not surprisingly, these developments antagonised Norwich's hard-line Protestants, who, derided as puritans, saw themselves as the persecuted Godly. They perceived royal policies as popish innovations, and established their ministers in rival city lectureships. Matthew Wren's aggressive style of church government irritated both the city's more moderate aldermen and the Norfolk gentry alike. Even the royalist earl of Clarendon reflected that Wren's 'exorbitant acts' and 'great pride and insolence provoked all the gentry, and in truth most of the inhabitants' of his diocese. Defamed as 'Little Pope Regulus' who introduced idolatry and devil-worship into the church, Wren was probably the most unpopular bishop the diocese has ever had.[2] Soon after his appointment, he ordered his chancellor, Dr Clement Corbet, to conduct a full visitation of the diocese. Equally committed to enforcing Laudian uniformity, Corbet condemned Godly lecturers as 'false jugglers', who 'will onely promise, for Restitution, to do as the Canons and Constitutions require them, but performe nothing'. He recommended: 'If His Majesty shall in his princely care abolish that Ratesbayne of Lecturing out of his Churches, the virulency wherof hath intoxicated many thousands of this kingdome we shall have such a uniforme and orthodoxe Church, as the Christian world cannot shew the like.' Wren's visitation provoked local resistance, as some ministers and churchwardens sought to evade his injunctions. On 9 June 1637, his commissioners reported that the church-wardens of St Andrew's, St Benedict's, St Clement's, St Helen's, St Peter Hungate and St Michael-at-Plea were proving the most troublesome.[3]

Wren stifled criticism by removing lay patronage for Godly lectureships and ejecting nonconforming ministers. He deprived eight Norwich clergy-men, including William Bridge and Thomas Allen, who migrated to Holland and Massachusetts respectively.[4] The largest migration of Norwich citizens occurred during Wren's episcopacy. It numbered up to five hundred, the majority of whom crossed to Holland.[5] On 17 June 1637, William Grant reported that a silenced Godly minister, a 'Mr Sheaphard', had said that the people of Greenwich had cursed Wren to his face and 'bad the divell take him, the divell goe with him', adding 'it is God's mercy that he is hated of the people'.[6] Richard Gastricke dismissed Chancellor Corbet's warrant more robustly, 'sayinge that he would wipe his arse withall and that he cared nott a turde for itt'.[7]

The Laudian drive for conformity included enforcing censorship through the consistory courts and the court of High Commission. In February 1637, Edward Penton was arrested in Norwich for smuggling illegal books written by the Puritan activists Henry Burton and William Prynne, and was sneeringly described as a 'Sanctified Brother', who 'hath bin already at New England'.[8] Later that year, Corbett informed Wren that yet more illegal books from Holland had arrived at Yarmouth and had been conveyed to Norwich 'sent from some of their Holy friends from Delph'. It then emerged that the Toft family, living at Fye bridge and Tombland, had received them. Mrs Toft confessed that one of the books came from her maid in Delft, and Corbett urged Bishop Wren that 'if the lawes permitt, bothe the authors and despensers of such scandalouse and sedetiouse bookes were committed to the hangemans despatch, the state woulde be at muche quiet'. Thomas Toft's family was also reported for attending conventicles 'of simple and ignorant people more fitter to be taught then to teache'. By the outbreak of war they had become ardent parliamentarians.[9]

The Laudian style of churchmanship intensified discord between leading puritan aldermen and cathedral clergy in 'a common pattern of factional conflict' discernible in other cathedral cities, including Canterbury, Chichester, Gloucester, Worcester and York. Points of disagreement usually arose over the corporation's seating in the cathedral, the preaching of sermons and the immunities enjoyed by people living in cathedral precincts.[10] Yet Wren did not completely unite Norwich's corporation against him. Important evidence for lay initiatives by future royalist sympathisers to beautify the churches of St Peter Mancroft and St Gregory in the 1620s that clearly anticipate the Laudian style has been unearthed. In 1636 Henry Lane, a select vestryman at St Gregory's, led nine aldermen in writing a letter supporting Wren just when the puritan mayor had formulated a petition against the bishop. By the following year Wren had received written pledges of support from fourteen Norwich ministers. City magistrates from the Anguish family (later destined to support the royalist cause) became enthusiastic enforcers of Wren's policies. By 1638 there were signs that Wren had worn down opposition, even that Norwich's puritan movement had reached its low point.[11]

In 1638 Wren was translated to Ely, but bitter memories in Norwich lingered on, and his enemies awaited the opportunity for revenge. On 23 December 1640, a petition against Wren in the name of Norwich's inhabitants was sent to the Long Parliament. It complained that he had 'laughed att their request being for the restoring of week day lectures', and that Godly ministers had been excommunicated simply 'for not obeying the Bishopps unconscionable commands'. It claimed many clergymen had fled overseas leaving behind a ministry 'altogether unworthy of that holy calling', and that many employers in the cloth trade had also emigrated, increasing unemployment among Norwich's poor.[12] Clarendon later endorsed this argument, notwithstanding Corbet's rebuttal of it as 'a most impudent lie'.[13]

Norwich's corporation also complained that Wren had enforced a royal order of 14 March 1636, which stipulated that all the city officers should attend Sunday morning services in the cathedral.[14] Not only did these officials, many of them aged and infirm, endure three and a half hour services without relief in cold seats, but:

> By reason that there be many seates over our heads wee are oftentymes exposed to much danger as alsoe to have many scornes and contempts (vizt) as in the maioralty of Mr Christofer Barrett a great bible was lett fall from above and missed very litle of hitting him upon the head & broke his spectacles ... And not long before the tyme of Mr Barretts maioralty some made water in the gallery over the Aldermens heads and dropt downe into their wifes seats who sate close att their backs ... That in the tyme of the present maior that now is upon that Sunday the day before the knights of the shire was chosen in October last Alderman Shipdham justice of peace and sitting next the maior some body most beastly did conspurcate and shitt upon his gowne from the galleryes above. And the Sonday imediately after some from the galloryes lett fall a shooe which narrowly missed the maior's head And att another tyme one from the said gallery did spitt upon Alderman Barrett's head.[15]

Far from being puritan propaganda, this petition was signed by four aldermen subsequently ejected from the corporation for royalist sympathies. Such humiliations were not unusual; the residents of Exeter's cathedral close in 1638 also went out of their way to bait the city authorities.[16] It is within this context, rather than one of ill-informed, impulsive condemnation, that subsequent iconoclasm in Norwich cathedral needs to be reconsidered.

After Charles I called the Long Parliament in November 1640, the position of the cathedral clergy and Laudian party in Norwich came increasingly under threat as their opponents' confidence grew. Complaints against clergy who had supported Wren became vociferous. Thomas Knyvett wrote to his wife from Quidenham on 17 January 1641:

> Heers like to be such a purgation of black-coates, as, if the Parliament intertaines all the complaintes of the Brethren, I knowe not wher they will finde newe ones to put in. Conventicles every night in Norwich, as publickely

knowne as the sermons in the day time, and they say much more frequented. Ther is but towe preaching ministers that goes for currant Amongst them in the whole cittye vidz. Carter and Hall, the rest all Praters. The country is nowe full of warrants for certifycates againste Bishop Wrenn, sent out by justices by command from the Parliament.[17]

When the city's charge against Wren was delivered to the House of Commons on 22 February 1642, the House replied that proceedings had been in hand for some time. On the same day, the corporation organised a petition condemning Charles I's attempt to arrest the Five Members.[18]

One newsbook reported that, on Shrove Tuesday 1642, anxious cathedral clergy raised an armed party to defend the close from feared riots. Allegedly one apprentice informed the dean that 'the [communion] rayles, and [organ] pipes, and other Innovations was against the Protestation, and he had sworne against all Innovations and he would pull them downe whereever he saw them'. The tract declared that the cathedral courts had been 'the cause of many a sorrowfull heart in Norwich'. It ridiculed the dean and chapter, declaring 'to the world the sillynesse of these Cathedrall blades: It is a signe that they have no law for the maintenance of their pipes, that are so afraid of the pulling of them down by boyes'.[19] This tract heralded the vengeance inflicted upon the Laudian cathedral once parliamentarians secured control of Norwich in 1643.

Fear of Catholics and popish plots was a critical factor stimulating parliamentarian recruitment in 1642. Clarendon noted that 'the imputation raised by Parliament upon the King, of an intention to bring in, or ... of conniving at and tolerating Popery, did make a deep impression upon the people generally'.[20] Norwich was no exception, and an anti-Catholic panic occurred in September 1640 when it was feared that Catholics intended to fire the city. The privy council reported to Sir William Denny (d. 1642), steward and former MP for Norwich, on 12 September that Alexander Pritchard, foot boy to Sir William Thexton, had lodged with Edmund Bedingfield, a recusant of Kirkeby, and had been heard to say 'that there was twelve thousand comeinge (not nameinge of whome) and that Norwich should be burnt within a weeke. And that the howses by Bracondell [Bracondale] beinge reeded howses would burne bravely.' The council ordered Denny and Henry Lane, mayor of Norwich, to examine Pritchard, and was concerned that 'speeches and rumors together with some other of like nature in theise troublesome times have much distracted and disquieted the common sort of people'.[21]

These fears intensified in October 1641 with news that Irish Catholics had risen in rebellion and massacred Protestant settlers. Historians

increasingly recognise this as the principal immediate factor causing civil
war in England, since it raised the crucial question of who was to control
the English army to be sent against the rebels. Although command of the
militia was lawfully within the crown's prerogative, there were doubts over
entrusting it to the duplicitous and religiously suspect Charles I. Thousands of Protestant refugees fled from Ireland into England to escape the
slaughter, spreading terror with tales of torture, rape and murder. Another
anti-Catholic panic occurred in Norwich soon after. One London newsbook reported that on 27 November there was a 'great uproar in Norwich
concerning the papists arising there, they being intended to burn the whole
city'.[22] The ensuing pages reported the trickery and grisly murder of a
Protestant by his Irish Catholic neighbour who then proceeded to pillage
his house, the tale providing a bitter foretaste of what Norwich's citizens
could expect if Parliament and Protestantism were not safeguarded. Some
local authorities were suspicious that Protestant refugees were actually Irish
rebels infiltrating England, and on 10 June 1642 the mayor's court expelled
a party of Irish refugees from Norwich for vagrancy.[23] When the taking of
sides became critical in late August of that year, parliamentary propaganda
in London newsbooks alleged that Cavalier horsemen were looting Norwich's outlying villages, exploiting a popular mentality that often identified
Cavaliers as plunderers.[24]

Parliamentarians consolidated their control of Norwich over August and
September 1642. On 5 August the Assembly Book zealously recorded orders
from Parliament to secure the city, to implement its Militia Ordinance and
to confine papists to their dwellings. A committee of the assembly was
formed just ten days later 'to consider of all fitt wayes and meanes for the
better securinge of the Citty' and specifically to contemplate the drastic
step of 'imployinge of such poore men as they can arme to be exercised in
armes and to be otherwise imployed for the good of the Citty'.[25] Parliamentarian deputy lieutenants met at Norwich on 6 September and took
control of the county militia. Then, within less than a fortnight, twenty-
four militia captains pledged themselves to support Parliament's lord
lieutenant for Norfolk, the earl of Warwick, and on 29 October a military
engineer was paid for advice about fortifying the city.[26]

It has been pointed out that twenty of the twenty-two towns where parliamentarians first recruited were established centres of Godly preaching,
some even with traditions of pre-Reformation heresy.[27] Norwich clearly
conforms to this pattern. In the 1630s its inhabitants had watched puppet
shows depicting the fall of Nineveh and the destruction of Jerusalem, no
doubt applauding gleefully as proud priests and princes were struck
down.[28] Ministers such as William Bridge, who Wren had ejected from his

parish of St Peter Hungate, also exposed Norvicians to Godly sermons and lectures. Bridge was restored to a lectureship at St Andrew's church in 1643, having preached an inflammatory sermon to parliamentarian volunteers from Norwich and Great Yarmouth at the very start of the year (Figure 24):

> should the *Ammonites* prevaile (I mean that malignant Jeusuiticall party prevaile) in the Kingdome, what a dark and blacke day would it be upon *England*? ... what would they do, yea what would they not do? ... and me thinks every one should sit down and think with him selfe, what shall I give or do, that my person should not be enslaved? that my wife and daughters be not abused, that my poor children be not massacred, that my house be not plundered, that my Country be not betrayed?[29]

Declaring that Parliament's volunteers were the bulwarks of England and the Protestant faith, he posed what for them was the ultimate question: 'who would live when Religion is dead?' Bridge assured the volunteers that they were marching into a promised land where the tables would be turned, and they would rank far above the royalist gentry: 'The mercie of those that are in authority may let the houses of Malignants stand, yet I make no question, but the doors of their houses shall be made so low, that they shall alwayes stoop, as a note of their subjection; whil'st you that stand for the cause, and Countrey, and Cities of your God, shall have the doors of your houses enlarged.'[30] This rhetoric of godliness was easily turned towards parliamentary propaganda, but it radically raised volunteers' expectations of a new and improved status in the post-war settlement.

Whereas parliamentarian recruitment was encouraged by a powerful combination of anti-Catholicism and rousing sermons, royalism's potential was stifled in Norwich by lacklustre commitment from royalist aldermen, poor coordination with Norfolk's royalist gentry and the city's isolation from royalist-held regions. Captain Moses Treswell discovered this on 28 July 1642, when he vainly attempted to read the commission of array to recruit royalist volunteers in Norwich. The next day the mayor's court forbade him from beating his drum. Letters were sent to the king explaining the corporation's actions.[31] On 5 August the assembly recorded that Treswell had actually been arrested and sent to London to be dealt with by Parliament because he did 'unlawfully trayterouslye beate drumes and use his endevors for the raysenge of forces against the Parliament'.[32]

Nevertheless, there were royalist sympathisers in Norwich. Rumours that Parliament might go too far circulated that summer. Citizens drank the king's health and sang verses against leading parliamentarians. For example, John Baldwyn, William Symonds and Robert Riches allegedly met

A
SERMON

Preached unto the Voluntiers of the
City of *NORWICH* and also to the
Voluntiers of Great *YARMOVTH* in

NORFOLKE.

By *William Bridge* Preacher of Gods Word.

Judges : 5. 9.
*My heart is towards the Governours of Israel that offered them-
selves willingly among the People. Blesse yee the Lord.*

IT is Ordered this thirtieth day of January, 1642.
by the Committee of the House of Commons in Parliament concerning Printing , That this Booke intituled
A Sermon preached unto the Volunteers of the City of
NORVVICH &c. be Printed.

JOHN WHITE.

London, Printed by *J. F.* for *Ben. Allen*, and are to be sold
at his shop in *Popes-head* Alley. 1 6 4 2.

FIGURE 24. Godly rhetoric was easily turned to the purposes of anti-royalist
propaganda in sermons sponsored by the emerging parliamentarian corporation.
*A Sermon Preached unto the Voluntiers of the City of Norwich and also to the Vol-
untiers of Great Yarmouth By William Bridge Preacher of Gods Word* (London,
1643). (*University of East Anglia Library*)

in the Turkey Cock tavern, on 24 August 1642, when they claimed, with some prescience: 'If the king should go to the Parliament they would take away his Prerogative and commit him to prison and take off his head.' The company drank a health to King Charles and confusion to 'factious Pym'. Alarmed by such potentially dangerous sedition, Parliament ordered the mayor and JPs to proceed against the ringleaders at the next sessions.[33]

In early August the royalist lord lieutenant, Lord Mowbray, arrived at Kenninghall on the county border, near Diss. Despite summoning the commissioners of array, he failed to rally Norfolk's royalist gentry and avoided the summer assizes. Many Norfolk landowners, such as Sir Jacob Astley of Melton Constable and Sir Thomas Corbet of Sprowston, left independently to join the king's field armies, thereby depriving local adherents of organisation and leadership. It is maintained that counties such as Norfolk were largely 'abandoned to the Parliament by the organisation of the royalist war effort', and that 'Norfolk's royalism found its fullest expression away from the county in the king's fighting armies'.[34] Expressions of royalist sentiment looked increasingly like futile bravado, foreshadowing the Jacobite outbursts of Norvicians in the 1720s. On 3 December 1642 information was presented against the brewer, Robert Holmes, and one William Hardingham for abusing the city watch. Declaring that they were themselves the king's watch, they exclaimed 'what Jackanapes are you', and jeered that 'they would not be confronted by such a company of yonge fellowes'.[35]

Deep as pre-war divisions had become, the local authorities were unready for armed conflict and tried to avoid partisan language. Norwich's MPs and deputy lieutenants advocated moderate policies; and parliamentarians on the corporation were similarly restrained.[36] One newsbook reported a letter from Norwich explaining that, because of the trade depression, 'we can scarce keep the poor from mutiny, and [it] filleth us with fears, such as hasten on apace even to desperation, and make many people to mutter'.[37] While the memory of Kett's Rebellion still haunted them, Norfolk gentry and city aldermen were cautious about countenancing popular activism.[38] Sir John Potts, a deputy lieutenant for Norfolk, wrote to Sir Simonds D'Ewes on 19 August 1642:

> I concur with you in your fears of ungovernable numbers from whence, my thoughts alwaies apprehended ye most remediless dangers, which God avert. My own endeavours heer have been for peace and hitherto wee are quiet, whensoever necessity shall enforce us to make use of ye multitude, I doe not promise my self safety.[39]

The roving crowds in the Stour valley and around Colchester that August may have unnerved Potts, who probably felt it was only a short step from their sacking the mansions of Catholic and Laudian gentry to plundering parliamentarian ones. On 27 August the annual sermon 'in commemoration of the overthrow of Kett and his confederates' reminded the propertied classes of the dangers of popular violence. Doubts over encouraging such activism usually militated towards a royalist allegiance, and Potts needed to reassure D'Ewes of his loyalty. He accordingly wrote again on 2 September: 'Doe to your friend right against scandalous tongues which I heare blast me with report that I decline the service of the house [Parliament] and encourage the commission of array; Sir I assure you my conscience leads me to uphold the Comonwealth to which I will prove noe changling.'[40] There were many on both sides who shared Potts's priority of limiting the war's impact on their localities and thus safeguarding their own estates rather than becoming committed activists. The earl of Dorset echoed Potts's fears, writing to the countess of Middlesex: 'I wowld ... my children had never binn borne, to live under the dominion of soe many Cades and Ketts, as threaten by their multitudes and insurrections to drowne all memory of monarchy, nobility, gentry, in this land.'[41]

From January to March 1643, aldermen sympathetic to the royalist cause became increasingly isolated and passive. Their lingering influence was finally extinguished when Lord Grey of Warke arrived in Norwich late in February. As Parliament's major-general of the new Eastern Association, Grey enforced the Militia Ordinance and 'finally shattered the uneasy peace in Norfolk'. On 2 March the mayor, William Goslyn, a royalist sympathiser, refused to approve orders to requisition malignants' horses, so Grey had him arrested and removed to Cambridge. Sir John Potts, demoralised because of his failure to keep the county peacefully on the side of Parliament, prepared to leave the next day.[42]

The spring of 1643 saw increasing activity in Norwich. On 7 March Captain John Fountain led a contingent of civic volunteers to arrest royalist gentry at Augustine Holl's house in nearby Heigham. These included Sir Thomas Richardson, Thomas Aldrich, Augustine Cullier, Sir William Denny, Augustine Holl and John Payne. Possibly plotting to seize Norwich, they had written to other county gentry. Parliament ordered that they should be dealt with as Colonel Oliver Cromwell, shortly expected with five troops of horse, might see fit. Supported by a company of Norwich dragoons, Cromwell then captured another group of royalist gentry at Lowestoft on 17 March.[43] The next day four Norwich aldermen, John Daniel, John Osborne, Richard Rosse and Henry Lane, were ejected from the bench. The city elections began on 20 March, the day Cromwell triumphantly returned from Lowestoft. A parliamentarian, John Thacker,

was chosen as mayor elect, along with five new aldermen of similar per-
suasion, including Livewell Sherwood and Matthew Lindsey. On 27 March
a sequestration committee was formed in Norwich to confiscate royalist
estates.[44]

Yet even with its victory complete, the parliamentarian corporation continued to fear Norwich's potential for popular royalism. The quarter
sessions dealt with many cases of residents verbally abusing volunteers.
Nicholas Wymer, a joiner, was prosecuted for taunting one Major Wild,
'sayeing that he and his company would be made fooles before they came
home', while others mocked Captain Sherwood, suggesting his volunteers
were horse thieves.[45] On 13 July Sherwood was ordered to guard against
'any stire or tumults that may arise, in regard that the vowe and Covenant
is then to be taken'. He was authorised temporarily to arm and train a further hundred volunteers to ensure security.[46] Norwich's magistracy
remained anxious, fining a mason, Martin Morley, the remarkable sum of
twenty pounds 'for sayeinge they were all for sworen [perjuers] that had
taken the Covenant', while also imprisoning and fining John Rogers no less
than one hundred pounds for speaking against the earl of Manchester.
Robert Drake was prosecuted 'for sayeinge that if all the Roundheads,
Anabaptists and Brownists were hanged we should have a true church in
England'.[47]

A pattern of allegiance among leading citizens may be discerned from a
list of voluntary subscriptions towards the cost of regaining Newcastle-
upon-Tyne for Parliament in 1643 (Table 4.1). There were 229 contributors
and 275 refusers. This evidence must be treated cautiously, as refusals
may have been neither politically nor religiously motivated and contributions may simply reflect a desire to liberate Newcastle's coal from royalist
control. Yet the contributors included nearly all the corporation's parliamentarians. While 69 per cent of common councillors in Wymer and
Over-the-Water (Ultra Aquam) contributed readily, only 18 per cent did so
in the more conservative Conesford and Mancroft wards. This impression
is reinforced by statistics concerning the Solemn League and Covenant in
1644 (Table 4.2). Those taking this oath swore to adhere to a Presbyterian
church settlement which emerging sectaries and, in far greater numbers,
adherents of a non-Puritan Church of England would alike have found dis-
tasteful. The significant proportion of refusers may reflect an attachment
to the Caroline church, or at least hostility to Parliament's drive for further reformation. Once again, the largest numbers of refusers are strikingly
located in Mancroft and Conesford wards, and spectacularly in the wealthy
parish of St Peter Mancroft itself. Interestingly, the market was situated
there, as were the anti-parliamentarian riots staged between 1646 and 1648.

TABLE 4.1 The subscription for regaining Newcastle-upon-Tyne
for Parliament, 1643

Ward	Contributors	Refusers	Sum raised (£)
Coslany	52	18	90.00
Colegate	25	37	50.00
Fyebridge	33	35	115.00
West Wymer	24	47	30.00
Mid Wymer	38	53	97.10
East Wymer	8	29	22.00
St Giles	–	–	–
Mancroft	7	31	13.00
St Stephen	6	–	54.15
Ber Street	3	–	3.00
North Conesford	13	9	36.00
South Conesford	3	16	5.00

Source: F. R. Beecheno, 'The Norwich Subscription for the Regaining of Newcastle', *NA*, xviii (1914), pp. 149–60; Evans, *Seventeenth-Century Norwich*, pp. 132–4.
Note: Most of the donation from St Stephen's ward was provided by Sir John Hobart, who gave £40. Without it, Over-the-Water's contribution would have been larger than that known to have been raised south of the Wensum.

Statistical analysis of taxation records tends to confirm enthusiasm for the parliamentary cause in Wymer and Over-the-Water and a strong royalist presence in Mancroft and Conesford.[48]
On 13 March 1643 the assembly appointed a committee to recruit and equip a company of fifty dragoons. Within a matter of weeks two further volunteer companies were established for civic defence under Sergeant Major Sherwood and Captain Thomas Ashwell.[49] The young men and maids of Norwich raised £240 and Colonel Cromwell wrote to them on 2 August advising them to buy pistols and saddles for a troop of horse. Cromwell himself undertook to provide eighty horses and declared: 'Pray raise honest godly men, and I will have them of my regiment'.[50] The recruits rode out under Captain Robert Swallow to become the eleventh troop in Cromwell's own regiment.[51] They were ridiculed by the royalist newsbook, *Mercurius Aulicus*, on 3 September 1643:

> Another sub committee of the Maids of *Norwich*, who by all meanes will give money and plate to raise a Troope of eighty Horse for the Two pretended houses; and this they will have called (forsooth) the *Virgin Troope* ... Now if

Table 4.2 The Solemn League and Covenant in Norwich
by parish, 1644

Parish	Great Ward	Takers	Refusers
St Peter Mancroft	Mancroft	305	182
St John of Sepulchre	Coneford	73	52
St Andrew's	Wymer	175	37
St Peter Southgate	Conesford	74	20
St Simon and Jude	Wymer	43	17
St Michael at Plea	Wymer	80	15
St Peter Parmenter	Conesford	206	8
St Swithin's	Wymer	86	5
St Martin at Oak	Over-the-Water	175	3
St John Maddermarket	Wymer	113	2
Eaton	–	24	3
St Michael Coslany	Over-the-Water	206	1
St Helen's	Wymer	84	1
St George Tombland	Wymer	132	Unknown
St Julian	Conesford	71	Unknown
St Lawrence	Wymer	123	Unknown
St Michael at Thorn	Conesford	26	Unknown
Trowse and Carrow	–	26	Unknown

Source: NRO, NCR, 13C/2, The Solemn League and Covenant in Norwich; 13A/43,
Militia Records.

these busie girles shall hereafter live to be stale Virgins (for men I presume
will suspect those women to falsifie with their husbands, who are not true to
their Prince) let them take notice it is their owne fault.[52]

On 8 January following, the newsbook continued that 'no less than five of
this Virgin Troope are now greate with childe, but by whom it is not yet
signified'.[53] The troop served throughout the wars and took part in the Protectorate's occupation of Scotland in 1655.[54]

Recruitment to foot companies serving outside Norfolk became increasingly difficult and desertion common. Robert Dall lost eight of thirty-four
recruits he took from Norwich to Reading and on 8 July 1643; John Wynne,
a deserter from Captain Ashwell's company, was sent to the Bridewell,
whipped and ordered back again. By November 1643 impressment was permitted, but the mayor's court tried to limit its impact. Although it ordered
forty-four men to be pressed, at least fifteen were servants or from outside

the city. Norwich's Dutch and Walloon Strangers also mustered a foot company to join the earl of Manchester at Cambridge in March 1644.[55]

After the local royalist capitulations at Heigham and Lowestoft, the greatest threat to Norwich came from outside the region and may thus, at first, have seemed remote. After the victory of the earl of Newcastle's royalist army over the Fairfaxes at Adwalton Moor, near Bradford, on 30 June 1643, the situation changed dramatically, as it was feared that his army would sweep through Lincolnshire and invade the eastern counties. Newcastle's forces comprised the largest and most feared royalist army of the entire civil wars. Heavily officered by Catholics, it was popularly known as the 'Popish Army of the North'.[56] In June four city gates were earthed up and river traffic restricted. On 26 July the deputy lieutenants were granted leave to fortify the castle yard and bridge.[57] Thomas Knyvett wrote ominously to his wife a few days later, referring to other royalist successes at Bristol and Exeter and an anticipated one at Gloucester: 'These three westerne cittyes have bledd deeply to save plundring. A good looking glass for Norwich to bethink themselves in time for their peace and security, for their turne will certainly come if the King and Parliament does not speedily Agree.' On 11 August a letter to the deputy lieutenants of Essex warned against the 'approach of the Northerne force soe neere threatning ruine ... soe formidable yet Popish enemy'.[58]

Newcastle's royalists advanced to Stamford in July and threatened Wisbech. On 13 August King's Lynn declared for the king, swayed by a number of local gentry led by Sir Hamon Le Strange of Hunstanton. This was strategically important as it offered a gateway into the Eastern Association for Newcastle's forces. Notwithstanding earlier refusals, on 6 September 1643 the mayor's court permitted Sherwood to beat his drums for Norwich volunteers to join the siege of King's Lynn. Fortunately for Norwich, Lynn surrendered on 16 September and Newcastle's attentions returned towards the resurgent Fairfaxes in Hull.[59]

The Godly laity exacted terrible vengeance on the cathedral as soon as Parliament passed ordinances against superstitious images and idolatry. Ironically, the bishop of Norwich was now Joseph Hall, who was certainly no Laudian. Considering Parliament's abolition of episcopacy and the imprisonment of Laud and Wren in the Tower, the harassment he endured was comparatively mild. He retired to Heigham and later recalled the fate of his chapel in the Bishop's Palace:

> Another while, the Sheriff Toftes and Alderman Linsey, attended with many zealous followers, came into my chapel to look for superstitious pictures

and relics of idolatry; and sent for me, to let me know they found those windows full of images, which were very offensive, and must be demolished. I told them they were the pictures of some ancient and worthy bishops, as St Ambrose, Austin [Augustine], etc. It was answered me, that they were so many popes (Plates 2–4).[60]

He vividly described the most unruly day of iconoclasm at the cathedral in his work *Hard Measure*:[61]

It is no other than tragical to relate the carriage of that furious sacrilege, whereof our eyes and ears were the sad witnesses, under the authority and presence of Linsey, Toftes the sheriff, and Greenwood. Lord, what work was here! what clattering of glasses! what beating down of walls! what tearing up of monuments! what pulling down of seats! what wresting out of irons and brass from the windows and graves! what defacing of arms! what demolishing of curious stone-work, that had not any representation in the world, but only the cost of the founder, and skill of the mason! what tooting and piping upon the destroyed organ-pipes! and what a hideous triumph on the market-day before all the country; when, in a kind of sacrilegious and profane procession, all the organ-pipes, vestments, both copes and surplices, together with the leaden cross which had been newly sawn down from over the Green-yard pulpit, and the service-books and singing-books that could be had, were carried to the fire in the public market-place; a lewd wretch walking before the train, in his cope trailing in the dirt, with a service-book in his hand, imitating in an impious scorn the tune, and usurping the words of the litany used formerly in the church. Near the public cross, all these monuments of idolatry must be sacrificed to the fire; not without much ostentation of a zealous joy, in discharging ordnance, to the cost of some, who professed how much they had longed to see that day. Neither was it any news, upon this guild-day, to have the cathedral, now open on all sides, to be filled with musketeers, waiting for the mayor's return; drinking and tobacconing as freely as if it had turned ale-house.[62]

The eminent physician, Sir Thomas Browne, later confirmed much of this account, and recorded that about one hundred brass inscriptions were removed: 'Hereby the distinct places of buryall of many noble and considerable persons, becomes now unknowne.'[63]

Such was the extent of the destruction, there was no need for William Dowsing, Parliament's iconoclast general, to visit Norwich. Not surprisingly, given their experiences in the 1630s, leading city officers were fully prepared to take the initiative. A century later Francis Blomefield blamed

the forwardness of TOFT, who was ringleader of the rabble, [since] but little escaped his felonious hands, when he had once got a taste of the value of the brasses he had pulled off, the cathedral alone affording him above a hundred; all which he seized, thereby defacing the memory of the ancestors of many of the most ancient and worshipful families in the county.[64]

Thomas Toft was a grocer of St Clement's parish, residing at the corner of Fye bridge and Fishergate. As we have seen, he had close links with English exiles in Holland and his three sons were appropriately named Daniel, Samuel and Joseph in the best Old Testament tradition. He was sheriff of Norwich in 1643, an Independent in religion and a committed political radical. Mayor in 1654, he was still conducting civil marriages in 1657.[65]

On 23 January 1644 the mayor's court appointed a committee headed by Toft to take information about royalist ministers and to destroy 'all such scandalous pictures cruceyfixes and images as are yet remayninge'.[66] That same month, an informant declared that Charles Davill, minister of the parish church of St Lawrence and St Mary Coslany, had preached a fast sermon that 'rayled on them that were the executioners of parliament ordinances in demolishing scandelous pictures and said they were base domineering fellows which scandalised the ministers of god and abused the temples of the lord'.[67] The mayor's court ordered further popish pictures from St Swithin's and the cathedral to be publicly burnt in the market place a few weeks later.[68] The stump cross at St Saviour's was demolished on 17 July.[69] On 1 March 1645 the rulers of Norwich demanded the removal of what few pictures and crucifixes still remained in the cathedral and the repairing of windows where stained glass had been destroyed.[70] The founder's tomb was levelled and the high altar replaced by the mayor's seat.[71] The aldermen's seats were also transferred to the east end, providing a concrete and unambiguous reminder of the parliamentarian corporation's victory over the cathedral and its Laudian innovations.

Some aldermen were uneasy with this triumph. Thomas Ramsey, the vicar ejected from Repps in July 1642, wrote to the sympathetic John Utting on 17 December 1647: 'I doe approve of an orderly reformation, but not of a tumultuarye; there is a difference betweene a reforming what is amisse, and a transforming of the whole into a new shape: the one, is as the pruning, and lopping of the vine, when it is too luxuriant, and the other, a digging of it up by the rootes.' He added: 'The Christians at first suffered by Crosses, and now Crosses suffer by Christians.'[72] The cathedral was not completely abandoned; the corporation's ministers used it for civic thanksgivings for Parliament's victories and Sunday morning sermons, and one of the chapels was set aside as a parish church for the close. But the buildings as a whole did not assume a new role, as, for example, did York

Minster, which became a well-funded preaching centre for Godly clergy fully integrated in the life of the city.[73] On 31 May 1650 the corporation of Great Yarmouth petitioned the Rump Parliament 'to grant us such a part of the lead and other usefull materialls of that vast and altogether useles Cathedrall in Norwich towardes the building of a works house to employ our almost sterved poore and repairing our peeres [piers in the harbour] or otherwise as you shall thinke fitt and sufficient'.[74] Yet the petition failed, as even Norwich's Puritan aldermen were reluctant to bestow a valuable resource upon their commercial rivals.

A memorial in the cathedral highlights its uncertain future during the interregnum. Bridget, the wife of Thomas Gourney, died on 26 September 1652, but her husband refrained from burying her there for a decade. An inscription explains that he sought to preserve her remains from desecration by fanatics and, therefore, both the living and the dead awaited Charles II's return.[75]

Stories of the cathedral's mistreatment featured in post-Restoration royalist propaganda. One account declared that Captain Garret had exercised his troopers there one Christmas day. It also claimed that Major Sherwood's volunteers 'marched up to the altar and turned their backs upon it in great derision lifting up their bumbs and howlding downe their heads against it in a deriding manner'. The account's reliability is, however, thrown into doubt by its claims that, cursed for their misdeeds, Sherwood, two of his sergeants and his clerk all hanged themselves, while another sergeant died mad and his lieutenant 'was smitten with sudden death'.[76] Norwich was not unique, and iconoclasm occurred in other cathedrals where deans and chapters had acted similarly in the 1630s.[77]

Even while the war was still raging, Norwich's parliamentarians, as elsewhere, proved themselves more united by what they opposed than what they supported. In 1646 the most powerful group advocated a national church along Presbyterian lines with the power to enforce conformity and obedience. This faction was probably connected to the peace party at Westminster. Opposing them, Norwich's sectarians had already established a meeting in the city and advocated the independence of individual congregations.[78] These divisions found coherent expression in August 1644 when a petition to Parliament for reorganising the city parishes and funding a Godly ministry was prepared. It remained unsent, however, as disagreement emerged over how to proceed. On 25 September 1645 the House of Commons directed the mayor and aldermen to divide the city into classical presbyteries.[79] Those parliamentarians who were hostile towards a rigid national church opposed this; and their anonymous pamphlet, entitled *Vox Populi*, compared the Presbyterian system to the episcopal tyranny of Wren in the 1630s. On 2 September 1646, the mayor's court declared the work scandalous and demanded the author be brought to justice. It had criticised Norwich's leading Presbyterian ministers for seeking to force compulsion in matters of religious conscience and clearly demanded a riposte.[80] Another pamphlet, designed to raise *An Hue and Cry after Vox Populi*, duly countered by accusing the Independents of 'Jesuiti-ciall practises' and declaring themselves freeborn subjects 'according to Lilbourn's [John Lilburne's] president'.[81] The county committee failed to resolve this dangerously divisive dispute and ordered both factions to desist from petitioning Parliament.

Parliament's financial demands gradually shifted from voluntary donations to compulsory taxation. On 11 September 1643 the mayor's court ordered the city aldermen to collect 'voluntary' contributions to relieve Lord Fair-fax in the north. As had been the case with the subscription for regaining Newcastle, the names of refusers were listed.[82] On 14 April 1645 a voluntary payment by the mayor, ten aldermen and various city officers raised £500 as Norwich's first two months' rate towards funding the New Model Army. Contributions of this kind were especially welcome, since by January 1644 Norfolk and Norwich's weekly assessment ranged from £1250 to £1850, and in October 1643 an additional £6000 had been demanded towards the cost of paying Parliament's Scottish allies. There was simmering disagreement over how the quotas between city and county were divided, the city being charged £366 and the county £7070 per month. Parliament demanded tax-ation of a weight and frequency hitherto unknown. This was to have grievous implications.[83]

The most unpopular levy of all was the excise. Introduced as a value added tax on essentials, from November 1643 it was administered at Alder-man Adrian Parmenter's house. It proved a heavy burden on the poor, particularly after its imposition on meat and beer. By the autumn of 1646 opposition among Norwich's butchers had reached flash-point. When James Sheringham was arrested for agitating against it, the butchers in the market rioted and assaulted his captors. On 26 November Parliament ordered the detention of four butchers, William Sheringham, James Sher-ingham, William Gaywood and John Phillips.[84] Alderman Parmenter and Sheriff Richard Wenman complained on 17 December that two excise offic-ers had been disarmed and beaten, as well as having their clothes torn off. They also alleged that 'one Holland a poore butcher ... rode about the Citty crieinge along the streets as he rode Arme, Arme, Arme: if you intend to save your lives & estates'. The tumult at the excise office itself was only diffused by some women, 'who interposed themselves betweene the assaulters and the gate'. Parmenter lamented that his officers were now too frightened to collect the excise and 'we our selves are threatened to bee chopt in peeces'.[85]

The underlying mood of unrest behind the riots was worsened by natural disasters of plague and flood. The flood that November was so severe 'that boats were rowed in St Edmund's, Magdalen, and many other streets in the city'.[86] On 28 December the butchers were 'still as abusive as ever, and none of them will pay a penny, but give revileinge languadge to them when we send to take notice what they kill'. One excise officer was threatened by James Sheringham's wife, who 'tooke upp a cliver [cleaver] & threatened to clive his head if he came into her shopp'.[87] Emulating the prowess of Samson, one butcher struck another official on the head with the jawbone of a beast.[88] Parmenter and others warned that the butchers and brewers in the surrounding countryside were also refusing the excise. On 8 January 1647 Sheriff Wenman reported that Norwich's butchers had paid no excise since June, and that their ill example was spreading: 'They dayly growe worse and are nowe come to the boldness and groune soe desperate that our officers dare not visit their howses to take noatice what flesh they kill, and say they will loose their lives before they will paye any more excise.'[89] On 9 February 1647, Thomas Atkin, MP for Norwich, hinted that some of his colleagues in the Commons blamed the mayor, Henry Watts, for a lacklustre handling of the crisis. One month later Atkin warned him outright that if the butchers were not brought to heel Norwich would be fined and troops quartered upon it. He reported, ominously, that 'the house is so incensed and some say if the magistrates did but theire duties the unruly persons durst not so do'.[90] Parliament increasingly doubted that Norwich's corporation was united behind its ordinances and plans for further reformation.

Alongside their demands for increased taxation, Norwich parliamentarians insisted upon stricter Sabbath observance, and on 25 April 1646 appointed two men in each ward to enforce 'dewe observation of the Lord's day'. Popular festive culture was attacked as popish, idolatrous, superstitious and unruly. Toft, Greenwood and Lindsey had attracted widespread support in ransacking the cathedral, but reforming the traditional celebrations which punctuated the working week was another matter. Guild days were neglected and shorn of the usual ceremonies, 'least any uproar might follow'. The St George's Company ordered in 1645 'that at the procession on the next guild or feast day, there should be no beating of drums or sounds of trumpets; no snap dragon, or fellows dressed up in fools' coats and caps; no standard with the George thereon, nor no hanging of tapestry cloath, nor pictures in any of the streets'. Likewise the mayor ordered ministers to 'forbeare to observe to morrow beinge the 25th of December as a festival daye'.[91]

A reaction in support of the old traditions gathered strength, especially among royalists barred from public life and retailers resentful of the excise. On 8 September 1646, the recalcitrant freemen elected Robert Holmes as sheriff. Having abused the watch in 1642, he was a known royalist. Another malcontent, Richard Turrell, allegedly remarked in April 1648 that 'if sermons were done it would be a better world then it is'. On 1 December 1647 apprentices gathered in the castle yard and petitioned the mayor, John Utting, for the observance of Christmas Day. Utting was a Presbyterian and churchwarden of St Peter Mancroft who was becoming increasingly inclined to royalist sympathies. He was accused of permitting royalist clergy to preach in Norwich churches, countenancing popular festivities on Charles I's accession day, and allowing the election of the royalist, Roger Mingay, as alderman in Mancroft ward in March 1648.[92]

The disturbances leading to the 'Great Blow' began when a petition to the mayor's court criticising the city authorities for becoming lax in their pursuit of further Godly reformation was ignored. Frustrated by their lack of progress, Sheriff Ashwell and Thomas Barret travelled to London to present information against Mayor Utting before Parliament. On 22 April 1648 a messenger arrived in Norwich to convey Utting to Parliament, with orders that Christopher Barret should forthwith replace him in office.[93] Remembering Mayor Goslyn's fate in 1643, Utting's friends, including six aldermen, prepared a petition to keep him in Norwich, testifying to his good government. As further signatures were solicited, support for Utting grew riotous and the messenger was smuggled out of Norwich. On the morning of 24 April, over a thousand people gathered in the market and looted the houses of parliamentarian leaders, seizing arms from Sheriff Ashwell's house and sacking the excise office at Alderman Parmenter's. They captured the committee house, which contained the county arms magazine and ninety-eight barrels of gunpowder. Seeking to destroy unpopular sequestration and taxation records, they 'cast out great bundles of writings att the wyndowes'.[94]

One Master Garret brought news of the tumult to East Dereham, where Colonel Charles Fleetwood's regiment was based. The men had just dispersed to their nearby quarters, but Captain Richard Sankey gathered his own troop and twenty more of Captain Stephen White's and rode to Norwich on 'a furious march'. Arriving at four in the afternoon, these eighty soldiers were later joined by Captain Griffith Lloyd's troop.[95] Undeterred by the rioters' verbal abuse, they soon quelled resistance in the parishes of

St Peter Mancroft and St Stephen's. A firefight developed around the committee house, where the rioters were careless with the gunpowder, one allegedly sweeping it up from the stairs and another taking a hatful home.[96] The ensuing explosion ranks among the largest of the century. At least forty rioters perished and a further 120 people were injured, some of them mortally, as timbers, tiles, plaster and human remains were scattered in the vicinity for miles around. Two of the city's most beautiful parish churches lost their windows and, in addition, a staggering £20,000 worth of estimated damage was inflicted upon nearby houses (Figure 25).[97]

A remarkable set of 278 written examinations survives, detailing the subsequent investigation. The affair had been planned the previous night in taverns, particularly the notorious White Lion. The evidence is full of reported anti-Roundhead street slogans and accounts of verbal abuse heaped upon parliamentarian sympathisers. How far it represents committed royalist sentiment is debatable. Richard Buddery allegedly declared that he hoped to see one hundred 'roundheaded rogues' and troopers hanged.[98] Although the rioters bragged loudly enough, facing New Model troopers was another matter. Some of them drank to the king. Most did far more drinking than fighting. The troopers probably regarded Norwich's infamous butchers as the ringleaders. James Sheringham, the butcher prominent in campaigning against the excise, had certainly solicited signatures for the mayor's petition. An informant further claimed to have seen him 'come ridinge from Berestreet gates and said every one bringe out his armes', while one of his confederates had warned of 'trooping rogues' and declared 'we will have the gates shut up and take them alive'. The latter had, moreover, incited further violence with cries of 'now for theise roundheadly rouges and whores'.[99] Another informer accused Thomas Cubitt of saying he had taken three or four score names of individuals who would be for the king. This tantalisingly suggests that, if the troopers had not arrived so swiftly, the riot might have developed into a rising.[100]

Christopher Barret wrote to Speaker Lenthall on 4 May observing that, as 'the petition was carried about by some in the very time of the height of the tumult, so that we conceive they were both birds of the same feather ... I doubt not time will evince there was a greater plot in it, and a design further off than we are yet aware of.'[101] Barret sought to implicate Mayor Utting and the resurgent opposition in order to further reformation within Norwich's corporation, and avidly reported the evidence of one Nicholas Dawes to the effect that several committee men 'had sayde to the people doe you the work as for us we have estates to loose you have none and we will assist you'.[102]

Most of the rioters were lesser tradesmen. Few of the accused were

A true
RELATION
O F
The late great Mutiny which was in the
City and County of NORWICH, April 24. 1648.
WITH
That accident that befell those Mutiniers that day:
there being as is thought, above 200. slaine by the fireing of 98.
Barrels of Powder; being truly related in a Letter from the
City of *Norwich*, to an honourable Person of the honourable House of Commons, with the Votes of
the House concerning the same, and ordered
to be printed, to prevent misinformation.

In foveam quam foderunt &c.

FIGURE 25. News of the explosive termination of the riots in Norwich was swiftly published in London as a further sign of God's support for Parliament's cause. *A true RELATION OF The late great Mutiny which was in the City and County of NORWICH, April 24, 1648* (London, 1648). (*British Library*)

freemen, but, as Barret was quick to point out, several gentry ringleaders escaped unpunished. Robert Cooke testified that his barber told him, while cutting his hair, that at The White Lion there were 'several men of quality who said they had lost nere two parts of their estate and would now win the horse or lose the sadle'. Master Thomas Palgrave, a merchant with the infamous address of White Lion Lane, bought rounds of drinks for the rioters, while Master Christopher Bransby urged others on and shut several city gates. The chamberlain's account book mentions a thanksgiving day 'for the great and wonderfull deliverance of this Citty from Brannsby and his confederates'. Intriguingly, the last four words were crossed out and 'the muteny or insurrection' inserted instead.[103]

The city paid the troopers a £250 gratuity and voted them money for quartering. Three troops remained in Norwich for the municipal elections that May.[104] Over one hundred accused rioters were tried in the guildhall in December 1648. Twenty-six were fined thirty pounds, seven imprisoned, two whipped and eight hanged alongside two witches in the castle ditches in the following January.[105] The main political consequence was that, by 1649, all those tainted with the affair had either been removed or prohibited from ever holding office. A third of the common council was purged, and Aldermen Utting and Tooly fined and imprisoned.[106]

With the outbreak of the Second Civil War, small-scale risings ensued at Thetford, Bury, Stowmarket and Newmarket. In early summer Norwich's security was again threatened as the parliamentarian fleet mutinied in the Downs and there were rumours that the Prince of Wales and 2000 royalists had landed at Great Yarmouth. On 9 June the earl of Norwich and his Kentish royalist insurgents reached Colchester. On 23 June, the Norwich assembly requested General Fairfax's aid and pledged that it would defend the city 'against any forces whatsoever raysed without authority of Parliament'.[107] This proved unnecessary, as Fairfax's victory at Colchester and Cromwell's triumph over the Scots at Preston ended the matter with dire consequences for Charles I and his supporters.

Norwich was not conspicuously active in the events leading to the regicide, although the assembly ordered a congratulatory letter thanking Cromwell for his solicitude towards the city to be dispatched in January 1649. Yet the petition addressed by leading citizens to the House of Commons on 25 December 1648 was considerably less restrained.[108] Not surprisingly, given its potentially treasonous content, this petition was not recorded in Norwich's Assembly Book. It requested: 'that he himself and all such as have been the most notorious incendiaries and instruments in shedding blood, may without further delay be brought to due and impartial justice'.[109] It

also argued that henceforward laws should be written in English according
to 'the true birthright and privilege of *English* Men', and demanded justice
against those 'that had any hand in the mutinies in Norwich, Kent, and
other Counties'. Norfolk's own regicide, Miles Corbet of Sprowston, later
reflected upon the king's crimes, among which he numbered: 'the horrid
rebellion and bloudy massacres of the Protestants in Ireland, the levying
warr against the parlement and the good people in England'. Even after
1660 he steadfastly regarded the execution of Charles I as God's will and
rejoiced that the Lord had raised up the 'weak things of the world to con-
found the things which are mighty & this is wonderful and glorious in our
eyes'.[110]

Outraged by the regicide, the Scots prepared to invade England again
and restore his son. The parliamentary forces were, however, more than
ready for them. Thomas Atkin wrote in April 1650 'that the Jockies intend
againe to see England ... wee shalbe provided to give them as good a welcome as they had the last time they came'.[111] That autumn, with the New
Model Army engaged in Scotland, Norfolk royalists plotted a rendezvous
at Easton Heath, about three miles outside Norwich. Suspicious hunting
parties and a disorderly crowd awaiting a football match unnerved the
authorities.[112] The conspirators hoped to be let into Norwich once they had
raised enough men, but support failed to materialise. Their muster around
28 November of no more than perhaps fifty was 'nothing answerable to
expectation' and they dispersed, as did similar gatherings at Downham
Market, Swaffham and Thetford. Many were apprehended through the evidence of an informer. Philip Jermyn and John Pulleston presided over their
trials at the shire house in Norwich on 20 December and thereafter at the
new hall. Six of the ringleaders were executed in Norwich market on 23
December, allegedly crying out 'God Save the King' upon the gallows. A
local clergyman named Thomas Cooper was also found guilty of involvement. His rectory at Little Barningham had been sequestered in 1644, and
he had subsequently found employment as Holt's schoolmaster. James Paston's account of the affair records that Cooper was 'tried on Christmas
Day, partly to show their dislike of the observation of that day and partly
to add to his affliction'. He petitioned for a reprieve, but was condemned
on 25 December and executed 'at Holt before his Schoolhouse door'.
William Hobart, one of his confederates, who had turned evidence against
him, was hanged at Dereham the next day.[113]

Paston's account claims that twenty-four royalists were condemned and
executed and that 'the court acquitted not one', but pardons were subsequently granted on 17 January 1651 to John Disney, David Dobbes, Thomas
Hill and Andrew Pope.[114] There were also executions at Downham Market,

Fakenham, Holt, King's Lynn, Swaffham, Thetford and Walsingham. No county gentry were executed. Most of those who died came from parochial gentry or the ranks of the middling sort. Among the latter, Francis Roberts and John Barber, citizens of Norwich, were hanged in the market place, Roberts allegedly outside his own door.[115] Barber was a Norwich brewer of Magdalen Street who had served as a lieutenant in the king's army and surrendered at Powderham castle in Devon in January 1646. He had recently been warned at Norwich quarter sessions in August 1648 not to assist royalist forces. His father had refused the Newcastle subscription in 1643, and Barber pleaded that because of his extreme youth he had been 'unhappily drawn to take up arms for the King against Parliament'.[116] The Norwich Mayor's Book recorded: 'Major Francis Roberts and Leivetennant John Barbor were publiquely executed in the market Place of this Citty on a gallowes there erected.' A different and far later hand continued: 'It may appeare to posterity they were not executed legally nor for any Notorious Crimes vide the order of the court the 4th of December 1675.'[117] One nineteenth-century commentator utilised the still bitter memory of Civil War to stir loyalist outrage against the acquittal in recent treason trials of republican activists: 'For a similar offence *against* royalty in 1795, the conspirators experienced better luck, and afterwards exulted in being called *Acquitted Felons*. One of these *gentlemen*, soon after his trial, came to Norwich, where he was *shown off* as a prodigy of persecuted patriotism!'[118]

The execution of King Charles brought to power a clique of Independents who lacked widespread support. Conservative undercurrents gathered strength in Norwich from 1653 onwards. John Hobart and Barnard Church were returned for the city to the Protectorate Parliaments in 1654 and 1656. Although not royalists, they opposed the army's influence in Parliament and worked to restore the traditional ruling order. In 1656 Hezekiah Haynes, Cromwell's major-general for East Anglia, warned Secretary Thurloe that Norwich was controlled by 'persons notoriously disaffected upon the worst principles [and that] the city was as bad as any other in England'. In 1658 the royalist Roger Mingay was elected mayor, and by 1659 those favourable to a restoration of the monarchy were once more a majority on the aldermanic bench.[119]

In January 1660, fourteen Norwich aldermen and twenty-five common councillors signed the Norfolk Address to General Monck desiring a free parliament. On 10 May Charles II was solemnly proclaimed king. The occasion was marked by several days of bonfires, feasting and an official thanksgiving on 24 May. One month later, Norwich assembly voted to restore to the crown its fee farm rent, which it had purchased in 1650, and

FIGURE 26. The Norfolk regicide, Miles Corbet, was captured by royalist agents while hiding in Holland. Brought back to London to face trial, he was unrepentant, and was executed alongside his colleagues, John Okey and John Barkstead, in 1662. His last confession survives among the holdings of the Norfolk Record Office. (*Cromwell Museum, Huntingdon*)

donated £1000 to Charles II. In August the aldermen and common councillors agreed to take the oath of allegiance and supremacy, reflecting their desire to remain in power. On 20 September, the soldiery in Norwich was at last disbanded.[120]

Not everyone in Norwich welcomed the Restoration. Independents and Presbyterians alike were gradually purged from office. By 1662 Robert Allen, John Andrews, Thomas Ashwell, William Barnham, Edmund Burman, William Davy, Adrian Parmenter, William Rye and Thomas Toft had been ejected from the aldermanic bench. Much of the assembly's legislation since 1642 was renounced as 'inconsistant with and derogatory from the constitucons of a well ordered monarchicall government'. Robert Swallow, captain of Norwich's Maiden Troop, was arrested in November 1662 and committed to the Tower.[121] Norfolk's regicide, Miles Corbet, was captured in the Dutch Republic in 1662 and brought back to face trial. In his last days he wrote a confession of faith that not only justified the regicide but lamented the Godlessness of the Restoration:

> And now the enemy cast iniquity upon us and they reproach all the footsteps of god & all his glorious appearances that been amongst us and they say where is their god and where is their reformation, and oh what a deluge of

profanes of whoredoms swearing cursings drunkenness poperie prelacie malice raige and bitternesss broken out.

Shortly after this remarkably accurate prediction of what was to be
expected from Charles II's court, Corbet was hanged, drawn and quartered
alongside fellow regicides, John Okey and John Barkstead, on 19 April 1662.
His remains were exposed on London Bridge (Figure 26).[122]

It has been argued that Norwich escaped 'the revolutionary excesses of
London' and that the victory of the 'parliamentary-puritans in capturing
the Norwich corporation had been gradual, peaceful, legal and non-
provocative'. In stressing the absence of divisions caused by class,
occupation, age or wealth it is further maintained that 'None of the prominent trades overwhelmingly favoured one side or the other'.[123] These views
ignore the well-documented correlation between parliamentarian allegiance and the cloth trade in Yorkshire, the West Country and East Anglia.
Strong popular support for Parliament was exhibited by Norwich's numerous cloth-workers who congregated in the poorer wards of Wymer and
Over-the-Water, the two districts which were most strongly Puritan and
parliamentarian.[124] Six of the sixteen new aldermen elected between 1649
and 1653 resided in Over-the-Water, whereas after 1660 only one in twelve
did so.[125] The contention that the parochial neighbourhood was the major
factor in determining alignment has received strong support from research
on allegiance formation in Devon. Comparisons between Norwich and
Exeter, another cloth making city, make clear that the opposing factions
were based in different parishes in each city.[126] Royalists, and subsequently
Tories, enjoyed support from the retailers and merchants of Mancroft
ward, while parliamentarians and dissenters were supported in Wymer and
Over-the-Water. These recent explorations of parochial allegiances, largely
based on the study of local office-holding and religious culture, provide a
promising historical framework for uncovering popular activism in the
civil wars and documenting political affiliations thereafter.

   The memory of the civil wars shaped Whig and Tory rivalry well into
the eighteenth century. In 1703 the monument to Dean Henry Fairfax was
covered with a cloak until the offending words 'Nasebiani' and 'Pii' had
been erased. It was felt that the monument's commemoration of the
deceased dean's parliamentarian cousin Sir Thomas Fairfax gloried in
rebellion and would provoke a riot by a Tory mob.[127] The arch-Tory *Norwich Gazette*, damned the English Republic and derided local Whigs: 'They
can with a *Puritanic* modesty deny their Sovereign's right and title to his
very face, and with *Oliverian* loyalty murder him to make him a *glorious*

Prince.'[128] In its vitriolic response to the events of the French Revolution, a handbill of 1796 invoked the memory of civil war: 'Remember OLD NOLL, let no sect whatever tempt you to rise against the Church, by Law established ... under the support of God let me advise you to shun all Democrats and factious discontented parties.'[129] Norwich's parliamentarian past, like that of the camping time of 1549, was not to be celebrated.

5

Health and Sanitation to 1750

Margaret Pelling

When shall the Muses by faire Norwich dwell,
To be the Citie of the Learned Well?
... Or when shall that faire hoofe-plow'd Spring distill
From great Mount-Surrey, out of Leonards Hill?

Michael Drayton, 'Epistle of the Lady Geraldine
to Henry Howard, Earl of Surrey'[1]

Early modern observers seem to have agreed that Norwich was a clean and healthy city. At the end of the seventeenth century Celia Fiennes contrasted well-paved Norwich, Ipswich, and Colchester with Ely, which she thought damp and filthy.[2] Many, like John Evelyn, conducted around Norwich by its most famous physician, Sir Thomas Browne, linked Norwich's size, its cleanliness, and the ample and agreeable spaces within its walls.[3] Some might also give credit to the major influxes of immigrants from the Netherlands, whose national stereotype at the time included cleanliness as well as drunkenness, or to Norwich's tendency to 'godliness', especially in the late sixteenth and early seventeenth centuries when a range of public health and welfare measures were experimented with, although each of these hypotheses is questionable.[4]

Modern commentators have tended to see such cleanliness as impressive only when compared with other places at the time. Any given society tends to think that there is only one way – its own – of being clean. In general, it has been assumed that the Tudor and Stuart periods were dirtier either than the middle ages or the eighteenth century.[5] In fact, historians of periods before the Industrial Revolution have not given much attention to basic sanitary arrangements, or to the physical relationship of ordinary people to their environment.[6] Thus, even for a well-studied city like Norwich, with published work on housing and the built landscape generally, as well as on social policy, there seems to be very little on such essential features as rivers, streams, drainage and wells. Partly because rivers have been so thoroughly superseded by a system of transport based on roads, the major role of water in shaping movement and experience for early modern people is not now given the prominence it deserves. Some exceptions to this are archaeological surveys, studies of regions particularly influenced by water levels, such as the Fens or the Kent marshes, and work on London, where logistics and environmental pollution alike demanded a response from contemporaries.[7]

Was Norwich indeed healthy? Given continued uncertainty about population totals in the early modern period, this question can be quantified only in terms of epidemic outbreaks. For plague especially, 'excess' mortality can be measured in parish registers and in the Bills of Mortality which Norwich was one of the earliest provincial towns to introduce. Regrettably, the bills did not record causes of death, although plague deaths were distinguished after 1590.[8] Chronologies of notable local events give some indication of epidemic outbreaks, as they do of fires and floods.[9] Norwich shared the experience of major urban centres at this period in terms of the gradual shift from plague and sweating sickness to smallpox and acute fevers, especially typhus (gaol fever, prison fever). Of almost equal importance, but comparatively neglected by historians because it did not register in the same way in the mortality figures, was venereal disease, predominantly what was later called syphilis. In the Tudor and early Stuart periods 'the French pox' was coupled with plague by contemporaries as a threat to the social order and a problem particularly among the vagrant poor. Norwich's five lazar houses were adapted to deal with this problem, a process involving a degree of municipal control. Norwich's other hospitals included some provision for sick inmates, but their strictly medical role was limited. The necessary functions of segregation and medical care were carried out by the lazarhouses or farmed out to individuals paid by the municipality. Although small and relatively fragile as institutions, and essentially private rather than public, the lazarhouses continued to take in sick people well into the seventeenth century, and had a more prominent and enduring role in the life of the city than any of the 'pest-houses' provided for plague.[10]

Behind these more dramatic events, and far more elusive historically, lies the experience of accidents, childbirth, malnutrition, old age, disability, chronic illness and the everyday toll of sickness not ending in death. Notable among painful and chronic diseases was the stone or calculus, which was prevalent in East Anglia until the early twentieth century. To this we are given some access by the correspondence of the literate elite, for example Humphrey Prideaux, dean of Norwich from 1702.[11] But the poor, and children, also suffered from the stone, and Norwich experimented with reducing the high cost of treating this condition by retaining the services of a lithotomist. For similar reasons the city also employed the services of bonesetters, an experiment which was more successful, and which involved a dynasty of practitioners over about a century. Norwich does not seem to have retained any midwives, although individual parishes may have done so; some impression of the circumstances of childbirth among servants and the poor is given by filiation proceedings, although these tended to be formulaic.[12] The best source for the state of health of a substantial proportion of Norwich's population, or indeed for the population of any early modern English city, remains the famous Census of the Poor of 1570. About 7 per cent of the 2359 men, women and children listed in the census were recorded as ill or disabled, suffering from a range of conditions, including broken or sore legs, gout, limb loss, dumbness, fistula, 'French pox', rupture and lunacy. This survey represents a minimum, partly because children and adolescents were under-recorded, and partly because both the census takers and the poor themselves are likely to have concentrated only on the conditions which were severe enough to prevent the person, or his or her relatives, from working; a specific diagnosis was not usually necessary.[13] As ever, the nature of the record affects the information we are given.

Towards the other end of the period, the same is true of the information offered by a series of verdicts of coroners' inquests, mainly for the parish of St Julian. These cases, sixty-one in all, are concerned with suicides, deaths by accident or violence, possible infanticide, and deaths in prison. The suicides, 'not having the fear of God before their eyes', hanged themselves indoors, threw themselves into the river, or, more rarely, used poison ('ratisbane or astnicke') or a knife.[14] Two of the total of seven suicides were 'lunaticke' or troubled in mind.[15] The prisoners, thirty-two in all and mostly debtors, were recorded as dying from either a 'visitation of sickness' or a restricted range of conditions: smallpox (1687), dropsy (alone and with other conditions such as a swollen throat), violent or hectic fever, black jaundice, scurvy, consumption, 'a paralitick distemper', a fit, violent pain in the stomach, and gangrene following a blow.[16] There is no indication that expert medical evidence was taken in these cases. By contrast, evidence from a surgeon, John Booth, was sought in 1688 to decide whether William Harper, aged eight, died of smallpox or from blows during a game called 'Salt Ele', 'usually plaid att with boyes', involving the hiding of a rope end.[17] The accidental deaths included several people killed by carts, a man of around sixty-six who fell downstairs onto a 'thicksell' he was carrying, and a labourer aged forty smothered when the well he was working on collapsed.[18]

Water-related circumstances were predominant among the accidental deaths, pointing to their ubiquity in everyday life. The victims included a child of five playing with a hoop in his father's yard in St Martin's at Oak; Temperance House, singlewoman and servant, aged around forty, washing dishclouts on the staithe at her mistress's house at Heigham; a woman of about eighty putting off in a boat early in the morning to rinse clothes; Robert Dixon, in his fifties, going home late in the dark; the four-year-old daughter of a Yarmouth waterman, playing on the 'key' in the parish of St Simon and St Jude; a younger child, 'being sett upon a seate in a house of office ... next over the river' at her father's house; an apprentice aged fifteen who went wading in midsummer; and a man in his twenties angling from a boat, were all accidentally drowned.[19] In the case of Temperance House, 'the barr of the said stath being insufficiently fixed did fall downe', so that she fell into the river. Even in the case of a girl suspected of infanticide, we find an explanation of her condition in terms of an injury she allegedly suffered from the crank wheel of a well in the dark.[20]

Emphasis on environmental measures, the imposition of forms of quarantine, and, indeed, the extent of lay authority exercised over health and disease in Norwich might lead to the conclusion that contemporaries had little or no faith in the power of medicine to heal or cure. This was far from being the case. Evidence from Norwich is especially valuable in demonstrating a high demand for medical care, and the proliferation of practitioners called upon to provide it.[21] Estimated ratios of practitioners to population in Norwich are as high as 1:200 for this period, though this should be set against other features, such as the wide range of practitioners (male and female), the part-time character of much practice, and the nature of patient-practitioner relationships. Sick people or their friends and relatives habitually used a number of different practitioners or were highly selective in their choice, depending on their own estimate of the condition in question. This pattern of high levels of consumption combined with selectivity was particularly noticeable, and perhaps predictable, among the elite – families such as the Pastons, living outside Norwich, expected practitioners to travel to them from the city – but it is also apparent in the attempts by the authorities to provide medical care for the poor. It was characteristic for poor women to be employed to care for, and treat, the poor, in order to solve two problems at once; this was also typical of what was then seen as an appropriate moral symmetry, but might now be called hypothecation, whereby fines for offences against the residents were used to pay for poor relief or improvement schemes. The Norwich authorities, however, saw it as both fitting and cost-effective to employ the full range of practitioners, including academically qualified physicians, to treat

the poor, depending upon the nature of the condition. They were even prepared to bring in specialist advice from a distance, just as Norwich was
included in the itineraries of oculists and other specialists.

Norwich was a relatively open city, so that, while many of its barbers,
barber-surgeons and even physicians were organised into a gild or company,
an almost equal proportion of Norwich practitioners cannot be connected
with these companies. The apothecaries traded in the market-place – the
spiceria – but their organisational affiliation remains uncertain.[22] It was
comparatively unusual in the early modern period for a Norwich barber-
surgeon to enrol an apprentice, which seems to have been the determining
factor in taking out the freedom, except when the municipality made a
concerted effort to improve the organisation of occupations. The idealised
progression, evident in the middle ages, whereby an apprentice born in
Norwich went on to become a master and to take on apprentices in his
turn perhaps became the exception rather than the rule. Norwich practitioners could be licensed by a range of authorities, or not licensed at all;
lack of a licence or company connection did not deter the city from
offering employment. It is clear that faith in one's chosen practitioner,
based on the widest possible choice, was an aspect of both public and private medicine in Norwich, and environmental regulation should be seen
as complementary to this. Both involved predominantly lay control.

Similarly, the attempt here to capture 'lost' aspects of Norwich's experience
should not be seen as implying that the city did not participate fully in
what might be called progressive tendencies. There were few municipal
building initiatives over the period in question, but the fifteenth century
had seen considerable activity; features such as the New Mills (water-mills
on the Wensum near Heigham gates) and the Old and New Common
staithes (in Conesford, south of Bishop's bridge) were well established by
1500.[23] Similarly, major aspects of Norwich's environment – its walls, the
numerous and extensive open spaces within them, its bridges, the broad
outlines of its housing – remained remarkably stable over the period, but
this was in part because in these respects Norwich was unusual or developed early. The walls, in place by the mid-fourteenth century, then
encircled an area as large as London, but with only a quarter of the population. London made do with a single bridge across the Thames until the
mid-eighteenth century; Norwich, in part as a reflection of its having set-
tlements of more equal size on either side of the river, as well as the extent
of its trade to the north, had five bridges in place by 1300, as well as a
ferry; and, apart from replacements, no more were built until the early
nineteenth century.[24] There were, likewise, four bridges across the Yare to

the south in the medieval period, transport to London by road developed early, and Norwich was credited with one of the earliest turnpikes in England, established between Norwich and Attleborough in 1707.[25] The perspective map of 1558 by the physician William Cuningham, said to be the first such record of the appearance of an English provincial town, gives the impression that Norwich's 'great rebuilding' had already occurred (Figure 3).[26]

That the open spaces within the walls survived so long is perhaps more puzzling, and undoubtedly had consequences, good and bad, for health. Commentators from the sixteenth century to the twentieth noted that increased population, particularly among the poor, led not to encroachment on the open spaces but to infilling and the proliferation of crowded courts, even though Norwich's burgage plots are said not to have been large. Part of the open land can be assumed to have been subject to flooding, even though marshland was progressively reclaimed and the river deepened and narrowed over the period; otherwise, the explanation is presumably in terms of land ownership and the requirements of major occupations like cloth-making, which needed extensive tenter-grounds.[27] The river meadows also allowed for transport canals, and for the creation of a new swanpit in the grounds of the Great Hospital, rebuilt in brick by William Ivory in 1793, with a connection to the river. The swanpit was a semi-public institution, and claims have been made for its rarity (Plate 5).[28] The orchards within the walls were evidently valued, and animals continued to be grazed in the open spaces and even in lanes, although intra-mural agriculture is not seen as significant for the city in economic terms.[29] In 1671 there was a complaint that 'immoderate campings and dauncings' were spoiling the pasture at Gildencroft.[30] The meadow on the river in the south part of the cathedral grounds leased by Sir Thomas Browne from 1669 was evidently used as an adjunct to his garden in the Haymarket; part of it was subsequently built upon, but the rest became a clerical vegetable garden, then allotments, until, in a manner characteristic of the late twentieth century, it became a car park.[31]

None the less, as with Chapelfield, which, besides providing pasturage, was also the site of the city's artillery ground and, later, of parts of the water-supply system, the public gardens seen as essential to gracious living, health and entertainment in the eighteenth century were created just within or outside the city walls.[32] Markets for livestock were gradually transferred from 'plains' at the junctions of streets to areas such as the castle dikes, and the stalls of butchers and fishmongers were also improved or relocated.[33] By the end of the eighteenth century, middle-class opinion, in the name of 'airiness', convenience, regularity and uniformity, was demanding the taking down of street signs in favour of numbers; demolition of the remaining walls, gates, and older housing; and the straightening and opening up of frequented streets, by the removal of houses if need be. Water channels in streets were denounced, as were water-spouts (which presumably emptied roof guttering). Associated recommendations, such as closing the city graveyards, long preceded the better-known campaigns of nineteenth-century sanitary reformers.[34] In general, change occurred in terms of uses rather than physical infrastructure until the nineteenth century, although, as we shall see, aspects of water supply constitute an exception to this.

The developments sketched above give some indication of the balance between water and land in Norwich's consciousness in the period in question, but with the emphasis on the latter. It is desirable to redress the balance. Norwich was not a coastal city; and, even though the Wensum remained navigable into the modern period, Norwich was already losing its port and fishery functions to Yarmouth by the thirteenth century. The conjunction of Norwich and Yarmouth, however, remained unusual, even unique, and the river system was essential to this.[35] Forms or tokens of shared responsibility for the Yare and the Wensum persisted until the 1880s, the jurisdictional boundary being fixed at a confluence of rivers at Hardley Cross.[36] The Wensum was both an amenity and a vital asset – 'a faire river' in the language of the earlier period, 'a quiet English stream' according to later observers.[37] But it was inevitably compromised by its urban setting, being disparaged by John Evelyn and Thomas Baskerville, according to seventeenth-century notions about great estates, as unfit to border a nobleman's residence. For Evelyn it was a 'very narrow muddy [river], without any extent'; for Baskerville, the site of the duke of Norfolk's palace was a 'dunghole', and the river fouled by the effluent of dyeworks.[38] Celia Fiennes, travelling in 1698, found the vicinity of Norwich relatively damp: from Beccles it was 'low flatt ground all here about so that the least raines they are overflowed by the river' and she approached Norwich, apparently *via* Bishop's bridge, on 'a high causey ... which lookes somewhat dangerous, being fenced with trenches ... pretty deep', the trenches being to drain the low ground so that it could be used for bleaching cloth. From Norwich she rode south west, towards Wymondham, 'mostly on a causey the country being low and moorish'. Ditches, rather than fences or hedges, were a common and effective means of marking boundaries or keeping in stock, especially if they were filled with water.[39] The ferry house at Surlingham became an island in flood time even at a much later date.[40]

Rushes, reeds and sedges were cut for thatching, rushlights and other purposes, a process that continues into the present day. Norfolk's comparative lack of woodland meant a demand for peat fuel, thus creating the pits which, once abandoned, became the Broads; these were not recognised as artificially created until the 1960s, but the term was used from at least the Jacobean period and has been claimed as peculiar to Norfolk. The ground begins to level out after Bramerton, 'the goal of the usual evening's row' in the nineteenth century.[41] One of the Broads nearest to Norwich, Surlingham, about six miles away, marked the boundary for the cutting of the river carried out each year by Norwich's city authorities.[42] Many of the Broads lie on the Bure, but those on the Yare between Norwich and Yarmouth meant that these wide stretches of water were part of Norwich's experience. The Broads did not become one of the favoured English 'playgrounds' until the late nineteenth century, after the advent of the railways, but they provided hunting-grounds as well as raw materials for early modern people. Norwich's barbers and barber-surgeons produced some of the game-nets used to catch fish and birds. 'Decoys' – curved and netted tunnels for luring and catching wildfowl – were used on the Broads from before the Civil War, perhaps earlier than anywhere else. Even the Wensum as it passed through the city centre was fished on a commercial basis.[43] Sir Thomas Browne, a naturalist as well as a physician, wrote with great enthusiasm about the teeming supplies of pike, tench, bream, roach and other fish to be had in the waters between Norwich and the sea (Figure 27).[44]

It was self-evident to Norwich's citizens that a balance had to be struck in the uses made of the river. The state of the river, like that of the walls and 'the king's highway', was seen as an aspect of local responsibility devolved by the monarch; defence was ostensibly a primary issue until at least 1452, and arose again during later crises. The very detailed accounts of Kett's Rebellion provide illuminating reflections on the topography of the city and its river.[45] What we might see as the lyricism of Thomas Fuller is a device to imply the need for control, partly in the interests of defence: 'The river Yere [i.e. Wensum], so wanton, that it knoweth not its own mind which way to goe, such [that] the involved flexures thereof within a mile of this city, runneth partly by, partly through it, but contributeth very little to the strengthning thereof.[46] Running water in large quantities was vital for a number of trades besides millers, including brewers, dyers, skinners, parchment-makers and slaughterers, but most of their activities were also highly polluting, and the rights of householders, especially to water for washing, had to be protected.[47] A widow, Anne Appelton, was presented in 1623 'for annoying the new stath called St Anns Stath with washing ther neats wombs or bellys to the great annoyance of the poor people whoe have

FIGURE 27. Nineteenth-century sketch of Bishop's Bridge showing a fisherman on the left and a waste-pipe on the right. (*Trustees of the Great Hospital, Norwich*)

no other place to fetch watter at'.[48] This, and the proper disposal of 'muck', are evident concerns in the surviving medieval records, as one part of the legal concept of nuisance, which largely governed this area of civic life until the nineteenth century. Norwich's lanes, which tended to be multi-purpose but semi-private spaces, provided access to water but were also convenient for muckheaps, which could affect the river. Bargains were regularly struck between the city and individuals or parishes to ensure a combination of private use, public access and the proper supervision of lanes. Decayed walls, lanes and even muckheaps could be seen as offering opportunities for criminal elements, especially at night.[49]

Commissioners for Sewers – a term then connoting water systems more than artificial drainage – were promulgated by central government authority from the early fifteenth century, but records of proceedings do not begin for Norwich until 1615. The 'river and street accounts', on the other hand, are complete from 1556, four years after reforms were first instituted, until they become unreliable in the 1710s.[50] Throughout these accounts, although it is rent from lands which provides the income, the emphasis in terms of action taken and paid for is on the river rather than on the streets. It is not possible here to examine the accounts from the financial point of view.[51] Instead, they will be used, with other sources, to gain some impression of Norwich's combination of water and place.

The first point to note is that Norwich's commitment to river and water management appears to have produced a terminology peculiar to the locality. The first such term is 'didall', meaning a (metal) net on the end of a pole, or a sharp, triangular spade with a long handle, used for clearing out rivers and ditches. There was a related verb, to dydall, or didle. This term was in regular use from at least 1490, when it appears in city records, to the 1890s.[52] A second is the verb to fye, not unique to Norwich but identified by the antiquary, Walter Rye, as a dialect word, and used very frequently in the accounts, as in fyeing or feying the river, a drain, a ditch, or a well. This word carried a more definite meaning of 'to cleanse'.[53] 'Bottom-fyeing' implied a thorough, and therefore less frequent, process than 'croming'.[54] It is not clear whether 'fyeing' is related to the name of Fye bridge, the point of termination of watersheds and the most frequently used route to the north.[55] A third term, possibly unique to Norwich and important to its early modern topography, is cockey, the derivatives of which included 'cockeyfyer' and 'cockey keepers'.[56] This term occurs from the medieval period but is ubiquitous in the early modern accounts.[57] Norwich's historians have differed over its meaning, in such a way as to reflect their preconceptions about Norwich's sanitary condition at earlier periods. Kirkpatrick took the cockeys to be gutters or kennels, or sewers in the modern sense; this was later contradicted by Harrod and Hudson, who argued strongly that the cockeys were natural streams flowing towards the river, which ran not just along streets but across them, and had been detected flowing underground even when they were built over. On the basis largely of documents about property, Hudson produced major amendments to Kirkpatrick's account. The lines he traced for the principal cockeys were followed by Campbell in the authoritative Atlas of Historic Towns, although the courses in some respects remain probable rather than certain.[58]

The most important of these streams or creeks was the Great Cockey, which rose from Jakkes or Jack's Pit at the junction of Surrey Street and All Saints Green, and ran north and west of the castle through the parishes of St Stephen and St Peter Mancroft, along Back of the Inns or London Lane, west along (Great) Cockey Lane, then north again through St Andrew's and St John Maddermarket, to enter the Wensum west of Blackfriars bridge. The Great Cockey retained a more precise definition partly because of its size, and partly because it served as a parochial boundary (Map 1). A shorter cockey south of the river rose from another pit at the end of Pit Lane on the hill near St Giles's church, then descended along

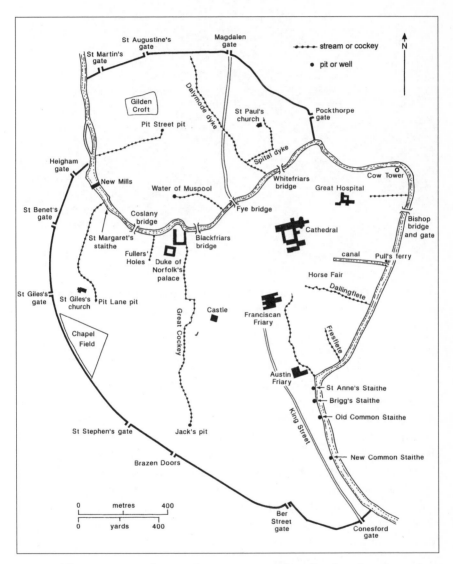

MAP 1. The streams, cockeys and watercourses of medieval and early modern Norwich. (*Phillip Judge*)

FIGURE 28. The New Mills, River Wensum and cockey as they appeared in 1818, by John Crome. (*School of World Art Studies, UEA*)

the line of Willow Lane and St Swithin's Lane, crossing Upper and Lower Westwick to enter the Wensum between the New Mills and St Margaret's staithe (Figure 28). To the east, three shorter cockeys arose in the vicinity of Rose Lane, crossing St Faith's or St Vedast's Lane to enter the river as it curved around the parishes of St Mary-in-the-Marsh and St Peter Parmentergate. The most northerly of these ran under 'the Stone Bridge' near the Horse Fair, and in earlier documents was called Dallingflete; it was also known as Grey Friars creek.[59] The middle one of this group was called Fresflete or 'ffreslet'; the most southerly entered the river at the bend just above St Anne's staithe, near the church of St Michael in Conesford.[60] A fourth cockey arose near the Great Hospital and ran parallel to Bishopgate, entering the river just north of Bishop's bridge (Figure 27).[61] The major cockeys to the north of the river are more obscure, and seem to have disappeared from view earlier; the longest, called Dalymond Dyke, has been traced from outside the city walls near the parish boundary of St Augustine's and St Paul's, thence through St Saviour's and St Edmund's to enter the river west of Whitefriars bridge. As it flowed through St Edmund's, this stream connected with another, called Spiteldyke, which arose near St Paul's church, crossed Norman's Lane, then bent to cross Rotten Row before joining the Dalymond. The 'water of Muspool' was a short but apparently broad and open cockey rising from a pool near the church of St George Colegate, running along Colegate Street through St Clement's and entering the Wensum between Fye bridge and Blackfriars bridge.[62]

Between them these streams traversed large areas of the city. Some records suggest that, like the river, they were essential for carrying away effluent, especially where they were covered over, but that they were not meant to be used indiscriminately for the wholesale disposal of muck.[63] It might be inferred, therefore, that the city was simply concerned with keeping its watercourses clean and free-flowing, whether covered or not, for the sake of the air as much as the water itself. The authorities paid for 'dydalling of the ... cockeys mouthes at the rivers side', for example; 'cockey mouths' could be the same as the 'cockey heads', which are also referred to.[64] But there are discrepancies: a second Cockey Lane, for instance, which ran between King Street and the river just north of the Old Common staithe, by the ground of St Clement's church in Conesford, has no connection with any of the streams just described.[65] Similarly, there was another cockey nearby in Conesford, 'Mr Briggs's cockey', presumably associated with Mr Briggs's staithe.[66] There were cockeys at the gates: one is recorded at Heigham, where the cockey, or cockeys, were associated with a drain and the dike, or long ditch, running along the city wall between Heigham and St Benet's gates, which the accounts suggest was still 'wet' at this period.[67] There was yet another at St Benet's gates, possibly 'new made' in the late fifteenth century, and associated in the accounts with both a drain and a cistern.[68] At St Stephen's gates, further south on the western wall, and on the main route to London, there was a 'great cockey', apparently outside the gate and perhaps similarly connected with the mural ditch, part of which may still have contained water to a late date.[69]

Other subsidiary cockeys, known by their parish names in the more detailed lists kept in the accounts in the seventeenth century, are more difficult to distinguish from the major cockey streams: St Andrew's, St Anne's, St Clement's, St Edmund's and St Paul's, St Faith's, St George Colegate, St Giles's, St Gregory's, St James's, St Lawrence's, St Martin-at-Palace, St Michael Coslany, St Paul's, St Simon's and St Swithin's.[70] Further cockeys took the names of the bridges, especially Blackfriars and Fye bridge, but also Whitefriars.[71] At Bishop's bridge, the accounts refer only to a drain or gutter on the outer side.[72] Cockeys were given place-names, too: those at the back gate of the Angel and the White Lion (presumably on the line of the Great Cockey along the Back of the Inns), 'the Friars cockey', the hospital dike or cockey between Rotten Row and Colegate, the cockeys by the mills, the common staithe cockey, 'the Bull cockey'.[73]

Personal names occur with greater frequency: Mr Sheriff Anguish's cockey, Mr Briggs's (already mentioned), Elmeham's cockey, the cockey near Sir Henry Gaudy's house, Mr Goldman's cockey, Mr Hassett's, Mr Hornsey's, Mr Howse's, Mr Layer's, Mr Mingay's, Mr Norrys's, Mr Pitcher's, and Mr (Edmund) Toft's.[74] Most, but not all, of these names belong to families prominent in Norwich's affairs. Occasionally a longer entry provides some elucidation of a short one: Anguish's cockey is more fully described in 1639–40, when payment is made for fyeing the cockey in St Faith's Lane running through Mr Anguish's ground at the Friars, sug- gesting that this cockey and the Friars' cockey could be one and the same.[75] Elmeham is identified as a barber, who was reimbursed in 1594–5 for keep- ing the cockey by his house.[76] Robert Howse was paid in 1615–16 for carrying away muck from his cockey, and a namesake was still 'keeping' it in 1645–6.[77] Mr Goldman's cockey was known by that name from at least 1609–10 to 1679–80. The accounts also mention scouring of the drain by Mr Hassett's, and bottom-fyeing the river at the same place.[78]

This plethora of cockey names might be thought to reflect the well- known subdivision of responsibility for street-paving, rubbish disposal and even river maintenance among urban householders and parishes.[79] Cockey names therefore proliferated as a result of changes in property ownership or responsibility. On this reading, with certain important exceptions already indicated, the cockeys were simply sections of the cockey streams, divided up and allocated to the property-owners most concerned. It should be stressed, however, that, in all the cases mentioned, the costs of fyeing or cleansing the cockeys were borne by the city on a regular basis. Moreover, the river and street accounts also indicate that the system of cockeys was more elaborate, and more artificial, than is suggested simply by tracing their courses as streams. This is reflected in Kirkpatrick's usage, and in Rye's alternative definition of a cockey as the trap leading to a drain. It does not seem that a cockey head in Crouch Lane, for example, can be identi- fied with the Great Cockey's mouth at the river further north, although a grate at the 'head' of the Great Cockey was replaced by a new large iron grate in the early Tudor period. By the 1650s the two cockeys in St Michael Coslany also had grates.[80]

Drains are mentioned with frequency in the accounts, either in connec- tion with cockeys or separately. There were 'cisterns' associated with the cockeys from at least the 1630s; four or five are recorded by the early eigh- teenth century, identified in 1719–20 as being at St Anne's staithe, by Mr Godfrey's, at St Andrew's, by the Three Privies (of which more later), and in the parish of St Swithin, Coslany, near the river. If, in terms of rough proximity, the location at Mr Briggs's staithe can be conflated with that at St Anne's staithe, and the Three Privies with St Martin-at-Palace, this list, with the exception of St Andrew's, can be matched with another compiled a few years later, which locates 'Mr Godfrey's' in St Swithin's parish.[81] Judging by a transaction from the early Tudor period, when one Thomas Large obtained a lane near the New Common staithe by paying for a cistern for the mud and soil washed up there, these cisterns seem to have been for clarifying the water flow and accumulating muck to prevent its silting up the river; this mud, once extracted, could be useful for other purposes.[82] It seems likely that such sediment would have included a rich admixture of sewage.

At least one other cistern, however, seems to have been part of a water supply system. King's Lynn possessed a drinking water pump built at a water mill in 1578.[83] At about the same time (1582) the rulers of Norwich had water conveyed from the New Mills (which was upstream of most of the built-up area) via St Lawrence's steeple to the arcaded cross in the marketplace, where there was also a common well or pump until around the early eighteenth century. The new supply was designed in part to improve the state of the nearby cockeys (Map 2).[84] The accounts mention a 'new Ingen' from 1643–4, but since this engine was movable – eight men were paid in 1648–9 to pull it from Coslany bridge – it cannot have been part of the water supply system. It was worked intensively for several years and was most likely used for dredging the Wensum. It employed 'great cable rope', an 'ancor', a 'great bucket' and three boats to service it. Rope was obtained from Yarmouth for it, and a 'Yarmouth man' was employed to work on it. Blomefield, writing from a royalist perspective, interprets these works not so much as defensive measures to protect the city from attack as being designed to prevent fugitives from escaping across the river to join the king.[85]

The main waterworks seem to have been run by lessees from the sixteenth century, an arrangement continued when new ones were built from 1699. Reservoirs were located first at Tombland and then in Chapelfield, the former also being described, somewhat confusingly, as a cistern.[86] References from 1652–53 to 'the cistern' may concern the one at Tombland. It must have been the Tombland works, a large red brick structure with a reservoir on the roof, that Celia Fiennes described in 1698 as

a great well house with a wheele to wind up the water for the good of the publick; a little farther is a large pond walled up with brick a mans height

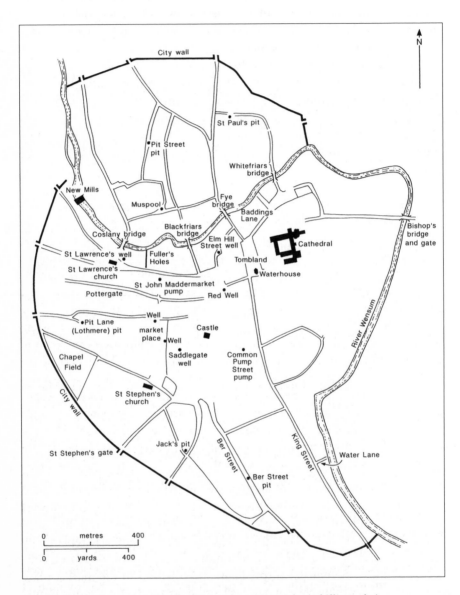

MAP 2.. The pits and wells of early modern Norwich. (*Phillip Judge*)

with an entrance on one end, a little farther was a building on which they were at work design'd for a water house to supply the town by pipes into their houses with water, at a little distance was another such a pond walled in … these things fill up the middle of this spacious streete which is for use and also ornament, the spaces each side being so broad.[87]

The Tombland waterhouse was condemned as a 'filthy building' in 1783, and was taken down in 1786, being replaced by a tower or obelisk enclosing an aqueduct, and a hydraulic machine or engine.[88]

The main waterworks may have supplied piped water to select households which could pay for it, but it was probably as important for fire-fighting as for water supply.[89] Norwich's citizens also got their household water from local sources. Water in any quantity is very heavy, and easy access was essential, although it should be noted that water sources had at this period an individuality which has now largely been lost. For drinking and for healing more distant sources might also be valued, as with the 'spring of pleasant water, formerly much resorted to', beyond Bishop's bridge, over which Sir John Pettus built a protective conduit in 1611. Customs relating to wells are, however, comparatively rare in East Anglia as a whole.[90] References to domestic, privately owned wells crop up only incidentally in the early modern city records (although they proliferate in medieval deeds and accounts), and it is archaeological evidence which demonstrates how routinely they were sunk and replaced, a process continuing into the twentieth century.[91]

Easier to locate, but still not straightforward, are the common wells: in the market place, already mentioned; in Elm Hill Street; in Ber Street; the Saddlegate well, in White Lion Lane, 'disused, in common, a long time' when Blomefield was writing;[92] St Lawrence's well, reached from Lower Westwick Street; and the Red Well in the parish of St Michael-at-Plea or Muspol. The last is said to have been a replacement for a pool, and was itself replaced by a pump and another well in 1629, only to be condemned as an obstruction in an overly narrow lane in 1783. Red Well Street ran west on the south side of the river, giving access to both the well and 'Red Well Plain' from Tombland.[93] The Elm Hill Street well was similarly replaced by a pump in 1639; the Ber Street 'common draw well' had likewise been converted by 1814.[94] Somewhat surprisingly, the situation in the market place does not seem entirely clear: a new well at the northern end was apparently built in 1591, which Starkings interprets as a necessary complement to the waterworks installed nearly a decade earlier; Blomefield implies the existence of a late medieval well on this site, rebuilt in 1453, and railed in 1679, but entirely demolished by his own time; Browne, on the other hand, locates a well at the opposite end of the market place, in the Haymarket, built in 1591, which was still represented in 1814 by a pump.[95]

Campbell's reconstructed map of *c.* 1789 identifies a further pump in Common Pump Street, on the parish boundary of St Michael-at-Thorn and St Peter Parmentergate, and another a little way east from St Lawrence's, just north of the church of St John Maddermarket.[96] As was commonplace with respect to locations where people, especially women, gathered to wash or draw water, Pump Street became 'somewhat notorious'.[97] Kirkpatrick evoked a once-damp area in St Stephen's or Nedham Street, where there was a 'little void place', with a common well, near St Stephen's Plain or Nedham Slothe, which he explained as denoting a slough or 'deep miry place' made from the confluence of water from kennels before the streets were paved.[98] The St Lawrence well had a more individual history. This was a common well from the medieval period; in 1547, the parishioners were granted the well and the lane leading to it provided they gated the lane and kept the gate closed at night. In 1576 or 1577, Robert Gybson, a wealthy beer brewer and later sheriff, acquired the lane on the proviso of installing a pump bringing water from the well for the parishioners through a lead cock or conduit. 'Gybson's pump', and the doggerel inscribed above it, was eventually reinstalled on the wall of the Anchor Brewery in Lower Westwick Street (Figure 29). Gybson's claims to being a champion of the public health are undermined not just by the nature of the bargain he made but by his defiance in 1602, when he was an alderman, of precautions against the plague.[99]

Much less well defined than the wells are the pits. As already indicated, this name was in common use during the early modern period, when Jack's Pit, at least, was already a long-established feature.[100] The latter, and the pit at the end of Pit Lane, mentioned above, stood in the middle of major thoroughfares; another two have been located, St Paul's pit, at the junction of All Saints Street and Rotten Row, and one near St Olave's church, north of the river, in Pit Street.[101] None of them appears to have then been a 'pit' in the modern sense, however. The first two, and possibly the third, marked the source of cockeys or creeks, and Jack's Pit was described as a 'large piece of water' in the parish of All Saints, long since filled in, and partly built over, in 1814. Kirkpatrick stated that the one in Pit St (or St Olave's) was a 'common' pit, filled up 'a few years agoe'.[102] It could be surmised that these pits were the site of springs, but they must also, given their location, have been partly artificial. Moreover, as we have seen with respect to cockeys, many others appear in the civic records: a 'new' pit, with a drain, so described between 1656–7 and 1679–80; one in the parish of St John of the Sepulchre, which, complaints alleged, had not been fyed in

FIGURE 29. St Laurence's Well and Robert Gybson's pump as they appeared in the early nineteenth century, by John Sell Cotman. (*School of World Art Studies, UEA*)

1694; a third, in St John Timberhill, similarly presented in 1694 and 1695, for which the city chamberlain was responsible; and a pit on the west side of St Stephen's gates, which by 1814 was seen as a nuisance and was to be filled in.[103] Ber Street, another main thoroughfare, had a large pit of water, similarly removed by this date.[104] 'Lothmere', a medieval survival, is apparently identical with the pit in Pit Lane (near St Giles's), which Kirkpatrick knew before it was filled up and paved.[105]

Other neighbourhood pools are harder to identify.[106] Probably more industrial in origin was Fuller's Hole, linked with Fye bridge in the accounts and possibly related to Fuller's Lane, which met the river on its south bank between the bridges of Coslany and Blackfriars. It had its own cockey, and was fyed or cleansed by the city between at least 1643 and 1690.[107] The pits may have served for watering animals, being in most cases near livestock markets or entrances to the city, but there were also designated common watering places on the river: one in Conesford, at the end of Water or Watering Lane just south of the second Cockey Lane, between the Old and New Common stathes, and 'near the sign of the Ship' in 1706;[108] one or perhaps two near the New Mills and Lower Westwick, also identified as being in the parish of St Martin over the Water, Coslany, and as having later become a staithe;[109] one in St Clement's parish, also superseded by a washing staithe, in the early Tudor period;[110] and another just to the east, in the lane linking Fish Gate Street to the river alongside St Edmund's church. The last was for horses in Kirkpatrick's time, and had previously been a quay.[111] We should note that, as with the wells and staithes, this list relates only to the common watering places, not those available on private property.

Much the same point can also be made about privies, or houses of office. In common with so many ideas about cleanliness in general, it is assumed that, if anything, the Tudor and Stuart period saw a decline from monastic or medieval standards, but such questions cannot be settled without a serious search for whatever information is available for sites other than major public buildings. Like wells, domestic cesspits and related arrangements are accorded some of their true importance by archaeology. Excavations in Norwich have revealed relatively sophisticated 'garderobe' structures in quite modest houses in fifteenth-century Pottergate. In 1585 it was made clear that landlords were expected to provide 'jakes' for their tenants, although the nature of these structures is not specified.[112] Incidental references, such as the case of drowning mentioned earlier, suggest that, whenever a house or its garden abutted a watercourse, there was the temptation to install a 'house of office' which would not require a cesspit or cesspool. The state of the 'Normans crick' was giving concern in the 1630s, possibly because of its proximity to the Children's Hospital. There was some division of responsibility between the city, which had the creek fyed at this time; the surveyors of the Hospital, who were asked to suggest remedies for its condition; householders on the banks, who were requested both to fye the creek and to pull down the houses of office erected over it; and the commissioners of sewers, who were to be brought in if the house-holders failed to co-operate. This creek was still being inspected by the city in 1651.[113] With respect to common privies, a cluster of them was evidently provided in or near what became Three Privy Lane or Baddings Lane, which connected St Martin's Plain with Fye bridge quay and the river. The river and street accounts confirm that there were indeed three, first mentioned in the 1650s, and associated with a cistern by about 1720.[114]

It is not possible here to do justice to the incidental details that crop up in Norwich's rich surviving records, or to tackle systematically the nature and extent of the city's investment in water-related measures. The importance of water in the life of rich and poor alike is reflected in the ubiquity of street and place names derived from the wells, pits, pools, cockeys, creeks and privies which were such a salient feature of the urban landscape, and in the rich legacy of dialect words to which they gave rise. Even a preliminary survey of the kind just made involves a laborious collation of small items of information, and numerous topographical and other ambiguities remain. As in so many other, related areas, Norwich, with its developed civic consciousness, provides an excellent opportunity for revising our assumptions about the conditions under which early modern people lived and wished to live, and the part that water, and a watery environment, played in early modern lives.

6

From Second City to Regional Capital

Penelope J. Corfield

Of all the cities I have seen
(And few their numbers have not been)
This Norwich is the oddest; whether
View'd in its parts, or altogether.

Anon, *A Norfolk Tale*[1]

Norwich in all its glory was an impressive sight to see. Visitors admired its relative size, its urban density, its attractive site, its busy industry, its famously lively population, and its long history – which was visible in the city's glittering black flint-stone walls, its ancient castle, and in its many town churches of medieval origin. But how exactly did they 'place' Norwich? Their verdicts differed. George Borrow, who came to live in the city as a young man in the 1810s, described it both as 'fine' (an understated East Anglian compliment) and 'old', with a genuine urban antiquity. 'There is a fine old city before us, ... A fine old city, truly, is that, view it from whatever side you will; ... perhaps the most curious specimen at present extant of the genuine old English town.'[2] By contrast, the anonymous poet, who visited in 1792 but did not stay long, thought it 'odd' and unlike other places, although his doggerel verse did not specify the precise nature of its oddity.

For the historian, these comments suggest two rival ways of looking at urban history. One technique is to consider typicality. How does a town fit into the urban pattern of its day? With what other centres can it be compared? What was normal and unsurprising about its role, whether locally, regionally, nationally or even internationally? The second technique highlights the opposite. What was unique and special about each place and how did it differ from other towns? After all, however widespread or otherwise the extent of urban development, each urban centre occupied its own distinctive place in the world that belonged to it and to none other.

These two contrasting approaches serve to highlight the simultaneous 'normality' of Norwich and its 'oddity'. And, as will become apparent, both these features of its history were crucial for its long eighteenth-century transition from England's second city into well-established regional capital.

A traveller in western Europe in 1700 would have had little difficulty in finding urban centres that were on a par with Norwich in terms of population size. It was not one of the giant metropolitan cities, like London or Paris, whose growth had been so rapid in the sixteenth and seventeenth centuries. Instead, Norwich and its approximately 30,000 inhabitants matched other places like Amiens and Rennes in France, or Utrecht in the Dutch Republic, or Padua in northern Italy. All these were medium-sized regional centres, sited inland and powerful within their own hinterlands, where they were easily distinguished from the smaller market towns that were scattered around them. One visitor in 1698 thought that Norwich, verdant with its many trees, resembled a Dutch city. Another seventeenth-century writer compared the East Anglian capital to Constantinople. That was based on the happy assertion that both places abounded with orchards and gardens, making each 'a City in a Wood, or a Wood in a City'.[3] The comparison was doubtless not the first that sprang to mind on the banks of the Bosphorus; but, for home consumption, it placed sylvan Norwich in an international league. Local authors obviously enjoyed the phrase, because it was applied with many variants, for example as 'a city in a grove', 'a city in a garden', or 'a city in an orchard'.[4]

Added to that, Norwich by 1700 was clearly well rooted, with its own history and traditions. It was no sudden newcomer in the English urban hierarchy. Its medieval town walls, which, unlike those of many places, had survived intact after the seventeenth-century civil wars, proclaimed its independent jurisdiction as a city and county in its own right. Norwich in the early eighteenth century visibly guarded its own, as did other fortified places like Chester, Chichester and York in England, and great number of cities across Europe. Its fortifications were by no means as massive and militarised as those of places like Carcassonne in France or Avila in Spain. But the Norwich walls, adorned by forty towers, were sturdy and spacious, enclosing a central area larger than that of any other town in England, including the City of London. For many years, the twelve main gates were closed at night and on Sundays, leaving determined travellers to use the postern gates instead. Norwich therefore looked like what it was: proudly and self-containedly urban. In September 1662, a youthful citizen, returning from travels with his brother, was impressed to see his birthplace again:

> That famous city of Norwich presents itself to our view; Christ Church high
> spire [the cathedral], the old famous castle, eight and thirty goodly churches,
> the pleasant fields about it and the stately gardens in it, did so lessen our

opinion of any [other city] we had seen, that it seemed to us to deride our
rambling folly and forced new admiration from us.[5]

Popular traditions also contributed a mythic dimension to genuine
antiquity. Norwich was not a city that dated back to pre-Roman or even to
Roman times. In urban longevity, it could not compare with, say, York or
Winchester. Undaunted, however, local legends gave Norwich castle a historic ancestry. It was said to have a pre-Roman foundation and a founding
monarch, to boot. He was the ancient British King Gwytelinus, or Gurguntus. The castle mound (actually built by the Normans in the later
eleventh century) was rumoured to be 'the grave heap of an old heathen
king, who sits deep within it, with his sword in his hand, and his gold
and silver treasures about him'. So reported George Borrow, recounting
the story with relish but adding with a shade of scepticism 'if tradition
speaks true'.[6] When Queen Elizabeth I visited the city in 1578, she was
greeted not only by the mayor and corporation but also by a player dressed
as King Gurguntus, who was ready to give a versified loyal address but,
alas, 'by reason of a shower of rain, Her Majesty hasted away, the speech
not uttered'.[7] A century later, however, enthusiasm for this story was
already dimming. King Charles II, who visited in 1671, was not introduced
to a proxy Gurguntus; and the tale dwindled from quasi-history into total
legend.

Mythically, Norwich joined a number of old-established cities with
claims to a pre-Roman monarchical foundation. Bath, for example, was
allegedly created by King Bladud; Colchester by Old King Cole (the 'jolly
old soul' of popular song); Canterbury by King Rudhudibrass; Leicester by
King Lear; and Northampton by King Belinus. It seemed manifest to the
local enthusiasts who first circulated these myths that the early monarchs
must have been enlightened town planners, who would have known just
where England's regional capitals properly ought to be.

Elevated fiction and real history thus located Norwich firmly within the
established urban scene. What then rendered it 'odd'? Here a word of definition is required. 'Oddity' in this context really refers to 'distinctiveness'.
It does not mean that Norwich was strange or incomprehensible. Not all
visitors liked the place, although many, perhaps most, did so. None, however, found it beyond their powers of description. It was recognisably both
urban and civic.

None the less, among any given category, it is always possible to be distinctive for one reason or another. Within the genus of the 'old English
town', Norwich was unusual in being relatively populous over a long
stretch of time – so much so that for many years, until well into the

eighteenth century, it held pride of place as England's largest provincial town. How had that happened?

Evidence of the relative size of Norwich came from a local population enumeration in 1693, recording 28,881 residents then living in the city.[8] No census is perfect, of course; and the origins of this one are unclear. Very probably, it was prompted by municipal concerns over the rising cost of poor relief, resulting from population pressures; and, in the eighteenth century, this enumeration was cited as a civic listing. It appears to have been made carefully, on a parish by parish basis; and it can therefore be taken to provide a reasonably reliable benchmark. A population of approximately this magnitude was additionally confirmed by independent estimates by the pioneering social statistician Gregory King. He calculated the Norwich inhabitants at 29,332 and 28,546 in 1695 and 1696 respectively, multiplying the number of households by an average figure of 4.2 inhabitants to provide a grand total. As the city saw a surge of growth in the later seventeenth century, it is entirely probable that its population had reached 30,000 by 1700. That made Norwich easily England's largest inland town and, after London, its second city.

At this point, it is useful to recollect that the meaning of urban population size depends on context. Norwich was not particularly large in absolute terms. Moreover, like all provincial towns, it was insignificant besides England's own great metropolis. Nor was Norwich very massive when compared with the contemporary range of leading towns across western and central Europe. In 1700 there were thirty large urban centres with resident populations of 50,000 plus. Of those, only two were located within the British Isles, and they were the capital cities of Dublin (60,000) and mighty London (c. 575,000) – already one of the largest cities in the world. Norwich was therefore relatively modest in population terms. It just scraped into the next category of Europe's thirty medium-sized urban centres, with populations of between 30–49,000, as shown in Table 6.1.

On the other hand, it is also apparent that the urban hierarchy was steeply graded. At the top, there were only eleven really large cities (six of them seaports) with more than 100,000 inhabitants apiece and another nineteen (nine of them seaports) with more than 50,000. The European countryside was not at all densely urbanised at this date. Tiny hamlets and scattered villages dotted the landscape, interspersed by thousands of very small towns, some hardly larger than villages themselves.[9] The entire population of the total of 201 cities with populations of 10,000+ (still a low threshold in absolute terms) was no more than 8.7 per cent of Europe's population in aggregate. In this context, Norwich in 1700 appeared much

Table 6.1 West and Central European towns and cities (10,000+) in 1700, grouped by population size[1]

Population Size	Number of Cities	Aggregate Population	Towns 10,000+ as % of all Population
500,000+	2	1,085,000 [2]	1.33
100,000+	9	1,305,000 [3]	1.60
50,000+	19	1,263,000 [4]	1.55
30,000+	30	1,094,000 [5]	1.34
10,000+	141	2,313,000	2.84
All towns 10,000+	201	7,060,000	8.66
Total population		81,400,000 [6]	

Source: Calculated from data in J. de Vries, *European Urbanisation, 1500–1800* (London, 1984), pp. 269–78. Figures are best estimates, based upon local enumerations if available.

Notes: [1] Comprising all countries in West and Central Europe from the Atlantic to, and including, Austria-Bohemia and Poland; but excluding Slovakia, Hungary and the Balkans.

[2] In size order (1) London; (2) Paris.

[3] In size order: (3) Naples; (4) Amsterdam; (5) Lisbon; (6 jointly) Rome, Venice; (8) Milan; (9) Vienna; (10) Madrid; (11) Palermo.

[4] In size order: (12) Lyon; (13) Seville; (14 jointly) Brussels, Genoa; (16) Marseilles; (17) Florence; (18 jointly) Antwerp, Copenhagen, Hamburg; (21) Rouen; (22) Bologna; (23) Dublin; (24 severally) Berlin, Leiden, Lille; (27) Ghent; (28 jointly) Bordeaux, Danzig, Valencia.

[5] In size order: (31) Rotterdam; (32 jointly) Liège, Stockholm; (34) Barcelona; (35 severally) Cologne, Nantes, Turin; (38) Verona; (39 severally) Dresden, Edinburgh, Messina, Nuremberg; (43) Prague; (44 jointly) Bruges, Toulouse; (46 severally) Brescia, Konigsberg, Parma; (49 jointly) Haarlem, The Hague; (51 severally) Amiens, Malaga, *Norwich*, Orléans, Padua, Rennes, Strasbourg, Tours, Utrecht, Zaragossa. [Note: Jan de Vries lists Norwich's population as 29,000, whereas here it is taken to be 30,000. The difference in terms of calculating Europe's aggregate urban population is minimal.]

[6] As estimated by De Vries, *European Urbanisation*, p. 36.

more impressive. It ranked with thirty medium-sized towns with populations of 30,000–49,000 that had themselves emerged from the larger ruck of another 141 small-medium towns (mostly situated inland) with populations of 10,000–29,000. In other words, it stood poised between the significantly large towns on the one hand and the long tail of smaller places on the other. It was an urban intermediary, a linkage point between the centre and peripheries, and between 'rural networks and urban hierarchies', as aptly noted of the urban role in a twentieth-century African case study.[10]

It may be observed, too, that most of the medium-sized and small-medium towns at this period were located inland. While Europe's urban leaders consisted of great sea-ports as well as magnificent capital cities (and some, like London, Lisbon, and Copenhagen, were both at once), a sizeable majority of the middling cities were situated away from the coast, commanding the countryside via their local networks. Norwich fits that pattern well. It was, in fact, a small river port, as were a number of inland towns. But it was sited at the heart of an encircling hinterland within Norfolk, in a classic 'central-place' location. One precondition for Norwich's urban success was thus its prime location within a fertile agricultural terrain.

Within this immediate region, its nearest urban rival, in terms of population size, was the port of Great Yarmouth, located twenty miles away, at the mouth of the River Yare. There was always a certain competitiveness between the two places. The region was, however, amply able to sustain both. Indeed, if Norwich and Yarmouth are considered together as a 'split town' or an 'urban consortium', then the urban development of east Norfolk in 1700 was even more notable. At that date, Yarmouth housed another 10–11,000 inhabitants and was itself the seventh city of England in population terms. It was a busy entrepôt, sending bulky raw materials and coals up river to Norwich; and it was also the home port of the North Sea herring fleets. These provided a regular source of cheap and nutritious food. Lightly-smoked red herrings – the celebrated Yarmouth bloaters – thus became standard fare for the poor in Norwich, filling 'many a hungry bellie'.

Fortified by these agricultural and maritime contacts, the city was readily able to recruit population, especially when its economy was booming. Throughout the eighteenth century, many migrants into Norwich came from within East Anglia, and especially from Norfolk and east Suffolk. At the same time, a subsidiary stream of newcomers travelled from further afield, attracted by the city's size and reputation. In addition, Norwich had longstanding overseas contacts. Many citizens were descendants of the massive influx of sixteenth-century Dutch and Walloon settlers, and of the smaller number of French Huguenots who came in the early 1680s. In addition, numerous Norwich merchants had trading links with their counterparts in Holland and Germany. As Map 3 indicates, the city in 1700 was part of a distinctive North Sea urban 'cluster'.

So sustained, Norwich continued to grow until the mid 1780s. It is true

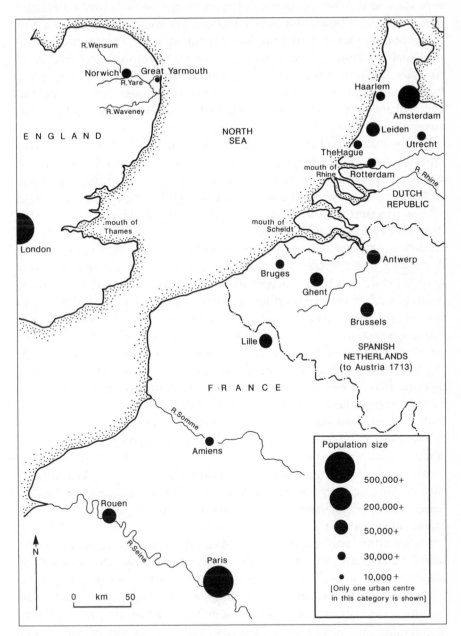

MAP 3. Major urban centres and the North Sea economy in 1700. (*Phillip Judge*)

that its mortality rates remained high for most of this period.[11] As the city expanded, so did the silent toll of deaths within its walls. There were, however, no overt plagues and their attendant panics. As in all cities at this time, mortality levels were especially high among the very young; and in one local epidemic (probably smallpox) in 1747, almost 70 per cent of all fatalities in Norwich involved children under the age of ten – most being babies in the first year of life. These grim urban penalties, however, did not halt the city's expansion, as long as buoyant hopes of work continued to attract new recruits.

The special factor that accounted for the emergence of inland Norwich into the front ranks of England's provincial towns was ultimately not demographic but economic. It sprang from the city's capacity to combine its longstanding trading role, as a centre of distribution and consumption, with a specialist industrial role as a centre of textile production. This strategic multiplication was clearly distinctive.

Important as was its manufacturing sector, the Norwich economy was by no means so specialised that the city had shed its traditional functions as a regional, county and ecclesiastical centre. On the contrary, all these different strands worked together. Norwich's famous markets continued to flourish and were frequented by wholesalers and retailers alike. It was a major regional centre for shopping, with both luxury goods and staple wares available in abundance.[12] Professional and financial services were also located in Norwich, as a nodal point where clients and providers could meet readily. Much business came to the city through its role as county capital, as headquarters of the Anglican diocese, as a centre of religious Dissent, and as a 'leisure town' where people came for recreation and consumption. The town walk in Chapel Fields, smartly laid out with trees and gravel paths, was deemed likely to become the veritable '*Mall* of Norwich',[13] in a flattering allusion to metropolitan amenities. And ancient Cockey Lane ('cockey', or watercourse or drain) was renamed as London Lane, later London Street, upgrading its nomenclature as it turned into a fashionable shopping parade.

Such commercial and leisure activities undoubtedly created work and wealth in the city. They did not in themselves, however, account for the relatively large size of Norwich by 1700. The example of the city of York provides an instructive contrast. Its long-term role as a regional centre of commerce and of conspicuous consumption very much paralleled that of Norwich. Yet York, 'the ancient and venerable capital of the North', had ceased by the mid seventeenth century to grow with any rapidity. Housing around 11,000 inhabitants in 1700, it was only a little over one-third the size of Norwich. And for many years in the eighteenth century

York – majestic and well frequented as it was – did not make any net population gains.

Some other factor was impelling the growth of Norwich. That was its continuing success as a textile town. As one local historian reported proudly:

> By their industry and ready invention, the [Norwich] manufacturers have acquired prodigious wealth in the art of weaving, by making such variety of worsted stuffs, in which they have excelled all other parts of the kingdom; which trade is now [1728] in a flourishing condition.[14]

Even in the era of pre-mechanised industrial production, manufacturing could be very labour intensive. That was particularly notable in the case of textiles. It took much application to transform the shaggy hanks of untreated wool into massive bales of finished fabrics, ready for market. An official computation in 1719 estimated that labour accounted for 'more than' five-sixths (83 per cent) of the total production costs in the Norwich industry, and in 1785 a very similar figure was reported to the younger Pitt, in response to a government enquiry.[15] The location of the workforce was thus poised between centrifugal forces, seeking cheaper costs in the countryside, and centripetal forces, seeking specialist urban production skills. The Norwich industry exemplified this tension. There was a rural sector to the industry, clustered in villages within an approximate twenty mile radius of the city, where simpler and plainer stuffs were woven. And pre-mechanised spinning always remained a low-pay, low-skill preparatory process that was widely diffused across the countryside, generally carried out by nimble-fingered women and children as a by-employment. However, the need to dye the yarn, once spun, so that the Norwich weavers could create their beautiful designs in the weave, and then to finish the woven textiles by hotpressing, to give them a characteristic glazed and shiny surface, all encouraged an urban location. That permitted the workforce to respond quickly to news of changing fashions; and also helped the merchant manufacturers, who organised the distribution networks, to get the stuffs speedily from the loom into the markets.

One name for the stage of cottage industry for mass markets at a distance from the point of production is 'proto-industrialisation'. The concept has been much criticised; and rightly so.[16] Stress upon rural or 'peasant' industries, migrating into the countryside to evade restrictive town guilds and there becoming precursors of industrialisation, oversimplifies the paths of economic development. Some pre-mechanised production was indeed based in the countryside; but far from all. The case of Norwich indicates that 'cottage' manufacturing could still be very urban in its location; and that medieval guild controls had generally lapsed. Historians who follow Mendels too closely, in assuming that pre-industrial towns were centres of commerce and distribution but not of production, miss a vital element of town life. An instructive analogue to Norwich was Leiden, its Dutch counterpart, which made similar textiles with similar success in the later seventeenth century.

Locations for pre-mechanised industrial production in fact depended very much upon the nature of the product and of its market. Among hand-loom textiles, for example, the simple, low-cost linens were characteristically made by a dispersed rural and small town workforce. By contrast, luxurious silk manufacturing was concentrated in London's Spitalfields, close to fashionable consumers, while its lighter, cheaper half-worsteds, combining worsted yarn with silk, were gradually dropped from production by the mid eighteenth century. These metropolitan producers catered for the really volatile upper end of the market. The worsted stuffs made in Norwich, however, were not ultra-stylish products. Instead, they were smart items for middling purchasers, whose pockets were not endlessly deep.[17] That made the Norwich industry also highly cost- and fashion-sensitive. A location in a reasonably accessible provincial centre with low production costs accordingly made good sense: it avoided the great expense of London but, at the same time, it retained an urban workforce that was sufficiently skilled to produce quality goods and sufficiently nucleated in location to get speedy news of changing market conditions.

During the period from 1680 to 1780, therefore, the East Anglian capital grew large and rich on the strength of its famous textiles. It already had a long weaving tradition, that went back to medieval times.[18] This staple industry had shown itself to be very adaptable, shifting to the lighter, brighter 'New Draperies' in the later sixteenth century, under the stimulus of Walloon knowhow, and refining its fabrics in the later seventeenth century, with some contribution from Huguenot expertise. The urban economy thus specialised in production for distant markets. And, by way of proof, the hand-loom worsteds that were produced in both the city and its rural hinterland became known generically as 'Norwich stuffs'.

Combining many roles created a spirited urban ambience in Norwich. Its way of life yoked the busy intentness of trade and manufactures with the polish and public jollity of a social and leisure capital. Writing in 1802, John Thelwall the radical orator, who had lectured in the city in 1796, lamented his self-imposed exile in south Wales, which kept him mired in rural ignorance, far from the urban stimulus of places such as 'the friendly, the enlightened, the animated circles of Norwich'.[19] Something of what he was missing was indicated by another visitor in 1805. The artist John Opie confided that his late summer stay with his wife's family in Norwich had prepared him for the rigours of winter, 'through the medium of beef, dumplings, wine, riding, swimming, walking and laughing'.[20]

Local authors regularly chorused their praises. To a clerical poet in 1774, Norwich was the 'faire nurse of industry and wealth'.[21] In 1783, the city's first Directory agreed that the place was 'abounding in opulence and fashion'.[22] There was an element of the formulaic, of course, in such commendations. But it is always interesting to see what was said or left unsaid. Another local poet in 1730 celebrated the social excitements of the 'Norwich Assembly', that attracted county society each summer to visit 'happy Norwich'.[23] And a Norfolk-born visitor in 1800 expressed satisfaction with the total effect. 'Norwich, the industrious, commercial, and prosperous Norwich, is certainly a very lovely spot', adding that nothing could equal the view of this 'happy seat of affluence and industry' from its castle hill.[24]

Characteristic sounds then recorded the city's busy diversity. In the weaving parishes, the pervasive background noise was a rhythmic 'click-clack' which signalled that the wooden hand-looms were being set vigorously to work. Aloft could be heard birdsong from the caged canaries, kept in many a weaver's garret.[25] This vied with the ringing of church bells from the city's thirty-three medieval churches (Norwich had its own Society of Ringers); and with the street cries of the itinerant vendors, offering goods and services for sale.[26] Horses and carriages clattered on old cobbles and new paving stones alike, although the traffic clogged when carts laden with hay got stuck in the narrow medieval gates. Everywhere snatches of laughter, song and talk were audible from the urban inns and alehouses. These were the venues for the many clubs and societies that formed the bedrock of this intensely clubbable city's social life.[27] And attentive listeners could distinguish among the cacophony of voices the 'broad Norfolk' of the countryside and the sharper vowels of 'Narrich's' own citizens.

Animated conservation was an urban staple. As the city's livelihood depended upon the ready circulation of news and views, it was no surprise to find that Norwich was the first provincial centre to gain its own weekly newspaper, launched in 1701. Indeed, for most of the eighteenth century, the city sustained two rival journals – one Whig and one Tory – in circulation. Venues for discussions were plentiful, from boozy inns and taverns to more sedate club rooms, lecture halls, informal salons, and to the new coffee houses, clustered around the market-place. It was in one such establishment in 1697 that a young Norwich-born cleric, Samuel Clarke, debated the new Newtonian physics with William Whiston, then chaplain to the bishop of Norwich.[28] This chance encounter in a coffee house was a classic example of the urban circulation of ideas. The meeting began a long friendship between these two unorthodox thinkers, whilst leading to clerical preferment for Clarke, who was introduced by Whiston to the bishop. It also indicated that some Norwicians were *au fait* with the latest scientific ideas. Indeed, it transpired that Clarke and his father, one of the city aldermen, had been studying Saturn's rings through a seventeen-foot telescope. The episode serves as a reminder, therefore, that Norwich was sizeable enough to sustain its own 'intelligentsia', renewed in each generation.[29] This informal network of men and some women furnished a vivid sequence of local historians, topographers, antiquarians, essayists, poets, scientists, medical men, lawyers, theologians, hymnodists and clerical polemicists.

What else would strike a visitor to Norwich? In terms of immediate olfactory impact, the city was not exceptionally notorious. Some low-lying parts of town, abutting the sluggish River Wensum, were indeed disagreeable: the duke of Norfolk's former palace was reported as 'built in a low stinking place', which helps to explain why the ducal family finally abandoned its delapidated Norwich residence after a quarrel with the corporation in 1708. The river was also clogged by discharges from numerous private 'bog-houses'.[30] Furthermore, the best behaviour among polite society was not enforced in the male territory of the city's alehouses and taverns. Each room had its own pewter chamber pot, ready for use: 'there it stands stinking till it is full, and often till it run about the room in a very nasty manner',[31] noted William Arderon, a Yorkshireman who had moved to Norwich in the 1740s. These things, however, were widely tolerated. Above all, the urban production of hand-loom textiles did not have a seriously blighting effect, unlike the smoke-stack industries that choked some other places. Thus, on its ridged site in East Anglia's breezy lowlands, the city was considered to be generally salubrious. On hearing in 1757 of the death of John Clarke (Samuel Clarke's younger brother and dean of 'vile, damp' Salisbury), a friend claimed that had Clarke 'wintered at Norwich, as he used to do, he might have been alive & bonny many a day longer'.[32]

This aura of healthiness, which was quietly belied by high urban mortality rates for most of the eighteenth century, was fostered not only by the city's many trees and gardens, but also by the abundance and quality of foodstuffs in its markets. Taste-buds in Norwich, those of the well-to-do at least, were well treated. There were plentiful North Sea fish on sale; as well as good agricultural produce from the city's fertile and 'improving' hinterland; there were the plump ducks, geese and turkeys for which the region was famous; and sturdy cattle, brought from afar to fatten on the marshlands between Norwich and Yarmouth. All that, washed down with the hearty local drink, the 'humming brown beer' known as 'Norwich Nog'. Other cities enjoyed their own favoured beverages too: a ballad saluting the virtues of Nottingham ale promised that it would cure all ills and drive women wild with lust.[33] Drinking songs in Norwich did not claim quite so much. But they enthused over their brew and its brewers, who provided some of the city's great urban dynasties:

> May Weston's name shine, in Numbers divine
> And his malt and hops never cog;
> May Tompson have store, with Morse and some more,
> And live long to brew Norwich Nog.[34]

Bright lights too signalled a busy as well as a sociable urban world. Viewed after dark, when the weavers were working late in their garrets by candlelight, Norwich was a glimmering beacon of activity: 'every winter's evening exhibited, to the traveller entering its walls, the appearance of a general illumination'.[35] And, from 1701 onwards, oil-lamps were ablaze in the city streets until 11.00 p.m. at night. Norwich did not have a separate 'red light' district (here unlike most port cities) but there were many venues for night life including the sale of commercial sex. While the city had a public reputation for Puritanism, in practice tolerated a range of behaviour. A scandalous divorce case in 1707–8 revealed that a group of Norwich 'middling sort' spent their evenings in drinking, card-playing, and sexual games, that included group sex, bi-sexual flagellation, and voyeurism.[36]

Meanwhile, by day there were many respectable sights to be seen, registering both the antiquity and the modernity of the city. 'Old' Norwich was visible in the medieval walls, the town gates, the Norman castle on its bulky mound, the cathedral with its elegant spire, its thirty-three medieval parish churches, the flintstone guildhall in the central marketplace, the venerable half-timbered town housing and the great public inns. The 'modern' city was interspersed within the older framework, with new buildings, rebuildings and fresh frontages (Plate 7). Indicators of change were to be found not only in the smart brick and stucco housing, coffee houses, shops, pleasure gardens and, after 1756, dignified local banks; they also included dedicated buildings such as the substantial New Theatre (1758; enlarged 1800), the grand Assembly Rooms (1754) providing a venue for balls, concerts, and dinners, the Unitarians' striking Octagon Chapel (1754–6) 'one of the most spacious, noble, and elegant buildings of this kind in the kingdom', various discreet Nonconformist meeting houses, a new concert room (1816), and, just outside the walls at St Stephen's gate, the new Norfolk and Norwich Hospital (1771).

Significant urban atmospherics responded also to the dynamics of people as well as the statics of the built environment. The streets of Norwich
were good indicators of the state of urban economic and social life. When
trade was busy, the weavers – with the characteristic pale faces of indoor
workers – toiled inside at their looms, leaving the weaving parishes in West
Wymer and the northern ward apparently deserted. But in the evenings
and at times of holiday, people quickly reappeared. Saturday nights were
the busiest time of the week, and Sundays the quietest days, in due deference to Protestant tradition.

Crowds, however, were never far away. On special occasions, the
townees were always augmented by visitors from further afield. Observing
the public celebrations in October 1746 to laud the defeat of the Jacobite
rebellion, William Arderon noted that: 'We had the greatest part of the
nobility and gentry of ye country [Norfolk] here, as well as multitudes of
people of lower life'.[37] There were also annual festivities that regularly
brought people into Norwich. The Tombland fair, held on Maundy Thursday, just before Easter, had shifted its role from commercial event to a
popular festival, with vendors selling toys and gingerbread. It also coincided with the annual horse fair, held in the castle ditches. And the late
summer assize week, when the judges arrived on circuit and festivities were
organised, attracted huge crowds, making this 'the gayest period known to
the inhabitants of Norwich'.[38] On such an occasion, in August 1783, the
new bishop preached before a 'brilliant and crowded audience'; and, at an
assembly in the evening, 'the wives of some of the richest people in the
county shone with diamonds at least'.[39]

People did not come to town solely for special events. Touring the sights
of Norwich on a late Sunday afternoon, an aristocratic visitor in mid
September 1732 commented: 'I think I never was in so mobbish a place,
we could scarce walk the streets for the numbers of people that flocked
about us'.[40] Market days, especially on Fridays and Saturdays, were always
thronged. Country farmers and their wives came to sell; and country as
well as town residents to buy. The ensuing bustle was highly characteristic (Plate 6). One traveller rhapsodised specifically about Norwich's great
central market as a forum for the easy mingling of rural and urban society. It is notable, however, that this 1800 account, written in wartime, did
not list the city's weavers, whose industry was then in crisis, among the
promenaders:

> At the bottom [of the central market] is another space of parade-like appear-
> ance, emphatically called the Gentleman's Walk. This walk, on the market
> day, is thronged with a collection of very interesting characters; the merchant,

the manufacturer, the magistrate, the provincial yeoman, the militia officer, the affluent landlord, the thrifty and thriving tenant, the independent farmer, the recruiting officer, the clergy, faculty, barristers, and all the various characters of polished and professional society. In short, [a] proud scene of bustle and business, health and wealth, prosperity and pleasure – proud let me call it, as it is the true criterion of provincial and national glory.[41]

References to the social confidence of the leading Norwich citizens were commonplace. Politically, the place had long maintained its independence. Although it was frequented by Norfolk bigwigs at times of festivities, Norwich was no 'pocket borough' under the sway of aristocratic patrons. Instead, the city's two MPs were chosen by a large electorate of urban freemen, including many craftsmen and weavers, as well as merchants and professional men. The urban grandees in Norwich accordingly walked tall in their own bailiwick; and they were readily saluted as urban 'gentlemen', as shown by the 1783 *Norwich Directory*, which was significantly sub-titled *The Gentlemen and Trademen's Assistant*.[42] Civic dignity was confirmed annually, with a pageant to celebrate the mayoral election. This was the 'Guild-Day', held in June on the Tuesday before midsummer: with a procession in full regalia, civic music, a service in the cathedral, a public oration, an official swearing-in, a gunfire salute, a corporation dinner, and the parading of the Norwich 'snap-dragon' (a brightly painted beast, of wicker and canvas) with an attendant fool to add to the fun and whifflers (sword-bearers) to clear a path through the crowds.

Events like this provided an outward signal of urban solidarity and community. Of course, in practice there were often divisions among the Norwich population. Religion and politics were sources of argument, sometimes ritualised, sometimes heated.[43] The diversity of the city's economy, however, meant that Norwich society did not appear riven between a few great masters, on the one hand, and a large number of journeymen, on the other. A variegated middle band of citizens interposed between the very rich and the very poor; and, because the staple industry was known to require a certain skill and application, the workforce was mentioned in respectful terms (except when it was rioting). In 1763, for example, the mayoral court referred routinely to the city poor as the 'industrious' class.[44] Among their number were several self-taught men, such as Daniel Wright and an amateur mathematician John Barnard. The eccentric scholar and tutor John Fransham (1730–1810) also sustained himself for a time by weaving in a garret.

Collectively, the Norwicians had a reputation for being assertive and disputatious. They were 'the most wrangling, mischievous, envious, malicious people that ever I came amongst', a Quaker complained in 1655.[45] They were 'a little self-conceited, and prone to Discords', ran another verdict in 1718, although adding rather more kindly that people were also quick-witted and friendly.[46] Opinions were commonly expressed with force and sometimes via direct action. In 1751–52 the plebeian adherents of a controversial Methodist preacher, James Wheatley, were repeatedly attacked by hostile crowds, who also mockingly shouted 'Baa, Baa' at his 'dear lambs of God'.[47] Arriving in Norwich to minister to his own followers in August 1759, John Wesley faced 'a large, rude, noisy congregation'.[48] He fretted that, after the sermon, people gathered in knots to talk, turning the 'place of worship into a coffee house'. In 1764, Wesley was still upset by the fickleness of his flock: 'I have seen no people in all England or Ireland so changeable as this'.[49] Deference was certainly not the habitual style in Norwich. It may have been that urban directness as well as the severity of his tutor that caused the Norfolk-born William Godwin – then a precocious eleven-year-old sent in 1767 for his schooling in the great county capital – to bemoan the 'odiousness of the Norwichers'.[50]

Weavers were known as particularly forceful lobbyists. As evidence of that, in May 1765, Horace Walpole in London was on the verge of panic when he heard that a disaffected contingent from Norwich was marching upon the capital city. This was to support the Spitalfields campaign for legislation to protect the silk industry. 'A large body of weavers are on the road from Norwich, and it is said have been joined by numbers in Essex', he wrote; 'guards are posted to prevent, if possible, their approaching the city. Another troop of manufacturers are coming from Manchester.'[51] In the event, the reports were quickly contradicted. The mass march of weavers never occurred. But the episode was instructive. Legislation duly followed to exclude foreign-made silks, just as earlier in 1722 combined protests from Norwich and the Spitalfields had gained protectionist laws against the wearing of printed calicoes. The city's assertiveness in its own cause was allied also with its reputation for radicalism. Again, that can be exaggerated, as political views were never unanimous in Norwich. Nonetheless, common repute did not worry about such qualifications. A loyalist satire in 1795 thus envisaged the Norwich population as chorusing proudly:

> Since the days of old Kett, the republican Tanner,
> Faction has always seen us lost under her Banner;
> From our country's best Interests we've ever dissented,
> In War we're disloyal; in Peace discontented.[52]

With its size, success, and reputation to safeguard it, Norwich appeared outwardly unassailable. In particular, the years of the mid eighteenth century, from the 1730s to the 1770s, seemed in retrospect a gilded era, when trade was buoyant, food was relatively cheap, dire poverty was held at bay, visitors were appreciative and the city was embellished with new amenities. Norwich's industrial specialism had not ousted its other functions. In 1780, for example, it was the sixth most substantial 'residential leisure town' in England (after London, Bath, Bristol, York and Newcastle upon Tyne), as measured by the presence of thirty or more elite families employing menservants.[53] Such a role as a resort for the conspicuously rich was clearly not just a matter of urban size. The huge metropolitan region of London, to be sure, easily took first place, followed by Bath. Yet the much smaller city of York, the traditional capital of the north, was also a significant home for menservants and their employers. Norwich's role therefore reflected its historic regional placement rather than merely its size. However, not all wealthy people employed menservants (upon whom tax was due), so this data provides only partial evidence about the very rich. In practice, social leadership in Norwich came from its affluent working elite. This included families such as the Pattesons (brewers), the intermarried Ives and Harvey families (worsted merchant-manufacturers), the Kerrisons (bankers), and the Quaker Gurneys (who had moved from textiles into banking).

Details of these urban bigwigs were publicly listed in the 1783 *Directory*. This was a pioneering volume, confident in the city's fame but also ready with suggestions for environmental improvements. Its business information demonstrated once again the importance of textiles to the urban economy, while confirming that commerce and specialist services provided long-term ballast. Table 6.2 shows that 546 of the 1323 people with stated occupations (41.3 per cent of all occupations) were in manufacturing, compared with 370 (28 per cent) in 'dealing' and 192 (14.5 per cent) in the professional sector. At this date, most businesses were headed by one person, but there were 118 firms, including a number of family concerns. Another 268 people featured in the *Directory* by name only, without apparent occupation (16.8 per cent of all entries). These individuals may have been rentiers, living off private income, but some did have thriving businesses, such as John Morse, the brewer (twice mayor of Norwich in 1781 and again in 1803) and the banker Bartlett Gurney. These men were sufficiently well known to be recorded without further description, so that the *Directory* listing must be taken as indicative rather than absolutely comprehensive.

Women, who formed a majority of the urban population (as in all large towns at this date), also had a public presence among the urban elite in 1783. At least 208 were listed in the *Norwich Directory* (13 per cent of all names).

Table 6.2 Occupations of the social and business elite in Norwich in 1783

Occupations by Economic Sector[1]	Number	% of All With Occupations	% of All Listed
Agriculture	31	2.3	1.9
Mining/Quarrying	5	0.4	0.3
Building	102	7.7	6.4
Manufacturing	546	41.3	34.3
Dealing[2]	370	28.0	23.2
Public Service/Professional	192	14.5	12.0
Transport	10	0.8	0.6
Industrial Service[3]	5	0.4	0.3
Domestic Service[4]	62	4.7	3.9
All Occupations	1,323	100.1	82.9
None Given	268		16.8
Not Classified	3		0.2
TOTAL LISTED	1,594	99.9	

Source: Figures calculated from entries in Anon., *The Norwich Directory: Or, Gentlemen and Tradesmen's Assistant* (Norwich, 1783), pp. 5–46. The assistance of Serena Kelly in compiling this data is gratefully acknowledged.

Notes: [1] This economic classification sub-divides occupations into separate groups by type of product or service. The schema (known as Booth/Armstrong) was derived from the nineteenth-century occupational censuses, following the Registrar General's own categories, by Charles Booth in 1886; and has since been adapted by historians from W. A. Armstrong onwards: see C. Harvey, E. Green and P. J. Corfield, *The Westminster Historical Database* (Bristol, 1998), pp. 87–112.

[2] 'Dealing' includes all occupations involved in the sale and distribution of goods, whether wholesale or retail. There is an unavoidable overlap with 'manufacturing' where the same individuals both made and sold goods (a problem highlighted long ago by Booth). In the Booth/Armstrong classification, the schema follows the main meaning of the occupational title, so that those listed as '-maker' are classified as manufacturers: Harvey, Green and Corfield, *Westminster Database*, pp. 89–91.

[3] This category relates to occupations that serviced industry, broadly defined. It is a hybrid and not very satisfactory grouping, that ranges from bankers and brokers to labourers and porters.

[4] This category relates to occupations that serviced the household. It includes not only domestic servants (not usually listed in Directories) but also occupations providing services for the individual or for the home, such as hair-dressers, cleaners, chimney sweeps and rubbish collectors.

A majority of them had been married ('Mrs': 143; 'Widow': nineteen) but nineteen were unmarried and another twenty-seven gave their name only. Most did not have any stated occupation and probably lived on private incomes, as seems likely in the case of the twelve ladies dwelling in the cathedral close. But at least ninety women owned their own businesses, including not only thirty-eight commercial dealers, twenty-five specialist makers and dealers in clothing, seven proprietors of 'boarding schools for young ladies', and seven miscellaneous, but also thirteen working in the staple manufacturing sector. One was Susanna Hardingham, who lived in unfashionable Cowgate Street, in the weaving ward of Fye bridge, north of the river. With her son, she ran a business as a scarlet dyer. Two more, Mary Powell and Mrs Towler, were skilled hotpressers. The presence of all these women, without fanfare, indicated that economic imperatives were quietly eroding the old cultural and legal barriers to women's business careers.

Throughout all this, Norwich's population continued to grow for most of the eighteenth century: not rapidly but steadily, reaching a total of some 41,000 by the third of its three local enumerations in 1786. No fears were expressed in the city that its urban predominance was under threat. A local history in 1728 had already noted – correctly – that Norwich had been overtaken by Bristol and was thus by that date the third, rather than second, city in England and Wales. But without regular censuses before 1801, all population figures were hazy. In 1795 another local commentator had reviewed the demographic history of eighteenth-century Norwich and concluded cheerily that, in population terms, the city 'has something to boast of, and nothing to fear'.[54] Indeed, old reputations died hard. In 1792 a national guide to parliamentary boroughs still named Norwich as 'in point of opulence, commerce, manufactures, and number of inhabitants', unequivocally 'the second [city] in the kingdom'.[55]

Imperceptibly, however, things were changing. It was not that Norwich was not growing, at least before the 1790s, but that other places were expanding more rapidly. The 1801 census provided a snapshot of the process. Norwich was still one of the urban leaders, the tenth largest urban place anywhere in England and Wales (see Table 6.3).

It was more populous than the fashionable resort city of Bath, which was the classic eighteenth-century urban success story. That indicated the scale of Norwich's historic lead. But a new urban-industrial world was clearly emerging. The new provincial power-houses were Manchester, Liverpool, and Birmingham. Even Bristol, which had surpassed Norwich to become the second city by 1750, was being overtaken in turn by 1801. In addition, the number of places with populations of 10,000 and over

Table 6.3 Leading towns and conurbations[1] in England and Wales, in 1700, 1750 and 1801

1700	Population in thousands
Metropolitan London	575
Norwich	30
Bristol	22
Newcastle/Gateshead	18
Exeter	14
York	11
Great Yarmouth	10
7 towns over 10,000[2]	680

1750	Population in thousands	1801	Population in thousands
Metropolitan London	675	Metropolitan London	948
Bristol	50	Manchester/Salford	88
Norwich	36	Liverpol	83
Newcastle/Gateshead	29	Birmingham	74
Birmingham	24	Bristol	64
Liverpool	22	Leeds	53
Manchester/Salford	18	Sheffield	46
Exeter	16	Plymouth/Dock	43
Leeds	16	Newcastle/Gateshead	42
Plymouth/Dock	14	Norwich	37
Chester	13	Bath	35
Coventry	13	Portsmouth	33
Nottingham	12	Hull	30
Sheffield	12	Nottingham	29
Worcester	11	Sunderland	25
York	11	Oldham	22
Great Yarmouth	10	Bolton	18
Portsmouth	10	Exeter	17
Rochester/Chatham	10	Great Yarmouth	17
Sunderland	10	Leicester	17
		Rochester/Chatham	17
		York	16
		Another 27 towns	
20 towns over 10,000[3]	1,012	49 towns over 10,000[4]	2,079

Source: Best estimates for 1700 and 1750, derived from local enumerations where available, plus 1801 census returns.

Notes: Because figures in Table 6.3 refer to entire conurbations (such as Manchester/Salford), the size order of English towns differs slightly from that shown in footnotes to Table 6.4, which show rankings of single municipalities.

[1] Conurbations of contiguous urban development are here counted as one unit, even if they contain more than one municipal authority: these include Manchester/Salford; Newcastle/Gateshead; Plymouth/Dock; Rochester/Chatham; and metropolitan London (including the cities of London and Westminster, plus the borough of Southwark, and all contiguous urbanised parishes).

[2] Containing 13.1 per cent of total population in England and Wales estimated at 5.2 million.

[3] Containing 16.6 per cent of total population of England and Wales estimated at 6.1 million.

[4] Containing 23.4 per cent of total population of England and Wales of 8.9 million at 1801 census.

was fast multiplying – from only seven in 1700 to forty-nine in 1801 – as the general urban infrastructure gained depth. As a result, Norwich was no longer head and shoulders ahead of all rivals. Instead it was very noticeably experiencing a relative eclipse, as was its East Anglian partner, the port of Great Yarmouth, if to a lesser extent.

Specialisation was and is no guarantor of automatic urban growth over the long term. Everything hinges upon the fortunes of the special economic function. Many towns have faced serious problems when a key trade or industry gets into difficulties. In periods of crisis, individuals may leave to search for work elsewhere. Yet towns by definition must stay put. They gain continuity and identity from a settled location but, by the same token, they have to cope with problems on the spot.

Manufacturing towns, especially single-industry towns, are vulnerable to downturn if the markets for their staple products collapse, or if their wares are undercut by cheaper competitors elsewhere. Leiden, just across the North Sea, already offered a warning. Norwich's Dutch counterpart saw an outright population decline of remarkable proportions, from perhaps 55,000 in 1700 to 31,000 in 1801. Its famous university could not attract sufficient labour-intensive business to counterbalance the collapse of its stuffs manufactures. An English visitor in 1769 accordingly noted: 'As Leyden consists chiefly of people in trade, which is at present, greatly on the decline, you may suppose the town to be, what in fact it was, extremely dull.'[56] Its population loss was much the steepest to be found anywhere in eighteenth-century Europe, at a time when most towns were growing. Leiden's problems, as a particularly painful part of the readjustment of the Dutch economy, put those of Norwich into perspective; but that was little consolation in Norwich when the crisis came.

Disaster struck as a result of the long wars between Britain and France from 1793 to 1815. In the early eighteenth century, the city's textiles had been sold chiefly in domestic markets. Over time, however, Norwich merchants had turned their attention overseas, in response to competition at home from new fabrics such as Manchester cottons. Some exports did go to North America, especially before the American War of Independence. From the mid century, however, the big surge had been in sales of Norwich stuffs to mainland Europe, moving into markets vacated by the declining Leiden industry. But this business was severely curtailed by the French wars and consequent trade embargoes. In 1798, the city's staple industry was said, with exaggeration but genuine anguish, to be 'effectively ruined'.[57] Many weavers simply left the city and the total population declined.[58] Those who remained lounged in the streets, pale-faced and despairing. In May 1799 a commentator urged onlookers 'rather to commiserate than reproach these emaciated and inactive wanderers' amidst their 'empty looms, uninhabited houses, and unwanted work-rooms'.[59]

In fact, Norwich's famous textile industry was not dead. It hung on and eventually enjoyed a revival, following the peace of 1815. Many in the city fervently expected the 'immediate return of our manufacturing grandeur', as a commentator noted,[60] although old hands advised against excess euphoria. And the eventual decline of the handloom industry, which followed from the later 1820s, was very protracted.

Starkly revealed, however, was the vulnerability of the urban economy and the extent to which its staple livelihood was dependent upon factors far beyond the city's direct control. This was a deeply worrying portent. Norwich was gradually losing its earlier locational advantage. It drew its raw materials from afar, and its finished goods were sent to distant markets. Moreover, river transportation was slow to its regional port at Yarmouth, which had a difficult harbour and was in turn losing its own competitive position. Why should worsted weaving have continued to be located in Norwich at all? The industry relied upon the accumulated knowhow of its skilled workforce, but Norwich weavers had little scope for cost-cutting, in the event of competition from cheaper rivals. Moreover, a new domestic challenger was emerging in the form of Bradford, located on the West Yorkshire coalfield, where from the late 1790s machine-spun yarn was beginning to be supplied cheaply and close at hand. In fact, the emergent 'worstedopolis' of the north, with a population of some 13,000 in its four townships, was still much smaller than

Norwich in 1801. For all that, the signs of change were apparent; and some worsted weavers left East Anglia for Yorkshire.

Citizens in Norwich, meanwhile, had not been silent in their anger and consternation. Already in January 1795 the city corporation, despite its general support for the Pitt government, had petitioned urgently for an end to the war, 'which has nearly annihilated the manufactories and trade of this once flourishing city'.[61] The poverty of the weaving workforce dampened purchasing power throughout the urban economy, which was plunged into depression. One obscure artisan, a member of the tiny sect of Muggletonians surviving quietly within the shelter of Norwich's eclectic Nonconformist tradition, wrote to his co-religionists in London in May 1794, hoping that they could find him work. He explained in simple English: 'I am sorrow that I have not rote to you all before this time, the reason wich is I havae bin disstred in my buisness ... the treade is so bad that in Norwich my friends can not meet so often as we would.'[62]

Radicals meanwhile called for political overhaul at home. Norwich brimmed with urgent debate. A young trainee lawyer, Thomas Amyot, confessed in May 1794 that 'I am so pestered with Aristocrat and Democrat, Royalist and Jacobin, Pitt and Robespierre, Prussian Hussars and French Sans Culottes that I almost sicken at the sight of a newspaper'.[63] Numerous radical artisan clubs in Norwich pressed for peace and constitutional reform. They were in contact with similar societies in London and Sheffield. Some 'Sons of Liberty' were bitter. In November 1793 inflammatory handbills were circulated. 'Ninety Thousand Guineas is taken out of our Pockets every week for the expenses of this cruel, unjust and destructive War! Oh, ye sons of Liberty, why will you suffer it? Haste and revenge your Wrongs. Let us all join and Rebel', urged one. Another was even more specific: 'He who wishes well to the cause of Liberty, let him repair to Chapel Field at Five O'clock this afternoon. There he will meet with Hundreds to begin a Glorious Revolution.'[64] There was in fact no uprising. None the less, the sheer extent of discontent, however diverse in its political aims, was sufficient for Norwich to be known as 'that city of sedition'.

Famously in 1796, moreover, the urban electorate gave the government an anxious moment. Bartlett Gurney, a respectable Quaker banker from a leading Norwich family, boldly stood against William Windham, the sitting Whig MP for the city, who was Secretary of State for War in Pitt's wartime cabinet, no less. The result was highly dramatic. Windham kept his seat, but only just. He had a majority of eighty-three votes, surviving only through support from 321 'out-voters' – freemen who had left the city but returned to support the sitting candidate. Within Norwich itself, Gurney actually won the suffrage. He obtained 122 more votes from the city freemen than did Windham. None the less, the Secretary of State had survived.

Further excitements followed six years later, when the electoral battle resumed. During the 1802 campaign, Windham still expected to win. 'All that system and organisation and malice and activity and Jacobinism and puritanism can do against us here is doing, but I think upon the whole that we shall prevail against it', he wrote, showing a vivid sense of the multiple forces ranged against him.[65] Yet this time, it was he who lost. His opponent, the dissenter William Smith (son of a London merchant) gained – with fine appropriateness – precisely eighty-three more votes than did Windham. It was a political sensation that was described, exaggeratedly, as a veritable 'Jacobin triumph'.[66] In fact, however, the Norwich electorate had embraced moderate reform; and Smith retained his seat, with one short break only, until 1830. But his success did not stop the war, which resumed after a brief truce in 1802. One radical pamphleteer, naming himself as '(in the modern acceptation of the word) a Leveller, Jacobin and Revolutioner' had hoped that the city's vote would be decisive. 'A *disaffected* place so formidable as Norwich, rejecting a war-minister in disdain, would in all probability have put an end to the war.'[67] Such calculations were, however, wide of the mark. The hard truth was that Norwich, with or without the hapless William Windham as its MP, was not so important to those outside the city as it was to those who lived and worked there.

By the end of the eighteenth century, there were already clear signs of change in Britain's urban configuration. Norwich was no longer the provincial leader. Instead, it was more than ever described as 'old', 'ancient', 'venerable' and 'odd' rather than thrusting, 'modern' and go-ahead. The corporation itself made an ill-considered decision to permit the destruction of the city's medieval gates, chiefly in 1792–94, and then to allow the old city walls to decay, on the grounds that the cost of their upkeep was too great in hard times.[68]

Survival was, however, still the great theme in the city's history. Norwich was sustained by its long-term role as the regional capital of East Anglia. It had no new competitor nearby to provide a new challenge. Unlike Coventry (say), Norwich did not have to face a Birmingham in East Anglia. The city's hinterland, however, was itself changing. East Anglia had been a mixed agricultural and industrial region; but increasingly it was coming to specialise in the former role. Norwich played a part in that, as the commercial, administrative, social and financial capital of a rich and highly developed farming terrain.[69] Insurance and banking featured among the city's new growth sectors in the early nineteenth century. In particular, the Norwich finance houses were one of the key mechanisms whereby capital from East Anglia was invested into the fast-growing industrial north and Midlands. This was a new regional specialism in a new regional dispensation. Henceforth Norwich was, as it were, 'locked' into agrarian East Anglia, in a way that it had not been before. But, if it isolated the city in one way, its regional role also sustained it. Only in the later twentieth-century growth of Ipswich has a substantial rival emerged within Norwich's own heartlands of East Anglia – a new challenge for the future.

Returning therefore to the question of urban typicality or otherwise, onlookers in 1800 would not face any difficulty in 'placing' Norwich. The city's long-term decline was, after all, slow and relative. Moreover, urbanisation has historically been fuelled by a range of urban specialisms, and not by the fate of manufacturing alone. At the end of the eighteenth century, Norwich still ranked among the leading urban centres not only of Britain but also of Europe as a whole, where it was the sixty-eighth largest (jointly with Magdeburg in Germany). A comparison of Tables 6.1 and 6.4 shows that between 1700 and 1800 demographic growth had greatly multiplied the number of towns with populations of 10,000 plus; but that still only relatively few had surpassed 30,000 by the later eighteenth century.

If Norwich in 1801 no longer stood out from its British peers in population terms, it kept its status among Europe's medium-sized inland towns – with counterparts in places like Amiens, Nîmes, Frankfurt-am-Main, Magdeburg (on the Elbe) and Parma. Interestingly, even an urban rising star like Munich, capital of the emergent Bavaria, was still at this date smaller than the East Anglian metropolis.

Norwich also had by no means shed its distinctive qualities. It stood out, among Europe's medium-sized commercial centres, for the exceptional vitality and 'outreach' of its urban culture, as seen especially in its literary and artistic flowering. Comparisons with classical Athens in its glory were made not only in the case of late eighteenth-century Edinburgh, at the heart of the Scottish Enlightenment, but also with reference to Norwich. It is true that there was an element of local flattery in this latter attribution.[70] Yet it paid tribute to the city as a cultural capital in its own right, and as a cultural intermediary with northern Europe. Thus in the 1790s the essayist William Taylor, the leisured son of a Norwich textile manufacturer, was a key translator of German literature into English; as was Anne Plumptre, daughter of a prebendary of Norwich. With her markedly pro-French views, she was a particularly controversial member of the city's literary and political circles. 'Oh for the good old times! when females were satisfied with feminine employments ...', groaned one traditionalist cleric, shocked

Table 6.4 West and Central European[1] towns and cities (10,000+)[2] in 1800, grouped by population size

Population Size	Number of Cities	Aggregate Population	Towns 10,000+ as % of All Population
500,000+	2	1,446,000[3]	1.18
100,000+	15	2,531,000[4]	2.06
50,000+	33	2,307,000[5]	1.88
30,000+	42	1,538,000[6]	1.25
10,000+	268	4,345,000	3.54
All Towns 10,000+	360	12,167,000	9.91
Total Population		122,700,000[7]	

Notes: [1] Comprising all countries in West and Central Europe from the Atlantic across to and including Austria-Bohemia and Poland; but excluding Slovakia, Hungary and the Balkans.

[2] Following the source, the figures here relate to individual municipalities and not to conurbations, with the exception of London and Paris. That affects the rankings of some cities (Manchester with Salford would rank above rather than below Liverpool) but does not seriously affect the overall urban profile.

[3] In size order (1) London; (2) Paris.

[4] In size order [newcomers in this group in bold type]: (3) Naples; (4) Vienna; (5) Amsterdam; (6) Lisbon; (7) **Dublin**; (8) Madrid; (9) Rome; (10) **Berlin**; (11) Palermo; (12) Venice; (13) Milan; (14) **Barcelona**; (15) **Copenhagen**; (16 jointly) **Hamburg, Lyon**.

[5] In size order [newcomers to this group in bold type]: (18) Seville; (19) Genoa; (20) Bordeaux; (21 jointly) **Edinburgh, Turin**; (23 jointly) Florence, Rouen; (25) Valencia; (26 jointly) **Liverpool**, Marseilles; (28 jointly) **Glasgow, Prague**; (30 jointly) **Cork, Stockholm**; (32 jointly) Brussels, **Nantes**; (34) Bologna; (35 jointly) **Cadiz, Manchester**; (37 jointly) **Birmingham, Bristol**; (39) **Warsaw**; (40) Antwerp; (41 jointly) **Königsberg**, Lille; (43) **Rotterdam**; (44 severally) **Dresden, Grenada, Liège**; (47) **Wroclaw** (Breslau); (48 jointly) **Leeds, Livorno**; (50) Ghent.

[6] In size order [newcomers in this group in bold type; declining towns returning to this group in *italics*]: (51) Strasbourg; (52) **Sheffield**; (53 jointly) **Catania**, Toulouse; (55) Messina; (56) Orléans; (57) **Plymouth**; (58) Cologne; (59) Verona; (60 severally) **Cordoba**, *Danzig*, **Murcia**, Nîmes, Zaragossa; (65 jointly) **Limerick, Metz**; (67) The Hague; (68 jointly) **Magdeburg**, Norwich; (70 severally) Amiens, **Bremen**, Malaga; (73 jointly) **Frankfurt-am-Main, Jerez**; (75 severally) **Caen, Munich**, Parma; (78) **Cartagena**; (79 severally) **Bath**, Bruges, **Leipzig**, Padua, **Portsmouth, Toulon**, Utrecht; (86 severally) **Graz**, *Leiden*, **Montpellier**; (87) **Reims**; (90 severally) **Clermont Ferrand, Ferrara, Porto**.

[7] As estimated by De Vries, *European Urbanisation*, p. 36.

to find such a 'totally Frenchified' person emerging from the Anglican calm of the cathedral close.[71]

Both Anne Plumptre and William Taylor were members of Norwich's radical intelligentsia who contributed in 1794–5 to their own literary and political magazine. Named *The Cabinet, by a Society of Gentlemen*, this innovative venture attempted to sustain a reform culture. It published not only political articles, discussing constitutional change (one author advocated votes for women), but also poems and general essays.[72] Appearing fortnightly, it was an ambitious project to launch in a troubled city of 37,000 inhabitants – the successful Whig journal, the *Edinburgh Review*, which followed in 1802, was published quarterly within the much larger Scottish capital with some 82,000 inhabitants. In the event, The *Cabinet* was voluntarily ended in 1795, at a time of political clamp-down. A weekly newspaper supporting reform, named the *Iris* and edited by William Taylor, followed in 1802 but, again, did not last long. The circumstances were not propitious. Yet a snooty visitor in 1812 still noted the 'astonishing' enthusiasm for literature in the city, despite the fact that it had no university and was 'merely a manufacturing town'.[73]

Equally ambitious but less political and more successful was Norwich's celebrated Society of Artists, founded in 1803. Their skills were fostered by urban traditions of artistry, and nurtured by the city's rich textile heritage of expertise in colour and design. In addition, the artists were sustained by an affluent urban clientele, willing to support local art. Here there were noted similarities with the commercial context of seventeenth-century Dutch art, which was well known to East Anglian collectors. It took, however, the mutual organisation of the city's artists into their own society to consolidate their *de facto* identification as a 'school'. Nothing as formalised was to be found anywhere else, outside London; and nowhere else in Britain was the urban connection so cultivated directly by the artists themselves.

Admittedly, none of the painters made great fortunes. Nonetheless, from 1805 onwards, the society's annual exhibitions, held in the busy assize week, kept their work in the public eye. Thus were bolstered the careers of modestly born artists like John Crome, son of a Norwich journeyman weaver and publican, and John Sell Cotman, son of a Norwich hair dresser who later kept a small draper's shop, as well as those of lesser luminaries like James Stark (1794–1859), the son of a Scottish dyer who had come to work in Norwich, and George Vincent (b. 1796), another son of a Norwich weaver.

Between them, they painted the serene enduringness of the Norfolk countryside, that framed the long-term survival of the city.[74] They also depicted the busy life of the winding river, gracefully linking Norwich to Yarmouth and the wider world. And they painted the city too: in evocative panoramas and detailed vignettes, featuring street scenes, old housing (but no weavers at their looms), the cathedral, the water mills, the river backs, and the central market, beautifully shown in its combined hubbub and harmony by Cotman in 1806. So there survives a visual record of distinctive urbanity by those who witnessed it, capturing the 'fine old city' of Norwich amidst its historic transition – from second city to regional capital.

7

Politics, 1660–1835

Mark Knights

Never was a city in the miserable kingdom so wretchedly divided as this.

London Post, 14 May 1705.

For much of the period between 1660 and 1835 Norwich was a divided city.[1] In 1681 Humphrey Prideaux, dean of the cathedral, described the city as riven 'into two factions, Whigs and Torys ... and both contend for their way with the utmost violence'. In the following year the splits were said to 'appear in all public businesses'. A London newspaper reported in 1705 on the contests and remarked: 'Never were such divisions carried on with such feud, such malice, such magisterial tyranny and such defiance of laws of government.' This turbulence was still the case in 1727, when a riot followed the general election:

> after the mixed multitude had commenced the fray by thowing dirt, oyster shells, stones or whatever else their fury could lay hold on, a warm engagement ensued amongst the staffmen, who laid on all that stood in the way with passion and violence ... some of the mob cried out 'kill the sheriffs, D—n 'em, kill 'em and then we shall get the election.'[2]

A century later, in 1830, the strife was even more palpable. An election parade brought 15–20,000 inhabitants on to the streets, and at the poll there was 'ringing of bells – the rattling of coaches – the shouts of the assembled multitude and ... a large "Blue and White" [Whig party banner] floated majestically in the air, over a group of happy individuals, who testified their approbation by the waving of their handkerchiefs'. The festive atmosphere soon changed and 'symptoms of angry feelings [appeared] till at length stones were thrown, and with such effect, that many persons were dangerously wounded'. Even after peace had been restored groups of men 'made dreadful havock, knocking down friend and foe; it was most appalling', one observer wrote, 'to see in the space of a few minutes fifteen or twenty men extended on the pavement in front of the booth'. After the declaration of the poll the participatory nature of city politics became clear:

> persons of all descriptions began to congregate, by the hour ... every window in the market appeared filled with spectators. The balconies were also crowded, and the very roofs of the houses had their share of anxious gazers. The roof of the Guildhall and St Peter's steeple, were actually studded with heads; while the extensive area of the marketplace was equally crowded.[3]

Such eagerness translated into verifiable allegiances. In 1840 it was said that the 'party to which every man in Norwich belongs, from the highest to the lowest, is as well known as if he daily wore clothes of the colour by which it is designated'.[4] These remarks highlight the city's longstanding appetite for political conflict and participatory politics. Norwich's political culture between 1660 and 1835 was vibrant, exuberant, partisan and sometimes violent.

To be sure, part of the explanation is peculiar to the city, which shaped and sometimes distorted national party politics. Divisions after 1780 were literally coloured, as we have already seen with the banner of the 1830 election. The party of blue-and-white, which wanted reform on local and national issues and took an independent stance towards the government administrations of the period, was pitted against the orange-and-purple pro-ministerialist and pro-church party. These divisions roughly corresponded to a Whig-Tory split, but the match was never exact, not least because Whiggery came in many different varieties. Nevertheless, the local dimension of the struggles should not obscure their connection with national movements.[5]

At the outset it is worth reiterating the peculiarly open – some have called it democratic – structure of the city's local government, for it was this that was responsible for much of the vitality of Norwich's political life.

Unlike other large cities, such as Bristol and Exeter, Norwich's civic structures were remarkably open and popular – but also complex. At the heart of the citizenry were the freemen. There were about 2000 freemen voters in 1690, rising to over 3300 by the mid 1730s. The number of freemen was linked to trade apprenticeships but was also politically manipulated for electoral purposes – for example, as many as 231 were created just before the 1702 election, and 341 in 1714, as against an average of between thirty and sixty a year. The number of freemen contracted slightly in the mid eighteenth century, with fewer than 2300 voting in 1761, but again expanded to about 4000 in 1831. Only after 1750 did the expansion of the electorate fail to keep pace with demographic growth, so that by 1800 only

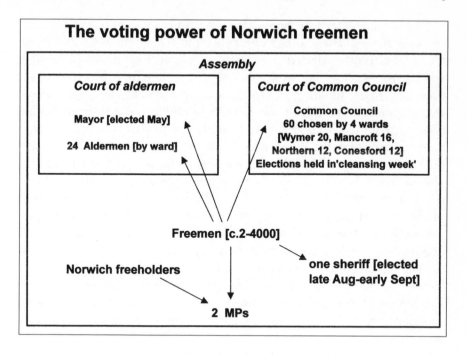

The voting power of Norwich freemen

Assembly

Court of aldermen

Mayor [elected May]

24 Aldermen [by ward]

Court of Common Council

Common Council
60 chosen by 4 wards
[Wymer 20, Mancroft 16,
Northern 12, Conesford 12]
Elections held in'cleansing week'

Freemen [c.2-4000]

Norwich freeholders

one sheriff [elected
late Aug-early Sept]

2 MPs

22 per cent of the adult male population were eligible to vote, compared with a third earlier in the century. Even so, turn-out among those who had the vote was high, with some 3800 (of 4327 potential voters) polling in 1833. The freemen had a number of occasions on which to exercise their franchise, and civic elections were perhaps even more important in dividing the city than parliamentary ones. A Norwich citizen in the early nineteenth century remarked that 'the prosperity of the city and private intercourse of society are poisoned by party spirit, engendered at the municipal elections. I attribute these consequences to their frequency and the nature of the constituency. We have three elections every year; and there is no cooling time.'[6]

The municipal elections were for mayor (in May), sheriff (late August or early September) and common council (in the week before Easter), and each attracted a huge amount of interest. In 1710 more than 3000 freemen – more than in the general election of that year – voted in a mayoral election; and in 1716 the mayoral election ended in riot, with both sides throwing 'brick ends and great paving stones' at each other. Turn-outs for shrieval elections was generally smaller but on occasion, as in 1797, there could be great struggles, especially as the sheriff acted as returning officer for the parliamentary elections. Moreover, only ex-sheriffs could qualify as mayoral candidates, so this apprenticeship was essential to attain high office. The freemen elected sixty common councilmen each year in what was known as 'cleansing week', and also in their wards chose (when the occasion arose) the city's aldermen, a body of twenty-four men whose election was for life. At least twenty-three of the thirty-six aldermanic elections between 1699 and 1722 were contested, with particular heat in 1705, a dispute in which the Whigs allegedly spent £600–700. Later in the century common council elections were again fiercely contested. Yet the obvious rewards were meagre: 'we can only express ... an utter astonishment at the strength of the motives which can impel gentlemen to so profuse an expenditure of time, money, personal exertion and fatigue', observed the *Norwich Mercury* in 1829. The contests also gave ample opportunity for bribery and corruption, which became an especially notable feature of late eighteenth- and early nineteenth-century political culture. In 1808 it was reckoned that the cost of contesting one ward was nearly £3000; and in the early nineteenth century an increasing reliance on bribery pushed them towards £10,000. These were enormous sums for municipal elections. In addition to straightforward bribery, votes could also be induced by judicious use of corporation charity – the Great Hospital alone had £6000 annually to dispose of. Yet whether such bribery altered, rather than confirmed, allegiances is doubtful; the electorate continued to show independence, even if it was rewarded through a party system.[7]

This system of elections produced two bodies. First, the mayor's court, consisting of the mayor, sheriffs, and aldermen; and secondly, the assembly (the mayor's court and common council joined). The latter had a complex system of committees – only three in 1700, but twelve by 1835. There was also provision for freemen to call a common hall, which could confirm petitions and addresses from the city. The structure of local government thus afforded, even encouraged, a high degree of political involvement. Moreover, the parish and ward system also fostered concentrations of power geographically in the city. The affluent ward of Mancroft had a Tory bias in the early eighteenth century. Even between 1730 and 1750, when the Whigs largely monopolised parliamentary and civic offices, Mancroft remained a Tory stronghold. The Whigs, on the other hand, did much better in the Northern and Wymer wards. So it is worth remembering that the sheer variety and scale of legitimate participatory platforms, in terms of number, together with the nuances of different zones within the city, mean that the following generalisations about shifts in political power have to be treated as broad-brush strokes painting an overall picture.

The period from the restoration of the Stuart monarchy in 1660 to the establishment of a Whig oligarchy at both local and national level witnessed bitter contests. Norwich showed early signs of partisan politics around three issues: religion, civic independence, and rivalry between aristocratic factions in the county. These tensions came to a head, and were to some extent fused, in the early 1680s. In 1678 the earl of Yarmouth, who sought to dominate county politics over his rival Lord Townshend, thought 'Norwich would be the loyallest city in England if a few were out of it, who infect a party with anti-monarchical principles. I am in quest of them all'. Two days later he wrote to the chief minister of state asking for permission to 'purge this bench of the goats' or 'fanatics', whom he regarded as seditious in politics and religion. Yet it was not until 1682 that those 'loyal' to king and church were in a position to threaten the city's independence. In that year, despite opposition from over eight hundred citizens, the city's charter was surrendered to the king, allowing the crown to nominate sympathetic personnel, who were now being styled 'Tories' by their enemies, the 'Whigs'. Once in power, the Tories, many of whom believed in strict adherence to the creed and ceremonies of the Church of England, initiated a campaign of prosecutions against the city's numerous dissenters. Serving on the remodelled council and participating in the repression of dissent marked and fixed officeholders' allegiances and drew the lines of conflict for a number of years to follow. Ironically, the high church Tory grip on the corporation was temporarily relaxed by the crown itself, for after 1687 the Catholic James II sought an alliance at local and national level with nonconformists who might support his religious policy of toleration for Catholics and dissenters alike. This forced the crown to weed out Tories who would not comply. James's experiment was short-lived and his overthrow was popular – about 1000 'boys' rioted in the city on 14 October 1688 and the Catholic chapel was pillaged. Even so, the revolution of 1688 had profound consequences in the city, for the high-church Tories found the coronation of William and Mary as king and queen to be unpalatable and even objectionable.[8]

Norwich Toryism after the Revolution was thus tinged with Jacobitism – adherence to the exiled Stuarts. Bishop William Lloyd, who had helped lead opposition to James, nevertheless found himself unable to take the oaths of allegiance to the new monarchs and after 1692 headed the 'nonjuring' clerics. But sympathy for James and his heirs went beyond the clergy. In 1693 the Whigs drew up a list of those 'disaffected to the government', concluding that 'the eighth part of this city is ill affected to ye gover[n]ment and that way inclyning'. In 1704, for example, it was alleged that at Fowler's alehouse the landlord, 'with a glass of beer in hand, went down [on] his knees and drank a health to James the third, wishing the Crowne well settled on his head', and there were many other similar reports. High church militancy was thus one of the factors responsible for Tory successes, such as those of 1710 when local and national energies focused on the trial of Dr Sacheverell, whose prosecution by a Whig-dominated parliament unleashed cries of 'the church in danger'. So at the city's general election that year Sacheverell's picture was 'hung at out a window' facing the city hall and after the poll the Tory victors 'were carried three times round the market cross in a triumphant manner ... the pictures of the royal martyr, King Charles I, Her Majesty Queen Anne and the Reverend Dr Sacheverell being all three put on boards together were advanced on a pole and carried all the time before them'. The divisions, between stout adherents to the church and Stuarts, on the one hand, and passionate defenders of the revolution, on the other, split the city. The 1710 and 1715 poll books show voters almost invariably voting on party tickets. Indeed, from 1689 until the death of the last Stuart monarch in 1714, politics in Norwich was hard fought between two parties ideologically opposed about the nature of the Revolution settlement in church and state. As one partisan put it, 'the City of Norwich is at present distracted with party rage, Whig and Tory, High Church and Low Church, or to give it to you in our dialect, Croakers and Tackers make the two contending parties'.[9]

For the later seventeenth and early eighteenth centuries the Tories had control of the city's civic bodies, but in terms of general elections the parties were quite evenly matched, indeed so balanced that under a hundred votes could swing a result. In 1734 a mere 218 votes separated the two parties, out of a total of 3363 votes; and a difference of 400, out of 3246 voters, in 1735 could be counted a large margin. Even in 1710, when the Tories were strongest, they only had 54 per cent of the freeman vote. Nevertheless, the accession of George I in 1714 weakened the Tory hold and in 1715 the Whigs gained 56 per cent of the vote. The Tories thereafter struggled to retain control of the corporation. By 1717 they had lost their majority on the assembly and in 1720 the Whigs controlled the court of mayoralty too. Yet the Tories were not routed – indeed in 1721 and 1722 they won a parliamentary seat and the mayoral election – and this so alarmed the Whigs that they set out to rig civic elections in their own favour. In January 1723 the assembly, which was still in Whig hands, successfully petitioned parliament for a new Election Act that would force all adult males engaged in the textile industry to take up the freedom (on the correct assumption that they were more likely to vote Whig), regularise electoral polls (after those in the city gaol had been dragooned into voting), and specify property qualifications for sheriffs. Some Tory support seems to have been won for the bill, perhaps because its ostensible reason was to reverse a decline in the city's revenue. In any case, the Tories shocked the Whigs by winning majorities in 1728 in two wards, again giving them control of the assembly. The Tory mob was so 'elevated' by this news that they rang bells, fired guns and 'were so insolent as to insult gentlemen of the contrary party in the streets and at their own doors'; the guildhall was invaded and the Riot Act had to be read. One report claimed Norwich 'seem'd one continued scene of riot and madness'. After a further Tory mayoral victory, the Whig aldermen refused to attend the assembly, a boycott that lasted over a year. Their revenge took the form of the Norwich Elections Act of 1730, which instituted a novel bicameral legislature modelled on the 1725 London Act, which had curtailed popular elections in the capital.[10]

The Norwich act attempted to circumscribe the independence of the electorate in two ways. First, it required voter registration and attempted to bar the purchase of the freedom for poor men in return for their votes. Secondly, the number of councillors to be chosen by each ward was reduced to three, a triumvirate who were then empowered to co-opt others.[11] Moreover, in the wake of the act the aldermen and common council henceforth met separately, a recipe for further dissension since both bodies felt able to veto the decisions of the other. The Whigs now controlled the corporation. They only just secured victory in the ward elections of 1730 and 1731; but the Tory spirit had been temporarily broken. Thus, although the excise crisis dented Whig fortunes at a national and county level, they scraped home in Norwich at the 1734 general election and the following year achieved a far more convincing victory at a by-election. In part this loyalty was due to the personal influence of 'prime minister' Sir Robert Walpole, a Norfolk man with a county seat at Houghton, whose support for the local textile industry endeared him to the city. Indeed, it granted him its freedom in 1733 at a ceremony conducted in the market place. In the following year, Walpole was able to insert his brother, Horatio, as MP for the city.[12] Norwich had been temporarily tamed.

Rampant Whiggery and anti-populist civic measures consequently boosted the city's popular Jacobitism, which became a means of protesting against both Hanoverian and local Whig domination. After 1714 there was a flurry of popular demonstrations of sympathy for the ousted Stuarts or hostility to the incoming Hanoverians. In January 1716, for example, the proclamation of the 'Pretender' at a play staged at The New Inn was cheered, and the audience hissed when King George's name was mentioned. Days associated with the Stuarts were commemorated with what has rightly been called 'audacious enthusiasm'. The Whigs saw such

Jacobitism as seditious and even treasonous; but those who flirted with it saw in it an opportunity to cock a snook at dissenters or their allies and to display their loyalty to a faded concept of a powerful national church. On 29 May 1717 – 'Restoration day' for the Stuarts – bells were rung until midnight and 'musketeers and wheel-guns kept firing all day in the streets', while many sat 'drinking prosperity to the CHURCH'. The city even produced its own Jacobite plotter, Christopher Layer, whose list of supporters included five aldermen and the former MP, Richard Berney. In 1722 it was reported that supporters of the king were 'hiss'd at and curst as they go in the streets'. In 1731 Jacobite elements were again blamed for disturbances. A 'Tory mobb, in a great body, went through several parts of this city, in a riotous manner, cursing and abusing such as they knew to be friends of the government' and threatened the life of one man who had uncovered a Jacobite tract. A strong non-juring tradition encouraged a language of defiance. The contests within Norwich thus continued well into a period in which 'political stability' has often been discerned at a national level. Yet the Jacobite invasion of 1745 proved devastating to the Tories. When the news reached Norwich, citizens mustered themselves into an association whose signatories promised to defend the city against internal and external threats. Some Tories did sign but others refused to do so and the vestry of St Peter Mancroft resolved that it would not ring its bells. Undaunted, the Whigs organised a sumptuous thanksgiving in October, outdoing 'any city in England', with a magnificent triumphal arch erected in the market place, covered with some ninety-six yards of Persian silk so that the candles inside the structure illuminated both the kings arms and mottos such as 'Religion and Liberty' which were painted on it (Figure 30).[13]

Although in the late 1750s the naturalist William Arderon observed that 'the city for many years hath been split into two factions or parties', the bitterness of such conflicts had subsided from the mid 1730s onwards, in Norwich and in the nation as a whole. After 1741 there was no parliamentary contest in the city until the 1760s; and the excitement of 1745 confirmed rather than established the Whig predominance that had been won the previous decade. Contests for common council elections were rare between 1750 and 1780. Between 1760 and 1779 councillors sat on average for over fourteen years, nearly twice as long as the average tenure in the 1720s. The mid century was thus a period of relative concord and stability.

Although this stability is interesting in itself, offering a marked contrast with the first rage of party, it is also possible to see the mid century years as ones of important transition. Although the Seven Years' War (1756–63)

FIGURE 30. The 1745 triumphal Arch erected for a thanksgiving after the defeat
of the Jacobite rebellion. (*Norfolk Heritage Centre*)

was very popular in Norwich, as it was elsewhere in Britain, it promoted patriotism and a sense of independence from government, both of which could undermine government credibility in the following decades, especially when George III appeared to have made an unsatisfactory peace and to be intent on increasing royal power. Just as in London such popular sentiments were exploited by John Wilkes, so in Norwich there were toasts to the 'friends of liberty'. A parliamentary candidate in 1768, Thomas Beevor, duly promised to oppose 'all attempts upon the liberty of the Subject and every other UNCONSTITUTIONAL measure'. In order to prevent Beevor's election, attempts were made to persuade the sitting MP, Harbord Harbord, to abandon his independent stance in order to join with ministerialist Whig Edmund Bacon; but a group of five hundred freemen formally protested at this 'conspiracy' and a satirical print, 'The Junction', depicted a crowd crying 'Beevor forever' and protesting against the proposed stitch-up (Plate 8).

In 1768 a group of freemen duly published a 'letter of instruction' for the MP to direct his conduct in parliament. It contained twelve demands, including triennial parliaments, the exclusion of officeholders and pensioners, the release of Wilkes and his recognition as MP of Middlesex; it also attacked the 'secret influence of that undermining favourite', Lord Bute. Beevor lost, but not without a spirited fight. Since Harbord maintained his independent stance, and Bacon appeared on occasion to join it, the independents might be said to have put enough popular pressure to direct how their MPs behaved; and reform was now on the public agenda.[14]

Another factor polarising opinion was the war with the American colonies. A city subscription to raise money for a regiment listed 144 names in 1778. Yet this was condemned by William Windham, a young critic of the government, as 'unconstitutional', and in the election of 1780 he stood with Beevor on an anti-war platform.[15] As Edward Crane, the son of a Unitarian minister, put it,

> our city had for a long time been slave to two families of the names of Ives and Harveys [eminent manufacturers], who had nominated all the members of the corporation, though by the charter of the city, every freeman has a right in his separate ward to vote for aldermen etc. However, we had been so long tame that they thought to impose a member of parliament upon us ... known to be a ministerialist.[16]

Such compliance could no longer be guaranteed under the pressure of new forces. Indeed, the independent vote was to be described two years later as consisting of 'a considerable proportion of manufacturing interest and tradesmen together with a warm attachment of the inferior class of freemen'. This trend was facilitated by the fact that political and economic power in the city did not necessarily coincide. In the 1750s only one in four of the wealthiest residents chose to take up civic office.[17]

Embedded in this new independence was religious dissent. Between 1740 and 1760 half of the serving mayors came from nonconformist backgrounds; indeed, by the 1750s the core of the 'civic elite' was predominantly dissenting. A powerful set of leaders was thus drawn from outside the ranks of the Anglican Church. This phenomenon needs to be set in a longer tradition. Nonconformity had been strong in late seventeenth-century Norwich too. The Presbyterian minister John Collinges was said to have headed the Whig party in the city in 1682, and in 1687, shortly after the declaration of indulgence, to grow 'very pert and pragmatical'. The Toleration Act of 1689 allowed dissenters freedom of worship so long as their meetings were licensed. By the early eighteenth century Norwich had four meetings, in the parishes of St James, St Paul and St Giles. The chapel built off Colegate in 1698 still survives as one of the oldest in the country. The rise of the political power of nonconformity was soon visible in political terms too. In 1696 one of the leaders of the Presbyterians, Robert Cooke, was responsible for organising an association of loyalty to the king in the wake of an assassination plot, and a host of fellow dissenters signed alongside him. Cooke had been an alderman and had risen to become mayor in 1693. Between 1720 and 1750, in fact, twenty five Presbyterians assumed civic office. If we take 1734 as an example of the relationship between Dissent and politics, we find that both the mayor and sheriff were Presbyterians and that the Quaker John Gurney acted as electoral agent for the Whig MP Waller Bacon. And in general the Whigs did well in Northern and Wymer wards, where there was a high concentration of dissent.[18]

Yet in the early 1750s the religious culture of the city appeared to be becoming more overt with the impact of 'New Dissent'. Soon after James Wheatly began preaching a brand of Methodism in 1751, a 'church and king' mob staged a riot and shouted 'down with the meeting houses'. Dissenters now began to take over buildings which had previously had other uses – the Foundry in St Stephen's was licensed in 1755, the Malthouse in St Paul's in 1756, and the Old Playhouse in St Peter Mancroft in 1758. More significant was the building, begun in 1753, of the Octagon chapel. The Unitarians (rational dissenters rooted in Presbyterianism) who met there were to become key to the city's political radicalism, even though numerically they were the smallest dissenting group. After the 1780s the Unitarians were elected to council in significant numbers – five in 1791, eight in 1800, thirteen in 1818, and six in 1827 (Plate 9).[19]

In theory, dissenters were denied access to civic office by the Test and

Corporation Acts. In practice, when political tensions were low, the religious test could be ignored. Until 1801 known dissenters were elected to the common council and even then, when the Tories challenged the legality of those evading the Corporation Act and secured a verdict in King's Bench to require a new election, four of the five dissenting councillors were simply re-elected. Moreover, some dissenters 'occasionally conformed' to the church, thereby qualifying themselves. Elias Norgate, for example, the chair of the dissenters' meeting in 1789, also took Anglican communion. This situation may explain why Norwich was not at the forefront of attempts to have the Test and Corporation Act repealed. Indeed the Unitarian John Taylor went so far in 1806 to say that he cared not 'two straws about the matter'. We therefore need to be cautious about seeing religious polarity as the sole explanation for political divisions; but we must certainly count it as a major factor contributing to them. The blue-and-whites were bank-rolled by the Gurneys, who had prospered to become one of the wealthiest dissenting families in England; and certainly the party contained many dissenters and low churchmen. Indeed, by 1829 about one in seven of the adult population in Norwich was a dissenter. The bedrock of the orange and purples, by contrast, were churchmen.[20]

In order to explain the evolution of political culture in the city two more of its general features need to be taken into account, the role of the press and the rise of political clubs and societies. The political press in Norwich had a long history, for Britain's first provincial newspaper, the *Norwich Post*, was published there in 1701. A second, the *Norwich Gazette*, began in 1706. The latter was edited by Henry Crossgrove, a deeply partisan Tory but also an innovative journalist, whose paper not only carried news but also a correspondence column for its readers. A third paper, the *Norwich Postman*, also began in 1706. It evolved into the *Weekly Mercury* in 1714 (becoming in turn the *Norwich Mercury* in 1726), and was edited by William Chase, a Whig who gave Crossgrove a run for his money both commercially and politically. Both Crossgrove and Case served as common councillors, the former as a Tory for Mancroft between 1728 and 1744 and the latter as a Whig for Wymer in 1714, 1718 and 1734. Crossgrove was defiantly anti-Hanoverian and did all he could to promote the Jacobite cause. 'Norwich is not altogether Germanized', he wrote, for it still had 'persons who are real Englishmen and can never cease to be so'. He suffered for such views by a number of Whig-inspired prosecutions and attacks. It is difficult to assess the impact of such partisan polemic, but by the 1780s there was a sufficiently vibrant local press to influence popular politics. In mid century, about three-quarters of males in some parishes were literate, though rates fell to below a half in the larger sprawling parishes. And there

were two newspapers between 1761 and 1790 (the *Gazette* altered its name
to the *Norfolk Chronicle*) and in the 1770s both carried columns of letters
from readers. Moreover, the quantity of political print published locally
seems to have increased markedly from the mid eighteenth century
onwards.[21]

Some of the print was rather parochial and, as one collection of election
pieces admitted, could be 'understood only by such as know the circumstances that produced them'. Nevertheless, a good deal of the polemic drew
on language that had national resonance, as illustrated by *The Narrative of
the Proceedings at the Contested Election* (1780), which sought to collect and
preserve 'the hand-bills promiscuously distributed' during the general election. It included one, in favour of Sir Harbord Harbord, that attacked 'the
undue influence of the Crown and the corruption of parliament', and
noted that the 'voice of the people called loudly for a reform in the expenditure of the public treasure', claiming that £40 million had been spent on
a war with America to 'establish tyranny, oppression, slavery and other
modes of coercion'. Moreover, when Harbord announced that he would
not contest the seat, it was the press that kept up the barrage of opposition.
This did not go unchallenged, again by further prints. Thus a 'Genuine
Protestant' urged support for rivals Bacon and Thurlow, rejecting the alle-
gations against them as 'meer bugbears, to terrify the ignorant into an
opposition'. This prompted a reply from 'Junius', who attacked the ministry
as 'weak, or wicked or remarkably unsuccessful', citing the famous resolution of the House of Commons that 'the dangerous influence of the Crown
has increased, is increasing and ought to be diminished'. Just as the
national government was depicted as insidious, so the local junto of 'two or
three wealthy families' was also attacked for being 'ministerial tools'.
Further handbills roused those 'who dare to be free in the worst of times'.
Unless the freemen acted against those who undermined their birthright, it
was said, they would have to 'wear the chains of slavery, unrepining, for
ever!'. When Alderman Robert Harvey circulated a handbill claiming that
the 'duplicity of the Quakers and the cant of the Presbyterians' might carry the
day, an embarrassed Bacon and Thurlow had to issue another denying any
involvement in its publication so as not to alienate potential supporters.[22]

This type of printed exchange was to characterise politics thereafter.
Electoral print was even directed 'to the ladies' in a handbill from
'Boadicea' asking them 'to exert YOUR persuasive influence on the mind
of a father, brother, husband, lover. Tell them, NOT to seek filial duty,
congenial regard, matrimonial comfort, nor tender compliance, till they
have saved YOUR country from perdition!' Print played a part in ensuring
that Harbord won. Although his partner Windham came bottom of the

poll, it is significant that he immediately placed an advertisement in the
Norfolk Chronicle to thank his supporters and indicate his future hopes.
The sheer variety of ways in which print could influence politics is indicated in the subtitle of *The Election Magazine* (1784), which proclaimed it
a 'repository of wit and politics being an impartial collection of the essays,
songs, epigrams, cards, reasons, strictures, prophecies, letters, questions,
answers, squibs, queries, addresses, replies, rejoinders etc that were distributed during the canvas and election' of 1784. Moreover, flurries of print
now surrounded civic elections too. The shrieval election of 1781, for example, provoked 'papers, advertisements, questions, verses etc', when Thomas
Colman stood on 'constitutional principles' against the war with America.
Shortly afterwards Colman again forced a contest for an aldermanic seat,
opposing a man who had subscribed toward the American war, prompting
one tract to note that 'never was there a greater struggle for Parliament-
men than on this occasion for an alderman … promises, treats, menaces,
obligations, interests, and whole phalanx of corruption was opposed to the
genuine sentiments of freemen'. Print was by then both an integral part of
the political process but also an agent for reform; and its use in Norwich
was perhaps unparalleled outside London.[23]

Independent politics was also facilitated by the proliferation of clubs,
societies and associations. Again, these had a longer history. Associations
before 1750 were often communities of subscribers bound by oaths. Thus
the 1696 association oaths that recognised William as 'rightful and lawful'
king, after a Jacobite attempt to murder him, were signed by about 7000
men. To put it in some perspective, this number represented nearly all the
adult males in the city. Two different texts were promoted – one by the
corporation and one by the dissenting weavers – who felt that the official
version was too weak in merely promising to *punish* those who had
attempted to kill the king – and these split the city; only about 3.5 per cent
of the signatories signed both versions. This type of mass oath-taking was
again repeated in 1723 in the wake of another Jacobite plot, though women
were included this time. Nevertheless, there was a shift towards smaller voluntary associations and societies that attempted to represent sectional and
secular interests. There were at least sixty clubs formed in Norwich
between 1715 and 1745, and seventy-eight between 1750 and 1785. These
found homes in the city's numerous alehouses – there were some 281 in
1702, roughly one for every hundred inhabitants – and in the coffee houses
that sprang up after the first opened in 1676.[24]

The clubs could mobilise political pressure. One of the most important
such societies in the early eighteenth century was a development of the
association of 1715, the Artillery Company, which became an armed tool for

the Whigs and dissenters. In 1716 the company burnt an effigy of the Stuart 'Pretender' and sought to confront any displays of Jacobite loyalty; but it was also active at the mayoral election that year, inflicting 'bloody noses and broken heads' on opponents. The rival camps 'began to pelt each other with sheeps horns, brick ends, and great paving stones by which many people received cuts and contusions. Several constables had their heads crack'd and their staves broke'. The Artillery Company, with over a hundred members, held an annual feast in St Andrew's hall and between 1715 and 1745 six mayors were drawn from its ranks. Other, less militaristic, societies also emerged. The Loyal Society of Worsted Weavers, formed in 1717 primarily as a benefit society, was devoted to the Hanoverians – if any of its members voted Tory in local or parliamentary elections they could be thrown out. The Constitution Club was also formed in the early 1740s in support of the Whigs, and held dinners, such as the one in 1744 when it unveiled a portrait of Walpole. In 1745, in the wake of the Jacobite threat, the Constitution Club joined with the Artillery Company for demonstrations of loyalty, including a dinner attended by over two hundred of the local gentry.[25]

In the 1750s there were a number of short-lived partisan political clubs, such as the Society of True Protestant Britons, the Anti-Gallican Association and the Brethren of the Society of True Blues, which met at the White Horse. A Corporation Club began meeting at The Blue Bell, mimicking the official corporation by electing a 'mayor' and other parallel officers, and survived until the 1790s. The Blue Bell was owned in the early eighteenth century by the high church Tory Helwys family, who were suspected of Jacobitism, and the tavern remained a venue for Jacobite and then radical clubs. Loyalist clubs were active too. The Hell-Fire Club, for example, was responsible for the riots in 1751–52 against Methodists. But in the 1760s a number of clubs appeared with explicitly reformist agendas. In September 1769 there was a report of a meeting of the 'Free and Easy Society', which made toasts to 'Annual Parliaments' and a 'Speedy Redress of American Grievances', as well as to the Middlesex freeholders. Two months later, the 'Sons of Liberty' were said to have celebrated John Wilkes's victory against general warrants, an occasion at which a toast was made to 'the independent commons of the city of Norwich'. In April 1770 Wilkes's release from prison was celebrated by a number of 'purse clubs' in Norwich, who 'marched in procession' and rang bells. And in 1780 the Independent Club was established in order to build on the momentum achieved at the general election victory and to co-ordinate opposition.[26]

By the 1780s Norwich had a politically active group of dissenters, a strong local press, and a tradition of associations, clubs and societies. These made for a lively political culture, in which independence from governmental lines was particularly strong, evident in campaigns against the war with America and for reform. From the 1780s onwards these developments flowered into full-blown party conflicts, with a return to the violence and popular politics that had characterised earlier divisions. These divisions were, again like earlier ones, ideological; but they were also the result of a powerful cocktail of issues, in which trade and the impact of war with revolutionary France were key ingredients. The open and contestable structure of local government, the press, the clubs and societies, and dissent all ensured that politics overlapped with communities bound by economics, religion, ideology and print in a world in which public opinion could not be ignored. We can best explore this culture by identifying the various strands of conflict and then piecing together the fortunes of the different parties.

The issue that became the focal point for division was the Revolution across the Channel and the subsequent war with France. In Norwich's reformist circles the Revolution was greeted with enthusiasm. In April 1789 Sir Thomas Beevor proposed a toast at the Independent Club to 'the friends of freedom all over the world and success to the third estate of France in their noble struggle for liberty'. In November that year the Norwich Revolution Society was formed. At its core were dissenters such as William Barnard, the Taylors, Elias Norgate, the Reverend Mark Wilks and John Cozens, a grocer who was considered its 'great mover'. A glimpse of their attitudes can be gained from Mark Wilks's sermons. On one remarkable occasion he claimed that 'Jesus Christ was a revolutionist', that 'the French Revolution is of God, and that no power exists, or can exist by which it can be overthrown'. Another member, William Taylor, actually visited France in May 1790 and read his translated version of the decrees of the French National Assembly to the society. Norwich's dissenting intelligentsia was powerful, founding the *Cabinet* in 1794 in order to conduct a 'liberal investigation into the nature and object of civil government' and to protest against the war. But the Revolution Society also had a proselytising mission, aiming to found and coordinate subsidiary clubs among the populace. During 1792 the movement flourished, with membership claimed in excess of 4000 and as many as forty confederated clubs in Norwich, each sending delegates to meet at a central club at The Blue Bell inn in the city centre. In March 1792 delegates from the political societies joined together as the United Constitutional Societies, and established contact with the London Society for Constitutional Information. Men of the 'lowest description' were read extracts from Thomas Paine's *Rights of Man* and other popular radical works.[27]

Did the Revolution Society want revolution in Norwich? In 1792 the society stressed that 'riot and disorder are no parts of our political creed'. Rather, it sought 'an equitable representation of the people' and had little concept of class conflict, declaring that 'the interests of all the industrious from the richest merchant to the poorest mechanic are in every community the same'. It optimistically believed that 'men need only be made acquainted with the abuses of government and they will readily join in any lawful means to obtain redress'. Yet as the violence of the revolution in France became more apparent after 1792, and trade was again disrupted by war, the Norwich clubs lost their mercantile leaders and adopted more radical solutions. By early 1793 the Norwich clubs were in contact with the London Corresponding Society and declared for universal suffrage, claiming that landowners and merchants 'eat up the people as they eat bread'. Norwich even sent a representative, Maurice Margarot, to the radical convention in Edinburgh. When the authorities broke it up and sentenced Margarot to transportation, the Norwich society sent £20 for his defence costs and condemned the government action. But the execution of Louis XVI and England's declaration of war against the revolutionaries had turned sympathy for France into sedition. In March 1794 the secretary of the Revolution Society, Isaac Saint (publican of The Pelican inn), was arrested and the society, which had been one of the largest in the country, was disbanded.[28]

Even so, the formation of reformist clubs and societies continued. In April 1795 the Norwich Patriotic Society was founded to agitate for parliamentary reform. Within a year, it had twenty-seven branches, drawing its members primarily from the city's shopkeepers and craftsmen. Such popular political enthusiasm contributed to demands for universal suffrage and annual parliaments. In 1797 the society published a manifesto, whose probable author, Richard Dinmore, believed that 'the first grand principle, from which all others flow, is equality'. But the society was now up against acts of 1795 which restricted the press and freedom of assembly, and though it invited the radical John Thelwall from London to lecture to a crowd of over four thousand in 1796 and again in 1797 (provoking a riot when soldiers intervened), it appears to have vanished by the end of the century.[29]

This radical activity did not go unchecked by loyalists. In December 1792 the mayor, John Harvey, a merchant and banker, presided over a dinner at which loyal toasts were made. He then warned against those who:

disperse innumerable hand bills and cheap publications, the false reasonings of which are meant to delude and ensnare the lower class of the people, from whose useful labours our manufactures thrive and commerce flourishes.

Missionaries are sent from club to club to disseminate these detestable
opinions, that the poison of sedition may be more copiously diffused.[30]

An armed loyal association was formed, but when the justices met in
November 1796 to raise the number requested by the government under
the terms of the Supplementary Militia Act, a mob broke up the meeting
– the people's minds having been 'inflamed by various hand bills published
by ill designing persons'. Just over a week later effigies of Pitt and Windham (who had abandoned independent politics and was by then minister
for war) were burnt when magistrates tried to meet again. Even so, a loyalist momentum emerged as fears of a possible French invasion grew and
parishioners from each of the city parishes resolved to offer their services
to the government. By 1797 the *Norfolk Chronicle* was declaring that 'to
defend our country against the common enemy is now the only measure
left to us and no man, whatever his political opinions, will hesitate to take
his share of danger and fatigue'. That month a voluntary militia, the Norwich Loyal Military Association, was formed and about the same time the
Norwich Light Horse Volunteers offered gentlemen a similar opportunity
to enlist. Fears of invasion the following year boosted the associations,
though there were some who feared that the loyalty of the volunteers was
suspect and that they wanted only to avoid government compulsion to
serve outside their home city.[31]

The press encouraged loyal sentiments with patriotic songs – one was
composed to the tune of God Save the King – and the city's Tories took
advantage to head this wave of popular loyalism. But the press reflected
bitter exchanges between the parties. At his charge to the Norwich grand
jury in 1793 Alderman Charles Harvey urged prosecutions against libellers,
for he feared that 'writings and libels of the most seditious and inflammatory tendency have been industriously circulated, not only over this city
but over every part of the kingdom', promoted by societies which circulated cheap tracts. These made men 'dissatisfied with the present
constitution' and put forward 'a visionary and impracticable equality,
founded on some pretended rights'. Thus, while claiming not to want to
interfere with free speech, Harvey argued that this should not extend to
slandering the government. So 'every freeman has an undoubted right to
lay what sentiments he pleases before the public; but if he publishes what
is improper, mischievous or illegal, he must take the consequence of his
own temerity'. A collection of 'election squibs' for the 1796 general election
shows how rich the printed contest was. Windham, who had appeared to
have changed his liberal spots, was described as 'stained all over with mur-
derous crimes, like a scarlet leper' and voters were asked 'will you vote for
tyranny, war and corruption?'(Figure 31)[32]

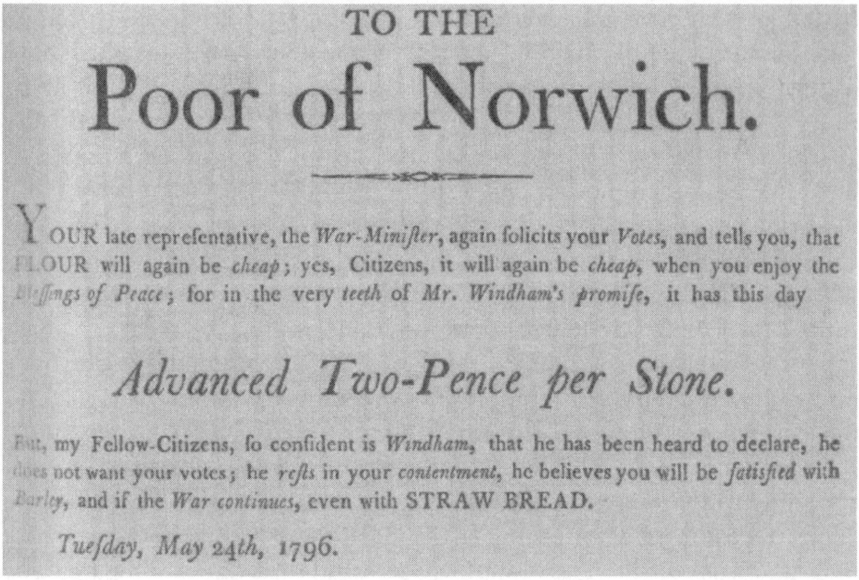

TO THE
Poor of Norwich.

————⪻⪼————

Y OUR late reprefentative, the *War-Minifter*, again folicits your *Votes*, and tells you, that
FLOUR will again be *cheap*; yes, Citizens, it will again be *cheap*, when you enjoy the
blefings of Peace; for in the very *teeth* of Mr. *Windham's promife*, it has this day

Advanced Two-Pence per Stone.

But, my Fellow-Citizens, fo confident is *Windham*, that he has been heard to declare, he
does not want your votes; he *refts* in your *contentment*, he believes you will be *fatisfied* with
Barley, and if the *War continues*, even with STRAW BREAD.

Tuefday, May 24*th,* 1796.

FIGURE 31. A simple but effective anti-Windham handbill showing how the impact of war on food prices was a political issue used by both sides. (*Norfolk Heritage Centre*)

One 1796 handbill, 'To the Poor of Norwich', made the price of flour an election issue. Poverty was not, of course, a new political controversy. In February 1699, following a major shortage of coin and bad harvests, there had been a grain riot in Norwich, and frustration over food had been linked to politicking. Thus one John Hall, when asked who he would be for in the parliamentary election, said that he would vote for the Whig dissenter Robert Cooke and not Thomas Blofield 'because he sen[t] away corne'. A petition of 1719 claimed, with some exaggeration, that 120,000 of the city's 'poor people' had previously found employment through trade, but that this had been 'gradually decreasing till it is almost intirely lost', forcing expenditure on poor relief to £6000 a year. Failure by Parliament to agree to protectionist measures, and an overseas recession which affected markets, led to riots that year. Moreover, the administration of poor relief had by then become politicised. Legislation for a city workhouse was passed in 1712 and the law allowed the corporation to impose a special tax and to set the idle poor to work. The resulting board of guardians included a number of dissenters who had been behind the scheme, and the managers of the Bethel workhouse represented an alternative corporation. The workhouse could, however, also focus resentments. In 1730 the corporation inserted an advertisement into the local newspapers promising a reward for information about a 'scandalous letter' that had been 'thrown into the house of one of the magistrates of this City full of notorious falsitys reflecting upon the conduct and management of the guardians of the poor in the workhouses in this City and threatening to burn his and others houses and also the Workhouses'. There were more food riots in 1766 and 1772, and the city's expenditure on poor relief again rose to over £17,000 in 1785. Nevertheless, it was the poverty of the 1790s that gave the distress real political meaning. The war against France disrupted the Dutch, German and Italian trade routes. As even a staunch supporter of the war admitted, 'this languid trade has doubled our poor rate and a voluntary subscription of above £2000 is found inadequate to the exigencies of the poor'. Poverty had become an acute political issue.[33]

Poverty, of course, was linked to more general issues of trade.[34] Indeed, appealing to the weavers had always been crucial to political success. The Whig victory in 1715, for example, was not due to a shift in the attitudes of civil officials or the gentry, but to a successful turn-out of Whig weavers. We can see the importance of appealing to the weavers in an election tract of 1734, *A Letter from a Weaver at Norwich to a Member of Parliament Concerning the Present State of our Woollen Manufactures* (1734). This expressed despair at parliament's refusal to aid the woollen industry, despite numerous petitions. Walpole was forced to announce his intention to enact legislation to facilitate the wool trade, declaring that 'the supporting the woollen manufacture was what he had ever at heart'. The surviving poll-books for 1734 and 1735, when correlated with other data, show that in terms of wealth there was little to choose between the two parties; but, since about two-thirds of the electorate were artisans involved in the textile trade, securing the votes of weavers, combers and hot-pressers was vital for any party. By the mid 1730s the Tories were losing their manufacturing support, though they did retain support among the retailers and so did well in the market precinct of St Peter Mancroft and neighbouring parishes. The parishes with high concentrations of weavers – such as St Peter Parmentergate, St George Colegate, St Michael Coslany, and St Clement's – were predominantly Whig in the first half of the eighteenth century. Trading interests were thus key to explaining popular political allegiances. Whereas in other cities the celebrations for Admiral Vernon's victories in 1740 could boost anti-Walpolean factions, in Norwich the festivities were appropriated by the Whigs.[35]

Peace rather than war favoured Norwich's trade. In 1780 the Baptist minister Rees David preached against the American war, blaming it for causing the decay of trade so that 'men of property, and once of great property, find it very difficult to live. The poor by this suffer exceedingly'. Although there was recovery in the 1780s, there was no return to full employment. In 1785 it was reckoned that the city's economy was operating at three-quarters of its capacity. The outbreak of war against revolutionary France then proved catastrophic. From 1793 to 1802 the city endured a painful recession. With prosperity so obviously related to war it is not surprising that anti-war, and hence anti-ministerial, feelings should have run high, particularly when the war minister, Windham, was the parliamentary candidate. The day before the 1794 election James Mingay, a barrister, threw his hat into the ring on an anti-war ticket and his supporters declared that 'by the prolongation of such a war our trade has been entirely destroyed, and all commercial intercourse obstructed and endangered'. Windham is alleged to have said 'perish commerce', provoking fury from commercial interests. Although insufficient on that occasion to unseat Windham, this hostility became more obvious in 1796. The opposition candidate, Bartlett Gurney, again only had one day of canvassing but secured a majority of the resident voters, beaten only by Windham's marshalling of eligible voters from London. There were just eighty-three votes between them. Windham was canny enough to realise that the impact of war had created 'a new division of parties', but also that it was better to fight against revolutionary principles rather than in favour of war. Thus while his critics played up the devastating impact of war, his party attacked them as Jacobins. Earlier in the century the textile trade was a support for the government; by the 1790s it offered a rallying cry for opposition.[36]

The 1790s also highlighted another feature of political culture: the petition or address. The rebirth of independency in Norwich had been marked in February 1762 by contests over an address of thanks to William Pitt the Elder, whose conduct of the Seven Years' War had made him popular but who had resigned because of George III's lack of faith in him. The address had been passed only after heated debate. Afterwards some councillors snubbed official city celebrations of peace by dining separately to toast the reduction of the national debt, those MPs who opposed the cider tax, and 'the Patriots and Heroes of the Nation' Pitt and Wilkes. This ability of petitions and addresses to focus and highlight division was to become a common feature in the following years.[37]

In 1775 citizens petitioned against the treatment of the colonists, declaring them to have been 'condemned and punished without examination' and three years later 5400 citizens of Norwich and Norfolk signed a petition against the war. In 1780 a county meeting was held in Norwich to draw up a petition in favour of parliamentary reform, emulating the Association movement elsewhere. Between 1782 and 1785 the city sent several addresses of an independent nature, including one in support of William Pitt the Younger's plans for limited parliamentary reform. But again it was the 1790s and beyond that saw this contest between addresses intensify. A petition of 1793 in favour of annual parliaments and an adult male suffrage attracted over 3700 signatures and was presented to parliament. In January 1795 the city petitioned against the war with France, 'a war which has nearly annihilated the Manufactories and Trade of this once flourishing City and consequently reduced the majority of its inhabitants – the industrious poor – to a state of extreme distress'. Common hall was summoned the same year, producing a 5,000 strong petition against legislation restricting the freedom of speech and assembly. In 1797, at a meeting where one speaker claimed that Prime Minister Pitt called Norwich the 'Jacobin City', another petition against the government was passed. Petitions and addresses thus highlighted differences and ensured that the independents had a public voice.[38]

By contrast with the 1790s, the period of the war against Napoleonic France was much less marked by contention. Indeed, the years between 1802 and 1815 saw some degree of unity against a common threat and a sharing of the parliamentary representation. In 1802 the blue-and-whites achieved victory, when the Unitarian William Smith's platform of reform, abolition of the Test Acts, anti-slavery and peace appealed to most of the independent interests in the city. Smith's opponent Windham described his loss that year as 'the triumph of … Jacobin Politics' but the gain was secure, in the sense that at least one opposition MP continued to be returned until 1818.

Two issues served again to ignite political division after 1815. The first was economic dislocation. In 1815 Thomas William Coke of Holkham, MP for Norfolk, was pelted with stones in the city during rioting directed against the new Corn Law, by a mob alleged to be 10,000 strong. The four years between 1816 and 1820 saw economic unrest again converted into serious political protest and intensified when 1825 witnessed the start of the city's longest depression. In 1822 the city's journeymen had set up a committee to defend their interests, and between 1826 and 1827 this organised well-attended meetings and petitions. Economic agitation also focused minds on the maladministration of poor relief, which became a significant factor in the 1827 election. A victory here and in elections to the board of guardians (an innovation introduced by act of Parliament), encouraged the Whigs to embark on fundamental reform of poor relief. But this backfired. In 1829–30 there were riots in the city when over three thousand weavers blocked access roads to the workhouse and threw its looms into the river. Suspicion that the blue-and-white dominated guardians of the poor were colluding with employers to bring down wages led to purple-and-orange victories in all four wards at the common council elections in 1830. The last five years of the old-style corporation were thus ones of Tory domination.[39]

The second issue that inflamed political passions was parliamentary reform. By 1816 there were thirteen Hampden clubs in the city, each with about 150–200 members, devoted to participating in a national campaign for reform. The Tory Castle Corporation Club was concerned enough to report to London that they had met to consider

> the best means of counteracting the evil designs of these clubs. The result was a determination to encourage the revival of the old Church and King and Constitutional Clubs which had pined away. As these clubs consist chiefly of the lower order, who require a little pecuniary assistance, we are now raising a subscription for that purpose. The principal encouragement, however, which they want, is the presence and countenance of respectable men at their meetings.[40]

In order to resist such blandishments and manipulation the Norwich Electoral Union had been formed by 1826 to obtain pledges from freemen not to accept bribes: 'It will be a new era in the annals of electioneering, tending to cement the necessary virtues and at once to form an irresistible barrier to corruption', boasted one tract.[41]

Abolition of bribery and the Corn Laws, and support for parliamentary reform tended to become fused demands by 1830, but also created a movement at times only loosely tied to the Whigs. Thus the Norwich Political Union was active in 1831 and 1832, largely independent of the city's Whig leaders, demanding repeal of the Corn Laws, the abolition of tithes and parliamentary reform. Indeed, this shifted even further from the Whigs when George Burrows, disgruntled at what he considered to be its moderate stance, formed the Union of Working Classes and even invited a radical lawyer, William Eagle, to stand at the parliamentary election. As one supporter put it, 'This is not a question of Whigs or Tories – we detest both. We, of the middle classes, introduce a man who will support measures for the benefit of us'.[42] Yet the bulk of reformists backed the Whigs. The 1830 and 1831 elections thus witnessed ranks of reformers against conservatives. Indeed, as *The Times* noted, the victory of the reformers in Norwich would 'vitally affect many, if not all those places where any spark of independence exists: it will become a beacon to show those who, like Norwich, have become or are about to be sacrificed to the place hunters'.[43] Nearly 3000 attended a reform meeting on 19 January 1831, which promoted a petition calling for shorter parliaments, universal suffrage and the ballot as a means of alleviating distress, and in March another petition, in support of the reform bill, was presented. At the May 1831 election placards proclaiming

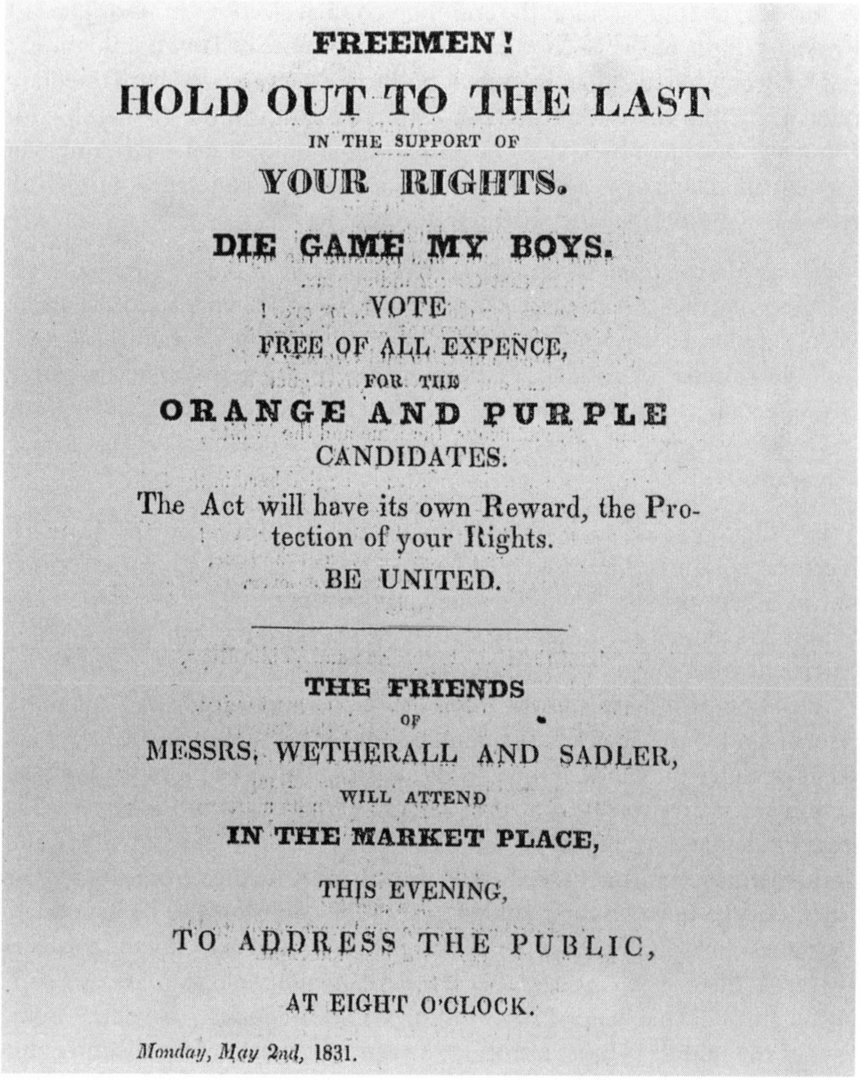

FREEMEN!

HOLD OUT TO THE LAST

IN THE SUPPORT OF

YOUR RIGHTS.

DIE GAME MY BOYS.

! VOTE

FREE OF ALL EXPENCE,

FOR THE

ORANGE AND PURPLE

CANDIDATES.

The Act will have its own Reward, the Protection of your Rights.

BE UNITED.

THE FRIENDS

OF

MESSRS. WETHERALL AND SADLER,

WILL ATTEND

IN THE MARKET PLACE,

THIS EVENING,

TO ADDRESS THE PUBLIC,

AT EIGHT O'CLOCK.

Monday, May 2nd, 1831.

FIGURE 32. (above and opposite) Contrasting appeals, for and against reform: both sides claimed to be defending voters' rights. (*UEA Archives*)

'reform', 'liberty' and 'social order' were part of the blue-and-white campaign, opposed by the orange-and-purples. The crowd demolished their rivals' poll booth and tore up the poll books. The Riot Act was read, but a huge crowd over 20,000 met again to 'chair' the victors (Figure 32).[44]

The Whigs thus won a crushing parliamentary victory that reversed their

REFORM.

ELECTORS OF NORWICH,

REMEMBER! it is your SOVEREIGN who calls upon you to rally round him. HE has done HIS Duty nobly, and expects you will do YOURS. Be resolute, but generous Be brave, but merciful.

REMEMBER! the CAUSE in which you are now engaged, is one for Life or Death to the Rights and Privileges of Englishmen!!

THEREFORE SUPPORT

GURNEY AND GRANT.

GOD SAVE THE KING !!

municipal losses. They were able to build on their success. A petition in favour of the Reform Bill attracted as many as 11,352 signatures in September 1831; their opponents could muster only 1300.[45] And when the final Reform Bill was jeopardised by the king's opposition the Norwich reformers again met to petition and 2000 signed a declaration of support for their MPs, both of whom backed the measure. The years 1830 to 1835 therefore saw Tory control of the corporation but real rivalry at the parliamentary level, with Whig victories in 1830 and 1831, largely because of the agitation for reform. The end of the corporation was thus certainly not due to a sterility of city politics. The Tory majority in the assembly even tried to rally other corporations into resisting abolition, denounced the parliamentary commissioners as 'irregular, vague and arbitrary', and sent a committee to the House of Lords to oppose the Municipal Corporations bill. But they proved powerless to stop its passage and hence the major changes to the corporation's structure.[46]

As a tract of 1833 remarked, Norwich had been:

> most unhappily for its real interests, split into two factions i.e. the purple and orange, and blue and white. These two parties have at various periods, when political feuds ran high, not scrupled to use the most offensive and insulting language, denouncing each other as robbers, tyrants, and oppressors.[47]

Moreover, voters had exhibited a remarkably consistent attitude to the parties – about 80 per cent of freemen polled both their votes for a single party between 1760 and 1802. For sure, as the corporation commissioners insisted, municipal politics had become corrupted in the early nineteenth century by bribery and malpractice (including the practice of 'cooping' voters and keeping them inebriated until required to stagger to vote); and the proportion of householders who were freemen did fall to a fifth. The reform of local government and of the franchise duly changed the context in which city politics worked. What is striking about the political culture of the eighteenth century is how civic and parliamentary politics, in overlapping with issues to do with dissent, the constitution, the succession, the economy, poverty, war and reform, resulted in an educated, sophisticated and involved citizenry. In the process many citizens made themselves heard through frequent elections, ritual and display, and through print, petitions, addresses, clubs, associations and societies. For much of the period Norwich had been a vibrant world of contest, strife that was sometimes blamed for the city's economic decline but that more probably reflected the city's vitality and vigour.[48]

8

An Enlightened and Polite Society

Angela Dain

I ... found it a place where the arts are very much cultivated. The people are active and public-spirited in the highest possible degree. Some branches of knowledge, chemistry, botany etc. are carried a great length. General literature seems to be pursued with an ardour which is astounding when we consider that it does not contain an university, and is merely a manufacturing town ... Music and painting too are equally cultivated.

Andrew Robertson, a Scottish artist, who visited Norwich in 1812 [1]

Commenting on the centenary of the Glorious Revolution, the *Norfolk Chronicle* maintained that the following hundred years had introduced:

The most illustrious and happy era in the British annals ... Hence agriculture, manufactures and commerce have risen to a height which has surprisingly increased the wealth of the community. Hence science, polite literature and the arts of social life have been improved in a manner that ... cannot be equalled in any part of universal history. [2]

This was the essence of the English Enlightenment, a whole new way of progressive thinking, that lauded rational religion, experimental science and economic progress and dismissed the puritan and catholic extremes which had produced the upheavals of the seventeenth century. [3] It was a profound shift in thought based on a rapidly expanding print culture, a new consumerism and an extension of leisure, once exclusive to the elite, to the 'middling sort'. At its heart, as popularly expounded by Addison and Steele in the *Tatler* and *Spectator*, and developed by David Hume, David Hartley and Adam Smith, Enlightenment thought centred upon the potential of the individual to produce men and women who were educated, sociable and polite. Translated from 'Closets and Libraries, Schools and Colleges' to the 'Clubs and Assemblies ... Tea Tables, and ... Coffee Houses' which were universal in the Georgian city, knowledge was the foundation of improvement both for the individual and society generally. [4]

The roots of Norwich's post-Restoration sociability extended into the past. The city waits, established in 1294, and retained continually by the corporation from the early fifteenth century, had a long tradition of performing concerts.[5] The genteel custom of public promenading in Chapel Field, on the south-west fringe of the city, dated from at least the sixteenth century. Since then Norwich had been an acknowledged centre of theatrical activity, with performances being regularly staged at the Red Lion, in St Stephen's, and at St Andrew's hall.[6] The city boasted one of the earliest provincial public libraries, and the first under municipal control, when a repository was set up over the south porch of the Blackfriars' church, now St Andrew's hall, in 1608.[7] Furthermore, an annual Florists' Feast, comprising a flower show and a play, had become an established feature of city life by the 1630s.[8]

What differentiated polite forms of sociability before and after the English Civil War was the fact that they flourished and became commercialized to accommodate ever-increasing numbers of the middle ranks who sought to register a cultural claim to gentility rather than one based solely on pedigree. Social mobility and status found their fullest expression through participation in the network of institutions directed towards the transmission of useful knowledge and corporate pleasure. Prominent among these were the coffee house, the promenade, the assembly, theatre, pleasure garden, concert, museum, exhibition, lecture, book club and circulating library. All were inextricably linked, and attracted rapidly expanding audiences, both of men and women alone and of both sexes together.

Learning and knowledge spread more widely in published form after an act restricting printing to London, Oxford, Cambridge and York was allowed to lapse in 1695.[9] The reintroduction of printing to Norwich in 1701 and the setting up of the first provincial newspaper, the *Norwich Post*, not only fostered reading, but also provided an advertising medium which encouraged the fledgling commercial leisure sector. Throughout the eighteenth century Norwich supported at least two newspapers. Coffee houses, synonymous with the circulation and distribution of the press, also served as agencies for burgeoning leisure enterprises. Tickets for assemblies at Chapel Field House could be obtained from Braithwait's and Blomfield's coffee houses in the 1720s, and from Gray's, Hunn's and Johnson's in the 1760s and 1770s (Figure 33).[10] Similarly, when Archibald Spens sought to gauge potential support for a fourth series of lectures on experimental philosophy in Norwich in 1738, he requested subscribers to leave their names at Braithwait's Coffee House.[11]

The fact that Norwich supported nine booksellers by 1750 and no fewer than seventeen in 1820 affirms the impact of publishing, indeed of the

1. The Market Cross built between 1501 and 1503. Almost seventy feet high, it was, after the Guildhall, the most striking feature in the market. Subsequently altered and extended, it was demolished in the 1730s. (*Norwich Castle Museum and Art Gallery*)

2. (left) This graffito in Norwich cathedral, close to the high altar, was possibly left by parliamentary soldiers or civic officials during their occupation of the cathedral. (*Andrew Hopper*)

3. (below) This musket ball lodged in the tomb of Bishop James Goldwell (d. 1499) is said to have been discharged by a parliamentary soldier during the civil wars. (*Andrew Hopper*)

4. The Seven Sacraments font now in Norwich cathedral reveals signs of civil war iconoclasm, the heads of its carved figures having been struck off. (*Andrew Hopper*)

5. Having, from the middle ages, kept its own game of swans on the River Wensum, the Great Hospital subsequently built a special pond, where the birds could be fattened for the market. (*Trustees of the Great Hospital, Norwich*)

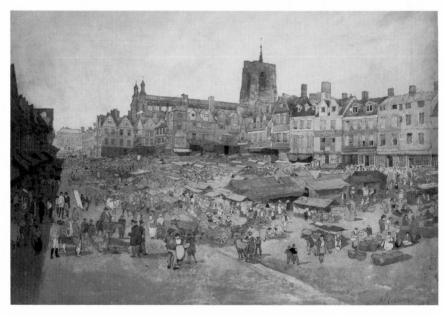

6. Norwich Market Place from the north, in the 1807 water-colour by John Sell Cotman (1782–1842), showing the crowded Saturday morning market in full swing, with people from both town and county meeting, trading, chatting and promenading on the Gentleman's Walk (east frontage, half shadowed). Note the military man in his regimentals (front left); the female as well as male traders (centre); and the middle shop (west frontage, centre right), which advertised itself as a bookshop and corculating library. (*Abbot Hall Art Gallery, Kendal, Cumbria*)

7. Detail from *The Haymarket* by John Thirtle (1777–1839), showing the juxtaposed legacies of Norwich's long history: the medieval church (east end of St Peter Mancroft), the high gables of the seventeenth-century shops, and the stately Georgian town house. The old, narrow street in between is crammed with wheeled traffic, pedestrians (on a pavement protected by low posts), and hanging shop signs. (*Norwich Castle Museum and Art Gallery*)

8. In this satire of 1768 angry freemen outside protest against insider deals to deprive them of independent-minded MPs. (*British Museum*)

9. The Octagon Chapel, engraved here by James Sillet in the early nineteenth century, was described by John Wesley as 'perhaps the most elegant one in all Europe', and its Unitarian congregation was at the heart of independent and radical politics. (*Trustees of the Octagon Chapel*)

10. The mural monument to William Rolfe (d. 1754) in Norwich Cathedral by Thomas Rawlins. (*Jonathan Finch*)

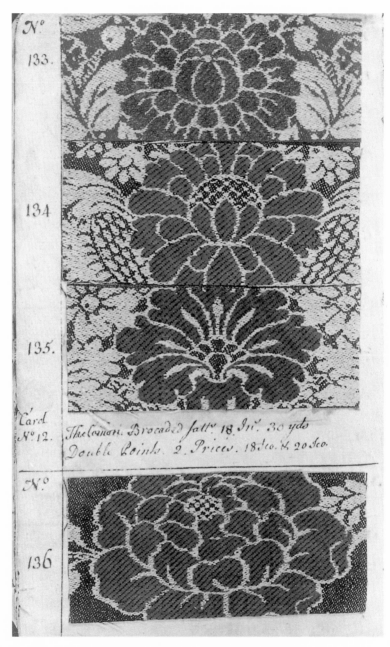

N.º
133.

134

135.

Card
N.º 12.
The common Brocaded sattin 18 Inc. 30 yds
Double Points. 2 Prices. 18 d.co. & 20 sco.

N.º
136

11. Samples 133–136 taken from 'Mr John Kelly's counterpart of patterns sent to Spain and Portugal, Norwich 1763'. Common Brocaded Sattin double points. Sample 136, Fine Brocaded Sattins: Mosaic and Rose figures. (*Trustees of the Victoria and Albert Museum*)

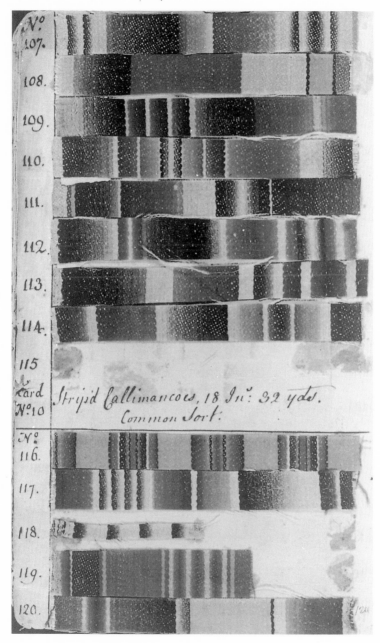

Samples within the figure bear the handwritten numbers: Nº 107., 108., 109., 110., 111., 112., 113., 114., 115, Card Nº 10, Nº 116., 117., 118., 119., 120., and the inscription *Striped Callimancoes, 18 In: 32 yds. Common Sort.*

12. Samples 107–20 taken from 'Mr John Kelly's counterpart of patterns sent to Spain and Portugal, Norwich 1763'. They show striped callimancoes, popular for European peasant dress, of the common and (samples 116–120) second sort. (*Trustees of the Victoria and Albert Museum*)

13. A Norwich drawloom shawl of the 1840s in silk and wool, probably made by the firm of Towler and Camplin.) (*Norwich Castle Museum and Art Gallery*)

14. St James's Mill, 1839. Built for the Norwich Yarn Company to house 1000 power looms and 65 spinning frames. Manufacturers could hire both space and power on its six floors, but thirty years later it was running at less than half capacity. Until recently it housed Jarrold's printing works. (*Norfolk Museums and Archaeology Service, Bridewell Museum*)

15. The Norfolk and Norwich Hospital, 1772, by James Sillett (1764–1840). (*Norwich Medico-Chirurgical Society and Dr Anthony Batty Shaw*)

16. The consultant medical staff, Norfolk and Norwich Hospital, in the 1860s. Standing: Sir Frederic Bateman, W. Cadge, T. W. Crosse, Sir Peter Eade. Sitting: E. Copeman, W. R. Nichols, G. W. W. Firth. (*Norwich Medico-Chirurgical Society and Dr Anthony Batty Shaw*)

17. Norfolk and Norwich Hospital nurses, 1876. (*Norwich Medico-Chirurgical Society and Dr Anthony Batty Shaw*)

18. An upper floor ward in the Norfolk and Norwich Hospital, *c.* 1890. (*Norfolk and Norwich Hospital*)

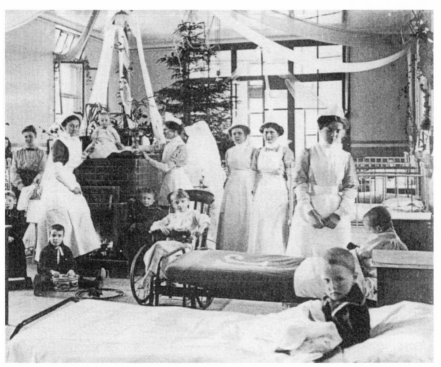

19. Nurses on Gannon Ward, Jenny Lind Hospital for Children, Christmas, 1913. (*Norwich Medico-Chirurgical Society and Dr Anthony Batty Shaw*)

20. Students at the Diocesan Training College, then in College Road, *c.* 1890s. (*School of Education, UEA*)

21. Duke Street Higher Grade School, 1888. Created by the Norwich School Board for post-elementary education. (*Norfolk Heritage Centre*)

22. A woodworking class for children in the Junior Technical School, *c.* 1919. (*Handbook of the Education Week* held in Norwich from 17 September to 3 October 1925)

23. Girls in a chemistry class at the Municipal Girls School, *c.* 1925. (*Handbook of the Education Week* held in Norwich from September 17 to October 3 1925)

24. The first students arrive in the Village at the opening of the University of East Anglia, October 1963. (*UEA Archives*)

FIGURE 33. The Assembly Rooms in 1828. They were enlarged and altered by Thomas Ivory and Sir James Burrough in 1754–5 to provide one of the finest sets of public rooms in England. (*Norfolk Heritage Centre, photograph by Terry Burchell*)

Enlightenment, in the city during the eighteenth century. This impact was further promoted by the growing number of circulating and subscription libraries in the city after 1780. The former, run by tradesmen, had existed in a small way for sixty years, but now a rapid rise in book prices and the ever-accelerating publication rate of books and periodicals brought an increased demand for borrowing facilities. In Norwich and Yarmouth at least twenty-four different circulating libraries are known to have existed in the first quarter of the nineteenth century. The more prestigious subscription libraries were much fewer in number. The Norfolk and Norwich Literary Institution founded in 1822 had a panel of local experts and a selection committee to draw up its impressive list of acquisitions.[12]

The effect of the written word was extended in other ways. Since newspapers generally carried no illustrations, other than simple sketches to accompany advertisements, until the second half of the nineteenth century, models, panoramas and waxworks were among the various devices that broadened intellectual horizons and served as contemporary newsreels. In 1746 a 'Curious Philosophical Optical Machine', affording perspective views of cities and the London pleasure gardens of Vauxhall and Ranelagh, went on display at the grand jury chamber in the guildhall in Norwich.[13] The popularity of the panorama, at its height in the half century after 1770,

lay in its sheer size, stimulating the pleasures of the imagination by engul-
fing the spectator in an experience as amazing as it was didactic. In 1779,
on the occasion of the annual celebration of the victory of William III over
James II in July 1690, a panorama depicting the burning of the Boyne and
the fleet's 'miraculous escape' from the flames, was removed from the
Assembly Rooms to St Andrew's hall, the former having proved 'too small
by one half for the purpose'.[14] A panorama depicting Nelson's funeral was
exhibited at Ranelagh Gardens, Norwich, in 1807, although one of Waterloo (1815) was somewhat dated by the time it went on display in 1821.[15]
Short guidebooks priced at 6d., which outlined the historical and geographical importance of the scene, not only provided a tangible souvenir,
but also underpinned the educational aspect of the spectacle.

   Waxworks were another visual medium which engaged public interest
and exploited it for commercial gain. 'An inimitable collection' of waxwork
by one Geidinger was to be seen at Abraham's Mall in the hay-market in
the mid eighteenth century.[16] The most notable exponent of the art was
French *émigrée* Marie Tussaud (1761–1850), who twice visited Norwich during her years of touring between 1802 and 1835. Although she took the
largest room at the Angel on her first visit in 1819, it was not an unqualified success, since the cramped conditions prevented her from displaying
her seventy to ninety figures to best effect. Her return in 1825 proved far
more successful. Not only had she managed to procure the use of the more
spacious Assembly Rooms at Chapel Field House, but also the attendance
of a band had become an established feature of her entertainments as her
patrons promenaded among the life-sized, accurately dressed, brightly
illuminated wax figures.[17]

The proliferation of clubs and societies was a more permanent element in
the cultural renaissance of Norwich than models, panoramas and waxworks. Trade guilds, which had numbered more than one hundred in
Norwich under Elizabeth I, dominated associational activity until the
emergence of the masonic, pseudo-masonic, political, ethnic and social
clubs in the third decade of the eighteenth century.[18] Following the setting
up of the Grand Lodge of England in London in 1717, freemasonry rapidly
gained a foothold in the city. By the time Edward Bacon became the first
Provincial Grand Master for Norfolk in 1759, no fewer than twelve lodges
existed in Norwich.[19] The Maid's Head lodge, constituted in 1724 and the
first of the fifty-two to be founded in Norfolk, remained the most prestigious in the county, the first four Provincial Grand Masters for Norfolk
being members.

   The best known of the pseudo-masonic groups in Norwich was the

Society of United Friars. Founded in 1785 on 18 October, the feast day of St Luke, patron saint of artists and physicians, the society moved to rooms in St Andrew's parish in 1791 from premises it had initially occupied at Crown Court, Elm Hill.[20] Espousing the ideals of enlightened sociability, it provided a forum for the exchange of useful knowledge, an environment conducive to good fellowship and a collaborative platform for philanthropy. Its ceremonial dress was mock medieval, each member wearing the habit of the monastic order to which he had been assigned, together with a rosary comprising twenty-four beads, each representing a moral, social or intellectual attribute. Members, including the artists William Beechey and John Sell Cotman, and the landscape gardener, Humphry Repton, presented papers at their meetings, amassed a library and created the nucleus of a museum over the society's forty-three year history. The society was also a trailblazer in instituting large scale emergency charitable relief. In 1793, for example, it organised the first of a number of soup kitchens to operate in Norwich.[21] During the severe winter of 1813–14, when upwards of £2600 was subscribed to relieve hardship in the city, it distributed 28,170 quarts of soup and an equal number of penny loaves among the poor.[22]

The Scots' Society, founded on St Andrew's Day 1775, was the precursor of a sister institution founded in London in the late 1780s.[23] Renamed the Universal Society of Goodwill in 1784, it had emerged from an informal circle of Scottish expatriates who met to celebrate their patron saint each year on November 30.[24] Having established a fund in 1777 to assist native Scots settled in Norwich, it soon began helping distressed English and foreign nationals as well. Despite the adoption of an open-door policy for membership from 1779 onwards, some vestige of its Caledonian roots remained, in so far that Scottish songs predominated at benefit concerts staged between 1783 and 1789 to support its charitable work.[25] In the summer of 1784 a thirty-four year old Swedish seaman, Pieter Niclaus Boline, shipwrecked off Norfolk the previous winter, was found begging in Norwich, almost naked and nearly starved. His case was referred to the Scots' Society, which promptly clothed, fed and provided him with lodgings until 'proper opportunity' arose to return him to his homeland.[26] In similar vein, over a twenty-year period ending in 1796, French prisoners-of-war as well as German emigrants en route to America were among the 1644 beneficiaries of the society's charity.[27]

In retrospect, the Society of Artists, which met for the first time in 1803, was much the most significant of the city's numerous clubs. The brainchild of John Crome and Robert Ladbrooke, it stands as a testament to the importance of Norwich as an artistic centre. Members were selected by ballot, on evidence of their work. An entrance fee of three guineas, together with an annual subscription of one guinea, further ensured exclusive membership. With a library at its disposal and fortnightly meetings at which members read papers and studied casts, drawings and prints, the society provided another enclave of intellectual and social fellowship. Public exhibitions, held until 1833, and staged to coincide with the summer assizes, aimed not so much towards finding buyers as nurturing an interest, appreciation and emulation of art, an indispensable attribute of politeness. Thus, at the first exhibition in 1805, staged in Sir Benjamin Wrench's Court, off Little London Street, only nineteen out of the 223 items were offered for sale, a trend which persisted until the late 1820s.[28] Members of what was to become known as the Norwich School were bound not so much by a collective vision, or a shared theory of art, as by a common location which sustained a range of landscape genres ranging from the flat patterning mannerism of John Sell Cotman to the naturalism of John Crome.

It would be misleading, however, to convey the impression that all clubs were bastions of enlightened sociability, fostering individual and civic improvement. For some, the consumption of alcohol was their raison d'être. Many inns in Norwich acquired their own drinking clubs, where bacchanalia were *de rigueur*. The King's Head, demolished to make way for Davey Place, was the regular hostelry of Parson Woodforde and the rendezvous of the Thumb Club.[29] On one occasion Woodforde was delivered from a disturbed overnight stay when revellers staggered from the room below at eight o'clock the following morning, having 'hallowed and hooped all night, [and] broke above 12 shillings worth of bowls and glasses'.[30]

Although this world of association was predominantly male, there were a few female societies, mainly benefit clubs, and a number of mixed gatherings.[31] A friendly society, formed in April 1802 and run by sixteen stewards, who were 'ladies of Norwich of the first distinction', disbursed £1207 5s. 6d. to women in times of sickness and old age during its first eleven years.[32] Women were the main beneficiaries of an expansive model of sociability spread by the civilising principles of the European Enlightenment. Previously, social contact between the sexes rarely extended beyond the obligatory attendance at church, or sortie to the local barn or inn for entertainment by a troupe of strolling players. Since, however, spinsters and widows owned around a fifth of all property in eighteenth-century England, and women constituted a majority of the adult population in all cities except Oxford, they provided an important market for learning and leisure in the post-Restoration town.[33] The presumed moral superiority of women and the acknowledgement that men became more complaisant in their company, coupled with the acceptance that women's powers of reason and judgement needed fostering, endorsed the companionable world of the public lecture, promenade, assembly and concert room as the embodiment of polite sociability.

Since the architects of the European Enlightenment regarded natural philosophy, broadly translated as science, as an essential attribute of politeness, the elite of Norwich supported a long succession of resident and itinerant lecturers in this field. Polite learning involved the scientific study of nature and human society in order to lay secure foundations for religious belief and greater material prosperity. Although the Enlightenment has been characterised as propagating a more secular vision of society, its underpinnings were spiritual, based on the supposition that it was through scientific demonstrations, observation and the contemplation of nature, rather than the abstract interpretation of scripture, that God and his works would be revealed.[34] The pursuit of science as an alternative and more rational path to achieving religious insight was exemplified, among others, by the physico-theologists, who held that the perfection of scale in nature was evidence of the glory of the Creation. Dr John Taylor (1703–1770), occulist to George II, presented a series of lectures entitled 'Physico-Theological Declamation in Praise of Sight' to the social elite of Norwich at Francis Christian's dancing room in 1748.[35]

The growing assumption that knowledge and politeness were synonymous was articulated by the Chichester schoolmaster and scientific instrument maker, Benjamin Martin (1704–1782), who delivered two courses on natural philosophy during his stay in Norwich in 1750.[36] 'Knowledge is now become a fashionable thing, and philosophy is the science à la mode: hence to cultivate this study, is only to be in taste, and politeness is an inseparable consequence.'[37] James Ferguson (1710–1776) likewise offered several courses on astronomy and natural philosophy on his four visits to the city between 1752 and 1763.[38] Martin and Ferguson were respected enthusiasts, seeking an enlarged audience for empirical science, more especially as both were manufacturers and retailers of scientific paraphernalia.[39] The increased use of optical instruments, such as the microscope, encouraged an aesthetic as well as a scientific aspect of the contemplation of nature, and had an especial appeal to women. Another celebrated lecturer to visit Norwich was Adam Walker (c. 1731–1821). Famed as the teacher who inspired Shelley with a love of science, Walker expanded the market for science by devising an enlarged orrery, the eidouranion, a fifteen-feet square mechanical device for projecting an illuminated model of the solar system, which proved effective in reaching mass audiences in auditoria. Parson Woodforde was among the 'great deal of Company' to see the eidouranion and hear the 'excellent' accompanying lecture at the Assembly Rooms at Chapel Field house in 1785.[40]

A series of lectures in natural philosophy, priced at one guinea, or a single event, costing 2s. 6d., inevitably precluded all bar the upper echelons of civic and county society. However, the lower ranks shared the intellectual *frisson* of the Enlightenment through the practice of lecturers charging reduced fees, and also by associational activity. In 1761, for example, a course of electrical experiments, which had been presented in the daytime to 'most of the Gentry' of Norwich, was staged the following week in the evenings for 'Journeymen, Servants, and others' for the moderate charge of 3d.[41] A society founded by Peter Bilby in 1754 for 'men of original minds and small incomes, for their improvement in Mathematics and Experimental Philosophy' afforded another channel for the diffusion of Enlightenment rationality among the populace of Norwich.[42]

Exhibitions of automata spanned the cultural divide which separated the lecturer in natural philosophy from the mechanic who was able to apply technical ingenuity to industrial production. There were two types of automaton: the composition, activated by a central power source, usually clockwork, in which action was repetitious, thereby negating any concessions to realism; and the independent life-size figure which attempted something far more natural. Parson Woodforde admitted himself 'highly Astonished' at the wax doll on display at St Stephen's in 1786, which, complete with trumpet, answered every question put to it, and even posed its own. The deception, wrote the diarist, 'is wonderfully ingenious'.[43] Automata exemplify one of the many contradictions of the Enlightenment: namely, desire for mystery rather than elucidation, and the accompanying perception of science and technology as magical rather than empirical disciplines.

The freak show stimulated and reflected public demand for science while also pandering to baser motives. Satirised by Jonathan Swift in *Gulliver's Travels* (1726), the raree show capitalised upon growing popular interest in biology and the current preoccupation with reproduction. Exhibitions of abnormal gestation, presenting dramatic reversals of nature's laws, defined the normal and endorsed orthodox teaching about the overwhelming power of divine creation. It embraced an eclectic audience ranging from the incredulous gaper to the disinterested seeker of rational knowledge, whose presence was vindicated by the fact that few of the freaks exhibited in Norwich during the eighteenth century escaped mention in the hallowed pages of the *Philosophical Transactions of the Royal Society*. John Coan, the Norfolk-born dwarf, was the subject of a paper read to the Royal Society following several weeks on show in the city in 1750.[44] There were many others exhibited. Anne Farro from Framlingham, in Suffolk, two feet three inches tall, was hailed in 1741 as 'the wonder of the world' when she was showing at The Star in the hay market for eleven hours a day for an entrance fee of 3d.[45] The limbless Miss Beffin, thirty-seven inches high, could in 1811 sew, draw landscapes and paint miniatures with her mouth.[46] 'Count' Joseph Boruwlaski, two inches taller and a cultured Pole who had travelled throughout Europe, gave private concerts on his guitar at his lodgings in St Stephen's in 1788. Visitors paid a shilling each; in London his tariff had been ten shillings six years earlier.[47] In contrast, in 1753, a sixteen-year-old youth, Cornelius MacGragh, seven feet and three inches tall, from Munster, 'who for his gigantick form far exceeds any ever exhibited ... and has grown eight inches and a quarter the last year', went on display at The Bear in the market place.[48]

Exhibits of natural history, especially rare animals, were a fashionable diversion and a further manifestation of the transmission of knowledge in an essentially social context. When a red buffalo went on display at the Bear in 1750 the Norwich public were not spared the customary hyperbole. Not only had its capture engaged the natives of Madagascar for 'fifteen days and four hours', but its subjection had been effected by beatings 'night and morning instead of victuals' so that a beast, once capable of carrying 'one ton a thousand miles in twelve days without rest', could now be handled by genteel patrons 'as they pleased'.[49] In 1788 a tiger, valued at two hundred guineas, was exhibited at the same inn. The spectacle came to an abrupt end, however, with the premature death of the animal. Having broken loose, the tiger swallowed his brass collar and chain, then proceeded to feast on two hapless monkeys. Recaptured, it died when gangrene set in.[50]

The variety of creatures deemed amenable to instruction and commercial exploitation increased during the eighteenth century. The Learned Dog appeared at the Red Lion playhouse in St Stephen's in 1753.[51] The most prodigious of talents, however, was arguably the Learned Pig, immortalised in contemporary prints by, among others, the caricaturist Thomas Rowlandson (Figure 34). Parson Woodforde, always inclined to view a well-published spectacle in the city, considered his one hour and one shilling well spent in its company when the pig was shown in Norwich shortly after making its London debut in 1785:

> It was wonderful to see the sagacity of the animal. It was a Boar Pigg, very thin, quite black with a magic collar on his neck. He would spell any word or number from the letters and figures that were placed before him.[52]

When Signor Polito brought his travelling menagerie to the aptly named Hog Hill for a week in 1807, he received 'great encouragement' because

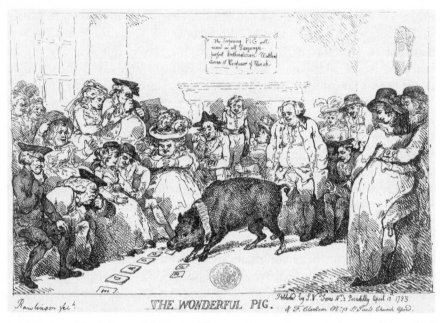

FIGURE 34. The Wonderful Pig (by Thomas Rowlandson, 1785), a much travelled exhibit shown in Norwich in December 1785. (*British Library*)

'knowledge of natural history ranked as a polite acquirement' and served as a medium 'naturally inciting contemplations of the Divine wisdom'.[53] Exhibitions of natural history, rarities and unusual phenomena, so common during the eighteenth and nineteenth centuries, not only expanded – and exploited – the public culture for science, but also superseded sacred writings and holy relics as an acceptable, if sometimes questionable, source of knowledge and spiritual experience. To the less credulous spectator, they reflected Enlightenment Deism and its creed of salvation through rationalism.

The Natural History Society, founded in Norwich in 1747 by William Arderon (1703–1767), two years after his election as a fellow of the Royal Society, provided a forum for acquiring and disseminating knowledge about fauna and flora.[54] Proposals to establish a botanic garden in the city, first broached in 1779 and revived in 1824, offer a further example of the didactic purpose and spiritual undertones of scientific ventures in the polite social sphere.[55] It can hardly have escaped the advocates of this scheme that many female members of the royal family and aristocracy were enthusiastic botanists, the subject being deemed more suitable than zoology for such delicate sensibilities.[56] Investors in the garden, which was projected to cost £1500 in preparation and planting and £380 in annual maintenance, were certainly conscious of the wider lessons to be learned from botany:

> to favour a useful habit of observation in the young; and to produce in the mind an admiration of the beauties of the creation, and of the wisdom and beneficence of the Divine Creator ... a botanical garden was most desirable, not only as it regarded the amusement and recreation it would afford, but ... the increased store of information it would lay open to all the community. The greater the diversity of those stores of knowledge, the more general the happiness that would be diffused throughout society.[57]

In this way children as well as women were beneficiaries of an enlarged model of sociability advocated by proponents of the Enlightenment. Polite society now provided a kind of supplementary public tuition for the young. As the *Norwich Mercury* commented in an editorial in 1821: 'Balls ... at once afford the means of carrying forward in a good degree the education and of forming the manners of youth.'[58] When Roger Kerrison (1740–1808), the banker, was inaugurated mayor of Norwich in 1778, his children, two daughters and a son 'the eldest not more than eight', attended the feast at St Andrew's hall.[59]

Polite social commerce also carried with it the prospect of a more enlightened approach to matrimony. In an age when arranged marriages were on the wane and young people were permitted a greater freedom of choice, public gatherings afforded an enlarged selection of partners. The dance enabled both sexes to demonstrate their social graces, but was especially important for women, who otherwise had fewer opportunities to communicate with non-family members in public and display their attractions than men. Further, it afforded an acceptable means of physical contact not permitted elsewhere. Partners for the evening and partners for life were seen as synonymous. Thus, Elizabeth Fromanteel remarked in a letter to her cousin, John Patteson, of an evening at the Assembly Rooms in 1778: 'Our assembly on Tuesday was the largest ever seen in Norwich. I wish you had been there. You might have chosen a pretty partner, I think even for life.'[60] Assemblies continued to function as marriage markets well into the nineteenth century. Girls were displayed to their social group at large, as the lithotomist John Green Crosse (1790–1850) observes somewhat cynically of his attendance at the sessions ball at the Assembly Rooms in October 1815:

> crowded for three to four hours through a genteel mob of 700 persons ... it struck me as a sort of market for stale as well as fresh goods ... so many

mothers leading their bare-necked daughters about. The whole affair went
dully and the market was certainly overstocked; besides there was not half room
enough for showing the goods off ... Four of Dr Rigby's grand-daughters
were there – three upon sale hill and one who kept retired. I pushed my way
down two dances with a comfortable partner – sat and saw two rubbers of
whist played, without knowing all the while what was trumps – took a cup of
tea and coffee at three or four different tables and made my escape at 1 a.m.[61]

Music meetings and concerts were another integral aspect of enlightened
sociability and by the 1730s Norwich was among the eight or nine provincial centres to have staged commercial public concerts.[62] Norwich, the
home of one of England's largest and most politically active dissenting
communities, was not inherently predisposed to church music or oratorio
performances.[63] The cessation of sung services during the Civil War and
Commonwealth was more damaging to the musical heritage of Norwich
than either the destruction of the cathedral organs by a mob in 1643 or a
directive of 1651 that the organ of St Peter Mancroft be sold.[64] A considerable number of organs removed from churches were, however, set up in
inns where they generated a subsidiary business which activated the concert tradition. Weekly concerts, sometimes concluding with a ball, were,
for example, held in the music room in The King's Arms from at least the
mid 1740s.[65] Shared musical experience was seen as improving morals and
manners, as well as promoting individual and corporate harmony. At the
conclusion of a meeting of the Anacreontic Society, for example, one of
several music clubs to flourish in the city during the eighteenth and nineteenth centuries, the seventy to eighty gentlemen who departed the White
Swan, were reported to be 'highly gratified with this feast of *reason*, and the
flow of soul'.[66]

Although concerts were staged in certain inns and also in the premises
of dancing masters from at least 1712, musical festivals, synonymous with
large-scale charitable fund-raising, came belatedly to Norwich. The initial
impetus was provided by the opening of the Norfolk and Norwich Hospital in 1772.[67] In 1773, a year after the inaugural anniversary sermon, music
was added to the service, which became an annual event for the next
fifty years.[68] Parson Woodforde, and his niece, Nancy, were among the
congregation in 1792,

I drove Nancy to Norwich to be at the Musical Meeting at the Cathedral, for
the Benefit of the publick Hospital. We got to Norwich by 11 o'clock we went
immediately to the Cathedral, I gave at the entrance of the Church £1 1s. 0d.
for the Charity, which is reckoned handsome but we were some time before
we could get Seats, the Church being so exceedingly crowded. Nancy got a

seat under the Orchestra and very little after I got a most excellent Seat along with the Stewards of the Charity ... We had very select and grand Pieces of sacred Musick from Handels Compositions before and after the Sermon. All together it was not only delightful but seemed heavenly and gave us Ideas of divine Musick. It finished about half past two o'clock.[69]

A campaign to replace the anniversary sermon with a triennial musical festival, on the model of the annual Three Choirs Festival established by 1720, began in 1818.[70] In 1824 the first Norfolk and Norwich Musical Festival, held over a four day period, proved an unqualified success. It was attended by 8652 persons and generated remarkable profits of £2400 for the hospital.[71] In its first seventy years, the twenty-four festivals produced aggregate receipts of £121,000, from which £13,520 was disbursed in charitable causes. The commercial advantages were also considerable. The *Norwich Mercury* claimed in 1827 that the local economy benefited to the tune of at least £50,000 during festival week.[72]

Although she never appeared at the festival, the celebrated Swedish soprano Jenny Lind (1820–1887) gave two charity concerts in St Andrew's hall in January 1849. The profits provided the substantive capital to establish a children's hospital, initially located in Pottergate, subsequently in Unthank Road, which bore her name and is now part of the Norfolk and Norwich University Hospital.[73] Among other internationally renowned musicians to visit Norwich were the Italian violinist Nicolò Paganini (1782–1840) and the Hungarian pianist and composer Franz Liszt (1811–1886). The former gave performances at the Corn Hall and Theatre Royal during assize week in 1831, while the latter delivered two concerts at the Assembly Rooms and the theatre in the afternoon and evening of 1 September 1840 (Figure 35).[74]

Pleasure gardens were intrinsic to enlightened sociability, providing the staple fare of refreshments, promenades, the occasional concert of vocal and instrumental music, theatre, firework displays, exhibitions, sporting contests, public breakfasts and assemblies. Although London possessed more than sixty pleasure gardens in the eighteenth century, no other provincial town in England could compete with Norwich, where as many as four such establishments were at times in competition until the mid nineteenth century. The earliest known commercial garden in the city, complete with bowling green, was My Lord's garden, laid out between King Street and the River Wensum in 1663 by Lord Henry Howard, brother of Thomas, fifth duke of Norfolk. Cater's garden in St Faith's Lane, taken over by George Nichols in 1728, and by John Moore in 1739, when it was renamed 'New Spring Garden' and subsequently Vauxhall, afforded

FIGURE 35. The hand-bill advertising two grand concerts to be given in the
Assembly Roooms by Franz Liszt in September 1840. (*The Assembly House, Norwich*)

tree-lined gravel walks interspersed with triumphal arches, and water frolics on the adjacent Wensum.[75] The *Norwich Mercury* in 1750 provided a
glimpse of this pastoral idyll in verse:

> The lucid Lamps that shine between
> The bending Boughs, all fresh and green;
> The sweetness of the vernal Showers;
> The vivid Dyes that paint the Flowers.
> Their fragrance floating on the Breeze;
> The Songsters warbling midst the Trees;
> Describe the soft expiring Notes,
> As o'er the Stream the Musick floats.[76]

The popularity of pleasure gardens can be gauged by the enduring con-
course of patrons who continued to frequent these resorts. In 1775 Vauxhall

gardens were advertised as having attracted upward of 2500 visitors a night for many years during assize week, each paying 1s. a ticket.[77] The last known tenant, John Keymer, announced regular gate takings in excess of £300 for assize week alone, while Ranelagh gardens in St Stephen's were able to attract 9000 visitors during the corresponding period in 1819.[78] The elite of Norwich liked to keep abreast of metropolitan fashion, even if the naming of their gardens suggests a degree of provincial insecurity.

Norwich pleasure gardens seized the opportunity to exploit the balloon mania following the first successful public ascent by the brothers Jacques-Etienne and Joseph-Michel Montgolfier in France in 1783. James Bunn constructed a balloon, ten feet in diameter, which went on display at the Pantheon in his Vauxhall gardens in mid January before its unmanned launch on 1 March 1784.[79] The following year James Decker made the first manned flight over Norwich when he ascended from Ranelagh, touching down in a meadow near Loddon.[80] Later that summer, 'a large and brilliant assembly of the first and most distinguished personages in the city and county' gathered at the same garden to witness the launch of another balloon, this time to raise money for the Norfolk and Norwich Hospital.[81] The most eventful flight, graphically described by the earl of Orford, involved the intrepid Major John Money (1752–1817), who lived just outside the city at Crown Point, Trowse.

> I am sorry to inform you that a Major Money ascended alone under the British Balloon at four o'clock yesterday afternoon. The balloon rose to a great hight and took a direction towards the sea. It was seen entering over the Ocean about a league south of Lowestoff at a very great hight at Six of Clock. By which circumstance I am greatly apprehensive for his thus continuing in the air, but that by some accident perhaps the String which connects the valve was broken or by the collapse of the lower part of [the] balloon (for it twas not half full) the string would not act upon it.[82]

Having lifted off from Ranelagh on 22 July 1785, the balloon finally ditched in the North Sea. There Money remained five and a half hours, chin deep in water, before being rescued by a passing cutter eighteen miles off the coast at Southwold.[83]

The Enlightenment witnessed a surge of aesthetic sensibility to embrace the human form as well as the fine arts. Social attributes such as appearance, conduct, etiquette, deportment and philanthropy increasingly came within the purview of aesthetics. It was the assembly, the embodiment of polite society in Georgian England, which raised sociability to the level of art. A 1751 definition of an assembly, as 'a stated and general meeting of polite persons of both sexes, for the sake of conversation, gallantry, news and play', describes some of the features of these gatherings.[84] The importance of one's personal appearance increased not only because it was an integral facet of selfhood or being, but also a manifestation of taste, manners and morals, each of which contributed to civilised behaviour. Sartorial conventions and codes of etiquette served to contain and express public opinion within fairly narrow boundaries. This shared sense of propriety was evident, for example, in 1793 when the Norwich subscription assembly met at Chapel Field house in the wake of the execution of Louis XVI:

> It ought not to pass unnoticed that the company at the Assembly on Tuesday night (with very few exceptions) appeared in mourning dresses for the melancholy death of the unfortunate King of France; setting these exceptions aside, which we are persuaded arose purely from the unconsciousness of its propriety or *etiquette*, we were happy to see all parties unite in testifying their respect for the memory of a virtuous, though ill-fated monarch.[85]

External display served not as an end in itself, but as an emblem of the inner being. Polite society was not merely an outlet for vulgar consumerism, as a report of the October sessions ball at the Assembly Rooms in 1817, attended by upwards of six hundred persons, makes plain:

> Many of the County Ladies were most splendidly attired, and appeared with diamonds, pearls, rich cameo necklaces etc. Indeed, the display of fashion and of personal charms, of elegant dresses and of costly ornaments, was as complete as bountiful nature and ingenious Art could possibly combine.[86]

Existing crafts and skills which claimed to enhance appearance were absorbed among the emergent trades and professions catering for fashionable leisure. By 1758 hair cutting and dressing had become so common in Norwich that 'every Pretender to this Art' had forced down the cost to as little as 2d. a head.[87] It was imperative, however, to be *au fait* with the tempo of fashion. Norgate, a ladies' hairdresser on Surrey Corner, returned from London in 1792, complete with the fashions worn at court to celebrate the queen's birthnight ball, ready to dress heads for the guild day ball 'cheap as in London'.[88] So great was demand at peak times in the social calendar that the services provided by Norwich's resident hairdressers were supplemented by peripatetic craftsmen such as Woollard and Davis from Bath and Semmence and Bull from London. All four were in Norwich for the summer assizes in 1771, 1773 and 1778.[89]

Perhaps on account of the paramount importance now accorded to teeth in beautifying or disfiguring the face, the most notable profession to emerge during the eighteenth century was dentistry. There were seven known tooth drawers, operators for the teeth or dentists resident in Norwich during the period 1720–80, as well as a cadre of peripatetic practitioners.[90] Driven by a combination of hygiene, fashion and snobbery, the aesthetic appearance of the teeth had become an established feature of polite social commerce by the 1780s. When the surgeon dentist Samuel Crawcour visited Norwich in 1801, he stressed the social benefits of attractive teeth:

> We every Day observe the irreparable damage that Beauty sustains by the Loss of a Tooth; the oratory of the Pulpit and the Bar, and above all the Arts of pleasing in Conversation and social life, are matters of the highest Concern to Individuals.[91]

Sound teeth were required, not only to enhance the appearance of the mouth and face, but also to effect correct enunciation, another facet of personal beauty. Clear enunciation, proper syntax and the use of standard received English were integral to the process of cultural refinement, and became assimilated into the canons of aesthetics and fashionable behaviour.

The incompatibility of speech impediments with polite discourse was the stimulus behind the emergence of another profession, speech therapy, during the eighteenth century. William Penry, on a visit to Norwich in 1744, was one of several practitioners who undertook to cure stuttering, stammering and lisping, each of which offered audible proof that a person was unfit for polite conversation.[92] Samuel Angier had a broader, and potentially more challenging, remit when he arrived in 1751. He undertook to cure speech impediments *and* eliminate provincial accents, proposing:

> to Teach ... the Art of Pronunciation; the learning of which will enable any persons, if diligent, to speak or read in an elegant Manner in one Month. The price is One Guinea Entrance, and Two Guineas a Month, the learner to attend him three times a week: or the price is One Guinea the first time, and Five Shillings every time afterwards.

Further, Angier acknowledged women's role as guardians of proper speech when he addressed twelve lectures on the 'Art of Pronunciation' in the grand jury chamber in the Guildhall, 'to the Ladies who have the Principle care in bringing children to Speak'.[93]

The increased importance of standard pronunciation to an enlightened society is confirmed by the expanding market for published works on the subject; for money was to be made, and personal publicity furthered, by the authors of self-help literature for the upwardly mobile. In 1735, for example, *A New General Dictionary* 'to prevent a vicious Pronunciation' was advertised in the *Norwich Mercury* on the day of its publication.[94] The Reverend John Herries, author of one of the most important tracts on orthoepy, *The Elements of Speech* (London, 1773), delivered a series of seven lectures on the 'Art of Speaking' at the Assembly rooms in Norwich, at a cost of 10s. 6d. to subscribers for the whole course, or 2s. 6d. to non-subscribers for each lecture.[95] John Collins, a former actor with the Bath Company, exemplified a change in standards from easy-going acceptance to ridicule of dialect when, in 1775, he concluded a lecture on 'Modern Orators and Modern Oratory' at the Assembly Rooms with a comic rendition of provincial accents.[96] Teachers of various accomplishments helped their unpolished patrons to function with ease in polite society. Edward Christian (1743–1804), whose family had practised as dancing masters in Norwich for three generations, established 'an oratorial academy' at his concert room at St Michael-at-Pleas in 1780, with the aim of promoting public elocution at the modest admission price of 6d. for gentlemen, but free of charge to ladies.[97] A private theatrical society, founded under the aegis of James Bunn in 1785, provided another setting for the perfection of spoken delivery.[98]

Commercial schooling, established during the seventeenth century, expanded in the eighteenth century. Norwich stood particularly high in the provision of day and boarding schools for both girls and boys, where elocution was a cornerstone of the curriculum intended to prepare pupils to take their place in the world of fashionable leisure.[99] Thus, when he opened his school in St John's Maddermarket in 1771, William Harmer assured his patrons that 'Due Regard will be had to Pronunciation, Emphasis, Cadence and Pauses, Orthography and Grammar.'[100] Similarly, at Mr and Miss Smyth's school for girls in St George's Colegate, the curriculum centred on teaching 'the French and English Languages grammatically, and with their respective *proper* Pronunciation'.[101] Norwich demonstrated its claim as an enlightened community through its support of teachers of the French language, the *lingua franca* of the European elite. When Monsieur de Roullon advertised classes in the French language, his long-term aim, once his pupils had acquired the rudiments of syntax and phonology, was to nurture the elements of conversation and elocution.[102]

Just as important as improvement of speech was attention to deportment. It created an agreeable and engaging first impression, which, in turn, contributed towards social success. Dancing and fencing furnished those who sought acceptance by the polite and leisured elite with the correct manner of presenting themselves and of receiving others in company. Dancing masters advocated training at an early age so that deportment which, when first corrected, might appear artificial, would become increasingly natural with time. The Norwich-based dancing master Francis Lambert argued that children should be taught dancing between the ages of five and eight when their bodies were at their most supple, to prevent the onset of postural defects.[103] The role of the dancing master as a teacher of deportment remained paramount until the mid nineteenth century, and was emphasised by Lambert in 1815:

> The intention and use of the dancing room is to improve the manners and external appearance; the etiquette of it obliges a respectful behaviour; the curtsey and bow is observed in entering and quitting the room, and frequent practice enables a person to make them in a graceful manner. These are the chief advantages to be considered in learning to dance ... The object of learning steps and dances is perhaps the least part of it. It is to improve the carriage and give a confidence in entering and quitting a room.[104]

Possibly because the code of chivalry had traditionally equated dancing and soldiering, many dancing masters taught the use of the smallsword, a difficult, aristocratic skill, slowly acquired, which aided proper carriage. In 1751 Norwich was able to support two fencing masters, Bayol and Johnson, whose services, like those of dentists and hairdressers, were supplemented by peripatetic instructors, notably from the theatrical fraternity.[105]

Dancing not only served to facilitate correct carriage and deportment but also to engender social cohesion. Demand for dancing lessons and assemblies increased as a result of the growing belief that aesthetics were personified in the human, especially the female, form, which was itself best displayed in the dance.[106] The status of dancing within the sphere of cultural refinement was assured by the enthusiastic patronage of Louis XIV (1638–1715) and further enhanced when it acquired a scientific language of its own, dance notation, which permitted courtly styles of dance to be communicated across Europe. The symbols, letters and characters that comprised this notation enabled dancing, like natural philosophy, to be recognised as an indispensable body of knowledge for those with aspirations to join polite society. Two Norwich-based dancing masters, John Bosely (d. 1739) and Francis Christian (c. 1676–1754), were among the subscribers to the first English translation of a system of notation published by Feuillet in 1699, and produced by John Weaver in 1706.[107]

A change in social climate, whereby dancing became a necessary rather than an optional accomplishment, encouraged several dancing masters in Norwich to address the adult market. Charles Gosnold, Joseph Guérin, Francis Veron and Francis Metcalf in the 1750s, 1760s and 1790s and the third decade of the nineteenth century, respectively, offered ladies and gentlemen who had received no previous instruction 'the opportunity of being qualified for the first Assemblies'.[108] The eighteenth and early nineteenth centuries may, indeed, be regarded as the golden age of the dancing master, since the social dances of the period were not only constantly changing but also extraordinarily complicated, requiring much investment of time and money to achieve the required competence before a person could confidently put him- or herself on display at a ball or an assembly. In an age when appearances counted for so much, the dancing master became an important conduit and arbiter in matters of etiquette, deportment, behaviour and social instruction.

Norwich's aspirations to cultural refinement can be gauged by its connection with the internationally renowned Noverre family over four generations. Evidence of the family's first link with the city is to be found in 1765 when the Norwich-based dancing master John Brown returned from London, having received dancing lessons from the 'celebrated' Augustin Noverre (1729–1805), brother of Jean Georges Noverre (1727–1810), dancing master to Marie-Antoinette.[109] Noverre is commemorated in a rhyme which was current in Norfolk until the First World War:

> Mr Noverre came from France
> To teach the natives how to dance.[110]

In 1794 he retired to Norwich, having established his son, Francis (1773–1840), as a dancing master in the city the previous year.[111] Francis not only followed the family profession until 1837, but also served as a director of the Norwich Union Fire and Life Insurance Societies. His son, Frank (1806–78), another dancing master, built the Noverre ballroom, opened in 1859, which remained a popular venue for dances until 1901.[112] He further enriched the cultural life of the city as a founder and honorary secretary of the Norwich Philharmonic Society (1841–78), honorary treasurer of the Norwich Choral Society, and prominent committee member of the Triennial Musical Festival. Two of his sons, Frank William Bianchi Noverre (b. 1843) and Richard Percival Noverre (1850–1921), the former being founder of the Norwich Ladies' Orchestral Society, were organisers of the festival and fourth generation dancing masters in the city. They cut imposing figures, as one former pupil recalls:

> the Noverre brothers wore tail coats and knee breeches, silk stockings and buckle shoes, and we certainly did learn to waltz and reverse beautifully. Also, we knew at the time that their ancestor had been ballet master at the French Court.[113]

Philanthropy was another manifestation of this personal aesthetic and, although it had the deepest roots in the medieval past, Enlightenment values encouraged the elite in new, more sociable forms of charitable effort, such as the Norfolk and Norwich Hospital. Founded by voluntary donations, it was largely sustained by annual subscriptions from men and women of all persuasions.[114] Thereby the scores of similar institutions, built across England in the eighteenth century, also eased the ever-present threat of political and religious division even in matters of public charity.[115] A further reflection of Enlightenment ideals was the building of the Bethel Hospital in 1713 by Mary Chapman (1647–1724), the widow of the Reverend Samuel Chapman. She was induced to build this early asylum when relations of both herself and her husband suffered mental incapacity; she was horrified by the treatment meted out to them. The Bethel was founded, and by her will endowed, for 'the convenient reception and habitation of poor lunaticks', defined by her as those 'afflicted with lunacy or madness (not such as are fools or idiots from their birth)'. By 1753 the inmates numbered twenty-eight; almost two decades later the governors planned accommodation for a total of thirty-three females and twenty-two males.[116] This city centre foundation was daily testimony to a more humane care of the insane.

Much charitable effort was naturally centred upon the city's textile industry. It had always known periods of recession when journeymen were thrown out of work for weeks on end. If these coincided with sharp rises in food prices then riots would periodically erupt, as in 1720, 1756–57, 1766, 1772 and during the long years of inflationary French Wars (1793–1815), unless staved off by the easing of poor relief, the generous distribution of soup, and subsidising of flour and meal supplies. Immersed in the city's great worsted industry, the elite were well aware of their social responsibilities. At times they would integrate these into their social calendar. In 1757 a crêpe ball was held in the new Assembly Rooms to promote the Norwich stuffs industry at a time when it was coming under increasing pressure from printed calicoes. Another, in 1826, served a twofold purpose: to advertise the fashionability and variety of Norwich crêpes and to donate the profits (£79 5s.) to a fund affording relief work to unemployed weavers macadamising Ber Street.[117] If a rational society is gauged by deeds of practical humanitarianism and the desire to render society more reasonable and humane, then Norwich might be considered one of the more enlightened centres in Europe. Certainly, some contemporary commentators – and testimony comes from a rival town – thought so. 'No place enters more warmly into acts of kindness towards the poorer part of their fellow citizens', believed the *Ipswich Journal*, when the Benevolent Association for the Relief of Decayed Tradesmen, their Widows and Orphans was established in 1790 'by the opulent inhabitants of Norwich'.[118]

What mark did the aesthetic vision of life promoted by the Enlightenment have upon the design, appearance and convenience of the city's
architecture and landscape? Most visitors, at least before 1750, would have
answered very little. Celia Fiennes, who approved of all that was spanking
new, wrote in 1698, 'all their buildings are of an old form ... and their
building timber and they playster on laths which they strike out into
squares like broad free stone on the outside'. Only a few houses 'beyond
the river' were built of brick.[119] An anonymous tourist in 1741, a disciple of
the new Palladianism, was equally disappointed. He reckoned 'the buildings which have anything of grandeur in them are all Gothic'.[120] But there
was much rebuilding in brick after 1700. Old houses were given classical,
usually astylar fronts, their rooms reordered and repanelled, new staircases
inserted. Some, like Sir Thomas Churchman's major remodelling of his
father's earlier house in St Giles's (itself on an old foundation) in 1751, were
impressive with decorative schemes encompassing tip-top plasterwork and
chimneypieces.[121] Another mayor, John Patteson, engaged Robert Mylne,
an up-and-coming architect and engineer, to build him a more restrained
but stylish and expensive house in Surrey Street in 1764–5.[122] There were
other houses built or extensively remodelled by the elite, especially in
St Giles Street, Colegate and All Saints Green.[123] And if Norwich had no
need for a Palladian church, the Old Meeting House off Colegate (1693)
and the Octagon Chapel, Colegate (1754–6), are testimony to the wealth of
England's second city, as impressive dissenting places of worship as any
built in the period. Indeed, John Wesley thought the latter 'probably the
most elegant in Europe' (Plate 9).[124] Yet there was no new lay-out of any
section of the city on classical principles, as in London, Edinburgh or Bath.
The medieval imprint of walls, streets, buildings and plots was too fixed.
The engine of growth was insufficient to support new streets, terraces and
public buildings on anything like the scale of those in Edinburgh's New
Town or even Leeds's West End for example.

Except for individual houses, there were only two schemes which might
be said to be generated by enlightened concepts of leisure and classical
architecture. The first was the redevelopment of the Chapel Field estate as
a superior neighbourhood for leisure in the mid eighteenth century.
Although promenading and impromptu assemblies at Chapel Field had
been a feature of the diversions of assize week in early August each year
since 1688, the redevelopment of the area afforded a setting commensurate
with the new urban consumption of leisure.[125] The tone for the site was set
in 1746 by planting three avenues of trees, themselves an aristocratic
symbol, to provide the perfect shaded promenade for the display of dress
and status (Figure 36). A new bowling green was opened three months

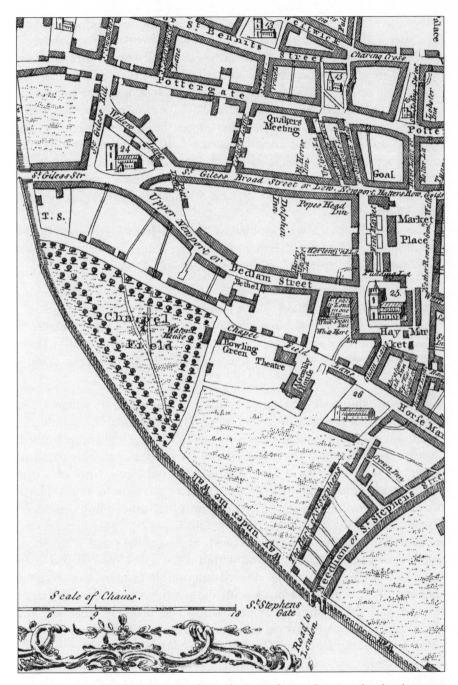

FIGURE 36. A detail from Samuel King's map of 1766 showing the development of Chapel Field with its avenues of trees, bowling green, theatre and assembly rooms. Note the city walls. (*Norfolk Heritage Centre, photograph by Terry Burchell*)

before the remodelled assembly rooms were inaugurated during the summer assizes of 1755.[126] Designed by the Norwich architect, Thomas Ivory, and the Cambridge arbiter of polite architecture, Sir James Burrough, they provided an enfilade of 143 feet for dancing when the three richly decorated rooms were opened up. They were 'esteemed by good judges to be as commodious and elegant as any in England'.[127] Ivory, a builder, speculator and timber merchant as well as architect, built the adjacent Theatre Royal, designed on the model of London's Drury Lane and capable of housing an audience of a thousand in 1757–8.[128] For many years it attracted for brief seasons the capital's leading actors and actresses. Sarah Siddons pocketed staggeringly high fees of £423 for her nine-day engagement in 1788 (Figure 37).[129]

The second scheme was another of Thomas Ivory's ventures. In the decade after 1761 he built a terrace of imposing houses in Surrey Street, as the *Norwich Mercury* described them in 1766:

> The homes make a most noble appearance, and are furnished in such taste as does honour to the architect ... The projector, we hear, will have ten more elegant houses, with every necessary conveniency for genteel private families, as coach-house and stables, etc, to each dwelling, with proper offices ... The whole when executed will greatly contribute to the elegance of that part of the city.[130]

Building on this scale was not continued. The impact of schemes like Thomas Ivory's ventures in Surrey Street and All Saints Green, and the smart refronted houses of St Giles Street and Colegate, was always limited. Visitors saw the city as old-fashioned and crowded, increasingly confined within its walls. In 1783 William Chase, who published Norwich's first directory, advocated pulling down the city gates and walls to improve both the circulation of air and prospects out into the surrounding country.[131] The removal of the gates along the city walls began in 1792, when the corporation ordered five to be demolished. St Augustine's and King Street gates followed two years later and within a few years the rest had been taken down.[132] With the walls allowed to crumble further, their dismantling marked a significant break with the medieval past. Enlightenment thought had always stressed modernisation and progress. Therefore the Georgians could be unthinking about their heritage. Certainly, all prospect of conserving a future mecca for tourists was jettisoned.

And in other ways improvements, already evident in other cities, came late to Norwich. Dorothy Wordsworth, who spent five years of her early life in the rectory at nearby Forncett St Peter, thought Norwich in 1788 was 'an immensely large place, but the streets in general are very ugly, and they are

FIGURE 37. The Theatre Royal, Norwich (1828). Originally built by Thomas Ivory in 1757–8 it was rebuilt by William Wilkins in 1800 and again in 1826. (*Norfolk Heritage Centre, photograph by Terry Burchell*)

so ill-paved and dirty, as almost entirely to take away the pleasure of walking'.[133] This was not simply a woman's reaction on a wet day. The well-travelled Maximilien de Lazowski, although impressed by its size, considered 'like all ancient cities, Norwich is badly planned and built. It is not that there are no good or beautiful houses, but a well-built house on a bad site or in a narrow street can never appear more than very moderate.'[134]

Only in 1800 was there a public meeting to address problems such as those Dorothy Wordsworth voiced. Even so progress was slow. Another six years passed before there was an act of Parliament obtained for 'The Better Paving, Lighting, Cleansing, Watering and otherwise Improving the City of Norwich'. But the large body of commissioners named to raise a rate and put the act into practice appear to have been remarkably inefficient. In forty years they had spent £300,000, incurred debts of £17,000, and yet, in A. D. Bayne's view, had left Norwich the worst paved town in England.[135]

The impact of an Enlightenment-driven modernisation in Georgian Norwich is therefore not clear cut.[136] Yet all its attributes, as listed by Peter Borsay, John Brewer and Roy Porter, in their path-breaking surveys of eighteenth-century thought and action, encapsulated in the terms 'English Enlightenment' and 'urban renaissance', are evident enough in the city – a vibrant print culture, music, assemblies, a vast variety of clubs, a calendar of leisure and sociability all underpinned by the growing consumption of the city's grandees and 'middling sort'.[137] Perhaps in Norwich it is now best recaptured in the fine sets of marble monuments which crowd the walls of the cathedral, the city's churches and principal chapels. No other provincial city possesses a finer collection of monuments or a more active group of sculptors than Robert Page, Thomas Rawlins and John Ivory (Plate 10).[138] The eulogies to the dead they commemorate, so carefully composed, laud the merits and aspirations of men and women who have imbibed Enlightenment values. In their splendour they also underline the wealth of a city well able to support an impressive network of architects, sculptors and craftsmen.[139]

If the gauge of cultural refinement is measured by the opportunities afforded for social commerce, the diffusion of rational and useful knowledge and the availability of schemes for improving both the individual and society, then Norwich experienced an era of unprecedented enlightenment between 1680 and 1830. Sociability, philanthropy and what, in the fullest sense, might be described as public education endowed the upper reaches of Norwich society with a degree of rationality and cohesion absent during the political conflicts of the seventeenth century

9

The Textile Industry

Richard Wilson

If the energy and thoughts of the men of Norwich had not been absorbed in party politics; long before now the town would have had an efficient police force and the majesty of the law would have attained respect; enterprising men would then have ventured to establish machinery in their manufactures, which they have not dared to do. The probability is that, under such circumstances, the vast space of ground now empty within the walls; and much land in the vicinity, would have been covered with buildings, and the population instead of 60,000 or 70,000 would have been 120,000 or 180,000; the ground would be yielding a rental many times what it does at present; there would have been many more opulent manufactures and tradesmen of every description, and Norwich would have been one of the chief places in the empire.

Reports of the Assistant Commissioners
for Hand Loom Weavers (1839–40)[1]

The difficulty in envisaging the extent and appreciating the fame of the Norwich textile industry is that there is so little left to remind us of its eighteenth-century heyday. There are, with one exception, no vast mills and chimneys such as those which haunt the landscapes of Lancashire and West Yorkshire and the steep valleys of Gloucestershire and serve as perpetual prompters to a great industrial past. Yet it is this seemingly strange lack of physical evidence of the city's worsted industry which provides a key to it. The Marchioness Grey, *en route* to view the Palladian splendours of Holkham and Houghton in 1750, at the very height of Norwich's fame as a textile centre, was as puzzled as a tourist might be now. She logged her frustration:

I was disappointed in not being able to see any of their Manufactures at Norwich. I expected to have seen some kind of Public buildings for carrying them on, or large work-rooms belonging to the several weavers, but there is no such thing, and the workmen I was told have all their separate looms in their own houses; and mounting up into a Garret to see a single Loom was not worthwhile.[2]

Others recalled the strange lack of people in the streets by day, of weavers' attics dimly lit on a winter's night, and everywhere the constant clack of shuttles.

Clearly what Lady Grey had wanted to see were cloths piled high on trestle tables, to note the numbers sold and the proceeds realised, much as Daniel Defoe had recorded them in wonder thirty years earlier at the bustling cloth markets of Exeter and Leeds.[3] Her puzzlement was in a sense echoed by those first generations of twentieth-century economic historians preoccupied in charting the precise role of the wool textile industries in Britain's industrialisation. When they came to the Norwich industry, very few business records had survived. There was little conspicuous industrial archaeology, no continuity of manufacture, no factory masters or textile workers to talk to since the industry was on its last legs by the 1880s and latterly run by an aged workforce. Little surprise they concentrated upon tracing its decline.[4]

In the last thirty years the interests of historians have shifted. They have come to see Britain's industrialisation as being far less cataclysmic and much more a process (eventually no less path-breaking) taking place over a much longer period. In these accounts, pushing the emergence of an increasingly dynamic economy back into the seventeenth century, the Norwich industry slots more readily. Now historians have begun to explain the success of England's second city in terms of its vitality as the centre of a remarkable industrial network which stretched across Norfolk and Suffolk into neighbouring Cambridgeshire, Huntingdonshire and Bedfordshire. Researches on a wide front into inventories, early insurance records, port books, parish, freemen and apprenticeship registers, and the few surviving pattern books of some of its leading manufacturers, are bringing a much fuller understanding to the history of the city which at first sight provides so few traces of the pinnacle of its industrial past.[5] How had Norwich's pre-eminence, to quote Macaulay in his famous account of the economy and society of late seventeenth-century England, as 'the chief seat of the chief manufacture of the realm' come about? What were the chief features of its prominence? How long did leadership in and the prosperity of the industry continue?

Of course, the worsted industry in Norfolk had a long history.[6] Why the county specialised in the production of lighter, cheaper worsted cloth woven from long combing wool, as opposed to the traditional cloths of England, made from short carding wool with good felting properties and invariably fulled, is not clear. Some broad cloth was turned out in Norfolk and the making of coarse linens was widespread, but it was the manufacture of worsteds, often incorporating carded yarn to produce 'union' cloths or those with linen warps woven by dornix weavers and famed for bed coverlets, which led the way in textile manufacture in the county. On balance, it was easy contact with the Continent, the home of fine worsteds, that proved a more cogent reason for Norfolk's concentration upon them than either the properties of its native wools or its lack of water power to drive that great thirteenth-century innovation in cloth production, the fulling mill.[7]

Norwich came not only to dominate the weaving of worsteds in the county, but also emerged as the centre where all cloths were sent for the vital finishing stages, for inspection or 'searching', and for sale. But the fortunes of the industry fluctuated wildly between the fourteenth and sixteenth centuries. A peak in exports seems to have been reached as early as the fourteenth century. Long periods of decline occurred during the fifteenth century, before recovery took place during the early Tudor period. Then, towards the end of Henry VIII's reign and into the 1550s, real recession set in. Exports, facing crippling competition from the Continent, were negligible after 1540. The industry was over-regulated. Even Norwich market was reported to be overgrown with weeds in 1544. Increasingly, the city's prosperity came to rely, not on its industry, but on its role as the administrative, social and shopping centre of the prosperous agricultural regions of Norfolk and north Suffolk.[8]

Aid for Norwich's ailing worsted industry came from an unexpected and controversial quarter. As early as the late 1540s and early 1550s a few Flemish weavers were brought to Norwich to improve the making of some of the city's finer cloths. Their numbers were soon entirely swamped by a flow of immigrants, Dutch and Walloon alike, fleeing the religious persecutions of the duke of Alva in the 1560s and 1570s. Their presence in Norwich was not unique. They could be found in Sandwich, Canterbury, Colchester and, above all, in their assembly point, London. Nowhere, however, in provincial England were they more numerous than in Norwich, nor their influence in the wool textile industries more pronounced. If a head count was deeply impressive, their integration was fractious and slow.[9] By 1582 there were 4679 'strangers' in the city, forming it seems over a third of Norwich's population.[10] Many of them found work in the worsted industry. Their impact on its revival has, none the less, been disputed. Some historians argue that the so-called 'New Draperies', itself a term never accurately defined, but essentially embracing a whole variety of light worsteds blending in mixed yarns, were already to be found amongst the city's range of cloths before the Strangers arrived.[11] Again one of the arguments is that weavers in Norwich were already in close touch with developments across the North Sea. In truth, the contention is difficult to resolve. We are simply unsure about the precise qualities of Norwich cloths before the 1560s.

By the mid sixteenth century the Low Countries produced finer and better-finished worsteds than those manufactured in Norwich, Coventry or London. Their superior know-how seems to have been transferred by the Strangers in two ways. The Dutch, who formed the majority of immigrants, arguably made the lesser contribution. They wove chiefly bays, a heavy cloth of plain weave with a carded wool weft, a cloth more akin to woollens and a product which became a famed Colchester rather than a Norwich speciality. Indeed, by the 1630s the manufacture of bays, always sold in a 'white' or undyed state, seems to have disappeared from the city. The influence of the Dutch was possibly of more moment in the better finishing of the simple, traditional Norwich goods, camlets and says, both cloths widely used for dress and hangings. The contribution of the Walloon Strangers appears to have been much more significant. Again like the Dutch, the dyeing and finishing of their goods was superior to those of the Norwich craftsmen. They used scoured, dyed yarns and introduced silk thread to produce much lighter cloths which when finished achieved a lustrous effect (the new worsteds were known collectively as *caungeantry*). It was these innovations, combining worsted with jersey, cotton, linen as well as silk yarns, which formed the basis of what later became known as Norwich stuffs, England's premier worsted for the next two centuries.[12]

There are no firm series of statistics to chart the course of the worsted industry in Norwich in the seventeenth century. Although there were periods of difficulties in the 1620s, the 1640s and again in the 1660s, the historian of the Norfolk worsted cloth industry in the Tudor and Stuart periods maintains that these were only temporary interruptions in its growing prosperity throughout the century.[13] A number of factors underpinned this expansion. First, the city's native practitioners of the art of cloth making led the marked revival of the 1600–20 period. The high standards of the Strangers had clearly been emulated and absorbed. Indeed their influence gradually waned as their numbers declined after 1620. Archbishop Laud's harassment of their places of worship in the 1630s was pivotal. Some returned across the North Sea, others braved the Atlantic to America. By 1650 their number in the city probably did not exceed 1500.[14] Activity in the first two decades is indicated by a surge in population growth (checked by a serious outbreak of plague in 1625–26) and an impressive increase in the number of freemen engaged in every aspect of cloth making.[15]

Secondly, the industry seems to have been better regulated. There were the usual perpetual complaints: of workers evading apprenticeship controls; of shoddy cloth; of the fraudulent reeling of yarn; and of the falsification of measurements and embezzlement generally. But in 1613 rules were drawn up to monitor every aspect of the Norwich stuffs industry which took into account the innovations of the previous half century and which applied to both native and foreign craftsmen alike. They were further refined in Acts of 1650 and 1672. Observation of their strict letter, through the agency of the corporation and the Company of Weavers, as with all industrial regulation, was fitful.

Thirdly, there appears to have been an important shift in the marketing of Norwich stuffs. In the home market, much the most important sector for sales, they had been vended by chapmen, mercers, drapers, even grocers, and by general merchants. The trade continued to expand. The New Draperies were generally cheaper than the old worsteds, and inventories reveal that Norwich goods were to be found across a broad spectrum of society in Stuart England. A great variety of dress and furnishing materials made up from them is recorded in the probate valuations of the landed and professional classes. Even in those of much less well-to-do farmers and craftsmen Norwich stuffs are to be found, though they were far more limited in range and lower in cost.[16] Simultaneous with growth in the home market was greater activity in the export trade, especially to southern Europe. Informed guesses reckoned around a quarter of Norwich goods found their way overseas by 1700.[17] They did so through London merchants who bought directly from the Norwich weavers. The latter, by an edict of the privy council in 1638, had obtained exemption from the required inspection and sale of their goods, unlike the clothiers of the west of England and Devonshire, through Blackwell Hall, the great metropolitan cloth market. It was an important freedom. By the late seventeenth century wagons loaded with cloth were departing four days a week from Norwich to meet the orders of London merchants. Surprisingly few cloths found their way to the capital by the circuitous river and sea route via Yarmouth, or for that matter were exported directly to the Continent without the intervention of the metropolitan merchants.

Lastly, the Norwich industry successfully overcame its raw material supply problems. Around the mid sixteenth century the combing wools of Norfolk and Suffolk deteriorated in quality. East Anglian sheep seemed no longer to produce the finest, longest wools which when spun were essential to obtain the required lightness and sheen of the New Draperies in their almost infinite variety. Instead yarn markers and wool combers throughout East Anglia turned to the graziers of Lincolnshire, Northamptonshire and Leicestershire for their supplies. It was generally accepted that these counties produced the best combing wools in Europe. As the Norwich industry expanded, yarn was obtained from an increasingly wide area, running into Cambridgeshire, Huntingdonshire and even Bedfordshire, in essence an extended East Anglian proto-industrial region.[18] And, as the Norwich industry grew, its dependency upon an enlarged spinning network was compounded by the fact that it had to procure other yarns, of carded wool, jersey, linen and, above all, silk, to produce assorted Norwich stuffs. By the last thirty years of the seventeenth century the city had become famed in Britain and Europe for the novelty, variety and quality of its worsteds. It was an ascendancy and reputation which was to endure for a further century.

The linchpin in the organisation of the Norwich industry was the master weaver. It is a curious description for a business leader in that weaving in the popular imagination was associated with long hours of laborious, poorly paid labour. In the Yorkshire textile industries the dominant figures were more grandly designated 'merchant', in the west of England cloth industry, 'clothier'.[19] At the top of the tree, both could abut on gentleman status. In Norwich no other term than 'master weaver' was used until the 1770s, when the largest amongst them became known as 'manufacturers'; even then 'master weaver' still signified status, while 'merchant' was more sparingly employed, often simply describing general dealers.

Around 1700, it is reckoned there were about 500 master weavers in the city controlling a total of about 6000 looms.[20] But evidence both from the 181 probate inventories of master weavers to survive for the 1650 to 1750 period and 571 recorded apprenticeship fees paid to them between 1710 and 1745, together with the view that the industry was largely in the hands of around thirty firms by the 1780s, suggests that the term master weaver is somewhat meaningless when applied uniformly to as many as five hundred masters.[21]

Already by the 1670s there was a handful of master weavers possessed of considerable capital (the gross estate of one was valued for probate in 1679 at £9699), totally different in the scale of their operations from those at the bottom of the ladder, who were little better off than the thousands of journeymen weavers with whom they lived cheek by jowl.[22] The national apprenticeship registers reveal a similar picture for Norwich.[23] Premiums paid to train as a weaver in the city (usually for seven years) ran from as little as 5s. to as much as £80.[24] The majority of fees paid were under £10. Again, a handful were over £40 and always point to training with a top worsted weaver (never described as a master weaver in the registers). The

FIGURE 38. An eighteenth-century drawloom used for complex weaves such as worsted damask. The weaver sat on the narrow bench on the left to throw the weft shuttle; the draw boy seen here pulled up the warp threads in a pre-arranged sequence. From Diderot's *Recueil des planches sue les sciences, les arts libéraux et les arts mechaniques avec leur explication* (Paris, 1763)

premium of £157 10s. paid in 1718 to Richard Gildart by Edward Parkinson, clerk in holy orders of Louth, Ireland, for the completion of his son's training was quite exceptional, but it reflects the standing of those apprentices who trained with the city's leading weavers.[25] Their fees of £40 and more, compared with the run of the mill two to five pounds, clearly marked out the status of the master and the far greater opportunities training with him appeared to secure. Yet the inventories show that few weavers, whatever the scale of their operation, owned more than four looms each.[26] And as we have seen, Lady Grey was disappointed in 1750 at the absence of 'large work rooms belonging to the several Weavers' for her to appraise. This puzzling lack of both large-scale loom ownership and large workrooms in which many weavers were gathered and supervised is explained from a study of the letter books of Philip Stannard and the early insurance policies of the leading weavers. It is evidence which begins to tease out the extraordinary organisation of the Norwich industry at the height of its fame.

The firm of Philip Stannard was at its zenith in the 1750s. It could blow its own trumpet most effectively: its fabrics had been 'very well known ... throughout all Europe, for many years', Stannard's partner claimed on New Year's day 1763.[27] When trade was at its briskest, Stannard employed three hundred journeymen weavers across the city making top of the range stuffs 'in the flowered way only' – satins, florettas, taboretts and, most expensive of all, fine brocades in imitation of silk (Plate 11). His orders at this stage (he later disastrously ventured into the export trade) were from 'most of the merchants in London'.[28] They ordered goods in quantities large and small; some were for as many as three hundred pieces at a time. When he carried out his annual stock taking he often had over two thousand cloths in store. It is clear, however, that the London merchants called the tune. To keep pace with metropolitan changes in fashion they constantly demanded new goods. One wrote: "Tis not the quantity, but quality and newness which I ask. As to the old patterns, I have had enough'.[29] Therefore Stannard had to have new designs made up, draw looms (Figure 38) expensively reset and keep the closest eye on the finishing of his goods, putting them out to reputable hot pressers who added the characteristic high gloss of the Norwich stuffs, but, if the utmost care was not taken, could cause spotting and variations in colour. To keep the London merchants continually appraised of his goods, like all the big Norwich weavers, he had pattern books made up for them.[30]

As with so many pre-industrial systems of manufacture, the production of Norwich stuffs seems both complex and full of potential problems. Stannard was at the mercy of hard-nosed London merchants, ever watchful of quality and price. Moreover, there was no question even in the simplest lines of producing anything like a standard product. Sorting variable, handspun yarns, setting up 'tows' for the weavers' draw looms in his workshops, chivvying weavers, checking and packing goods after dyeing and finishing were constant occupations. The closest supervision of every stage of manufacture was vital. Yet it had one strong point from the manufacturer's perspective. When any slackness of trade descended, seasonal or cyclical, the army of weavers could be laid off, the whole process of manufacture squeezed. Then problems of credit and payment became uppermost. This see-saw of prosperity and recession in the Norwich trade and the ease with which the principal element of its workforce could be laid off led to acute problems of unemployment. This is reflected in the city's famed reputation for both its high poor rates and its notorious radicalism.

The policies of the Sun Insurance company throw further light on the structure of the Norwich worsted industry. Running from 1714, they provide little detail and no valuations before the early 1720s.[31] Then, better-recorded policies between 1721–22 and 1750 (there are 209 in all), taken out in the city by worsted weavers, wool combers, dyers, hot pressers, wool and yarn factors and twisterers alike, show a marked increase in value.[32] Seldom more than a conventional £300 or £500 at the outset, they run to as much as £3000 by 1750. There is an element of under valuation in the policies, and they do not necessarily include all the property of the insurer. Their great merit is that they allow a comparative view of the East Anglian textile industry, since they include policies (in total far fewer than those for Norwich) of enterprises across the region. Again, although they provide further confirmation of growth in the industry, the policies chiefly covered stock-in-trade or goods-in-trust, those being made up in the garrets of journeymen or the workshops of dyers and hot pressers. Often the dwelling house is included, but the valuations of warehouses, workrooms and utensils does not suggest a heavy fixed capital investment in either premises or machinery. Joseph Hannant the younger, of St George's Colegate, was a large-scale worsted weaver who, most unusually, combined wool combing in his business. In 1742 his dwelling house and its contents were valued for insurance at £450, his warehouse for £50, his utensils and stock in it for a further £500. He possessed additional workrooms (probably his combing shops) valued at £200 and their contents at £600.[33] Peter Columbine, a famed Norwich manufacturer, insured his house and workrooms for £450, his domestic goods and furniture for £350. But it was a policy taken out in the following year which discloses the true scale of his operations. George Mann, his hot presser, insured his utensils and the goods he held in trust for Columbine for £1000.[34] Sometimes valuations include property let out to other masters and journeymen and the occasional public house, such as the endearingly noted *Flower de Lice* of John Brett in 1728. Thomas Brady, worsted weaver, rented out no fewer than twenty tenements, valued together at only £180, in three parishes a decade later; he also insured 'his goods and stock for £120'.

The various masters in the Norwich stuffs industry were insuring their houses and contents, their utensils, warehouses and workshops (invariably in the yard adjoining their dwelling), and sometimes cottage property let to their journeymen. Crucially, the policies were for protection against the

loss of valuable goods in various stages of completion, not for the insurance of vast workshops or large quantities of expensive machinery.[35] The
policies represent a cross-section of leading masters. Again, their enterprises varied in size from this evidence, showing, as with the Stannard
letters, the surviving inventories and the apprenticeship registers, the dominant position of a quite small number of master weavers and, to a lesser
extent, wool combers. This is not surprising. Given the sheer variety of
Norwich goods and the need to make up big orders to the exacting
demands of the London export merchants, it is clear that only the largest
weavers, such as Stannard, could provide this range and manage the necessary credit mechanisms in the many stages of their manufacture. Men
who once might have been styled master weaver, or were independent
dyers, hot pressers and twisterers, were increasingly working to the direct
order of the larger master weavers.

The Sun Insurance policies suggest that the only other weaving centres
of any importance were Dereham and, to lesser extent, Aylsham. The number of country policies, always registering smaller sums covered, fell away
sharply after 1730. Indeed, all the sources underline that by 1750 weaving
was becoming increasingly concentrated in Norwich itself. All the more
complex patterns of mixed yarns were made up in the city because skills
and expertise in both the manufacturing and commercial aspects of production developed, coral like, there. The example of Norwich perfectly
illustrates how, in contradiction to the claims of the early advocates of a
proto-industrialisation theory who argued that European pre-factory
industries were located in the countryside, industry in its pre-mechanised
form had the strongest *urban* presence. The city was not simply a service
and commercial centre; it was a great pre-industrial manufacturing town.[36]

If the Norwich master weavers relied upon a host of journeymen owning their own looms and working in their own homes, and upon teams of
well-paid dyers and hot pressers, men whose skills were internationally
recognised, how did they organise their supplies of yarn? In some ways this
was the most difficult aspect of the whole cloth-making process. Contemporaries reckoned that as many as between six and nine hand spinners
were necessary to keep one weaver constantly supplied with yarn.[37] In Norwich alone there were reckoned to be 12,000 weavers in and around the city
at the peak of the industry's prosperity in the mid eighteenth century
employing on these calculations a vast army of between seventy-two thousand and ninety-six thousand spinners. The task was chiefly women's work
and poorly paid; at full stretch, the earnings of the most adept were less
than half of those of male labourers. Young girls, rewarded with a miserly
penny or tuppence a day, were raised in the art from an early age. Even

these pittances were an important contribution to the earnings of labouring families and the occupation could be fitted into the annual calendar of agricultural tasks, especially during the summer months.

Yet the organisation of spinning was not as casual as this glimpse of it might suggest. As already noted, Norwich was the weaving centre of the East Anglian worsted industry, its large consumption of yarn drawn from a wide area stretching across Norfolk, Suffolk, Cambridgeshire and Bedfordshire. The key figure in maintaining supplies over such long distances when communications were slow was the wool comber-cum-yarn merchant. Although they might be found in towns scattered across the region, the insurance registers suggest they were increasingly concentrated in Bury St Edmunds and in Norwich itself.[38] Fortunately, the diary of one has survived.[39] James Oakes inherited a flourishing business in Bury from his uncle in 1768. It was a profitable affair, yielding a net return of around £1650 on its large capital of £20,000. He bought the finest, glossy, long combing wools from the East Midlands, Lincolnshire and Kent, either at the wool hall in Bury or at various wool fairs including Stourbridge outside Cambridge. It was then sorted into as many as a dozen categories, scoured and combed on the premises behind his fine house in Guildhall Street. Oakes employed no fewer than fifty highly paid and skilled combers in his shops, as well as a dozen sorters and warehousemen.[40] The tops were then despatched to four depots in High Suffolk and one in Cambridgeshire to be put out to spin, either with individuals or the inmates of the big poor houses of the incorporated hundreds to the north east of Bury. Oakes was himself possibly the largest wool comber and yarn merchant in Suffolk. He reckoned, perhaps too neatly, that there were 120 yarn makers in the county employing 1200 combers and 36,000 spinners.

Most of his yarn was sold 'white' in Norwich to the leading firms of master weavers, who put it out for dyeing the myriad colours which the brighter Norwich stuffs demanded. He had other, lesser outlets in Colchester, Spitalfields in London, even the midlands and the north. The real difficulty, besides the constant one of embezzlement prevalent at almost all stages of cloth production, came in sorting yarns. Whether they were spun on the Saxony wheel, as in Suffolk, or to produce the finest yarns, often in Norfolk on the traditional distaff and spindle, there were great variations in quality.[41] Oakes himself concentrated upon superior yarn suitable for camblets.

Oakes was clearly at the top of the wool combers' tree. His tightly run organisation, which reveals exactly how this key aspect of pre-industrial textile manufacture worked, was not untypical of the larger wool combing firms in Norwich and Bury. It was this complex, labour intensive, widely scattered organisation of combing, spinning, dyeing, weaving and finishing, exploiting the division of and, at least in spinning, the cheapness of labour and the nurturing of sparse capital, which underpinned the development of the great Norwich worsted industry in the eighteenth century. It was the archetype of pre-mechanised industrial organisation, supporting agriculture and rural earnings, encouraging urban development, expanding labour markets, supplying home and overseas trade alike.

This system of cloth manufacture in East Anglia must have been at full stretch in the decades between 1740 and 1770, when it was at its zenith and population growth in the region was only slowly recovering from a virtual standstill over the previous hundred years. Certainly, in the second quarter of the eighteenth century Norwich began to secure increasing quantities of yarn from Ireland as well as from Yorkshire and Cumbria.[42] Restraints upon the import of Irish yarn were removed by Parliament at the entreaty of the Norwich manufacturers, who constituted a powerful lobby. Duties were removed in 1739 and thirteen years later a customs concession allowed yarn to be shipped through Yarmouth. Previously it had been expensively transported overland from Bristol, since to prevent its export abroad only a handful of west coast ports were allowed to import it.[43] Then the trade really flourished, with yarn merchants such as the Gurneys becoming prominently involved. Although the consensus was that Irish yarns were not as fine as the better East Anglian ones, nevertheless, because they were based on good quality wool, they were prized in the making of calimancoes, one of the most popular Norwich lines. Such yarn was also cheaper, the price of labour in Ireland being around two-thirds of English rates.[44] Yet, despite these advantages, in the long run reliance upon Irish imports had serious consequences for the Norwich industry. It was a significant factor in the city's neglect of the key innovations in machine spinning, which revolutionised all the textile industries after the 1770s.

As we have seen, the Norwich worsted industry was principally supported by domestic markets. Prized for women's and children's clothing and for furnishings, Norwich stuffs were widely sold. In their variety, their lightness and cheapness in comparison with woollen cloth, in their use of silk threads, and in their colour and finish they had no match in Britain or on the Continent. The domestic market grew more in response to rising incomes than population growth, at least before the 1780s. The making of cloth in the home, even in the remoter north was on the wane in the eighteenth century. More and more cloth was bought from retailers and chapmen, more and more outer garments made up by tailors and mantua makers. Even the clothing of the labouring poor included stuff dresses (taking six yards of cheap stuffs at 1s. 6d. a yard and lasting two years, or so Sir Frederick Eden reckoned in 1797), petticoats and cloaks, often bought second-hand or institutionally supplied.[45] Yet in spite of the popularity of Norwich stuffs, the city's position in the manufacture of English textiles was, to a greater or lesser degree, exposed.

Threats came from two main quarters. First, there was continuous competition in the eighteenth century from cotton goods. Initially these took the form of imported Indian calicoes (partly stemmed by the Calico Act of 1721), then of printed fustians, a linen and cotton mix made in Lancashire, which could thereby evade the provisions of the Act. Eventually, after the removal of all restrictions in 1773, the full-blown, rapid expansion of the domestic cotton industry posed an even more serious challenge. Its products were cheaper, lighter and more readily washed. They were very quickly a major threat to Norwich stuffs. It was not that the climate warmed up to increase the consumption of cottons, but coal-heated, less draughty rooms, hung with wallpaper, required fewer heavy hangings. Women in summer sported cotton gowns, muslin becoming the fashion rage of the late eighteenth century. Secondly, even in worsteds there was competition. That from the Devon industry making serges, a mixed cloth with a worsted warp and woollen weft, became less and less serious as the century progressed. A cheaper and lighter substitute for woollen cloth, it was increasingly outsold by the even lighter weight patterned Norwich stuffs.[46] After the mid century, the threat from Yorkshire was much more serious. Increasingly, its large-scale worsted clothiers made cheap, plain worsteds which undermined some of the best-selling, more basic Norwich lines. The finish of the Yorkshire worsteds improved, although little attempt was made to imitate the more intricate Norwich goods dyed in the yarn – calimancoes (Plate 12), satins and brocades. Nevertheless by the mid 1770s output in the West Riding was believed to have overtaken that of East Anglia.[47] Yorkshire stuffs and Lancashire cottons were pushing the Norwich manufacturers into the more restricted sectors of highly volatile export markets.

Norwich cloth before around 1750 seems principally to have been sold to London merchants for both the home and export trades. Then after 1750 the larger Norwich weavers, perhaps no more than the majority of the leading three dozen firms, broke directly into the export trade. The reasons are difficult to determine with precision. Early nineteenth-century commentators tended to cite the competition of cottons in domestic markets.[48] The chronology is thirty years out. More recently it has been suggested that the Norwich weavers turned to foreign markets when domestic sales became static or even declining.[49] On the other hand, the collapse of textile production in Leiden may have provided the leaders of the Norwich industry with a window of opportunity on the Continent. Possibly, they were increasingly frustrated with the stranglehold of London merchants, themselves not necessarily fully committed to vigorously promoting cloth sales abroad, although they had pushed the exports of stuffs very successfully between the 1700s and 1730s.[50] Norwich men must have envied those thriving merchants in Leeds, Wakefield and Halifax who traded directly abroad. As their resources grew, the Norwich manufacturers believed they had the necessary capital to finance the complexities of foreign sales – shipping, customs, insurance, and, above all, extended credit and terms of payment. Virtually no records of this trade have survived. A stray account of the leading firm of Ives, Basely and Robberds for 1791 shows that their trade in Europe and to China accounted for no less than a massive and untypical £109,282. For forty years Norwich's direct cloth exports, chiefly via Yarmouth, flourished. The newspapers listed ships sailing from there to Rotterdam, Hamburg, the Baltic, the Iberian Peninsula and the Straits (largely to Italy). William Taylor, a distinguished German scholar and one-time Norwich manufacturer, looked back on the trade's heyday in 1798 as the wars which were ravaging the Continent throttled cloth exports from the city:

> Their travellers penetrated through Europe, and their pattern cards were exhibited in every principal town, from the frozen plains of Moscow, to the milder climes of Lisbon, Seville and Naples. The Russian peasant decorated himself with a sash of gaudy calimanco, and the Spanish Hidalgo was sheltered under his light cloak of Norwich camblet. The introduction of their articles into Spain, Italy, Poland and Russia, soon made the manufacturers ample amends for the capriciousness of fashion in their own country.[51]

The export trade was never as plain sailing as Taylor suggested. There were disruptions even before the catastrophic French wars (1793–1815). The impact of the American War of Independence was European wide. In 1781 Parson Woodforde succinctly noted its impact on the Norwich economy: 'Trade at Norwich never worse. Poor no employment'.[52] Ironically, the Norwich manufacturers never effectively broke into the American trade itself, much the fastest growing sector of Britain's export markets in the late eighteenth century. Norwich faced the wrong way for the Atlantic. In the United States, Yorkshire merchants, operating through Liverpool, pushed both their woollen and worsteds with vigour and success.[53] Moreover, competition from the French, whose worsted manufacturers were consistently improving, was keen in Portugal and the Levant. Commercial rivals were constantly adjusting tariffs and enforcing embargoes on trade. As a consequence the export trade was extremely cyclical. The tendency to venture goods that were not sold to the usual direct orders from overseas merchants fuelled this. Arthur Young, writing in 1771, was of the impression that the city's bigger manufacturers had so overstocked the Europe market with these speculative goods at the conclusion of the Seven Years' War (1756–63) that their export trade had never quite recovered. The state of the industry was, he noted, 'neither brisk nor very dull'.[54]

The experience of Philip Stannard in the export market highlights its hazards. His business as a leading weaver of top quality stuffs had clearly flourished since the late 1720s. Several times in the 1750s he stated that he had no wish to export cloth himself; he was entirely satisfied with his London connections. When he had put a toe in the Norwegian market, in 1755, the results had been disappointing. But by 1763 the success of some of his fellow Norwich weavers in export ventures, and his own slackness of business, 'brought [him] to a resolution to follow our neighbours and to seek for correspondence abroad'.[55] He acquired a thrusting new partner, well versed in the European cloth trade. They attempted to seek orders on a wide front especially in Spain. Three years later speculative cargoes were despatched via Seville for Buenos Aires, Lima and Vera Cruz. By late 1769 Stannard, an old man out of his depth, was bankrupt. Martha Patteson wrote to her son in Leipzig:

> We have had a very melancholy affair happened in Norwich which has taken up the whole attention of the city for this fortnight past. Messrs Stannard & Taylor are broke for above 50 thousand pounds ... Many Families, Widows and Orphans will suffer prodigiously by [it].[56]

Bankruptcy on this scale was exceptional, and clearly there were firms of leading manufacturers, such as members of the Ives, Harvey and Patteson families, who did well in the four decades after the early 1750s. But the impression is that, in comparison with the West Riding and London, merchants who specialised in marketing but not in manufacturing cloth, Norwich master weavers struggled when they took on the burdens of overseas sales as well as of manufacture. Their resources were stretched, their product increasingly undercut by cottons and cheaper West Riding worsteds, their entrepreneurial drive somewhat weakened by close involvement in the political and cultural diversions of Norwich itself, distractions less evident in the textile centres of West Yorkshire.

When eighteenth-century political economists and pamphleteers came to reckon the national wealth of England, a central feature in their calculations was the size of the wool textile industries. Their zeal in making estimates, literally an academic version of sheep counting, is easy to understand. The manufacture of woollen and worsted cloth was by far the country's largest industry. Its exports accounted for no less than 70 per cent of all foreign trade in 1700.[57] The prosperity of the industry was vital to England's well being. Everyone understood this. Statistically, these commentators approached the question from three angles: the export of cloth (reasonably accurate figures, but providing few clues to the extent of the home trade); the number of sheep (a basis for estimates of the growth of the industry and necessary because the export of wool was absolutely prohibited); and the number of people employed in the industry (figures almost as variable as the number of sheep).[58] Arthur Young's estimates about the size of the Norwich industry in 1771 are a good example of the species and provide the best starting point for a brief discussion of its growth during the eighteenth century.[59]

Young was knowledgeable about trade and industry in East Anglia; he had served his apprenticeship as a merchant in King's Lynn and lived near Bury St Edmunds. He clearly talked to some leading manufacturers in Norwich before he wrote down his account. He gauged the size of the industry by making three calculations: estimating the export and inland trades via Yarmouth, London and other places (the most dubious method); adding up the annual returns of the city's manufacturers (presumably made available because trade was in the doldrums); and totting up the number of looms. He reckoned, presumably on good authority, that there were 12,000 looms which 'each ... employs six people in the whole'. These 72,000 people, ranging in every aspect of manufacture from scouring fleeces to packing bales of cloth, supposedly generated a total output valued at £1,200,000, a sum Young believed 'very near the truth'. It suggests that the output of the Norwich worsted industry was rather smaller than that of its Yorkshire counterpart, reckoned to be worth £1,404,000, which in turn was an estimated three-quarters of the county's woollen cloth industry.[60] In terms of value the Norwich industry was probably very similar to that of the west of England broadcloth manufacture. Young believed that output in Norwich had increased three times since 1700. This is certainly an exaggeration. More likely, it had doubled, since the number of looms had been somewhere in the region of 6000 in 1700.[61] In the early 1720s an eminent weaver of Norwich assured Daniel Defoe with a long 'Account ... Curious enough, and very exact' that the stuffs manufacture of Norwich and its region employed 120,000 people.[62] It is easy to read too much into such figures, and thereby to create periods that are both artificial and arbitrary. Three essential points do, however, emerge from them. The Norwich industry had flourished since the Restoration; it was the greatest employer in Norwich and, through spinning, across East Anglia. The city had enjoyed a century of industrial prosperity. Indeed, it was one of the three flourishing centres of the country's great wool textile industries. The third quarter of the eighteenth century marked its zenith.[63] Young had been told in 1771 that the twenty years after 1743 was its 'famous era'.

When John James came to write his magisterial *History of the Worsted Manufacture in England* (1857) he compared Norwich at its peak with Manchester in the 1850s.

> During the middle years of the eighteenth century the manufacturers of Norwich attained the greatest prosperity ... Between the years 1743 to that of 1763 Norwich reached the palmy, the highest state of its greatness as the 'chief seat of the chief manufacture of the realm'. Undoubtedly in these times it occupied ... the position of the present Manchester.[64]

James could have made no bolder claim on Norwich's behalf. Almost a century ago, Sir John Clapham wrote that the transference of the worsted industry from Norwich to the West Riding raised 'questions of fact and problems of causation of the first interest'.[65] Although a good deal has been written about the subject since, it still does. Let me begin with the easier half of the discourse Sir John suggests, before I speculate about the causes. Although the Norwich industry was in some difficulties after 1780, and 1792 was perhaps the last year of unalloyed prosperity, its decline, in comparison with the great Lancashire cotton industry, or indeed the West Riding worsted industry, after 1945, was protracted. But it was not a gradual, uniform erosion, relentless as it must have seemed at the time, for the periods of marked recession were punctuated by years of moderate revival, at least down to the 1850s. Undoubtedly, the French Wars (1793–1815) did incalculable damage to the Norwich industry. European markets were thoroughly dislocated. As early as March 1793, James Oakes wrote after a wasted journey from Bury to sell yarn, 'The trade of the City in the most distressed state I ever remember to have seen it'. In 1798 William Taylor reckoned the output of Norwich stuffs was no more than £800,000 a year and that the war had 'effectively ruined' the city's industry.[66] Taylor had his ear close to the ground in Norwich. Besides, other commentators corroborate his view. Sir Frederick Eden, a year earlier, was informed that 'Trade in Norwich has for some years been in a declining state', an opinion reiterated by Crutwell in 1801, who ascribed its causes to 'rivalship of the cotton branches and ... prohibition in foreign countries'.[67] Poor relief, always a sound indicator of the city's economy, burgeoned: in 1803 one in seven of its inhabitants was receiving payments.[68] Taylor's assessment of trade in 1812 was brutally succinct, 'the sunset of Norwich is arrived'.[69]

His prediction was a little premature. When peace at last came in 1815, there was optimism that trade in the city would revive. In the next decade this optimism was not entirely misplaced. There was an extraordinary surge in the city's population between the censuses of 1811 and 1821.[70] Many immigrants from the neighbouring countryside were seemingly attracted by prospects in the worsted industry. Certainly, new lines were introduced and old ones revived: shawls (embroidered, woven on the draw loom, and block printed), bombazines, 'modern', light mourning crêpes and silk gauzes. 1819 was a particularly brisk year, with as many as 10,000 looms at work in the Norwich area.[71] But beneath the surface optimism there were causes for deep concern. The European export trade for Norwich stuffs did not recover. This was a particular blow to the calimancoe and camblet trades which had been the pillars of production in Norwich. The former especially fell out of fashion, but even demand for the superbly dyed camblets, which draped so attractively and which had been so popular on the Continent before 1793, declined. In part, the camblet trade was sustained by orders from the East India Company to supply the Chinese market for Mandarin dress. But the years between 1811 and 1813 saw even this branch, which it was reckoned kept a tenth of the looms in Norwich busy, reach its peak.[72] Thereafter the monopoly of the East India Company was gradually eroded and finally suppressed in 1833. More worryingly, the Yorkshire industry, flourishing in Halifax and Bradford after 1800, seemed to undermine virtually every Norwich line – moreens, camblets, crêpes, damasks and other figured stuffs. Even the secret of dyeing bombazines a true black was given away to Yorkshire through 'the villainy of a confidential servant' of Messrs Stark, the most innovative firm of dyers in Norwich.[73] Whether cloth was manufactured in Halifax or Bradford, trade was captured by the most keenly priced competition as the quality of their goods, using superior machine-spun yarns and better dyeing and finishing techniques, improved. The Norwich industry was increasingly forced into the specialist market of articles for ladies' dress – shawls (Plate 13), challis and mourning goods, such as heavy bombazines and crêpe trimmings.

If a somewhat shaky recovery did take place in the decade after 1815, the Norwich industry undoubtedly underwent a protracted recession from late 1825 through to 1837. The national financial crisis of 1825–26 hit all manufacturing districts hard, none more than Norwich. 1826 was a terrible year in the city. Matters barely improved during the following decade. At the pit of the recession as few as 1500 looms were at work, and even when orders temporarily picked up underemployment was rife.[74] Most commentators reckoned that in the 1830s the average weaver was likely to be out of work for as long as three months in the year. Not surprisingly, labour relations were at a low ebb. The years between 1822 and 1829 saw constant attempts to reduce weaving rates in line with severe price falls generally. In the latter year a reduction of 20 per cent was generally enforced. Another stratagem which the Norwich manufacturers pursued, leading to riot and intimidation, was to put weaving out into the surrounding countryside (Wymondham became the chief centre with three hundred looms in 1838) to secure lower piece rates.[75] The real underlying cause of the Norwich industry's difficulties, however, was competition from Yorkshire. By 1835 it is estimated four-fifths of the British worsted industry was concentrated in the West Riding.[76]

A vivid insight into the plight of the Norwich industry at the end of this period of recession is provided in the reports of the Assistant Commissioners on Hand Loom Weavers.[77] Of course, the sorry condition of the hand-loom weavers was desperate everywhere in Britain in 1838, as the power loom in the cotton and, increasingly, in the worsted industry carried all before it after the mid 1820s. But the evidence presented from Norwich illustrates the peculiar difficulties of the stuffs industry. Both the commissioner and the manufacturers blamed the intransigence and 'violence' of the weavers and the deleterious effects of 'party spirit' which flared around every election to every office, however petty, in the city. But beneath this familiar, well-rehearsed rhetoric was a profound unease about the impact of machinery in Yorkshire undermining every general line of manufacture in Norwich. The statistical survey of weaving in the report highlighted both the decline of the industry and the response manufacturers had been forced to make.[78] There were now only 4054 looms in operation. Many of these (1648) were worked by women weaving, at cheap rates, light goods with a high silk content, such as the 500 looms weaving gauzes or the 727 producing challis. Indeed, in some cases the task had become so deskilled that 195 children were listed as weavers. Otherwise the traditional pattern of the industry remained much in evidence. There were still 3398 looms in weavers' houses, a mere 656 recorded in factories. Not quite all was gloom. At last in 1834 the Norwich Yarn Company (Samuel Bignold of the Norwich Union was its leading light) had established a yarn mill in the parish of St Edmund's, and a year after the hand-loom commission took its evidence in Norwich a large weaving factory at St James's with capacity for 1000 looms (Plate 14) was opened. Altogether there were eight textile factories (one cotton, three worsted, two woollen and two silk mills) employing 1285 persons and utilising 151 steam horsepower.

The next detailed snapshot of the industry was supplied by A. D. Bayne in 1852.[79] He was incensed that the Norwich industry had been ignored in publications about the Great Exhibition of 1851 while at the same time

Bradford's triumph was trumpeted abroad. Bayne made out a case that manufacture in Norwich had retained both its variety and vitality. He estimated that its annual value at £2 million, a sum probably 'under the mark', whilst maintaining that it still employed as many as 15,000 hands. Somehow he managed to turn a blind eye to the poor relief returns of the 1840s (in 1845, of the 2500 on out-relief in the city three-quarters were weavers),[80] or the awkward fact that the census returns of 1841 and 1851 listed no more than 5637 persons engaged in textile manufacture in the city. What might more plausibly have been argued was that the industry still maintained a steady state. Then, in the 1860s, a serious contraction set in. In 1869 Bayne reckoned that there were only 500 power looms at work 'when trade is good' and at least 500 hand-looms together producing goods valued annually at 'in round numbers £200,000'. Even this relentless optimist could only gloomily conclude the chapter on Textile Manufacturers in his long history of the city, 'We are sorry to state ... that the manufacture of textile fabrics in Norwich has for some time past been declining and cannot compare with former years'.[81]

Fashion was one explanation. The replacement of the crinoline by the bustle meant that short jackets ousted the shawl, and the gradual easing of rigid Victorian mourning customs hit the traditional bombazine and crêpe markets hard. Even in the early 1850s much of this had been forecast. The constant shift of fashion was dizzying. The old worsted goods disappeared, ones with cotton, silk, mohair and alpaca mixtures took their place. As White's *Directory* of 1864 put it,

> Many articles formerly made here entirely of worsted, are now not heard of, and new ones are introduced yearly, the manufacturers being constantly on the alert, either to anticipate changes of the public taste, or to copy, and if possible, to sell at a low price, some prevailing article of recent introduction.[82]

By 1870 this treadmill had become intolerable for the majority of manufacturers in Norwich. In 1901 there were only 1331 people (of whom around 85 per cent were female) engaged in textile manufacture, a mere 2.6 per cent of the city's working population. A few hand-loom weavers were still at work on the eve of the First World War; two silk manufacturers were recorded as late as 1937.[83] But contemporaries realised that the industry was dying in the third quarter of the nineteenth century. By 1861 boot and shoe manufacture had taken its place as the city's prime employer.[84] And in comparison with Bradford, in the forefront of those spinning, combing, weaving and dyeing innovations which transformed the industry after the 1830s, decline looked terminal even earlier. Any complacency was misplaced.

Providing a convincing analysis of the demise of Norwich stuffs, from leadership of the wool textile industries in the 1750s and 1760s – the Manchester of the eighteenth century in James's account – to the pitiable remnant Bayne described in 1869, is a task which has intrigued historians for a century and more. Whether they are looking at the question in terms of Britain's curious route to industrialisation, comparing rates of nineteenth-century urban growth, assessing its contribution to the debate about whether proto-industrialisation automatically led to vigorous, factory-based growth, or indeed studying the textiles themselves. From these different standpoints there has been little agreement about either chronology (or more precisely the date when decline set in) or causation.[85]

The chronology, bar interpretations of degree, now seems settled enough. Yet, however late we place the date for the industry's final demise, we must look much earlier for the causes of its eclipse. These must focus upon developments in the industry itself, rather than on locational factors or, a favourite with nineteenth-century writers, the obvious lack of coal, iron and water power in East Anglia. Sir John Clapham believed these issues to be important but not necessarily decisive. Recent historians would contest his assertions. They maintain that coal was not only vital in replacing the old organic energy economy by coal-fired steam power but also that its ready availability prompted a whole cluster of technical innovations in a variety of industries. Norwich, far from any coal fields, was at a marked disadvantage.[86]

Setting the important question of cheap coal supplies aside, other significant causes of the industry's problems after the 1780s appear to be disclosed in an account of its distinct development. We have seen that Norwich imported increasing quantities of yarn from Ireland, besides depending heavily upon those of a widely-defined East Anglian region. This was no problem so long as manufacturers could rely on supplies and compete in price and quality with their northern rivals. Yet, when the successful mechanisation of worsted spinning by the throstle (an adaptation of Arkwright's spinning frame) occurred in the 1800s, this key phase of industrialisation completely bypassed East Anglia and Ireland. Their great hand-spinning and combing networks collapsed with dire results for the economies of both. Machine-spun yarn was far more consistent in quality than the hand-spun hanks. After 1810 the Norwich manufacturers turned almost entirely to West Yorkshire for their supplies. When trade was busy, it was with cap in hand.[87] No effective attempt was made to manufacture machine-spun yarn locally before 1834. This was a fatal delay. The city had missed out on one of the key innovations in the mechanisation of the industry.

It also missed out on the second stage, the adoption of the power loom after 1825. The usual argument is that the complex Norwich weaves were unsuited to the early power looms. But the production of many plain worsteds was lost to Yorkshire in the 1820s and 1830s, where they were woven by power loom from the outset. Some hand combing was re-established in Norwich after 1834, but the great inventions of the late 1840s and 1850s, the last stage in the integrated machine production of worsteds, which fully mechanised the process, were completely centred upon Bradford.[88] From the late 1850s what yarn spinning there was in Norwich contracted sharply. Already, from the 1820s, the industry was increasingly driven into a narrow corner of the textile market – silks, shawls, mourning goods and the short-runs of high-fashion materials. Even here there was fierce competition from Paisley and from foreign silks after import duties were removed in 1825. Clapham concluded his celebrated essay on the transference of the industry from Norfolk to the West Riding with a final flourish of figures. Of the 850,000 spindles and 32,600 power looms at work in the English worsted industry in 1850, Norfolk possessed 19,216 and 428 respectively.[89] From the Norwich angle, it is a gloomy comparison.

Who was to blame for the failure to mechanise? The manufacturers held the weavers wholly responsible. Those who gave evidence to the Hand Loom Commission in 1838 were in no doubt that the failure to introduce the power loom in Norwich put them at an untenable commercial disadvantage.[90] The 20 per cent reduction of wages in 1829, after half-a-dozen years of attempts, was a central event. Several manufacturers suffered 'personal outrage' from the active Weavers' Union. One lost the sight of his eye when vitriol was thrown at him. Henry Willett, a leading shawl manufacturer, had had the windows and lower floors of his factory in Pottergate demolished in 1824 when he attempted to put work out into the countryside. Unabashed, five years later he had tried to introduce the power loom. He was stoned and only saved by the unlikely intervention of Prebendary Wodehouse, the cathedral's grandest canon, who stood robustly at the entrance to a narrow court to protect Willett, and from this vantage point 'addressed the people'. Certainly, in 1838 the commissioner, Dr Mitchell, believed it was the weavers' hostility to machinery which led to a failure to invest in the industry and to the loss of many lines to West Yorkshire. Contemporaries linked this reluctance to mechanise with the 'utterly amazing' extent of party spirit.[91] Every office in the city was contested, often with violence and always, it was maintained, with bribery. Far too much entrepreneurial effort was dissipated in the process. Since many weavers were amongst the city's freemen and members of parish vestries, the manufacturers who sought office were afraid to confront them on the issue of mechanisation. Mitchell believed it was the 'party spirit' which poisoned political life in Norwich and was doubtlessly the 'chief obstacle to the prosperity of the city'. Few in authority, however, appreciated the weavers' concerns – constant under employment, declining piece rates and the threat to their centuries old way of life which the power loom presented.

And what of capital? Was there a serious shortfall of enterprise and investment in the city? In terms of enterprise there is not a clear-cut answer, since, although there was a fatal delay in spinning and weaving, in hot pressing, dyeing and in the introduction of a constant stream of new cloths, there appears to have been no stem in the flow of innovations.[92] With investment the explanation is simpler. Many leading manufacturers took a rational decision as difficulties mounted in the industry, very sharply after 1793. Prominent merchants such as the Gurneys, John Patteson, John Morse and James Oakes in Bury St Edmunds were quick off the mark to move into banking and brewing. William Taylor persuaded his father, another leading export manufacturer, to withdraw his capital from the industry in 1791, when 'their joint property appeared adequate to afford them the comforts and even the elegancies of private life, and they retired from the cares of business to possess and secure to themselves these enjoyments'.[93] This exodus was numerous during the French Wars. According to the Norwich and London banker Hudson Gurney (1775–1861), writing in 1843, this 'higher class of men keeping up County and City Society' became 'a Race totally extinct ... these old merchant manufacturers ceased with the Decline of Norwich. Some of them became Squires and some became Bankrupts'.[94] He was clearly thinking of the city's three leading manufacturing families of the 1780s: the Ives, Harveys and Pattesons.[95] The new men who replaced them making bombazines (there were 156 bombazine manufacturers in 1824), shawls and crêpes were far less affluent, probably with difficulties in raising capital and securing credit networks.[96] Still less were they capable of exporting directly abroad. Increasingly they relied on a narrow niche of the domestic market. All this was in sharp contrast with the expansion of the West Riding worsted industry or Norwich stuffs a century earlier. Bayne wearily concluded in 1869, 'Norwich weavers have not the energy of those in Bradford'.[97] The region became a clear case of early deindustrialisation in the first half of the nineteenth century. Its famous stuffs manufacture did not provide the foundation of a major industrial region, a prediction which might just have easily been made about it in 1750 as for either the West Riding or South Lancashire.

10

Population, 1700–1950

Alan Armstrong

> Cold statistics only become vital and significant when brought into
> relation with other facts about life and work in Norwich.

C. B. Hawkins, *Norwich, A Social Study*, 1910[1]

Population history seeks to find patterns in a myriad of individual events
revolving round birth, marriage, sex, migration, illness and death. In order
to produce an intelligible account of developments in Norwich over two
and a half centuries it is convenient to divide them chronologically into the
eighteenth and early nineteenth centuries, the Victorian and Edwardian
era, and the four decades following the onset of the Great War in 1914.[2]

In the first period local enumerations and national censuses are used to
trace the extent and phasing of the city's growth. These and other sources
are brought to throw light on the time-honoured question of how far natural increases were promoted by falling death rates or, in accordance with
recent reappraisals of national changes, by rising birth rates. The second
era saw the accession of Queen Victoria coinciding with considerable
improvements in the sophistication of the censuses, and with the advent in
1837 of a comprehensive system of civil registration. The demographic
regime of Norwich during these years – extended, by convention, to 1914 –
was by no means set in stone, and we shall trace variations over time
and from the national experience. The decades after 1914 are commonly
seen as establishing a new demographic era, based on extended longevity
and on the full flowering of modern behavioural norms with regard to
procreation. Much interest attaches to the disturbances arising from two
world wars and to the effects of social policy measures on the welfare of
the people of Norwich.

Recent years have seen major advances in the analysis of national population trends, incorporating new methods of back projection from
nineteenth-century data (such as demographic forecasting in reverse) and
the application, to carefully selected parish registers, of the technique of

family reconstitution, originally pioneered in France.[3] These approaches are notoriously greedy of time and effort, and it has yet to be shown that they can be made to work in any town of significant size. What follows in this section is based upon contemporary estimates of total population, supplemented from 1801 by the national censuses; and on work carried out a generation ago on the aggregated record of baptisms and burials by J. K. Edwards and by Penelope Corfield, whose research findings have been the most authoritative guide to the demographic features of Norwich during the period.[4] Some adjustments, however, to their figures and commentaries are suggested in the light of later research findings which were not available at the time when their work was completed.

According to a local enumeration carried out in 1693 and calculations made two years later by the political arithmetician, Gregory King, the population of Norwich stood at 29,000 (give or take a few hundred) in the mid 1690s. It was the largest of English provincial cities by some margin. Half a century on, an apparently careful count compiled by William Anderton arrived at a population of 36,169, and a third, prompted by concern with problems of poor relief in 1786, showed the population to have reached 40,051.[5] So far, so good. The historians who have commented on these figures agree that most of the growth was concentrated within the walls with, as yet, little sign of expansion beyond these limits. We then run into differences of opinion. The next benchmark, that of the first official census in 1801, indicated a substantial fall to 36,854, though subsequent censuses suggested that this was halted by 1811 (37,256) and that subsequently Norwich showed rapid growth through 1811–21 (to reach 50,288) and 1821–31 (61,116 in the latter year). Edwards, the first author to appraise the figures, was sceptical of the completeness of the early censuses, that of 1801 especially, where he substituted a figure as high as 41,764 based upon a projection of earlier growth rates; and, with further adjustments to subsequent census figures, he proffered instead a smooth growth curve through 1786–1821.[6]

By contrast, Corfield maintained that there was insufficient evidence to support such drastic revisions: there was, she insisted, a strong case for a very real check to population growth in the 1790s when the onset of the French wars depressed the market for textile manufactures. Diminishing totals of both baptisms and burials, the existence of a high proportion of uninhabited houses in 1801 (747, or 4.3 per cent of the stock) and a marked rise in poor relief were consistent with a set-back to population growth. In the second decade of the nineteenth century, however, these adverse conditions were alleviated and Norwich enjoyed a boom reflected in a rapid rate of house construction, lasting until the late 1820s. Between 1811 and

1831 the aggregate population of a series of 'hamlets' adjacent to Norwich (Earlham, Eaton, Heigham, Hellesdon, Lakenham, Pockthorpe, Thorpe, Trowse) had increased by no fewer than 10,421 souls. Thus, the substantial population increases of Norwich in these two decades are seen by Corfield as entirely plausible. Yet, already by the late 1820s there were clear signs that growth was coming to a halt: for in 1831 no fewer than 1050 houses were recorded as uninhabited, a fourfold increase on the figure for 1821.[7]

In short, Corfield is of the view that throughout 1786–1831, population growth in Norwich, perhaps uniquely among large British towns, was decidedly erratic and should not be represented as a smooth upward trend. Her conclusions are adopted in Table 10.1, which consolidates the various figures given in this section and also takes advantage of correction factors for the early censuses, which were not available at the time she was writing.

Table 10.1 Revised Population of Norwich, 1695–1831

	Population
c. 1695	c. 29,000 (see text)
1752	36,169 (local enumeration)
1786	40,051 (local enumeration)
1801	38,502 (official census, x 1.0449)
1811	38,795 (official census, x 1.0413)
1821	51,645 (official census, x 1.0270)
1831	62,552 (official census, x 1.0235)

Sources: For 1695–1786, see text. Adjustment factors from 1801 are those proposed by Wrigley and Schofield for correcting national population totals to take account of under-registration of 0–4 year olds and the armed forces. See *Population History*, p. 595.

In the 1690s, according to Corfield's estimates, mortality in Norwich stood at 35.8 per thousand population, and at 35.7 in the 1740s, with children aged under ten accounting in 1750–51 for nearly half the burials and the infant (0–1) age group, alone, for 45 per cent.[8] Although the plague had made its final appearance in 1665–6, Norwich continued to be visited frequently by epidemic disease, notably smallpox. Particularly grim years, based on the Bills of Mortality, included 1680–81, 1710, 1728–29, 1737, 1741–42 and most notably 1747, which saw the highest total of burials in any single year in the eighteenth century (2065, a figure not reached again before the 1850s, by which time the city's population was twice that of the 1740s).[9] There is a suggestion in the returns, endorsed by both Corfield and Edwards, that years of high mortality bore some relationship to food shortages and high prices. The two authorities agree, however, that although the second half of the eighteenth century was by no means disease-free (there were further mortality peaks in 1764, 1770, 1773, 1776, 1781, 1786 and smallpox attacks in 1805, 1807 and 1819), none of these outbreaks occurred on the same scale as hitherto, and that their relationship to dearths became weaker.[10]

While year by year fluctuations in mortality continue to attract interest from both an academic and the 'human interest' angle, arguably more significance attaches to the trend of death rates over time. Until a few years ago, it was presumed that the principal motor of British population growth in the century following 1750 was a fall in mortality rates, and the contributions of Edwards and Corfield lean strongly towards this view, which was conventional at the time they were writing. Using the bills of mortality and relating these to his adjusted population figures (see above), Edwards discerned a linear fall in the burial rate, from 34.2 (1751–60) to 18.6 (1821–30).[11] Corfield noticed that averages drawn from the Bills could mislead, in that they covered only the area over which the jurisdiction of the corporation ran, meaning, to all intents and purposes, the intra-mural parishes. From the 1780s she preferred the information gathered in the parish register abstracts, published alongside the 1801 and subsequent censuses – which was drawn from a slightly wider range of registers and, in principle, came closer to embracing the whole of Norwich. However, her burial rates showed the same favourable trend as those of Edwards, albeit to a lesser extent, as follows: 34.3 (1750–59), 30.0 (1780–89), 28.9 (1790–99), 26.3 (1800–9), 22.5 (1810–19) and 23.1 (1820–29).[12]

Both authorities, it will be appreciated, relied on data originating at the parish level, which has long been suspected of increasing deficiencies arising from a variety of causes, including haphazard record-keeping, the use of private, non-Anglican burial grounds and the omission of entries for the dissenting population – one that was very considerable in Norwich.[13] Unfortunately, no local multipliers to compensate for these inadequacies and to convert burials into deaths can be calculated, but we can now invoke and apply a series of (national) correction factors calculated by Wrigley and Schofield which are likely to be minima so far as Norwich is concerned; and also present their English mortality rates for comparative purposes (Table 10.2).

The chief observations to be made are that – as would be expected – Norwich death rates exceeded the national level throughout; and that, on the basis on these figures, it is probable that Edwards (especially) and Corfield

Table 10.2 Revised estimates of Norwich mortality rates in the eighteenth and early nineteenth centuries

	(1) Bills of Mortality	(2) Parish Register Abstract	(3) England
1707–11	38.0		26.6
1728–32	38.4		36.9
1750–54	37.7		25.9
1784–88		33.7	27.0
1799–1803		32.8	27.1
1809–13		30.9	25.5
1819–23		31.4	24.1
1829–33		26.2	22.0

Sources: Bills of Mortality as given in Edwards, 'Norwich Bills', pp. 110–12; Parish Register Abstracts, 1801–31; and, for England, Wrigley and Schofield, *Population History*, pp. 139, 533–4.

Notes: i Base populations in these calculations are as follows: 1710 and 1730, estimates by Corfield, 'Norwich 1650–1850', p. 33; 1752, local enumeration. In each of these cases, because the Bills are used, deductions have been made for the extramural hamlets (7.2 per cent). From 1784–88, no such subtractions are made. All census data, from 1801, are inflated by the factors given in Table 1.

ii Throughout, the numbers of Norwich burials are adjusted using the nearest available multipliers of Wrigley and Schofield, as reported in their *Population History*, p. 111, and (from 1771) as implied by their recent recalculations of numbers of deaths in Wrigley et al., *English Population History*, p. 530. The successive factors are as follows: 1.039 (1701–10); 1.051 (average of 1721–30 and 1731–40); 1.074 (1751–60); 1.123 (1781–91); 1.202 (average of 1791–1801 and 1801–11); 1.316 (average of 1801–11 and 1811–21); 1.364 (average of 1811–21 and 1821–31); 1.288 (average of 1821–31 and 1831–41).

exaggerated somewhat the extent of the fall in mortality in the years after 1750. Nevertheless, Table 10.2 confirms a moderate fall in the mortality rates of Norwich from the second half of the eighteenth century, interrupted only briefly about 1820, against the background of exceptional population growth since 1811 (see Table 10.1). The improvement was occasioned by factors which remain mostly conjectural. Edwards looked to the expansion of health facilities, inoculation against smallpox and some alleviation of the condition of the poor arising from improved relief practices.[14] For her part, Corfield had little time for environmental betterment, Norwich having inherited from earlier times a number of housing and sanitary problems in the old city centre and gaining some new ones in the unplanned districts of growth beyond the walls; it was thus, in the early nineteenth century, a 'crowded, smelly and insanitary city'. However, like Edwards, she was impressed by intermittent campaigns against smallpox through inoculation and, later, vaccination; and she also allowed a role for the argument that there may have been autonomous changes in the nature and ferocity of epidemic diseases. Moreover, although Norwich experienced problems arising from unplanned urban growth, it did not encounter simultaneously those associated with uncontrolled industrial development, i.e. there were no especially noxious or polluting industrial processes.[15]

Despite their name, the locally generated bills of mortality also included yearly totals of baptisms, while the parish register abstracts associated with the early censuses included retrospective annual baptism figures reaching back to 1780 (and each tenth year, as far as 1700) as well as yearly marriage totals from 1754. Arranging this information in decadal averages, Edwards was unimpressed by the marriage and baptismal rates of eighteenth century Norwich. If anything, they tended to decline during the second half of that century, showing signs of revival only after 1811 (marriages) and 1821 (baptisms).[16] Using the same source for the first half of the eighteenth century, Corfield noted that baptisms fluctuated less wildly than burials and calculated a baptismal rate of only 27.8 per thousand population for the 1740s. Transferring to evidence drawn from the parish register abstracts, she compiled rates running at about 24 from the 1780s to the 1810s, before rising in the 1820s to 33.6. This upward shift she was inclined to ascribe to a changing proportion of young adults in the population, arising from immigration, for the ratio of baptisms to marriages fluctuated only within narrow limits, at around three.[17] Thus, neither authority was inclined to put much weight on the contribution that rising fertility might have played in promoting the population growth of Norwich. In the light of more recent work on national population trends, especially that of Wrigley and Schofield, it is timely to reconsider this issue.[18]

As a first step, it is worth emphasising that marriage rates in Norwich were comparatively buoyant in the later eighteenth and early nineteenth centuries. Marriage totals are not considered to need much in the way of adjustment, and a five year average for the city centred on 1786 yields a rate at least equivalent to the English national average, now available from the work of Wrigley and Schofield (9.2 marriages per thousand population, against 9.0). Moreover, similar rates centred on 1801, 1811, 1821 and 1831 show both a rising trend and very significant higher rates in Norwich than for the English population at large.[19] For good measure, it can be added that at its peak (11.6 in 1819–23) the Norwich rate approached that attained in late eighteenth-century Nottingham (12–12.5) and was if anything rather higher than a comparable figure from Leeds (10.2 in 1796–1801).[20] In view of these findings, there is a strong presumption that the baptismal rates advanced by Edwards and by Corfield fall well short of the true birth rates applying to Norwich, a possibility that both acknowledged.

Once again, there is no basis upon which local multipliers can be calculated, but we can turn to the national inflators used by Wrigley and Schofield to move from baptisms to births. Table 10.3 presents the results of this exercise, together with national birth rates for comparison. The national rates, it will be seen, show a consistent upward trend until 1829–33. Those of Norwich, down to 1784–88, show no such linear progression and their variability is likely to have been influenced by migration flows and by the economic conditions prevailing in the several quinquennial sub-periods taken. Thereafter, the modest reduction in the birth rate featured in 1799–1803 is consistent with Corfield's assessment of the local economic situation during the war years, although a distinct recovery followed by 1809–13, and in 1819–23 the Norwich birth rate actually outpaced the still ascending national rate.

Thus the quite substantial multipliers adduced here – which, if anything, may be insufficient to connect Norwich baptisms fully – have the effect of lifting aggregate births considerably and, by implication, the contribution made by higher levels of fertility to the increasing population of Norwich.[21] The point can be made quite simply. If, between the mid 1780s and the early 1820s the population of Norwich rose by about 29 per cent (Table 10.1), the absolute number of deaths rose by 2 per cent and births by some 60 per cent (as is the case using the adjusted figures), it is probable that, after all, a rising birth rate played a more significant role than Edwards and Corfield allowed, at least in the later eighteenth and early nineteenth centuries. To what extent births were boosted by increases in illegitimacy, and how far they were generated chiefly by a downward shift in the age at marriage and by a rise in the proportions ever-marrying – as Wrigley and Schofield show was the case nationally[22] – are matters which still await research in the case of Norwich.

From Tables 10.2 and 10.3, it appears likely that the contribution made by falling death rates, or rising birth rates, varied at different stages of the city's chequered population history between the 1690s and the 1820s. Uncertainties in the figures, however, should not be allowed to obscure a transformation of the urban demographic landscape during the course of the eighteenth century. Whereas towns had hitherto tended to experience more burials than baptisms, and were thus dependant upon streams of

Table 10.3 Revised estimates of Norwich fertility rates in the eighteenth
and early nineteenth centuries

	(1) Bills of Mortality	(2) Parish Register Abstracts	(3) England
1707–11	35.2		29.1
1728–32	32.6		32.3
1750–54	39.2		33.9
1784–88		36.9	37.5
1799–1803		35.1	37.7
1809–13		40.1	39.5
1819–23		47.1	40.7
1829–33		38.6	35.7

Sources: Norwich Bills of Morality, as given in Edwards, 'Norwich Bills', pp. 110–12;
Parish Register Abstracts, 1801–31; and, for England, Wrigley and Schofield, *Population History*. pp. 138, 533–4.

Notes: i Base populations are as outlined in Table 2, note i.

ii Throughout, Norwich baptism totals are adjusted using the nearest available
multipliers of Wrigley and Schofield, as reported in their *Population History*, p. 140
and (from 1771) as implied by their recent recalculations of the numbers of births
in Wrigley et al., *English Population History*, pp. 528, 530. The successive factors are
as follows: 1.099 (1701–10); 1.141 (average of 1721–30 and 1731–40); 1.143 (1751–60);
1.204 (1781–91); 1.279 (average of 1791–1801 and 1801–11); 1.367 (average of 1801–11
and 1811–21); 1.420 (average of 1811–21 and 1821–31); and 1.391 (average of 1821–31
and 1831–41).

immigrants to replenish or augment their populations, a novel situation
now arose whereby baptisms normally exceeded burials, that is towns
began to generate their own natural increases. Some well-documented
cases included York, Exeter, Nottingham and Leeds; and Norwich was no
exception.[23]

There is, however, some scope for debate as to the timing of the change.
Relying on unadjusted data from the bills of mortality, Edwards delayed
the crossing of the divide until the beginning of the nineteenth century,
from 1802 on.[24] Corfield, however, gave the matter much closer attention.
Using the same source (the bills), she noted that in all but nine of the years
1707–50, burials exceeded baptisms and on the average they did so in every
decade between 1720 and 1750. But her use of the parish register abstracts
for the later years has the effect of placing the watershed some twenty years

before Edwards supposed, that is, in the 1780s.[25] Indeed, there is some reason to believe it may have occurred even earlier. If we examine the adjusted absolute numbers of births and deaths which underpin the quinquennial averages in Tables 10.2 and 10.3, a surplus of births over deaths was apparent even in 1750–54, although of course we cannot assume that it was yet a regular feature. At all events, it is clear that by the time rapid population growth was in train in 1811–21, a regime very different from that obtaining in the seventeenth and early eighteenth centuries had emerged. Henceforth immigration would do more than replenish numbers and, to a greater extent than ever before, be a factor tending to swell them. The achievement of surpluses of births over deaths did not, however, mean that Norwich was capable of holding such increases in their entirety. If Corfield's suggestions are correct, some losses had already occurred in the depressed years of the 1790s;[26] and, as we shall see, nineteenth-century Norwich frequently tended to lose substantial fractions of its natural increases, so calculated.

The new system of civil registration that commenced in 1838 was not without its flaws. In particular, the returns of births, in the early years, were quite seriously deficient. Even at its worst, however, the civil system was 'far superior to its predecessor in every respect' and the case for introducing correction factors is nowhere near so compelling because, over time, the efficiency of the system undoubtedly improved.[27] In the case of Norwich, the civil returns are easy to use, on account of the neat coincidence between the boundaries of the post-1835 municipal borough, the poor law union and the registration district.[28] Our starting point will be a brief analysis of the situation in the late 1830s and 1840s.

Following a disappointing decade of economic recession and population stagnation in 1831–41, when the population grew by only 5 per cent, there were signs of renewed growth in the decade that followed, though it was modest by national standards (9.5 per cent against 12.7 for England and Wales). Through 1841–50 a total of 17,375 births was recorded for Norwich, a figure which, related to the population at risk (mean of 1841 and 1851), yields a rate of 27.8, somewhat below that of England and Wales (32.6). In neither case were the high birth rates characteristic of the second and third decades of the nineteenth century fully sustained, but at Norwich the retraction was particularly marked. The low level of the Norwich birth rate in 1841–50 is, however, somewhat puzzling in view of the fact that the city's nuptiality, also established from early civil registration data, was still comparatively buoyant, amounting in 1839–43 to 9.0 marriages per thousand population and 10.4 in 1849–53 – rates which ran at nearly one-fifth above national levels and one-third higher than those prevalent in the rural parts of Norfolk. Part of the explanation may lie in differentials in the efficiency of birth registration; while the recording of births was defective across the board, the shortfall may have been especially marked at Norwich. In the early Victorian period, however, the Registrar General was not much interested in questions of human fertility or in pursuing local peculiarities; rather his attention was given over to tracing, in ever-increasing detail, mortality variations and their environmental causes.

Norwich in the 1840s was much investigated, by the Health of Towns Commission (1844–45), in the famous *Morning Chronicle* reports of 1849, and in William Lee's *Report to the General Board of Health [on] the Sanitary Conditions of the Inhabitants of the City of Norwich* (1851). All found much to criticise, noting the city's crowded courts and lanes, inefficient scavenging, want of drainage, a dirty and insufficient water supply, and the state of burial grounds and lodging houses.[29] Reflecting these conditions, Norwich remained vulnerable to outbreaks of disease resulting in noticeable fluctuations in deaths. A major outbreak of smallpox in 1839 produced 418 deaths in the city, while the same cause accounted in 1845 for 233 predominantly young persons and was blamed, along with the fate of others who were 'blinded, maimed or deformed for life', on 'the negligence of the parents in the application of the protection discovered by Jenner'.[30]

Cholera accounted for 129 deaths in 1832, although fortunately the city escaped comparatively lightly in 1849, occasioning a service of thanksgiving in the cathedral for its deliverance. From such evidence, it is easy to infer that early Victorian Norwich was a hotbed of squalor, disease and premature mortality. Indeed, the years 1838–44 featured a male death rate of 26.9 and for females, 23.1 (weighted average, 24.8). This suggested only a negligible, if any, improvement in Norwich mortality since 1829–33 (see Table 10.2), The city's mortality was significantly higher than the comparable rates for rural Norfolk (19.7) and the nation at large (21.4), with 29 per cent of male babies, and 19 per cent of females, still failing to reach their first birthdays. On the other hand, it should be emphasised that the annual mortality fluctuations were nowhere near so dramatic as in the seventeenth and early eighteenth centuries, and that the Norwich death rates were by no means exceptionally high in comparison to the largest towns of the time.[31]

Such were the main demographic characteristics of Norwich in the years following the accession of Queen Victoria. By the end of her reign, and even more decisively by the close of what historians commonly refer to as the long nineteenth century much was to change, and on the whole for the better. Table 10.4 illustrates the movement of mortality rates from 1851–55,

Table 10.4 Crude death and infant mortality rates,
from the mid nineteenth century to 1905–10

	(1) Norwich Rates	(2) Ratio to Norwich: England and Wales	(3) Ratio to Norwich, rate in 1851–5
Crude death rates (deaths per 1000 population)			
1851–55	25.3	111	100
1856–60	24.2	111	96
1861–65	24.8	110	98
1866–70	23.7	106	94
1871–75	24.2	110	96
1876–80	22.5	108	89
1881–85	20.0	103	79
1886–90	19.8	105	78
1891–95	19.4	104	77
1896–1900	18.2	103	72
1901–05	17.2	107	68
1906–10	15.2	103	60
Infant mortality rate (deaths per 1000 live births)			
1851–55	205	131	100
1856–60	190	127	93
1861–65	192	127	94
1866–70	184	117	90
1871–75	194	127	95
1876–80	183	127	89
1881–85	158	114	77
1886–90	161	115	79
1891–95	180	122	88
1896–1900	182	117	89
1901–05	171	124	83
1906–10	127	109	62

Source: Armstrong, Population, pp. 49, 55.

and Table 10.5, the course of the birth rates. Behind the variations in these statistical determinants of population change lay a wide range of influences and it is advisable to pursue each development in turn.

In the wake of the plethora of sanitary reports in the 1840s, there were some modest attempts at environmental betterment. In the early 1850s, parliamentary sanction was given to a bill to create a new water company drawing on the Wensum above its more notoriously polluted stretches. Approximately one-sixth of the city's houses had acquired water closets by 1864, and in 1867 an Act for the Better Sewering of Norwich was passed and partly implemented by 1871. There was, however, considerable opposition to undue expense and what was achieved was far from revolutionary. The early water closets discharged straight into the Wensum, and the new sewers of 1871 were inadequate in design and in construction materials.[32]

Epidemic diseases continued to make their mark. The cholera resurfaced in 1853–54 (193 deaths, half of all those occurring in Norfolk), while among infants and small children measles and scarlet fever appeared on several occasions. Norwich was regarded by the Registrar General as one of a number of places of moderate size which were 'conspicuous for their summer insalubrity', showing increases in deaths from diarrhoea during particularly hot summers, such as 1857, 1868 and 1870. The city's infant mortality rate, running substantially higher than that of Portsmouth, or even London, was held to reflect 'much ignorance ... among the poor classes as to the proper way of bringing up infants'.[33] Not surprisingly, the overall death rate of Norwich improved only very slightly by the early 1870s (Table 10.4), a conclusion that echoes recent research on urban mortality trends in general, which detects little or no improvement in the third quarter of the nineteenth century.[34]

From the later 1870s, however, definite progress was made in the reduction of mortality rates. At Norwich, there was a fall of over one-third in general mortality (if the crude rates of 1871–75 and 1905–10 are compared), which mirrored and even exceeded slightly the concurrent diminution in the national rates (Table 10.4). Infant mortality – a major statistical component of the total death rate – showed clear signs of decline through the 1880s but rose again in the 1890s before resuming its downward path, especially after 1905. Close inspection of the causes of death in these years shows the final disappearance of smallpox (the last incident was an outbreak among prisoners in Norwich castle in 1876) and typhus; and a perceptible diminution in deaths from typhoid, scarlet fever and tuberculosis. Although other diseases demonstrated few if any signs of decline (measles, diphtheria) and cancer fatalities tended to rise, overall the expectation of life at birth in Norwich definitely increased, showing a significant gain of seven years if data from 1861–71 and 1891–1900 are compared.[35]

Historians have no difficulty in identifying the various influences that lay behind these national and local improvements. Where they differ is over their relative significance. Reacting against a tendency to attribute too much to the role of the medical profession and hospitals, Thomas

McKeown has expressed strong doubts as to their impact upon national mortality rates, given the limitations in their expertise and armoury of techniques.[36] On the local level, the researches of Michael Muncaster and Steven Cherry tend to endorse this view, the latter drawing attention particularly to the pressures which the Norfolk and Norwich hospital encountered by the 1870s. In-patient mortality rates were not improving in the later nineteenth century, and, although this and other institutions were treating rapidly increasing numbers of out-patients, and the city's small army of doctors doubtless offered sound advice regarding rest, or lifestyles, it is improbable that medical intervention was a major determinant of the downward course of mortality in the late nineteenth century.[37]

Another view is that the decline should be attributed chiefly to improvements in the quantity and quality of food available. Economic historians have long been aware that, from the mid 1870s to the mid 1890s, there were very significant increases in real if not money wages, enabling the purchase of more and a wider range of foodstuffs, including meat, fish, eggs, butter, and so forth. To be sure, Norwich was and remained a low wage city, by contemporary standards. In 1886 the hourly wage rates of building workers were exceeded in a large number of provincial towns and cities, among them Birmingham, Cardiff, Dover, Leicester, Nottingham and Oxford, as well as a string of northern towns; and Hawkins, writing in 1908, laid much stress on the existence in the city of a sub-stratum of the male population which depended heavily on casual work in the cattle market and on building sites.[38] On the other hand, the city was not vulnerable to cyclical fluctuations to the same extent as export-led towns, and it offered a good deal of work for women, thereby supplementing family incomes. Above all, unless it can be shown that money wages were actually falling in the later nineteenth century – and no one has suggested this – consumers in Norwich, as elsewhere, can scarcely have failed to benefit from the fall in the cost of basic foodstuffs at that time, with most of the benefit, in all likelihood, accruing to older children and to adults. Again, however, this is only a partial explanation, for the growth of real wages was checked after 1900 – almost certainly in Norwich as in the nation at large – yet mortality rates continued to decline.

This leaves us with environmental improvements, chiefly in the field of public health, an explanation that recently has been much favoured among historians. At Norwich, new housing from 1858 was subject to by-laws which regulated minimum dimensions and also – by insisting on open spaces behind new dwellings – effectively forbade the creation of any more back-to-backs. The first tentative attempts to engage in slum clearance, in the benighted parish of St Paul's, date from the 1870s; and water supply and sewage arrangements were gradually improved.[39] A national system of urban and rural sanitary districts came into being as a consequence of the Public Health Acts of 1872 and 1875, and Norwich appointed, for the first time, a medical officer of health. His reports are a rich source of information, permitting year by year monitoring of public intervention, and incorporating details of the activities of his colleagues, the public analyst and the sanitary officer. Thus, vaccination was accounted well looked after by 1875; the notification of infectious diseases was reckoned almost complete by 1885; and inspections of foodstuffs revealed a gradually improving situation, especially with milk, for by 1905 only one in five samples were condemned.

Although as late as 1893 one quarter of the city's population still depended on wells for water, only three years later 84 per cent enjoyed piped supplies, and 98 per cent by 1906. In 1893 fewer than 5000 houses had water closets, the majority still depending on bins and privies, but a transformation in this respect was effected by 1914 when 96 per cent of houses possessed water closets. In short, Norwich was becoming a much cleaner, more hygienic place; and, in a further manifestation of municipal initiative characteristic of the times, the appointment of two lady health visitors, Miss Hatton and Miss Stevens, in 1906 surely had a direct influence in helping at last to bring down infant mortality rates. In 1907 they paid over 10,000 visits, especially targeting mothers with young children, and seeking to get bad feeding practices substituted by better. A little later, in 1909, two more ladies were appointed, and visits ran to over 17,000 in 1914. Most confinements were, by now, handled by nine registered midwives, who by 1908 may have managed up to 60 per cent, in addition to those attended by doctors.[40]

To be sure, there remained much to be done. By present-day standards, mortality rates were extremely high, and the infant death rate especially remained vulnerable to extreme climatic conditions, such as occurred in the blazing summer of 1911 when it soared nationally and locally, reaching 135 in Norwich. All the same, we should not be distracted from taking a longer view. Owing to a concatenation of favourable circumstances, death rates had fallen very significantly since the 1870s, and expectation of life at birth had advanced to reach 51.6 years for males, 57.1 for females, by 1911–12. What this meant was that a young male, having survived to fifteen, could expect another fifty years, in round terms, and his female counterpart, fifty-four.[41]

Norwich marriage rates in the 1850s remained brisk, still running at a level higher than in the nation at large and much higher than in the surrounding rural districts. For the first time, using data on the proportions ever-married from the increasingly sophisticated census returns after

1851, we are able to calculate the mean age at first marriage which, for 1861, yields a figure of 24.9 for males, 25.2 for females; and for 1871, 25.0 and 25.3.[42] This suggests a somewhat unusual feature: Norwich males tended to marry over a year younger than men in the nation at large, and females a shade later. Moreover, the proportion of Norwich females ultimately marrying was distinctly lower than in the nation at large, or in rural Norfolk. Such differences are in part explicable in terms of a skewed sex ratio, which enhanced the marriage chances of males and reduced those of females. This much was fact. We can also surmise that the availability of paid work for females in Norwich, in factories and in the home, acted as a positive incentive to young men to offer marriage; and possibly conferred a modicum of independence that would limit enthusiasm for early marriage among Norwich women.[43]

In the later nineteenth century, the national age at first marriage rose by about a year, to 27.7 (males) and 26.3 (females) by 1911. This was mirrored at Norwich, where the average age of males at first marriage advanced by over two years between 1871 and 1911, and among females by some seventeen months, to reach 27.3 and 26.7 respectively. These developments are usually linked by historians to the defence of living standards and the Victorian quest for respectability; however, delayed marriage was not the only avenue for pursuing these goals for there was also, eventually, a noteworthy decline in birth rates, to which subject we turn next.

Table 10.5 gives a comprehensive view, based on a series of measures. The crude rate of fertility recorded for 1859–63 (33.8) suggests a recovery from the level quoted for the 1840s, though this may be due in part simply to improved registration of births. It was stable until the 1880s and then embarked on a decline which broadly matched the national downshift until 1899–1903, and thereafter began to exceed it. Much the same pattern holds for the general fertility rate, which makes allowance for variations in the age-sex composition, Norwich having a relative abundance of females aged fifteen to forty-four. Most interest, perhaps, attaches to the other aspects of Table 10.5. Norfolk in general had become notorious for its high incidence of illegitimate births, and the rate ruling in the city, though a little lower than in the countryside, still stood well above the national norm in the mid nineteenth century.[44] It was set on a declining trend, however, falling two-thirds in just fifty years, by 1911–13. In explanation of this tendency, which was universal, it has been suggested that the social norms governing the degree of intimacy between partners before the marriage ceremony were gradually changing. Moreover, an increased appreciation of the value of legalised marriage may have led to a decline in consensual unions and also affected the intensity of sexual activity during courtship.[45]

Yet, after all, most births occurred in the context of marriage, and the section of Table 5 that covers marital fertility is particularly important.

Table 10.5 Fertility from the mid nineteenth century to 1911–13

	(1) Norwich Rates	(2) Ratio, Norwich: England and Wales	(3) Ratio to Norwich, Rate in 1859–63
Crude fertility rate (births per 1000 population)			
1859–63	33.8	97	100
1869–73	33.2	94	98
1879–83	33.9	100	100
1889–93	31.5	102	93
1899–1903	28.8	100	85
1911–13	22.3	91	66
General fertility rate (births per 1000 females aged 15–44)			
1859–63	131	88	100
1869–73	135	88	103
1879–83	139	94	106
1889–93	128	98	98
1899–1903	111	97	85
1911–13	87	89	66
Illegitimate fertility rate (illegitimate births per 1000 unmarried or widowed females aged 15–44)			
1859–63	26.1	139	100
1869–73	21.6	129	83
1879–83	19.5	138	75
1889–93	13.1	125	50
1899–1903	9.6	113	37
1911–13	8.7	109	33
Marital fertility rate (legitimate births per 1000 married women aged 15–44)			
1859–63	251	89	100
1869–73	266	91	106
1879–83	278	97	111
1889–93	260	98	104
1899–1903	231	98	92
1911–13	185	94	74

Source: Armstrong, Population, pp. 107, 117.

Norwich fertility rates of 1859–63 and 1869–73 stood marginally below national levels, and one is tempted to surmise that the rather numerous female factory workers of the city, like their counterparts in places such as Keighley and Bradford in Yorkshire, sought to space out their pregnancies in order to keep in employment and conserve their strengths.[46] Over time there was no noticeable change before the 1890s when a sudden fall set in; one, moreover, that was greater than could possibly be accounted for in terms of the trend to later marriages. Ultimately, it was changes in procreative behaviour within marriage that contributed most to the reduction of birth rates in Norwich, as in the nation at large.

Since so little can be said with certainty about the techniques involved in deliberate family limitation, the attention of scholars has tended to be given over to finding underlying explanations for this major change (or at least the beginnings of it) in human reproductivity. These include arguments from demographic necessity (parents were reacting to falling infant and child mortality); economic considerations, mediated through enhanced aspirations, initially among the 'middle classes'; a vast range of ill-defined social factors including a rise in the status of women, and the declining hold of religion; reduced opportunities for children to earn incomes as longer periods of schooling became established; greater literacy; and last, but not least, the way in which desirable careers were becoming increasingly meritocratic in their pattern of recruitment, inducing among professional parents a disposition to plan their families accordingly.[47]

We may be sure that there was no single, master-cause at work, and that the blend of influences varied over time, and between different localities. No doubt all or most of these factors affected patterns of procreation in Norwich, but because it is difficult with the sources currently available to identify *which* couples were limiting their fertility, the range of suggestions that can be made about the progress of birth control in Norwich is decidedly narrow. It is clear that neither the city nor the county were in the vanguard of change, but neither did they lag much behind the national trend. It is also striking that sophisticated Norwich, with an above average proportion of professionals and low numbers of labourers (that is, in comparison to rural Norfolk), did not give a lead to the country districts. From the 1880s marital fertility fell by as much in rural Norfolk as in the city, and illegitimate births to nearly the same extent.[48] However, this is less than surprising in the light of recent work on the European experience generally, for it has been remarked that:

> if urban and rural people within regions exhibited similar fertility behaviour
> it is partly because these were the *same people*, part of the same regional

network of economic opportunities and constraints, a system of shared
knowledge and ramifying kinship networks ... given that kin and friends
spanned rural and urban areas, cities and their hinterlands, we can expect that
urban and rural people would exhibit similar fertility behaviours.[49]

It would scarcely be possible to find a better illustration than that of Norwich and Norfolk, given that, as late as 1911, no fewer than 86 per cent of
the population of the city had been born within the county.

The continued capacity of Norwich to generate substantial natural
increases is clear from a comparison of the birth and death rates given in
Tables 10.4 and 10.5. In the early Victorian years, despite the problems
besetting the city, its natural increases were augmented by net immigration
to the tune of 4.5 thousand in 1841–51 and 890 in the ensuing decade.[50] Very
probably this was an inflow of poor people from the surrounding countryside, whose conditions at this juncture were dire and who were looking
to the city's more generous relief provision.[51] Otherwise, only in the 1880s
did the city succeed in making a small net gain by migration. More often,
that is in the majority of inter-censal decades, Norwich lost some part of
its successive natural increases; by 1891–1900 and 1901–11, some 2000 per
decade, or approximately one-fifth of the surpluses of births over deaths.[52]
To some extent these losses reflected only 'leakage' across the city boundary into neighbouring villages, although this type of suburban colonisation
was not extensive around Norwich at this time. Quite commonly, however,
longer distance moves were implied. Most Norwich adults of 1911 would
remember siblings and childhood friends who had moved away to London,
the northern towns and coalfields, or crossed the oceans in their search for
betterment.[53] On the other hand, although the city no doubt continued to
draw in immigrants from local sources, it did not attract influxes from further afield. Consequently, as we have just seen, the Norfolkness of Norwich
remained very pronounced.

Finally, the outcome of the interplay of the vital rates and these migra-
tory propensities is summed up in Table 10.6. By 1911 Norwich accounted
for virtually one-quarter of the entire population of Norfolk (24.3 per cent,
as against 14.9 per cent in 1841), and people of a certain age – say, seventy
– would have witnessed approximately a doubling of the population during their lifetimes. Growth on this scale was, indeed, much greater than
had at one time seemed likely. In an era of spectacular urban population
expansion, however, it did not save Norwich from falling back from ninth
position in the hierarchy of British towns in 1831 to thirtieth in 1911.[54]

The coming of the Great War brought extensive movements of population and the system of civil registration was driven to various expedients

Table 10.6 Growth of the population of Norwich, 1841–1911

	Norwich (000)	Percentage growth since previous census	England and Wales
1841	62.3	2.0	14.5
1851	68.2	9.5	12.7
1861	74.9	9.8	11.9
1871	80.4	7.3	13.2
1881	87.8	9.2	14.4
1891	101.0	15.0	11.8
1901	111.7	10.6	12.1
1911	121.5	8.8	10.9
Overall increase (1841–1911)	59.2	95.0	126.7

Source: Armstrong, Population, pp. 5, 7.

in order to monitor the situation.[55] Local population estimates depended upon data generated by the National Registration Acts of 1915 and 1916 and these were used to arrive at two base figures, year by year. Death rates were quoted in relation to civilian populations only, but birth rates were related to total populations because, as the Registrar General put it, 'married men in the services who are given occasional home leave remain an effective element in the population, so far as the birth rate is concerned'.[56] The evolving situation in war-time Norwich can be summed up as follows. There was a huge increase in marriages in 1915, of no less than 59 per cent compared to 1914, though this later tailed off rapidly. Birth rates were upheld to the 1914 level (20.5) for a couple of years, then saw quite a sharp fall to 15.9 in 1917 and 1918, despite a modest increase in the number of illegitimate births, which by 1918 accounted for 9.8 per cent.

Meanwhile, concern over venereal disease was voiced in the medical officer's annual reports, the Norfolk and Norwich Hospital handling 511 cases by 1919. More happily, although there were signs of increasing mortality from tuberculosis, the general death rate among the civilian population showed no tendency to increase, which was probably due, locally as well as nationally, to the effects of fuller employment (including that of women), and higher real wages, influencing standards of nutrition. War-time meals may have been starchier and less appetising but, apart from a decline in sugar consumption, pre-war calorific levels were upheld. The influenza pandemic of 1918, extending into 1919, certainly affected Norwich, accounting for a total of 429 deaths in these years; however, principally because of its world-wide character, it is not now reckoned to have been related to any deterioration in civilian living standards.

Most strikingly, in Britain at large the mortality of infants continued to decline, a feature unique among the combatant nations. This reflected a drive to provide better health care for mothers and infants, involving the provision of ante- and post-natal care in a context where, as the Bishop of London observed, 'The loss of life in this war had made every baby's life doubly precious'. Other factors deemed to have played a role include a decline in parental alcoholism and the increased use of condensed and dried milk (less likely to carry the tubercle bacillus), followed later in the war by the rationing of fresh supplies, thereby ensuring regular quotas to families.[57] These are 'national' explanations, but presumably all were at work in Norwich, where the activities of the health visitors, monitored in the medical officer's reports, continued to expand, reaching 19,550 visits or revisits in 1919. The outcome in respect of infant mortality was a pro- nounced if somewhat erratic fall, moving from 115 per thousand live births (average of 1914–15) to ninety-six (the lowest figure ever recorded) in 1916, and eventually to eighty-four (1919).

Another substantial leap in marriages occurred in the immediate after- math of the war, as demobilisation took place. At Norwich, the average number for 1919 and 1920 was 1,303 (against 927 in 1917 and 1918) and the birth rate rose briskly, peaking in 1920 at 26 per thousand population. But a fuller assessment of the outcome of these dramatic years could not be made until the publication of the results of the 1921 census. It was then revealed that the total population of the county borough, despite regular surpluses of births over deaths, had declined by 829 souls (0.7 per cent) since 1911. In part this reflected the deaths on active service of no fewer than 3544 Norwich males, a figure equivalent to 15.8 per cent of the male age group of fifteen to thirty-nine in 1911. Among the consequences of this loss, the same census showed, over 2500 Norwich children aged 0–14 (8.3 per cent) were fatherless, while, in the age-range of twenty-one to thirty, the surplus of females – always a marked characteristic of the city – now reached one-third, thereby limiting the marriage prospects of a generation of young women.[58]

After the flurry of marriages in 1919–20, and of births in 1920–21, fertility in the inter-war years resumed its tendency to decline. The average birth rate for 1922–30 was 17.4, and for 1931–39, 13.9. Within these figures, the proportion of all births that were illegitimate was fairly steady, at about one in twenty; a little above the national average, but now only marginally so.

With the absolute numbers of marriages fairly steady through 1923–39 (varying between 1022 and 1178), the implication is that the control of births within marriage continued to gather pace in Norwich, as indeed it did nationally. This owed nothing to official encouragement, for little was done to promote contraception. While advice and information on the topic was obtainable from 2–4 p. m. on Thursdays at the city's maternity home, it was confined to married women and then only to cases where there were medical grounds for deciding that further pregnancies would be detrimental to their health. According to the medical officer of health, Victor Soothill, only four women made an appearance in 1934 and, in 1935, even after the dropping of the medical justification, only thirty-one. His 1934 report expressed the view that any support of the birth control movement by official authority was fundamentally wrong, and he was no doubt pleased when in 1937 this service was discontinued and left to a voluntary clinic in Pitt Street, to which the council subscribed £5 per annum.[59]

Consequently, the spread of contraception must have rested upon individual initiative. Of course, the decline in the birth rate was not uniform. A scrutiny of birth rates applying in the various wards of Norwich in 1931 suggested to the medical officer that they ran rather lower in 'our more aristocratic areas' (Mancroft, Eaton, Thorpe, Town Close), hinting that 'in Norwich, as elsewhere, the birth rate in the higher social class is not as great as in the other classes', while in 1937 he worried that professional males and clerks were scarcely in a position to contemplate a wife and family before reaching twenty-eight, twenty-nine or thirty, 'by which time the full vigorous desires of youth may have started to disappear and certain ductless glands be slightly less active'.[60] He was also of the view that women's work 'offended against all the canons of mammalian biology', and detected the existence in Norwich of a sub-normal group comprising the 'feeble-minded', and even 'the dull and backward', who were not desirable progenitors. These people, he suggested at one point, might with advantage be incarcerated in a sort of barracks or hostel, featuring a supervised regime of daily baths, compulsory work, the cultivation of vegetable plots and no alcoholic drink (though smoking might be allowed as a reward), the premises to be locked by 10 p.m. His views fell just short of the advocacy of sterilisation, in that people should be given the chance to improve before 'selection'.[61] Illiberal though Soothill's opinions might appear to later generations, and lacking in adequate supporting evidence, his views on these matters reflected widely held contemporary prejudices. He was equally capable of making shrewd points, such as his recognition that in part the birth rate of the county borough was being affected by the growth of suburbs; thus, he noted (without tracing in detail) the effects on

Norwich fertility rates of the building of a large number of houses just out-side the city boundaries which were accommodating 'a considerable number of Norwich inhabitants of child bearing age'.[62]

Despite their reputation for severe economic depression, the inter-war years featured a further decline in British mortality rates, and Norwich was no exception. To be sure, there were persistent signs of ill-health in Nor-wich during this period. Year by year variations in the incidence of measles, scarlet fever, diphtheria, influenza and other infectious diseases were still considerable, but the extent to which these unpleasant experiences trans-lated into actual deaths was definitely on the wane locally, as it was nationally. Thus, in the medical officer's report for 1923, 1095 cases of scar-let fever were noted and 248 of diphtheria, but there were only thirteen and thirty-one deaths respectively; and in 1934 a major epidemic of measles (1301 cases) brought only twelve fatalities, and there were thirteen from a similar outbreak in 1936. Indeed, we are concerned in this chapter only with accounting for lower mortality levels.

The infant mortality rate (in which stillbirths were included for the first time in 1926) continued its downward progression in most years, moving from seventy-five in 1920 and 1921 to fifty-two in 1935, when it stood at a level 12 per cent below the average of a group of provincial boroughs with populations lying in the range 100–200 thousand. This improvement applied also to illegitimate births, and the maternal mortality rates of Nor-wich, running usually at two or three per thousand births (that is not more than four or five cases per annum), stood, if anything, below the national average.[63] The crude rate, it is true, showed little variation from one decade to the next, averaging 11.8 in 1922–30 and the same in 1934–39 but the introduction of 'areal comparability factors' by the Registrar General, seek-ing to allow for variations in age and social comparison, housing density and even latitude, showed that the improvement in the city's overall mor-tality between 1911–14 and 1931–34 was typical of that achieved in eighty-two county boroughs (twenty-eight fared better, eight the same, and forty-two worse); and that mortality, so standardised, was in 1935 and 1936 24 and 22 per cent below the average of the large provincial boroughs. The same source shows also that the city's excess of mortality over that of rural Norfolk had fallen from 18 per cent in 1911–14 to 13 by 1931–34.[64]

Again, historians have found it easier to list the contributing causes of this development than to decide on their relative weighting. Autonomous factors (shifts in the virulence of infectious disease organisms) may have played a part, particularly in connection with scarlet fever. Dietary improvements, a consequence of the fall in the cost of living, probably also contributed though this is thought to be less likely for the inter-war years than for the later nineteenth century.[65] Locally, some backing for the nutritional case might be found in a decline of deaths from tuberculosis, which in 1921–22 averaged 316 in Norwich, but only 145 in 1938–39. On the other hand, an enquiry into the condition of 12,002 elementary school-children in 1939–40 revealed that 27 per cent were still malnourished to some degree, most, however, 'slightly'.[66] As is argued elsewhere in this book and in the general literature on the subject, advances in medical therapy and surgical techniques – at least before the discovery and application of chemotherapeutic drugs in the late 1930s – are not considered crucial.[67] To the extent that these factors are downplayed, we are left with environmental improvements, on which information is relatively abundant, certainly for Norwich.

The momentum of the war-time movement to improve the survival prospects of mothers and infants was not lost. There was a considerable expansion in midwifery services and a proliferation of infant welfare centres offering advice and antenatal services, even if it was not easy to persuade pregnant women to attend them. A rather disappointing proportion (equivalent to 35 per cent of births) did so in 1933, which was deemed significant, in that neo-natal deaths in the first four weeks of life were not falling in line with the infant mortality rate as a whole. Closely associated with these measures was a move in the 1920s by the health department to provide milk for selected households, initially in the form of packeted, dried supplies, and later fresh milk, the quantity distributed rising eight-fold to reach nearly 400 thousand pints between 1925 and 1932. This was supplemented by a drive to encourage breast-feeding: in 1935 it was reported by the health visitors that 75 per cent of babies were so fed, up to nine months, and that only a quarter remained bottle-fed, including – the medical officer remarked – twenty-nine out of thirty-five who had died under the age of four weeks.[68]

More general improvements in hygiene included the continuing conversion of privy pans and bins. Even during the war progress had not entirely ceased, and in 1919 there remained only 943 (against 30,692 water closets), a figure reduced still further to 116 by 1931. The city's health department chivvied away at a range of other measures designed to improve hygiene, introducing galvanised dustbins by 1935, using its powers under the Norwich Corporation Act of 1933 to register all sellers of preserved meats and ice-cream, and by 1937 giving attention to ventilation in cinemas and providing free washing accommodation in all public conveniences.[69] Moreover, a major benefit stemmed from improvements in the housing stock. The number of new houses, which averaged 367 in

1897–1912, had slowed to a trickle during the war (eighty-six in all, through 1914–19), with the result that scarcity compelled Norwich, according to the medical officer in 1923, to 'tolerate the continued existence of undesirable habitations'. Through 1921–29, however, the number of new houses averaged 417 per annum, and for 1930–9, 780. Although some of these, particularly in the 1930s, were privately funded, the vast majority were planned and executed by the corporation.[70] Already, by 1931, the census suggested that Norwich was better placed, in terms of persons per room, than the general run of county boroughs.[71]

Quite a lot of the corporation's activities entailed slum clearance, for example a number of unwholesome yards in the vicinity of Pitt Street and Coslany Street in 1931. The policy allowed 3238 houses with 9873 residents to be dealt with over the next seven years. Without question, commented the medical officer of health, these new houses offered improved social conditions. Rejecting in 1938 a common complaint that the occupants would use their baths only to keep coal in, he regarded improved housing, along with evidence that the population was cleaner, better dressed and better fed than ever before, as a boon: 'a little more sunlight is getting into the lives of the people'.[72]

Despite the changes that have been described, there is a sense in which inter-war Norwich was merely marking time. The aggregate surplus of births over deaths amounted over 1922–31 to nearly 7000, but the population of the borough grew only modestly between the two censuses, by 5575 or 4.7 per cent. This was a smaller increase than that of the population of England and Wales (5.5 per cent), and the rise in numbers was concentrated chiefly in the Thorpe, Lakenham, Eaton and Catton wards, with actual decreases occurring in those already affected by property demolition (Conesford, Ber Street, Westwick and Coslany). Meanwhile, significant increases were now appearing in a number of locations lying outside the borough boundary. These included, in the ten year period, Thorpe (+948), Costessey (+1452), Cringleford (+391), Hellesdon (+1315) and Sprowston (+1117), as well as – a little further afield – Brundall (+362).[73] Unfortunately, owing to the absence of a census in 1941, it is not possible to monitor these developments in detail for the 1930s. They certainly accelerated, for, despite the continuation at a lower level of surpluses of births over deaths in the county borough, its estimated population in 1939 was put at only 121,700, representing an absolute decline of 4.5 thousand since 1931.

Once again, national registration data and food office records were pressed into service at the General Register Office as a basis for producing demographic statistics during the war years. The estimates for Norwich show the civilian population falling to a nadir in 1943 of 101,160, thereafter recovering slightly to 103,540 in 1945.[74] On the mortality side, the published death rates excluded civilian war fatalities, which in the case of Norwich amounted to sixty-three in 1940, twenty-two in 1941, and 244 in 1942, a year of heavy air raids, but only eleven in the rest of the war years. Although food supplies were tolerably well upheld, and more children took school meals, a number of factors detrimental to health and, potentially, life expectation, were mentioned at one point or another in the medical officer's reports. These included the virtual cessation of house-building, as attention shifted to the construction of shelters and the repair of war damage, leading to a situation whereby, in 1943, some previously condemned tenements had to be reoccupied; and to the emergence of a major accommodation shortage by 1945. There were considerable difficulties in maintaining standards of hygiene. Flies and hence dysentery were prevalent by the time it took to clear up foodstuffs damaged in air raids (1942), and the quality of milk supplies was another area of retrogression. Levels of personal cleanliness were threatened by shortages of soap and cotton goods, such as sheets, pillowslips and underwear (1944), one consequence of this being a noticeable increase in the incidence of head-lice; while shelter life, by its very nature, was less clean and therefore conducive to the spread of infectious diseases.[75] Despite these adversities, commented the medical officer of health in 1944, 'it speaks well for the general conditions in Norwich that we have been able to avoid an epidemic of disease'. Although there were signs of an increase in tuberculosis in 1943 and 1944, in the round the civilian death rate rose little, if at all, and further modest improvements in infant mortality were recorded. Whereas in 1940 this rate soared temporarily (due, it was suggested in 1944, to the diversion of health visitors to ARP duties at first aid posts), subsequent years revealed a fall to thirty-seven in 1945.[76]

Meanwhile, the war also had a significant impact on the side of procreation. In 1939 and 1940, perhaps in anticipation of call-up into the armed forces, there was a pronounced leap in marriages; one of no less than 40 per cent, in fact, on the 1938 level, though they later fell away until the cessation of hostilities in 1945. An echo of this was a rise in legitimate births, running by 1944–45 at 1758 against 1555 in 1938–39, a 13 per cent increase. But there was a far greater one (355 per cent) in illegitimate births, where the averages for the same years were 369 and eighty-one respectively. In effect, the proportion of births on the wrong side of the blanket, in contemporary terminology, had risen from 5 to 17 per cent. Commenting on the early stages of this increase, the medical officer of health remarked, 'I have had reports that even a few married women are being more promiscuous than usual', and the fact that no fewer than 996 men and women were attending venereal disease clinics in 1945 was another indication, perhaps, of disturbances to pre-war habits of sexual behaviour.[77]

The demographic profile of Norwich in the years immediately following the war can be traced from the reports of the medical officer and the Registrar General, coupled with the results of the long-awaited census of 1951. Notwithstanding some concern about a revival of bottle-feeding, mentioned by the medical officer in his 1950 report, infant mortality rates continued on their downward path and by 1950–52 stood at 23 per thousand births. Among adults, there was a perceptible increase in cancer deaths, which he was disinclined to link with smoking. More happily, mortality from tuberculosis halved in just five years following 1946. This was associated with the coming of mass radiography and BCG vaccinations of contacts, but probably influenced also by smaller families, implying less scope for the spread of infection, as the medical officer suggested in 1947. The situation was further improved by the resumption of house-building at a rapid rate and by the advent of the National Health Service.[78] At all events, the great majority who survived the first year of life could now expect – on reaching the age of one – another seventy years of life.[79]

Marriage rates were especially brisk in the years 1945–48, and a falling age at matrimony was implicit in the rise in proportions ever-married in the age group 20–24: by comparison with 1931, the percentage had moved by 1951 from 15.3 to 27.8 per cent for males, and from 23.5 to 57.0 for females. Norwich was sharing in the increase in 'marriage intensity' that the Registrar General remarked on as a characteristic of these years.[80] Even though there was a significant increase in the incidence of divorces and the number of illegitimate births declined rapidly after 1945, there was a marked recovery in fertility which reached its peak in Norwich in 1946 (nationally, 1947), a year which featured a birth rate of 22.2, a level not seen since 1920. This trend was universal, but the Royal Commission on Population, which sat between 1945 and 1949, did not expect the flood of births to last.[81] Indeed it did not, either nationally or locally, for by 1950 the Norwich rate was reduced once again to 15.6. This, commented the medical officer of health – in line with his earlier views on the matter – was 'only to be expected so long as many women, including married women, are spending their energies in gainful employment'.[82]

The same sources can be used to make an historical and comparative summary of the experiences of Norwich in the first half of the twentieth century. The infant mortality rate of 1950–2, though halved since 1932 and no more than a quarter of that prevailing in the Edwardian years (see

Table 10.4), nevertheless still stood at a level which placed Norwich in only 112th position among 157 large towns in England and Wales. The birth rate of 1950, though still a shade higher than that ruling in the 1930s, was fractionally lower than the national rate and also than that of an average of 126 large towns.[83] Some long-entrenched features of the demographic profile of Norwich were still present in 1951, notably a surplus of females over males (1,130:1,000, contrasting with 951 in rural Norfolk); and the birth place origins of the population were still overwhelmingly local, in that 85 per cent of the city's inhabitants were Norfolk born. The age composition featured – at least marginally – a higher proportion of persons aged sixty-five and over (12.2 per cent) and a lower proportion of children aged nought to fourteen (21.8 per cent) than the national norm (11.0 and 22.1 respectively). Above all, despite a 17 per cent increase in the population of the county borough between 1945 and 1951, to reach 121,236, the aggregate population had yet to recover fully to its 1931 level. Indeed, in respect of total population change, 1931–51, Norwich occupied only 133rd position among 157 towns.[84]

These features, set against the progress of other towns and cities, hint at a situation of relative stagnation in the case of Norwich. But it is important to emphasise that the figures relate to the county borough, which was extended only to a minor extent in 1950. A careful comparison made in the 1951 census drew attention to the expansion of population in the contiguous registration districts of St Faith's and Aylsham, Blofield and Flegg, and Forehoe with Henstead. These showed, respectively, population growth of 46.7, 30.7 and 25.2 per cent, amounting altogether to over 24,000 persons between 1931 and 1951, and in each case these increases were very significantly greater than those arising from surpluses of births over deaths.[85] In other words, Norwich was moving out – not, of course, to cover the whole of these extensive registration districts, but certainly extending developments in the satellite villages or suburbs mentioned earlier. Reflecting this, the 'job ratio' at Norwich (the population working in the area in relation to the resident population) stood in 1951 at an index figure of 121, placing the city as high as fourteenth among 157 large towns. Moreover, while the medical officer of health observed in the year of the Festival of Britain that there was 'a general feeling of being hard up', *per capita* retail sales in 1950, reflecting the city's status as a commercial and shopping centre, were such as to place the city in twentieth position.[86] In short, what might be termed greater Norwich was by no means in a state of demographic or economic inertia.

11

Medical Care since 1750

Steven Cherry

A bewildering variety of agencies ... work for health mainly by attacking specific diseases and disabilities as they occur and by maintaining
the sufferers.

Political and Economic Planning,
Report on British Health Services, 1937[1]

Although perceptions of illness and well-being change, the fact that everyone succumbs to sickness or disease at some point in life is one of the few
universal experiences. People did not suffer equally, however, and some
were better placed than others to record or address their ill health. Over
time, responses to illness increasingly involved the seeking of professional
medical attention, which, in turn, improved in its proficiency. This is not
to ignore the importance of lay care or to understate the contemporary significance of other forms of healing, which might later be regarded as
unqualified or unorthodox. But the growth of a medical market and the
increasing emphasis placed upon scientific knowledge is a notable feature
of the past three centuries.[2]

In a city as important as Norwich, a local medical hierarchy and signs of a
developing medical market were only to be expected. Attempts to control,
define and benefit from medical practice in the early modern period began
with the Royal College of Physicians of London, which from 1518 granted
licences and imposed fines. Yet the physicians were unable to establish a
monopoly over the care of the wealthy and had little direct interest in any
others. Records dating from the early fourteenth century indicate that the
barber-surgeons served a wider clientele, though the formation of the separate Company of Surgeons, later the Royal College of Surgeons, in 1745
marked their efforts to delineate skills and emulate the market position of
the physicians. In turn, the Society of Apothecaries specified minimum
conditions of training and expertise by legal statute in 1815. Until then, the
main form of medical regulation in Norwich was through episcopal

licensing, which was extensive and certainly lasted until the 1790s.[3] Physicians, surgeons, apothecaries and midwives were granted bishops' licences,
as were occasionally wise-women, phlebotomists, bonesetters, toothdrawers,
herbalists and the purveyors of empirics or cures. It has been suggested that
there was one such 'healer' per 200 city dwellers in the late sixteenth and
early seventeenth centuries and that a relatively developed service for the
sick poor, based upon medical practitioners, already existed.[4]

Sir Thomas Browne, who practised in Norwich from 1636 until his death
in 1682, was a great humanist physician, but the blurring of traditional professional divisions can be seen among his local contemporaries. Thomas
Havers (1659–1719) was a clergyman licensed to practise as physician and
surgeon and was a lithotomist of repute. Benjamin Gooch (1708–76), a distinguished surgeon apothecary, acquired a national reputation for the
treatment of fractures, enhanced by his three-volume text on surgery and
his development of a light, supportive leg splint.[5] Gooch was also associated with the establishment of perhaps the first English cottage hospital at
Shotesham and then the Norfolk and Norwich Hospital, where he was the
consulting surgeon. Not all 'regular' practitioners, however, were sharply
demarcated from the 'unorthodox'. There was no distinct body of 'scientific medicine' and the whims of moneyed patients could not be ignored,
even by the bearers of new knowledge from centres of medicine such as
Padua, Leiden or Edinburgh. Lesser figures might promote their skills by
advertising and entrepreneurship. Thus Agabus Molden, son of a barber
surgeon, informed his public in 1734 that he 'cleans teeth to great perfection ... to prevent their decay and aching ... takes out teeth and stumps,
be they ever so decay'd, or broken by unskilful persons'.[6] His advertisement
also drew attention to his dealings in whale oil and the hairdressing skills
of Mrs Molden. Early trade directories also indicate the emergence of prototype general practitioners and new claims to medical expertise by the late
eighteenth century. Norwich had six physicians and twenty surgeons,
including five surgeon apothecaries, two surgeon druggists and a man mid-
wife in 1783.[7] Their numbers increased modestly to 1830, perhaps reflecting
the city's uncertain economic development, when there were eight physicians and twenty-four surgeons, but two qualified apothecaries, five
opticians, four dentists and at least twenty-nine chemists and druggists
were also listed.[8]

Charitable bequests from the medieval era to the late seventeenth century were expressed in institutional medical facilities, which illustrated
continuity and change in modern Norwich. Certainly the city was exceptionally well endowed in this respect, reflecting both its wealth and
deep-rooted charitable effort. The Great Hospital in Bishopgate, managed

since the Dissolution by the mayor and sheriffs until 1712 and then by the Norwich corporation of guardians, was essentially a hospice. Candidates for admission were nominated by the aldermen and suitable entrants were required to bring 'a featherbed, blankets and ten shillings for a coffin'.[9] Extensions in 1826 and 1850 doubled the eighteenth-century accommodation to provide for two hundred persons, nominated from the aged and infirm, rather than drawn from the poorest or the sick. In 1850 their average age was no less than seventy-five years and the period of residence was typically eight or nine years.[10] The hospital was well endowed with land, which produced an average rental income of £7500 in the late nineteenth century. Boys and girls at the children's hospital endowed by Thomas Anguish in 1618 were accommodated on different sites after 1649 and the hospital was clearly a school by the nineteenth century. Thomas Doughty's bequest of £6000 in 1687 provided a hospital for thirty-two men and women aged over sixty, and thirteen more when it was restored and extended in 1869. The smaller Cooke's Hospital, opened in 1692, housed ten elderly women. In the same philanthropic tradition, Thomas Tawell's Hospital and School for the Indigent Blind in Magdalen Street was only the fourth of its kind in England when established in 1804. It provided an industrial training for up to fifty blind children from the age of twelve, whilst maintaining twelve elderly blind people. By the 1830s these endowed institutions had attracted further donations or legacies which generated a combined annual income of approximately £9000; and in 1836 their administration passed from Norwich corporation to an independent body of twenty-six Charity Commissioners appointed by the Lord Chancellor.[11]

Donors determined new philanthropic provision, however, and perceptions concerning popular need and the utility of more medicalised institutions were changing. The Bethel Hospital at Norwich, founded by Mary Chapman in 1713 and administered as a public charity from 1724, was virtually alone in attempting to treat forms of mental illness or disorder in a period when sufferers were frequently dehumanised and incarcerated. For much of the eighteenth century it accommodated over forty persons, mainly private patients charged at four shillings per week, along with ten or more charitable cases and some others maintained by the corporation. Records for over 800 of the 1300 Bethel patients between 1760 and 1880 suggest that one-third were pronounced cured or relieved, but the average residence of those who died in the hospital over the first half of the nineteenth century was typically fourteen years.[12] Another unique institution was Shotesham village or cottage hospital, founded some time before 1754 by William Fellowes, the local squire, who equipped it with around a dozen beds at the disposal of Benjamin Gooch.[13] This rural prototype was supplanted by the Norfolk and Norwich Hospital, but it predated similar cottage hospitals by more than a century.

The need for poor law medical effort was also acknowledged, although provision was uneven. Under the 1712 Norwich Workhouse Act an elected court of guardians assumed the supervision and control of indoor relief to the poor, establishing workhouses at New Hall (now St Andrew's hall) and in Bridge Street, St Andrew's parish. Outdoor relief to the sick poor ranged from items of food to provision for lying-in women and surgical cases, and a former lazar house in St Augustine's was converted in 1712 for use as an infirmary.[14] In adverse economic conditions the court struggled with the rising costs of poor relief and the availability of workhouse accommodation for only 1300 people in 1802 compared with 5000 persons, or roughly one-seventh of the city population, on relief.[15] A vaccination programme from 1805 helped, however, to restrict the 1819 smallpox outbreak in Norwich.[16] Distinctions between deterrence of the able-bodied pauper and aid for the sick were maintained in the Norwich Guardians Act of 1827 and its 1831 amendment, which established district provision based upon part-time poor law medical officers and a central dispensary. As will also be seen, institutional provision for chronic sick and insane paupers remained poor indeed, though limited arrangements for the acute sick were offered in association with the Norfolk and Norwich Hospital.

A wave of general hospital building occurred in provincial England from 1736, following the establishment of new London hospitals in addition to St Bartholomew's, St Thomas's and the Bethlem. Voluntary hospitals, with their respectable donors and poor but deserving patients, embodied humanitarian and religious expression, but also reflected other motives.[17] For example, they provided their honorary medical staff with opportunities to extend their own medical knowledge and practice, to teach pupils, to gain status and to acquire a potential patient clientele among the hospitals' more affluent supporters. In so far as hospital treatments could restore the sick and reduce poor rates, they also offered the prospect of value for charitable effort.

The trinity of promoters – clergy, landowners and doctors – often seen in cathedral towns where hospitals were established, might have produced earlier results in Norwich had not Bishop Thomas Hayter, a leading advocate, been translated to London in 1761. But delay also brought advantages. A key argument for establishing the Norfolk and Norwich Hospital a decade later was that 'sufficient practical experience ... had been obtained to confirm the prevalent opinion that such institutions must confer great advantage on the public'.[18] Considerable thought went into the choice of an open site, (now St Stephen's Street) well beyond the city walls and on the edge of the rural Town Close estate, and into the design of buildings (Plate 15). Rather than adopting the model of a large rectangular block, it was decided that 'a building in the form of an "H" would be most convenient for the purpose as admitting the freest circulation of air; provision of which had, by the Gentlemen of the Faculty of Physic, been earnestly recommended'.[19] Consequently, the hospital was less affected by overcrowding, cluttered extensions or hospital diseases than many similar institutions. The prison reformer John Howard, visiting in 1789, noted: 'this spacious infirmary was perfectly neat and clean, the beds not crowded, the wards quiet and fresh ... there are about ninety beds ... fifty-two were occupied'.[20]

The hospital remained central to the needs of the city and county sick poor, although smaller hospitals developed from dispensaries at Yarmouth in 1825 and at Lowestoft and King's Lynn, both in 1838. Hospital treatment differed little from that offered in domiciliary visits by physicians or the basics of kitchen table surgery. An average six weeks' stay in hospital, with rest, a good diet and nursing, however rudimentary, probably benefited poor patients considerably. But such care was conditional. Subscribers were issued with letters of recommendation in return for their annual donations – one guinea for two outpatients and two guineas for one inpatient was the early rule – and prospective patients had to obtain one of these, unless they were accident or emergency cases. Hospital rules precluded the admission of paupers unsupported by parish subscriptions or those able to pay for medical attention. Patients felt to be incurable, suffering from infectious diseases or forms of mental illness were also excluded, as were women about to give birth and smaller children. A transfer to the local workhouse, its infirmary ward or the county asylum was likely to follow any inadvertent admission, though older children were treated before and after the establishment of the Jenny Lind Children's Hospital. Seemingly harsh, such policies focused upon the curable, for the hospital needed to demonstrate both medical and economic efficiency to attract continuing financial support.

In such circumstances, the meaning of a hospital 'cure' might be questioned, particularly given inadequate aftercare or the patient's return to a poverty-stricken or insanitary domestic environment. 'Relief' might be no more than temporary, as in the draining of fluid or removal of a tumour. As charitable and medical 'cases', patients had no rights and risked discharge for 'irregularity' if they did not comply with hospital rules. Those 'not likely to benefit' were often discharged because the hospital authorities, relying upon subscriptions and donations, were hesitant to record their deaths as inpatients.[21] This said, the Norfolk and Norwich typically claimed cure rates approaching 55 per cent, with a further 10 per cent 'relieved', and inpatient mortality rarely exceeding 5 per cent before the 1840s.[22] It acknowledged high risks in operations carried out before the introduction of effective anaesthesia or antisepsis: for example, one in four leg amputations ended fatally. Major operations were relatively few in number, but still significant. Between 1771 and 1820 there were some six hundred operations to remove bladder stones, almost all of them lateral lithotomies. These required an incision and exposed the patient to infection. A total mortality rate of 12.8 per cent for this hazardous procedure seems to reflect good surgical practice with relatively low levels of infection from the surgeon, operating instruments or hospital environment.[23] Given the constraining economic and social contexts, the fact that in any one year before 1870 between six and eight per thousand of the city's population were hospital inpatients suggests a positive contribution to health care and even to reduced mortality (Plates 16 and 17).

The very success of the hospital contributed, however, to growing difficulties by the 1870s. The city had begun to encroach upon the previously open hospital site and more inpatients were admitted. Overcrowding both in the wards and the outpatients' department rose, even though more inpatients were transferred to outpatient or convalescent status. Following the introduction of anaesthetics, the number of serious surgical cases more than doubled in the 1850s and 1860s. Outbreaks of hospital infection occurred, notably in 1873 and 1877. Neither antiseptic procedures nor reduced surgical workloads could remedy a defective operating environment and, following investigations of finances, nursing and sanitary conditions, the decision to rebuild rather than to extend and refurbish was taken in 1877.[24]

Two acres of adjacent land were purchased and the new buildings were rapidly completed at a cost of £52,000. Again the "H" shape plan was preferred, using pavilion design principles. The western pavilions, central administrative buildings and operating block were completed in June 1881, with the remaining eastern pavilions and an outpatients department rebuilt from a wing of the former building being finished in 1883.[25] There were now six wards of twenty-four beds each, and two of seventeen beds, with smaller special or acute rooms (Plate 18). By 1914 the hospital had 220 beds; and the acquisition of the twenty-six bed Fletcher convalescent home at Cromer in 1893 allowed the transfer of post-operative and recovering cases. Table 11.1 illustrates the surge in twentieth-century patient numbers. Almost half of the inpatients came from outside Norwich in the late nineteenth century, although roughly three-quarters of the outpatients lived in the city. A surprising 18 per cent of inpatients were children aged under ten years, despite the existence of the Jenny Lind Children's Hospital from 1854. Bed provision had doubled to 440 by 1939 and facilities were used more intensively, the average inpatient stay falling from thirty-one to nineteen days between 1900 and 1939.[26] Outpatient numbers increased still more rapidly, though the focus was upon consultations rather than dispensing facilities, and medical staff were reluctant to treat large numbers of people who were, arguably, the responsibility of the state national health insurance scheme.

Table 11.1 Patients at the Norfolk and Norwich Hospital:
annual averages, 1800–1947

	Inpatients	Outpatients		Inpatients	Outpatients
1780s	500	400	1880s	1,100	3,300
1800s	600	500	1900–4	1,900	7,300
1820s	750	650	1920–4	3,650	10,500
1840s	750	900	1935–9	7,200	21,350
1860s	1,100	2,400	1946–7	8,000	28,350

Source: NRO, Norfolk and Norwich Hospital Annual Reports, numbers rounded to nearest fifty.

Hospitals like the Norfolk and Norwich were not provided with financial resources to match the increasing numbers of patients referred by general practitioners or school medical officers for more advanced forms of treatment or care. To safeguard its financial position as treatment costs rose, the hospital introduced outpatient charges in 1907 and inpatient charges in 1921. It remained dependent upon major bequests and legacies for capital projects, such as the building of the Leicester and Alexandra nurses' homes, but new sources of income became increasingly important. The Hospital Saturday organisation, an offshoot from Sunday church or chapel collections in support of the hospital, developed after the First World War into a contributory scheme, under which regular weekly payments exempted contributors and their dependants from hospital charges. Some 70 per cent of hospital inpatients were members of the scheme in 1923 and 80 per cent in the 1930s, their contributions representing over 80 per cent of the hospital's treatment and maintenance costs and 55 per cent of its annual ordinary income. Such self-help perpetuated voluntarist traditions but was now the product of quasi–insurance provision rather than simple donations.[27] As the merits of hospital treatment became appreciated by the better off, private patients were admitted to the former Eye Hospital buildings from 1925. New accommodation for them in Brunswick Road increased from twenty to thirty beds during the 1930s, as a private patients' insurance plan was developed.

Hospital expansion also included new specialties. The electrotherapeutic department, formed in 1904 as X-ray technology was increasingly utilised, grew and separated into orthopaedic, X-ray and neurological departments. An ear, nose and throat clinic dating from 1912 became a full department in 1921 and was accommodated in a new twenty-eight-bed block from 1930. A twenty-two-bed building opened for eye patients in 1930, and a thirty-bed block was added for maternity and gynaecology patients in 1935. By 1939, with a dermatology department and radium treatment for cancer underway, 'the Norfolk and Norwich was as well-equipped for its tasks as any in the country'.[28] During the years 1900–39 the nursing staff increased exponentially from forty-five to 204 and the medical staff, excluding assistants and dental surgeons, from twelve to twenty-five. This growth of specialist hospital staff reflected scientific, professional and economic developments. The nineteenth-century hospital had a small honorary staff, just three physicians and three surgeons, supplemented by juniors and assistants, many in general practice. Consultant numbers were not a reflection of expertise but were:

> sufficient for the wards and ... as many as the district could provide a living for as consultants ... the poor have always required more specialist services than practice among the well-to-do pays for. By appointing as assistants men in general practice and therefore not dependant on their earnings as specialists, the evil of overloading the ranks of specialists is avoided.[29]

Contrary to national interpretations, which focus too closely upon teaching hospitals, hospitals like the Norfolk and Norwich obtained predominantly consultant staffs and excluded general practitioners only when their finances were secured, first by the contributory schemes and private wards and then by income from the wartime Emergency Medical Service and later National Health Service.

The growth of voluntary special hospitals is conventionally associated with forms of medical entrepreneurship, as ambitious doctors founded institutions to make their reputations and dominate a particular part of the medical market.[30] Undoubtedly they also reflected medical advances for, as John Green Crosse put it, 'the assemblage of the medical sciences is too vast for the mind to cope with even during a lifetime: the way to excellence is to work in a particular department'.[31] In East Anglia, however, small general and cottage hospitals predominated and just two special hospitals were established, both in Norwich.

It was 'chiefly through the exertions of the medical gentlemen' that the Norwich Eye Infirmary was set up in 1822 with eight beds, later extended to fourteen, at a house in Pottergate.[32] Over three hundred patients were treated annually in the first fifty years, many as accident or cataract cases; of these more than two-thirds were pronounced cured.[33] In the early 1900s the Eye Hospital had moved to St Stephen's and it admitted more than 150 inpatients per year. With the new county school medical service referring over a thousand children in 1909, workloads increased rapidly and the physician, two surgeons and assistant refused to treat further schoolchildren without financial assistance. The Jenny Lind and Norfolk and Norwich also claimed financial support for 'education committee' patients and, as their medical staffs overlapped considerably, the Eye Hospital eventually merged with the Norfolk and Norwich in 1925, followed by the opening of the above-mentioned twenty-two-bed eye block there in 1930.

In contrast, the Jenny Lind Infirmary, later Hospital for Sick Children, was a provincial pioneer in 1854. This special hospital dealt with a population group rather than a discrete part of the body. Its establishment after concerts by the 'Swedish Nightingale' herself reflected civic and philanthropic effort, rather than the promptings of would-be medical specialists. The infirmary opened with twelve beds in a house in Pottergate and was intended for 'children between the ages of two and ten years, suffering from any disease not contagious or infectious ... as inpatients, and children from birth to the age of twelve years ... admissible as outpatients'.[34] In the 1860s it treated more than five hundred children annually and 1150 two decades later: this on a total income representing less than £1 per patient. Nearly one-fifth of the children were inpatients and two-thirds of them were pronounced cured or relieved.[35] The Jenny Lind notably encouraged parental attendance and assistance in caring for child patients and broke its own rules to admit babies with their mothers.[36] Moreover, its reported 'constant drilling of parents as to the general management of their offspring' suggested a novel health educational role.[37] Although children suffering from infectious diseases were not knowingly admitted, wards were closed because of scarlet fever in 1894. Four years later the hospital temporarily relocated to Tombland while buildings were constructed in Unthank Road (Figure 39 and Plate 19).[38] Its resident medical officers included Drs Lucy Muir and Mary Bell, who were among the first qualified women practitioners in Norwich. With the growth of the Schools' Medical Service and the transfer of children from the Norfolk and Norwich in 1914 the hospital expanded further: in the 1920s it had eighty beds and treated 1300 inpatients

FIGURE 39. The Jenny Lind Hospital for Children, Unthank Road, 1898–1976. (*Norwich Medico-Chirurgical Society and Dr Anthony Batty Shaw*)

annually. These were joined by some two thousand outpatients when this department transferred from Pottergate in 1929. Patient numbers rose by two-thirds in the next twenty years, but full nurse training could only be offered conjointly with the Norfolk and Norwich. This feature, overlapping consultant staff, and financial pressures were all prominent when the Jenny Lind was incorporated with the St Stephen's site from 1975.

Sharing premises with the Jenny Lind between 1854 and 1886, the Norwich Lying-In Charity demonstrates traditional philanthropic effort, the processes of medicalisation and of assimilation into twentieth-century local authority services. Established in 1832, it provided midwives for married women confined at home, one-half of these domiciliary attendances being organised by local clergymen rather than directly by subscribers.[39] The process whereby female midwives were partly displaced by man midwives, surgeon accoucheurs and eventually obstetricians reflected the medicalisation of childbirth and the influence of doctors upon wealthier families. Midwives continued to attend poor women, but the Lying-In Charity, based in St Benedict's from 1886, also became a training centre for midwives under the direction of two consultants with fifteen years' experience in midwifery practice and three surgeon accoucheurs with seven years' or more. In 1894 it became the Norwich Maternity Charity with a small maternity home in Bethel Street, the qualified midwives attending over five hundred births annually.[40] With state regulation of training and encouragement of local authority services beginning under the 1902 and 1918 Midwives' Acts, the institution was the obvious base for local maternity services and was in effect municipalised in 1919. An earlier charity founded in 1815, the Norwich Society for Relieving the Sick Poor in their own Homes, focused upon married women with children. It offered money, goods or medical aid for roughly 250 women in 1818 and over 1200 eighty years later.[41] If associated with the moral overtones of 'lady visiting', this body also provided a model for the Norwich District Nursing Society, which employed six nurses on domiciliary services in 1900, and for municipal health visiting services from 1907.

Another undervalued source of primary care was the Norwich Dispensary, whose medical officers diagnosed illnesses and prescribed the medicines to be issued. It was established in Pottergate in 1804, moved to larger premises in the Maddermarket in 1843 and was further extended in 1856. Treating roughly 700 people annually before 1820 and 1600 in the 1830s and 1840s, the dispensary was dogged by financial difficulties. It was also regarded with suspicion by the Norfolk and Norwich Hospital and by wary medical practitioners, keen to maintain their market position and status. As a medical charity operating on the principles of subscriber-recommendation, the dispensary competed with the hospital. Attempts by the apothecary and two attending physicians to add surgical facilities and beds in 1819 brought public condemnation from hospital staff; and a later domiciliary service fell foul of local doctors, who resented the competition.[42] Like these prototype general practitioners, the dispensary's resident medical officer was a surgeon-apothecary in 1850 and at least one-tenth of his increasing workload over the next decades involved surgery. (Map 4)

Under pressure from its patient clientele and because of financial difficulties, the dispensary was reorganised in the light of national concern with charitable abuse and efforts to promote self-help in the 1860s and 1870s. Patients were asked to contribute towards the costs of their treatment and those 'in a position to help themselves [or] in receipt of district or parish relief' were refused. The medical officer was also dismissed in 1875 because of 'the lax and extremely careless mode in which the books of the institution were kept'.[43] Five years later the dispensary was reorganised on a provident basis. Monthly contributors were offered the choice of doctor from a paid medical staff of three, rising to six by 1898, and Norfolk and Norwich Hospital staff were now willing to act as consultants. A vestige of the charitable service remained, but over 4100 members were enrolled by 1887 and a midwifery service was also offered. It is difficult to estimate the dispensary's workload: the 'total served' exceeded 30,000 in the early 1900s but 60 per cent of these were 'medicine only' patients and repeat prescriptions counted as new cases.[44] However, the advent in 1911 of compulsory state health insurance, offering sickness benefit as well as general practitioner

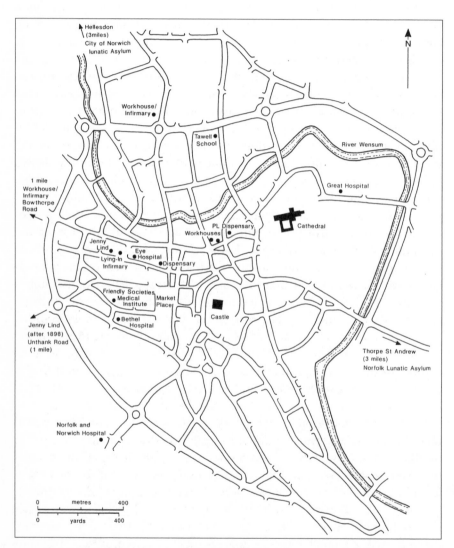

Hellesdon
(3miles)
City of Norwich
lunatic Asylum

N

Workhouse/
Infirmary ●

Tawell ●
School

River Wensum

1 mile
Workhouse/
Infirmary
Bowthcrpe
Road

Great Hospital
●

PL Dispensary
Workhouses ●   ● Cathedral

Jenny
Lind ●
          ● Eye
●   ●Hospital
Lying-In
Infirmary   ●Dispensary

Friendly Societies
● Medical   Market
     Institute   Place

●Bethel
Hospital   ■ Castle

Jenny Lind
(after 1898)
Unthank Road
(1 mile)

Thorpe St Andrew
(3 miles)
Norfolk Lunatic Asylum

Norfolk and
Norwich Hospital
●

0   metres   400

0   yards   400

MAP 4. Medical Institutions in and around Norwich, c. 1880. (*Phillip Judge*)

care to manual wage earners, greatly damaged the dispensary. Its income fell by a quarter in 1912. An attempt was made to attract family dependants, excluded from the state scheme, but expectations that 'many women and children will join the Provident department' were optimistic.[45]

The late eighteenth-century surgeon-apothecary valued his apprenticeship, medical lectures, anatomy classes and hospital ward experience. His early nineteenth-century equivalent claimed that scientific knowledge, acquired at university medical school and hospital, differentiated the qualified from irregular competitors and those 'in trade'. The 1858 Medical Act established procedures for formal qualification and a register of those suitably qualified, but it did not prohibit the unqualified. Table 11.2 suggests either that the registration of qualified practitioners under the 1858 Act, or the compilation of accurate local information, was delayed. From an apparent peak in 1845 the numbers professing formal qualifications fell, although seven 'medical botanists', two of them 'practical', appeared along with the chemists and druggists. A handbill from the 'doctress' Mrs Wesby informed her readers: 'I prepare ointments of different kinds for green wounds ... sores, oils for the rheumatic sprains and weaknesses of the limbs ... I cure all sorts of precarious diseases ... jaundice, weasing of the chest, trembling of the heart ... ulcers, sores and all manner of wounds'.[46] Even with the rise of patent medicines, Norwich still had at least five 'medical botanists' as late as 1925.[47]

Qualified medical practitioners usually worked as family doctors, though their documented competence in midwifery was not legally required until the Medical Amendment Act of 1886. There were about fifty such generalists in 1900, including Ethel Louise Starmer, a graduate of the Edinburgh School of Medicine for Women in 1897 and the first woman doctor in Norwich. Only a few described themselves as 'physician and surgeon' and physicians were now more associated with hospital-based or private consulting work. Yet their standard medical fees remained too costly for most of their potential patients. Depictions of an 'overstocked' late nineteenth-century medical market, with individual doctors in competition with each other, threatened by homeopathic, charitable and club practice, and frequently undercut by druggists retailing patent medicines, offer an incomplete picture. In practice, many doctors ran their own sick clubs or supplemented their income with club or poor law work and, for a time, club practice may have shaped the profession in the city.

By the mid nineteenth century Norwich and Norfolk were well known for their low wage rates, but they also had relatively high levels of friendly society provision. It was generally recognised that sickness entailed the

Table 11.2 Medical practitioners and others from Norwich Directories, 1783–1952

Date	Physician	Surgeon	Total qualified	Chemist/ druggist	Midwives	Dentists
1783	6	20				
1802	6	17				
1830	8	24		29		4
1845	10	37		35		
1854	8	36		34	8	8
1868	7	36	43	40		14
1883	4	30	34	35		13
1900	4	45	49	30	9	17
1914	4	55	60	31		23
1924	5	57	62	35	12	35
1937	5	69	74	41	14	34
1952	6		83	40		36

Sources: Chase (1783), p. 47; Peck (1802), p. 42; Pigot (1830), pp. 567–87; W. White (1845), p. 202, 207; W. White (1854), pp. 223–4, 255; Harrod (1868), pp. 479–510. Remaining entries are from Kelly's Directories for Norfolk (1883), pp. 764–5; (1900), pp. 649–777; (1914), pp. 582–603; (1924), pp. 522–763; (1937), pp. 843–6; (1952), pp. 766–806.

Notes: Surgeons were surgeon-apothecaries or general practitioners by the late nineteenth century and 'physicians' were consultant physicians. Directory entries represent minimum figures of active practitioners.

triple penalty of trauma, loss of earnings and the cost of medical attendance. In giving evidence to the 1905–9 Poor Law Commission, friendly societies stressed their low cost provision and indicated that over 40 per cent of the city's working population were members.[48] A number of societies collaborated in 1872 to establish the Norwich Friendly Societies Medical Institute with three full-time medical officers (later six) in Lady Lane, off Bethel Street. By 1906 approximately 7000 contributors, including over 1000 with families and at least 1300 single working women, obtained additional medical cover for one penny a week.[49] Although the dispensary and friendly societies provided work for qualified doctors, this was not on terms approved by the British Medical Association. Consequently, seventeen BMA members, including Dr Mary Bell, established their own Public Medical Service in Norwich, encouraging doctors 'who hold contract appointments at a rate of payment lower than that of the

PMS ... to raise such rate up to that adopted by the Service'.[50] This was open to families with earnings below 30s. a week, offering them a choice of doctor and domiciliary visits, and attracted 3270 enrolments by 1904.

William Bell, who had established the Norwich Homeopathic Dispensary in 1852, presented another challenge to medical orthodoxy. Bell and his colleague, F. A. Hartmann, were adroit publicists and soon claimed 2000 consultations annually at the dispensary. Their *Norwich Homeopathic Journal* played upon the invasive measures and pain associated with allopathic medicine, whereas 'homeopathy sheds not a drop of blood, administers no emetic purgatives or laxatives, prescribes no warm baths nor medicinal clysters, nor mustard plasters ... burns not with moxa nor red iron to the very bone'.[51] Bell, however, falsely described himself as a fellow of the Royal College of Physicians and, to compound his offence, advertised and offered consultations at the premises of druggists, which outraged the local medical profession. Following the death of a young woman in 1858, for example, the coroner's inquiry suggested misdiagnosis of a strangulated hernia by the homeopathic doctor and regretted the delay in surgical intervention. Nevertheless, the dispensary held its ground after the 1858 Act. Claiming 5000 consultations annually in the early 1900s, its medically qualified staff who chose, to the consternation of orthodox colleagues, the homeopathic system, included Dr Flint and Dr John Roche, whose son Eleazer was the dispensary medical officer until 1924.[52]

With its lack of heavy industry and comparatively low population growth, Norwich projected itself as 'a healthy city', though the consequences of urban decline were being noted as early as the 1820s.[53] Clusters of housing around small yards and closed courts were nationally associated with overcrowding, poor sanitation and ventilation; and Norwich possessed numerous examples of both within the city walls. Outside them, early nineteenth-century working-class housing was cheaply built with poor sanitation. Overcrowding was characteristic of many of these unplanned developments. Epidemics were potentially devastating in this situation and the smallpox outbreak of 1819 accounted for 40 per cent excess mortality that year. As in the middle ages, they reflected poverty and low bodily resistance to disease as much as defective sanitation, although the latter feature attracted more public attention. Dirt, miasmas and spectacular killer diseases were the compelling subjects of the day, rather than deficiencies in sanitation and water supplies or ever-present 'background' diseases such as tuberculosis. During the decades before and after the 1831–2 cholera outbreak in Norwich, for example, 'between 1500 and 1600 persons had been attacked by smallpox, measles, scarlet fever and typhus'.[54] Only 30 per cent of the city's houses had piped water in the 1840s and the majority relied on shared pumps, shallow wells and the river itself. The Wensum was also the main repository for sewage and industrial waste, and neighbouring cesspools and privies often contaminated wells. In 1845 the Health of Towns Commission referred to the lack of water and in the poorer districts of Norwich noted bizarre sanitary arrangements: 'here until very lately were distributed throughout the city no less than nine hundred jars ... for the reception of stale urine; the poor inhabitants being bribed ... about £200 annually, to endure these nuisances'.[55]

Although Norwich suffered relatively lightly from the cholera outbreak of 1848–9, one consequence was the establishment in 1849 of a new water company, pumping comparatively clean water west of Heigham to a reservoir at Lakenham, thus affording more effective distribution. The General Board of Health enquiry of 1851, however, chaired by William Lee, noted a continued deterioration in public health and drew attention to the amount of preventable sickness in the city.[56] Its report focused upon inadequacies in water supplies, drainage and sewerage, and overcrowded burial grounds. The last problem was tackled by the closure of burial grounds inside the city walls and the purchase of a thirty-five acre site between the Earlham and Dereham roads in 1856. Work to improve and channel drainage on the northern side of the city commenced in 1858, but its expense and any sign of central government coercion generated considerable opposition. Thus, when Thorpe residents complained to the Board of Health of pollution levels in the Yare, remedial plans were attacked. A modified version of a scheme by the celebrated sanitary engineer, Sir Joseph Bazalgette, to bypass the river using north and south drains as far as Whitlingham began in 1867. Hampered by defective materials and leakages, this took twenty years to complete and cost £206,000, funded mainly by Local Government Board loans.

No medical officer of health was appointed in Norwich until 1872, some twenty-six years after Liverpool had established a precedent. Even then, T. W. Crosse was employed on a part-time basis before H. Cooper-Pattin held the post full time from 1893 until 1925. In the early 1900s 30 per cent of houses were still 'without effective water carriage' for waste and sewage disposal, and it was felt that 'enteric fever [typhoid] has been rather endemic than epidemic in its character with us'.[57] As we have seen in chapter ten, until 1914 Norwich mortality rates exceeded national averages because of high infant mortality, another consequence of poverty, underemployment and the high incidence of home-work as much as defective sanitation. Crosse believed that one-sixth of infant mortality arose from the inadvertent administration of opiates, used to quieten babies;

Cooper-Pattin later linked one-third of infant deaths with poverty, but also to the ill health of mothers, who were 'underfed ... unwisely fed [and] working during the later stages of pregnancy'.[58] Even as death rates declined, particularly from infectious diseases, those associated with chronic and degenerative illnesses in a longer-living population rose: by the 1930s cancers and heart diseases caused over one-third of all deaths. Such evidence confirmed the continuation of incurable illnesses and suggests that medical effort was a rearguard action against the underlying causes of ill health. But, given that people continued to encounter illness and that there was some scope for its medical management, the issue of popular access to medical expertise remained important.

On the eve of the introduction of state health insurance, friendly society membership in Norwich was extensive: 'on the lowest estimate at least half of the adult wage earning male population provide against sickness in this way', although arrangements for women and families were less developed.[59] Additional hospital, charitable and poor law medical effort was consider-able, but there were gaps in provision and degrees of social stigma involved. The 1911 National Insurance Act compulsorily extended health insurance to most male manual workers, formalising arrangements made by 'approved societies', including friendly societies, trades unions and commercial concerns. Although the scheme offered general practitioner care, it was initially resented by most doctors because it resembled 'club practice' and they disputed the level of capitation payments. In fact, it secured their economic and professional position, as only qualified med-ical practitioners could act as panel doctors and authorise sickness claims. More men and some working women thus obtained access to primary care, but the scheme neglected hospital treatments and excluded the dependants of contributors. Many sought to remedy these defects by joining hospital contributory schemes and enrolling their dependants in sick clubs.

A local insurance committee represented local authorities, doctors and the insured, and its records suggest that over 42,000 people were registered when the scheme became operative in December 1913, the great majority of them enrolled on doctors' lists.[60]

The scheme expanded slowly, reflecting the modest growth in the work-ing population and the inclusion of 3400 young workers in 1937, but its main defects were not corrected. Tuberculosis sufferers were formally enti-tled to treatment, although only eighteen beds were available at Kelling hospital on the north Norfolk coast and many other victims remained at home or in workhouse wards.[61] Additional domestic shelters were pur-chased and child patients were sent to Holt hospital, while the Stanninghall farm colony was established jointly with the Red Cross for civilian and

Table 11.3 The National Health Insurance Scheme in Norwich, 1911–48

Date	City population	Date	NHI members	Numbers on doctors and FSMI[1] Lists	Number of doctors participating
1911	121,478				
		1914	46,297		
		1919	49,542		
1921	120,661				
		1927	54,761	51,032	
1931	126,236				
		1932	55,668	52,834	39
		1939	58,986	56,539	43
1940	115,400[2]				
		1947	62,090	58,302	
		July 1948 NHS	116,770	112,625	57
1951	121,236				

Source: NRO, NEC, Norfolk NHI Committee Minute Books, 1/1–2, 1912–49.
Note: [1] Friendly Societies' Medical Institute
[2] Estimated

soldier sufferers in 1919.[62] Medical access was another persistent problem: there was a supposed national average of 1000–1100 panel patients per doctor, but the Norwich average exceeded 1500. Some local doctors concentrated on private practice, others stacked up panel patients, and in poorer areas 'there were four or five doctors whose lists numbered about 3000 patients'.[63] In either model, the panel patient received little individual attention. Rising unemployment and the national economy measures of 1931 prompted fears of disqualification through lack of insurance contributions, and formerly employed married women were actually being struck off in 1932 and 1933.[64] Although the scheme was a landmark, its lack of comprehensiveness became clear with the registration of NHS patients, included for comparison in Table 11.3.

For those excluded from state health insurance, access to medical care was chiefly determined by income. Poor law provision was a last resort, although the emergence of proto-public sector health care can also be charted through sanitary improvement, the provision of isolation hospital facilities, the inspection of workplaces, and finally the development of personalised health services. Historically, the isolation of the infectious was adopted mainly to protect the wider public and almost any accommodation, including gate towers in the city walls at St Stephen's and a former lazar house in Salhouse, was deemed appropriate. Later facilities included the Bowthorpe Road 'iron hospital', used for smallpox cases and, briefly, as emergency operating rooms for the Norfolk and Norwich Hospital during the 1870s. Provision of a new isolation hospital in Bowthorpe Road 1893 (now the Julian Hospital site) was a significant response to health legislation and the detection of 'dangerous diseases' by the medical officer of health along with his staff of sanitary and schools' inspectors and health visitors. Over sixty beds and forty-eight cots were provided by 1900. With the decline of smallpox, the hospital focused increasingly upon scarlet fever, diphtheria and measles, although the number of beds for tuberculosis sufferers doubled to twenty-four by 1929.

The development of diphtheria anti-toxin boosted preventive medicine in the 1890s and was followed by the use of salvarsan, an essential in the treatment of venereal diseases, which was offered as a public service from the Norfolk and Norwich Hospital under the VD Act of 1917. But other infectious diseases, once contracted, could not be arrested until the advent of sulphonamide drugs and antibiotics in the late 1930s. Isolation thus remained an important defensive procedure, but the hospital's facilities were periodically swamped, for example by outbreaks of measles in 1918, influenza in 1919 and scarlet fever in 1922. It was also traumatic and haphazard: the absence of co-ordination with the poor law meant, for example, that pauper children with measles went to the workhouse whilst friends with scarlet fever went to the Isolation Hospital.[65]

Infant mortality in Norwich was considerably higher than national or county averages in the nineteenth century and there was no pronounced fall before the twentieth. Each year in the early 1900s ten qualified midwives attended roughly 2500 births, one-eighth of these at the maternity charity home. In response to the 1907 Notification of Birth Act, the city's public health committee appointed two health visitors to monitor infant welfare and dangerous diseases. This was an arduous and sometimes thankless task but, along with the provision of a pure-milk municipal depot and vitaminised milk for babies, it helped to reduce infant mortality rates. In 1919 the city council took control of midwifery services and, like the county council, began to send maternity cases with complications to the Norfolk and Norwich Hospital. Ten infant welfare centres offered antenatal clinics, babycare advice and monitoring for many children to the age of five. By 1938 four-fifths of births were either 'supervised' by fifteen district midwives, or seventeen private registered midwives, or took place at the overworked and inadequate city maternity home.[66]

Arrangements for schoolchildren were also flawed. By 1913 the Norwich medical officer of health aimed to inspect starters and leavers: 4700 children were examined and over 800 needed treatments, though barely half received them. Eight years later, the number of inspections had doubled and treatments were provided in 80 per cent of cases. Both the city and county councils provided block grants towards the cost of surgery or medical care at local hospitals, in parallel with the model for surgical obstetrics cases. But inspection was no guarantee of improved standards of child health, and important hospital treatments did not address fundamental problems. Roughly 14 per cent of Norwich elementary and secondary schoolchildren were malnourished in 1938, for example, compared with the national average of 11 per cent.[67] Following medical inspections, almost 30 per cent required treatment, in addition to those pronounced 'unclean' or in need of dental care.[68]

Medical provision by the mayor and corporation, formerly considered reasonable, attracted growing criticism by the 1830s. Some sick paupers remained in the workhouse because most of the infirmary beds were occupied by ninety or so elderly and infirm patients, but all were nursed by able-bodied paupers. At the infirmary just twenty-four sick beds were available and 'all the rooms appropriated for smallpox and other patients, and for lying-in women are so low and limited in their dimensions as to be utterly unfit for the purposes intended'.[69] The surgery and convalescent rooms were also 'quite useless', with cross-infection a constant hazard.

Provision for pauper lunatics was even worse. When it opened in 1814 with facilities for 104 patients, the Norfolk Lunatic Asylum was only the second provincial example of its type and, at a cost exceeding £35,000, it represented a substantial undertaking.[70] This was the county institution, however, and Norwich had separate, wholly inadequate, provision. A few city patients were sent to the Bethel hospital, but most were left in the workhouse until a makeshift asylum was added to the infirmary at St Augustine's in 1828. The accommodation for over a hundred inmates allegedly available by 1850 outraged the Commissioners in Lunacy and was acknowledged as 'hopelessly bad, and ... a disgrace to the city'.[71] Over fifty patients were later transferred to the county asylum, pending the construction of the City of Norwich Asylum at Hellesdon, three miles north west of the city. This opened in 1880 but became grossly overcrowded as a result the reception of additional patients from the county asylum, which served as a military hospital during the Great War. Even with peacetime re-conversion completed, the retitled Hellesdon Hospital contained nearly 700 patients and the county's St Andrew's Hospital had more than 1200. In 1930 the opening of Little Plumstead Hospital, mainly for mentally handicapped children and adults, was a belated development by national standards. Worse, the use of former workhouse accommodation at Swainsthorpe and Heckingham for senile and infirm patients suggested an economy-minded approach to their needs which persisted into the National Health Service.[72]

There was limited improvement in other local poor law arrangements for the sick. In the years between the 1831 Guardians' Act and the 1929 Local Government Act, Norwich was divided into eight districts, each with a part-time poor law medical officer. These doctors also attended the workhouse and infirmary for a period of six months by rotation. Their initial salary of £25 per year did not have to cover the cost of prescribed medicines, made up by a resident apothecary at the Elm Hill dispensary. Roughly £1000 was spent annually on mid nineteenth century poor law medical relief, salaries and the infirmary-asylum, so earlier criticisms that 'the care of the sick poor [was] undertaken as cheaply as possible' still applied.[73] For all the growth of provident and charitable services, over 2300 people in Norwich still relied upon poor law medical outrelief in the early 1900s.

A much-needed city workhouse and infirmary, costing £33,000, opened in 1859 on Bowthorpe Road. This accommodated over 600 inmates initially but by 1900 was increasingly used for aged, infirm or mentally ill patients. Most of the 170 infirmary patients were then described as 'feeble', though there were some child patients and a number of male tuberculous victims were placed in shelters. Although the available beds were reduced to 400 by 1925, three-quarters of these were infirmary beds in constant use, confirming the institution's changing role. The female wards had room for 117 beds, but thirty-two child beds and five cots were added and patients suffered 'intolerable overcrowding'.[74] Under the 1929 Local Government Act former poor law institutions could be utilised as public hospitals and some co-ordination of their facilities with the voluntary sector became possible. Funding shortages, however, were accentuated by the 1931 financial crisis and there was 'no official consultation ... with representatives of the voluntary hospitals'.[75] Infirmary facilities only improved after an additional ninety-bed block opened in 1939 and the need for use by the general public under wartime emergency measures finally led to municipal control. From 1941 the infirmary was known as Woodlands Hospital before it became the West Norwich Hospital under the National Health Service.

If medical provision in Norwich had developed markedly by 1939, it was not comprehensive in terms of the services supplied or the population covered. Many primary care services originating in philanthropic effort, such as maternity and nurse visiting, were now under municipal control, but they remained underdeveloped. Arguably, voluntary arrangements were flawed in that older endowed institutions had been designed for care rather than treatment – though care was also vital – and expanded very slowly, while newer hospitals often had slender financial resources. State medical insurance was now extensive but neglected family dependants and hospital provision. These restrictions were partly overcome by reorganisation on a quasi-provident basis. Significant numbers of family dependants relied upon sick club arrangements: 7550 with the Norwich Friendly Societies Medical Institute in 1936, for example. The former Norwich-based hospital contributory scheme expanded throughout the county (excepting west Norfolk), and into north Suffolk. It boosted hospital incomes, covering over 160,000 members, the great majority of whom were wage earners, and their dependants, for treatments by 1939.[76] But general practitioner referral to hospital was a precondition of financial support and not everyone could afford primary care. Services for the poorest were limited, particularly for women and children, who were also most likely to lack the adequate nutrition or accommodation deemed essential to well-being.

Inadequate peacetime health services might collapse in wartime, particularly under aerial bombardment. Proposals to evacuate 'routine' hospital patients were modified in 1936 so that the Norfolk and Norwich Hospital could handle casualty cases, while retaining 125 'civilian' beds. All child patients moved to the Jenny Lind and up to three hundred others were attended nearby, at St Andrew's and Hellesdon hospitals and the former poor law infirmaries at Wayland and Bowthorpe Road. Under the Emergency Medical Service, state funding now covered patient care, subject to availability, but was otherwise offered as of right. In the event, 340 people were killed in air raids on Norwich and over 400 of the 1092 recorded civilians injured were hospitalised. Moreover, the Norfolk and Norwich Hospital was itself badly damaged. More patients were evacuated and surgery was performed at outlying hospitals, with nurses accommodated at Bethel hospital, which had been cleared.[77]

As plans for the post-war National Health Service emerged, Norfolk and Norwich Hospital authorities hoped to secure financial assistance and independent status. They welcomed proposals for a £400,000 county-wide hospital fundraising effort and the prospect of contract work for government and local authorities, arguing that 'the best individual hospitals ... should be allowed to retain as complete autonomy as possible, provided they discharge their duties to the state satisfactorily and so earn the subsidies which everyone agrees must be paid to them by the government'.[78] Immediate post-war attempts to establish a university and medical school in Norwich, replicating the efforts of John Green Crosse in the 1820s, were forestalled by a lack of funds and the rival claims of Addenbrooke's Hospital and Cambridge University.

Primary care under the National Health Service closely resembled the old 1911 insurance scheme, now made universally available, and its greatest deficiencies removed. General practitioners henceforward referred the seriously ill to free, but tax-funded, nationalised hospitals. By December 1948, 96 per cent of the city population, including 55,000 new women and child patients, were registered with a National Health Service doctor. In the preceding six months 260,000 prescriptions were issued, 14,000 sight tests undertaken and 9850 pairs of spectacles supplied in Norwich. Evidently, 'the rush by the public on the health services has been quite beyond expectations ... the services at present were being strained to the utmost ... what would be the position in a winter epidemic?'[79] Particular problems, such as hospital waiting lists and inadequate facilities for maternity care, were being addressed by 1950, but these pressures on the new service constituted a legacy of deprivation, much of it economic and social in origin, which is still with us.

The development of medical services in Norwich over three centuries reflected a diversity of interests; it embraced a wide range of organisational forms and affected a considerable proportion of the city population with varying degrees of success. In many respects such provision was impressive; and, as one historical coda, we may note that attempts to establish a university and medical school in Norwich, originating with John Green Crosse in the 1820s have finally succeeded. Less optimistically, and over fifty years on from the establishment of the National Health Service and the Welfare State, fears that medical effort alone cannot guarantee health for all are only too evident.

12

Education since 1750

Michael Sanderson

> Norwich has, throughout its long history, been closely identified with the successive educational movements of the past and their impress is yet traceable in its ancient records and buildings, and even in its present institutions.
>
> The Handbook of the Education Week Held in
Norwich from September 27th to October 3rd 1925 [1]

The earliest education in Norwich probably goes back to pre-conquest times, when the church of the Holy Trinity is thought to have had a school.[2] In the later middle ages there were almost certainly song schools which taught reading and writing at St Giles's hospital, the church of St Peter Mancroft and the cathedral priory. In the fourteenth century the four friaries ran schools, as did some chantry priests in the city. But the main focus of educational activity was the cathedral, with its cloister school run by the Benedictines from the twelfth century. Also important was the episcopal grammar school founded by the first bishop of Norwich, Herbert de Losinga, shortly after his arrival in 1096. This was joined in 1311, if not before, by the almonry school. So three schools, if not more, were certainly operating in the vicinity of the cathedral in the first half of the fifteenth century. In 1540 the episcopal and almonry schools possibly merged as the king's grammar school with twenty boys still attached to the cathedral. Then, seven years later, the school was separated from the cathedral and refounded as King Edward VI's Grammar School (now the Norwich School).

The extent of this provision was fitting for a city of Norwich's culture and prominence as England's second city. That it was focused around religious institutions was partly an expression of Christian charity. It was also a means by which children of ability could be identified and developed for service in the church as one of the major highways of advancement in the world. But this was not a time when the 'education of the people' was seen as a necessary or realistic goal.

A secular initiative in this direction was Thomas Anguish's Childrens' Hospital of 1620.[3] This was not a hospital in the medical sense but in the older meaning of a place of care. Education was provided for the orphans who lived at Anguish's hospital at Fishergate. Ten boys and two girls were initially admitted, clothed and educated. By the eighteenth century the boys and girls lived in separate buildings at St Edmund's and Golden Dog Lane, about twenty in each. The realisation of a similar vision was intended by John Norman, mayor of Norwich in 1714. When he died a decade later, he left a considerable estate to charitable uses but devised it by an odd will. His intention was to create a school which would provide an education for thirty boys in literacy and the classics. But such were the complications of his will that it was not until 1839 that the school was actually built in Cowgate Street.[4]

Education prior to the eighteenth century had depended on these ecclesiastical foundations, a few secular charities, and presumably some teaching at home and by private schoolmasters about whom very little is known. The beginnings of a sustained attempt to create a more widely available education system date from the early eighteenth century.

From the early eighteenth century there was a strong charity school movement.[5] Nationally the movement had been started by the Society for the Promotion of Christian Knowledge (SPCK), founded in 1698. Starting as a tract-publishing organisation, it began to create schools in London and encourage their formation in the provinces to increase the readership of Christian literature. The first Norwich charity schools were founded in 1700, with four churches teaching poor children basic literacy and finding apprenticeships for them.[6] It is suggested that the SPCK made its first contact in Norfolk through Thomas Ibbot, the master of Swaffham grammar school, who 'communicated the designs' of the Society to the bishop of Norwich in July 1700.[7] Then in 1707 Bishop Trimnell raised more funds to establish further schools and in 1711 a committee was formed which by the following year claimed to have twelve schools in association.[8] They were regularly visited and the children clothed as well as educated. Sums of money were given for the schools, although their donors are not known (Figure 40).

After 1760 these donations were not recorded, possibly reflecting a diminution in financial support, itself a national trend. The money was invested variously in the Lottery and the Old South Sea annuities, and the income used to pay teachers' salaries, and to provide pensions and some clothing for the children. The schools were run by a committee of trustees in Norwich. The SPCK central committee in London, based on

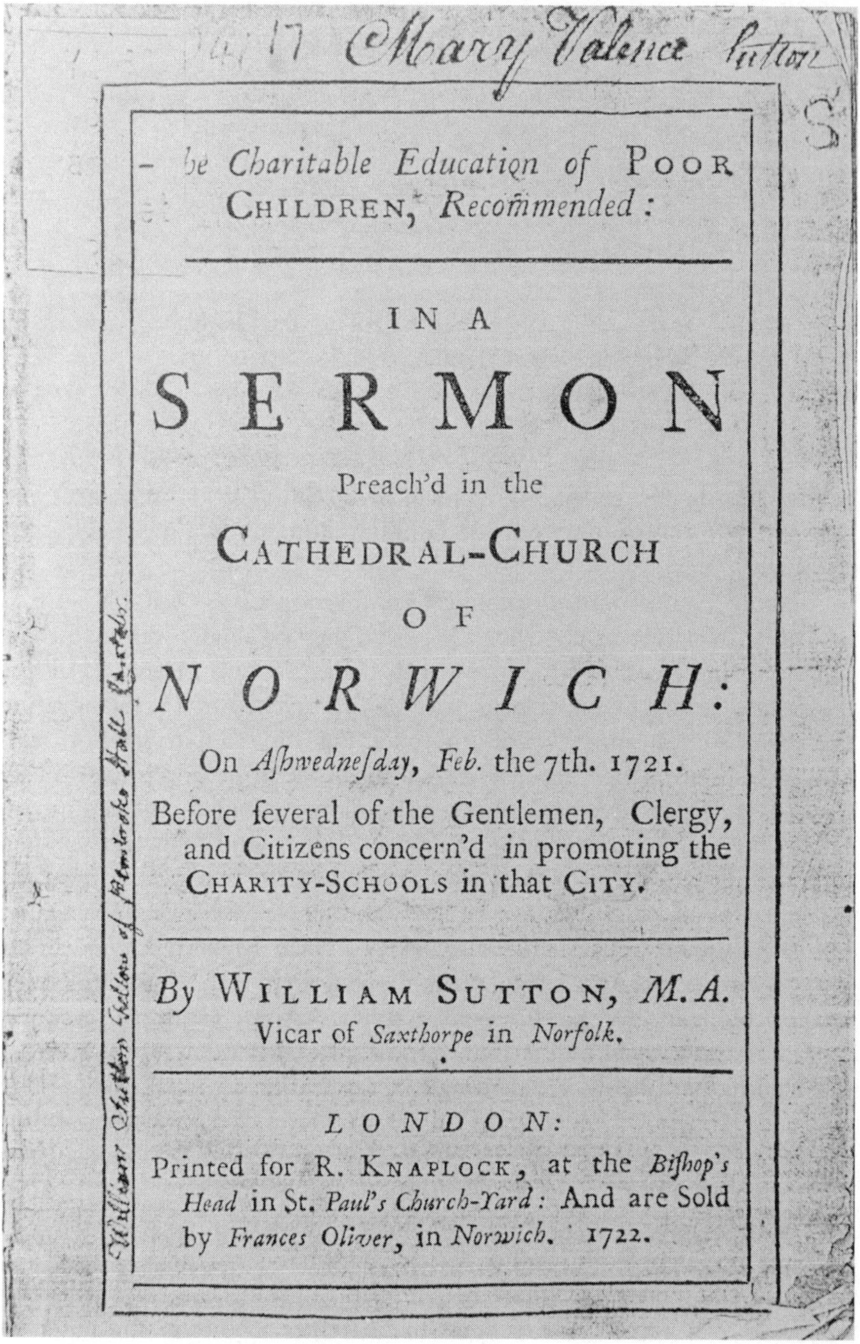

Mary Valence Sutton

William Sutton, Scholar of Pembroke Hall, Cambridge

be *Charitable Education* of POOR CHILDREN, *Recommended*:

IN A

SERMON

Preach'd in the

CATHEDRAL-CHURCH

OF

NORWICH:

On *Aſhwedneſday*, *Feb.* the 7th. 1721.

Before ſeveral of the Gentlemen, Clergy, and Citizens concern'd in promoting the CHARITY-SCHOOLS in that CITY.

By WILLIAM SUTTON, *M.A.*
Vicar of *Saxthorpe* in *Norfolk.*

LONDON:
Printed for R. KNAPLOCK, at the *Biſhop's Head* in St. *Paul's Church-Yard*: And are Sold by *Frances Oliver*, in *Norwich.* 1722.

FIGURE 40. A Charity School Sermon in Norwich, 1722. Such sermons encouraged the raising of funds for this early form of working class education. (*UEA Archives*)

Table 12.1 Donations to Norwich Charity Schools, 1711–60
(totals in £s per decade)

Date	Donations (£)
1711–20	802
1721–30	426
1731–40	820
1741–50	30
1751–60	775

Source: NRO, DN/NDS/1, A Book for the Charity Schools in Norwich, vol. i, 1711–1759; C/314/7, 703 XI, vol. ii, 1759–1815.

St Marylebone church, had no control over schools in the provinces and gave no financial support outside London, although it did provide text-books nationally.

Anglican control and the political complexion of the schools were as evident in Norwich as elsewhere. Whereas they originally were suspected of harbouring Jacobite sympathies, with the accession of George I in 1715 they came firmly to be seen as part of the defence of the Hanoverian Protestant succession. It was clearly stated that the schools were for 'educating children of the City of Norwich in the doctrine and liturgy of the Church of England'. As in London, the children paraded on the anniversary of the king's coronation in their new clothes, and their teachers had to be regular attenders of their parish churches.

There was also the intention in Norwich that the charity schools would not only support religion but also help to create an industrious labour force. A Norwich charity school sermon preached in 1722 stressed the value of the schools in 'training up so many poor destitute creatures to honest callings in the ways of industry' and urged those that stood 'at the Head of the Trading part of this Flourishing City' to see the advantage of training youth in 'Honest Diligence and Principles of Virtue'.[9] Yet instruction was not intended to expedite social mobility, for 'these poor children are born to be daily labourers'. It was believed that 'to qualify them for a rank to which they ought not to aspire ... would be injurious to the community'.[10]

In the late eighteenth century the charity schools took a new direction, reflecting the increasing industrialisation of England. The Norwich committee in 1784 agreed it 'expedient to introduce labour in the mode of education in the charity schools' and set up a spinning sub-committee two years later. Parents resented this unremunerated labour, especially since they were foregoing similar earnings by sending their children to school. By 1788 the children were being paid, and in the 1790s the basics of shawl making were introduced into the curriculum. The early eighteenth-century charity school ideals of education for the defence of church and state had been replaced by those of education for industry. The latter had serious shortcomings in that academic work, notably arithmetic, was neglected and the spinning school was closed in 1803.

This left 206 children in five schools by 1804, which were seemingly in good order. The final phase was presaged in a proposal of 1809 to establish a school on the plans of Joseph Lancaster and Andrew Bell. Lancaster and Bell were founders of two nationwide societies to build schools for the increased juvenile population. The British and Foreign School Society, founded in 1810, developed from the activities of the Quaker schoolmaster, Joseph Lancaster. This was followed in 1811 by the National Society, founded by the Reverend Andrew Bell, a former East India Company chaplain in Madras. Both devised monitorial systems whereby large numbers of children could be taught by monitors. The acrimonious difference between them was that the British Society was originally non-denominational but increasingly seen as nonconformist, whereas the National Society was firmly Anglican. In 1812 the Norfolk and Norwich National Society was established and offered £300 to the charity schools. New premises were bought in the parish of St Peter Hungate in 1812 (paid for partly from National Society funds and partly from the old charity school assets). In effect the charity school movement had merged with that of the new National Society.

The Norfolk and Norwich National Society had been formed at a meeting at the shirehall in July 1812. This took over the activities of the earlier charity school movement and tried to expand its provision. Growth was slow in Norwich. Only two schools – St Peter Mancroft and St Martin-at-Plea – claimed to be National by 1818.[11] Intriguingly, St Peter Hungate, noted above, no longer had a school by 1818. The poor simply went to adjacent schools. This tardiness is attributed to the priority given to rural areas by the society in the Norwich diocese. Also there was no great urgency in Norwich. In 1818 a parliamentary select committee on the education of the poor obtained evidence from all the parishes in England on the state of education. Most replies from Norwich to these 1818 returns suggested that poor children in the city already had ample access to schooling without much further expansion. 'There are so many schools in Norwich that all the poor children may be taught', claimed the vicar of St Augustine's, and many of the Norwich clergymen replied in the same vein. These 'many schools' would have been a mixture of endowed, charity and National

Schools and some schools run by private schoolteachers for the working class. Nevertheless there were renewed efforts in the 1820s, and by 1839 twenty-eight day schools enrolled some 2632 children.[12]

The new National Schools were supplied with teachers from the diocesan training college from the 1840s.[13] This was part of a nationwide movement whereby dioceses were expected to train their own teachers for National Schools and not rely on the central training college in Westminster. Accordingly, the Norwich college started in a house in the cathedral close in 1840, the students undertaking teacher training in National Schools in the city. After various locations in Norwich, it moved to College Road in 1892 and, following wartime bombing in 1942, to Keswick Hall in 1948. In 1981 it became the School of Education of the University of East Anglia (Plate 20).

Rivalling the National Society was the British and Foreign School Society. Its founder, Joseph Lancaster, visited Norwich in 1810 to lecture at the Theatre Royal and The Maid's Head. In the following year a Lancasterian school was established,[14] supported by leading nonconformists of Norwich. At the national level there were two Gurneys on the finance committee of the Lancasterian Society and three others as life governors. It was unsurprising that the younger J. J. Gurney, a Quaker banker, brother of Elizabeth Fry the prison reformer and resident of Earlham Hall on the outskirts of the city, should have taken a close interest in the Norwich school. He visited it daily, checked absentees and inspected similar schools in London for new ideas.[15] Likewise ,Jeremiah Colman, the founder of the mustard firm and a leading Norwich nonconformist, was on the committee of 1810 to establish the school in the parish of St Martin-at-Palace which also served as a Congregational chapel until 1819.[16]

As well as the Lancasterian school, non-Anglicans supported other educational initiatives. The Presbyterians ran a school with money left to the predecessor of the Octagon Chapel in 1709. This was maintained until 1902. Eight years later its funds were channelled into the new City of Norwich School. Similarly, the Roman Catholics occupied a chapel in St John's Alley from 1794 (now the Maddermarket theatre), which also served as a school. A subsequent chapel in St Swithin's Lane in 1801 became a school in 1828 after the opening of Willow Lane chapel in the same year. The 1818 returns referred to an evening school and a girls' school supported by the Gurneys, and to those maintained by Methodists, Quakers and other unspecified dissenters, besides the Lancasterian school and Presbyterian schools. Altogether this was a remarkable dissenting contribution to Norwich education.

Of particular interest was the school created by James Jeremiah Colman,

the great-nephew of Jeremiah Colman.[17] He inherited the family mustard
business in 1854 and developed it as a major source of employment in Norwich. He was also Liberal MP for the city. A Sunday and evening school had
already been started at the firm's mustard mill at Stoke in the 1840s, and a
new, purpose-built school was erected after the firm's subsequent move to
Carrow.[18] The school was non-sectarian and covered the usual elementary
subjects, together with history and geography. Its particular *forte*, however,
was practical handicrafts, both to cultivate manual dexterity and so that
pupils could learn the means of gaining a livelihood. Organisationally the
school remained independent, entirely supported by the firm until 1900,
when it was transferred to the Norwich School Board. Between 1887 and
1900 it had also served parents through evening classes in a range of technical subjects. It was one of the best schools in Norwich, an expression of
Colman generosity and an exemplar of practical elementary and technical
education.

By 1871 there were nineteen National Schools, nine British, two Roman
Catholic and three endowed schools in Norwich. The end of expansion of
the voluntary church school system occurred at the point where the new
Norwich School Board was established that year as a secular, elected, local
government body for education.[19] But as late as 1906 there were still fifteen
church schools in Norwich – three Anglican, eleven still described as
'National' and one Roman Catholic – educating over 5000 children.[20]

As well as these charity, National and other religious school movements,
other charities relevant to education were created or continued from the
past. The schools supported by Anguish's charity instructed boys in reading, writing and accounts before they were apprenticed, and girls in the
same subjects plus needlework before they entered domestic service. In
1864 the charity opened an industrial school for girls in Lakenham, teaching poor girls basic literacy, needlework, cooking and laundry work. The
boys' school was sold off in 1885. John Norman's endowed school, envisaged in his will of 1724, was at last built in 1839. It survived until 1934, when
its funds were used to provide educational grants for descendants of the
benefactor, known as claimants. A specialist educational charity was the
School for the Blind in Magdalen Street founded in 1805 by Thomas
Tawell, a wealthy one-time iron merchant.[21] Tawell, himself blind, was
influenced by similar schools in London, Liverpool, Bristol and Edinburgh.
He purchased a house and grounds in Magdalen Street and provided an
endowment of 1000 guineas. This was to create both a school for the young
blind of Norwich and Norfolk where they would be educated and taught a
trade, and also a hospital or asylum for the old.

Of particular importance in the history of education in Norwich is the

Town Close Estate Charity (NTCEC).[22] From the middle ages Norwich had been a city distinctive in the strength of its body of freemen, who were payers of taxes with the right to trade in its markets. In 1524 a long standing dispute with the Benedictine community was settled when the 'mayor, aldermen, citizens and commonalty of Norwich' relinquished grazing rights over lands claimed by the cathedral priory on the outskirts of Norwich in exchange for the Town Close, a triangle of land between the present Ipswich Road, Newmarket Road and Eaton Road. With the reform of Parliament in 1832 and municipal government in 1835, the freemen's role changed from one of exercising political power to that of a charitable body deriving its income from the ownership of the Town Close. The value of the close greatly increased in the nineteenth century as it gradually became the site of high-quality housing, and, after various legal disputes, the Charity Commissioners established the Norwich Town Close Estate Charity in 1892. It now became relevant for education, since it disbursed its funds not only in pensions and the support of freemen in hospital but also in educational grants to freemen's children to attend 'a place of education higher than elementary'. The recipients had to be residents of Norwich who had attended a public elementary school and who could pass an examination set by the charity. So restrictive did these conditions prove that only two pupils had qualified by 1909.

Accordingly, a further scheme in 1923 allowed the extension of grants to pupils in private schools in the city, and to students attending universities and teacher training college or engaged in professional training. Expenditure rose steeply from 1924 and usually exceeded that on pensions. After 1945, however, there was less need for educational grants and pensions since both were now more widely provided by the Welfare State. The Charities Act of 1960 therefore widened the purpose of the NTCEC even further, so that it was able to make a grant of £2000 to the new University of East Anglia in 1963. In the 1970s and 1980s the charity adopted a policy of selling property in the triangle and investing the proceeds in commercial property elsewhere. This greatly augmented the funds at its disposal. Another scheme in 1977 extended the scope of support to virtually all kinds of education and vocational, professional and physical training; and in 1983 to even wider academic and cultural activities in the city – theatres, the Triennial Festival, museums, church buildings and, for example, the production of this book. From being a narrow concern of freemen, the NTCEC has evolved into a generous benefactor of local education and culture in the widest sense.

Beyond these charities the poorest children were also provided for. A ragged school was formed in 1848. The purpose of ragged schools was to give a totally free education for those too poor to afford the fees required by the National and British Schools. In Norwich it took the form of a Sunday school teaching writing and arithmetic in the evenings on Sunday school principles. At one level it was successful, as numbers rose to seven hundred. But there were problems, as the support was largely nonconformist and the Anglican Church showed little interest. Also, the unmanageably large number of pupils were from the poorest families. Rowdiness was prevalent. On one occasion, the superintendent was 'grossly insulted' while trying to break up fighting between boys who displayed 'a degree of hardihood and want of shame scarcely credible'. There were no defined ages at which children and young people could attend such ragged schools. They included both the very young and rowdy teenagers, which explains the problem of large numbers and the disorderly behaviour in the Norwich establishment. It was closed in 1857.[23] The other agency educating the very poor was the workhouse school established by the New Poor Law after 1834. It educated and boarded children who were orphans or whose parents were in the workhouse. Usually about forty boys and forty girls attended the school. The practical benefits of their curriculum were apparently encouraging. In 1849, for example, three boys found occupations as trainee shoemakers, three went to sea, two became haberdashers, a couple went into hotel work and three left to seek jobs as watermen, carpenters and bricklayers. Of all the seventy-one boys educated between 1847 and 1851, only two had failed to become independent of the workhouse; most obtained their own livings, 'some in very respectable situations'.[24]

As in the rest of Britain, Norwich had an active Sunday school movement to supplement the work of the day schools. The first was started in St Stephen's parish church in 1785.[25] It was rapidly followed by others at St John Maddermarket, St Paul's, St James's, St George Colegate, St Clement's and St Michael-at-Thorn in the early months of 1786. The nonconformist Sunday schools seem to have been established rather later. The Methodists opened the first in 1808; James Martineau started (or revived) Unitarian Sunday schools attached to the Octagon Chapel.[26] The Congregationalists followed with their Prince's Street Sunday school established in 1820, with satellites in the nearby villages of Trowse and Thorpe formed in 1821 and 1839. The parliamentary enquiry of 1818 had listed thirteen Norwich Sunday schools educating some 698 children. Pupils were usually taught in the pews of churches and chapels, and partly for this reason it was regarded as inappropriate to provide instruction in secular subjects such as writing and arithmetic on Sundays. Accordingly, many Sunday schools taught these skills on weekday evenings, and confined Sunday education to reading and reciting chapters from the Bible. The attractions of the schools were

enhanced by the provision of sick benefits, boots, cakes and ale, and out-
ings such as that enjoyed by 1600 Sunday scholars on the newly opened
railway to Great Yarmouth in 1846.[27] Nonconformists placed great value on
the schools – James Martineau, J. J. Gurney and J. J. Colman being deeply
committed to their respective Unitarian, Quaker and Congregational
schools. Over half the children attending Sunday schools in the city were
nonconformists. The Sunday school movement in Norwich was rather less
important than in northern industrial cities, but more so than in comparable cities such as Exeter, Worcester or Shrewsbury. Certainly, its growth
in Norwich was impressive. The Sunday schools were popular institutions in the fullest sense, with the number of children in them increasing
from 698 in 1818,[28] to 5861 by 1835, and 7000 by 1851.[29]

This development of education to 1870, largely driven by religious and
charitable motives and organisations, was remarkable. Nationally about
8000 schools had been built, most by the National Society, making up
nearly a third of the public stock of schools in England and Wales today.
By 1870, however, it was thought necessary to make a more comprehensive
provision of elementary schools, built and run by local government bodies, on non-sectarian lines, with the power to exert compulsory attendance.
The 1870 Act created some 2000 school boards to bring this about.

The Norwich school board first met on 19 April 1871.[30] The members of
the first board were four gentlemen, three clergymen, a Catholic priest, and
a banker, printer, brewer, headmaster and wholesale confectioner. It found
that there were 10,644 children aged between five and thirteen years in Norwich of whom 8522 (80 per cent) were attending school and 2122 were not.
The reasons for non-attendance were chiefly the poverty of the parents,
girls looking after younger children and boys at work. The board decided
that attaining full attendance was as important as increasing the provision
of education. Accordingly, it decreed (as the 1870 Act gave it the discretion
to insist) that education for *all* children aged between five and thirteen
should be compulsory. The members also made classes virtually free at a
nominal farthing a week, although this was raised appreciably to three pence
after a dispute with the Education Department in London. The Norwich
school board made little attempt to recover unpaid fees, since it appreciated that wages in the city were lower than in nine other comparable towns
for which similar information existed. It made the important point that it
wanted children to receive an education virtually regardless of cost.

By the late 1890s the social composition of the board had become wider,
with working-class, female, nonconformist and professional membership.
It was also extending its activities well beyond elementary education (as

was common with boards throughout the country). Thus it ran evening classes, provided swimming lessons, bought pianos to provide basic musical education in schools, and built a physics laboratory in Duke Street. The Higher Grade School it opened in 1889 was its boldest innovation (Plate 21). This in effect was a working-class secondary school, as the plaque on its wall celebrating literature, science and the arts indicated. By 1894 sixty-three towns had similar higher grade schools. Sir George Kekewich, the secretary of the Education Department in London, whose clandestine policy was to encourage this drift from elementary into secondary education, looked on approvingly at these events in Norwich.

These surreptitious policies were rudely overturned by the Cockerton judgement in 1899, which declared pseudo-secondary schools such as Duke Street illegal. It presaged the complete reorganisation of education in England, replacing the Education Department in London with a Board of Education, and over 2000 school boards nationwide with 140 local education authorities. This was brought about by the 1902 Education Act. Already the Norwich school board had begun to see that its own days were numbered. On 11 February 1901 it urged the government to create a thorough system of secondary education and provide unified education authorities in local government. It held its last meeting on 28 September 1903 under Sir George White (chairman 1890–1903), by which time it was responsible for 14,589 children in nineteen schools. It had not only provided mass literacy for virtually all Norwich children but also in the process widened the horizons of narrow lives.

The consequence of this expansion of education, charitable, voluntary and municipal, was an inevitable rise in literacy in Norwich.[31] Between the mid eighteenth century and the 1880s there had been a good doubling of the literacy rate in the city. From 1839 it is possible to compare the Norwich figures with reliable national ones (see Table 12.2). They are in line with each other, the Norwich figures being somewhat above the national ones. The dip in the 1820s is more typical of industrial towns experiencing rapid population growth. Yet in Norwich it was comparatively slight. By the 1840s most people marrying were in occupations which demanded literacy and which reflect the importance of skilled crafts in the Norwich economy. Only hawkers, labourers, chimney-sweeps and husbandmen were generally illiterate. This is in sharp contrast to many northern cities, where most factory work could be undertaken by illiterate workers. In consequence Norwich was a more socially mobile society than that of towns in Lancashire. Sons of Norwich labourers who became literate were more likely, in comparison with their northern counterparts, to rise to better jobs than those of their fathers.

Table 12.2 Percentage literacy in Norwich and England, 1760–1884

	Norwich (Per cent)	England (Per cent)
1760	44.5	
1812	54.0	
1820	49.9	
1830	55.4	
1840	59.6	58.4
1850	69.2	61.4
1860	75.5	69.2
1870	79.1	76.5
1880	84.8	83.7
1884	86.9	86.7

Source: Smith, 'Education and Society' , pp. 254, 257, 269.

Following the Cockerton judgement of 1899 and the 1902 Act, education was restructured. The policies behind this were engineered by Sir Robert Morant, permanent secretary of the Board of Education in London and creator of the 1902 Act. His aim was to limit the transition of elementary schools into post-elementary education (the policy favoured by his predecessor Sir George Kekewich). Instead he wanted education authorities to develop properly structured systems of secondary education influenced by French and German models.

Norwich responded accordingly. First, the Duke Street higher grade school was reorganised as Norwich Municipal Secondary School in 1904, providing for both boys and girls. Secondly, the city had to create a new municipal grammar school. It was the plan of James Stuart, Sir George White and Alderman E. E. Blyth to merge together the Edward VI Middle School (a commercial school created in 1858 and called the Middle School from 1886),[32] the new Duke Street boys' department, and the old Presbyterian school, into the City of Norwich School (CNS) in 1910. This became a splendid example of the new kind of municipal grammar school envisaged by Morant. Meanwhile Duke Street became a girls secondary school, the city counterpart of the Norwich High School for Girls, and the precursor of the Blyth School of 1929. The new Norwich Local Education Authority, which replaced the school board, now provided five hundred secondary school places including forty scholarships to enable ex-elementary school pupils to attend secondary schools.[33]

A third aspect of Morant's policies was the creation of junior technical schools to focus on training for mid-teenagers preparing for the engineering and construction industries.[34] There were claims at the time that such a school would be especially appropriate for Norwich to offset the problems caused by boy labour in dead-end jobs.[35] In Norwich one was eventually created in 1919 in the Technical Institute (Plate 22). Finally, Morant was also keen to pioneer the social welfare aspects of schooling. Accordingly, attention was also paid in the 1910s to Norwich children with special educational needs. In 1908 an open-air school was set up, and moved to Colman Road two years later. Another was started in 1912 on the Clare House estate, specialising in children with tubercular tendencies; and the East Anglian Institution for the Blind was opened at Gorleston (near Yarmouth) to take blind children from Norwich.

Norwich was well provided with 'middle-class education' as the Victorians called it. The Edward VI School in the Cathedral close should have been the crown of Norwich education. Its quality and progress were, however, very patchy.[36] When it was functioning efficiently, its numbers were usually between 100 and 150, but in adversity they collapsed to eight in 1811 and thirty in 1859. In Georgian times it had enjoyed two prosperous periods under Dr Samuel Parr (1778–85) and the Reverend Edward Valpy (1811–29).[37] But the buildings were generally dilapidated and the trustees of the Great Hospital, who preferred to spend most of their £7000 a year income on the poor, provided a mere £300 for the school. In the mid nineteenth century there were attempts at reform. A chancery scheme in 1858 extracted £1000 from the Great Hospital and created the Commercial School, as an offshoot of the Edward VI School to train boys for careers in industry and trade. It was located in the precinct of the Blackfriars on the west side of the cloisters.[38] But the endowment income was insufficient to support both schools and the Commercial School drew off fees and pupils. The Edward VI School benefited from the headmastership of the historian Augustus Jessop (1859–80), one of the great Victorian reforming headmasters. He was determined to make the grammar school into a leading public school with prefects, more boarders, team sports and a military cadet force. Languages and science were to flourish in a scholarly sixth form. Yet in the late nineteenth century, since four-fifths of the endowment income came from land, the income of the school was seriously depleted by agricultural depression and the collapse of rents. The Commercial School (called the Middle School from 1886) suffered competition from the Higher Grade School in Duke Street. It must be admitted that for most of its history the Edward VI School was not worthy of a city of Norwich's standing.

The parents were not prepared to pay higher fees and they seemed neither to need nor value a good academic education for boys destined for family farms and firms. Only in the 1960s did it achieve standards truly appropriate for the city.

As in all cities, however, there was a tradition of private schooling run on commercial lines. Advertisements for no fewer than sixty-three private schools appeared in the *Norwich Mercury* in the seven years between 1749 and 1756, and the *Ipswich Journal* carried seven advertisements for Norwich schools between 1743 and 1747.[39] Their curriculums ranged from ordinary subjects to languages, navigation, accounts and Dutch for merchants. Some were clearly commercial academies. Dr William Enfield of the famous Warrington Academy came to Norwich in 1785 to teach from his home. The grandfather of J. H. Tillett (a Norwich MP and newspaper proprietor) 'kept a school of an old-fashioned sort' sometime in the eighteenth century.[40] J. J. Gurney attended a boarding school in Norwich kept by one Simon Browne from 1796,[41] whereas J. J. Colman went to the engagingly named Sarah Pigg's infant school in the parish of St Martin-at-Palace from 1837 before progressing to a private tutor in Norwich, John Dorman, until he was seventeen.[42] The rapidly increasing population of all towns in the early nineteenth century put pressure upon existing, publicly provided education and led to an expansion of private schooling. Those who failed to gain entry to the grammar school found places at the new Theatre Street House Boarding and Day School (1810), where Mr W. K. Farnell prepared young gentlemen for the professions and agricultural and mercantile pursuits. It was opposite St Stephen's churchyard and was destroyed by the widening of Theatre Street in the 1950s.[43] The tradition of small scale, somewhat hand to mouth private education continued, largely unrecorded, through the nineteenth century. In the late 1890s, for example, Ebenezer House was founded in Pelham Road and run by two sisters teaching young children whose parents regarded their offspring as socially superior to the entrants of board schools (Figure 41).[44]

A leading private school in Norwich in the nineteenth century was the Pottergate Street Academy. This was run by Charles Turner (1789–1861) in a fine Georgian mansion at 63a Pottergate.[45] Turner was a man of substance, and sheriff and mayor of Norwich, whose portrait hangs in St Andrew's hall. The curriculum was serious, with a classical department taught by his clergyman son to prepare boys for university. There were classes in mathematics and natural philosophy, practical courses on agriculture, commerce, bookkeeping and French, and a gentleman's social refinements were encouraged by lessons in dancing, music and drawing. Surviving work from the 1840s, offering beautiful copperplate writing, detailed commercial

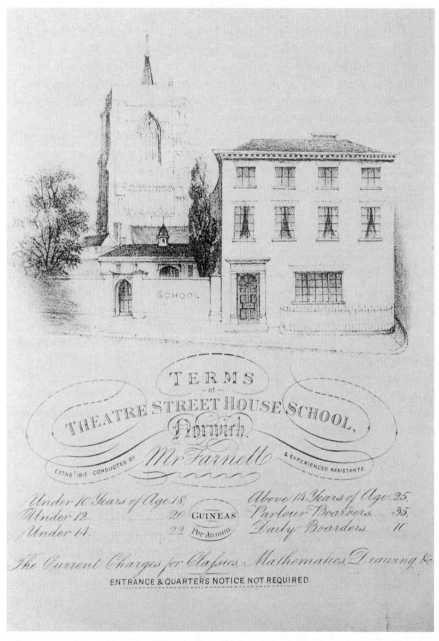

FIGURE 41. Prospectus for Theatre Street School, 1815. This was typical of private fee paying schools catering to the rising middle class population of the time. (*Norfolk Heritage Centre*)

arithmetic, and even a poem, suggests a first-rate middle-class private school. A later example was Paragon House, started in Earlham Road by a Dr Wheeler in the 1880s before moving to Bracondale in 1897. R. H. Mottram, the distinguished Norwich novelist, remembered the school with affection and saw it as part of a wider context in which 'there was every sort of establishment opened by any sort of gentleman who thought he would keep school in order to earn a living'.[46]

The Victorians had to face the specific problem of middle-class girls' education. In the early part of the century such girls attended private schools. By 1818 there were five ladies' boarding schools in Norwich.[47] The city, salubrious and cultured, had obvious attractions. Lonsdale House in Earlham Road, which opened in the 1820s and closed only in the early 1990s, was the most long lived of this type.

In the 1870s, however, two major permanent schools were established. In 1869 six sisters of the Roman Catholic order of Notre Dame came to teach at Ten Bell Lane school and in the next year founded the Notre Dame Boarding and Day School for girls.[48] The non-Catholic middle class of Norwich quickly saw the need for secondary education for their daughters. A Social Science Congress meeting in Norwich in 1873 focused these demands. Maria Grey, a founder of the Girls' Public Day School Company, was invited to Norwich and in consequence the Norwich High School for Girls was opened in February 1875 in Churchman House, in the parish of St Giles.[49] It was the first GPDST school outside London, one of six such provincial schools opened in that year. The Norwich school began with sixty-one girls, daughters of professional middle-class city families. In 1877 it moved to the Assembly Rooms with 350 pupils, finally transferring to its present site in Newmarket Road in 1933.

The curriculum was suitably rigorous, with classes in Latin, French, German, English and history. Science was tentatively introduced but, for lack of a laboratory, botany remained the only scientific subject until 1897 when it was joined by biology. The rapid development of science waited until the inter war years. Yet, in keeping with the social status of the pupils, afternoons were devoted to ladylike pursuits – music, dancing, drawing – with shorthand for those seeking future work in the 'white blouse' secretarial revolution of those years. The physique of the girls was not neglected. Initially they were drilled by a sergeant major from Norwich Barracks, then games were introduced; tennis from the 1880s, cycling and hockey from the 1890s, physical training in 1914 and lacrosse a year later.[50]

Technical education in Norwich had numerous roots. In 1825 a mechanics' institute was founded, at the same time as in many other towns in Britain.

It grew out of the Norwich Penny Library of the previous year. Situated in St Andrew's Street, it provided lectures, a library and a collection of scientific apparatus. There was also Norwich's famous artistic tradition, which reached its finest expression in the work of the Cromes and J. S. Cotman and in the foundation of the Norwich Society of Artists of 1803. On a commercial front, those struggling to run Norwich's declining textile industry saw the need for industrial design. Accordingly, John Barwell, a local wine merchant, secretary of the Norwich Society of Artists and vice-president of the mechanics' institute, organised a Norwich polytechnic exhibition in 1840 as part of a movement to create a school of design. The Norwich School of Design was established in 1846 in St Andrew's hall, one of twenty-one schools created nationally in the decade between 1842 and 1852.[51] Although the school's committee consisted of four textile manufacturers and a draper, a confusion of purpose arose. There were complaints that the school was insufficiently relevant to the manufactures of Norwich. When drawing became compulsory in National schools in 1853 and in training colleges in the same year, the training of teachers became a major purpose of the school. It also depended financially on fees paid by amateur ladies for drawing lessons. The teachers and the ladies quite outnumbered the artisans. As manufacturing fancy textiles gave way to the production of beer and boots in Norwich, the Art School seemed to have less industrial relevance. It survived on the top floor of the new public library opened at the corner of Duke Street and St Andrew's Street in 1857.

In 1886 the school changed its name to the Norwich School of Science and Art and included more practical tuition in the building trades. Between then and 1891, of the total 1120 pupils, 312 had entered trades, 312 became teachers, 210 were 'middle-class pupils' and 286 comprised 'boys and girls of the industrial classes at school'. Undoubtedly its most celebrated pupil was Alfred Munnings, a brilliant advertising artist for Caleys, celebrated painter of rural life and irascible president of the Royal Academy.[52] He remembered with affection the 'pleasant studious atmosphere' of the school. Munnings's early career combined both the commercial and fine art aspects of the school. When the new Technical Institute was built between 1899 and 1901 the School of Art became part of it in the latter year.

Following the Technical Instruction Act of 1889, the Norwich Technical Instruction Committee was formed in December 1890 to consider its implementation, along with that of the subsequent Local Taxation Act of 1890.[53] The initial technical instruction committee consisted of eight people under the chairmanship of George White, the shoe manufacturer (Plate 47). The occupations of the other members were medical practitioner, two solicitors, a manufacturing clothier, a tailor-outfitter, a tea and coffee merchant and a 'gentleman'.[54] Recommending that a technical school be built, they then came to form the core of an expanded committee. They were joined by another tea and coffee merchant, a provision merchant, a watchmaker and silversmith and another gentleman of unknown occupation. Most were clearly businessmen, but with a bias towards commerce rather than manufacturing.[55]

There was thus a good deal of disparate technical education provided in Norwich, at the Art School, at Duke Street Higher Grade School, and in the science and art department classes at the Presbyterian school. But in a city of Norwich's size a fully-fledged, purpose-built technical college was badly needed. Early teaching began in temporary premises in St George's Street, moving to Bethel Street after 1892, before the building of the Technical Institute by St George's bridge was undertaken between 1899 and 1901. Student numbers increased from 460 in 1895 to 1140 by 1906. Yet there were disappointing elements about the 'Tech'. Older workers, fearing it would erode their skilled exclusivity, ridiculed the idea that trades could be learnt in college. And, surprisingly, the boot and shoe industry did not engage more with the institute. There were more (women) students in dressmaking and cookery than men in the boot and shoe classes. As a proportion of their workforces, far more masons and plumbers (between 10 and 17 per cent) took courses than did boot and shoe makers (1.5 per cent). C. B. Hawkins deplored the fact that few ex-elementary school pupils went on to further technical study. He believed that one problem was that evening classes were too tiring after a day's work. Moreover, the subject matter was either already taught in elementary schools or appeared to offer 'strictly bread and butter subjects' which did not attract adults.[56]

In the interwar years education in Norwich underwent significant restructuring. The Hadow Report of 1926 advocated an advance on the pre-1914 situation whereby most children went to elementary schools and stayed there until they left at thirteen. Sir Henry Hadow wanted more children to receive a secondary education; indeed, 'secondary education for all' became a slogan of the time. There were to be more grammar schools and, for those who could not attain entrance to them, senior schools for children over the age of eleven were to be distinguished from the elementary schools for younger children. Norwich responded to these challenges in various ways.

In 1919 a junior technical school was created to diversify post-elementary education. It provided a full-time, two-year course to prepare boys for the construction trades. This became the main daytime activity of the

Technical Institute in St George Street. To it was added a junior art school in 1925 and a junior commercial school in 1937. They closed in 1951 and 1957 respectively, with the junior technical school becoming the Hewett School in 1958. In addition two central schools, in Angel Road and Nelson Street, were formed in 1924 to provide less academic children with the elementary curriculum, a lot of craft work and, even, French. Pupils stayed until sixteen and the curriculum was given a strong commercial bias in their last terms. In 1930 the central schools transferred from Angel Road and Nelson Street to Duke Street as the girls' Municipal Secondary School moved out to become the Blyth School.

The fall in the birth rate changed elementary education. The number of children on the registers of elementary schools fell from 19,129 in 1920 to 14,076 in 1940, and the number of elementary schools contracted from seventy-one in 1924 to fifty by 1940. This easing of pressure enabled the age of admission to be reduced from four to three years. Conditions of schooling also improved. Of the seventy-eight acres of playing fields owned by the LEA in 1939, fifty-four had been acquired in the last four years. Altogether there was a greater emphasis on play areas, grass and flowers, school pictures and large windows.[57]

For those children not in secondary (grammar), junior technical or central schools, post-elementary education was provided in senior schools. Five schools were built for senior girls and three for boys. Most prominent among these was the Alderman Jex Senior Boys' School, completed in 1939. These senior schools taught the academic curriculum as well as a good deal of practical crafts and domestic science. By 1939 Norwich was proud that all children over eleven were taught in secondary or senior schools. The rise of the senior schools occasioned the closure of the central schools in 1937, since their purpose and curricular distinctiveness had become less evident.

Norwich was also rightly proud of its recreational evening institutes which were held in four schools across the city. They provided meeting places for youth for worthwhile recreation – physical training and games, arts and crafts hobbies, and amateur dramatics. 'The primary concern is the welfare and happiness of the members', noted the director. Certainly the evening institutes were a much appreciated feature of education in the city in the interwar years.[58]

At the peak of the municipal system were the two grammar schools. The City of Norwich School (CNS), as we have seen, was founded in 1910. It rapidly became the foremost school in Norwich and one of the best in the country under its headmaster, W. R. Gurley (1910–29), the former head of the Edward VI Middle School.[59] Academic success was remarkable in the

1920s. In each year between 1921 and 1925 its boys gained more Cambridge school certificates than any other school in the country. By 1928 the school had sent fifty-three pupils to university, including amongst them five future graduates with double firsts and PhDs. The school's contribution, however, was not only academic. The school magazine was full of articles introducing boys to the professions, law, banking, accountancy and insurance. Most boys did not then go to university but entered the commercial and industrial life of Norwich. The CNS perfectly exemplified the hopes of Morant's 1902 Act in providing academic and career opportunities for a social class below those attending the old endowed schools. Its counterpart for girls, the Blyth School, was created in 1929 from the Municipal Girls' School, which had occupied Duke Street since the removal of boys to the CNS in 1910. Accordingly the number of girls receiving a municipal secondary education in Norwich rose from 336 in 1920 to 563 by 1937 (Plate 23).

The reorganisation entailed school closures and new building. Between 1926 ands 1939 no fewer than twenty-seven schools closed. These were old buildings in the centre of Norwich where populations had been reduced by slum clearance. In the same period twenty-two schools were built on new housing estates as the population moved out. By 1939 over 8000 children, more than half the total, were accommodated in new schools on the outskirts of the city.[60]

These developments were impressive and Norwich's position was favourable by national standards.[61]

Table 12.3 Number of children in grant aided secondary schools, per thousand population, 1925 and 1937

	1925	1937
England and Wales	9.7	11.8
Norwich	11.9	16.5

Source: NRO, N/TC/ 35/5/9, fo 495, Post Primary Education in Norwich, 24 February 1940.

Yet there were problems and criticisms. Of children who qualified for admission to secondary schools, 15 per cent did not take up scholarships owing to economic circumstances. Some never got the chance to sit the examination.[62] Yet HMIs thought that Norwich's secondary schools more than amply provided for the population. This had fallen from 126,000 in

1931 to 119,000 by 1940. It therefore seemed unnecessary to increase provision further. Indeed, the LEA proposed reducing the streams to the CNS and the Blyth School. It also believed that there was too much academic education and not enough vocational training. The Blyth School therefore started a commercial sixth form preparing girls for work rather than university. Conversely, there was probably too much concentration on domestic subjects for poorer working-class girls whose time would have been better spent learning to make a living.[63] Finally, there were uneasy relations between the maintained and non-maintained sectors. The Edward VI School and Norwich High School for Girls appealed to the LEA for increased subventions but were firmly and rightly refused.

The schools provided Norwich with a well-prepared supply of labour. Elementary school children in 1939 went into the following occupations:

Table 12.4 First occupations of pupils form Norwich elementary schools, 1939

Boys	Per cent	Girls	Per cent
Distributive trades	27.9	Boot and shoe factories	33.1
Boot and shoe factories	25.5	Chocolate and cracker factory	14.2
Engineering	9.3	Shop assistants	10.4
Joinery, carpentry	8.7	Tailoring	8.0
Sheet metal workers	8.0		
Others/unknown	20.6	Others/unknown	34.3
Total	100.0		100.0

Source: Rackham, *Education in Norwich*, p. 27.

Those of secondary school pupils 1931–39 are presented in Table 12.5 below. Pupils in the Norwich junior technical and junior commercial schools were more vocationally targeted (see Table 12.6).

In the immediate post-war years educationalists in Norwich had to respond to the 1944 Education Act.[64] Their proposals are summarised in Table 12.7.

The grammar schools, both independent and municipal, carried on as before. Indeed, Norwich was much better supplied with these than the country at large. The city's education committee did not contemplate comprehensive schools at this stage. Its strategy was to turn the senior schools of the 1930s into the new secondary modern schools. The overall balance

Table 12.5 First occupations of pupils from Norwich secondary schools,
1931–39

Boys	Per cent	Girls	Per cent
Commercial clerks	24.7	Clerical	45.9
Local government	10.3	Shop assistants	13.0
Professional clerks	7.4	Training College	4.8
Shop assistants	7.3	Factory	4.1
Industry	6.8	University	2.8
Engineering	5.5	At home	2.9
H.M. Forces	3.2	Commercial school	2.6
University	2.3	Nursing	2.6
Employed by father	1.7	Civil service	1.8
Printing/journalism	1.5	Hairdressing	1.8
Pharmaceutical chemist	1.4	Laboratory assistants	1.1
Student teachers	1.1	Student teachers	0.8
Building	1.0	Tailoring/dressmaking	0.8
Commercial school	0.9	Domestic servants	0.5
Railway clerks	0.8	Library	0.5
Transferred	3.7	To other schools	5.8
Unknown/unemployed	11.4	Others	8.2
Others	9.0		
Total	100.0		100.0

Source: Rackham, Education in Norwich, p. 28.

Table 12.6 First occupations of pupils from Norwich Junior Technical
and Junior Commercial Schools, 1939

	JTS (per cent)	JCS (per cent)
Engineering	32.0	1.6
Clerical	–	88.5
Building	13.9	1.6
Printing	8.6	–
H.M. Forces	17.2	–
Boot and Shoe	7.5	1.6
Shop assistants	–	3.2
Commercial	7.5	–
Other/unknown	13.3	3.5
Total	100.0	100.0

Source: NRO, N/TC/35/5/9, fo. 495, occupations entered by
pupils from Norwich Secondary and Technical Schools, 1939.

Table 12.7 Norwich proposals for the implementation
of the 1944 Education Act

School	Number	Places	Per cent	National comparison (per cent)
Voluntary	1	360	4.1	10.0
Independent and direct grant places	–	500	5.7	1.0
Grammar	2	1,800	20.7	13.0
Technical	3	950	10.9	7.5
Modern	13	5,080	58.4	51.0
Comprehensive	0	0	0	12.5

Source: See note 64, below.

was to be forty-six to forty-seven infant streams, forty-five to forty-seven junior, thirty-seven to forty-five secondary modern and ten secondary grammar and technical streams. The Norwich plan was held up by the Minister of Education until 1951, since he and the HMIs insisted on a secondary technical school for Norwich, which J. W. Beeson, the chief education officer, was resisting. Eventually it was agreed to build such a school in conjunction with the City College (the new name of the Technical College since 1941). Some Labour Party members hoped the deadlock would lead to the complete rejection of the plan, thereby opening the way for one based on comprehensive education. As part of the implementation of the 1944 Act twenty-one new schools were built by 1961 – nine infant, seven junior and five secondary. Advocates of comprehensives got their way in the 1970s when Norwich followed national policy. Hence the Blyth (grammar) and Jex (senior then secondary modern) were merged as Blyth Jex, and the old Junior Technical School became the Hewett School under the notable headmastership of Walter Roy. In 1974 control of Norwich's schools passed to Norfolk County Council.[65]

The creation of the University of East Anglia (UEA) was another of the major post-war educational developments in Norwich.[66] It was part of a wider expansion of universities in the 1960s, including Sussex, York, Essex, Warwick, Kent at Canterbury and Stirling. They all arose from certain national pressures. More children were staying on in sixth forms, the birth bulge of the end of the War was scheduled to arrive in universities by the mid-sixties, and without expansion there would have been a shortfall of places for 25,000 young people capable of, but denied, university education. There were also concerns to increase working-class participation in higher education and to redress the neglect of technology. Above all, there was a belief that more higher education would improve Britain's post-1945 economic growth performance.

Norwich had long-standing claims to a university. The Norwich University Extension Society had been running university lectures since 1901, and the Technical Institute was preparing students for London University degree work. But the city had no hope of gaining a university in the 1900s when the major civic universities were chartered. Its population was too small; agricultural depression and lack of industrial development had left it poor; and, apart from the new Technical Institute of 1901, it had no upgradable institution. After the Great War an attempt was made to create a university as a war memorial, but it failed for lack of resources. Twenty years later, the intention to make the Technical College the basis of a university was thwarted by the outbreak of war. The ending of the war brought yet another unsuccessful initiative in 1947. Then, under the impact of the national changes indicated above, proposals for a University of Sussex were accepted in February 1958, which reactivated the Norwich movement. Lincoln Ralphs, the director of education for Norfolk and a leader of the 1947 movement, and Andrew Ryrie, vice-president of Colmans, both independently made speeches calling for a university in Norwich. The arguments were undeniable. No other city and no other regional aggregate population of 500,000 was so far from a university. Norwich would be an ideal centre for curricular development in biology, chemistry, and the food sciences – all related to agriculture. The Universities Governing Council agreed to a university in April 1960 and it opened three years later under its first vice-chancellor, Frank Thistlethwaite (1963–80). Under him and four successors it has thrived and expanded to over 13,000 students (Plate 24).

The achievements of the UEA have been considerable. In the sciences it has developed strengths in environmental sciences, now boasting the premier department in Britain and arguably in Europe, its interests ranging from the Norfolk Broads and North Sea gas to the global climate, especially problems in the Arctic, Brazil and the Vietnamese coastline. The university has always been prominent in biology and chemistry and is now a leading centre for biochemistry and metallobiology. This is strengthened by the university's being part of the Norwich Research Park, home of the John Innes Centre and various food and agricultural research laboratories of international standing. It also contains the Norfolk and Norwich University hospital, a vital concomitant of the new medical school of the university. In the Arts and Social Studies UEA has undoubtedly the leading social work school in Britain and is strong in history, art history (supported by the Sainsbury Centre for Visual Arts) and creative writing (led at various times by two knighted professors and the poet laureate). UEA has always faced the dilemma of how far it is an international research university and how far it should serve Norwich and the region. In practice it does both. Its global concerns are evident in environmental, climatic and development studies. Yet is provides a regional service through the Centre of East Anglian Studies and its commitment to local history, and by virtue of the expertise UEA academics have brought to regional environmental, social work and medical matters. Its last vice-chancellor, Vincent Watts (1997–2002), also served as chairman of the Eastern Region Development Council. It is, moreover, also one of the most architecturally noteworthy of all new campuses, with prize-winning buildings by Sir Denys Lasdun, Norman Foster, Sir Bernard Fielden and Rick Mather. Sir Timothy Colman, the county's long-serving lord lieutenant, regarded the creation of the university as the most important development in Norwich in the second half of the twentieth century.

On a parallel track, the Norwich City College (the former 'Tech') moved into its completed buildings in Ipswich Road, begun in 1937 but not officially opened until 1953. Its numbers increased from 5000 students, including only 205 full timers in 1948, to 7500 (with 715 full timers) in 1965, to 13,000 (with 2500 full time) by 1991. Expansion has been accompanied by curricular change. Junior departments were hived off in the 1950s as the college became a totally post-school institution of further education. Advanced subjects relevant to industry continued to develop, including business and management studies, mathematics and computer studies, electrical and production engineering, while its hotel school with its much appreciated public restaurant opened in 1953. The relevance of the college to local industry was further emphasised after the Education Act of 1988, giving a predominant voice on the governing body to local employers. Degree work was encouraged and facilitated by a link with the Anglia Polytechnic University from 1991.[67] An independent survey found Norwich City College 'one of the most cost effective Further/Higher Education Colleges in the country', which attracted 'a general chorus of approval from employers for the training services provided by the College'.[68]

The fourth noteworthy development was the revival of the King Edward VI Grammar School under its headmaster Stuart Andrews (1967–75), the most outstanding head since Jessop. Andrews forced the parents to support the school by raising fees. In 1975 he disengaged the school from the last state link of the direct grant system to make it totally independent. The increased finance facilitated the expansion of creative arts, computing, the library and science laboratories. It also provided more scholarships and assisted places for the able but less affluent. The school was at last made worthy of the city, parents now being more concerned about academic results, so that their offspring could enter good universities and competitive professions.[69]

The path of educational development in Norwich has mirrored that of the nation. It responded to voluntary movements – charity schools, National, British and ragged, had its own stock of endowments and inevitably complied with national legislative policy through the Acts of 1870, 1902 and 1944. This gives the pattern an expected predictability. Yet educational achievement and provision in the city often appears rather better than normal. The rise of literacy was slightly above the national trend. Norwich's 1818 returns, for example, were remarkable in suggesting ample provision well received. Lord Brougham, who was expecting to use negative responses to convince Parliament of the need for state intervention, must have regarded the Norwich evidence with mixed feelings. Norwich's gradual population rise and lack of social problems attendant on rapid heavy industrialisation did not place unmanageable demands on education. Facilities in the city also benefited from the strong religious influence both of the Anglican Church and prominent nonconformist families. The number of British schools, the survival of church schools after the 1870 and 1902 Acts, and the pioneering activity of the Colman family were very evident. The Norwich School Board was as progressive as any, with its attempts to enforce compulsory, virtually free education, its post-elementary school in Duke Street, and its provision of swimming lessons and pianos.

The first generation of pupils from the City of Norwich School was outstanding as an example of the new municipal grammar school. Likewise, Norwich was a famous provincial pioneer of girls' secondary education. The Hadow reorganisation in Norwich was good, providing more secondary places than the national average and replacing elementary schools with genuine senior schools. Moreover, the targeting of pupils to appropriate local occupations seemed successful.

On the more negative side, it is surprising that the King Edward VI School was not more successful until recent times, even accepting an inferior role to the CNS which provided its science teaching. Also, while the Technical Institute itself seems to have been eager to relate to local employers, the use of it by Norwich's main industry of that time – footwear – was remarkably slight. There was a mismatch between the late Victorian rhetoric of the need for technical education for industry and the reliance of 'The Tech' on women artists and cookery classes. It was conversely a pity that Norwich did not develop a secondary technical school after the 1944

Act, to the exasperation of the Ministry of Education and HMIs, who refused to authorise Norwich's implementation plan until remarkably late. It was also regrettable that the University Grants Committee advised the new UEA not to have relations with the burgeoning City College. This decision contributed to the deficiency of vocational education at the university until recent years.

Yet overall what impresses is the normality of the development and that quality above the norm is so recurrent. Norwich has been a well-educated city, a feature which has contributed greatly to its culture and prosperity.

13

Architecture since 1800

Stefan Muthesius

Norwich has a rich history and a significant and purposeful past. Her present is significant too, in so far as it shows that, unlike her bygone alter ego, she has failed to recognise the potentialities of the age and the need for progressive change.

City of Norwich Plan, 1945[1]

Architecture is not only the most impure of the visual arts but, unless of a venerable age, it has also been subjected to the most diverse evaluations. Judgments are liable to change and to clash much of the time. It is not enough to ask one simple question: is it good architecture? We not only want to know: is it a good building? is it a building that corresponds to national standards? but also, is it a building that suits Norwich? Today, around the year 2000, architecture is enjoying perhaps a better press than it has done for a long time, new buildings, that is. But it has to be 'famous'. The buzzword 'signature architecture' speaks of the pressing need, the compulsion even, to employ a great name. What may also help with fame is notoriety – witness a number of the most prominent recent buildings in London, designed by world-renowned practitioners. It would have been impossible for the city of Norwich to turn to somebody less celebrated than Sir Michael Hopkins for its new library. Will, in addition, something soon go wrong, will there be some harsh criticism, as well as praise? The University of East Anglia (UEA), with its sequence of famous architects, has long received a constant alternation of praise and criticism.

This chapter seeks to remind readers first of all of some of the immense diversity of Norwich's architecture. But the main points of contention that run through this whole account are the diverse ways of judging those buildings of Norwich and the ways these judgements were arrived at. There is, above all, a division between judgements made from inside and from outside. There is the issue of ordinary user versus the specialist critic. In each case judgements might constitute polar opposites. As ordinary local users we might be content with a building, but the critic from outside tells us that it is dull architecture – or vice-versa. The desire for the 'signature architect' starts at the architectural end, so to speak; at considerable cost we engage a big name designer, most likely from the capital or even from abroad, because this promises unusual and striking shapes. We are then unhappy when we find deficiencies in its practical usefulness. Strictly speaking, though, all this is not a new problem. We may simply take it as a new version of the oldest definition of architecture, valid from ancient Greek and Roman times: any building may be 'divided' into the mundane and the decorated. The Victorians and the Modernists added one important further critical dimension: a new building must be stylistically advanced. 'Advanced' and 'backward' are more often than not linked to the evaluation 'backward-provincial' versus 'metropolitan-advanced'. As time went on the question of the region's, or of Norwich's own character gained prominence, but the old polarity of inside-outside or local-national still applied: who was in the best position to recognise the character of Norwich, the locals or those from outside?[2]

One way to simplify the problem is to begin with an assessment of some buildings in purely 'architectural' terms. We may hereby disregard their practical use; we may in fact arbitrarily pick out just a few decorative features of a building. What the buildings meant to those who financed and built them, that is, to its patrons, is of secondary importance. There is little concern for any local specificity. It is likely that the building was designed by an architect of note, but not even that is a stringent condition. It is also not relevant whether the building is considered advanced or retrogressive in stylistic terms, whether it is ahead of or behind its time. We are, in short, taking an architectural enthusiast and tourist point of view, or simply engaging in a search for uniqueness, as well as diversity (Plates 25–34)

The second and major part of this contribution proceeds quite differently. We must now scale down our postulated values of 'outstanding art' and our demands for uniqueness and enter a world of more 'normal' kinds of architecture. A building should, first of all, be understood in its entirety. Buildings are now taken as locally specific, they were primarily built not for tourists or for the architectural critic, but for the citizens of Norwich, for their day to day users. This account must restrict itself to major buildings, those which concern the town as a whole, hence neither minor commercial architecture nor private domestic building can be considered here.[3] And yet, our previous criteria are not given up altogether. Virtually all the buildings discussed here also belong under the classical definition of architecture; they, too, carry decoration, they were subject to the law of necessary decorum, according to each building's exact social status. Furthermore, these buildings have a part in nationwide discourses of architecture; hence they are to a greater or lesser extent subject to considerations of provinciality versus metropolitan-centredness. But the local specificities and the social and economic contexts come first.

We must begin with what appear to be some facts of general economics. If we take the later eighteenth century as a starting point, hardly any major town, or even medium-sized country town, showed a slower growth than Norwich. True, one has to be aware of the way in which private building, for example, palatial country houses, far outshone any urban municipal activities well into the nineteenth century. But it was the large terraces of the smartest residences that began to transfer some of the country estate splendours into the towns, or at least to the suburbs. Yet the mass of the urban populations still did not count as patrons or recipients of 'architecture'. In many towns we witness the beginnings of an industrial architecture, but although impressive in their size, the buildings normally showed just bare walls and were thus, at the time, not classified under the category of architecture. Even so, town halls and some other corporate buildings began to catch up during the 1820s and 1830s, especially in the industrial north. What did Norwich have to show in terms of these considerable new opportunities for architecture, even by 1850? Very little indeed. The building of large suburban terraces and architecturally ambitious villas hardly happened here, for which an added reason may have been the way in which the Norwich elite tended to stay in their small country seats nearby. As regards early small mass housing, Norwich developed rather on the lines of midland industrial towns, with a plethora of back to back and court layouts, while later in the nineteenth century its neat rows of the regular small terraced house type developed more on southern English lines.

There was one kind of architecture that served everybody, almost by definition, and that was of course the church. A new church or chapel we are sure to find wherever there was a growth in population, or a new suburban development.[4] The first of a new group of buildings for the Established Church were mostly large in order to cater for the new 'masses', the so-called Commissioners' Churches, starting around 1820, which benefited directly from assistance by the state. Norwich followed only from the 1840s. Christ Church, Catton, consists mainly of a copious and low nave. It is kept in the Early English style of Gothic, or, to use a less academic term, the 'Lancet Style', which meant that expensive window tracery could be avoided. Christ Church sports no tower, another saving, but the massive pinnacles and the prominent bell turret together make up an effective west façade (Plate 35). The next church, St Mark's, City Road, Lakenham (1843) was given a modest tower which extends the townscape of Norwich's medieval churches and might thus be taken as the first sign of respect for the city's medieval heritage. The last of this group, all designed by the county surveyor, John Brown, St Matthew's, Thorpe (1851), was in the even cheaper round-arched lancet style. Again there was no tower.

Those three churches served the less affluent new districts, St Mark's being close to the very poorest agglomerations of new suburban housing. They were followed by four churches closer to the better districts. Holy Trinity, Trinity Road (1859–61), forms a large preaching box again, but there is also an elaborate ritual east end with a massive tower and spire, all in the strong, 'muscular' High Victorian Gothic style of the day, designed by an otherwise unknown architect, William Smith of London. There was also St Philip's, Heigham Road (1871), by the equally unknown Edward Power of London (now destroyed) in a similar vein. Further out, amongst Norwich's richest suburban residences, came Christ Church, Church Avenue, Eaton (1873–79), by the local architects J. H. Brown and J. B. Pearce, in a rich High Victorian style, too; yet, there is lack of a tower again. The church is, in fact, almost invisible amongst the trees. Extremely low contours also characterise St Thomas's, Earlham Road (1886), by the London architect Ewan Christian, best-known for his designs for the National Portrait Gallery. Thus, not counting St John's Roman Catholic church (later to become a cathedral) (Plate 36),[5] it was really only Holy Trinity which fulfilled the demands made upon a prominent and prosperous Victorian suburban church. In the twentieth century building for the major churches was, counter-cyclically, more vigorous in Norwich than usual. But shapes remained 'traditional', that is, they continued Victorian patterns.[6]

Nonconformist churches in the south of England mostly kept a modest face until about the middle of the nineteenth century. The 'meeting house' looked, literally, like a somewhat better class urban or suburban house from the outside. Calvert Steet Methodist chapel (1810, destroyed) was a case in point. There seemed no way in which the splendours of the interior of the Octagon chapel of the previous century could be kept up, although the Quaker meeting house in Upper Goat Lane (1825–6 by J. T. Patience) showed at least a rich façade, using a massive amount of expensive freestone (Plate 37). What was new was the great increase in the number of chapels, each reflecting the size and needs of their district. Although somewhat more ambitious than the rest of the other 'nonconformists', the domestic palatial features of the Jesuit chapel in Willow Lane (1827) by J. T. Patience, Norwich's first Roman Catholic Church since the

Reformation, also belongs in this context. Thus far, nonconformist church design had remained architecturally on a local level. Chapel Field Congregational church (1856; demolished by the city authorities in 1972) marked the beginning of much bolder nonconformist architecture for Norwich (Plate 38). Neo-Romanesque, with two prominent towers, it was designed by the denomination's busy London architect, John James. Not far away stood the Trinity Presbyterian church, Theatre Street (c. 1880, blitzed), also in an ornate Neo-Romanesque style with one short tower. The contemporary chapels designed by Edward Boardman, on the other hand, at that time Norwich's most important architect, namely the prestigious United Reformed church in the city centre (1869) and Chapel Field Methodist church (1880), continued an older, simpler tradition of an arrangement where the gabled front provides the main façade. Late in the century, A. F. Scott chose a more elaborate Gothic style, and with their red brick the firm's chapels stood out more prominently in the street scene. There are few examples of elaborate twentieth-century non-conformist buildings. The Presbyterian church, Unthank Road, of 1954–56, seemingly inspired by Scandinavian municipal Modernism, was by Bernard Feilden who was to become Norwich's most important architect and to whom we shall return.[7]

The tradition of the church as the single architectural focus of a residential area continued well into the twentieth century. It would be hard to postulate distinctive elements for Norwich. The national norms of these institutions were too strong, especially as regards the rules for new buildings. Major and minor church architects travelled out from the capital to build even small village churches or devise restorations in the remotest areas of the country; Norfolk, as a whole, was an exception in that it simply did not need many new churches. Apart from St John's Roman Catholic cathedral, there are very few Victorian churches and chapels in Norfolk which merit the attention of today's Victorian architecture enthusiasts.

Into a similar category of nationally directed building types we may put most schools – excepting the private ones. Moreover, school buildings provide a precise reflection of the fundamental changes in patronage in the nineteenth century. 1870 marks the crucial date; before that it was invariably the churches which built their usually small but ornate structures in a style akin to their places of worship.[8] Thereafter it was the municipality, and the look of the building and the styles of decorations changed, as with the Duke Street School of 1888, which adheres to the 'secular' Queen Anne style of the London School Board (Plate 39). After the middle of the twentieth century, under the direction of city architect, David Percival, a strict modernism reigned, combined, however, also with a spirit of experimentation. From the late nineteenth century secondary education experienced a strong municipal input which manifested itself in very large and very ornate buildings, witness the Technical Institute (now the School of Art) by W. Douglas Wiles and A. E. Collins, the city engineer.[9] It was supplanted by an even larger structure, City College (1937–53), in Ipswich Road, by the city architect, Leonard Hannaford, rivalling even the City Hall in size. A more friendly look was chosen for the late Victorian Norwich Diocesan Training College on the pleasant western edge of the city at College Road (blitzed).[10] The list of municipal buildings for mundane purposes might include also burial grounds; here, too, every town followed the new legal stipulations and Norwich's large Earlham cemetery, begun in the 1850s, with its pretty Gothic chapels and gatehouses, is no exception. Rather more haphazard in English towns was provision for the military. With the striking castellated Drill Hall in Chapel Field Road (by city surveyor J. S. Benest, 1866, demolished)[11] and the Britannia Barracks, Norwich in this respect must call itself lucky in architectural terms.

There was one group of structures one might call 'public buildings' which were mostly founded from the early nineteenth century onwards by public authorities, namely workhouses, asylums and prisons. Yet the term 'public building' hardly seems appropriate within the traditional terms of architecture, as these buildings usually lack decoration. The explanation, until after the middle of the nineteenth century, was simple: they only served the poorest sector of the population. Moreover, prisons and workhouses were invariably built out of town and thus remained largely out of sight, as in the case of the borough lunatic asylum off Magpie Road, demolished long ago, and the Norwich Union Workhouse on Workhouse Lane, now Bowthorpe Road (1856–9, by architects Medland and Maberley of Gloucester and later incorporated into the West Norwich Hospital).[12] A much more conspicuous structure, however, had appeared earlier just outside St Giles's, the Norwich City gaol of 1822.[13] However, not giving these buildings an urban public building status did not entirely preclude their effectiveness; ordered layout and good construction, in conjunction with strict regimes, were aiming to impress and 'educate' their inmates.

The second half of the nineteenth century brought a vital change in respect of decoration: even the most utilitarian structure, even those buildings which provided charity for the poorest, moved up the ladder of decorum, representing the continually growing state and corporate provision for health care. 'Public' in the new terminology of 'public health' meant precisely what it said: it concerned everybody. The new Norwich Lunatic Asylum at Hellesdon of 1877 shows a splendid array of linked pavilions carrying a modicum of decoration (Plate 40).[14] This new development was, however, also reflecting back to the way in which a related type, the 'hospital', had always been one of the most prominent buildings of a town. The Norwich and Norfolk Hospital's new buildings of 1874–83 became indeed the city's most prominent new structure, maximising its impact in its situation close to the best residential quarters of the town and its main entrance. The local sponsors of the Norfolk and Norwich called in T. H. Wyatt from London, one of the country's busiest and most versatile practitioners, as consultant, to work with the chief local architect, Edward Boardman. The result was that, in Jeremy Taylor's words:

> Norwich provides an example of an up-to-date hospital that reflected both the new planning ideas of the 1860s – the pavilion approach – and also, at the same time, the equally new aesthetic ideals of the 'Queen Anne' movement which had only been given first expression over the same decade.[15]

Rather different is the situation with regard to 'public buildings' in the narrower sense of that term, buildings in which the practical purpose is less pronounced and the honorific element comes out more strongly. In contrast to the pattern of quasi-compulsory provision for asylums or schools, the patronage situation for buildings serving governmental purposes was much more volatile, both in the sense of the actual political situation and as regards establishing the real need for new buildings. A case in point was the buildings for the courts of justice. Britain differed strongly from most other European countries in the nineteenth century in that it did not seem *de rigueur* to build new courts of justice (which, on the Continent, were entirely separate from other government buildings). The public face of justice did not really seem to matter. In Norwich, at any rate, we can forget about state and county patronage in architecture until the later twentieth century – excepting the buildings for the military mentioned above. Until the 1960s many of the courts were housed in an amalgam of buildings at the foot of the castle. The latter had served as the state prison until the end of the nineteenth century. To what extent the citizens of Norwich continued to regard Norwich castle as the symbol and the stronghold of the central state needs further investigation. The county offices had gradually moved out of Shire House (the shire hall) into makeshift as well as some purpose-built accommodation in Thorpe Road and Stacey Road. Shire House itself (1822–4), by the Norwich-London architect, William Wilkins junior, could hardly rate as major public building. What looms large here is the story of abandoned plans: first those for a grandiose Neo-Classical structure for Judges' Lodgings and Law Courts of 1827 by a little known London architect, Thomas Nicholls, and at the end of the century those for trebling the building's size by the local architect, A. F. Scott.[16] A proper county hall had to wait until the 1960s, and a complete set of courts until the late 1980s.

A detailed history of all of Norwich's buildings for its municipal administration still needs to be written. The most salient fact is the prolonged lack of them, that is, the lack of a prominent city hall (if one discounts the old guild hall). It would be hard to find a major and even medium-sized English town without a monument to the nineteenth- and early twentieth-century democratisation processes in municipal decision-making, to which were added the more individual elements of patronage, showing the pride of the town's commercial elite. We only need to turn to nearby Great Yarmouth and Ipswich to find major examples of Victorian town halls. Among the early municipal structures in Norwich are the Free Library (1854–7) which also housed the newly founded Norwich School of Art, a medium-sized, but ornate Renaissance-style building, by city surveyor E. E. Benest,[17] as well as smaller administrative buildings near the market.

The account presented here is primarily one of types of building and of their patronage in order to understand why they were built in the first place. At the same time our concern is with the development of 'architecture', in the traditional sense of the term, that is, the development of large and ornamented buildings. It seemed characteristic for Norwich that neither the city nor the state were forthcoming in this respect. But who was? The short answer is commerce. Going on from here to commercial and industrial buildings we would appear to enter again a sphere of greater predictability. Surely a commercial building would only be erected as and when a precise need arose, and its size and degree of ornamentation would be an exact reflection of these needs and possibilities, in Norwich as anywhere else. We must, however, begin with an example of a building of great presence, but of an undertaking which never achieved the success its building was intended to show. Norwich yarn works, later called Jarrold's printing works (also called St James's Mill, or New Mill), built in 1839, fell foul of the general industrial climate in Norwich in those years and did not serve long as a textile mill. Although it probably was the most distinctive industrial building ever built in Norwich, its fame is largely owed to the way some architectural journalists of the 1950s, especially J. M. Richards and Ian Nairn, fell in love with what they called the 'functional tradition in industrial architecture'. However, as Bill Wilson points out, the building is not vernacular but Georgian utilitarian and mildly classical.[18] Norwich's most important assembly of industrial buildings from all phases of the later nineteenth century is no doubt Colmans' Carrow works. In conjunction with the development of the 'necessary decorum', in analogy to workhouses and prisons, as explained above, later nineteenth-century factories and also breweries (Bullard's Anchor brewery in Westwick Street, still standing, and the Steward and Patteson's Pockthorpe brewery in Barrack Street, demolished) had to show a public face, which meant the display of a considerable amount of decoration.

The pattern of development of industrial and commercial building in Norwich must be characterised as *sui generis* for a number of reasons. Unlike most northern towns, Norwich did not initiate any zoning, separating commercial, industrial and residential districts (apart from the traditional pattern of locating industries near the river). The mixture of all types of buildings continued until after the Second World War. Thus very large factories can be found in most parts of the town centre dominating the old small houses – much in the same way as high office blocks of the 1950s to 1970s dominate town centres now.[19]

And yet, probably more by chance than through plan, a specific business district did develop at Bank Plain and Agricultural Hall Plain (Plate 41). At one end stood the entrance to commercial London Street, faced by Boardman's office block, No. 5 Bank Plain (1899), at the other end we turn into Prince of Wales Road, a rare example of a unified commercial development, begun in 1860. Terminating the view of Bank Plain is a lavish, early pure office building, Harvey's Crown Bank (1866; later the Post Office and now Hardwick House) by one of London's top commercial architects, Philip Hardwick.[20] To be entirely faced with stone must have seemed wondrously extravagant in Norwich at that time – especially in view of the fact that the bank failed one year later.[21] Next to it, close to the vast auctioneering activities that went on in the centre of Norwich at Castle Hill until the 1930s, stands Agricultural Hall (now Anglia Television Centre), by the Norwich architect, J. B. Pearce (1882), somewhat conservative in its design, especially when compared to his picturesque town hall in Great Yarmouth. Apart from the hospital it was Norwich's most stately building at the time, fitting into a pattern of corn halls and exchange buildings, prominent in all the smaller towns of East Anglia. Norwich possessed another example, the Corn Exchange (1860) in Exchange Street.[22] Bank Plain is further linked with the Boardmans' *magnum opus*, the picturesque Royal Hotel (1896). This is again a structure which, in its size and ornamentation, evokes more than a faint echo of northern towns, such as Manchester's Midland Hotel. Finally, to Barclays Bank (opened in 1929) opposite, by Walter H. Brierley of York and Boardman, the last of the major buildings of Bank Plain. Designed by a disciple of Lutyens and with a certain Arts and Crafts orientation, the complex appears relatively modestly scaled from the outside, as the primary aim was to fit the irregular contours of the plot. The Royal, by contrast, made much more spectacular use of its equally awkward site.

Inside, however, the bank presents a highly unified and huge banking hall, a giant Roman basilica; a space almost as impressive as Skipper's Marble Hall.[23] In short, Bank Plain is a commercial ensemble creating an impression way above Norwich's 'station'. The real station down the road (Norwich Thorpe, 1886), the city's main railway building, making a good impact with a medium size, appears to correspond precisely to the city's rank. Stations usually get this right, because they were built according to the calculations of a national company, rather than according to local aspirations.[24]

This is not the end of the story of banks in Norwich. Norwich actually sported one of the first accomplished bank buildings in the country, stone-faced and in an Italian Renaissance style, the Norwich Savings Bank by J. Stannard (1844), in Rampant Horse Street, but it did not survive for very long.[25] English banks were invariably using white Portland stone, traditionally reserved for classical buildings of the highest status. Because of the greater preponderance of vernacular street façades of a modest kind, these Norwich banks stand out more than elsewhere; on the other hand, those from the inter-war period, such as the National Westminster bank at the corner of London and Bedford Streets and Lloyds bank in the Market Place, are cleverly adapted to their 'vernacular' sites.[26] Adding the banks and other business buildings by Skipper from the 1890s onwards in London Street and St Giles Street,[27] Norwich's commercial architecture presents a picture of high quality as a whole. Finally, Norwich contributed a most remarkable solution to the theme of department store façades: Skipper's Jarrold's Store at the corner of Market Square and London Street, of 1903–5 (Plate 42). Just to call it 'Baroque' (Bill Wilson) in no way does it justice. Skipper in fact provides a most sophisticated reflection on a problem which had bothered designers for many decades. Ever since technical progress made possible very large sheets of glass, store windows were made as large as possible to display the goods inside and to let the light in. But such a shop front might, in serious architectural terms, look flimsy. By way of a complex series of supports and arcades, Skipper gives the impression of a reasonably weighty construction, while still getting across that we are looking at and into a department store.[28] Lastly, its delicacy and relatively modest overall size were meant to distinguish it from the largish and squarish factory piles.

By 1930, then, Norwich's architecture, in the sense of large and stately buildings, was dominated by commerce and industry, in fact, almost completely so. Of public buildings that made an architectural impact, there would be very little to say. Norwich differed greatly in all this from most towns of its size. As so often, the northern industrial towns, with their large municipal buildings are brought in for a comparison. Their streets were, of course, lined with new and stately commercial buildings as well. In the last

resort, the differences between commercial and municipal are not that significant, because who else but the commercial elite could promote the
grand municipal structures? From that we may conclude that the crucial
difference in Norwich seems to have been simply the lack of interest on the
part of its citizens in grand municipal design, and their concentration on
their individual business premises.

It is around 1930 when we may finally resume, or actually begin, our tale
of municipal architecture in Norwich. The story of the 1932 competition
for, and the commissioning of, Norwich City Hall (C. H. J. Ames and
S. R. Pierce, built 1937–8) has been told, at least in outline, by George
Nobbs (Plate 43).[29] From the start, designers, especially in the pre-compe-
tition proposal by a major London practitioner, Robert Atkinson, took
account of the opportunities of the site, in order to maximise the building's impact. In purely architectural terms, the evaluation of Norwich City
Hall has for a long time been contradictory. Undoubtedly there is a
Swedish element; Stockholm City Hall of 1911–23 is usually mentioned. But
the main stylistic assessment oscillates between 'modern' and 'classical'.
That is, as such, no surprise, as there were many buildings at that time
placed on, or around the same borderline. Captain Sandys-Winsch's structures in Norwich's celebrated public parks demonstrate something quite
similar, a move from classical in Eaton Park (1924–8) to art deco-moderne
in Waterloo Park (1933).[30] What one may call modern, or rather art deco-
moderne in City Hall presents many of the smaller elements and decorative
features inside and out. As a whole and in its main aspect outside, City Hall
stands firmly in the classical, but especially in the nineteenth century, civic
hall tradition,[31] at which Norwich had finally arrived. A town hall should,
first, appear as grand as possible and dwarf any surrounding commercial
buildings. It should have a clearly marked central, ceremonial entrance. On
the first floor we find the classical *piano nobile* of the Italian Renaissance
palazzo and the French royal palace tradition. For the Victorians this meant
that it was externally obvious where to find the main rooms of civic government (though it was rare to place the council chamber in this position).
There must be a balcony on this first floor for the authorities to show
themselves to the 'people'. The view from this balcony over the city centre
is, indeed, incomparable. Finally, a tower must be added: the clock tower,
as such a nineteenth-century innovation, always reminiscent, of course, of
Big Ben, and, as in London, to be placed asymmetrically; at the same time
it was a motive which harks back to the *beffroi* of the commercial towns of
Flanders as well as to the civic towers of Tuscany. Thus a more narrowly
architectural term 'modern' does not really grip in the case of City Hall.
Clearly, it is a 'modern' building; connoting modern city government, the

building speaks as much as it looks. But the 'real' international modern only arrived with David Percival's City Library next door to City Hall (planned from 1956; destoyed by fire, 1994).

Another case of a monumentalised Modernism, now of the more narrowly speaking continental-international variety, we meet in our next giant building, Norfolk County Hall in Martineau Lane. Reginald Uren made his name with moderne municipal designs in London in the 1930s (Plate 44). Like City Hall, County Hall, too, was perceived locally as a late, and therefore all the more vigorous, effort to provide a building and a symbol for local government. The 1930s had witnessed 'old-fashioned councillors who believed it was a waste to spend money on offices at all'. The new building's £2.5 million cost certainly seemed prodigious in the early 1960s. But the architect was asked to provide a building 'of appropriate character and dignity' as well as 'business offices which are satisfactory, economic and adaptable in use'. Again, judgments clash, though there is one big contrast with the City Hall: County Hall has never received much comment in the first place and virtually no praise. To a contributor to the local press in 1966 it was not simple enough, given the magnificent site. According to Bill Wilson, however, it looks like 'an ordinary steel-framed office tower'.[32] County Hall does indeed occupy an attractive former parkland site which is open not to the city but to the country, although its long-distance effect is hampered by the ramshackle surroundings on the southern side. As an international modern building it should not be viewed from a fixed point but from many sides; and one has actually to experience the complex access up to the airy main entrance and reception lobby. The external treatment of the main block does not really repeat the usual office slabs of the time, but shows a vigorous modelling and rhythmic spacing with the help of coloured tiles. With its height, and through strong and repeated patterning, one may call this building a monumental and a 'formal' one, too. One only needs to compare this with Lasdun's studied new informality at UEA, built at the same time.[33]

We may finally see both City Hall and County Hall, together with the central government financed Lasdunian university, as thoroughly 'modern' manifestations of governmental power, placed in an environment remote from the capital, one traditionally ruled by a reactionary elite sceptical of those centralised forces and by a conservative yet sceptical urban population. Moreover, while one would not normally expect the architecture of these large institutions to fit in closely with the cherished local vernacular, the clash between the giant new buildings and 'old Norfolk' does seem enormous. We shall have occasion to return to the issue.

Our story of large buildings in the streets of Norwich began with commerce and industry and has continued with municipal grandeur. That grandeur was now also synonymous with modernism. But it was only from about 1960 that the international style version of modernism entered Norwich. It was commerce again which took the initiative – apart from David Percival's public library. Many of the new undertakings assume the name 'development', which indicates the ambitions of the time, not just to insert buildings into the existing street layout, but to rebuild whole quarters of the city. Two areas stand out: the first is the Norwich Union and its complexes along Surrey and St Stephen's Streets. It was a new post-war modernism of wide roads and high individual blocks of buildings. A further new modernism from the later 1960s, however, went for concentration: not wide open streets, but smaller pedestrian areas, squeezed between and placed underneath multilevel structures, as at Anglia Square.[34]

The evaluation of all this has now to proceed more cautiously. The high blocks of the Norwich Union's Surrey Street complex were criticised from the beginning in London circles, notably by Ian Nairn.[35] To him they did not fit the cherished old Norwich street scene. But one has to reflect once again generally on how Norwich wanted to appear to itself. One hundred years before, Harvey's Bank of 1866 certainly seemed similarly out of place in the small-scale Norwich streetscape. In 1945 the city brought out a lavish book, entitled *The Norwich Plan*, which as well as dealing with the problems caused by war destruction, demanded the renovation of many of what were seen as muddled and ugly streetscapes and their replacement with wide roads and squares, lined with buildings in solid façades of the City Hall kind (Plate 46). Debenhams department store of the late 1950s gives us an idea of what the city centre might have looked like. Norwich wanted to shed its market town image and replace it with the look of a *Grossstadt*, a face indicative of a city of several hundred thousand inhabitants. Given the size and national importance of the Norwich Union, the size of its buildings appeared entirely appropriate. Norwich, in fact, faced a dilemma: could a modern office town of some size retain a vernacular image – in itself an imprecise term – unless one opted for the rigorously old-world look of Aylsham, or Bury St Edmunds at the largest? And yet, if a look ahead is allowed at this point, from about the 1980s, these kinds of problems did not arise any more, as large commercial complexes were accommodated either on the outskirts of towns, or in buildings adopting a new kind of vernacularised style. As will be argued below, both might spell the end of the kind of centralised town as we know it.[36]

One must attempt to view the whole situation once more from a different angle, from that of the designers. How do we perceive the local *versus* national issue with regard to the architectural profession? At the beginning of our period we can assume an enormous contrast between the situation in the metropolis and that of outlying provinces such as Norfolk. In London a whole range of practitioners made their mark, from high class to hack while, the best architects extended their activities to distant country houses everywhere, north and east Norfolk included. In a city such as Norwich there was virtually no work for them. The number of 'architects' in Norwich in the early nineteenth century was minuscule. Norwich was one or two generations behind London as regards the separation of architectural and building activities. Even the great Skipper, at the end of the nineteenth century, occasionally undertook the speculative building of small houses. To most, 'architect' and 'surveyor' were near identical. Early nineteenth-century Norwich 'architects', such as J. T. Patience or J. Stannard junior, appear shadowy figures.[37] Of the slightly younger group, John Brown (1805–1876) was probably an exception, in the way he combined a great number of activities, such as the county surveyorship, with numerous church restorations, as well as work on the cathedral, church building (including large churches further afield, even in London), workhouses, and speculative developments in Yarmouth.[38] In Norwich, much of the important design work was done by those who filled the post of city surveyor or engineer. The post of city architect was established only in 1888. A maverick was Thomas Jekyll who had at least two distinct phases to his career: first, in the 1860s, his churches in Norfolk (for example, St Andrew's, Thorpe St Andrew, 1866) and secondly, during the 1870s, his activity as a kind of interior designer for the London avant-garde group around the artist, James McNeill Whistler. In addition he designed Japanese-style ironwork for the famed Norwich foundry of Barnard, Bishop and Barnard, which included the celebrated pavilion for the 1876 Philadelphia exhibition, later placed in Chapel Field Gardens and destroyed by the city authorities after 1945. But Jekyll, who went insane in 1879, clearly did not fit in with the evolving pattern of solid professionality and his name was rarely mentioned in Norwich after his premature death in 1881.[39]

It was the railways which exercised a decisive influence in our field, too. Church architects from London could now easily reach the provinces. Perhaps this also provided one of the catalysts for the establishment of Norwich's first proper architectural office in the modern sense, that of Edward Boardman. Founded in 1860, this firm lasted through three generations until 1966.[40] Edward Boardman learned his job during the 1850s while working for the builders, Lucas Brothers of London, who were engaged in what was by far the largest building undertaking in the region: the development of South Lowestoft with associated railways and the building of Somerleyton Hall, all under the entrepreneurship of Sir Samuel Morton Peto. Boardman then worked almost exclusively in Norwich, occasionally in the surrounding towns, though few jobs were to be had in the country as such. As would be expected from a large provincial practice, work proceeded in many styles. It seems that Boardman & Son took on every kind of job. A little later important firms could act probably a little more selectively; Augustus Frederic Scott specialised in Methodist chapels on the one hand – a connection he inherited from his father, the well-known preacher Jonathan Scott – and in reinforced concrete construction on the other.[41] Much later the firm became Lambert, Scott and Innes, who acquired a national, even international, reputation as consultants for the Moscow subterranean shopping centre, following their Castle Mall in Norwich (Plate 74).

For the late nineteenth century we may take Burgess's *Men Who Have Made Norwich* as a barometer of the state of Norwich's self-consciousness, if not actually in the case of architects, then in the analysis of the firm E. W. D. Potter, the stone specialists. First, Norwich's inferiority:

> It is worth noting here that although buildings of stone were first introduced in England as long ago as AD 670, it was not until the year 1887 that any Norwich citizen set himself the task of initiating, to any substantial extent, the industry connected with the actual working of stone in this city.

It was Potter's rapid adoption of breathtakingly advanced, automated electric machinery that made this possible, so that no longer 'in the erection of our large buildings the contractors had to go far and wide for responsible firms who would undertake the necessary stone work'. Moreover, professionalisation to Potter meant specialisation. In dealing with stonework only, he 'has never dabbled in the building trade' (in contracting). Potter was capable of dealing even with the £10,000 worth of work for Skipper's Norwich Union Surrey House. His new speciality was Portland stone and Potter himself must have instructed Burgess to write:

> It is a freestone which ... has been extensively used in London. Indeed, some of the most notable buildings in the metropolis are partially or entirely built of this stone ... St Paul's Cathedral and Somerset Houses ... Mr Potter has shiploads of Portland Stone brought direct from the quarries to Yarmouth.[42]

Finally, of course, there was George Skipper, far and away Norwich's most famous architect. Going strong from the early 1890s, he then won the largest commission the city could provide, the Norwich Union head office, in 1901. It is difficult now to gauge Skipper's fame in Norwich during his lifetime. The way he saw himself, as the gentleman designer amongst the building workmen, is depicted in unique fashion on a moulded brick panel on his office in London Street (Plate 34). He lived on to 1948, but his reputation was eclipsed during most of his later life, as somebody who rejected modernism. It was only the new attention given to all things Victorian and Edwardian by the likes of John Betjeman, and subsequently by Nikolaus Pesvner, which established Skipper as a national figure in Edwardian architecture.

Skipper appears to have been the only Norwich architect who did prestigious work in London, the Sackville scheme on and off Piccadilly, from 1928; to be outdone only by Feilden and Mawson in their work for Queen Mary College much later. It is understandable that this is far outweighed by the commissions which London architects obtained in Norwich. In fact, sometimes it was the Norwich clients who did not sufficiently trust the local designers and downgraded them to site architects, as in the case of the Boardmans at the Norfolk and Norwich Hospital and for Barclays Bank. In the case of City Hall there was national competition, and for County Hall the client took the customary step of asking the president of the Royal Institute of Architects to supply a short list of names. Against that we may cite the way in which more recent books on architectural history describe the Marble Hall as 'one of the country's most convinced Edwardian office buildings. It is by G. J. Skipper, a local architect but every bit as competent and inventive as any in London'.[43] One may conclude that the architecture of Norwich, largely directed, as it had been, from the metropolis, had been properly integrated – a long haul from 1800, when new 'architecture' was practically non-existent in Norwich.

It is only in the post-war revival, from the 1960s onwards, that we can speak, even if very cautiously, of a Norwich, or a Norfolk 'school' of architecture, or at least of a Norwich line of thinking on architecture. Its beginnings are complex. We are fortunate in having a long number of the *Architects' Journal* devoted to contemporary buildings, on the occasion of the Norfolk and Norwich Association of Architects hosting the British Architects' conference in Norwich in 1956.[44] At that date much of the debate turned around the question of progressive versus retrogressive. Many local practitioners, even some of those aged between forty and fifty, would stress their scepticism towards the modern. For instance, W. A. J. Spear (forty-seven), a Londoner by birth, maintained 'that the contemporary style in Norfolk would look like wearing grey flannels with a topper', whereas Alan Dennis Cook (thirty-nine), 'admires the "so called contemporary style", also Frank Lloyd Wright' – we saw him keeping it up at Anglia Square. C. H. Thurston (forty-nine), the county architect, was,

25. Canonry in the Cathedral Close ('Abbeyfield') (by John Brown, the County Surveyor, advised by J. C. Buckler, 1862). (*Sarah Cocke*)

26. HM Prison built as Britannia Barracks, Mousehold, 1886–7. This is an unusually elaborate building; no doubt, the varied skyline was thought appropriate for its position on a hill overlooking the city. (*Sarah Cocke*)

27. St John the Baptist, Roman Catholic Cathedral since 1976 (by George Gilbert Scott Junior and John Oldrid Scott, 1884–1910). (*Stefan Muthesius*)

28. Methodist Church, Thorpe Road. (by A. F. Scott, 1901–2). Its rostrum and front gallery were arranged on the usual nonconformist model, but the intricate handling of its curves probably had not too many equals. (*Michael Brandon-Jones and Stefan Muthesius*)

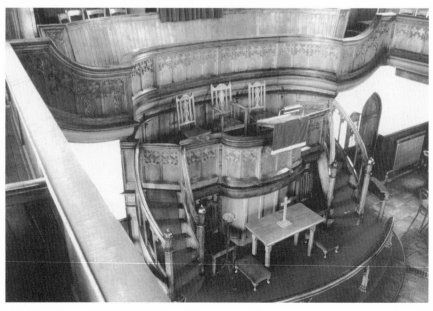

29. Former Norwich Savings Bank (then Barclays Bank), Red Lion Street (by George Skipper, 1905). (*Sarah Cocke*)

30. Norwich Union Insurance Headquarters, Surrey Street (by George Skipper, 1903–5). The Marble Hall, from an early photograph. This building (Plate 53), although it is not actually overlarge, has always been considered in a class of its own, chiefly because of the richness and heaviness of its decor. As a class above that again we must rate the Marble Hall inside which used diversely coloured Italian marble facings, originally destined for Westminster Cathedral. (From *Peeps into the Past*, Norwich, 1908)

31. Council Chamber, City Hall (by C. H. James and S. R. Pierce, (1931) 1937–38). (*Stefan Muthesius*)

32. University of East Anglia Library (by Denys Lasdun, 1966–68 and 1972–74). (*Stefan Muthesius*)

33. Queen Elizabeth Close, Palace Plain (by Feilden and Mawson, 1973–75). (*Sarah Cocke*)

34. London Street, Offices of George Skipper (now part of Jarrold's Department Store), 1896. (*Stefan Muthesius*)

35. Christ Church, New Catton, by John Brown, 1841–2. (*Sarah Cocke*)

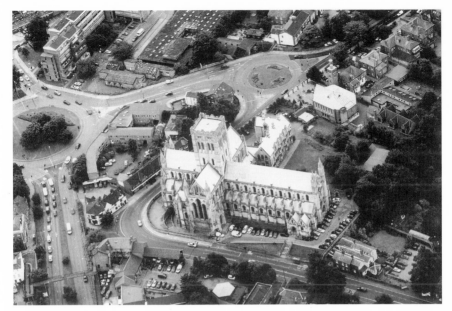

36. Cathedral Church St. John the Baptist, by George Gilbert Scott, jun. and John Oldrid Scott, commissioned by the Duke of Norfolk, 1884–1910. (*Eastern Daily Press*)

37. Friends' Meeting House, Upper Goat Lane, by J. T. Patience, 1825–6. (*Stefan Muthesius*)

38. Chapelfield Congregational Church, by John James, 1857–8. (*Stefan Muthesius*)

39. Norwich Board School (former), Duke Street, 1888. (*Sarah Cocke*)

40. Hellesdon Hospital (Norwich Lunatic Asylum), by R. M. Phipson (of Ipswich) 1877. (*The Builder*, 1877)

41. Agricultural Hall Plain, looking down Prince of Wales Road. Far left: Barclay's Bank (formerly), centre left the former Royal Hotel, centre right Crown Bank (later Post Office) and far right the former Agricultural Hall (Anglia TV, including Crown Bank). 1860s–1920s. (*Stefan Muthesius*)

42. Jarrold's Department Store, by George Skipper, 1903–5. (*Stefan Muthesius*)

43. City Hall, by C. H. James & S. R. Pierce, Competition 1931, built 1937–8. (*City of Norwich, The Norwich Plan, 1945*)

44. Norfolk County Hall, Martineau Lane, by Slater and [Reginald] Uren, 1966. (*Stefan Muthesius*)

45. Friar's Quay Houding, by Fielden & Mawson (David Luckhurst and Ray Thompson) 1974. (*Stefan Muthesius*)

46. Projected rebuilding, from *City of Norwich, The Norwich Plan* (1945).

FIGURE 42. Central Library (formerly Esperanto Way) destroyed by fire 1994, by City Architect David Percival (job architect J. Vanston), 1960–2. (*Architects' Journal*, 1956)

again, 'not strongly contemporary-minded'.[45] His counterpart in the city, however, David Percival, at the helm from November 1955, took the opposite view, coming from the then hotbed of civic-minded modernism, Coventry. While making his mark as an international modernist with his Public Library, he introduced the notion that council housing had to be in the forefront of the modernisation process (Figure 42). This involved a new kind of sociological-architectural thinking which, in turn, led to tower blocks and deck-access types, even in Norwich – on the whole, such housing has worn relatively well (Vauxhall Street, from 1958; Bowers Avenue, 1964).[46] Perhaps this was due to the way in which Percival and the numerous designers working under him tried to fit in with, or to augment, the already existing low-density patterns of council housing. The proportion of council housing in Norwich remained very high indeed, at well over 50 per cent.

Thus there was no way of stopping the contemporary; but what exactly did 'contemporary' entail? David Percival, when asked by the *Architects' Journal* of 1956, did not cite the elements of mainstream modernism he had imbued, but named as his special heroes 'Salvisberg of Switzerland, Kajmoeller (University of Aarhus), and Thomas Sharp'.[47] The latter had been an influential proponent not of the Modern as such, but of the adaptation of the modern with the English vernacular. What emerged from this was the practice of two styles side by side: flat-roofed modernist construction in schools and libraries and in some of the housing; and an old-world look, using conventional materials, with pitched roofs for infill housing, of

which Alderson Place, Fishergate (1959), was the first prominent example.
A new notion of a *genius loci* seemed to emerge for the city, whereas the
county had witnessed a wave of neo-vernacularism early in the twentieth
century, with the work of Lutyens, E. S. Prior and Detmar Blow. Yet there
seemed virtually no links between these members of the London avant-
garde and the architectural world of Norwich. The history of the
conservation spirit in Norwich itself still has to be written. It probably
began with the way the early nineteenth-century Norwich school of artists
led viewers to appreciate the charm of old walls, followed by the restoration campaigns for the cathedral and the castle. The recognition of the
picturesqueness of the old townscape, and a sense of the need to preserve
it, seemingly only developed in the twentieth century, the saving of Elm
Hill in 1927 being the first well-known case. But the real impetus came
from the 'townscape' movement of the 1950s, initiated largely by the *Architectural Review* and its architectural illustrator Gordon Cullen. In
conjunction with the novel attitude towards the 'industrial vernacular' discussed above, a new way of seeing had arisen, through which virtually every
grubby street of old Norwich could be called picturesque and thus appear
deeply attractive. It is crucial to note that this new townscape attitude to
the city was initially brought in from outside, and not developed in Norwich itself, although it was to be rapidly taken on by resident architects,
though chiefly by those who had come in from elsewhere.

We have, so far, traced the history of Norwich architecture in terms of
a constant process of modernisation, or, to use a less charitable expression, of trying to catch up with the main national trends. That is what
John Brown, the Boardmans, A. F. Scott and many other Norwich architects were striving for. Moreover, that is what they thought their clients,
and the users of their buildings, would expect. By the 1960s, Percival
worked with committee chairmen who fully supported his general drive
for modernism. When we come to the new trend of the late 1950s, it is
crucial to note that it was architect-directed. It evolved from developments within the architectural discourses of the period. The beginnings of
anti-modernism entertained by these circles were, significantly, not at all
linked with the residual general popular anti-modernism of the time,
neither in London, nor in Norwich. The new conservationist movement's
key figure, J. M. Richards at the *Architectural Review*, had been, just before
the war, a fervent, even a communist-materialist advocate of the international modern, but after the war he turned towards a gentle (though
not genteel) appreciation of what he saw as a general English vernacular,
while Nikolaus Pevsner advocated a nationalised modernism embedded
in the English landscaped garden. There was, lastly, a renewed interest

in Scandinavia, where, according to the English critics, one could find a successful combination of modernism and traditional local materials.

A considerable part of the new strength of Norwich architecture was provided by the work of Sir Bernard Feilden and the members of his large office, of whom David Luckhurst was probably the most outstanding figure.[48] Just thirty-seven when the Norwich Issue of the *Architects' Journal* came out in 1956, Feilden labelled himself as a 'moderate modern'.[49] During the 1960s Feilden and Mawson acquired a national reputation, not equalled by any Norwich firm before or since excepting, posthumously, Skipper. Feilden's neo-vernacular style first manifested itself in his own house, 17a Cathedral Close, where he chose, entirely untypical for the time, a very steeply pitched roof. Feilden's desire was to blend in with Norwich flint and brick (ironically, the local manufacture of the cherished Norfolk red brick was just about to be phased out and Feilden's brick here is not local). During the 1960s the firm was busy with many large mainstream Modernist works. But from the early 1970s the new vernacular element came to the fore, while Feilden himself embarked on his main career, the restoration of cathedrals as well as on his international conservation activities. The high-density group of terraced houses in Friars Quay gained the firm national, even international recognition (Plate 45).[50] It may have originated the 'maltings style', subsequently perceived to be an East Anglian mode, of which another prominent early example was the South Norfolk Offices in Long Stratton by Lambert Scott and Innes (1978–9). In the 1970s a number of Norwich practices (Wearing, Hastings & Rossi, Edward Skipper & Associates, Furze & Hayden, Cleary & Associates, Tayler & Green and others) used the new neo-vernacular particularly for small groups of housing and old people's homes, lending them a kind of intimacy which contrasted strongly with the openness of council, or, for that matter, most private suburban housing of the decades before.[51] As has already been stressed, much of Norwich's later council housing under Percival was in tune with this movement. With the designs for Bowthorpe in the 1970s (a mixture of private and council housing) we reach the peak of this development: a whole new town was created in the new vernacular style.[52]

We may end the story of post-Second World War architecture by referring back to what seemed an increasingly potent underlying question behind so many of the architectural decisions dealt with here: what style would serve Norwich and its inhabitants best, and, secondly, what can a Norwich architect contribute to the way the city is perceived from outside. In our account of the period *c.* 1930–1980 we met a strong reversal of judgement. The large modernist office block, whether used by official or by private bureaucracies, was first thought highly desirable, even a necessity, and was then strongly rejected, even abhorred. While the high blocks may have served the practical purposes of its local users, they did not seem to conform to what we like to think of as germane to 'Norwich'. The reaction resulted in a preference for small-scale, picturesque forms and an adherence to 'local' materials. However, if we take Bowthorpe as the culmination of this movement of neo-vernacularism, this may lead us into a striking contradiction. At this point architectural style ceases to be just a matter of the immediate environment and becomes part of much larger issues. It is precisely this kind of satellite settlement, in conjunction with out of town shopping and other kinds of commercial activities, that leads to the emaciation of life in the old centre of Norwich. Seen in this context, the 'old' Modern civic and commercial 'monstrosities' were, in fact, supporters, we may even say, the last protagonists, of the old self-centred town, increasing its density; they were the last contributors to what had always been an intensely centripetal place. The 'modest' neo-vernacular, on the other hand, as we see it in Bowthorpe, has now been placed in a locality and acts, in cahoots with modern mobility generally, to undermine the old urban structure, the old relationship between town and country, between centre and hinterland. While we find the city centre 'modern' blocks incongruous, we must realise that they actually do help to keep the old city together, while an architecture that is designed to be 'in keeping' with the old townscape has been placed in a position where it may help to detract from the central area. All of this is about to change the shape and the meaning of Norwich and its buildings, perhaps for ever. From the evaluation of buildings we must move to the evaluation of the city and the region as a whole.

14

Politics, 1835–1945

Barry Doyle

Norwich is not a city to which we should look in ordinary times for
any definite pronouncement upon a great political question.

Sir Wemyss Reid, 'Last Month', 1904[1]

Sir Wemyss Reid's characterisation of the political insignificance of Norwich is one which most modern historians have followed. At best it is a
short-sighted assessment of the situation, for the city has much to tell
about key developments in politics in the nineteenth and twentieth centuries. Over the past thirty years the central focus of political history has
moved from a concern with the actions of the governing elite and the ideological and institutional development of national parties to analysis of the
operation of political power at the local level. Within this new historiogra-
phy, four key elements have come to predominate: the structure of local
politics; the significance of the popular politics of the excluded; the boundaries of urban governance; and the importance of locality in the rise of the
Labour Party. Closer scrutiny of each of these aspects has questioned much
of the Whiggish interpretation of local politics, especially the smooth transition from private to public in the delivery of local services.[2] It has aided
our understanding of the part played by non-voters and non-party pressure groups,[3] revised accepted ideas about the social composition of parties
and elites,[4] and has illustrated the conditions most favourable to the
growth of effective Labour politics.[5] However, in exploring these issues,
historians have tended to focus on a relatively limited number of geographical areas, with Lancashire and West Yorkshire, London and the west
midlands predominating. This survey of Norwich's politics between 1835
and 1945 extends these studies to a less industrial but, nevertheless, major
provincial centre.

Despite its economic, social and political prominence in the eighteenth
and early nineteenth century, and its reputation as a 'Jacobin city',[6] the
political history of Norwich since the reforms of the 1830s has been rather
scant. The city's location in a predominantly rural region, away from the

centres of heavy industry, has made Norwich unfashionable with political and social historians interested in the link between economic and political 'modernisation'. Yet economic and social transformation during the nineteenth century,[7] supported by the growing strength of nonconformity, produced a variety of challenges to the traditional political elite, whilst the twentieth century saw the emergence of Labour as the dominant political force. Analysis of the political history of nineteenth-century Norwich is limited in both its municipal and national dimensions,[8] though the history of the twentieth century is rather better served, with studies revealing the complex nature of party politics, exploring the role of class and women and challenging accepted ideas about both the decline of Liberalism and the rise of Labour.[9]

The political structures in Norwich were important in shaping political outcomes. Prior to 1832 Norwich had the third largest municipal electoral roll in the country, but the abolition of the freeman vote and the introduction of strict qualification rules in 1847 meant that, unlike most boroughs, the number of municipal voters was significantly lower by 1850, and, owing to the exclusion of inhabitants who did not pay their rate directly to the local authorities, the municipal electorate grew only very slowly in the 1850s and 1860s. On the other hand, the proportion of the adult male population eligible to vote in parliamentary elections was, at just over 20 per cent, around the average for medium-sized boroughs.[10] The 1867 Reform Act increased the municipal electorate more than fourfold and the number of parliamentary voters threefold, bringing Norwich into line with similar-sized boroughs.[11] However, the fact that Norwich was too small and compact to be split into two constituencies – even after 1918 – yet was too large to be represented by just one Member of Parliament (with the suburbs hived off to county seats) meant that in parliamentary elections throughout the period the city returned two members for the one constituency, an ideal environment for political dealing and cross-party alliances. In many respects this was the single most influential factor in explaining both the rise of Labour and the relatively slow demise of Liberalism in the early twentieth century.

In municipal politics the formation of the new council in 1835 saw the city divided into eight wards, each returning two members a year on a three year cycle.[12] These wards became increasingly unbalanced in terms of population, with the suburbs significantly under represented from mid century onwards. A redistribution in 1892 saw the eight wards divided into sixteen, each electing one councillor *per annum*. Whilst these wards were a more accurate expression of the demographic profile of the city, they still privileged traditional property owning interests at the expense of the suburban working class, leading to a further redistribution in 1932 which acknowledged the shifting human geography of the city.[13] Reform in 1835 also brought a new mayoral and aldermanic system, with sixteen alder-men, a mayor and sheriff all elected by the council. Selection for these roles could provoke intense political controversy. As the Liberal victory in 1835 was not a landslide,[14] a monopoly of the aldermen was vital to ensure Liberal administration in the face of a strong Tory recovery. Although the Liberals did not blush at using their aldermanic majority to maintain their control, from the later 1840s they conceded aldermanic seats to leading Conservatives, whilst the obvious claim of the city's pre-eminent Tory, Sir Samuel Bignold, forced them to relinquish their stranglehold on the may-oralty in 1848. By the Edwardian period the civic offices were divided equally between Liberal and Conservative and remained so until the advent of Labour. The socialists secured aldermanic seats during the 1920s; and in 1927 Herbert Witard became the city's first Labour lord mayor, with Mabel Clarkson selected as the city's first Labour (and woman) sheriff the following year.[15]

Party politics dominated from before the age of reform and remained vitally important, bucking the expected patterns for parliamentary contests in borough elections, especially in the 1830s and again in the 1920s. Con-servatism was always strong and not infrequently predominant, fighting back in municipal elections in the late 1830s and sweeping to victory in 1872, following the introduction of the ballot. Conservatives also fared well in the later Edwardian period, coming to dominate anti-Labour municipal politics by the 1920s. For the Liberals the greatest periods of strength were found in the mid nineteenth century, and in the early years of the twenti-eth century when control of the council and parliamentary representation was once again secured. Liberal municipal strength declined after 1907, but it continued to play a major part in parliamentary politics, returning a member to parliament at every election until 1945, with the ironic excep-tion of 1923. This latter election was the only time in the first half of the twentieth century the Liberals fielded two candidates of their own as opposed to one candidate in a more or less explicit alliance with one of the other two main parties, suggesting Liberals were most effective in max-imising their vote in the sort of coalition facilitated by the double member seat. Liberal decline was mirrored by the rise of Labour. Before the First World War the 'Progressive Alliance' saw the return of a Labour MP in harness with a Liberal, yet in municipal politics the Independent Labour Party (ILP)'s progress was stalled by a Tory-Liberal alliance. After 1918 Labour successfully asserted its independence, winning both parliamentary seats in the 1923 election, gaining *de facto* control of the council in 1933 and sweeping to victory in the 1945 general election.[16]

Both parliamentary and municipal representation underwent a marked transformation during this period, driven by a changing economy and increasing democratisation. For most of the nineteenth century parliamentary candidates were middle- and upper-class men, subtly divided by class and status depending upon the party for which they stood. Represented in Parliament in the 1830s by the sons of the duke of Wellington and the earl of Mansfield (both Tories), in 1847 Norwich witnessed the election of the first 'modern' Liberal, Samuel Morton Peto, a Baptist railway promoter. Liberal control for the next ten years was ensured by fielding a Whig landowner and Liberal businessman in tandem, but this system of careful balance was disrupted in 1867. From 1868 Liberal representatives reflected the nature of the city's new middle class, as first a solicitor, J. H. Tillett, and then the mustard manufacturer, J. J. Colman, secured election in the radical cause. Similarly, rural Tories like Sir Henry Stracey were replaced by business, commercial and professional candidates, such as the self-made brewer Sir Harry Bullard and the county banker Sir Samuel Hoare (MP 1886–1906). The 1890s also saw the first efforts to secure the election of a working-class candidate with the failed attempt to field John Bedford as a working-class Liberal in 1892. More significant was the Labour representation committee's promotion of the trade unionist, George Roberts, in the by-election of 1904. Though his candidature was unsuccessful, an agreement was made that he would stand in tandem with a Liberal candidate at the next general election. Roberts became the first Labour and working-class MP for the city in 1906 (Plate 50). His triumph led the Conservatives to field their own working-class candidate in December 1910. But it was a strategy which proved unsuccessful. The key moment in the transformation of the city's parliamentary representation, however, came with Labour success in 1923 when Dorothea Jewson, Socialist daughter of a local Liberal grandee, was elected together with Walter Smith, a former Norwich shoe worker.[17]

Change amongst municipal representatives followed similar patterns. Unlike the situation in many other towns, the new corporation of 1836 was much like the old, being composed mainly of manufacturers, merchants and professionals, a significant number of whom were Tories.[18] However, the decline of the Norwich textile industry saw the disappearance from the council of this interest and a growing place for professionals, especially lawyers. By the 1870s the council was reflecting the transformation of the local economy as manufacturers and merchants associated with the new consumer industries came to dominate the Liberals, whilst among the Tories an alliance of lawyers, commercial interests and brewers held sway.[19]

Further change came in the 1880s and 1890s when working men candidates, such as the Lib/Lab shoe workers' leader, James Mason, began to enter the council.[20] The first success for a socialist working man was that secured by George Roberts in the school board elections of 1899.[21] The school board was also the body which first elected women representatives, the most prominent being Mrs Scott Pillow.[22] In the early twentieth century most municipal representatives were still drawn from the ranks of the middle class, with both Liberals and Tories tapping the same social groups, though with some sectoral divisions. Footwear, food processing (especially representatives of Colmans) and distribution tended to produce Liberals, whilst banking, insurance and brewing, and declining industries like silk weaving, Conservatives.[23] The council, however, was transformed by the arrival, from 1902, both of Labour councillors, most of whom were union officials and respectable working men,[24] and women candidates promoted by all parties. Mabel Clarkson (Liberal) was the first to enter the council in 1913. The number of women and working-class councillors continued to increase. By 1927 Norwich had seven women councillors and fourteen female members of the board of guardians (out of forty-eight), both relatively high numbers at this time. The advent of many more Labour councillors after 1919, the vast majority drawn from working-class occupations, especially the footwear industry and the railways, completed the reconstruction of the council.[25] As a result, between the 1830s and the 1940s the elected elite of Norwich was remade from one composed entirely of middle- and upper-middle class males, some with deep roots in the social leadership of the city, to one dominated by managers, clerks, manual workers and women, most owing their positions to party machines.[26]

Religion was the predominant element dividing the middle class until at least the 1910s. Nonconformity – dominated by the Congregationalists of Princes Street and the Baptists of St Mary's – played a disproportionate part in the social, economic and political life of the city and formed the backbone of elite Liberal activism. Though it was possible during the nineteenth century to find a significant group of Anglicans within the Liberal ranks, there was a mere handful of nonconformist Tories, the vast majority being Anglican.[27] Religious divisions reflected not just theological differences but fundamental cultural oppositions in which the free churches saw themselves standing politically against the Anglican old order in all its forms. This clash of world views manifested itself in the fields of church rates, education and social reform, as well as in the broader nonconformist conscience which added a moral dimension to all political issues. J. J. Colman led the witch-hunt against Parnell in the 1880s,[28] whilst George White's 1903 speech on 'The Nonconformist Conscience' reiterated the Liberal litany of land and housing reform, temperance, anti-imperialism, anti-militarism, religious equality and education reform (Plate 47).[29] The 1906 election was fought overwhelmingly on this nonconformist agenda, and the Liberal government's failure to satisfy these demands by 1914 is often seen as signalling the death knell for middle-class liberalism.[30] Yet social and political divisions between Nonconformist and Anglican remained at the centre of middle-class politics up to the 1920s, whilst the strength of elite dissenting culture underpinned the Liberal Party in the city and contributed to the slow realignment of the middle class after 1900.[31]

These religious divisions were strengthened by economic factors, especially free trade, which usually saw textiles and industries with close links to the agricultural community adopting a protectionist stance. Admittedly, not all business support for Conservatism was determined by protection. The temperance agenda pursued by Liberals and the strong links between the brewing industry and the agricultural interest – the latter in dire straits with the onset of the depression in the mid 1870s – pushed the brewing industry into the Conservative ranks by 1886. Yet brewers, bankers and insurers could be free traders. When tariff reform became an issue after 1903 the sitting Conservative MP, the banker Sir Samuel Hoare, refused to defend his seat at the 1906 election because of his commitment to free trade. Such sentiments were, however, more closely associated with the new consumer industries, many of which were dependent on both domestic demand and access to foreign markets.

Similar concerns were discernible amongst retailers, with drapers and publicans moving over to the Conservatives in a trend apparent across the country,[32] whilst grocers generally supported Liberalism, mainly because of free trade. Although by the 1920s some footwear manufacturers were willing to support tariffs, the residual commitment of some businessmen to the Liberal Party seen during the 1930s owed as much to free trade as chapel culture. Within the professions solicitors and doctors in the less fashionable specialisms were often Liberals, as were many of those associated with the new professions, in part reflecting tension between *arriviste* outsiders (both socially and professionally) and those in the more established professions. Furthermore, the increasing diversity of the local economy and the networks and strategies of the Victorian family firm saw some men from business backgrounds enter the professions, allowing them to extend business networks and provide ancillary services to the firm. Thus, the growth of professionals on public bodies did not necessarily reflect the decline of business involvement in public affairs, but the greater sophistication of the economy and the growing complexity of the business world.[33]

In the early nineteenth century most working-class political activists were weavers, though from the 1850s onwards shoe workers predominated, both generally operating through the ranks of the Liberal Party. Conservative working men were closely identified with breweries and friendly societies. From their ranks came the first working-class mayor, Henry Flowers, secretary of the local branch of the Manchester Unity of Oddfellows, who took office in 1904.[34] By the Edwardian period such traditional political alignments were weakening as working men, especially shoe, railway and print workers, became involved in the ILP, whilst those workers who stayed with the Liberals or Tories after 1904 tended to be the most skilled, such as the engineer W. B. Greenfield, who sat as a Liberal councillor for Ber Street. For women, class and marital status were most important, many of the Liberal women being the unmarried daughters of middle-class figures. Tories were more often wives. Labour's working-class women were wives or widows; those from the middle class were, in the main, unmarried.

The high proportion of women involved in local government in Norwich was partly attributable to the relevance of municipal issues to the social sphere women inhabited (housing, welfare, education), and to the enduring links between the middle class and the city. In the 1920s such links were typified by the Misses Colman who served as councillors, mayor and mayoress and charity leaders. But it was also due to the weakness of trade unionism in the city. Where Labour membership was dominated by strong unions, as in parts of Lancashire and in the north east, party leaders could be insensitive to the needs of women voters.[35] On the other hand, where unions were weak there were spaces in the party structure for women to carve out a career. Furthermore, the dominance of political over industrial issues in areas where unionisation lagged made the ideas of women, such as Mabel Clarkson, more acceptable to the rest of the rank and file. Overall, the rise of Labour challenged the primacy of the issues which had divided the middle class. Up to the First World War most Labour activists had been schooled in the educational and Sunday school organisations of the free churches where they acquired a moral and ethical approach to politics and commitment to free trade. By the inter-war period, however, free trade ceased to be an important issue for Labour. Although many Labour leaders remained puritanical on issues like drinking and Sunday leisure, and used the language of religious morality to attack capitalism, these elements gave way to a programmatic municipal socialism which, though moral and often puritan in tone, was essentially secular.

For much of the nineteenth century Norwich was synonymous with electoral corruption. Traditionally associated with elections to the unreformed corporation, with the passing of the Municipal Corporations Act the focus of such activities switched to parliamentary contests, an orgy of bribery characterising the election of 1837 when the candidates together spent £40,000. The crippling cost of this election led to a deal in 1841 which gave a seat each to the Liberals and Conservatives, Chartist attempts to field a candidate resulting in the blatant bribery of their leader, John Dover, and his humiliation at the hands of his erstwhile supporters.[36] Endemic in the 1840s and 1850s, corruption was most apparent at the high points of political partisanship in the city, as, for example, during the first few years after the Reform Act or during the Tory push for power in 1859–60. Furthermore, it was extensively practised by both sides – the Tories claiming the Liberals offered £20 to £30 per vote in the municipal elections of 1859.[37] T. O. Springfield, a charismatic businessman, and Sir William Foster, a traditional Whig, managed the Liberals corruptly, despite 'Radical objections'.[38] The key Tory figure was Sir Samuel Bignold, whose main vehicle was the Eldon Club, though by the 1860s his style was seen as a liability in comparison with the rising leadership of the brewer, H. S. Patteson.[39]

From the mid 1840s Jacob Henry Tillett (Plate 48), the city's leading radical, campaigned against corruption, setting up a vigilance committee and drawing support from the leading nonconformist minister, the Reverend George Gould of St Mary's Baptist church.[40] As mayor in 1859, Tillett exposed Tory attempts to bribe a councillor with £300 to vote for eight conservative aldermen,[41] and a Conservative councillor suggested that, 'by his peculiar influence almost a millennium had been brought about in the city, for they had had for the first time for hundreds of years a municipal election without drunkenness, without corruption, without bribery'.[42] Though it should be added it was also an election without contests! Ironically, it was Tillett who became the main victim of corruption after 1867. Although his defeat in 1868 was overturned when an enquiry found extensive Conservative bribery, his easy victory in the 1870 by-election was declared void on a technicality.[43] Far worse, his 1875 by-election success was found to have been secured by the practice of 'colorable [sic] employment' (where potential voters were given paid jobs of little importance by the party agents to secure their vote).[44] A subsequent Royal Commission to investigate bribery and corruption in Norwich elections concluded that such practices were indeed rife and suspended the writ until the next

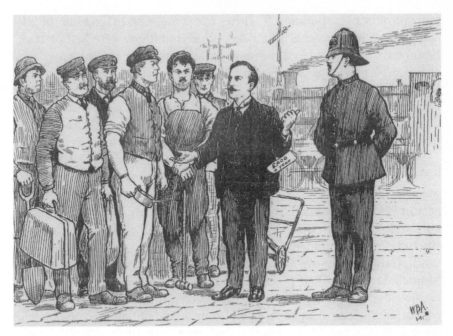

FIGURE 43. Labour logic: a Conservative attack on Labour MP George Roberts, 1914. (*Norwich Unionist*, May 1914)

election. Although Tillett was unimpeachably elected in 1880, he retired after one term, to be replaced in 1885 by the Conservative brewer, Sir Harry Bullard, who followed in Tillett's tradition by being promptly unseated. From this point open corruption ceased to be an important aspect of parliamentary politics in Norwich, though accusations of invidious influence continued through to the Edwardian period (Figure 43).[45]

Corruption initially owed much to the remnants of the wide pre-reform freeman franchise which, combined with the depressed state of the Norwich economy, created a pool of poor voters who expected treating at election time. Its reappearance after 1867 reflected attempts by the two parties to come to terms with the massively expanded working-class electorate, and the heightened state of political partisanship associated with the candidature of Tillett. Yet corruption was also an integral part of the popular politics which operated in the city.

Traditions of involvement in Norwich politics amongst both the included and excluded continued into the reformed era. In the early period this embraced intimidation and the practice of cooping – kidnapping political opponents on election day – whilst suburbs such as Pockthorpe maintained their custom of mock mayor making which had characterised the pre-reform corporation.[46] These manifestations of popular politics could shade into violence when economic conditions were bad or traditional ways of life menaced. In January 1887 a meeting of the unemployed attended by more than five hundred people threatened to take the mayor hostage before attacking shops and taking a ham, hence the naming of the incident 'The Battle of Ham Run'.[47] In the Edwardian period, suffragettes allegedly burned buildings, whilst the by-election of 1904 witnessed a number of disrupted meetings, especially those of the Tariff Reform League.[48]

Popular politics also adapted to the requirements of democratic politics before 1914. In the early years of Chartism, a central tactic of the excluded was the invasion of other parties' meetings, where they made speeches against Whig employers, Tory guardians, the poor law, the police, the corn laws and the church, besides pressing the inevitable vote in favour of the Charter.[49] More dramatic, however, was the Pockthorpe committee's unsuccessful twenty-five year campaign against elite attempts to empark Mousehold Heath. Their political impact was such that at the 1868 general election the Liberal candidates Foster and Tillett, who had both initially supported the idea of a people's park, trailed behind the Tory candidate in the Pockthorpe area, although this may have been the result of intensive treating and bribery by Stracey's agents.[50] In the later 1870s, however, resistance to the scheme was more openly supported by members of the local elite, headed now by Tillett, MP from 1880–5, for whom Mousehold represented another abuse by landowners of the rights of the people. Support also came from Edward Burgess's Independent Political Association, a ratepayer body whose opposition to the park on grounds of taxation was united with a populist defence of the people's rights against the grand designs of the municipal elite. Yet, this support from the middle classes did not imply they were controlling the people of Pockthorpe or using them for their own electoral ends, as both politicians and residents clearly depended heavily upon each other – as indeed they did in the case of corruption – in a complementary exchange of political, cultural and economic resources.

Mousehold revealed the multi-faceted dimension of popular politics in the mid to late nineteenth century. Defence of community rights was undertaken by traditional methods – violence, intimidation, occupation; by playing the party system – accepting bribes, supporting political sympathisers; and by exploiting the rules of modern civil society – organising committees, putting forward candidates, constructing and fighting lengthy legal cases. Yet when all of these tactics failed to secure a victory the people of Pockthorpe turned their backs on politics, choosing to revert to 'type' and to behave badly towards the new people's park. The large boards which displayed the bye-laws were repeatedly torn down, whilst evidence exists of boys throwing stones and playing tip-cat, girls behaving 'indecently' with soldiers from the barracks, and men fist-fighting, poaching, using obscene language, gambling and linnet-netting.[51] Although debate continues over the extent to which such popular politics was tamed after the First World War,[52] it would seem that political violence and extra-party activity were weakened. Forms of direct popular politics were apparent in the unemployed movements of the late 1920s and early 1930s, but Geoffrey Shakespeare's memory of taming a working-class audience during the 1929 election by appealing to reason, fair play and the love of a wager, suggests a civilising of the political process.[53]

This civilising process was most obvious in the development of pressure groups, not least because the boundaries of urban governance were fluid, allowing politics to find expression in other forms of organisation. Those formed to defend business interests often slipped into politics themselves – especially between 1875 and 1939 – stimulated by the growing intervention of local and national government in matters concerning business and the emerging power of organised labour. The 1890s saw the appearance of a chamber of commerce and the development of strong associations among master builders and footwear manufacturers. The chamber created a non-party environment where businessmen could unite against legislation which threatened their interests. During the 1920s its membership grew and in 1926 it launched a rates economy campaign with the support of businessmen from all parties. In the following year, chamber of commerce candidates contested local elections. Over the next five years it challenged the local authority, especially in 1933 over the municipalisation of the trams, but from this point the independent actions of business pressure groups declined as economic crisis and Labour control reunited the middle class along conventional party lines.[54]

The development of labour organisations was characterised by a generally weak trade union movement and a strong political wing. In the mid nineteenth century working men were prominent in campaigns to extend the franchise, but trade unionism remained fragile, with skilled unions such as the Amalgamated Society of Engineers having just forty-four members in 1862. The 1870s saw more effective organisation as conflict in the footwear industry and elsewhere led to the successful formation of unions, and in 1875 the foundation of a co-operative society which developed an educational and political wing. The transformation of industrial defence into political pressure came with the creation of the Trades Council in 1886, which provided a link between working-class organisations and politics. In 1901 its executive committee promoted a conference of trade unionists, co-operators and the ILP which agreed to field a labour candidate at the next election.[55] By 1914 it was managing the local Labour representation committee, promoting trade union activity and lobbying local government. But the role of labour organisations as pressure groups declined in favour of direct political action by the ILP and Labour Party. Even ex-servicemen initially chose a direct political approach, successfully contesting a number of wards in the 1919 elections, whilst the unemployed workers' organisations of the 1930s quickly became identified with the Communist Party.

In the early nineteenth century, organised nonconformity was prominent in campaigns against slavery and the Corn Laws and became embroiled in attacks on the Church of England. Thus, for example, the Baptists in St George's Colegate successfully prevented the levying of a church rate.[56] By the 1860s, education was the main battle ground, as a local branch of Chamberlain's National Education League became a major vehicle for dissenting political action. School board elections were conducted primarily on religious lines, with denominational (Anglican) and non-denominational (Nonconformist and secular) candidates contesting seats. When, in 1902, new legislation permitted the use of rate income for the upkeep of Anglican schools, the free churches organised opposition through the Norwich Citizens League, which involved Nonconformists in the non-payment of a portion of the rates, a campaign which contributed significantly to the victory of the Liberals at the 1904 by-election. In the sphere of housing reform leading Baptists, the Reverend George Gould and councillor John Willis, campaigned successfully in the 1870s for the application of the Cross Act to part of St Paul's parish. A more extensive housing crusade following the flood of 1912 found members from all denominations leading the drive for reform, many urging a return to the moral dimension of politics around the issue.[57] As this suggests, lobbyists from both church and chapel could also act together against their political masters, actively contesting the council's attempts to introduce Sunday opening of library reading rooms and cinemas. Similar unity could be found on the temperance issue, both sides of the Protestant divide coming together to defend the small gains made by temperance workers, such as the limitation of opening hours in 1872.[58] However, the power of anti-drink bodies was balanced by that of publicans and brewers whose economic clout ensured that Norwich never became too earnest in its pursuit of temperance.

As with most towns in this period, the expansion of local government was the central political concern and the arena which united formal and informal politics, private and state action. In tackling the problems of sanitation and disease in the late 1840s Norwich displayed many of the ambiguities of Victorian urban governance, with multiple agencies (improvement commission, voluntary board of health, city council) attempting to organise adequate services in the face of competing agencies, limited resources and strong public opposition. The setting up of a local board of health in 1851 helped, but it was only after the adoption of the 1872 Public Health Act that the city really began to tackle the problems associated with poor housing and high infant mortality. Though tardy on public health, Norwich proved in the vanguard of developments in education and recreation, being one of the first cities to adopt the Libraries and Museums Act of 1850 and to set up a free library and museums service, though both depended heavily on donations and subscriptions to provide their stock. This combination of donation and rate support also characterised the expansion of leisure facilities, where personal acts of philanthropy often blurred the boundary between state and voluntary activity.[59] The acquisition and development of open spaces, such as the castle, Chapelfield Gardens and Mousehold Heath, were driven forward by the personal zeal of individuals, although their actions were not always welcomed by the whole community, as shown by the ambiguous response to proposals for the emparking of Mousehold Heath. In education the scope for municipal action was more constrained by law. During the 1860s the city council used its ancient rights to transform the Grammar School and promote a new commercial school. It opened a Technical Institute in 1898, but until 1902 it had no part to play in elementary education, which remained the responsibility of the school board. The board built a large number of schools, yet even here the public and the voluntary sat uneasily together, with church and company schools existing alongside the board's own provision. The post-1902 system allowed the council to centralise all education from nursery to further education in one body and discharge new statutory responsibilities which brought health and welfare into the field of education through the introduction of school meals and inspections.[60]

The situation in education reflected the general trend towards the centralisation of urban governance in the hands of the borough council.[61] At the same time, improved economic circumstances and the democratisation of the municipal electoral system increased the importance of policy in local affairs. The emergence of a group of politicians more willing to employ the council as the vehicle for social change led to some progress on environmental issues, typified by the St Paul's scheme, whilst an important 1898 court case established the council's right to force owners of court and yard property to improve public areas at their own expense, heralding significant progress in paving, lighting and sanitation. Although, before the flood of 1912, the council was reluctant to close slums or build its own properties, between the wars it proved highly effective in both slum clearance and house building, erecting 7900 houses by 1939.[62] Yet this drive to modernise the urban fabric stimulated a powerful conservationist lobby led by the Norwich Society founded in 1923, whose aims included 'a vigilant opposition to all acts of vandalism', their greatest success being the preservation of Elm Hill, earmarked for demolition during the 1920s.[63] Environmental improvements were also affected by the expansion of the city's public parks and sports facilities, exemplified by Eaton park, with its eighty acres of pleasure gardens, sports pitches, a restaurant and yacht pond.[64] These were facilities for all – young and old, male and female, middle and working class – intended to meet popular demand without imposing an agenda of rational recreation. This change of purpose demonstates the evolving mission of the council by the later 1930s.

The municipalisation of public utilities was not so readily accepted. As late as 1900 the city council controlled none of the four main utilities (gas, water, electricity and trams). Having lost the right to provide water in the early 1850s, it failed to acquire the supply of gas and passed up the opportunity to operate the new electric trams.[65] There was a shift of emphasis in the Liberal group around 1900, however, with George White claiming in October 1901 that, as water, gas and electricity were natural monopolies, they could not be left 'safely in the hands of individuals, but should be administered for the good of all by the representatives of all, the community sharing the profit, if any, and also bearing the loss'.[66] Within two years the council had taken over the electricity supply, with an eye to achieving greater efficiency, profitability and potentially reduced costs to business consumers. The acquisition of water in 1920 drew a spirited opposition from ratepayer groups, easily defeated by a united council advocating public control of a 'natural monopoly'. But this was not the case with the attempt to municipalise the trams in 1932–33. On this occasion, the Labour group, along with some leading Tories and Liberals, were successfully opposed by the chamber of commerce, most Conservative council members and a number of important Liberals led by the Colmans. Together, they secured an easy victory in a referendum on the acquisition plan, defeating Labour's dogmatic proposal to acquire the trams and thus deliver control of the nascent bus service to the municipality.[67]

These developments in local government were accompanied by a significant growth in the size, power and professionalism of the municipal bureaucracy. Opening up the jobs monopolised by the old corporations through patronage networks was a central aim of the reformers of 1835, yet in the short term the incoming council simply replaced the old Tory jobbing of the corporation with a new form of Liberal corruption. The new town clerk, J. R. Staff, a Liberal with close connections to the rest of the Whig elite, drew large and questionable fees for his post. Moreover, corruption was uncovered in the surveyor's office; and the inspector of nuisances, Samuel Clarke, came under scrutiny for some of his financial arrangements.[68] Furthermore, until 1900 being a Liberal remained an important qualification for a senior post with the council. Staff's replacement as town clerk, Wace Mendham, was an active Liberal married to J. H. Tillett's sister. His successor was also a Liberal,[69] and in the early 1870s, the first medical officer of health and the new city treasurer were both sitting Liberal councillors when appointed. In the early twentieth century, social networks were added to these familial and political connections, most obviously in the case of the city engineer, A. E. Collins, who was a member of the Social Lodge of Freemasons along with a significant number of Liberals and a large group with interests in the construction sector.[70] Yet the role of these public figures was becoming more professional and managerial as recognised qualifications, national recruitment and the development of professional bodies, along with the growth of the municipal workforce, modernised the world of the municipal officer.[71] In 1900 the council employed twenty-two heads of departments, mostly professionals, and around four hundred other staff. By the early 1950s, the figure had risen to five hundred city hall administrators, as well as several thousand manual workers, public health practitioners, police officers, teachers and nurses.[72]

The relatively slow pace of municipal progress in Norwich owed much to the financial frailty of the borough. Even moderate spending was constrained during the middle decades of the nineteenth century by the poor state of the local economy and sluggish population growth, which together exacerbated the enduring problem of a perennially weak rates base. During the nineteenth century Norwich retained very generous compounding arrangements for the collection of the rates. Under this system, the landlords of small properties collected the rates as part of the rent and passed on a proportion to the local authority, so that in 1900 it was calculated as 'giving a loss of thirty per cent on the rates of two-thirds of the city'.[73] This practice combined with low rents (roughly half those in London in 1908)[74] and the large number of small businesses to give Norwich consistently one of the highest penny in the pound rates in England, the figure hitting 27s. in the pound in 1921. This bill reflected both the increasing burden of recurring expenditure and the substantial growth of debt in the last quarter of the nineteenth century, which increased eight fold between 1870 and 1900.[75] The figure continued to rise throughout the first half of the twentieth century, as first investment in the electricity undertaking, then purchase of the waterworks and the commencement of a substantial building campaign, each demanded extensive borrowing.

The effect of these financial constraints was to produce a constant urge for economy amongst the local electorate. The first enquiry into council finances came in 1856, followed by many others across the later nineteenth and twentieth century. Ratepayer groups, dominated by *petit bourgeois* elements, appeared sporadically to challenge local political leaders, sometimes promoting a radical or populist agenda, though increasingly sharing personnel and ideas with Tory activists in working-class wards. However, in the early 1920s, with depression and high unemployment in the city and the rates bill peaking, economy became a pressing issue for big business. Their support for the rates economy campaign stimulated an extensive enquiry into council spending, but their offensive was stonewalled by departmental chiefs who blamed high spending on the requirements of central government.[76] But a drive for economy was not the only business response. The 1929 general election saw many business leaders back Lloyd George's unemployment campaign, possibly as a way of sharing some of the cost of the expanding welfare bill. Similar schemes had been canvassed in the 1840s, when Norwich Liberals had advocated a national assessment to spread the cost of poor relief. And George White had supported national insurance to redistribute the cost of unemployment from the areas where it was most burdensome to more prosperous regions.[77] In the long run the rates issue brought Liberal and Conservative together and diminished their cultural differences. For most of the period there was little to choose between the parties on municipal policy. With the rise of Labour the gap narrowed even further.

The triumph of Labour was the most striking and surprising feature of twentieth-century politics in Norwich for, as a cathedral city, with a large middle class and no dominant single industry, it had few of the characteristics of a classic 'Labour' stronghold. There had been considerable radical activity in the early years of the nineteenth century, but by the 1830s the main feature of working-class politics was corruption. Chartism in the city was surprisingly weak given both the earlier manifestations of radicalism and the decline of the textile industry between 1825 and 1844;[78] and most skilled workers were closely tied to the Liberals from the 1860s. Control over the votes of the workers was challenged from the 1880s by a growing socialist movement, led by the Social Democratic Federation (SDF) and the ILP, whose members, by 1902, were mounting a sufficient challenge to force the Liberals to develop a progressive municipal programme.[79] This did not prevent the ILP breaking through in 1903 and securing variable successes over the next ten years, by which time they had six councillors and had secured victories in six of the sixteen wards (Plate 49). Furthermore, from 1908 onwards limited ILP success prompted the Liberals and Conservatives to institute selective local alliances to prevent three-cornered contests when Labour candidates entered the field, though in the short term this did not compromise the Liberal arrangement with the LRC at general elections.[80] Labour's post-war breakthrough at the municipal elections of November 1919 provoked a more solid and largely effective municipal anti-socialist coalition. The defection of the Liberal MP, Hilton Young, to the Tories in 1926, however, disrupted this tactical gambit and allowed Labour to capture a number of new seats. They became the largest party, and by dint of assiduous attendance at committees dominated the council, often forcing through radical policies in alliance with some Liberal councillors. With the eclipse of the Liberals in the early 1930s and the redrawing of the ward boundaries to give Labour eight safe wards, overall control was secured in 1933. Norwich had become a central feature of Labour's heartland.[81]

In explaining Labour's triumph, a general consensus has emerged that it was the weakness of the trade union movement which contributed to the considerable strength of political organisations in the city. In many of the towns where trade unionism was strong an industrial strategy was adopted by the labour movement, with organisational effort directed at challenging the elite in the workplace. However, in towns such as Norwich, where the industrial wing was weak, effort and personnel were concentrated on building up the electoral machine. The ILP were pivotal in radicalising both politics and trade unionism in the city to create a strong electoral culture built on a combination of ethical socialism and faith in the municipality's ability to deliver a better world for the workers.[82] Labour's strength may also have owed something to the failure of popular politics to defend the people's rights and the inability of the mixed economy of local governance to deliver improved services. Furthermore, though the argument regarding a weak trade union movement holds well for the growth of Labour in the Edwardian period, it does not explain the continued rise of the party in the 1920s and early 1930s. For this we need to look to the enduring strength of Liberalism and the continuing divisions this caused within the middle class.

Labour's advance was curtailed between 1920 and 1926, when a strong anti-socialist alliance operated, but over the next four years, during which conflict re-emerged within the middle class, Labour made significant gains. They also benefited from the rapid growth of council housing in suburban estates, which solidified 'safe' Labour wards and weakened the pan-class alliances which both Liberals and Conservatives had developed before 1914. Finally, advocates for Labour have emphasised their ability to shape the agenda and deliver improved services for the benefit of the working classes, especially in the field of housing. This was the advantage of a labour movement run by the political rather than the industrial interest, for, as has been shown in the case of Preston, trade union run parties lost touch with many of the local issues which were important to women voters between the wars.[83] In Norwich, Labour activists were more receptive to changes in voter demand, a situation assisted by the important part women played in the party hierarchy and its electoral strategy.[84] Thus, both the original foundations of labour success and the consolidation of power were built on the strength of a political wing atuned to the demands of ordinary working-class voters.

The political culture of Norwich in the nineteenth and early twentieth century was profoundly influenced by the legacies of the early modern period, as manifest in its tarnished popular politics and its economy, which fed corruption, divided the middle class and produced the environment which spawned a successful political Labour movement. Moreover, its religious *milieu* defined the boundaries of cultural politics. Party politics were always central, yet political alliances were frequently constructed, assisted by the maintenance of the double member constituency until 1949, which seems to have benefited the Liberals in particular. Similarly, local government was hampered by its weak finances and forced to rely heavily on a combination of public, private and voluntary agencies to deliver even the most elementary of services. Norwich was certainly unusual in the rapid rise to power of its Labour Party and the importance of women in local politics, as indeed it may have been in the enduring strength of its middle-class Liberalism, based on nonconformist culture and the persistence of the undivided borough.[85] Yet, despite the importance of locality and heritage in shaping the city's politics, many of the responses reflected processes occurring elsewhere in Britain, sometimes ahead of the national trend, at others behind. In particular, Norwich is worthy of attention for the early and strong advance of its Labour Party. Yet, paradoxically, the persistence of an electoral presence for the Liberals, also challenges accepted ideas about urban politics in this period.

15

Banking and Insurance

Roger Ryan

T. Bignold took up the firepan and tongs, and placing himself on a chair, declared that he would break the head of the first man that attempted to open the chest, and calling upon his son, John Cocksedge Bignold, desired him to get his pistol which he immediately did, and presenting it, threatened in a most positive manner to fire at any of the directors who should attempt to open the chest; the father at the same time standing by and encouraging his son to fire, saying, 'fire, John – I will protect you'. Finding both father and son apparently determined to make use of their weapons against them, ... the Directors thought it most prudent to withdraw from the office.

Anonymous letter from 'An Advocate for Truth and Justice', 1805[1]

The nineteenth-century expansion of the Norwich financial sector of banking and insurance sustained the city's national and, indeed, international significance through a period of relative demographic and industrial decline. This growth occurred despite legislative obstacles to financial innovation. Provincial banking was hampered by the statutory monopoly of joint stock banking held by the Bank of England from 1708. This meant that all other English banks had to be private partnerships restricted to six partners without limitation of liability. Insurance projects faced a similar atmosphere of official hostility towards corporate ventures after the 1720 Bubble Act excluded all but a privileged handful of existing institutions. In fact lawyers became adept at using the legal device of the deed of settlement as a means of attaining similar privileges to incorporation for insurance firms, including the absence of a limit to the number of partners.[2] This restrictive climate hindered the development of banking far more than insurance because the partnership limit ruled out extensive branch networks capable of internalising the costs of regional differences in business activity. Private bankers in London's west end and the 'City' around Lombard Street thrived despite these barriers by exploiting the rapid growth of metropolitan trade and finance. No provincial English town, however, could match the scale and diversity of London's financial districts which also housed large insurance companies such as the Sun, Royal Exchange Assurance and, from 1762, the mutual life assurance business of the Equitable.[3]

Provincial 'quasi-bankers', traders who handled funds for others, had existed for centuries. But the earliest country bank, at Bristol, only opened in 1716 and few others followed until encouraged to do so by gradual but sustained economic growth from the 1760s. Around three hundred country banks existed by 1797, when an abortive French invasion at Fishguard led the Bank of England to suspend cash payments to forestall panic withdrawals of gold. That decision triggered an expansion of easier credit and the flotation of many more country banks to a peak of over 650 before the 1810–11 financial crisis dampened activity by proving that there was no safety in numbers. The problem was that country banks were too small. Their survival depended on informal links with 'City' correspondent banks which transferred funds between those with surpluses to others seeking finance for local borrowers. Because this was profitable, correspondent City banks also helped their country bankers during crises by sending funds at short notice to quell panic withdrawals by depositors fearful of losing their money.[4] For their part, country bankers actively backed local fire insurance offices in towns as diverse as Norwich, Manchester and Newcastle,[5] although few, Norwich being a notable exception, risked the long-term commitments of life insurance. These 'country' fire offices were as vulnerable as country banks. Whenever a town's banks wobbled, the local fire office usually folded, at which juncture its business was likely to go to a London insurance company.

Despite their obvious inefficiencies, English banks coped with the borrowing needs of other sectors without further legislative intervention until the 1820s, when they were hit by the combined pressures of insolvent debtors ruined by speculative overseas investment and the Bank of England's deflationary return to cash payments in 1821.[6] In December 1825 the collapse of the reputable firm of Pole & Company, a leading correspondent bank, triggered panic and the closure of sixty country banks within six months.[7] Parliament promptly ended the Bank of England's monopoly of joint-stock banking beyond a sixty-five mile radius of London in 1826, while non-note issuing joint stock banks were allowed within that boundary from 1833. That still ruled out stable corporate banks with nationwide branch networks until the 1862 Companies Act permitted banks, and also insurance companies, limited liability.[8] Nevertheless, some country bankers had long since turned to informal networks partially to achieve the same end.

Most notably Quakers relied on ties of kinship and religion to form interlocking business partnerships of mutual trust and obligation. It has been
argued that this was vital to English finance because 15 to 25 per cent of all
English banks were founded by Quakers by the late eighteenth century.[9]

Of these, the Norwich Gurneys were by far the wealthiest in the
provinces and the most closely connected in marriage and business with
fellow Quakers in Lombard Street.[10] There is a family story that their 'Norwich Bank' was opened in 1775 to give Henry Gurney's son Bartlett 'some
employment on account of his dislike of the [worsted] manufactory'.[11] Perhaps the tale is apocryphal, since the Gurneys were already experienced
quasi-bankers.[12] Local resources were certainly being switched from
worsted production into finance as leading families such as the Gurneys,
active Whigs and Quakers, and the Tory Anglican Harveys and Kerrisons,
moved into banking and insurance. The first Norwich bank was actually
opened in 1757 by a brewer, Charles Weston, while Thomas Bignold, a
newcomer, opened Union Bank in 1804 specifically to handle premiums
from the Norwich Union Fire Insurance Society which he founded in 1797.
Otherwise, the city's early financial sector was dominated by the worsted
trade. Yarn merchants Allday & Kerrison started a bank in 1768. Then, in
1778, warehousemen Hudson & Hatfield became bankers, their partnership
splitting in 1792 when Hudson joined worsted manufacturer Robert John
Harvey, while Hatfield entered a partnership with Thomas Back junior and
Thomas Kett, a wealthy Quaker woolcomber related to the Gurneys. In
1820 this bank passed to Kett's sons-in-law Charles Tompson and Charles
Barclay with Jeremiah Ives junior, a worsted merchant, becoming the acting partner. After Ives died in 1829 the bank was taken over by Gurneys.[13]
Finally, Starling Day, a wool factor, had founded a Norwich bank by 1806.[14]

Although diversification from industry into country banking was widespread in England, increasing agrarian wealth brought funds into Norwich
on a scale unmatched elsewhere (Table 15.1). Roger Kerrison's bank gained
directly when his Tory Anglican loyalty obtained for him the receivership
of the land tax for Norfolk in the late 1770s. A knighthood followed in 1800,
but Kerrison was extravagant: when he died in 1808 his bank failed, with
tax arrears and other liabilities of £460,000.[15] Despite this blow to the city's
reputation, the wool merchant and brewer John Patteson used his influence as Tory MP for Norwich to secure this government business for
R. J. Harvey. Harvey & Hudson's banking partnership took on the title
'Crown Bank' and gained a permanent interest free balance of over £30,000
from collecting the county's land tax.[16] But the exclusion of dissenters from
this form of government patronage barely troubled Gurneys.[17] With their
Peckover, Birkbeck and Buxton connections they 'formed marriage

Table 15.1 Norwich country bank partnerships and joint stock banking companies, 1756–1896

Date founded	Date of key partnership changes	Bank	Date of closure	Reason and disposal of accounts if known
1756		C. Weston	1812	
1768		Alldays		
1777		Allday & Kerrison		
1783		R. Kerrison	1808	Bankrupt. Receivership of land tax to Harvey & Hudson
1775		J. & H.Gurney		
	1796	Gurney & Company	1896	A founding firm in Barclays & Company
1783		Hudson & Hatfield	1792	Hatfield joined Kett Hudson joined Harvey
1792		Harvey & Hudson		
	c. 1808	Known as 'Crown' Bank	1870	Bankrupt. Accounts to Gurneys
1792		Kett, Hatfield & Back		
	1820	Tompson, Barclay & Ives	1832	Ceased trading. Accounts to Gurneys
1795		Day & Company	1825	Bankrupt
c. 1805		Bignold & Son	1819	Ceased trading
1826		Norfolk & Norwich Joint Stock Bank	1836	Ceased trading. Accounts to East of England joint stock bank
1836		East of England Joint Stock Bank	1864	Bankrupt. Accounts to Provincial Banking Corporation

Sources: Bidwell, *Annals*, passim; M. Dawes and C. Ward Perkins, *Country Banks of England and Wales* (Chartered Institute of Bankers, 2000); Ryan, 'Norwich Union', pp. 100–5; H. Preston, *Early East Anglian Banks*, passim.

Notes: Dawes and Ward Perkins, *Country Banks*, p. 434, also refer to the bank of J. & J. B. Bolinbroke which opened and went bankrupt in 1788; while Preston includes R. Ball's 'Deposit and Discount Bank', *c.* 1838 to 1854, with its single office in Norwich. Neither had a significant impact on the city's financial sector.

alliances and partnerships that created the largest, and largely Quaker banking network of the nineteenth century'.[18]

Meanwhile, London insurance companies had used Norwich agents for their business from the 1720s with little success, and any attempt to establish local fire offices had failed until the Norwich General Assurance was formed in 1792. It sought to raise capital of £160,000 in £200 shares, £40 called. The risks were large but, as a consequence, religious and political differences were ignored and every Norwich bank helped raise this capital from some three hundred local 'Gentlemen of known property'.[19] Thomas Bignold became secretary. A yeoman farmer's son, born in Kent in 1761, he seemed ideal. Reputedly a former exciseman, he had become a Norwich wine and spirit dealer in 1785 after marrying a widow, Sarah Long, and taking on her first husband's grocery business (Plate 51). Bignold took Norwich General's annual premiums past £3500 within five years, while low claims allowed dividends of 5 per cent on the called capital. Cautiously satisfied, the directors saw premiums rise slowly to around £5,000 and from 1812 yields advanced to around 10 per cent until 1821 when shareholders got the windfall chance to take over the much larger Norwich Union Fire Society.[20]

They owed their good fortune to a quarrel in 1797 between the then directors of the Norwich General and Thomas Bignold, who was frustrated by the board's caution and left abruptly to found the Norwich Union Fire Society with himself as secretary. With every local banker supporting the Norwich General, Bignold had little chance of raising capital. He therefore formed a mutual society with all profits and liabilities being shared by policyholders as 'members'. Although mutual fire insurance of this kind was a novelty beyond London, it appealed to local radicals, who became directors even though they were better known for their Jacobin sympathies than their financial acumen. Bignold and twelve directors guaranteed £1000 each and started insuring without other reserves. The attraction for policyholders was that they could vote at general meetings and share profits, although these were only paid as bonuses after a policy had run for seven years. The question of liability was ignored because losses remained well below premiums while Bignold concentrated on East Anglia and built up reserves. From 1804, when the first bonus was paid at 50 per cent of premiums, Norwich Union was effectively halving the cost of fire insurance. Bignold's success enabled him to take on the London companies by establishing over 350 agencies throughout Britain. He also opened the Union Bank and, in 1808, founded the Life Society as the earliest provincial mutual life office, legally distinct from the fire business but sharing its management and agencies.[21]

Bignold's manic activities soon attracted press and pamphlet attacks on his humble origins as an 'Exciseman!' and retailer of wines and spirits.[22] His Union Bank was ridiculed in a pun-laden anonymous poem called the 'Geneva Banker'[23] which epitomises the tone of the rest:

> B – d two callings has combined,
> And shown no little merit,
> For *Banking* with the Gin-trade joined
> Must be pursued with Spirit.
> The scheme may answer in the lump,
> However absurd it looks,
> Keep but his *liquor* from the pump
> And from the *Fire* his books.[24]

Bignold capitalised on his notoriety by recruiting liberal-minded business-men and landowners as trustees or local committee members throughout Britain. Scores of public figures backed his remarkable plan so that by 1817, with annual premiums of nearly £79,000, the Fire Society was among the five largest of thirty-six British fire offices. Meanwhile, the Life Society's premiums had reached £78,000, making Norwich Union by far the leading provincial insurance institution.[25]

There was, however, another side to Bignold. Domineering at the best of times, he ousted his founding directors when they questioned his plans in 1806 and, abruptly burying his radical allegiances of a decade earlier, replaced them with local Tories. By 1817, he had even fallen out with his three sons after bringing them into the business and, ignoring their oppo-sition to further expansion, moving to London to run Norwich Union from its Bridge Street office. He chose the wrong moment. The post-war recession hit all fire offices with massive claims, some undoubtedly fraud-ulent, by policyholders verging on bankruptcy. London companies avoided bad publicity by paying up, increasing rates and declining new high-risk business. Norwich Union, however, had no capital and its reserves, although by then over £108,000, could not stand a run of bad years. With losses rising fast, the policyholders could not expect further bonuses, while rivals claimed that they were liable for the heavy claims. This was never put to the test because Bignold's sons rallied enough policyholder support in 1818 to call a special general meeting at Norwich and dismiss him from the Fire Office so that they could reduce risks. Even then he continued dis-rupting the Life Society and only compromised after he had been declared bankrupt and imprisoned for debt in 1823.

Of Bignold's sons, Samuel, the youngest, emerged as secretary to both societies. John Patteson backed him by chairing the crucial general meeting in 1818, reassuring policyholders about the societies' future without their founder. Personal financial difficulties probably motivated Patteson because by keeping the societies at Norwich he could sell them his mansion in Surrey Street. This became their new head office in 1820 (Plate 52).[26] Meanwhile, Samuel Bignold turned to the Norwich General directors who alone in the city could muster enough capital to save the Fire Society. He did not go empty-handed. London companies were on the prowl for *all* provincial insurance firms, and he offered Norwich General the chance to avoid being taken over by merging with the Fire Society, an immensely attractive deal for well-to-do directors who lacked entrepreneurial flair.

They agreed, and in 1821 the Fire Society became a joint stock company with £550,000 capital, £66,000 called as additional reserves. The Union Bank had already been wound up by 1820 and Day & Son were Norwich Union's treasurers. From 1821, the Fire Society shared the appointment of treasurer between the four Norwich banks in rotation.[27] By working with leading London fire offices Samuel Bignold also stabilised Norwich Union's market share,[28] joining five other companies in 1826 to establish Britain's earliest formal tariff. When such rating agreements were regularised by creating the Fire Offices Committee in 1868, these 'tariff' companies controlled 90 per cent of all fire insurance in Britain,[29] and Norwich Union still ranked fifth out of sixty-one offices in the British market, bringing annual premiums of £160,000 into the city.[30] Being the largest insurer of British farmstock, Norwich Union was known as the 'Farmers' Office'. When freak hailstorms ruined crops in eastern England in August 1843,[31] Samuel Bignold wanted to build on this reputation by insuring farmers against hailstorm damage, but his directors refused.[32] Probably anticipating this, he immediately became a founding director of the Norwich based General Hailstorm Insurance Company, with Charles Suckling Gilman as secretary. Furthermore, its success encouraged Gilman's son, Charles Rackham Gilman, to establish the Norwich & London Accident & Casualty Assurance Association in 1856 with Bignold as a director. C. R. Gilman expanded the company at home and overseas, particularly in the booming United States market, and absorbed General Hailstorm in 1898. By then Norwich & London was a target for any insurance company seeking to diversify and, fearing an 'external' take-over, the Fire Society bought it in 1908.

When Day & Son failed in December 1825, in the midst of the national banking crisis, other Norwich bankers, led by Gurneys, bolstered local confidence and survived. In 1827, however, Samuel Bignold used the 1826 Bank Act to found the Norfolk and Norwich Joint Stock Bank (N & NJSB)[33] and take over the Life Society treasurership which had been with Tompson, Barclay & Ives since Days' failure.[34] By then Bignold was the leading local Tory, so Whigs inevitably viewed this as a blatantly political move. Prominent Whigs such as John Cozens and R. M. Bacon, editor of the *Norwich Mercury*, attacked N & NJSB for handling Tory bribery funds during general elections. As Gurneys had done the same for the Whigs such cries of corruption fell on deaf ears,[35] although Bignold narrowly escaped more serious criticism when he hurriedly transferred N & NJSB's business to the new East of England Joint Stock Bank in 1835. Bacon claimed that £150,000 of bad debt was concealed among the assets passed to the unsuspecting East of England shareholders. What he did not know at the time, but a parliamentary committee investigating joint stock banks discovered in 1836, was that the Life Society had some £30,000 to £100,000 deposited with N & NJSB during this transfer. Incredibly, that committee failed to get a more precise estimate from either Thomas Nimmo, the bank's chief clerk, who 'could not remember the exact figure', or Samuel Bignold, who claimed that he 'had large other pursuits and therefore gave but little time to the banking business'.[36] Yet Bignold was still in trouble because the Life Society had been in difficulty since at least 1835. This became public in 1837 when he failed to produce the regular septennial bonus that was then due to policyholders. Proposals to dismiss him and move head office to London were discussed at a widely reported unofficial members' meeting in London.

This was a serious threat to the entire financial sector at Norwich. It is hard to compare life offices in the 1830s because there was no legal obligation to disclose information. But three impressive Life Society bonuses declared in 1816, 1823 and 1830 had boosted annual premiums to £170,000, putting Norwich Union among the largest of the seventy-four British life offices.[37] With so much at stake, Bignold needed his considerable political skills to survive. He could count on most local members and the agents, all of them policyholders with a vested interest in maintaining the status quo. He also unexpectedly found support from Daniel O'Connell MP, a member of twenty years standing. With about an eighth of the society's policyholders living in Ireland, O'Connell's backing at general meetings in London and Norwich was decisive. It foiled local Whigs because O'Connell's Irish MPs held the political balance of power to keep Melbourne in office, while his eloquence subdued other opponents. Ignoring the ambiguities of this Tory-Anglican, Catholic-Radical alliance, O'Connell dominated the decisive special general meeting at Norwich in November 1837 and at his suggestion three examiners were appointed to audit the society's finances. The meeting agreed to take no further action until they reported.

This gave Bignold time. Timothy Steward, a Life Society director since 1835, became an examiner together with Charles Farebrother, an auctioneer and former Tory lord mayor of London, and Francis Lloyd, a Birmingham banker implacably hostile towards head office. Bignold was lucky to get Steward, who was chairman of the East of England Bank and Steward, Patteson, Finch & Company's brewery, as well as a director, with Bignold, of the Norwich Yarn Company.[38] Bignold also worked on Farebrother, while regarding Lloyd as a lost cause. An interim report in August 1838 excluded fraud. Nevertheless the final report published early in November 1839 made dismal reading. The society's books and legal papers were in a mess, and until 1835, when it was too late, Bignold had failed to appoint trustees and directors to replace those who had died since 1808. New by-laws were needed to put all this right. Bignold had also assumed the society's investments were worth £1,172,813 in June 1836, whereas the examiners' valuation of £1,005,133 wrote off £167,680, meaning that the bonus declared in 1830 had been excessive. The worst mistake had been to lend over £200,000 on jerry-built Brighton housing. Smaller errors, coupled with N & NJSB's closure, confirmed that he had taken excessive risks in his drive for new business. Nevertheless, the examiners' report emphasised that the revalued assets covered future liabilities. For *The Times*, by now familiar with real insurance fraud, this was all that mattered. By 12 November it had already concluded that 'fears for the stability of the Office had been groundless'.[39] Even so, Bignold took nothing for granted at the special general meeting called on 26 November to receive the report and vote on his future. It had to be held in the Norwich Assembly Rooms because over five hundred members attended. It seems that Bacon was correct when he claimed that the meeting was 'packed'. He reckoned two-thirds of those present were 'agents, clerks and dependents of the Institution, together with mortgagors, debtors, and others with whom party considerations are paramount'.[40] Even the Tory *Norfolk Chronicle* reported that critics were silenced by hoots, jeers and stamping,[41] enabling Bignold to win his vote of confidence, although Bacon persisted in his attacks until 1842 when a fourth bonus was declared.

Almost unnoticed, the prominent Tories Sir Robert Harvey and Timothy Steward had joined the weakened Life Board in 1835, while their Crown and East of England Banks became joint Life Society treasurers, and East of England replaced N & NJSB in the rota for the Fire Office.[42] Although they supported Bignold publicly, it was on their terms that he continued as Fire and Life secretary until he died in 1875. For all that, he remained a very influential pillar of civic life. MP for Norwich 1854–7, he received a knighthood in 1854 through his patron, the second duke of Wellington;

then, following an earlier term as mayor in 1833, he went on to serve an unprecedented four times, in 1848, 1853 and 1872. As a firm advocate of working-class self-improvement he supported the Norwich Free Library,[43] and became a trustee of the Norfolk & Norwich Savings Bank.[44]

Charles Edward Bignold succeeded his father as secretary of the Fire Office until his premature death in 1895, when his eldest son C. A. Bathurst Bignold took over. Both were prominent in charitable and politic activities while, as managers, they ensured that Norwich Union recovered to stay among the ten largest British fire offices until the First World War. They achieved this largely by expanding foreign business. By 1914 three quarters of the society's fire premiums of £1,200,000 came from overseas, principally from the United States, which was also a leading source of Norwich Union's £467,000 accident premiums following the Norwich and London Accident purchase in 1908. By the 1890s annual dividends were yielding 4 to 5 per cent on a very secure investment. The resilience of the society's reserves was fully tested by the San Francisco earthquake fire in April 1906, which cost Norwich Union some £358,000, out of total claims on British fire offices of £10 million.[45] Its dividend and share price held steady.

Meanwhile, T. Muir Grant, a Scot with wide experience of life insurance, became life secretary in 1875. Samuel Bignold's nephew, C. J. Bunyon, remained actuary, however, while the directors opposed innovation, leaving Grant in a hopeless position. Bunyon's retirement in 1887 broke the deadlock because the directors appointed John James Deuchar as actuary *and* secretary in 1887. Backed by George Forrester, a director who served as Life Society president from 1888 to 1898, Deuchar reorganised staffing and marketing strategy, introduced modern endowment schemes, and persuaded the directors to expand overseas. When he took over, annual new business had been stagnant at around £200,000 since 1837. By 1890, it was £1 million, rising to £5 million in 1910, when he retired through ill health. From a ranking below at least twenty other British life offices in 1887, making the society ripe for take-over, Deuchar took its new business to second place behind only the massive Prudential. Continued growth in both societies needed more office space. In 1905 Surrey House opened opposite the original head office and the Life clerks crossed the road, leaving Bignold House to the Fire staff. Designed by George Skipper, this solid neoclassical building reflected the new mood of confidence in the Life Society (Plate 53).[46]

In 1728 the Quaker banker Joseph Freame bought premises in Lombard Street from a scrivener whose sign, the 'Black Spread Eagle', Barclays still use.[47] The Barclay connection arose when Freame brought his Scottish

Quaker son-in-law, James Barclay, into the partnership and began redis-
counting bills sent by provincial bankers. When Freame died in 1770, this
business was so profitable that Barclay headed an 'extensive cousinhood' of
Quakers linking Lombard Street with provincial banks throughout England. Gurneys' Norwich bank was easily the most important connection,
with Barclay and Gurney intermarriages dating from 1752, enabling Gurneys to invest through London for higher returns than was possible within
East Anglia.[48] As their deposits increased, Gurneys also turned to another
Quaker, Thomas Richardson from Yorkshire, who had become an independent bill broker in 1802.[49] In 1806 Richardson brought in a fellow
Yorkshireman, John Overend, followed the next year by Samuel Gurney,
elder brother of J. J. Gurney at the Norwich Bank.[50] By then there were
eighteen city bill brokers, but Richardson, Overend & Gurney overshad-
owed the rest,[51] and the Norwich Gurneys were their main source of funds
with £1,450,000 invested in bills through them by 1809.[52] Gurneys got their
first fright about this commitment during the December 1825 banking crisis. Of their total assets of £3.5 million, some £2.3 million were in bills from
Richardson, Overend & Gurney. J. J. Gurney, in charge on Bank Plain, only
survived on the strength of his Quaker reputation and a judicious granting
of more local credit.[53]

Behind the scenes, Gurneys had been trying to retrench for several
months. The Gurneys, like Richardson, were related by marriage to the
Quaker Pease and Backhouse families of Darlington. The Backhouses, as
bankers, and the Peases, as woollen merchants, were the prime movers in
the pioneering Stockton to Darlington Railway Company which overcame
hostile opposition from its inception in 1818 to gain parliamentary approval
in 1821. They were unable to raise sufficient capital from local investors
so they turned for help to fellow Quakers, of whom the Norfolk Gurneys,
with Henry Birkbeck and Robert Barclay, became prominent shareholders
holding about a quarter of the £100,000 share capital. Gurney & Company
also lent £40,000 in 1824 to maintain liquidity until traffic revenues
began.[54] In August 1825 the vulnerability of the Norwich Bank during the
mounting financial crisis in London became obvious from J. J. Gurney's
uncharacteristically abrupt request for the Stockton & Darlington Railway
Company 'to repay the whole of their loan ... within six months'.[55] It was
only after Gurneys had survived that winter's bank failures that they
relaxed their demand, allowing the company to repay over two years from
1827, a reprieve that proved crucial for Stockton & Darlington Railway's
survival into profitability.[56]

Yet this kind of direct investment was dwarfed by Gurney & Company's
holdings of foreign and inland bills of exchange. Alarm bells ought to have

sounded when Samuel Gurney succeeded Hudson Gurney as a partner at
Norwich in 1831, because he increased the funds sent to Overend and Gurney just as the Lombard Street firm was moving from brokerage into bill
discounting.[57] This was a high-risk market calling for careful judgement,
but Samuel Gurney died in 1856 and his experienced partner David Barclay
Chapman resigned the next year, leaving the firm to a new generation of
Gurneys and Chapmans prepared to take far greater risks overseas. Their
lapse from traditional Quaker business standards was mirrored at Norwich
where Samuel Gurney's successors on Bank Plain became, unlike him,
merely sleeping partners who lost track of the labyrinthine dealings of
Overend & Gurney.

Ironically, when the East of England Bank collapsed in July 1864, ruin-
ing many local shareholders and depositors, Gurney & Company was
hailed as a beacon of stability.[58] Even Norwich Union dropped its traditional hostility and appointed Gurneys in place of the defunct East of
England as joint Life Society treasurers with Crown Bank. Just as this was
happening at Norwich, though, the London partners of Overend & Gurney were discovering that they held £4 million in bad debt. Failure was
inevitable if depositors found out, bringing down Gurney & Company at
Norwich along with their Lombard Street cousins. In a move that betrayed
their Quaker origins, the London partners shored up Overend & Gurney
in 1865 by floating it on the Stock Exchange as a limited liability company,
hoping to trade out of trouble with new capital. But it was too late. They
failed with over £5 million liabilities on 10 May 1866, triggering 'Black Friday' in the City the next day. The crisis ruined Daniel Gurney, J. H. Gurney
and Charles H. Gurney at the Norwich Bank, who were also partners in
Overend & Gurney, and their estates had to be sold to cover losses.[59] Yet
Barclays had realised a month earlier that Overend, Gurney & Company
would collapse, and decided to protect Norwich Bank as one of their 'most
valued county connections'.[60] In April 1866, Barclay's initiated a rescue by
introducing new partners from the 'extended cousinhood' of Quaker families to back Edward Birkbeck, an old partner not connected with Overend
& Gurney, by injecting an additional £635,000 into the Norwich Bank.[61]
They included Henry Ford Barclay, the great grandson of David Barclay,
who had made a fortune from manufacturing gutta percha during the
boom in submarine telegraphic cable production.[62] Another new arrival
was Samuel Gurney Buxton, a grandson of Samuel Gurney, with the added
twist that he bought J. H. Gurney's Catton Park estate.[63] Assembling in
haste at the guildhall on Black Friday, a 'Meeting of Citizens of Norwich'
fully endorsed this transformation by declaring 'publicly and unhesitat-
ingly its unbounded Confidence in the House of Gurneys and Birkbeck'.[64]

Although the crisis cast a shadow over the Gurneys' reputation for sound judgement, the speed and scale of this rescue sustained the family's hard won status as part of the 'Norfolk Squirearchy'.[65] This sense of continuity was sustained a year later when John Gurney, another grandson of Samuel Gurney and by then head of the Earlham branch of the family, joined the Norwich Bank, while in the longer term Edward Gurney Buxton, eldest son of Samuel Gurney Buxton, became the first of the next generation of Samuel Gurney's descendants to maintain the connection when he joined the bank in 1886.[66] Of course, the Crown Bank did its best to poach some Gurney accounts, but that situation was reversed in 1870 when Sir Robert Harvey committed suicide after bankrupting the Crown (which had liabilities of £1.6 million against assets of only £1m), through share speculations that he had financed by secretly creating false accounts. Gurneys bought the 'goodwill' of the Crown for £42,000 before London joint stock firms like the Provincial Banking Corporation could step in,[67] as they had done after the East of England's collapse.[68] By the 1890s, however, amalgamations were creating joint stock banks with far more resources than even the wealthy Quaker private partnerships.[69] Barclays responded in 1896 by joining with Gurneys and J. Backhouse & Company to become Barclay & Company Ltd. Samuel Gurney Buxton became its first vice-chairman and with deposits of over £26 million the new company immediately ranked among the six largest banks in England.[70]

Banking and insurance clerks were the elite of a burgeoning tertiary sector in the nineteenth-century economy. Yet until the 1880s even top London firms, such as the Royal Exchange Assurance, still only had relatively small clerical establishments of fewer than fifty. Although their starting salaries were modest, clerks in the large insurance and merchant banking firms were recruited from public and grammar schools and could expect to be earning £150 a year by their mid twenties, and to remain in secure employment until their 60s with a salary of perhaps £600 even without promotion, while for some a clerkship was a stepping stone to higher levels of management. Unlike the vast army of clerks in commercial offices, most of those in banking and insurance also received a pension, even though these were mostly paternalistic arrangements until the inter-war years.[71] At the 1881 census there were still only some 31,000 officials, clerks and agents in banking and insurance in England and Wales. But this total had risen to 85,000 by 1901, a far higher rate of increase than for the workforce as a whole, owing to London's dominance of world finance.[72] Changes in census classification make subsequent comparisons difficult, but expansion continued until 1914, while the most significant changes during the next twenty-five years were the introduction of new technology – typewriters, telephones and calculating machines – and the growing recruitment of women. Quite apart from replacing male clerks during the First World War, female clerical workers had for no logical reason become associated with the introduction of typewriting. They were invariably employed on less generous salaries and conditions than men. It also seems that some, but not all, leading banks took advantage of mechanisation during the 1930s recession to reduce costs by laying off clerical staff,[73] so there was not another significant overall expansion of employment in finance until after the Second World War.[74]

Clerical employment at Norwich Union during the nineteenth century mirrored that of the London insurance companies and merchant banks, except that salaries tended to be around 30 per cent less. Until the 1880s there were no more than about forty clerks at Surrey Street, with numbers rising sharply to over 150 by 1914, by which time the Norwich Union was by far the city's largest employer in this sector. The Life Office staff remained all male, although a few women worked for the Fire Society, where there were more routine tasks because of the need for annual policy renewals. Local grammar schools were a favoured source of new recruits and the arrival of so many young men since the 1880s meant that most were still of military age in 1914. Furthermore, contributions to the Fire Society's staff magazine suggest considerable interest in military activities and a readiness to volunteer at the outbreak of war. In all, ninety clerks from head office served during the conflict. A total of twenty-two Norwich Union staff, including some from the branches, were killed in action.[75] The Life Society's business did slacken because the board were reluctant to issue policies to men in the forces. New life business peaked at £5.4 million in 1914, fell to £3.5 million in 1916, but then recovered sharply after the war to a new record of £7.8 million in 1919. Fire and accident premiums, however, continued to rise because Norwich Union had so much overseas business, especially from the United States. This cushioned it from events in Europe and during the next four years fire premiums rose to £1.6 million while accident business increased to £705,000.[76] Overall, therefore, both societies came through the war in good financial shape, although the loss of some of their most able employees was only partly resolved by recruiting more female staff. Even after four years of war, Surrey Street's clerical establishment remained predominantly male and middle-class. It offered few opportunities for women, a situation that changed little during the inter-war years.[77]

The brief post-First World War boom brought a new wave of insurance company amalgamations,[78] and firms like Norwich Union Fire Office and

Phoenix became targets for take-over by larger 'composite' companies. This prompted the Norwich Union Fire and Phoenix to agree to a defensive 'fusion' in 1919. In fact, the larger Phoenix offered to buy the Fire Society's 44,000 £25 shares (£3 called) by issuing 440,000 new Phoenix (Norwich Union) £1 fully paid shares. At the respective market values of the two companies' shares, this was a 30 per cent bonus and Norwich Union shareholders readily agreed. Sir Gerald Ryan, Phoenix general manager, became president of the two companies, with Ralph Sketch, Norwich Union's accident manager, becoming general manager. Strategically the deal suited both firms. Since buying Norwich & London, accident insurance had been an area of strength at Norwich Union, especially in the USA, while Phoenix had very little. Furthermore, although Phoenix commanded more fire business than Norwich Union, there were gaps within the UK and in Australia, where the Fire Society was stronger.[79]

Despite this harmony of overall strategy, the fusion foundered on details. For a start, because Norwich Union agents now acted for both societies, Phoenix agreed that any life business taken by the Fire Society would go to the Life Society and not to its own 'Pelican' Life office. Sketch knew that any attempt to alter this would result in the best Norwich Union agents going to a rival. Furthermore, Ryan was an autocrat who preferred action to discussion with his fellow directors. He soon convinced Sketch of the need for this secretive approach. This proved fatal in 1922. Without fully consulting either board, Phoenix bought London & Guarantee Accident Company to acquire the three quarters of its £5 million premiums coming from American casualty insurance. Whereas Norwich Union's United States business was backed by strong dollar reserves, London & Guarantee's finances were weak. By June 1925 Phoenix needed to transfer £650,000, in dollars, to cover Legal & General's losses and meet United States legal minimum reserve requirements.[80] Sketch proposed economising by merging some Norwich Union Fire Office and Phoenix branches, weakening links between the Fire and Life Societies. He also planned to give Norwich all United Kingdom business while Phoenix staff would handle the overseas agencies. None of this went down well in Surrey Street.[81] Sketch regarded that as the 'special problem of the Norwich identity',[82] but he knew that Phoenix's own reserve position was precarious. The only hope was that the wealthy Life Society might be tempted into buying its 'sister' Fire Society. With a figure of around £7 million in mind, this would transform the Phoenix reserve position, but Ryan and Sketch wanted Norwich to take the initiative so that it would not become obvious that Phoenix badly needed funds.

The Life Society directors had realised by 1924 that here was a chance to

purchase the Norwich Union Fire Office at a good price. It was unprecedented for a mutual life insurance society to buy such a large joint stock
company. This particular deal would tie up at least 25 per cent of the Norwich Union's invested life funds in one commitment, and the directors
were understandably worried that critics would interpret such a step as
irresponsible. It would certainly be highly unusual for the directors of a
huge life fund to switch such a large proportion of its assets at one meeting, particularly when the new investment was in the fire and accident
business, which was prone to runs of heavy losses. On balance, though, the
normally cautious Life directors at Norwich decided that it was a risk
worth taking in terms of future marketing potential. They knew that they
could only go ahead if the purchase could be completed without having to
seek the agreement of the society's policyholders at a special general meeting. Such an event, with its cumbersome preliminaries of issuing press
notices in advance to all policyholders, would undoubtedly attract publicity and scare off Ryan and his fellow Phoenix directors in London. The Life
directors got round this obstacle because they could use their existing powers to switch funds, which normally involved run-of-the-mill decisions, to
exchange over £6 million, some 60 per cent,[83] of the Life Society's holding
of gilt-edged stock for the 44,000 Fire Office shares without having to call
a general meeting. Acutely aware that critics and supporters alike would
regard this as an extraordinary investment decision, the Life board resisted
emotive considerations about bringing the Fire Society 'home' to Norwich
and concentrated on negotiating a lower price. By June 1925, despite Ryan's
secrecy, Sir George Chamberlin, Life Society vice-president and on all three
boards, realised that Phoenix could go no further when Ryan proposed
'£6.5 million, to be paid in gilts' and by July the deal was complete.[84] With
its usual caution, the Life Society discounted the premium paid for the
44,000 Norwich Union Fire Shares, writing them into its balance sheet at
£6,088,174.[85]

Phoenix got its stronger reserves. Ryan and Sketch, however, lived to
regret a loss of business which they never recouped during the inter war
years. Meanwhile, Surrey Street had no desire to appear reckless. Local
responses were predictably upbeat, with the *Eastern Daily Press* welcoming
the purchase. More significantly, hostile *Daily Telegraph* and *John Bull* edi-
torials were nullified by the *Financial Times*, which had already
pronounced that 'Norwich Life will be in a better position to get the
utmost value out of the Norwich Union Fire than the Phoenix could ever
hope to secure'.[86] The deal was also welcomed in Surrey Street. Most senior staff had the option to join Sketch, who understandably stayed with
Phoenix. Virtually all of them chose to stay at Norwich, a blow to Sketch,

who had relied heavily on their expertise. The most lasting benefit came, however, after the Second World War when Norwich Union Group found its diversity invaluable in a changed competitive environment.

Through the intervening changes of ownership and control, the Fire Society's fire insurance premiums rose to a peak of £2.3 million in 1927 before world recession took them to a low point of £1.6 million in 1935. Their recovery to £1.8 million by 1938 was painfully slow. This fluctuation was largely due to external factors because, in 1928, the Norwich Union still had the tenth largest fire premium income among all British companies and it had only slipped to eleventh place a decade later.[87] Furthermore, the Fire Society's overall expansion continued because personal accident, employer's liability and above all 'general' insurance dominated by motoring risks made an increasing contribution.[88] Following the purchase of the Norwich & London Accident in 1908, the society's accident premium had doubled to £840,000 by 1919. It then grew faster to an inter-war peak of £1.9 million in 1929 before world recession brought a reduction to £1.4 million by 1935.[89] On the other side of Surrey Street, new sums insured by the Life Society rose to £9 million during the 1920s, slipping to £8 million by 1933, before increasing to £12 million by 1938. One effect of the depression was that policy surrenders increased during the early 1930s. Surrey Street only once paid out more than £250,000 a year on surrenders in the 1920s, but they peaked at £425,000 in 1931 and stayed above £250,00 until 1936. Overall, though, the Life Society's funds rose from £17 million in 1919 to nearly £50 million by 1938, reflecting the sustained prosperity of Britain's middle classes during the inter-war years.[90]

Victorian advocates of working-class financial 'self-help' included government and local elites as well as trade unionists and others intent on self-improvement. Nevertheless, there was seldom unanimity about the scale of this kind of 'self-help', and government intervention invariably ran up against vested interests. When, for example, the Post Office Savings Bank (POSB), founded by Gladstone in 1861, proposed raising its maximum for depositors from £200 to £300 eight years later, the government faced the anger of the 'larger banking community' who saw it as a threat to their own interests and, incidentally, established an upper 'working class' savings threshold because the government backed down and the Postmaster General kept the £200 limit.[91] Of course, most POSB savers had far less, as revealed by a 1910 report showing that although one fifth of the population held accounts these only averaged £20. Even then, the POSB's national significance is evident from its total deposits of £170 million.[92]

Within that context of modest individual savings, but substantial total investments, the most prominent working-class financial institutions at Norwich before 1939 were the POSB and Norfolk & Norwich Savings Bank (N & NSB) which was founded in 1816 by John Hammond Cole.[93] Cole, a worsted weaver's son who became a clerk with Kerrison's Bank, started one of England's earliest working-class savings schemes in 1812. That success led him to raise support from local business leaders and clergy for N & NSB as a secure place where 'tradesmen, mechanics, labourers, and servants' could 'save from their earnings'.[94] Savers had no say in the management of the bank and it did not lend money to the public, because deposits could only be invested in government stock.[95] The next year N & NSB conformed to new rules for savings banks set by Rose's Act of 1817, the significant difference being that all savings now had to go to the National Debt Commissioners, who guaranteed the sum deposited and interest rate so that savers were protected from fluctuations in stock market prices. The rate guaranteed to Trustee Savings Banks (TSBs) was progressively reduced from just over 4.5 per cent in 1817 to around 3 per cent by the 1860s, but this then became a source of resentment for the newly created POSB, which could only pay 2.5 per cent. POSB officials also criticised the TSB for being a movement controlled by local elites of the 'principal employers of labour or the parochial authorities'.[96] Working-class savers therefore found themselves at the centre of a barely concealed ideological struggle between the centralising civil servants running the POSB and the diverse paternalistic bodies that controlled local TSBs through trusteeships. It was a quarrel that ironically increased choice for working-class savers and this influenced developments in Norwich as in other large cities.

Trustees and managers ran each TSB without drawing fees, although larger banks such as N & NSB had a salaried secretary and clerks. Depositors could save up to £100 in the first year and £50 annually.[97] A series of frauds led to the more stringent Trustee Savings Bank Act of 1863,[98] introducing inspections by the National Debt commissioners. Each bank also had to display a list of deposits, identified by number only, for savers to check against their passbooks, a procedure the N & NSB had employed since 1850.[99]

By 1895, however, N & NSB still only had 12,900 depositors saving £429,000, little more than mid nineteenth-century levels. This was partly due to competition, coming since 1861 from the POSB as well as agents for friendly societies, building societies and 'industrial' life offices like the Prudential.[100] By 1906 there were ninety-four friendly societies or society branches at Norwich, with nearly 21,000 members.[101] Another problem was the periodically high levels of unemployment in the city's industries and resulting low wages.[102] Furthermore, Norwich banking crises from 1825 to 1870 had on every occasion led to withdrawals from N & NSB: £60,000 after the Overend & Gurney collapse alone, and £27,000 in the aftermath of the Crown failure, as the hapless Sir Robert Harvey was also N & NSB treasurer. There had been some recovery in the late 1860s due to the 'exceedingly prosperous state of the factories employing as many as six thousand hands' in the shoe industry.[103] But most of those who withdrew money put it into what they regarded as the safer hands of the POSB and left it there. TSB interest rates were cut to 2.5 per cent in 1888, putting them on a par with the POSB. But that soon became a competitive rate in the early 1890s, and the net inflow of POSB funds nationally rose from £2.3 million in 1891 to £7.7 million for 1896, as the lower middle class also turned to this form of saving rather than to commercial banks.[104] The problem was that most TSBs missed this opportunity because their reputation was damaged by further scandals, among a tiny minority. This had led to the 1891 Savings Bank Act imposing stricter inspections of their accounts.[105]

N & NSB's difficulties could therefore be partly blamed on factors beyond its control. In 1897, however, the trustees decided that there was a need to appoint a professionally qualified manager as secretary. They were fortunate in their choice of James Fairburn, a chartered accountant who had previously worked in London for the central office of the Trustee Savings Bank Inspection Committee.[106] In reviewing past results, he was critical of N & NSB's paternalistic organisation. Cole had been succeeded by his son in 1828 who, being a clergyman, became honorary secretary. Then, from 1839, a succession of officials had managed N & NSB: William Herring, manufacturer and Norwich Union Fire Society director; Captain Thomas Blakiston RN, Fire and Life Society director, and a nationally renowned archaeologist; the barrister W. C. Hotson, also an expert auditor of poor law accounts and Fire Society director; and finally Major Henry Cubitt, director of the General Hailstorm Company, auditor for the Norwich Waterworks Company and 'a zealous supporter of the Church of England Temperance Society'.[107] Fairburn was not impressed. In his view, they 'appeared unable to give sufficient time and attention to the affairs and development of the savings bank'.[108]

His arrival coincided with N & NSB's move from the Haymarket, to make way for the electric tramway, to a purpose-built head office in Red Lion Street which, like the Norwich Union's head office, Surrey House, was designed by G. J. & F. W. Skipper. The architecture of its ornate 'Renaissance' exterior and impressive banking hall expressed confidence in the future.[109] But Fairburn was more interested in how the bank was run. He introduced modern methods of book-keeping, extended opening hours, reduced customer waiting times, distributed 'suitable pamphlets and leaflets in the working-class districts at the Factories, Workshops, and

Penny Banks',[110] and increased the range of savings plans. He put all of his energy into serving the bank's customers, a quite different strategy from patronisingly assisting the working classes to save. He emphasised the convenience of the bank's new location, 'immediate to Orford Place, the hub of the Norwich Electric Tramways System, … easily accessible to those resident in the city and its suburbs'.[111] He also actively promoted the idea of the penny banks being 'fostered' in local schools and using N & NSB as their treasurer. Within five years, seventy-one were opened to provide savings accounts for 'upwards of eleven thousand youthful depositors',[112] boosting a subsidised method of saving that had existed in Norwich since the mid-nineteenth century.

When Rollit's 1904 Act allowed the larger savings banks to open special investment departments,[113] N & NSB became one of the first to invest in local government stock offering higher returns for savers. By 1914 deposits had doubled to over £860,000 compared with 1895 and the number of accounts had exceeded 27,000. Rollit's Act also made amalgamations easier, allowing N & NSB to absorb the Great Yarmouth and North Walsham savings banks in 1917.[114] Fairburn died, only forty-five years old, in March 1909. But at the N & NSB's centenary the chairman, John Henry Fraser Walter – also a Norwich Union director – paid tribute to his 'marked energy and ability', which had ensured that 'the business of the bank increased more rapidly than in any previous period in its history'.[115] It was also the first time that N & NSB had grown faster than the overall level of British trustee savings bank deposits, which rose from £51 million in 1895 to £72 million by 1914.[116] Growth continued into the inter-war years. By 1927 N & NSB's 40,000 depositors accounted for almost £2.5 million, some 1.6 per cent of the national total of £150 million, after which Norwich more than held its own through the depression, with 50,000 accounts by 1935 and savings of £3.5 million, a rise to 3.5 per cent of the £233 million deposited nationally.[117] Walter was still chairman in 1927 when, to cope with this rapid growth, he opened N & NSB's new head office in Surrey Street (Plate 54). Ten years later the first branch was established outside Norfolk, at Ipswich, and the bank became the East Anglian Trustee Savings Bank. By then, the earlier rivalry with the Post Office Savings Bank had faded and the two organisations worked with the local National Savings Committee as part of the National Savings Movement.[118]

Did the eighteenth-century emergence of a financial sector reduce investment in the city's worsted industry? Norwich radicals were the most vociferous critics of the worsted manufacturers, and they blamed the costs of bribery at local elections for the failure to invest in new technology.[119]

It has been argued, however, that political bribery was a symptom rather than a cause of the city's industrial decline and this applies with even more force to financial activity.[120] Gurney's Bank channelled far more funds out of the region than was spent at Norwich elections because they could make higher profits investing through London, or lending directly to ventures backed by trusted fellow Quakers, like the Backhouses at Darlington, than giving credit locally where there was insufficient demand.[121] Local industry never relied on the Norwich financial sector for long-term capital. Quite apart from the lack of interest of the city's bankers, Norwich Union's Fire and Life funds were kept well away from East Anglian commerce and industry.[122] Of course, the banks did facilitate note circulation and attracted the deposits of small traders, manufacturers and farmers who could also rely on short-term credit. But the bank failures, especially East of England's collapse in 1864, ruined many of these middle-income savers. Such people only gained a local bank with impeccable security after 1866, when the chastened Gurneys took great care to cultivate their position as the last Norwich partnership capable of withstanding competition from the London joint stock banks. For their part, prosperous local industries like brewing showed little desire for long-term bank credit. The largest brewers, the family firm of Steward & Patteson, financed investment by ploughing back profits until 1895, when it decided to raise capital by floating as a joint stock company. Family control was retained by holding £300,000 of the £450,000 share capital. The fact that the remaining £150,000 was oversubscribed sevenfold and predominantly by local investors suggests that, as in the early nineteenth century, such people were were keener to employ their savings in Norwich than the city's industries were to tap this source of finance.[123]

Furthermore, the record of bank failures from Kerrison to Harvey hardly points to a drain of entrepreneurial talent from worsted production into banking, and none of the wealthy backers of Norwich General, or, from 1821, Norwich Union showed much creativity. Gurneys were better equipped than other Norwich banks to employ surplus regional funds. Even then, leading Norwich members of the family, including Hudson Gurney, R. H. Gurney and J. J. Gurney, evidently preferred religious devotion or the higher financial and social rewards of gentlemanly capitalism not only to the daily grind of 'the "vile and mechanical" world of manufacturing' but also to the more genteel demands of banking.[124] Although their integrity was never in doubt, their inattention to business cost them dearly in 1866.

Indeed, except for C. R. Gilmans's striking success with the Norwich & London Accident Association from 1856, the most significant advances in the financial sector relied on fresh talent. Thomas Bignold was unique. Without his remarkable achievements in an unregulated market, insurance at Norwich would have gone the same way as its banks. In total contrast, the late nineteenth-century accountant James Fairburn introduced management that was single-minded and highly professional. In modernising past practice, he undoubtedly improved banking facilities for a growing number of working-class savers. Deuchar was an exceptional manager who avoided extra-mural commitments. He reluctantly served as a Conservative councillor and was a freemason, while his Presbyterianism and membership of the Norwich Scots Society suggest a lingering loyalty to his home city of Edinburgh. When illness forced him to resign, he was the first Norwich Union official to become a Life Society director. His death, aged sixty, in 1911 marked the end of the most remarkable phase in the Norwich Union's history since the early days under Thomas Bignold.[125] But whereas the founder left turmoil, Deuchar laid the foundations for the emergence of a modern insurance group in the inter-war years.

Although the creation of Barclays & Company Ltd left Norwich without a commercial bank of its own after 1896, the continued growth of N & NSB and Norwich Union ensured that the city remained one of the leading financial centres in Britain. Furthermore, during the inter-war years Barclays' local board at Norwich was still ruled by descendents of those Gurney family members who had taken part in the post-'Black Friday' rescue in 1866. The Gurneys were still part of the Norfolk 'squirearchy' during the 1950s.[126] Nevertheless, Barclays had from the start insisted upon having local directors who were 'practising bankers', not 'part-timers representing the local business community'. In return, Barclays gave them far 'more local discretion than in other joint-stock banks', regarding their expertise as the company's 'most valuable asset'.[127] Under the Gurneys during the inter-war years, the Norwich branch provided invaluable credit to the hard-pushed farming community at a time when the risks of this type of lending were increasing. By 1935 Barclays had some 200,000 British farmers borrowing a total of £12 million, nearly 8 per cent of the company's advances, and the former Gurneys' branches in East Anglia were the most notable connection for this business.[128] Barclays' trust in their Norwich board's judgement paid off handsomely after the Second World War, when the renewed prosperity of Norfolk agriculture gave a valuable boost to the service sector in Norwich.[129]

Following the failure of the Crown Bank in 1870, Gurneys had also become the Norwich Union's sole treasurers and this link was retained during the 1896 amalgamation. Barclays' local directors at Norwich also continued the practice of serving on the Fire and Life boards, starting with Samuel Gurney Buxton's Fire Society directorship from 1873 until 1909, after which his son, Edward Gurney Buxton, took over until retiring in 1926. Meanwhile, Quintin Edward Gurney joined the Fire board in 1921; then in 1934 he was elected to the Life board. Frank Jewson, a member of the Life Society, emphasised the importance of this long-standing connection when he proposed Q. E. Gurney for election as a director:

> The name of Gurney was, of course, known in all business circles; he [Q. E. Gurney] was a Director of Barclays Bank, and that alone would be sufficient recommendation as a qualification for this Society. He was sure they would all agree with him [the speaker] that Mr Gurney's ripe experience in business matters and his special knowledge of finance would be of great assistance to the Board at the present time.[130]

With the Life Society's annual income from premiums and interest rising from £2.8 millions to £6.8 millions during the inter-war years, while the Fire Society's income reached £3.7 millions by 1938, Barclays had every reason to value its local board at Norwich.[131] Quite apart from the 150 Fire Office staff, and the 130 who worked for the Life Society,[132] Norwich Union was creating jobs for many other clerical employees in the city's financial sector, as well as in related professions such as accountancy, the law and surveying.

During the inter-war years, Norwich Union's provincial character became more distinctive as take-overs absorbed most other 'country' fire and life offices. From the late nineteenth century, Norwich Union directors were chosen for their expertise, rather than for their political influence which had been so important in the days of Thomas and Samuel Bignold.[133] For most of them, a Norwich Union directorship was their major commitment beyond their professional or business career. They also worked side-by-side in discharging such public duties as N & NSB trusteeships, school governorships, and the committees running bodies such as the Church of England Young Mens' Association, or the Jenny Lind Childrens' Hospital. Sir George Chamberlin's career, leading him to a knighthood, is a notable example. Son of Robert Chamberlin, a successful wholesale and retail draper, he retained responsibility for the family firm after his father's death in 1876. He served as mayor, in 1891–92, 1916–17 and 1918–19, as well as being a director of the Norwich Electric Tramways Company, president of the Chamber of Commerce, and manager of the N & NSB from 1892, becoming a trustee in 1897. But his main contribution to the city arose from his Norwich Union directorships, in the Life Society from 1892 and the Fire from 1896, until his death in 1929.[134] Chamberlin played the leading part in the Life Society's purchase of the Fire Office in

1925, which was undoubtedly one of the most important business decisions taken in Norwich during the inter-war years. As this example suggests, the financial sector had its share of leaders honoured for their political and civic activities. At least six of the ten mayors of Norwich between 1836 and 1939 who gained a knighthood – Samuel Bignold, Charles Rackham Gilman, Peter Eade, George Chamberlin, George Henry Morse and Robert Bignold – were prominent in the insurance business and had also served as N & NSB managers or trustees before they were honoured.[135]

Their peers in London might dismiss this as narrow provincialism, but there was no denying its effectiveness in sustaining one of the largest insurance businesses in Britain, with all that implied for local employment and prestige. Indeed, no other leading British insurance company used a locational symbol in the way that Norwich Union adopted the spire of the city's cathedral as its 'housemark' from 1877. By the 1930s it had become a familiar advertising device across the world, an instantly recognisable logo bonding Norwich Union, the city and its cathedral in a powerfully symbolic portrayal of tradition, strength and trustworthiness.

16

Work and Employment

Christine Clark

In a very large slice of England, to thousands and thousands of good sensible folk who live and work there, Norwich is the big city, the centre ... [It] is no mere jumped-up conglomeration of factories, warehouses and dormitories ... It is not a place in which to make money quickly and then to plan a sudden exit. It is not filled with people who are there because they have never been offered a job elsewhere. No, Norwich is really a capital, the capital of East Anglia.

J. B. Priestley, *English Journey*, 1934[1]

Norwich, as the regional capital of East Anglia, occupied a place of considerable importance in England's pre-industrial economy. Until 1750 it was surpassed, in terms of population, only by London and Bristol. Set at the heart of an agriculturally rich hinterland, it enjoyed good land and river communications and access, via the port of Great Yarmouth, to international markets. It acted as a distribution centre for a significant trade in agricultural products and was renowned for its wholesale markets in cattle, sheep and grain. The city's commercial role was matched by its strength in manufacturing. Many local industries had their roots in agriculture: brewing, vinegar distilling, malting and milling, while cattle fattened on the nearby marshes formed the basis of a substantial leather industry supporting a wide range of craftsmen including tanners, curriers, fellmongers, saddlers and shoemakers. Above all, the city was famous for its textile manufactures.[2] As we have already seen, from the fourteenth to the late eighteenth century Norwich enjoyed an almost unrivalled pre-eminence in the manufacture of high quality worsted fabrics. As late as 1800 the trade was estimated to have employed, directly or indirectly, about 100,000 people, and to have produced goods to an annual value in excess of £1 million.[3]

During the last decades of the eighteenth century, however, the pace of urbanisation and industrialisation in the midlands and north began to outdistance that of East Anglia's premier textile region. The focus of economic growth shifted to new and burgeoning centres such as Birmingham,

Manchester and Liverpool.[4] Mostly devoid of mineral resources and water power, East Anglia found itself increasingly isolated from technical change and innovation. The industrial revolution largely by-passed the region. In the process it was firmly nudged further towards specialisation in agriculture and the service industries. The economic status of Norwich declined: by 1801 it ranked as only the ninth largest city in England; by 1851 it was the fourteenth. Most harmful to its well-being was the slow decline of the worsted industry as the city was displaced by its main rival, the West Riding of Yorkshire. Thereafter, adjustment was painful and prolonged. The city clearly provides an early and prime example of industrial deceleration. After the middle years of the nineteenth century, Norwich demonstrated its capacity to diversify and, if it was never to regain its manufacturing pre-eminence, to recover at least some measure of prosperity.

The decline of the city's leading sector brought widespread unemployment and poverty for thousands of local spinners and hand-loom weavers. Certainly, by the early decades of the nineteenth century, most contemporaries stressed the depressed state of Norwich. One reckoned that in 1833 'the city was never in a worse state'.[5] Apart from the post-war boom – evident in the Norwich textile trade once foreign markets were restored – the two decades from the mid 1820s were dull years everywhere. This was particularly the case in the countryside, where the end of the Napoleonic wars had brought a slump in grain prices. This, coinciding with the loss of hand spinning, caused much distress in rural areas. Most commentators showed great concern about the constant downward pressure on weavers' wage rates and the social unrest which resulted. In 1830, for example, between three and four thousand weavers rioted and attacked the mills and manufacturers. By the great strike of 1838 wage rates varied between a net weekly income of 4s. for a plain weaver and 13s. 6d. for a skilled one: this was less than had been paid half a century before and was poor in comparison with workers in other industries.[6] An inquiry into the condition of handloom weavers the following year found that, of a total of 5075 looms in the city, 1021 were unemployed. Moreover, the 700 power looms at work in its mills produced more in aggregate than all the looms in the weavers' houses.[7] The mills now formed the heart of a leaner, more diverse (and prosperous) industry, and those employed there enjoyed better conditions. The trade which survived was still substantial, directly employing around 5000 in 1850.[8] It was, however, a shadow of the industry which had dominated Norwich half a century earlier.[9]

The region's isolation from the main focus of technical change and innovation was further reinforced during this period by growing weaknesses in its transport network.[10] Until the beginning of the nineteenth century, the natural system of roads and waterways had favoured Norwich over its main competitors. The fine, long-stapled wool required for the manufacture of worsteds was imported from Lincolnshire and Leicestershire through the network of inland waterways to Boston or King's Lynn and thence overland or by coaster to Yarmouth and, via the River Yare, to Norwich. Finished goods were dispatched overland to London, for the East India Company, or to Yarmouth for direct export to Europe. A range of the region's agricultural products, including wheat, flour, barley and malt, was similarly exported from Norfolk's ports to London and the north, the vessels returning with cargoes of coal and iron. The early decades of the nineteenth century, however, saw significant developments in the national transport system that critically shifted the comparative advantage away from Norwich. Norfolk roads none the less appeared to keep abreast of progress, being considered among the best in the kingdom by 1800. R. N. Bacon, writing in 1844, noted a great improvement, not only in those of the turnpike trusts but also in the lesser by-ways.[11]

The real blow to East Anglia's economic fortunes came with the construction of canals across the midlands and north, linking the main industrial regions with the ports of Liverpool, Hull, Bristol and London. Reduced freight costs impacted on the price of raw materials and finished products and gave the West Riding, in particular, a huge stimulus. The main response from Norwich was to make the city an inland port, linking it to Lowestoft by cutting across the marshes to the River Waveney. Besides avoiding the shallows of Breydon Water, which would thereby permit the passage of larger vessels, and shortening the route, the canal was intended to resolve several problems: theft *en route* (alone expected to reduce freight costs by one shilling a ton), high harbour dues and delays in transhipment. Despite bitter opposition from the corporation of Yarmouth, the Norwich and Lowestoft Navigation was begun in 1827 and completed six years later. Opened to great public acclaim, it nevertheless proved an expensive failure. The new canal suffered silting from sand and mud and the company was declared bankrupt in 1844, its assets being sold for £50,000.

To an even greater extent, the coming of the railways highlighted the difficulties faced by Norwich in maintaining its industrial status. Between 1830 and 1847, the north of England saw the construction of a railway network which linked the entire region with the major ports. Further benefits came from the fierce competition between the railway and canal companies which forced sharp reductions in freight rates. These developments, coupled with the revolution in technology, gave the north a huge advantage over the textile manufacturers of Norwich. Nevertheless, there was not

the same enthusiasm for railways in East Anglia as in the north, a reflection not only of the region's isolation and low level of urbanisation, but
also an innate conservatism. The promised ease of construction across
receptive terrain failed to encourage early innovation. Proposals in 1825 for
a horse-drawn tramway to London via Ipswich failed to secure an act of
Parliament. Subsequently the Eastern Counties Railway took seven years to
reach Colchester from London and then, in 1843, faltered. By the 1840s the
need for rail communications was seen as imperative by many industrial-
ists. Yet the response to local proposals remained lukewarm. One
commentator described the attitude of Norfolk people as one of 'apathy
and inertness to their own salvation'.[12] At the promotion of the North
Suffolk Railway in 1845 there were applications for shares from London, the
North, Dublin and Glasgow, but none from Norwich and Norfolk.[13] Initially, proposals in 1841 for a Yarmouth and Norwich Railway, in spite of
the dismal record of the Norwich and Lowestoft Navigation, also received
a poor reception. Not until 1844 was the twenty-one mile track across flat
terrain completed. The opening of the East Anglian Railway the next year
provided the first through train to London (via Brandon and Ely). Local
branch lines followed and, in 1849, the second route to London (via
Ipswich) was established. The railway network came relatively late to
Norwich.[14]

Throughout this period, some sectors of the Norwich economy enjoyed
more stable and prosperous conditions. The city, with its flourishing markets, acted as a distribution centre for an extensive rural hinterland. In 1821
William Cobbett painted a glowing picture of the 'beautiful' provisions
market, noting its cleanliness and order, and its vendors 'equal in neatness
to (for nothing can surpass) the market women in Philadelphia'.[15]
A. D. Bayne estimated that during the 1840s the value of groceries entering
the city alone came to £500,000 a year. The returns from the grain trade
averaged a similar amount, while a decade later the annual value of the
malt trade was said to exceed that of all the manufactured goods in Norwich.[16] The livestock market on Castle Hill, described by Bacon as 'the
greatest weekly fair of England', also went from strength to strength.[17] By
the 1860s (when the city had invested £50,000 on improvements to the
market) a further 120 acres, much of it around Trowse station, were needed
as lairage for cattle and sheep during the peak season from August to
November (Plate 55).[18]

Another important, old-established sector in the city, again with its roots
in agriculture, was brewing. By national standards, the industry was already
highly concentrated, with over three-quarters of Norwich's 558 public
houses in the hands of seven firms by the 1840s. Further consolidation

within the sector over the next two decades saw the emergence of four major companies which were to dominate brewing in Norwich for another century: Steward, Patteson, Finch & Company; Youngs, Crawshay & Youngs; Bullards; and Morgans.[19] With the continuing expansion of the Norwich Union Fire and Life Insurance Societies, the latter ranking as one of the country's leading life insurance firms by the early 1820s, Norwich also established a growing reputation as a leading provincial financial centre.[20] Finance, like brewing, encouraged the accumulation of wealth and capital in the city. These sectors did little, however, to resolve the problem of structural unemployment caused by the decline in textiles. ·

From 1841 the census returns provide the first detailed picture of the way in which the city earned its living and illustrate changing occupational trends (see Tables 16.1 and 16.2). The figures are not without their short-comings, especially with regard to women's employment, where undoubt-edly much part-time work was not recorded. This is particularly true in the case of the 1841 return: the great increase in the size of the female workforce (from 7907 to 14,797) relative to population between 1841 and 1851 suggests that the census for the latter year provides a more accurate picture.[21]

The stagnation in textiles (which employed 20.75 per cent of the total workforce in 1841) is immediately evident. So, too, is the large number of women engaged in domestic service, almost one-third of the female work-force by 1861. In fact, women clustered in a relatively narrow range of occupations. Besides domestic service, textiles and shoemaking, only cloth-ing, which included seamstresses, milliners, dressmakers and corsetmakers, besides those working for larger concerns such as Rivett & Harmer (who manufactured wholesale clothes), was of any real significance. Building and general labouring provided considerable male employment, as did transport after 1851, a reflection of the developments outlined above.

By far the most important sector in its ability to absorb surplus labour from textiles was boot and shoemaking. During the early decades of the nineteenth century, the industry was no more important in Norwich than in many other towns and cities. Being practitioners of a universal trade, small-scale craftsmen sewed bespoke orders. As early as 1792, however, one Norwich leather seller, James Smith, began to make ready-made shoes in various sizes for the wholesale market. Others followed, and slowly the trade assumed a greater significance. It did much to compensate for the decline in weaving: the same manual dexterity was necessary, and in many ways the structure replicated textile production. Much of the trade remained in the hands of small employers known as 'garret masters'. These men organised the 'clicking and pressing' (cutting out the uppers and soles) on their premises before giving out the materials to different sets of workers.

Table 16.1 Numbers employed and percentage of male workforce, 1851–1901

Sector	1851		1861		1881		1901	
	Nos employed	% of work-force	Nos employed	% of work-force	Nos employed	% of work-force	Nos employed	% of work-force
Shoemaking	2,753	13.01	3,167	14.26	3,286	13.11	4,931	15.38
Textiles	2,759	13.04	1,986	8.94	838	3.34	209	0.65
Clothing	869	4.11	788	3.55	665	2.65	1,025	3.20
Metals/engineering[1]	891	4.21	1,246	5.61	1,576	6.29	2,215	6.91
Food and drink[2]	2,136	10.09	2,449	11.03	2,477	9.89	3,531	11.02
Building	1,775	8.39	2,158	9.72	2,751	10.98	3,569	11.13
Transport	1,455	6.88	1,312	5.91	2,207	8.81	3,503	10.93
Commerce[3]	845	3.99	767	3.45	1,041	4.15	1,112	3.47
Professions	958	4.53	881	3.97	912	3.64	1,142	3.56
Domestic service[4]	389	1.84	347	1.56	736	2.94	623	1.94
Agriculture[5]	1,083	5.12	1,548	6.97	780	3.11	895	2.79
General labourers	1,117	5.28	1,008	4.54	2,795	11.15	2,409	7.52
Other[6]	4,133	19.53	4,546	20.47	4,997	19.94	6,890	21.49
Male workforce[7]	21,163	100.02	22,203	99.98	25,061	100.00	32,054	99.99

Source: Census returns, 1851–1901 (see note 21).

Notes: [1] Includes ironfounders, black and white-smiths, tool, engine and machine makers, wire weavers and tinplate workers.

[2] Includes maltsters, brewers, mustard and vinegar workers, butchers, grocers etc., publicans and boarding house keepers etc.

[3] Includes merchants, salesmen, travellers, clerks, auctioneers, accountants, insurance agents and shopkeepers.

[4] Includes domestic servants, coachmen, grooms etc., cooks, charwomen, laundry workers.

[5] Includes farmers, agricultural labourers, nurserymen and seedsmen.

[6] Includes several small categories each not accounting for more than 3 per cent of the workforce.

[7] The 1901 workforce is defined as those over ten years; previously it is unspecified.

Table 16.2 Numbers employed and percentage of female workforce, 1851–1901

Sector	1851		1861		1881		1901	
	Nos employed	% of work-force	Nos employed	% of work-force	Nos employed	% of work-force	Nos employed	% of work-force
Shoemaking	2,285	15.44	2,933[1]	17.04	1,772	11.15	2,539	13.72
Textiles	2,878	19.45	2,993	17.39	2,188	13.77	1,122	6.06
Clothing[2]	3,671	24.81	3,197	18.58	3,158	19.87	3,889	21.01
Food and drink	690	4.67	869[3]	5.05	541	3.40	1,286	6.95
Commerce	301	2.03	185	1.08	18	0.11	166	0.90
Professions	598	4.04	548	3.18	876	5.51	1,267	6.84
Domestic service[4]	3,736	25.25	5,458	31.72	5,773	36.33	5,456	29.47
General labourers	43	0.29	216	1.26	385	2.42	370	2.00
Other	595	4.02	809	4.70	1,181	7.43	2,416	13.05
Female Workforce	14,797	100.00	17,208	100.00	15,892	99.99	18,511	100.00

Source: Census returns, 1851–1901 (see note 21).

Notes: [1] Includes 833 'shoemaker's wives'.

[2] Includes milliners, seamstresses, dressmakers and corsetmakers.

[3] Includes 99 'innkeeper's wives'.

[4] Includes domestic servants, housemaids, nurses (non-medical), charwomen, laundry and workers.

The uppers were 'closed' (stitched) by women, returned to be 'lasted' (joined) to the soles by men, then passed to another group to be 'finished'. Many entire families were employed in the different stages of production, working in their homes exactly as the weavers had for centuries before them. Nevertheless, the scale of the industry should not be overstated during these years. In 1831 it employed no more than a total of 829 people.[22] The real growth came in the decade after 1841, when the numbers employed increased from 1740 to 5038 (14.0 per cent of the workforce). The trigger had been improvements in technology and the gradual mechanisation of production. Charles Winter, the grandson of James Smith, installed sewing machines for upper closing in the 1850s; those for sewing soles followed by the end of the decade. As a result, the women and girls were moved into factories. But unlike other shoemaking centres such as Northampton, where strikes lasted for two years, and in sharp contrast to the protests against the mechanisation of textile manufacture, there was little opposition to these major technical innovations.[23] Indeed, rather than reducing the numbers employed, the greater productivity enabled prices to be cut and, together with better standardisation and durability, increased demand and therefore employment. By 1861 the industry, by now the city's leading sector, employed in excess of 6000 workers.

Of the remaining sectors, engineering and metalworking were small but growing, surprisingly so, given the remoteness from their raw materials, coal and iron. In 1841 the various branches – ironfounding, blacksmiths and whitesmiths, ironmongers and agricultural implement makers – employed a total of 558 men (3.6 per cent of the male workforce). By 1851 this had increased to 891 (4.2 per cent) and ten years later to 1246 (5.6 per cent). As at Ipswich, where the industry grew even more rapidly, there were strong links with agriculture, both through the demand for agricultural implements and conspicuous consumption on the part of successful landowners. By the 1840s several firms were designing and exhibiting agricultural machines. At the 1849 Royal Agricultural Society's annual meeting in Norwich, Holmes & Sons (founded in 1827) showed 112 exhibits; subsequently the firm won medals for its threshing machines at the 1851 Crystal Palace Exhibition and at the London Exhibition of 1862.[24] Barnard & Boulton (the forerunners of Boulton & Paul) and Charles Barnard (Barnards Ltd), were also making a wide range of agricultural implements. The former was founded as early as 1793 by William Moore (d. 1839) of Warham, near Wells-next-the Sea, who had opened an ironmonger's shop in Cockey Lane. He had quickly specialised in the manufacture of stove grates. By the 1850s the firm, then run by John Hilling Barnard and William Boulton, offered an extensive range of products including hurdles, fencing, pallisading and park gates, besides greenhouses and hot-water systems.[25] Charles Barnard had similarly set up as an ironmonger in 1826. A farmer's son, Barnard was also aware of the huge demand for fencing to keep out rabbits and foxes. Experimenting initially with cotton reels and then pegged rollers supported on trestles, by 1844 he had developed a primitive loom for the weaving of wire netting. The rapidly expanding business – by 1861 Barnard & Bishop employed 163 hands – was equally well known for its decorative park gates. The famous Norwich Gates, winners of a gold medal at the 1862 London Exhibition, were subsequently bought by public subscription as a wedding present for the Prince of Wales and placed at the entrance to Sandringham House, a fine example of the company's work (Plate 56).[26] This sector, if never quite the equal of its Ipswich counterpart, had by the 1860s assumed a significant presence in the city.

The 1627 people employed in 1841 in the food and drink industries embraced a wide variety of occupations ranging from butchers, bakers and corn millers to brewers, maltsters and publicans. The significant increase to 3318 by 1861 is explained in part by the natural growth of the city. The 222 grocers of 1841 had become 483 twenty years later, the sixty-eight fish-mongers had risen to 180, while the 162 butchers by then numbered 260, along with an additional 119 'butchers' wives'. A considerable part of the growth was however accounted for by the rise of a single firm, one which was ultimately to become the largest employer in the city and achieve national fame: J. & J. Colman.

The business was founded by Jeremiah Colman (1777–1851), a Bawburgh miller who acquired a mill near the Magdalen gate at Norwich in 1804.[27] Ten years later he bought the small mustard business of Edward Ames and moved to Stoke Holy Cross. Apart from a mortgage of £6000 in 1825 for the construction of a windmill, and evidence to suggest that he employed a workforce of around thirty, there is little indication of the scale of his ini-tial operations. Yet as early as 1820 mustard was being dispatched to London to extend the firm's markets. In 1840 a young traveller was sent to America and Canada to appoint agents and establish an export trade. Mus-tard milling remained the principal part of the business, but the range of products was also widened, first by the introduction in 1830 of starch and, later, laundry blue. By the 1850s an innovative policy of branding and pack-aging saw the company advertising an impressive variety of mustards, flour and cornflour, starches and blues. The coming of the railways to Norwich, together with problems with the lease at Stoke, prompted the gradual removal of the business back to the city. Production began in the spring of 1852, the smell from the 'new and offensive manufacture' of cattle cake (a by-product of starch) immediately resulting in a court case for the

company. Over the next decade, however, the move from Stoke was completed and the great Carrow works of Colmans established (Plate 57). Some
idea of the rapid growth of the firm is evident from the significant increase
in employment, from fewer than a hundred workers in the mid 1840s
to 500 in 1863 and 1500 a decade later. By that time the partnership of
J. & J. Colman had already established itself as one of the leading British
manufacturers of starch and mustard; the firm had become a Victorian
household name.

By the mid decades of the century, an air of optimism once more pervaded
the city. Despite the continued population growth (from 68,195 in 1851 to
74,891 ten years later), A. D. Bayne reckoned the working classes were as
fully employed as in former years.[28] Periodically, short booms and slumps
continued to rock the economy. But, as Britain entered a long period of
unbroken growth, the worst was over. In fact, the real expansion which was
to transform Norwich from a city dependent upon a single sector to one
more broadly based was yet to come.

A marked feature of the half century after 1860 was the rapid and sustained growth of companies across several sectors. Shoemaking continued
to lead the way. Although much of the industry remained in the hands of
small-scale operators and garret masters, the number of wholesale manufacturers grew steadily from twenty-three in 1867 to seventy-seven by 1900.
At the same time, increased mechanisation, especially after 1890, brought
rapid concentration and the rise of five dominant firms. Of these, the case
of Edwards & Holmes puts the scale of expansion into context. Founded in
1891 in a four-roomed cottage, by 1912 it had outgrown its first modern factory in Esdelle Road and was forced to build new works on the outskirts of
the city. Similarly, Howlett & White (established in 1846) were said to have
the largest shoemaking factory in Britain (Plate 58), while the great firm of
P. Haldenstein & Sons (established in 1799) had branches in London,
Leicester, Kettering and Wymondham, and employed around two thousand workers.[29] These concerns, like the other leading firms, James Southall
& Company (the firm originally founded by James Smith) and Sexton, Son
& Everard, had specialised in the high-quality market, producing mainly
women's and children's shoes, although a wide range, including sports
shoes and the special *veldtschoen* slippers and sandals, was manufactured
for foreign markets. Exports, begun in the 1850s, accounted for between 30
and 40 per cent of all production by 1913.[30] By that time, Norwich had
established itself as the third largest centre of shoemaking in Britain.[31]

The engineers enjoyed mixed fortunes. Those who had specialised in the
manufacture of agricultural machinery and engines felt the full impact of

the depression in farming after 1880 and the resulting fall in demand. Their heyday was over within a decade and several, including Riches & Watts, Sturgess & Towlson, Sparke & Company and Holmes & Sons, subsequently ceased trading.[32] Barnards, more broadly based, continued to concentrate much of its production on wire netting and by 1906 controlled 12½ per cent of the British market. Again, a large proportion of goods was exported; one order in 1906 was for 900 miles of netting for the New South Wales government.[33] Boulton & Paul also entered the field of netting manufacture, especially after 1890 when the company advertised itself as the largest manufacturer in the country. The firm was probably better known for its construction of wood and steel buildings, an activity which received a tremendous boost during the Boer War from government contracts for field hospitals.[34] Other firms took advantage of new opportunities, particularly the growing use of electricity as a power source. The partnership between William Scott and E. A. Paris was formed in 1884, initially to fulfil a contract to supply electricity to Colman's factory. Registered as a limited company four years later, their enterprise expanded steadily (by 1910 it employed 550 men) specialising in the manufacture of electric motors for industrial and marine use.[35] In 1899 the company sold its electrical contracting business to Gerard Mann, who the following year went into partnership with Hubert Egerton. Besides developing the electrical engineering business, the two moved into another young and growing field: motor vehicles. As specialist coach-builders, the firm produced customised bodies for Rolls Royce chassis. By 1913 Mann Egerton had branches throughout the eastern counties and in London.[36]

The same growth was evident elsewhere. The firm of J. & J. Colman continued its unprecedented expansion, embarking on a programme of acquisition from the 1870s which culminated in the takeover of the London company, Keen Robinson (makers of the well-known patent barley and groats), in 1903, and of Farrows of Peterborough (who made mustard and ketchup) nine years later. In 1900 the company employed 2352 workers at Carrow alone[37] and, by the outbreak of the First World War, numbered among the one hundred largest British manufacturing companies.[38] If not on the same scale, other food companies had also grown rapidly. The firm of A. J. Caley (established in 1863) manufactured mineral waters, chocolate and crackers, and by 1904 employed 700 workers in its factory at Chapel Field.[39] R. A. Cooper, employing around 300, produced a wide range of confectionery, cakes and biscuits at the Albion Mill, the former yarn factory. Like Colmans and Caleys, Coopers exported their products world-wide.[40] In other sectors large firms emerged: the brush-making firm of S. D. Page & Sons employed around 300 people in its

Haymarket factory; the clothing manufacturers F. W. Harmer & Company became one of the largest employers in the city; and Jarrolds dominated printing. The general improvement in living standards during the last quarter of the century also stimulated a growing consumer market, especially among the middle classes. Consequently, several department stores flourished: Bonds, Curls, Jarrolds (Plate 42), Buntings (Plate 59) and Garlands. Chamberlins, one of the foremost, also had a large factory in Botolph Street for the manufacture of clothing.[41] Expansion was widespread. For what distinguished the economy of 1900 from that of a century before was its diversity. Gone was the dependence on a single sector. Instead, the factories which dominated the skyline of central Norwich, and increasingly its outskirts, were the most obvious sign of a city which had regained at least some of its former industrial wealth.

A key element in the successful diversification of the economy was the low wages paid to Norwich workers. This was a consequence not only of the region's isolation from the main industrial districts but of a ready supply of surplus labour in the surrounding countryside. Farming wages in East Anglia were traditionally amongst the lowest in the country. The depression in agriculture from the mid 1870s pushed rates down further, a development exacerbated in the city as unemployed labourers migrated in search of work. In the three decades after 1881, the population of Norwich grew from 87,842 to 121,478 (an increase of 38 per cent), while that of the rest of Norfolk rose by a mere 4 per cent. Moreover, much of the employment in the new factories, often packing consumer goods such as chocolates, starch and blue, was suited to women, resulting in an unusually high proportion – 43.2 per cent as against 31.6 per cent nationally – in the workforce.[42] In contrast, there was a shortage of regular work for men, and in many families the wages of women and young boys and girls supplemented the casual, unskilled work available to them. Again, this had a further depressing effect on wages generally.

In almost every sector, wages were below the national average. In 1877 the Select Committee on Intemperance was puzzled by the fact that, although Norwich had the highest proportion of public houses per head of population, it had the lowest incidence of drunkenness. In his evidence to the committee, Simms Reeve, a city magistrate, reckoned the chief reason was the low wages which were much below those of the main manufacturing districts. 'The men do not earn enough money to buy spirits'. He estimated an average wage of 18s. per week for an 'ordinary' shoemaker.[43] Certainly, by 1906 the rates in shoemaking, at an average of 25s. 11d. per fifty-four hour week for men, were below the national average of 28s. 8d.; for women the rates were 10s. 6d. and 13s. 1d. respectively.[44] Similarly, average wages in the Norwich clothing factories were 28s. 4d. per week for men and 10s. 9d. for women, against 31s. 11d. and 12s. 11d. nationally.[45] These workers were among the elite of the city workforce and many others earned less. Generally, labourers in a wide range of occupations from brewing, ironworking and warehousing to railway portering received between 18s. and 16s. for anything from fifty-four to over sixty hours work a week. For women and girls the amounts ranged from 9s. to 10s., then on offer in food factories (with between 3s. 6d. and 8s. being paid to girls under eighteen) to a miserly rate of 6s., which is all that a 'rough class of girl' employed in covering chocolates or working with mineral waters might expect to earn.[46] Much employment was seasonal and, although the numbers were decreasing, many industries, including shoemaking, brushmaking, hair weaving and tailoring, continued to rely on outworkers to maintain production. These men and women survived on the lowest rates of pay, usually on a piece-work basis. The social commentator, C. B. Hawkins, critical of their conditions of work, welcomed the Trades Board Acts of 1909 as a means of increasing the rates. The city, he reckoned, had 'an unpleasant reputation for undercutting'.[47]

Not surprisingly, given the weak position of labour, attempts by trade unions to improve conditions met with little success. Until the late 1880s, trade unionism in the city remained limited and quiescent.[48] The upsurge in activity in 1890–1 proved short-lived, with strikes in shoemaking, building and brushmaking resulting in, at best, partial, flawed victories. Apathy and poor organisation were apparent, but, given the region's isolation and the excess supply of labour, most employers were able in any event to undermine the efforts of local unions. Many firms, including Harmers, Haldensteins, Chamberlins and Boulton & Paul, adopted strict anti-union policies. At Caleys, all combinations were banned and workers sacked for attempting to join organisations. Jarrolds brought in scab labour from London to break strikes. Colmans, one of the better employers, was more accommodating, recognising the Gasworkers' and General Labourers' Union. Nevertheless, the firm adopted tactics to weaken its hold, transferring activists to less well paid jobs and giving pay rises to 'selected' workers.[49] Typically, the shoemakers, faced with increasing mechanisation and changing work practices, struggled for years to gain conciliation procedures and minimum rates of pay. A minimum wage had been achieved at Leicester as early as 1893, and between then and 1906 was secured at every other major shoemaking centre – even in small ones such as Aberdeen and Dundee.[50] In Norwich, a thirty-four week strike in 1897 involving 1500 workers failed to achieve its objective. Not before 1908, with the national union committed funds to the tune of £100,000 and determined to 'sort out' Norwich, was a minimum wage finally agreed. This victory was an isolated example; unions remained on the defensive, unable to improve pay and working conditions appreciably. Lacking the major unionised industries, the city played little part in the great national disputes of 1908–13. Until the outbreak of the First World War, wages in several sectors remained the lowest of those paid in forty-four towns surveyed by the Board of Trade.

Employers capitalised on the weak bargaining power of labour throughout East Anglia. Overall, however, the city maintained a good reputation for industrial relations. Despite those, like Haldensteins, who had notorious reputations as employers, others, such as Colmans and Howlett & White, were renowned for their social responsibility. Not surprisingly in a stronghold of nonconformity, many businessmen were influenced by their religious beliefs, often combining public service with an active philanthropy. Men such as Arthur Howlett and Henry Copeman, the wholesale grocer, served as city councillors and aldermen and played an active role in Sunday and adult schools and missionary societies. George White (Plate 47), chairman of Howlett & White and of the Norwich School Board, and Liberal MP for North West Norfolk, continued to teach at St Mary's Sunday school long after he was knighted and had received the freedom of the city. He outlined his philosophy when, in 1903, he spoke as president of the Baptist Union of England and Wales:

> our relationship with those in our employ should be fair and equal ... as citizens we should strive to have the best things common to all. This is not a question of dividing money or property, but of equality of opportunity, of destroying privilege and placing within the reach of the people 'without money and without price' the advantages of moderate leisure, recreation, social advantages and the best spiritual influences.[51]

Frequently such paternalism has been viewed as an expedient means of maintaining social control. Yet, in practical terms, White supported the unions and his workers' efforts to better their conditions. On one occasion during the great shoe strike of 1897, when union funds were delayed, he had advanced the money and thus enabled the strike to continue.[52] At Colmans, there was the same sense of social conscience. Jeremiah James Colman (Plate 60), who on his father's death in 1851 became sole managing partner of the enterprise, was, like George White, also a teacher at St Mary's Baptist church. Writing to the Reverend George Gould in 1861, in response to an invitation to become a deacon, he observed:

> A master has an influence among his workmen no one else can exercise, and

having now more than five hundred about me, I am sure you will feel with me that this is a sphere or congregation, one might truly say, where my time may often be employed.[53]

Labour policy at Colmans was driven by two objectives: first, the desire to provide employment at a time when Norwich was recovering from the loss of its leading sector; secondly, the promotion of the well-being of the workforce. The latter involved a wide-ranging welfare programme which by the First World War was on a scale almost comparable with that of such great philanthropic companies as Cadburys and Levers. Throughout, it rested in the hands of the women of the family, initially James's wife, Mary (1805–98), and then Caroline (1831–95), wife of Jeremiah James. The first schemes, introduced during the early days at Stoke, included the benefit society, started in 1842, a clothing club, and Sunday, night and day schools, it being a condition of employment that boys would be given a half day's schooling at the expense of the firm.[54] These schools were the forerunners of larger ones at Carrow, and in 1864 new premises, entirely financed by Colmans, were built at Carrow Hill. By 1870 more than three hundred pupils were on the register and in 1900, when the school was transferred to the Norwich School Board, as many as six hundred. In 1857, a works' kitchen, serving workers with hot midday meals at nominal cost, was opened, and seven years later a works' dispensary with daily attendance from a Norwich doctor. A trained nurse, Phillippa Flowerday, was the first industrial nurse to be appointed in the country. Sick visiting of workers' families was introduced following the addition of an assistant in 1878; and from this innovation emerged welfare for the pensioners and the provision of company housing. Much of the social work revolved around the care of the young female employees, who were placed under the supervision of a welfare worker; they were also provided with low-cost accommodation and a laundry. As a memorial to James Jeremiah Colman, a pension scheme was started in 1899. Lastly, the purchase of the Lakenham cricket ground in 1878 provided the focus for sport and recreation. A classic example of Victorian paternalism and self-help, the philanthropy at Colmans catered for every aspect of life, from health and education, pensions and housing, to sport and recreation. Even the unemployed were not forgotten, when, in the years before the war, the firm provided practical and financial help to enable young people to emigrate to Canada. These policies were matched, moreover, by progressive improvements in working conditions, by wages amongst the highest in Norwich, by steadily falling working hours, and, in 1918, by a works council as a forum for negotiations between workers and management, which was in many respects the culmination of these policies. There is little doubt that the firm gained; and in an age of minimal state support so, clearly, did the workforce.

The outbreak of the First World War, at a time of relative buoyancy, marked a watershed for the economy. Almost immediately, several firms lost their export markets. For example, Howlett & White's large orders for German sports shoes instantly collapsed. Many firms also experienced difficulty in obtaining raw materials. Boulton & Paul and Barnards relied solely on Germany for their supplies of drawn wire for net making and found it necessary to import at high cost from Canada and the United States. Industries such as clothing, shoemaking and food processing, which made consumer goods, were particularly hard hit. Unemployment rose sharply, especially among women; in silk weaving alone, two hundred were immediately suspended. In October 1914 the Distress Committee reported 523 female applicants for relief and, by the time the register closed the following March, this number had risen to 744. In response a workshop for unemployed women, funded jointly by the Local Government Board and local charities, was established. A special workshop was also set up for girls under eighteen. The girls, mostly silk weavers or former employees in brush or sweet factories, made a wide range of toys which were sold locally. As the war progressed, however, and men enlisted, shortage of labour rather than unemployment became the problem. Haldensteins lost 90 per cent of its male staff, while another shoemaker, S. L. Witton, was left with only four male employees over twenty-one years of age.[55] The national Union of Boot and Shoe Operatives was initially opposed to women and girls replacing men, but, following the Treasury Agreement of 1915 between the government, employer and union representatives, it was agreed women could be employed if no male labour was available. Subsequently much of the work formerly reserved for men was satisfactorily carried out by women.

Many firms turned to war work. The clothing trade ran at full stretch, most factories being occupied with military orders. As early as 1912 Harmers had been asked to contract for uniforms, and with the outbreak of war was immediately able to step up production. In addition, the company spent £50,000 on knitting machines and produced a mile of knitted fabric a day.[56] Chamberlins also turned its factory over to war work and, in November 1914, two hundred girls were making uniforms for the Fourth Norfolk Regiment.[57] Production of waterproof clothing and oilskin, in which the company specialised, was requisitioned by the Admiralty and War Office, while such was the demand for uniforms for government departments and munitions factories it was necessary to build a new factory to cope. In all, the 800 employees made about one million garments for the war effort.[58] As specialists in high-class women's and children's wear, the shoemakers found it more difficult to adapt quickly to changed conditions. Machinery had to be installed, production reorganised and operatives trained; and, initially, military orders went to other shoemaking centres which concentrated on the heavy end of the market. By October 1914, however, 30,000 canvas fatigue shoes had been made by Howlett & White. Soon, despite shortages of labour and raw materials and escalating costs, the problem was to satisfy demand. During the course of the war Howlett & White produced nearly half a million pairs of boots and shoes for the army as well as a further 32,000 pairs for the allied forces and 21,000 pairs of aviation boots. Haldensteins similarly made half a million pairs of army boots; Edwards & Holmes manufactured 'War Time' boots and shoes for the civilian market, besides Cossack boots for the Russian army; William Hurrell made shoes for military rest camps and hospitals.[59] As was the case with regard to clothing, the industry worked at full capacity and beyond.

The greatest challenge was that faced by the engineering companies in transforming Norwich into a centre of munitions and aircraft manufacture. Apart from the shortage of raw materials, the sector moved easily onto a war footing. Wire netting was in demand for revetments for trenches and desert roads; between them Barnards and Boulton & Paul made in excess of 12,000 miles. Most companies also produced a wide variety of other war goods. Boulton & Paul, for example, was awarded numerous contracts for military camps, a naval hospital at Dover, structural steel buildings for dockyards, and aircraft hangars and hospitals in France.[60] Nevertheless, early in 1915 several companies offered their spare facilities to the government for further war work. In response, some were asked to make shells, Boulton & Paul and Laurence Scott amalgamating their resources with Brookes of Lowestoft and Elliot & Garrood of Beccles for the task. Subsequently the request was for fuses, and a separate company, Norwich Components, was formed jointly by Boulton & Paul and Laurence Scott. Most significant was the request to Boulton & Paul, Mann Egerton and Howes & Sons to make aeroplanes. Mann Egerton acquired sixty acres of land at Hellesdon and at Aylsham Road, where it made in all ten different models of aircraft, ranging from De Havilland long-range bombers to Short seaplanes. Boulton & Paul and Howes joined forces, with the former supervising woodworking and commercial operations, and the latter assembly. An airfield was laid out on the old Cavalry Drill Ground on Mousehold Heath and the first aircraft – an FE 2B – was ready for trials in October 1915. Adjacent buildings along Salhouse Road were taken over by the Royal Flying Corps as a school of flying instruction and the complex was completed by a light railway linking the airfield with Thorpe Station. Inevitably, labour shortage posed problems, and to supplement the company's supply skilled engineers were recruited from local military units. Initially there was opposition to the use of women, but the firm was threatened with closure by the government authorities if it failed to employ them. Consequently, a school was set up to provide the girls with basic engineering training. So successful was the scheme that representatives of other firms came from all over the country to study the methods. With the workforce approaching 3000, production quickly outgrew the Rose Lane works and a new site on the opposite side of the river – the Riverside Works – was opened in the spring of 1916. Like Mann Egerton, the company made a wide range of aircraft, completing in excess of two and a half thousand during the course of the war.[61]

The end of the war again caused a sharp shock to the economy. War contracts ended almost immediately. Within days of the armistice, Norwich Components was closed and the staff of six hundred laid off. A large section of Harmer's clothing factory came to a standstill. Elsewhere women workers left their jobs to make way for returning servicemen. Throughout the war the Chamber of Commerce had shown great concern that conditions might not return to normal. Export markets had been lost, in many cases irrevocably, as other countries increased their self-sufficiency. Nevertheless, Norwich was quickly caught up in the general post-war boom (Plate 61). In its annual report for 1919, the Chamber reckoned business had never been so brisk. Yet almost as quickly as it had begun, the bonanza was over. Prices and profits fell sharply and by December 1920 there were ten thousand people out of work in the city. Reductions in wages were commonplace: Laurence Scott cut its wage bill by 40 per cent but by 1924 orders had slumped to only a quarter of their 1920 level.[62] The confectioners, R. A. Cooper, never recovered from the loss of export markets and closed in 1927. Slowly, by a series of economy measures and diversification, most sectors gradually recovered and by the late 1920s some stability had returned to the city's economy. Any optimism, however, came to an abrupt end with the onset of the slump. The Wall Street crash of 1929 and ensuing financial crisis echoed around the world to be matched by a massive fall in manufacturing output. Although Britain's staple export industries were particularly hard hit, few domestic sectors escaped. Unemployment soared everywhere. In Norwich, 14.8 per cent of the insured workforce were out of work by 1931, and by October the following year only Sheffield and Liverpool had a greater proportion of the population in receipt of poor relief.[63]

How did business respond? The greatest responsibility rested with the

Table 16.3 Numbers employed and percentage of male workforce, 1911–31

Sector	1911 Nos employed	% of workforce	1921 Nos employed	% of workforce	1931 Nos employed	% of workforce
Shoemaking	5,495	15.05	4,979	13.36	6,045	14.92
Textiles	176	0.48	118	0.32	133	0.33
Clothing	1,148	3.14	1,566	4.20	733	1.81
Metals/engineering[1]	3,018	8.27	3,858	10.35	3,781	9.33
Food and drink	4,133	11.32	1,934	5.19	1,407	3.47
Wood/furniture	–	–	2,422	6.50	2,159	5.33
Building	3,314	9.08	2,254	6.05	2,753	6.79
Transport	3,856	10.56	3,741	10.04	3,931	9.70
Commerce[2]	2,719	7.45	4,166	11.18	5,514	13.61
Clerks/typists[3]	–	–	2,068	5.55	2,702	6.67
Professions[4]	1,284	3.52	934	2.51	992	2.45
Domestic service	840	2.30	582	1.56	892	2.20
Agriculture	1,212	3.32	1,207	3.24	1,049	2.59
General labourers	2,525	6.92	3,244	8.71	4,537	11.20
Other[5]	6,794	18.61	4,188	11.24	3,899	9.62
Male workforce[6]	36,514	100.02	37,261	100.00	40,527	100.02

Source: Census returns, 1911–31.
Notes: [1] Includes electrical engineering
[2] After 1911 grocers etc were included as 'shop assistants' in the commerce category, accounting for significant differences in 1921 and 1931.
[3] The new category of clerks/typists/draughtsmen was introduced in 1921. Previously clerks had been included in commerce.
[4] Includes accountants from 1921; previously they were in the commerce category.
[5] Includes several small categories, each accounting for less than 3 per cent of the workforce.
[6] The 1911 workforce is defined as those over ten years, that of 1921, over twelve years, and 1931, over fourteen years.

increasingly dominant shoemaking industry. By 1931 it employed 17 per cent of the workforce (22.6 per cent of all women then in employment – see Table 16.4); and, as the Chamber of Commerce acknowledged, 'the prosperity of the city as a whole seemed to flag or flourish with its fortunes'.[64] And flag and flourish it did. The early 1920s proved to be difficult years, when most firms suffered from the loss of export markets not only

Table 16.4 Numbers employed and percentage of female workforce,
1911–31

Sector	1911		1921		1931	
	Nos employed	% of work-force	Nos employed	% of work-force	Nos employed	% of work-force
Shoemaking	2,902	14.54	2,853	14.50	4,655	22.62
Textiles	703	3.52	556	2.82	456	2.22
Clothing	3,614	18.11	2,757	14.01	1,364	6.63
Food and drink	1,907	9.56	932	4.74	697	3.38
Commerce	439	2.20	1,931	9.81	2,203	10.70
Clerks/typists	–	–	1,571	7.98	2,095	10.18
Professions	1,336	6.70	1,279	6.50	1,245	6.05
Domestic service	5,770	28.92	4,596	23.35	4,689	22.78
General labourers	606	3.04	307	1.56	773	3.76
Other	2,678	13.42	2,900	14.73	2,405	11.68
Total workforce	19,955	100.01	19,682	100.00	20,582	100.00

Source: Census returns, 1911–31.
Notes: See Table 16.3.

through greater self sufficiency but because many countries such as South Africa imposed high tariffs on British shoes. As many as thirty of the smaller firms were forced out of business.[65] On the other hand, fashion had assumed a much greater importance than in the pre-war era, and for some years Norwich enjoyed a virtual monopoly in the manufacture of the light-weight Louis heel shoe then in demand. Sextons achieved a major breakthrough with the introduction, in place of the turnshoe (where production costs were high), of light machine-sewn fashion shoes. Gradually, Northampton and Leicester followed suit, and the contest became one of the higher productivity (and therefore lower costs) of the Midland centres versus the superior designs of Norwich. But after the slump of 1929 it was again a matter of survival and of fierce competition both from home and overseas. By December 1930 over 50 per cent of the workforce were on short time and, as before, many small firms went bankrupt or ceased trading.[66] In 1933 Haldensteins was acquired by the Swiss firm, Bally. But generally the larger firms found it easier to adapt to the changed circumstances. Some companies looked overseas – especially to Bata at Zlin in Czeckoslovakia – at methods of mass production and organisation, and returned to implement new systems at Norwich. Most successful were those which developed branded, high-quality lines. Sextons, one of the most innovative firms, made American shoes under licence and then, in the late 1930s, pioneered the popular platform casual shoe. As early as 1914 Howlett & White began selling all its shoes under one brand name: Norvic. Further consolidation was achieved in the early 1930s through the Norvic concentration plan (a retailing scheme developed by an American firm), which encouraged agents to sell exclusively for the company. The culmination, in order to offer a complete range of products to the market, was the acquisition of a number of subsidiaries – the Nottingham Mansfield Shoe Company in 1919, Oakeshott & Finnemore of Northampton in 1922, and the Norwich firm, S. L. Witton (manufacturers of the famous Kiltie childrens' shoes) in 1934; and the formation the following year of the Norvic Shoe Company.

Merger and rationalistion were common trends throughout Britain during these years and Norwich was no exception. Steward & Patteson the brewers, maintained their regional dominance by means of a conservative policy of consolidation, acquiring Charles Pearse's Crown Brewery at East Dereham in 1922 and the more substantial brewery and properties of W. & T. Bagge of King's Lynn seven years later. Their rival, Bullards, followed the same course, buying up a number of small Norfolk breweries.[67] The brushmakers, S. D. Page & Sons, merged with a London company, D. Matthew & Sons, in 1920 to form the Briton Brush Company. Seven years later the outdated Haymarket factory was closed and production transferred to Wymondham.[68] Similarly, Laurence Scott, hard hit by the depression in shipbuilding, acquired the Manchester firm of Electromotors Ltd to enable the firm to move into the production of alternating current electric motors.[69] Two of the city's leading firms, Colmans and Caleys, also gained significantly from mergers. Colmans, with its reliance on basic consumer goods, had suffered less during the depression than many other firms. Nevertheless, some products were becoming old-fashioned and, despite the great success of the Mustard Club launched in 1926 to promote the firm's famous mustards, it was new products, such as complete baby foods and Robinson's fruit drinks, which now led the way. The merger with their old rival, Reckitts of Hull in 1938, the result of many years of negotiations, brought the greater technical expertise of Reckitts, by now the larger firm, which was so necessary in modern markets.

In contrast, the take-over in 1932 of Caleys by John Mackintosh & Sons of Halifax was very much a rescue operation. The business was initially acquired in 1918 by United Africa Ltd, a subsidiary of Unilever, but, despite its decision to build one of the most modern confectionery factories in the country on its Chapel Field site, the enterprise failed to flourish. Indeed,

when in 1932 Mackintoshes were considering a take-over they were sur-
prised that the firm was still trading because losses were so great and
'management over the last ten years had been so terribly bad'. After the
take-over, however, the company went from strength to strength, launching such well-known products as Quality Street and Rolo and recording
record profits.[70]

During his journey around England in 1934, J. B. Priestley noted that
Norwich had 'escaped the full weight of the industrial depression'. The city,
he thought, had a 'solidly prosperous appearance ... at once gay and
weighty'.[71] The cheerful throng Christmas shopping in London Street certainly bore little resemblance to the shabby, dispirited men he saw loitering
around the streets of Jarrow and Hebburn. Also, unlike those bleak northern towns, Norwich was never classified as a Distressed Area.[72] Yet, despite
the best efforts of business and the city council, unemployment remained
persistently high throughout the 1930s. After the recovery of the late 1920s,
unemployment peaked in January 1933 at almost 20 per cent of the insured
workforce. Improvement thereafter was short lived; by 1936 the unemployment rate of 12.3 per cent of insured workers was still above the
national average, and never fell below 10 per cent again before the outbreak
of war in 1939.[73] Throughout these years, unemployment in the city
remained, on average, a stubborn 5 per cent above the level recorded for
the south-east region as a whole.

In many respects, Norwich followed national trends: deep depression in
many manufacturing sectors in the early 1930s followed by sustained, if
slow, recovery. Certainly, this was the experience of many of the city's staple industries and major employers. Most, like the engineering firms, were
badly hit during the early 1930s. Laurence Scott suffered particularly from
the suspension of work on the great liner, the *Queen Mary*, while Boulton
& Paul felt the full impact of the depressed state of agriculture and building and the cessation of public works. Both companies were forced to cut
wages and reduce their workforces. By 1936, however, both were prosper-
ing once more. Boulton & Paul rationalised into three main departments:
structural steel, wood-working and wire-weaving; the aircraft division was
sold in 1934 and moved to Wolverhampton two years later. In each case,
approaching war played a part in recovery. Laurence Scott took on specialist work for the Admiralty, while Boulton & Paul produced steel for
'shadow factories',[74] and built training camps for the Air Ministry.[75] The
building sector also recovered from the mid 1930s. It received a significant
stimulus when in 1933 the Labour Party, having achieved a slim majority
on the council, revived its housing and redevelopment programme. Both
private sector building, such as the development of suburbs at Hellesdon

and St Faith's, and extensive corporation housing estates, including Catton Grove and Mile Cross, boosted employment, as did large public building projects: a new police station and fire headquarters in 1934, the football ground the following year, and City Hall in 1938. Additionally, six new cinemas were built in the 1930s, three in 1938 alone.[76]

Some sectors struggled to recover from the depression of the early 1930s. Jobs in the manufacture of clothes, for example, declined permanently, lost to foreign competition, mechanisation and the shift away from department stores producing their own ready-made clothes in favour of cheaper and more fashionable branded goods.[77] Nevertheless, some larger firms were able to adapt. Harmers expanded into the manufacture of ready-made suits, while Chamberlins built up a large export trade in oilskins. In contrast, Colmans, as we have seen, weathered the storm better than most companies and, following their successful merger, Caleys recovered strongly; the 750 staff of 1933 in 'very irregular employment' had increased by 1936 to 2250.[78] Most critical, however, given its position as the dominant employer in the city (see Tables 16.3 and 16.4), was the performance of the shoemaking industry. In January 1933 there were 1684 footwear workers unemployed, almost one in five of the total. But despite the subsequent slow recovery of the sector in terms of output, there was little improvement in employment. On average, between 1000 and 1500 shoe-workers remained unemployed each week throughout the rest of the decade. Much of the problem came, paradoxically, from rising productivity following the demise of turnshoe production – which involved skilled men – in favour of machine-sewn shoes – dependent mainly on female operatives. The result was a large pool of long-term male unemployed who were not absorbed by other industries.[79] Moreover, the main changes in the pattern of employment during the inter-war years did little to ease the problem. Most growth came in commerce (including retailing, finance and insurance), in clerical work and in the professions (especially nurses and teachers), where a high proportion of the recruits were female.

The steady recovery of much of Norwich's industry, together with the growth of the service sector and professions, was therefore not sufficient to resolve the problem of high unemployment, especially among men. What set the city apart from others in Great Britain by the later 1930s was its lack of new industry. Elsewhere in the midlands and south-east region recovery was boosted by the growth of nascent industries such as light engineering, cars and artificial silk. Yet, despite the encouragement of the corporation, including assistance to develop industrial sites, new firms were not attracted to Norwich.[80] Indeed, the one new post-Great War sector, aircraft, was lost to the midlands in 1936. The reasons were clearly evident when in 1932 Sir Harold Mackintosh carefully evaluated the prospects of acquiring Caleys. The costs of transport, labour, housing and rates were all considered. The main disadvantage was the geographical position of Norwich, which 'added forty-four miles to every ton going out'; an annual extra cost of £5000 in comparison with London or Halifax. Labour was cheap, but thought to be 'not so quick and snappy' as elsewhere.[81]

Generally, the structural imbalance in the labour market – a shortage of female labour and an excess of male – did little to help. Proposals to build an artificial silk factory were frustrated by the former.[82] The consequences were all too apparent. Whereas the city's rivals, Northampton and Leicester, suffered higher rates of unemployment in the first half of the decade, both improved substantially after 1934, not least because of the growth of new industries. Ipswich, with its more diverse economy, also fared better.[83] Norwich, isolated geographically, and set at the heart of a deeply depressed agricultural hinterland, had little to attract new enterprise. In fact the city was again faced with almost exactly the same problems that had hindered its development in the early nineteenth century: remoteness from expanding markets, poor communications and a growing dependence on one sector. By rationalisation and innovation, shoemaking, like the other leading sectors, had slowly recovered. Between them, however, they were unable to expand sufficiently to absorb the large pool of unemployed labour. Without new industry the Norwich economy stagnated during the second half of the decade and the city remained an 'island of depression' in the relatively prosperous south-east region. It was to take the repeated demands of war and its aftermath to stimulate a further period of expansion and extended recovery.

17

Church and Chapel

Clyde Binfield

This is not a bad record is it? For our Churches and the part they play in civic life.

Ethel Mary Colman to Sydney Cozens-Hardy, 29 October 1923[1]

It was generally agreed that 30 March 1851 was wet. Since that was the Sunday set aside for assessing 'the amount of accommodation for worship provided by the various religious bodies in the country, and the extent to which the means thus shown to be available are used',[2] the state of the weather was a pertinent factor. Horace Mann, the official who supervised the census for George Graham, the Registrar-General, was sure the weather was 'about average for the season', but in Norfolk it was decidedly wet, even if in Norwich it was only the St Clement's Baptists who complained of the rain.[3]

Perhaps the weather coloured the comments which found their way on to some of the returns. Most were defensive, some bravely so. 'We are exceedingly poor in temporal circumstances', confided Isaac Dixon on behalf of the New Catton Baptists, 'opposed to popery and all kinds of Error, lovers of our Country from our Dear Queen to the poor rustic, hoping you are doing all in the fear of the Lord through Jesus Christ.'[4] 'We are a New Sect', stated John Boyce, minister of Tombland chapel. 'Near the Gas works . . . and stiling ourselves independent Methodists and in our infant state'.[5] Another sect met in Coslany using a room set apart 'For Worship and Christian intercourse'. Their Robert Tillyard painstakingly explained how unsectarian they in fact were: 'The persons connected with this place of worship consider it unnecessary and unscriptural as members of the universal church of Christ to adopt any distinctive name or any narrower Creed than the whole Word of God'; and Tillyard made it clear that he wrote 'not in any Official Character but as one connected'.[6] Sectarianism had also been banished from Crow's Yard Church of Christ ('Formerly a Warehouse') although here defensiveness was dulled into resignation.

Henry Pitcher, deacon, Lobster Lane, explained the situation: 'In the room in Crows Yard ... there has been no public worship since April 16th 1850. The people have been disbanded and sent to worship in their parish churches; as in future it is very uncertain what use may be made of the room I do not feel I can make any other return.'[7]

These were dissenting voices. Anglican defensiveness was more irritable. A day of reckoning had crept upon a city whose parishes were too many and too small and whose clergymen feared they had been outmanoeuvred. 'This parish consists principally of working people engaged in the different branches of Norwich manufacture very few of which can be prevailed upon to attend any place of Public Worship', wrote the curate of St Edmund the King.[8] For W. S. Maturin, the curate who served both All Saints and St Julian, the problem lay in his non-resident rector, although he was too restrained to do more than let the fact speak for itself.[9] That double instance of non-residence was unique in Norwich. Dissent by contrast was everywhere. 'Perhaps there are more dissenters (in proportion to the other Parishes in the City) in this than in the other Parishes'; wrote the incumbent of St George Colegate,'and such has been the case for more than one hundred years as I have heard'. And he noted the close proximity of four dissenting meetings, two of them in his parish, adding that 'Both the church wardens are dissenters. There have been no church rates collected for near fourteen years; and, in consequence, the church (though one of the handsomest in the city) is in a disgraceful state; whilst the Tower is in such a dangerous condition that on a stormy Sunday I should think it my duty to keep the door closed, lest an accident should happen.'[10] It was little better at St Mary Coslany and St James Pockthorpe. At the former 'There have been no church rates ... for fifteen years and until recently the church in ruinous condition'. At the latter 'in consequence of opposition to a church rate the surplice falls on the clergyman'. Pockthorpe's parson enlarged on this inspired ambiguity: 'There is certainly no sufficient provision for the religious instruction of St James with Pockthorpe. The population is nearly 3000 and church accommodation is only for 459, and for Pockthorpe a church or chapel is much needed, with endowment for another clergyman – the whole district may be said to be the poorest in Norwich.'[11]

There were signs of hope. St Mary Coslany was in fact no longer ruinous: 'Private subscriptions have been late raised towards the repair'.[12] St Martin-at-Palace too was on the verge of restoration, again by private subscription; that would add 217 sittings.[13] Sittings were a vexed question. The shape of old and variably restored parish churches seldom lent itself to the mechanical computation of sittings. St Martin-at-Oak, for example, had 570 but, as the incumbent observed, 'The number does not convey a correct account of the room in the church which a congregation of 350 almost completely fills'.[14]

It was left to the cathedral to state several cases by implication. Its morning and afternoon congregations (1442 and 824 respectively) were the city's largest. But what did they signify? Dean Pellew's concise return was to the point: 'Number carefully counted in. Increased perhaps from one 3rd to one 4th by Presence of the Judges. Attendance depends much on the weather and the season.' And who knew how many such a building held? There were sittings for 810; of these there were 'free at twenty inches each 348, but as parties often sit closer say 400 ... Besides much open space which on occasion is supplied with Forms, Benches, Chairs etc. etc. as required'.[15] Clearly the judges' service was one which prompted those expedients. Only a minority of Norwich's places of worship returned such comments, but these are enough to demonstrate the ambiguity inherent in a census of accommodation and attendance which none the less was presented as a census of religious worship.[16] The quantitative had slipped insensibly into the qualitative.

The subjective often rings true. Take those dissenting comments. None came from a large congregation. Theirs were uncoordinated voices, Norwich's variant of the Lantern Yard which George Eliot would illuminate ten years on in *Silas Marner*,[17] transient yet curiously ineradicable, easily ignored, hard to trace, unsatisfactory to assess, but quite as representative of the dissenting temper as those of the bigger and better known battalions. They also expressed dissenting fissiparousness rather than dissenting dissidence. Indeed, Robert Tillyard and Henry Pitcher testify to the craving for union which motivated many dissenters. Theirs was the spirit which had led nationally to the Plymouth Brethren in the last thirty years, and to the Churches of Christ in the last ten. John Boyce and Isaac Dixon introduce contrasting elements.

Norwich was an old city, its rhythms enriched by long-established traditions. Its Dissent was part of that establishment, in confident counterpoint to those defining rhythms. But Norwich, though old, was not ageing and novelty was a precondition of much of its Dissent. Its Methodism, irregularly introduced in 1751, was a case in point. In 1851 there were still antique Methodists who in youth had glimpsed John Wesley, although probably not in Norwich, which he had last visited in 1769. Even so the Wesley brothers were lively memories for any family whose Methodism was two generations strong. For middle-aged Norfolk Methodists the past thirty years had seen exciting growth, but equally exciting disruption had allowed no time for consolidation. If Primitive Methodists largely complemented Wesleyans in a spirit of healthy competition, the same could not be said of the Wesleyan reformers who had been exploding since 1849 or of the Independent and assorted Methodists who had periodically erupted in earlier years. These were none the less the tensions of youth coming of age, natural even healthy for families which took discipline seriously.

This leaves Isaac Dixon, speaking for New Catton's Baptists apparently apropos of nothing. There is more, however, to his loyal anti-popery than the instinctive prayers of a certain type of evangelical, for Dixon's political world has clearly encompassed the recent papal aggression, the restoration of Britain's Roman Catholic hierarchy, the reported fury of the queen and the consequent Ecclesiastical Titles Act, all things to make a conscientious dissenter from the established church fear greatly and without undue inconsistency for the safety of that same establishment.[18]

So to some Anglican voices. Their tone is depressing. Here are professional men frustrated by crumbling fabrics and their failure to mend those fabrics by levying church rate. Dissenting tactics expertly mythologised and carefully politicised are depriving them of their birthright. Yet there remains their cathedral, blending all classes under the aristocratic command of Dean Pellew, even if more by instinct than design. It is still the spiritual focus of the body politic when on parade. In 1851 Pellew was into his third bishop. To employ a metaphor which would have spoken to his first, the whist-playing Whig, Henry Bathurst, the cathedral was the church's trump card.[19]

The religious census of 1851 reflected and fed the Victorian passion for statistics. It provided figures for accommodation and attendance which Victorians decided were profoundly suggestive. It offered strong indications of the social class of attenders and of their churchmanship. Crude and confident observers might also feel that it indicated their spirituality, but there were some matters which it could do no more than indicate. Strategies could be spun from what it implied; its prime value lay in its figures.

Norfolk was on the median for English counties; it stood twenty-first out of forty-two for attendance.[20] Norwich was par for the course for populous English towns; it stood forty-second out of sixty-five. Church attendance in Norwich was proportionately the same as in Norfolk, making due allowance for the apparently adverse impact of rapid recent population growth: 46.1 per cent of its inhabitants had attended church or chapel; 22.1 per cent had worshipped as Anglicans, 17.2 per cent as Baptists, Congregationalists or Methodists, 0.4 per cent as Roman Catholics.[21] All concerned had cause for both guilt and congratulation. The guilt related to the thousands who had failed to attend.[22] The congratulation was felt chiefly by

Dissenters, for whom parity with the established church had suddenly become statistically possible, even likely.

Yet many church buildings in Norwich must have seemed decently full, with the national church comfortably ahead.[23] The cathedral has already been mentioned, but there were adult morning congregations of 700 at St Peter Mancroft and 400 at St Mark's New Lakenham (built 1844) and St Stephen's; afternoon congregations of 780 at St Peter's, with 650 at St Mark's and 400 at St Stephen's; and an evening congregation of 600 at St Stephen's. Admittedly St Peter's, St Mark's, and St Stephen's sat 1000, 850 and 900 respectively and relatively few Sunday school scholars were enumerated to swell their adult ranks (fifty-eight, 100, and 100 for their respective morning and afternoon services). Yet they must have seemed encouragingly full, and the proportions were not so different in smaller churches: 300 at St John Maddermarket, 250 at St Gregory, 236 at St Giles, 450 at St Simon and St Jude (which sat 500).

Even the smallest, oldest and most vulnerable turned out valiantly. Whether a church were better described as half full or half empty at its best attended service surely depended on how it looked; it was a psychological judgment determined by the disposition of transepts and chancel, the bric-à-brac of pews and memorials, and how people seemed as they sat among them, and the proportion of children to adults. St Martin-at-Oak, it will be recalled, could accommodate 570, but apparently 350 'almost completely' filled it; on census Sunday its evening service attracted 262. At St George Colegate's evening service there were 171 adults and sixty-five children; the church held 500. At St Etheldreda, St Peter Southgate, St Helen, St Martin-at-Palace and St Michael-at-Plea the afternoon service was the best attended. Congregations were small (seventy, forty, 147, ninety, and 100 respectively) but available sittings were also few (150, 160, 363, 230, and 200) and at St Etheldred's, St Helen's and St Martin's there were children to be added to the total (seventy, seventy-one, and forty-seven). None was quite as meagre as St Edmund the King (300 sittings; twenty-nine morning adults and twenty children, fifty-two evening adults) or St Peter Hungate (280 sittings; fifty in the morning – it was explained that more attended the afternoon service on alternate Sundays).

Certainly the fact of the empty sittings, enumerated as never before, was as bracing as a douche of cold water. Far more suggestive, however, were the occupied ones. In Norwich, when all allowances were made and all glooms indulged, they announced life, variety, and a potential for mission which embraced all classes from the forty-six afternoon adults enumerated at Earlham, that quintessential village church, to the 126 morning adults at

Holy Trinity Heigham, a dozen years on from its consecration. The former held ninety, the latter 400. What did the future hold?

That question was hardly less pertinent for dissenters. They were free of parochial constraints unless they tangled with clergymen over burials or church rate. They were otherwise normally neither legally nor ecclesiastically tied into a parish. Their mission was thus free of boundaries. Where their buildings were preaching boxes (and there were few more efficient ways of hearing the word than in a boxy building), and even if their numbers were harder to compile, since dissenting chapel builders often allowed for fewer inches per person than Anglicans, their empty sittings were easy to see. There was a world of difference between the dignified pews carefully ranked in the body of the chapel and the sweeping rhythms of those raked and stacked in the galleries. The preacher then saw all.

There was, of course, more between church and chapel than shape of building, size of sitting or mode of operation, although few differences had more immediate effect than those. In most chapels the morning service was favoured by the core of the membership, the pews close-knit by family connection. Evening services were more evangelistic. They attracted the young, the single, the sermon-tasters, the clerks and assistants, the servants too. The Orford Hill Baptists, for example, whose chapel (seating 550) had been converted from a factory in 1833, attracted 350 morning adults (and sixty Sunday scholars) and 450 evening adults; but there was also an afternoon congregation of 150, 'chiefly attended by servants, invalids and persons who cannot attend on any other part of the Sabbath'. That suggests not just a solid congregation but also a shrewd eye to need and an equally shrewd ability to turn need into demand and meet both.

With some striking exceptions that reflected the whole range of Norwich Dissent, Old or New. The city's Unitarians, Quakers, Congregationalists, and General and Particular Baptists had a steadily traceable seventeenth-century ancestry. All had characteristically dignified buildings. The elegant yet irrepressibly opulent Octagon chapel, which celebrated the transition of Norwich's Presbyterians into Unitarianism, testified to their Augustan civic clout. A century later its morning congregation adequately sustained the solidity. The chapel claimed to hold 500. That number would have made it intolerably full. As it was its 250 adults and its surprisingly numerous 247 children peopled it comfortably, even if its evening congregation (126) disappointed. The Congregationalists' Old Meeting was Norwich's oldest large purpose-built meeting house (Plate 62). Its mercantile dignity witnessed more to enduring tradition than outdated fashion. It seated 700 but, notwithstanding its minister's six-month illness, its morning and evening congregations remained admirable: 442 and 337, with a further 369 morning children. The Particular Baptists of St Mary's worshipped in a newer and larger building than either the Octagon or Old Meeting. Theirs was 'one of the handsomest Baptist meeting-houses in the Kingdom', Norwich's 'fashionable watering place' of 1812.[24] It too was adequately filled and its morning preponderance spoke of social solidity (482 morning adults, with 103 children; 346 evening adults; 874 sittings). By contrast the General Baptists' continuity demonstrated tenacity rather than consolidation. Their chapel was small (300), with matching congregations (a hundred in the morning, fifty in the afternoon, with a hundred children on both occasions, and 150 in the evening). It was the Quakers, however, whose absences were the most telling. Admittedly the lack of a return for their Gildencroft Meeting depressed their numbers, but the ninety-three morning and forty-one afternoon Friends gathered in their imposing Goat's Lane Meeting showed that at best it was not even quarter filled.

Thus Old Dissent. Its Baptists and Congregationalists, however, had been rejuvenated since the mid eighteenth century by the waves of evangelical revival. Old Meeting's Congregationalists had been outpaced since 1819 by those of Prince's Street, which sat almost a thousand, and held Norwich's third largest morning congregation (573, with 191 children) and second largest evening congregation (452; there was no afternoon congregation). The Baptists – Pitt Street, St Margaret's (Pottergate Street), St Clement's , and Orford Hill – were more heterogeneous. Their congregations varied as much as their shades of Calvinism and were as likely to issue from internal doctrinal scruples as from external revival. The numbers at St Clement's (380 in the morning, with 125 children; 263 in the evening) rivalled those at Orford Hill; those at Pitt Street and Pottergate Street were much smaller. The St Clement's Baptists were children of the Whitefieldite revival; the Pottergate Baptists, popularly known as Johnsonians after their apologist, John Johnson of Liverpool, were a pragmatic distillation of high Calvinism with an unexpected General Baptist admixture. Their beliefs were a tribute to the flexibility of lay theology. They were now steadily returning to the Baptist mainstream, but their smallness should not be confused with weakness.[25] A fifth congregation might be added to this Baptist quartet: the undenominationalists gathered in Broad Street's Bazaar chapel. Their morning congregation (420, with thirty-nine children), midway between those of St Clement's and St Mary's, met in a smaller building than either (550). Formed in 1844, they characterised the latest phase of the Evangelical Revival. The census caught the representatives of that revival's earliest Whitefieldite and Methodist phases at their most vulnerable. Bare statistics of attendance and accommodation revealed past glories and present agonies. They could offer little guidance as to future directions.

Their oldest building, the Tabernacle, founded in turmoil a century earlier in 1751 and rebuilt two years later by Thomas Ivory, whose crowning monument, the Octagon, followed within four years, had passed into the hands of the Countess of Huntingdon's Connexion, a small evangelical denomination which for practical purposes marched with the Congregationalists. In some places, notably Brighton, it still attracted good congregations to hear superior preachers at services structured by the prayer book. Their Norwich Tabernacle seated 950 and held services each Sunday morning, afternoon and evening, but attendances were no match for sittings: 120 morning adults, with forty children; seventy afternoon adults and eighty in the evening. Methodism, by contrast, had until recently offered a more enduring tribute to evangelistic success.[26]

John Wesley had opened Cherry Lane chapel in 1769. In 1811 its people moved to Calvert Street, within the easiest distance of Old Meeting, the Octagon and St Mary's. Like the Tabernacle, it seated 950 and the thin glazing-barred gothick of its fenestration offered an apt, almost light-hearted, prelude to the nearby Baptists' 'fashionable watering place' which opened a year later. St Peter's, a tribute to Methodism's mahogany age, followed in Lady Lane in 1824, at which point it was claimed that Norwich's Methodist chapels had over 2000 worshippers. Since St Peter's seated 866, that left few surplus sittings. New City chapel, seating 570, came fifteen years later.

These were Wesleyan chapels. The Primitive Methodists arrived in 1820. Thirty years later their chapels in Lakenham, Cowgate and Dereham road (St Benedict's), seated 514, 330 and 210 respectively. Given the strength of Wesleyan and Primitive Methodism in Norfolk, their Norwich societies were of strategic importance.

Yet in 1851 all was in disarray. Like all children of revival, Methodists were prone to explosive tension. Between 1849 and 1852 the explosion was nationwide. In Norfolk and Norwich it was county and citywide.[27] The conflict concerned the relationship between Conference, Wesleyan Methodism's ruling ministerial body, the 'living Wesley', and local activists. It was a matter of authority dramatised by personality. Norfolk's rebellious personalities included men, such as W. H. Cozens-Hardy, of marked ability and considerable local prominence. They were openly supported by leading Baptists and Congregationalists and publicised by the local press's newest, liveliest and most radical organ, the *Norfolk News*. Tempestuous public meetings showed that there was no containing them. By March 1851 an established denomination had all but unravelled and a new denomination was in formation. The Wesleyans had already lost New City chapel. Calvert Street would follow within a few months. Nationally most of the Wesleyan reformers, as they became known, merged in 1857 with earlier Methodist seceders to form the United Methodist Free Churches, the third largest bloc within British Methodism. The census reveals the extent of disruption.

Norwich's Wesleyan bastion was now St Peter's, Lady Lane. Its return of 320 evening adults meant that it was almost two-thirds empty for its best attended service. Calvert Street had yet to be transferred to the reformers; on census Sunday morning and evening it was four-fifths empty, at its afternoon service there were forty. Yet the reformers' New City chapel was itself little more than half-filled at its best service (294 in the evening), and their Philadelphia chapel was still too new a cause for easy assessment (a hundred adults with seventy-five children at the afternoon service occupied the 180 sittings). The Primitives were in best shape. Their chapels were smaller but Lakenham's evening congregation was now Norwich Methodism's largest (353; 274 in the afternoon and 267 in the morning). That chapel was thus three-fifths full while Cowgate was almost completely so. But at their newest and smallest city chapel, opened in St Benedict's on Dereham Road in 1850, the congregations were promising rather than good.

The variety of Norwich's mid-century religious attendance is almost exhausted. Its Roman Catholic presence was certainly understated. There was no return for the Catholics' Maddermarket church and only a perfunctory one – a suspiciously rounded morning 200 – for their church in Willow Lane. For the rest there were Swedenborgians (106 evening adults for 132 sittings) and Mormons (181 afternoon adults for 400 sittings). These were solid enough clusters attracting not dissimilar types. There were also Catholic Apostolicals, or Irvingites. Alas, they made no return, yet socially and liturgically there was probably no more suggestive Norwich congregation. And there were Jews, enumerated the previous day. Their building, opened like that of the Mormons in 1848, seated eighty-nine; twenty-six morning and twenty-four evening adults met there on census sabbath.

There remains one significant group. Norwich presented all the challenges of an old industrial city. Its established denominations encouraged mission rooms. Thus Anglican services were provided for the workhouse inmates in the old Dutch church. Its tradition of cooperative missionary endeavour was most practically expressed, however, in the City Mission, formed fifteen years earlier and now with eight branches in densely peopled parts of the city. The mission was undenominational but its chief support came from evangelical Anglicans and nonconformists. The fact that five of its branches met in British schools points to a Nonconformist bias. Its accommodation ranged from Bull Close's sixty sittings to Heigham's 300 and its best attendances (all save Heigham's were in the evening) were gratifying.

Such a census was never officially repeated. It is, therefore, uniquely valuable, but its value is limited because it is unique. It has no comparitors. Each of its returns, however, gains significance from the fact that it is a local reflection of a national inquiry. Their concern was with physical rather than spiritual disposition. They recorded the number of seats and those sitting in them, making no presumption as to their state of mind or any consequent attitude. None the less they provided enough circumstantial evidence for assumptions to be made about much else. They did in fact offer insights to the moral and spiritual concerns of a community. They cast light on its mentalities.

For example, the returns reflected a range of different structures. Horace Mann was at pains to explain them in his report. Sometimes the structure was reflected in the name: Congregationalists; Society of Friends; Wesleyan Methodist Connexion. Sometimes it was a practice: Baptists. Sometimes it was a mode of belief: Unitarians. In telling of structures, therefore, the returns spoke of differing interpretations of authority and of its mediation. Each bred its own political temper, its own understanding of relationships and loyalties as well as its own network of relationships. Those networks, loyalties, relationships and interpretations had their national dimension. Here, however, was their local reflection; in some cases 'refraction' would be a better word, as (to change the metaphor) regional accents, even dialects, took over. Such matters help to explain any community but they have particular value when applied to an old, complex yet steadily changing place which was at once cathedral city, provincial capital and county town, long practised in the interlocking mechanisms of public life.

Yet how should such matters be read? One reading is that they reveal the fragmentation, indeed the disintegration, of the interlocking city just described. They uncover a culture of distrust and dissatisfaction. They display the dissidence of Dissent in tandem with a mentality of competition. Each can galvanise, each can paralyse. The census is thus a tribute to schism. But a tribute to schism might also be a tribute to principles upheld. It is a tribute to citizens who think and care. Seen thus the census signals the advance of pluralism rather than a stage in disintegration. The forcing of debate has led to the fostering of debate and thus to the accommodation of its apparently conflicting consequences. And such an accommodation can lead to a rediscovery, amounting to a reinvention, of co-operation. The 1851 Norwich Religious Census, its returns for Swedenborgians, Mormons, or Lady Huntingdon's Connexion as significant as those for the Cathedral, the Octagon, or Princes Street, is a testimony to two of the nineteenth century's key words: competition and co-operation. It is about accommodation in more senses than one. It casts light on a key agent in the developing temper of a city on the cusp of change.

Change is incessant. It tends as much to the cumulative as to the sudden, regeneration in parallel with age. At mid century, Norwich's population had increased, but the spurts of growth varied. Its textile industry had all but slipped away but its footwear, its mustard, cornflour and starch approached the brow of more than local significance. So did its financial services and its wholesaling. There was a lively press. All the activities of a significantly established town were rejuvenating. The prime agents of this were energetically innovative local businessmen, Theobalds, Colmans, Copemans, Tillyards, Howletts, Jarrolds, joined by Whites and Jewsons in the century's second half, people whose familial, commercial and religious interests intersected and enlarged their secular culture. The regeneration of a long-established culture was in process.

That culture's leading edge was Anglican. Its cutting edge was dissenting. For those whose youth had been fine-honed by it, the culture had been radical. By the 1850s the families which had contributed most to it, the Quaker Gurneys, the Unitarian Aldersons, Taylors and Martineaus, had conformed, died or moved away. One who had moved away reflected late in 1853 on 'the extinction of the celebrity of ancient Norwich, in regard both to its material and intellectual production. Its bombazine manufacture has gone to Yorkshire, and its literary fame to the four winds.'[28] Their allure, however, survived in enjoyable and carefully fostered myth. The Gurneys' Quakerism was steadily dwindling. It effectively ceased as a local and national force with the death of J. J. Gurney in 1847. Yet the family networks of Gurneys, Hoares, Barclays, Hanburys, Frys and Backhouses, and their fellow-travelling Buxtons, carried on county and country wide, with their Byzantine intricacy undiluted, long after the Quakerism had gone.[29] It could be claimed without undue ingenuity that nineteenth-century England's three best-known Quakers, Elizabeth Fry, John Bright and W. E. Forster, were Norwich by birth or easily charted family association.[30]

The same might be said of the Octagon families. Amelia Alderson Opie (1769–1853), the most celebrated surviving Alderson, had become a Quaker. Her London-based cousin, the lawyer Sir Edward Hall Alderson (1787–1857), was a firm churchman. His daughter Georgina, the future marchioness of Salisbury (d. 1899), nurtured a household of the strongest churchpeople.[31] By 1851 there were better known Unitarian Taylors and Martineaus in London and Birmingham than in Norwich; the musical

Edward Taylor (1784–1863), the Colegate ironmonger who so assiduously fostered the Triennial Festival, in fact lived in London from 1825.[32] None the less, nineteenth-century England's three best-known Unitarians, James Martineau, Florence Nightingale and Joseph Chamberlain, were as Norwich by birth or easily charted family association as its three best-known Quakers.[33] The linking of Bright and Chamberlain with Norwich, as indeed of Forster or Florence Nightingale, may seem far-fetched but it illustrates an important point. Local Dissenting networks had a national dimension quite as much as any more obviously established networks and sometimes more intensely so. Even so, the latter set the tone.

At the peak of the city's ecclesiastical society were the bishop and the dean.[34] The prebends and the canons residentiary (their effective successors as the Dean and Chapter Act of 1840 came slowly into operation) were its cream. The bishop was away from Norwich for long periods. In the House of Lords he trod a national stage. Four of the century's six bishops (Manners-Sutton, Bathurst, Stanley and Pelham) were aristocrats by birth or marriage, so were two of its four deans (Pellew and Goulburn), so were several of the chapter; others came from leading local landed, professional or commercial families.[35] They were also university men. Indeed there was long a particular association between the close and St Catharine's College, Cambridge. These were men of parts, like their bishops frequently absent, as cultivated men of the world had every right to be, but more than competent to manage the affairs of what later generations might regard as a sizeable property company and fully alert to their responsibility.

Nowhere in Norwich was the tensioned relationship betwen age and regeneration more evident than in the civilised, prosperous, characterful cathedral close, its society punctuated by those long rhythms of preferment which brought in bright young men, turning them as time passed into all the remaining ages of man, bringing into play all the accents of conservatism and intelligence, suitably nuanced by opportunity and responsibility. The nineteenth-century church, like the law, medicine, the universities, the civil service and the armed forces, the whole public world indeed, was administratively and vocationally up-ended. Its essence, however, was unchanged. Norwich shared fully in that miracle. The diocese that critics had once deliciously called the Dead See was now making waves.

In the nineteenth century its key periods were the episcopate of Edward Stanley (1837–49) and the deanship of Edward Goulburn (1866–89). The former was the Whig Bathurst's Liberal successor; the latter replaced Dean Pellew's offhand quarter-deck efficiency with the hyperactivity of a past headmaster of Rugby. The relationship between bishop and dean can be instructive, and that between the contrasting characters and churchmanship of Bishop Stanley and Dean Pellew, and Dean Goulburn and Bishop Pelham calls for further investigation. Under Stanley and Goulburn the cathedral became what it has remained, the parish church of an up-to-date diocese. Its fabric was restored and increasingly accessible. Its music and services were exemplary. Its practical influence was pervasive. The city's proliferating voluntary sector depended on the cathedral's stamp of approval. It is from this background, rippling through the city's other parish churches from St Peter Mancroft downward, that the rhythms of Dissent must be appreciated.

Those of Old Dissent are most instructively mediated through the Martineau family. In 1832 that indefatigably enquiring London Unitarian lawyer, Henry Crabb Robinson, whose East Anglian acquaintance was wide and who had known Norwich in the dangerous glory days of the 1790s, revisited the city. 'Went with Mottram to Octagon, Congregation very small – splendour of the old Octagon is gone – many families are dead or have left N. – but why no new ones?' [36]

Robinson clearly visited on a bad day, but his impression is exemplified by the careers of Norwich's most remarkable brother and sister, James and Harriet Martineau. James (1805–1900) passed his life far from Norwich after 1819. Harriet (1802–76) left the city in 1832, the year of Crabb Robinson's visit. James was a lifelong Unitarian, Harriet was not. James was, none the less, an increasingly unwilling Nonconformist. 'I greatly prefer the Church system', he stated in 1863, 'in spite of its obvious evils; and I believe that the real future of English Christianity is entrusted to it.' [37] Harriet, by contrast, could never escape the upbringing on which her autobiography cast so unblinking an eye. Her departure for London, marking the point at which Brougham's 'little deaf woman in Norwich' became 'the Queen of Modern Philanthropists', virtually coincided with her departure from Unitarianism. [38] From the financial security of an eminent middle age she recalled the provincialism of blue-stocking Norwich ladies whose manners and fashions were as painful as their French, cramming themselves 'from reviews and publishers lists in the morning to cut a figure in the evening, as conversant with all the literature of the day'. [39] Yet what better preparation could there have been for this inspired populariser of political economy?

Harriet's memories were naturally coloured by the circumstances which both released and necessitated her career as a professional writer: the financial collapse of her father in 1825–6, his death in 1827, and the family business's liquidation, debt free, in 1829. 'We had lost our gentility.' [40] An equally coloured retrospect allowed her to criticise the intellectual substructure of that generation's Unitarianism: 'it must have been from wonderful slovenliness of thought as well as ignorance that we could have taken Unitarianism to be Christianity in any genuine sense'.[41] Yet her writing career in fact began in Norwich with a contribution to the Unitarian *Monthly Repository*, followed by two tales which she preferred to forget and three prize essays sponsored by the Central Unitarian Association and aimed at the conversion of Catholics, Jews and Muslims.[42] Thus 'all was prepared for that which ensued – a withdrawal from the body through those regions of metaphysical fog in which most deserters from Unitarianism abide for the rest of their time'.[43]

But the personal links were less easily snapped, not least because of the towering influence on thinking people of her brother James. He mediated the transformation of British Unitarianism from its original biblicism to a 'religion of the free Spirit controlled by Reason and Conscience'.[44] The reach of his attraction may be gauged by the unexpected comment which Gladstone's death prompted from C. S. Horne, a leading young London Congregational minister who had married into another celebrated Norfolk and Norwich dissenting family: 'Dr Martineau alone remains who in greatness of intellect and character is akin to Gladstone.'[45]

James's influence on the Octagon remained considerable. Its congregation had adopted his *Common Prayer for Christian Worship* by 1866. He recommended J. D. Hirst Smyth to its pastorate in 1862 and his successor Alexander Gordon in 1872. By then the direct Martineau connection with the chapel had ceased. In 1839 two Martineaus had joined those who invited Joseph Crompton to the pastorate. The success of Crompton's ministry was reflected in the figures for census Sunday, but within a year of the census that success had resulted in secession led by the minister and with the last Octagon Martineau, James's cousin Fanny (1812–1877), among the seceders.[46]

Crompton's secession took him eventually into the Church of England. His predecessor, W. J. Bakewell, the minister whose services had so depressed Crabb Robinson in 1832, had also conformed, although that had proved to be a stage on his way to Rome.[47] Theirs were not insignificant pastorates, but it was their predecessor, Thomas Madge (minister 1811–25), who was the last Octagon minister to become a national force in his denomination, even if the historically-minded Alexander Gordon (minister 1872–77) was denominationally formidable.[48]

The Octagon's mid-century tensions may have been those common to any congregation at any time. They may also have reflected a more general unease discernible across the whole contemporary denominational spectrum. It ranged from the great disruption which split the church of Scotland apart in 1843 to the reform agitation which split Wesleyan

Methodism from 1849 and was so noticeable in Norwich. Congregationalists suffered less seismic but still well-publicised eruptions in the mid 1850s.
Issues of authority, practice, personality and belief combined explosively:
one unconsidered spark sufficed for an explosion. From February 1852 the
Octagon's Joseph Crompton was moving toward the Church of England.
Eight years earlier and from the opposite end of the theological spectrum
the Bazaar chapel's Robert Govett, formerly curate at St Stephen's, had
moved out of it. Govett's views on baptism had changed. That happened
frequently, but Govett was an unusual acquisition for Dissent in that he
was an Oxford man with an apparently assured future and an impeccable
pedigree: fellow of Worcester College and grandson of William Romaine.
He was also a prominent millennialist. His following was large, loyal but
personal. In 1854 he moved with them from the Bazaar chapel to Surrey
Road. The *Baptist Handbook* listed him as a Baptist minister but not his
people as a Baptist church.[49]

Norwich Baptists had other tensions. The minister of one of a county
town's leading dissenting congregations was from the first a man of mark
among his own people and he was expected to make his mark in what
was now his town. Called young, he would grow with his people unless
congregational dissatisfaction, or a more eligible opening elsewhere, ter-
minated his settlement. A successful pastorate consolidated his position
socially and opened out prospects for his family, especially if strengthened
by marriage with prominent chapel families. He may have been called into
a world of payment by results, rather than preferment or endowment,
but that world had its own gradations and expectations. The minister of
St Mary's Baptist church filled such a position.

Between 1849 and 1882 that minister was George Gould. He entered into
the inheritance of two outstandingly capable predecessors, Joseph Kinghorn (minister 1789–1832) and William Brock (minister 1833–48). Kinghorn
had built 'the fashionable watering place'; Brock had confirmed its dissenting pre-eminence. Brock's St Mary's was what the Octagon had been
in the previous century. It was under Kinghorn and Brock, for example,
that the leather-making Tillyards and Howletts and the mustard-making
Colmans became leading lights at St Mary's. Jeremiah Colman (d. 1851)
was sheriff 1845–46 and mayor 1846–47, with Brock as his chaplain; James
(d. 1854), Jeremiah's nephew, was sheriff 1849–50. They were the founding
Js of J. and J. Colman. Kinghorn and Brock had arrived young but not
quite untried. They were the intelligent, self-improved products of a craft-
cum-trade background, expert communicators and shrewd operators with
a keen political sense. They were at once solid and radical. Their names
appeared naturally as promoters of the City Mission, the Bible Society and

overseas missions and as opponents of corruption or unjustified privilege, especially if disguised as church rate. Kinghorn's ministry linked the fall of the Bastille to the passing of the Great Reform Act. He hailed both with enthusiasm. Brock's ministry embraced Free Trade and the arrival of the railways. The political horizons of both men naturally encompassed West-minster. The leading dissenting MP, the Unitarian William Smith, in Parliament almost continuously between 1784 and 1830, was one of Nor-wich's representatives from 1802, and his son Benjamin Smith likewise from 1837 to 1847, but from 1847 the dissenting emphasis shifted with the election of the Baptist contracting impresario, Samuel Morton Peto. Indeed it was Peto who lured William Brock from Norwich to London where, as minister of Bloomsbury chapel, with Petos and Havelocks in his pews, joined by Colmans when in town, he entered into his long prime.[50]

George Gould was an ideal successor, active, young, yet already a vet-eran of church rate controversy, a man of forensic and executive skills and of broad horizons. Under him the Tillyards, Howletts and George White turned their leather business into a nationally known shoe business, the timber Jewsons first made their mark, and the Colmans spread like the green bay tree. Gould's was, in fact, in almost every respect a pattern-book pastorate. He became president of the Baptist Union in 1879; his family steadily made its way locally and nationally in the older professions.[51]

Yet, although St Mary's radiated life and influence, its membership stalled for some years and its minister's energies were diverted by a law suit. The St Mary's chapel case hinged on the right of Baptists to determine their conditions of communion: was their table (and membership) to be open only to baptised believers? The St Mary's trust deed was on the face of it closed, but it was as yet untested. The matter had been coming inex-orably to the fore, reverberating in the denomination and confirming the growing division, especially marked in much of East Anglia, between strict and open Baptists.[52] Kinghorn and Brock, the former a closed but the lat-ter an open communionist, had avoided the issue. Gould confronted it. He was an open communionist. The tensions were profound. It was Gould's successor, J. H. Shakespeare (minister 1883–98), yet another young man in the now traditional mould, who truly took St Mary's into the age of the institutional church and the nonconformist conscience, upending its inte-rior accordingly and launching a career which took him to the general secretaryship of the Baptist Union and a briefly perilous eminence as rep-resentative national Free Churchman.[53] And it was Shakespeare's successor, Thomas Phillips (minister 1900–5), who completed an elegant encircling of history when he too left Norwich for London, to turn Brock's Bloomsbury into a Central Baptist church and mission.[54]

By then, however, the leadership in Norwich nonconformity had passed to the Congregationalists. For the first half of the nineteenth century Old Meeting and Prince's Street complemented each other. Andrew Reed, Old Meeting's minister in 1851, was in his way as pattern-book as George Gould: son of a famous London minister, brother of an up-and-coming London businessman and politician, and appropriately vocal on public platforms, Reed sustained Old Meeting's reputation for radical sociability.[55] A prime agent in this was the chapel's book club, 'a first-class assembly of leading men – lawyers, doctors, manufacturers – men of wealth and intelligence, who, besides uniting to circulate valuable and expensive books, held also a circulating dinner'. Its members, or so Reed recalled, 'were mostly Con- servative Liberals, and as we belonged to the advanced guard of public opinion, there were often sturdy disputes on criticism and politics. There was always, however, a gentlemanly restraint and good humour which prevented offence'.[56]

Such lightning conductors allowed life to proceed in the midst of much relished controversy. That is the significance of J. J. Gurney's account of the funeral at Old Meeting in May 1845 of his head clerk, H. J. Balls, 'my long respected friend and Christian brother'. Gurney went to it with his son:

John Alexander conducted the 'service', at the Old Independent Meeting House. I went in with my hat on; quietly kept my seat until he had finished, and then rose and bore my testimony to his truly Christian character. The large assembly of his friends and neighbours seemed much affected. He was buried in the 'Rosary'. There was a precious solemnity to be felt at the grave. I was engaged beside it in vocal thanksgiving and prayer.[57]

It would, of course, have been hard to gainsay a Gurney in Norwich, but this Congregational funeral, moving from Old Meeting to that evocative new symbol of how human affairs should be regulated – a public cemetery, the Rosary – so powerfully flavoured by the accents of Friends' Meeting, unites several layers of religious experience. John Alexander, who con- ducted that service in Andrew Reed's chapel, was minister at Prince's Street.

That cause began as a secession from Lady Huntingdon's Tabernacle, thanks to the high-handedness of its trustees. The Tabernacle never really recovered but Prince's Street flowered under two legendary pastorates, those of John Alexander (minister 1819–66) and George Barrett (minister 1866–1911). Like Kinghorn, Brock and Gould, so Alexander and Barrett were cast in a similar mould adapted to their generation:

There was the Revd. John Alexander, with an overflowing audience on the Sunday and an active vitality all the week, now dining at the Palace with the Bishop, or breakfasting at Earlham with the Gurneys, now meeting on terms of equality the literati of the place ... now visiting the afflicted and the destitute ...[58]

It was a matter of pride for local dissenters, stiffened with a nice ecclesiological sense, that Norwich had two bishops, one of them Stanley and the other Alexander, but something of the latter's standing is conveyed by the autograph book kept by his wife from 1827: in addition to the signatures of dissenting pulpiteers and famous missionaries, there are those of Baptist Noel (the aristocratic seceder from the Church of England), Elizabeth Fry, William Wilberforce, Fowell Buxton, J. J. Gurney, Amelia Opie and Edward Bickersteth.[59]

George Barrett's standing was that of a younger, more settled generation (Plate 63). The Barretts were firmly embedded in a cousinhoood of upwardly mobile dissenters. Missionaries, ministers and office-holders proliferated. Barrett's father was a minister; three aunts married ministers, a brother was a minister, and so was a brother-in-law. Barrett himself was a force on the platforms and in the committee rooms of the Congregational Union. But another brother was an academic knight (and a founder of the Society for Psychical Research); a nephew-in-law was a manufacturing knight; and a son-in-law was a medical knight.[60] When he came to Prince's Street, Barrett could claim a useful connexion with leading families at St Mary's: Josiah Fletcher (1806–1876), who had been baptised by John Kinghorn and whose firm printed the *Norfolk News*, was his mother's first cousin.[61] Another connexion shows the circular reach of the chapel world.

In the late 1860s George Barrett was newly arrived in Norwich, his younger brother William was working in London under Tyndall at the Royal Institution, and their mother, widowed in Pimlico, took in two lodgers, the Asquith brothers, William Willans and Herbert Henry.[62] They were Yorkshire boys whose father had died and whose uncles were paying for their education at the City of London School. One of those uncles had married, like Andrew Reed, into the Leeds 'Bainesocracy', a family of newspaper proprietors and members of parliament, and another uncle was to marry, twice over, into the Cozens-Hardy family of Letheringsett. Those marriages made him a brother-in-law of J. J. Colman and they made his nephews, of whose academic prowess and professional potential there could be no doubt, objects of increasing interest to an extended cousinhood.[63] It was at this time that Colman transferred his allegiance from the Baptists of St Mary's to the Congregationalists of Prince's Street, persuaded by love for his wife, Caroline Cozens-Hardy (reared a Methodist), and by friendship for its minister, George Barrett. It was at this time too that

Colman became a Norwich MP, suceeding to the mantle of William Smith and Samuel Morton Peto as a representative power on the back benches, commanding East Anglia's Liberalism and commerce, announcing its non-conformity. The leading edge of a distinctive culture was in process of reformation, its Unitarian and Quaker shading giving way to a mingling of Baptists, Congregationalists and Free Methodists, aptly symbolised by Colman's purchase in 1878 of Carrow abbey, for this had been a Martineau property since 1811, although tenanted since 1861 by Colman's occasional parliamentary running mate, the radical war horse J. H. Tillett.[64]

There were other such representative occasions. In November 1886 the Colmans were at a ball in Sandringham, followed by Bishop Pelham's musical At Home ('Wonders never cease! I can't fancy the solemn Bishop having such an entertainment') and then by Miss von Finkelstein's lecture on Palestine.[65] The crown of such eclectic occasions came a few years later when Gladstone visited Norfolk for a series of grand set speeches. The visit in May 1890 entered family lore. Gladstone stayed at The Clyffe, the Colmans' seaside house. While the statesman rested before an evening meeting, local notables gathered for tea, the bishop, the dean, and J. H. Shakespeare from St Mary's, rehearsing points which they wished to put to the great man and so straining the patience of Mrs Colman and Mrs Gladstone that the latter brought matters to a climax with: 'There's One above who can settle all these difficulties for us; he will be down directly!'[66] That story bears all the signs of frequent retelling and it has been told of Mrs Gladstone on other occasions.

Gladstone took care to balance church with chapel. In Norwich he visited the cathedral 'conducted by the Dean and experts'. At Yarmouth he 'Saw the noteworthy Church – School etc. The clergy very kind'. He worshipped in Lowestoft's parish church and on his first evening (spent with the Birkbecks at Stoke Holy Cross, so the once Quaker and still Liberal Gurney connexion was carefully cultivated) he 'Dined within the Old Abbey of Carrow'. For this was also Colman country. For three of their four Norfolk nights 'Mr Colman's charming sea place' at Corton was the Gladstones' home. There Gladstone drove, read, wrote letters, 'Saw Prof. Stuart' and 'Mr Shakespeare', had long talks with Lord John Hervey who was that now rare bird, an aristocratic military Whig. Then he walked ('conversation with Rev. Mr Barrett'), noting 'Large party: the only complaint'.[67] That surely locates 'the One above'.

With such members and such a minister Prince's Street must have seemed impregnable. No wonder, when the time came, it held a service in Gladstone's memory. Under Barrett its membership grew from 288 to 840, combining all the agencies of an aggressively missionary community with the interlinked cousinhoods of a prosperously rooted society.[68] Norwich, however, was noted for low wages. An expanding electorate encouraged the transition from radical Liberalism to Labour. A church membership of over 800 by 1900 reflected such tensions but suggested that they could be contained.

A pattern was thus set for much of the twentieth century: central churches with large memberships and strong ministries, a sensible degree of church relocation or of church planting, and considerable public spirit. Baptists and Congregationalists were level-pegging. At the turn of the century there were some 1500 Congregational church members in Norwich; at the outbreak of the Second World War there were around 1400, compared with 1300 and 1200 Baptists respectively. Sunday school figures had been less well sustained: Congregational Sunday scholars had dropped from 2600 to 1200 and Baptist ones from 2200 to 1150.[69] The Baptist churches at Unthank Road (1875) and Silver Road (1911) were old causes which had moved out; only that on Dereham Road (1890) was new. By contrast the Congregational churches at Chapel-in-Field (1858), Magdalen Road (1893), and Jessopp Road (1932) were new; Old Meeting, like Prince's Street, remained on its original site. In the light of retrospect these figures might suggest ageing memberships as well as changing patterns of Christian nurture, but they also reflect a remarkable stability.

Norwich Methodism shared in this. Its Free Methodists consolidated and expanded, with substantial new buildings on Chapelfield Road (1881) and Rosebery Road (1908). So did the Primitive Methodists, their consolidation best marked by Queen's Road (1872), which housed the Primitive Methodist Conference in 1892 and 1912, and Scott Memorial, Thorpe Road (1902). By the 1890s the Wesleyans too had not so much consolidated as recovered: hence St Peter's, Park Lane (1895) and Sprowston Road (1909). With the union in 1932 of Wesleyan, Primitive and United (as the Free Methodists had been since 1907), Methodists there developed a cumulative opportunity for reorganisation, subject to the strains of sentiment and personality but marked in that first decade by one of twentieth-century Norwich's most architecturally striking chapels, Cecil Yelf's church at Mile Cross (1934), and by the third Methodist St Peter's (1939).

The familial continuities were certainly marked. At St Mary's there were Jewsons in membership throughout the twentieth century. At Prince's Street for much of the century there were wholesale provision Copemans and *Eastern Daily Press* Copemans, architect Boardmans and solicitor Cozens-Hardys, all of them connected with each other and with the Jewsons too. There were also social, political and evangelistic continuities.

Thus Prince's Street had its missionary martyr, Oliver Tomkins, one of eight brothers 'actively engaged in the service of Christ'. The Tomkinses were related by marriage to the Copemans and a branch of the Colmans. J. S. Tomkins was secretary of the new church on Magdalen Road; Leo Tomkins was to go out to China; and Oliver Tomkins, in membership at Prince's Street since 1890, was ordained by Barrett to the mission field in New Guinea. That was in autumn 1899. In 1901 he was killed by head-hunters. Prince's Street was packed for his memorial service: Sullivan, Mendelssohn, Beethoven and Stainer, and the hymn, 'The Son of God Goes Forth to War'. Barrett preached from the Book of Revelation: 'May God kindle in some heart tonight the greatest of all ambitions – the ambition to be fellow labourers with Christ in the redemption of the world.'[70]

Ethel Mary Colman (1863–1948), the second of J. J. Colman's four daughters, was a director of the missionary society which sent Tomkins out to New Guinea. She was one of the first women deacons at Prince's Street, and thus one of the first in any Congregational church. She was also England's first female lord mayor, pointing out proudly to her youngest uncle that she was Norwich's eighth Liberal lord mayor, and that six of the eight had been nonconformist deacons: 'This is not a bad record is it? for our Churches and the part they play in civic life'. Since Ethel's lady mayoress was her younger sister Helen Caroline, and her elder sister, Laura Stuart, had briefly been a city councillor, it is clear that Norwich's twentieth-century Nonconformist women were fully the equal of their celebrated eighteenth- and nineteenth-century predecessors.[71]

Ethel Colman's father and great-uncle had also been mayors of Norwich; she followed a loyally Liberal tradition. Dorothy Jewson (1884–1964) was altogether more radical. She left Liberalism for Socialism and the Baptists for the Society of Friends. She was a suffragette, a trade union organiser, an advocate of birth control and a sociologist in the Rowntree mould, author of *The Destitute of Norwich and How They Live* (1913) and *Socialists and the Family* (1926). She did not become lord mayor, but she served on the city council from 1927 to 1936, and she was Labour MP for Norwich in 1923–4. Thus, like Ethel Colman, she scored a first. Miss Jewson was the first Girtonian MP in the year that Miss Colman was the first woman lord mayor.[72]

St Mary's maintained its parliamentary links for rather longer than Prince's Street. Sir George White, its most prominent Edwardian member, was Liberal MP for North West Norfolk from 1900 to 1912; Sir Geoffrey Shakespeare, son of J. H. Shakespeare, was Liberal and Liberal National MP for Norwich from 1929 to 1945; and Percy Jewson (1881–1962), Dorothy's cousin and the church's most prominent mid-century member, served as Liberal National Member for Yarmouth from 1941 to 1945.[73]

Prince's Street and St Mary's maintained their influence for at least the quarter century following the Second World War. At the former, Sydney Myers (minister 1942–70) was every inch a successor to Alexander and Barrett: he served on the city's education, library and youth service committees, and on the panel which prepared the first religious syllabus for Norwich schools; he helped found the Norwich Marriage Guidance Council and the Norwich Council of Churches; he wrote 'Free Church Notes' for the local press, and he too was not to be enticed from Norfolk.[74] At St Mary's it was Gilbert Laws (minister 1928–45) who most aptly filled the mantle of Brock, Gould and Shakespeare as a force in Norwich and an influence in national and international Baptist councils.[75] Indeed, the years following the Second World War saw an Indian summer for the city's Free Churches, with a fresh manufacturing name, this time Methodist, to be added to Norvic shoes, Jewson's timber and Colman's mustard: Mackintosh.

In 1932 Sir Harold Mackintosh of Halifax purchased A. J. Caley & Son, the Norwich chocolate makers.[76] Fifteen years later he moved from Yorkshire to Norfolk, and Norwich became his company headquarters. Shortly afterwards he was ennobled for his work for National Savings. Mackintosh was reared in the Methodist New Connexion (which united with the Free Methodists in 1907). In Norwich he worshipped at the recently built St Peter's Methodist church. He was to Methodists what J. J. Colman had been to Baptists and Congregationalists. Like Colman he bred cattle and collected 'Norwich School' pictures, and like Colman he was a generous supporter of the YMCA. In one other respect he filled Colman shoes: the man for whom 'the Sunday School was my university' was an energetic promoter of the University of East Anglia. He died shortly before he could be installed as its first chancellor.[77]

For most hearers, however, the prime accent remained that of the national church and in Norwich the physical dominance of its cathedral remained inescapable. Its personnel, like its fabric, adapted seamlessly to a more ecumenical age, welcoming tourists as much as the worshippers which some of them became. Its twentieth-century bishops and deans were more numerous than their nineteenth-century predecessors and they were generally less socially elevated.[78] More significantly, later deans, notably Webster (1970–78) and Edwards (1978–82), were scholarly men of affairs in the ecumenical world, to the fore in the British Council of Churches' glory days. Alan Webster had been fired in Bishop Hunter's wartime Sheffield crucible of social relevance and industrial mission. David Edwards's apprenticeship was with the Student Christian Movement in its prime before its sudden implosion; he became the Church of England's most versatile chronicler.[79] In their time the cathedral became socially and liturgically adventurous. It was the city's representative church.

The real marks of twentieth-century change, however, can be most representatively seen in four case studies. The first is pin-pointed by Percy Lubbock, driving as a boy into Norwich from Earlham and

> confounded by a large and splendid church, scrupulously Gothic ... not an ordinary church, it was a Roman Catholic Cathedral; and I looked at it, I well remember, with a shade of meek and mournful regret, puzzled and interested, wondering at so vast a monument of perversity and yet compelled to admire its insolence. But we scarcely spoke of it, the exotic upstart – we looked and passed: it could by no manner of means be regarded as part of our Norwich, and on the whole we ignored its intrusion.[80]

St John the Baptist was certainly no ordinary church. Begun by George Gilbert Scott in 1882, in the lengthening wake of the First Vatican Council and shortly after his conversion to Catholicism, and completed by John Oldrid Scott in 1910, it owed more to ducal *pietas* than pressing need.[81] It was, in fact, the grandest of the city's Strangers' churches, conceived by the fifteenth duke of Norfolk 'When shortly after my most happy marriage I wished to build a church as a thank-offering to God'. The duke chose 'the pure and noble Early English style' to distinguish his church from the cathedral, 'one of the noblest examples of the grand Norman architecture', and from the 'display of beautiful Perpendicular churches absolutely unmatched for the almost prodigal generosity which has scattered them about your streets in ever bewildering multiplicity'.[82] It was a commandingly conservative building, quite as satisfyingly dull as pious triumphalism should be, but it was not a cathedral. That status did not come until 1976, when English Catholicism bore a greatly changed relationship to the other English churches and Alan Clark, first bishop of the new Catholic diocese of East Anglia, and a veteran of the Second Vatican Council, was set in a new Catholic mould.[83]

In size, conception, and patronage, Norwich's Catholic cathedral stands apart. The other three examples are also set apart, yet interlinked. Christian Science is not in the Christian mainstream. It is an American sect notable for some fine architecture and some interesting converts. A society was formed in Norwich in 1911, followed by a church of twenty-nine members in 1921. Their building was opened in Recorder Road in September 1934. It was small but perfectly formed, a late Arts and Crafts masterpiece in streamlined Gothic, full of vernacular touches, most of them more Sussex than Norfolk, deft with unobtrusive symbol and far churchier than the general run of Churches of Christ Scientist (Plate 64).

There was good reason for this. The moving light in the building was Mrs Herbert Jewson, whose husband was an uncle of Percy and Dorothy Jewson. Jessie Jewson was a Leicester Congregationalist whose family, the Hewitts, were to the *Leicester Mercury* what the Copemans were to the *Eastern Daily Press*. In Norwich she became a Christian Scientist. Her architect was her brother-in-law, H. G. Ibberson of Hunstanton, who was both a Jewson and a Hewitt connexion.[84] Thus was another Strangers' church rooted in Norwich, the more so indeed when it was taken over, with minimal adaptation, by Norwich's Greek Orthodox community in 1997.

Norwich's Presbyterian church was also a Strangers' church.[85] The Presbyterian Church of England was formed in 1876 from two largely nineteenth-century branches of Presbyterianism. It owed both strength and accent to incomers from Ireland, Scotland and Wales, so its presence in English towns was natural. Its sole Norfolk congregation was in Norwich, formed in 1867 largely by families of Scottish credit drapers quickly supplemented by the inevitable professionals and then by a group of farming families who came to Norfolk between the wars. It was therefore a scattered congregation which met in its solid town-centre church in Theatre Street. Its membership peaked at 272 in 1907 but declined thereafter to 147 in 1947. When it was reduced to a shell in the air raids of June 1942, its future was clearly in doubt.

The impact of the Second World War on British churches included three obvious yet easily overlooked factors: war-damaged or destroyed church buildings enabled their congregations to start afresh, subject to two constraints. The first was imposed by the War Damage Commission, the second by the determination of local authorities to replan their town centres. Seldom can such fresh starts have been so determined by external regulation. Norwich was dramatically hit and the case of its Presbyterians may stand for many. Theatre Street was in the heart of the city council's plans for urban regeneration. Late in July 1945 the minister-in-charge wrote in alarm to Prince's Street's Sydney Myers: 'To judge by the published "City Plan", the site of this church is obliterated, and in its place appears a "Parking Place" ... It appears now that we are to be dispossessed.' But that is not quite how things turned out. Thanks to deftly cultivated relationships with the city engineer and the War Damage Commission's regional manager in Cambridge, the derelict 600-seater in Theatre Street was replaced by an up-to-the mark 250-seater on Unthank Road's city end. Its stonelaying took place in October 1954, in the presence of the lord mayor, the sheriff and the dean (Plate 65).

The new Trinity Church was as artful a little masterpiece as the Christian Science church, now twenty years old, in Recorder Road. It too was domesticated by vernacular touches, user-friendly for a scattered county congregation, yet dignified by as much symbol as Presbyterians could be persuaded to take. It too was for Strangers threaded into an ancient community. Its building committee of three makes that clear: one was the lord mayor's secretary, an indispensable figure who knew everybody and wrote the perfect letter; the second was a senior figure on the sales and publicity side of Caley Mackintosh – he was the stage Scotsman, president of the Burns Federation in 1952; the third was partner in a leading firm of quantity surveyors. If the second knew what he did not want, the third knew what could be done. There was, of course, the minister, Cameron Joyce, who settled in 1946. He had been an army chaplain, mentioned in despatches. He was the man who made the building work.

There was also the architect, Bernard Feilden, who had joined Edward Boardman & Son, then into its third Boardman generation, in 1950. The Boardman firm had designed the original church in Theatre Street. They had also designed the Baptist church in Unthank Road (stone laid by J. J. Colman), which had been vacated in 1941, used as a store by Caley Mackintosh, and offered to the displaced Presbyterians. Feilden was not a partner in the Boardman firm, but Trinity was to be his project and the firm allowed him to complete it even though he had by then set up on his own. The church was thus at once another Boardman church and the first Feilden one. Few churches can have been more suggestively sited than Presbyterian Trinity in the wingspan of Catholic St John, its particular allegiance affirmed by the Presbyterian symbols of the burning bush and the open Bible framed in palm leaves, and its overarching allegiance affirmed (against the better judgment of older members) by a Portland stone cross and a detached tower. Locals liked to see Trinity's tower as an obeisance to St Peter Mancroft and St John Maddermarket. Outsiders were convinced that it showed Swedish influence. The architect, however, had something else in mind: 'I was alluding to the early Christian Church of St. Appolinari in Nuovo near Ravenna, which I had seen during the war.'[86] Church and architect prospered. By 1967 Trinity had 380 members (and four of its elders were women). By 1967 Feilden was architect to Norwich cathedral and surveyor to York minster. His ecclesiastical portfolio would include work at St Paul's cathedral.[87] Five years later Trinity, like Prince's Street but unlike Old Meeting, became part of the United Reformed Church, thus healing an historic ecclesiological division.

The most dramatic casualty of wartime Norwich was St Mary's Baptist church. This provides my fourth example. The interior of St Mary's had been remodelled in 1886 for J. H. Shakespeare by Edward Boardman, senior, the founder of the firm and a deacon at Prince's Street. Since his son and partner, Edward T. Boardman, married a daughter of J. J. Colman, and his daughter Ethel married Percy Jewson, Boardman was a sensible as well as a proper choice. On Sunday 10 September 1939 the church's interior was seriously damaged by fire. War had been declared but this was not war damage and a year later an 'improved copy of the old' had reopened (Plate 66).[88] That copy was destroyed twenty-one months later by enemy action. Its rebuilding took ten years.

The constraints were identical to those endured by Trinity, but Gilbert Laws, St Mary's minister, Percy Jewson, his senior deacon, and Charles Jewson, his church secretary, who was Percy's son and Gilbert's son-in-law, were masterful men. Charles would be lord mayor in 1965–6; Percy had been lord mayor in 1934–5, and was now MP for Great Yarmouth. He could barely contain his frustration:

> To me it is a distressing thing – to use no stronger adjective – that a nomi-nally Christian country refuses to allow the rebuilding of the House of God and the premises essential for the work of the church. No wonder that our juvenile courts are hard-worked and our prisons crowded to overflowing. I cannot help thinking that if we had with us today J. H. Shakespeare or Dr Clifford they would by now have carried the fiery cross through the country to arouse the Christian community to indignant protest. Perhaps the hour may yet bring the man.[89]

That was old-fashioned rhetoric harking back to passive resistance and the Liberal landslide of 1906. The new St Mary's was traditional without being old-fashioned. Utility was the keynote of its multi-purpose hall, coffee-tiled to waist height to facilitate cleaning, with space for forty cycles, room too for 'badminton, plays, and lunches', and a deacons' vestry com-fortably seated and carpeted. The church itself took large congregations for granted. It was wide, lofty and light. Its heating was controlled by thermo-stats, its lighting was 'shadowless and partly concealed', its cleaning claimed to be labour saving, its planning took account of 'the sociable Nonconformist habit of standing about for a gossip after services'. The new St Mary's was quite unlike the old and yet, like the old, it was approached through a portico and, although its memorial tablets had been shattered beyond repair, the three tall windows which fronted St Mary's contained three coats of arms, spanning three centuries, one for the Wilkins, one for the Colmans, and one for the Jewsons.[90] As with Recorder Road's Christ-ian Scientists and Trinity's Presbyterians, the key to the building's interpretation was turned by its architect, Stanley Wearing.

Wearing had been a member of the Unthank Road Baptist church, where his brother-in-law had been minister. He transferred to St Mary's in

1941. In one sense he too was a Stranger, since his had been a Cotswold and midland formation. Chance had brought him to East Anglia. There he made his clubbable and professional mark as an efficient and competitive architect in the Arts and Crafts tradition. He brought the Georgian revival to Norfolk and Norwich; and in the 1940s this Baptist visited every one of Norfolk's 650 parish churches in his work for the National Buildings Record. He exemplified the tradition.[91]

St Mary's was to have been rebuilt in three stages. Only two were completed. From the 1980s the threat of numerical decline which had haunted church leaders since the religious census of 1851 became inescapable reality. In 1967, when Trinity Presbyterian church claimed 380 members, Prince's Street had 541, St Mary's had 468, Old Meeting had fifty-eight. In 2002 Trinity and Prince's Street, both now United Reformed, had 159 and 138 members respectively, St Mary's had 121 (Dereham Road Baptist church had 159), and Old Meeting, now part of the Congregational Federation, had six, worshipping on the second Sunday afternoon of each month. And the national press seized happily on a nugget revealed by the Census for 2001.[92]

For the first time since 1851 an official census had provided evidence of religious affiliation. In Norwich 27.8 per cent of respondents claimed to have 'no religion'. That was a national record.[93] But what did it mean? One could be a Christian and yet deny any denominational 'religious affiliation'. Perhaps the Norwich respondents were being more precise as well as more honest than most. Certainly their response concentrated churchly minds as challengingly as their ancestors' response in 1851. However reduced the percentages, the variety remained. And there were strategies still to be spun.

18

Sport and Games

Roger Munting

It would be very hard to show that the increasing sobriety of Norwich ... does not owe something to this new habit of watching football.

C. B. Hawkins, *Norwich: A Social Study*, 1910[1]

For long before the nineteenth century 'sport' and 'games' had images far removed from those we associate with them today. Sport frequently involved blood letting, of animals (in baiting, cock fighting, dog fights, hunting, shooting and fishing) or of men, and sometimes women, in prizefights. 'Games' conjure an image of disorder and mayhem, of violent village football, broken bones and drunkenness. Like many such images this is oversimplified. What to our modern eyes were crude and violent contests did take place, though they were not always quite as disordered as they might appear. There were also gentler pastimes, like bowls. But games as yet had no necessary association with healthy pursuit and the creation of good character; nearly all involved gambling. By the late Victorian period, however, games had not only developed into recognisable modern forms, with rules and governing bodies (the Football Association was set up in 1863, the Rugby Football Union in 1871, the Amateur Athletics Association in 1881, generally accepted rules for hockey by 1865, Queensbury rules for boxing from 1867), but they were also seen as valuable for engendering team spirit and mental and physical health, and as such were associated with the qualities of British character. It is reasonable to claim that in general modern organised sport was invented in Victorian and Edwardian Britain.[2]

There was, of course, no sudden break; traditional pastimes only gradually gave way to modern forms. Some, like coarse fishing, never did. In other cases (cricket, horse racing, golf provide examples) the organisation and rules were in place well before the age of Victoria. In the early nineteenth century public, or rather political, opinion became less tolerant of cruel practices for pleasure. The Society for the Prevention of Cruelty to

Animals was formed in 1824. The Cruelty to Animals Act of 1835, intended to put an end to such sports as baiting and cock and dog fighting, was testament to their efforts. There were other influences at work also. Many observers have noted the growing commercialisation of games (above all professional football) later in the nineteenth century. We should be wary, however, of seeing this as a new development. Commercial interest had long been evident. Sir John Plumb wrote of the eighteenth century as the commercial age of sport; publicans, for example, promoted games and contests (cock fights, fist fights, horse races) to attract custom; 'gentlemen' patronised them as a betting medium. It was the norm to compete for a prize, in cash or favours; some particularly successful sportsmen, such as jockeys and cricketers, might be retained by patrons. The 'gentleman amateur' was the creation of the Victorian age. None the less the later decades of the nineteenth century did witness a growth in the market for spectator sports, as real incomes rose and working hours slowly began to contract.[3]

There is also evidence of some paternalism – a sense of a need for public provision of recreation, if only to give useful occupation to otherwise idle hands and minds. Games, previously seen as occasions of disorder, could therefore be made orderly and absorbed into the social fabric. Some moral reformers, such as Charles Kingsley, went further in seeing sport and games as a way of bringing social classes together and thereby reducing potential conflicts. Many in positions of influence thus came to regard games not as a waste of time but as valuable in themselves. The idea of a 'healthy mind in a healthy body' grew in mid-Victorian Britain and was especially associated with the privileged public schools. Whereas in the early nineteenth century physical exertion was associated with manual labour and was not a pursuit of members of the middle or upper classes, around 1850 games had come to be seen as healthy, and prowess at sport as conferring social esteem. The pursuit of pleasure and profit, sport as entertainment (be it watching or playing) and games as healthy exercise were to characterise popular sport thereafter. Thus we can detect various influences on the pattern of sport and leisure which might readily fall under three heads: *custom* – the carry over of traditional practice; *commerce* – the ever present lure of money, particularly evident in the spectator sports; and a sense of 'paternalism' in the social provision of recreational facilities, often by local *councils* but also by private institutions. These were not mutually exclusive factors, nor were they sequential, though from time to time they exerted differing influence. Together they led to changes in the perception and pursuit of sport over the last two hundred years. Such gradual changes were associated with the process of industrialisation and urbanisation. As Norwich grew relatively slowly in the nineteenth century, it might therefore be expected that changes in its sporting culture would be similarly constrained. Some traditions were strong in Norwich, but the city was by no means isolated from broader developments.

Traditions of what we now regard as cruel sports were robust. The baiting of bulls, for instance, was well known and apparently popular in Norwich into the nineteenth century. One report of 1815 refers to a bull that had been frequently baited; 'but no dog has yet been found that can pin him down'.[4] Cockfighting was more popular and regular. A good many pubs in the city had cockpits (The White Swan, in the parish of St Peter Mancroft and The Lobster, in that of St John Maddermaket being particularly well known). The breeders and feeders of fighting cocks enjoyed high esteem and the birds often represented the city or county against others. The last report of a cockfight in the city was in 1823, though they might well have continued surreptitiously.[5] But it was probably for prize fighting that Norwich came to be especially known, again often linked to pubs. The Green Dragon in Little London Street and The Sun and Anchor in Lobster Lane were especially prominent in the sport.[6] The city had its own pugilistic club early in the century. Although gentry patronage began to fade in the 1820s, great public interest in these brutal encounters was maintained in the city and surroundings. Crowds numbering thousands, male and female, were often reported. Upwards of five thousand were said to have been present to watch a fight over seventy-two rounds at Kirby Park in 1819. Serious injury or deaths were not infrequent. In 1822 a weaver, Purdy, died after a fight with Grint, a dyer, at Bishop's bridge. Grint was tried (on what charge is not known) and sentenced to three months. Such was the popularity of these fights that they were sometimes relocated at the last minute to prevent intervention by magistrates. Where they did interfere it met with hostility. In 1826 a fight was prevented in Surlingham by magistrates, but 'the parish constable at Bramerton was almost killed attempting to stop it'.[7] As late as 1852 the police were put to flight by the mob in Bungay when they tried to stop a prize fight, though the participants were subsequently committed for trial. These were clearly the death throes of organised prize fights. In 1879 a contest with gloves (one of the precepts of the Queensbury rules) was staged at Norwich Corn Hall, between Walter Emms and Arthur Shaw. But even they and their seconds were summoned for unlawful assembly and bound over to keep the peace.[8]

Traditional or 'folk' football games have often been regarded as unruly and uncontrolled mayhem. The name of 'camping' (or camp football), for such a team game, persisted longer in East Anglia than elsewhere. The game was sometimes, but not essentially, accompanied by violence. It can be dated at least from the fourteenth century and persisted into the nine-teenth. It is also evident that by the eighteenth century there were established rules (though they varied in detail across time and space) and set team sizes – frequently about ten, though sometimes more. Games might, but would not necessarily, allow rough play, so called 'boxing camping', including hacking, 'wrestling' or 'pugilism', according to con-temporary reports. One match between Norfolk and Suffolk was said to have resulted in nine deaths![9] Games were regular and frequent; fields or 'closes' were either set aside for the play or became associated with the game through custom and practice.[10] In 1472 the rector of Swaffham had bequeathed a field adjoining the churchyard known as 'camping close'.[11] Thus the games had a 'pitch' which might be roped off, with marked goals; they lasted a set time (thirty minutes was common) or until an agreed number of goals had been scored. The ball could be kicked or passed by hand with the object of being thrown through the opposing goal. These were clearly well organised contests.

Because the game allowed handling the ball, parallels have been drawn less with soccer than with rugby; it is difficult, however, to see any con-tinuity with modern forms of the game. Camp football died out early in the nineteenth century. It has been suggested that there was a revival after the Napoleonic wars, implying that it was already disappearing.[12] The *Nor-folk Annals* record a 'boxing' camping match in 1818 at Kirby Cane, 'the first thorough boxing camping match that has taken place for the last thirty-five years'.[13] The last such record was of a match at Norwich cricket ground in 1831, which was said to have been a generally disappointing affair, displaying little skill. Employees of Colmans, when the works were based in Stoke Holy Cross, also played camp football about this time.[14] There is a distinct break before the first mention of association football in the city – in 1868 – when a Norwich football club was formed, to play at Newmarket Road. Since it is unlikely that anyone playing in the 1830s would be ready to resume thirty years later, this marks a new develop-ment, the establishment of a new game. It is not clear, though, how close this was to modern soccer; some variations on the official rules appear to have been followed locally. The formation of the County Football Asso-ciation in 1881 removed any ambiguity. Subsequently the signs are that the game quickly became popular with numerous players in the area. The distinctive handling game was served by the Norwich rugby club, which was set up in 1885. There was therefore a readiness to take part in team games with some characteristics and skills similar to traditional forms of football.

Cricket, on the other hand, displays clear continuity. The game had agreed rules and a managing body (the MCC from 1787) before the nine-teenth century, but it came to exemplify the moral values of Victorian England. It first appeared in the south-eastern counties. The first mention of 'cricket' was in early seventeenth-century Kent, though there were vari-ations elsewhere; 'bandy wicket' in East Anglia for instance. Cricket was a rural game that came to be patronised by the well-to-do, largely as a gam-bling medium (rules were first agreed to prevent gambling disputes), but the governing body sought to squeeze out gambling in the nineteenth cen-tury. The incentive associated with the wager, however, led gentlemen patrons to employ the best players as professionals to boost their fortunes. In 1813 a team of gentlemen of Bungay objected to Norwich gentlemen fielding three 'expert cricketers' – professionals – in a match at Prussia Gardens. Cricketers were amongst the first professional sportsmen in this country. In this way the game came to embrace social mix though the differences in status were never forgotten.

Several clubs in Norwich were known as early as 1788; matches with other local clubs for cash prizes and substantial bets were commonplace. Variations on the rules were by no means uncommon. Matches against the odds – that is with unequal team sizes, as a form of handicapping – were frequent in the 1840s and 1850s. There were also single wicket competitions; games were played on ice at Diss Mere in 1827 and Scoulton Mere in 1840. Women's matches also took place: one between eleven married and eleven single women in 1823, for instance. Although teams bearing the title of 'Norfolk' played at an early date (the first in 1797; one such challenged the MCC at Lords in 1820), the county club was formed in January 1827 and held a cricket week at Lakenham later that year. They also had a ground in Dereham and later played games regularly at Swaffham. They were, after all, representing the county not just the city. Indeed, the major teams were based on counties, rather than cities – a hangover from the eighteenth cen-tury, though most were established in the nineteenth. Norfolk quickly achieved success; the county was said to be second only to the MCC. In 1833, however, they lost to Yorkshire in Sheffield (this was Yorkshire's first county match), gaining revenge the following year by a substantial margin.

One of the best known of all batsmen in the century, Fuller Pilch, played in this latter match, as he had done at Lords in 1820. Though a Norfolk man, Pilch also played for Suffolk on occasions (including once against his own county), as he was, at the time, playing club cricket for Bury St Edmunds. He was a consummate professional, selling his talent to the highest bidder. Pilch moved to Kent in 1836 (allegedly for £100 or even £150 per annum). It might have been as a result of his transfer that Norfolk's fortunes began to falter. For although the game continued to be popular, the county club faced repeated difficulties. It collapsed in 1848 and experienced a see-saw existence in the next thirty years. The official history speaks of its revival in 1862 before collapse again (through debt) in 1869. Rejuvenation followed seven years later.[15] Colmans bought the ground in 1878, which no doubt helped solve financial problems. These did not, however, reflect the steady appeal of the game, which was probably attracting more players year by year. The All England Eleven (a professional touring side) took on twenty of Norfolk, 'against the odds' in 1849, and eighteen in 1853.[16] The first touring party from Australia, of aborigines, visited the Lakenham ground in 1868, defeating a side from the Carrow works.[17]

There was as yet no official county competition. The national press recorded an unofficial county championship from the 1860s; proper county qualification was instituted in 1873 and a rough idea of 'first class' matches can be said to date from this time. Norfolk, however, was no longer in the prime position that it had enjoyed earlier in the century and was not one of the recognised 'first class' counties. In 1895 Norfolk became a founding team in the Minor Counties competition instituted that year and proved to be one of its most successful sides before the First World War, winning the title in 1910 and 1913.

Although horse racing was followed throughout the country, it had relatively less appeal in Norfolk than neighbouring counties. The correspondent 'Ringwood' for the *Sporting Magazine* noted, in 1836, that 'in the populous City of Norwich not one copy [of Weatherby's Racing Calendar] would be found … the county of Norfolk is certainly less addicted to racing than any other in his Majesty's dominions.' He was particularly critical of racing at Yarmouth, though commending meetings at Swaffham.[18] For a few years some meetings were held on Mousehold Heath in Norwich, though it is clear that not all were under the governance of the Jockey Club (whose undisputed authority over all race meetings was not accepted until after the 1860s) and were not therefore recorded in the racing calendar, and hence regarded as 'private'. The first of the nineteenth century appears to have been in 1838 – the 'Coronation Races' – attracting crowds of 30,000 spectators; a level of interest that belies the comments in the *Sporting Magazine*. Subsequently two day (official) meetings were recorded annually to 1842, and of a single day in 1876.[19] Another meeting over two days took place on land near The Heart's Ease inn, Plumstead Road, in 1848. There were also annual steeplechases in the 1830s on Scole common, and one was recorded at Kirby Bedon, only just outside the city, in 1864, organised by the Norfolk hunt and the 18th Hussars. It is unlikely that this was the only year such races took place there, though they are not otherwise recorded. Steeplechasing had not yet come under the aegis of the

Jockey Club or any equivalent.[20] In the longer term Swaffham ceased to hold meetings and Yarmouth prospered under the management of the corporation. A steeplechase course was briefly set up at Hethersett, and in the 1920s Fakenham race club was established.

Foot racing or pedestrianism, invariably for money, was very much part of the sporting scene before the end of the eighteenth century. Like horse racing and almost all other sports, it was the subject of betting. Such races, however, seem to have become infrequent in the early nineteenth century. Some crowd-pulling novelty tests were irregular events. In 1818, for instance, a well-known Norwich pedestrian, Robert Skipper, undertook to walk 1000 miles in twenty days. He gave up on the ninth. In 1826 a Mr Gibson, for a bet, carried more than four stone of copper coins while walking from Norwich to Yarmouth in less than seven and a half hours; Charles Thurlow walked 1,000 miles in 1,000 hours in Norwich in 1841. Foot racing proper seems to have been revived in 1854 when a one mile handicap, open to All England, brought twenty-four competitors to the cricket ground.[21]

Some Norwich runners achieved fame. Brighten, the 'Norwich Milk Boy', ran in a series of matches in various parts of the country in the 1860s. Possibly his most famous contests were against 'Deerfoot' in 1862. Deerfoot was a north American Indian brought over by George Martin, an early showman-entrepreneur of athletics. Martin had taken a group of English runners to the USA in the 1850s who had beaten all comers bar some noted native American runners, who excelled, like Deerfoot, at long distances. Martin and his troupe of runners travelled the country with a 'stadium', apparently a fence, set up on suitable ground – a cricket pitch was ideal – while the public paid to watch, and no doubt bet on, the races. The group eventually became discredited as the same runners continually competed against each other, prompting suspicions over the authenticity of the competition.[22] In October 1862 Brighten ran against Deerfoot for £30 at Figg's cricket ground, Newmarket Road. To allay suspicions about fixing the result there was a preliminary announcement declaring that, because Deerfoot's career was coming to an end, this was to be a genuine contest. Brighten won.[23]

The fading of interest in these circus-like events and the dubiety over how genuine they were, especially where bets were concerned, contributed to a reaction against such overt commercialism. The influence of the 'gentleman amateur' was to become stronger in the last quarter of the century. The Amateur Athletic Association, in 1881, excluded any who had competed professionally in this or any other sport, along with those who had been in any way professionally employed as coaches or trainers. The strong implication is that such organisations were designed to be socially exclusive, to preserve some competitions and events (if not entire sports) for members of particular social classes or occupations.

Rowing, like athletics, was another sport where the amateur gradually pushed out the professional. The river was a place for amusement and trade; it was natural that some competition to test the sporting prowess of those commercially employed on the Wensum and Yare should take place. Individual or team contests for cups and cash prizes were regular. In 1803 a match was held between two well-known Norwich boats, the *Lion* and the *Dove*, over four miles from Carrow abbey to Whitlingham reach; a similar contest took place five years later in a match for 10 guineas a side between two six-oared boats, the *Britannia* and *Crown Point*.[24] There are many more such examples, apparently between teams with some professional link with the river. But the river was used for recreation as well. Competition for the Carrow cup, reputedly the oldest such event in the country, possibly began as early as 1813. The award of a silver cup was made in that year and again in 1816 and 1818.[25] Rowing contests and 'water frolics' were pretty much annual events to the 1840s on the river, near Carrow or Thorpe. There seems to have been much clerical encouragement. In the 1850s there were so many clergy involved in rowing in Norwich that a local poet adapted Tennyson's lines: 'a Canon to the left of them, a Canon to the right of them …'[26]

At a national level, rowing was taken up in public schools and the universities (the Oxford and Cambridge boat race began in 1829) and acquired a character of social exclusiveness. In 1841 a four-oared match between crews from Norwich and London, from Coldham Hall to Thorpe Gardens (which London won), gave rise to a parallel competition between amateurs. In 1842 a great rowing match was held on the Yare, open to all England, of four-oared boats to be rowed specifically by amateurs. Teams included Leander, King's College, London, Cambridge amateur club and Norwich amateur club. There was a prize of £50; but amateur status was determined more by social standing than the offer of prize money.[27] In later years the amateur clubs predominated. The Amateur Rowing Association of 1882, rather like the Amateur Athletics Association in 1881, effectively barred not only those who worked on the river but all manual workers or any in lowly occupations. Rowing thus became associated with social exclusion rather than bringing classes together. The National Amateur Rowing Association was set up shortly afterwards specifically to counteract this trend. In Norwich there were real efforts to open up the sport of rowing: the Norfolk and Norwich Rowing Club, which held its first annual regatta in 1867,[28] was open to all amateurs, excluding as ineligible only those who had previously competed in watermen's races.

Several business house clubs were formed in or around the 1880s (including the Norwich Warehouse Co., Greens, Chamberlins, Hope Brothers, Curls and Buntings) to provide recreation for employees; and in 1898 the Norwich Rowing Association was set up, 'to develop the pastime of rowing between the different business houses in the city'.[29] Tracing their history presents difficulties, as clubs were sometimes short lived or changed their names. The City and Carrow Rowing Club is recorded from 1882 but dissolved ten years later, selling its boats to the CEYMS club (founded in 1890). When this latter was closed in 1911, a Yare Rowing Club was established at Thorpe Gardens. In 1972 some members left to join the newly constituted Norwich Rowing Club (Plate 67).[30]

Opportunities for enhanced leisure and recreation were growing and many were exploited by enterprising businesses to serve the expanding market. Some historians have argued that in this way working-class culture became subordinated to leisure businesses and internalised into a broader commercial capitalism, a process that was to be extended in the twentieth century. And it did not seek to serve simply the spectator. It certainly appears that, far from bringing classes together, much sport was differentiated along class lines.

Whether or not it was really created in Scotland as a game of the common man, golf certainly found its early home there and was thence exported to England in the middle years of the nineteenth century. And here it became very much a game of the suburban middle classes. A club was set up in 1888 in Great Yarmouth some years before Norwich. In 1893 steps were taken to rectify the omission when land was acquired in Hellesdon; the Royal Norwich Club was opened in February 1894, and Eaton Golf Club in 1910. Subsequently golf expanded nationally and locally to become one of the most popular games played, at least for those with sufficient money, time and patience. Though hardly a new sport in any sense, archery underwent something of a revival, though it was arguably even more socially exclusive than golf. A club, within the cricket club, which permitted occasional use of the ground, was set up in 1828. In the 1860s there was further interest. A great archery fête was held in 1863 at Crown Point, and a national competition took place there three years later.

Among the sports enjoying great waves of popularity with broader appeal and participation, were skating and cycling. Cycling first became widespread in the 1870s. Bicycles, though not yet cheap and not therefore within reach of those on the lowest incomes, did bring enormous freedom to many, as well as opportunities for competition. The Norfolk and Norwich Bicycle Club held its first meeting in January 1877 and the first road race, over twenty-four miles, in April of that year, followed by a sports meeting in Chapel Field in October. Interest spread. An inter-county race with Suffolk (won by the latter) was held in 1879. The real boom, for day to day use as much as competitive sport, came in the 1880s with the development of the 'safety bicycle' with wheels of equal diameter and a chain drive. The invention of the pneumatic tyre, patented by Dunlop in 1888, made for a more comfortable ride and added to the popularity of the sport. Subsequently local clubs clearly affiliated with national organisations; the fifty-mile championships of the Eastern Counties centre of the National Cyclists Union were held at Earlham Road recreation ground in 1899. Roller-skating enjoyed a short lived bubble-like boom. A rink was opened in the parish of St Giles in 1876 but popularity began to wane within the year. Circus-like acts, including performing dogs, were introduced to try to maintain public interest but the rink closed in 1882.

As a spectator sport, football (soccer) became the most popular in these years and has been so ever since. It was also a popular game to play. As we have seen, there was a Norwich club from the 1860s, with sixty members, and numerous other districts had clubs. Several regular competitions were run with teams based on pubs, neighbourhoods or churches. By the end of the century the CEYMS (Church of England Young Men's Society) team was the most successful. In June 1902, following a public meeting, a new club, Norwich City FC, was formed at the initiative of two of the CEYMS players. They were ambitious to play at a higher level than that offered by local competition. It is likely that there was some commercial interest also. Elsewhere in the country, above all in the north of England, soccer had been a thriving professional game for twenty years, drawing large crowds as an increasing number of industrial workers now had Saturday afternoons free from work. Arthur Turner, the first manager, set about recruiting the best players he could, using sweeteners, such as the offer of jobs in the city, to attract them.

It was a successful search. The club fielded four regular teams, the first eleven playing in the amateur Norfolk and Suffolk League. This they won in 1905 and had hopes for the Amateur Cup. The Football Association and League had accepted the reality of professionalism in the 1880s. A spirited amateur culture, especially in the FA, remained, however, and an amateur cup competition had started in 1893–4. The FA challenged the club's amateur status over the payments of 'expenses' and various allowances to its players and required them to leave the cup competition. The club therefore decided to become openly professional. In 1905 it formed a limited company and joined the Southern League in the 1905–6 season (from 1920–1 this was to be the Third Division South). In 1908, growing out of the rudimentary facilities at their Newmarket Road ground, the club moved to a new and 'custom built' location on Rosary Road – 'the Nest'. This remained Norwich City's ground until 1935.[31]

By the close of the nineteenth century the 'modern' structure of popular sports and recreation had been established. The blood-letting of traditional animal-baiting had been eliminated, at least in law. Football had moved on from the casual, if far from chaotic, 'folk' game to have national rules and become the most popular spectator sport. Paradoxically, there was a reaction against the overt commercialisation of some sports. This was backed up by an element of social exclusiveness, of members of the growing middle and professional classes seeking to separate themselves from the rest. Thus, activities like golf, tennis, rowing and athletics came to be pursued predominantly by the relatively well-to-do. It has been suggested that even the new pastime of cycling and the very old one of bowls were more for the white-collared clerk than the rough-handed labourer, because of entry costs, and this despite many of the teams being based at pubs. On the other hand, a new wave of commercialism took advantage of the growing real wages and extension to leisure time now enjoyed by the common man (and much less frequently, woman). The years from the late 1880s and 1890s saw a general expansion of the home market, but the impact of this was more modest in Norwich and its surroundings than in many other parts of the country. In turn such a muted response was associated with the depression in agriculture. Professional football as a spectator sport came somewhat later to Norwich than towns and cities in the north and midlands. Nevertheless, some reduction in working hours with a slow but steady growth in real wages boosted demand for leisure activities.

It is difficult to judge the extent of popular participation in games like football, though the incidence of local leagues and competitions (many associated with factory teams) would suggest that it was great. Yet the most popular pastime in Edwardian Norwich was fishing. It could be undertaken by young and old alike and needed very little outlay to begin. Shortly before the First World War, there were at least one hundred clubs, most linked to pubs, with an average membership of thirty to forty.[32]

Certainly, the pub remained the single most popular resort for (male) working-class leisure time, although average beer consumption *per capita* began to decline after 1880, a phenomenon that has been attributed in part to the rival attraction of watching football. C. B. Hawkins, writing in 1910, believed the public house was still the 'centre of social intercourse amongst working men in Norwich'.[33] The city was famously supplied with an abundance of drinking places (Figure 44). In 1873 there were 596 public houses

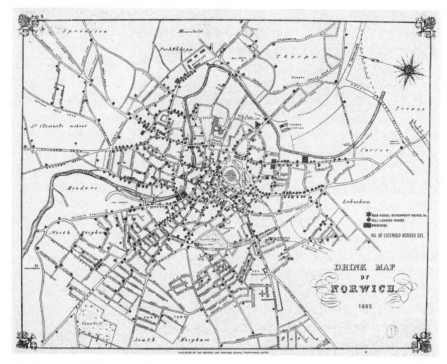

FIGURE 44. The Norwich 'drink map', 1892, which shows the breweries and 631 licensed proprerties in the city. (*Norfolk Heritage Centre, photograph by Terry Burchell*)

and forty-two beerhouses, approximately one for every 121 of the population. This was the highest ratio for any major urban centre in England recorded by the Select Committee on Intemperance. It was a surprising statistic. Yet, and this puzzled contemporaries, the incidence of drunkenness was by far the lowest. This was because wages were low,[34] and the beer consequently weak and cheap. Simms Reeve, a city magistrate, reckoned in 1877 that Norwich beer was:

> Very mild, so much so that a great deal of the beer that is drunk is not more than 3d. a quart, and is called 'straight', from it being supposed to go right down the throat and leave no effect behind it.[35]

Hawkins also described Norwich pubs as smaller and more homely than those in larger cities and commented on the extent to which they were a focus for a range of leisure activities.

Pubs were often the location for a variety of traditional sports: cock-fighting, bear-baiting, prize fighting. Many landlords were retired fighters.[36]

Pubs also offered billiards, bowls, skittles and a game peculiar to the region, logats. This was similar to skittles but the 'logats' (applewood pins about twenty-two inches long) were thrown at the jack. A particularly popular game in the eighteenth century, it was last played at The Hampshire Hog in St Swithin's Alley.[37] Bowls continued to flourish, though mainly among the better-paid workers: the Anchor Bowling League, of seven teams, was organised by Bullards' brewery. By the turn of the century the city had twenty-six bowling clubs, several affiliated to the Norwich Bowling Association. A 'working-class' interest, peculiar to the city, evident at the same time was canary breeding; there were about thirteen canary clubs. The pastime is said to have originated with Norwich's Flemish weavers, but there is no direct evidence to support this. The *Norwich Mercury* of 25 October 1729 advertised the sale of canaries 'brought over from High Germany' at The Bear Inn in the market place. The first recorded canary show was in 1846 at The Greyhound Inn, Ber Street.[38] This hobby was also a source of potential income, as around 30,000 birds were exported each year.[39] Before the First World War the price of a single bird could reach five pounds. As a shoemaker's wife said of the birds: 'Those are the boys that pay the rent'.[40]

The First World War had a great impact on all aspects of life. Although soccer continued for a time (in the face of significant criticism) some players and much revenue were lost to the Norwich club. They went into voluntary liquidation in 1917; two years later a new club was formed. The county cricket club ceased to play for the duration and competition was resumed only in 1920. Despite the losses of the war, the team was able to achieve consistent success (but not the minor counties title) through the inter-war years. In some other ways, though, the war brought more play, as war workers found new opportunities for organised games. Numerous teams, involving a wide variety of games, for both men and women, were formed, many based on the workplace, often with local inter-works competitions.[41]

The chance to take part in sport and leisure activities increased in the 1920s and 30s as the market expanded. Some believe that the inter-war years saw a new wave of the commercialisation of leisure.[42] Similar claims have been made about the eighteenth century and the years 1870–1914, but most would accept that it was the 1950s that signalled the start of a real leisure boom. It seems that throughout the modern period commercial interests have been in the forefront in organising sport and games. Despite the effects of depression, the poor state of agriculture having particular impact in the eastern counties, popular interest in leisure activities was maintained and extended in the inter-war years. Cinema attendances grew year by year, a new Theatre Royal was built in Norwich in 1935, and football remained by far the most popular spectator sport. Such was the interest in the 'Canaries' that the club outgrew the Rosary Road ground, 'the Nest' – helped by promotion to the second division in the 1934–5 season. In early 1935 a letter from the Football Association suggesting that the ground was unsuitable for large crowds accelerated the search for a new one. Negotiations with Colmans to take over the Boulton & Paul's sports club ground at Carrow Road followed quickly and a twenty year lease was signed in June. This site presented the great advantage of being a ready-made ground, though extensive adaptation for spectators was necessary. It was opened for the 1935–6 season and has been the home of the club, with many improvements, ever since.

The fastest growing spectator sport in the 1930s, and one which came to rival football for attendances, was speedway. A boom in the sale of motor cycles began in the mid-1920s and interest spread to watching them race. Grass track racing commenced in 1928 and a stadium was built on the Holt Road in 1930. Crowds as large as five to six thousand were attracted. The first dirt track was opened in September 1931, by which time a national league structure had been established. Norwich, as yet not participating in the league, relied on challenge matches to keep the crowds coming in. The local team faded quickly but was revived in 1937 as the 'Norwich Stars' took part in a provincial league. Crowds reached ten thousand. Although the sport was suspended in the Second World War it reached the peak of its popularity in the later 1940s.[43] Speedway had been able to share its track at the Firs for some time with another fast-growing spectator sport, though one primarily organised for regular legal betting, greyhound racing. A further, specialised track, affiliated to the National Greyhound Racing Society, was opened at the Boundary Park Stadium in 1932. This operated until 1962.

We should be cautious of observing only the forces of Mammon in sport. As well as the interests of commerce, there was a genuine sense that leisure and recreation could be usefully pursued. Many amongst the larger employers and community leaders began to see it as a duty to provide outdoor recreational facilities for their workforces and the general population. As we have seen, Colmans and some other employers in the city provided sports facilities for their workers in the nineteenth century. This was reinforced by the wave of 'muscular Christianity' which used games and sports to propagate the faith and keep boys, especially, off the streets (football and, paradoxically, boxing were used to spread the gospel). A cricket pitch was even laid down at St Andrew's asylum, Thorpe, in 1854, and the game became an essential aspect of life there. Many came to believe that leisure

47. Sir George White (1840–1912), managing director of Howlett and White, shoe manufacturers, leader of the Norwich Liberals in the 1890s and Liberal MP for north-west Norfolk, 1900–12.

48. Jacob Henry Tillett (1818–1892), solicitor, radical journalist and MP for Norwich, 1880–5. (*Norfolk Heritage Centre*)

49. ILP Public Representatives in 1914. Back row from the left: W. Savage (Councillor and Guardian), W. Hindes (Guardian), A. Keeley (Councillor and Guardian), F. Jex (Guardian), E. Manning (Guardian). Front row: W. R. Smith (Councillor and Guardian), Mrs E. Reeves (Guardian), H. Witard (Councillor) (*Norfolk Heritage Centre*)

TILLETT

IS

WILD

BECAUSE

ROBERTS

WINS.

BE ON THE WINNING SIDE.
VOTE FOR ROBERTS

G. H. ROBERTS,
THE WORKERS' CANDIDATE.

Printed and Published by
Chas. H. Myall, Pottergate Street, Norwich.

50. An ILP canvassing card from the 1904 Norwich by-election playing on the names of the Liberal candidate L.J.Tillett, the Conservative, E.E.Wild and the ILP representative George Roberts. Tillett won comfortably and Roberts was a poor third. (*Barry Doyle*)

51. Thomas Bignold, Senior (1761–1835), founder and first secretary of the Norwich Union Fire and Life Insurance Societies during the first two decades of their expansion to 1818. (*Norwich Union Archive*)

52. Surrey Street House, built by Robert Mylne for the worsted manufacturer and mayor, John Patteson in 1764–5. It was the head offices of the Norwich Union Fire Society and the home of Sir Samuel Bignold from 1819 to 1875. (*Norwich Union Archive*)

53. The Norwich Union's Life Society headquarters by George Skipper, 1901–5. The Recorder of Norwich, dismissing the Society's appeal against its rateable value, opined, 'I am sure the provinces contain nothing to equal it'. (*Norwich Union Archive*)

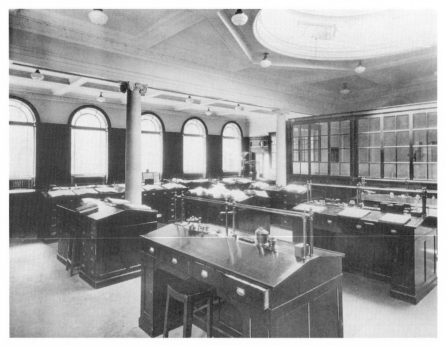

54. The interior of the Norfolk and Norwich Savings Bank in their new offices opened in Surrey Street in 1927. (*Lloyds TSB Group Archive*)

55. The livestock market on Castle Hill, late nineteenth century. (*Norfolk Museums and Archaeology Service, Bridewell Museum*)

56. The Norwich Gates made by Barnard and Bishop, presented to the Prince of Wales and erected at the entrance to Sandringham House. (*Norfolk Museums and Archaeology Service, Bridewell Museum*)

57. Colman's Carrow Works, 1905. Opened in 1852, in excess of 2,300 workers were employed here by the end of the century. (*Unilever Historical Archives, photograph by Terry Burchell*)

58. The machine upper closing room at Howlett and White's shoe factory, 1913. (*Coe of Castle Meadow and Norfolk Heritage Centre*)

59. Bunting's department store on the corner of Rampant Horse Street and St Stephen's, *c.* 1910. (*Coe of Castle Meadow and Norfolk Heritage Centre*)

60. Jeremiah James Colman (1830–1898), MP for Norwich, philanthropist and managing partner of J & J Colman during its period of rapid growth during the second half of the nineteenth century. (*Norfolk Heritage Centre, photograph by Terry Burchell*)

61. Workers leaving Francis Hinde's silk works in the 1920s – a daily scene outside Norwich's many factories. (*Norfolk Heritage Centre, photograph by Terry Burchell*)

62. Old Meeting (Congregational). The mercantile dignity of Norwich's oldest surviving purpose-built meeting house witnessed more to enduring tradition than outdated fashion. Its reputation for radical sociability was long reflected in its Book Club. (*Clyde Binfield*)

63. George Slatyer Barrett (1839–1916), Minister of Prince's Street Congregational (now United Reformed) Church, 1866–1911. Firmly embedded in a cousinhood of upwardly mobile Dissenters, his was the representative face of Norwich's late Victorian and Edwardian Nonconformity. He was also a respected hymnologist. (*Clyde Binfield*)

64. The First Church of Christ Scientist (now Greek Orthodox), Recorder Road, in 1935. This small masterpiece in stream-lined gothic, full of vernacular touches and deft unobtrusive symbol, was designed by H. G. Ibberson (1866–1935), of Hunstanton. (*Clyde Binfield*)

65. Trinity Presbyterian (now United Reformed) Church, Unthank Road. This church by Sir Bernard Feilden was built in 1955 on the site of a Baptist Church, but it replaced the Theatre Street Presbyterian Church, begun in 1867 and destroyed in 1942. (*Clyde Binfield*)

66. St Mary's Baptist Church as it was in 1940, restored after a serious fire to pro-vide 'an improved copy' of Edward Boardman's massive remodelling of 1886. (*K. Hipper, Archivist, St Mary's Baptist Church*)

67. Rowing and sculling became popular amateur sports in the nineteenth century with clubs on the Yare at Thorpe and, as with the Norwich Amateur Rowing Association here, pictured *c.* 1910, at Whitlingham. (*Neil R. Storey*)

68. Colmans were keen supporters of games for employees. Football had quickly become one of the most popular of games in the city following the formation of the Norfolk FA in 1881. (*Unilever Historical Archives, photograph by Terry Burchell*)

69. Hockey Team, Norwich High School for Girls, 1899, selected from its fifty-strong Hockey Club. The school included games in the curriculum from their opening in 1875. (*Norwich High School for Girls*)

70. League of Health and Beauty class at Carrow Club House, *c.* 1938. The League was founded in 1930 and quickly attracted many members. Demonstrations of 'natural movement' (their motto was 'movement is life') were held all over the country. (*Unilever Historical Archives, photograph by Terry Burchell*)

71. Car and pedestrian conflict: congestion in London Street, 1966. (*Eastern Daily Press*)

72. An urban environment to enjoy: The Walk, newly pedestrianised, 1988. (*Eastern Daily Press*)

73. An already shrinking industry at that time, the Closing Room, Norvic Shoes, in 1981. (*Eastern Daily Press*)

74. A new style of shopping: the first shoppers in Castle Mall, September 1993.
(*Eastern Daily Press*)

75. A tradition of valuable engineering skills, Laurence and Scott Electromotors Ltd, 1962. (*Eastern Daily Press*)

76. From fire disaster to institutional opportunity: The Forum, opened in 2001. (*Terry Burchell*)

should bring positive returns, with valuable and creative activities organised to marginalise idleness in the absence of work. In the nineteenth and even more so in the twentieth century religious organisations, enlightened (or paternalistic) employers, extended popular sport and leisure facilities. This was one of the most important mechanisms in the provision of opportunities in various sports and games at little or no cost to players and spectators. Colmans was probably the best known.[44] The company had supported angling and cricket from the 1840s. Jeremiah Colman believed cricket to be 'a harmless and healthful game and free from objectionable features'.[45] The family were keen cricketers themselves; the eleven sons of Robert Colman (d. 1867) made up a team that played in 1846.[46] An annual sports day was held in Whit week until 1877 when the number of workers grew too large. Thereafter the company used facilities at Lakenham cricket ground (which it acquired in 1878). In 1872 the company bought the Crown Point estate where, in 1907, it opened a new club house. The ground provided playing fields for eleven football teams (Plate 68), ten cricket teams (in local leagues) netball and hockey (for men and women), quoits, gymnastics and bowls, as well as accommodating various musical groups (Figure 45).[47] All gym equipment, even gym-shoes, was provided free; football and hockey jerseys at half price.[48] Colmans present an extreme example of a general trend. Records for other businesses have not always survived. Those known to be already offering similar facilities in the nineteenth century included the Post Office, Corporation Electricity Works, Caleys, Norwich Union and Boulton & Paul. The latter held a workmen's athletic festival in 1891. The works magazine in 1916 also refers to the cricket club as having 'long been formed'.[49] A football club followed in 1915. From the 1920s the pattern became a standard so that most large employers provided recreation facilities of some sort. A business house league in football was set up 1917;[50] similar contests for other games, including ladies' hockey, ran for many years, and in some cases still continue. Norwich Union opened their sports ground at Thorpe in 1921, but interest in the sporting activities of their employees long preceded this. The cricket club dated from 1881, with football in 1899, followed by bowls (1900), rowing (1905) and quoits (1906). There were regular matches within the company and against local clubs and sides.

Public schools had been the great propagators of sports in the middle years of the nineteenth century, both directly to the pupils and through subsequent dissemination by the alumni. King Edward's School for boys, Norwich, was able to take advantage of the river for rowing, as well as to foster the games ethic on the (rugby) football and cricket fields. Local

34   THE CARROW WORKS MAGAZINE.

Carrow Works' Social Scheme.

TIME TABLE.

The following Time Tables are for the winter months and are subject to slight alteration.

SUNDAY SECTION.

Sundays.
9 to 10.15   Carrow Men's First-Day School.
10.45 to 12   Carrow Sunday School (Senior, Junior and Infant Departments.)
2.30 to 4   Carrow Sunday School (Senior and Junior Departments).
2.45 to 4.15   Carrow Women's First-Day School.

Carrow Men's First-Day School.
Prayer Meeting on Friday evenings at 8 p.m.
Business Meeting on 2nd Monday in the month at 8 p.m. (except during the summer).

Carrow Women's First-Day School.
Business and Social Meeting held monthly during the winter months.

Carrow Sunday School.
Special Services held quarterly.
Monthly Prayer Meeting usually on 2nd Sunday in the month at close of afternoon school.
Mrs. Gaze's Preparation Class for Senior and Junior Teachers on Monday evenings at 8 p.m.
Miss Edith A. Cooke's Preparation Class for Infant School Teachers on Tuesday evenings at 8.15 p.m.

N.B.—The above Schools are not confined to Carrow Works Employees and their children.

WEEK-DAY SECTION.
MEN'S AND BOYS' SECTIONS.

Mondays.
8.30 to 9 a.m.   *Billiards, Skittles, Draughts, Football, etc.
1 to 2 p.m.   *   Ditto   Ditto
7 p.m   Military Band Practice.
8 p.m.   Gymnastic Instruction.
9 to 10 p.m.   Military Band Practice for Beginners.

Tuesdays.
7 to 9 p.m.   Gymnastics—Free Practice.
7 to 9 p.m.   String Band Practice.
9 to 10 p.m.   String Band Practice for Beginners.

Wednesdays.
7 p.m.   Military Band Practice.
8 p.m.   Gymnastics—Class Instruction.
9 to 10 p.m.   Military Band Practice for Beginners.

Thursdays.
7 p.m.   Physical Drill and Junior Gymnastic Class.
7 p.m.   Senior Gymnastic Class.
7.30 p.m.   Male Voice Choir Practice.

Fridays.
7 to 8 p.m.   Gymnastics for Boys.
7 to 9 p.m.   String Band Practice for Beginners.
8 to 10 p.m.   Gymnastics, Wrestling, etc., for Men.

FIGURE 45. Colmans had a strong commitment to company welfare. This programme of 1909 illustrates the extensive recreational facilities provided for employees. (*Unilever Historical Archives, photograph by Terry Burchell*)

Men's and Boys' Sections—*continued.*

Saturdays. Afternoons. Football League and Hockey Matches on Lakenham and Club Grounds.

2 to 6 p.m. Club House open for Billiards, &c., &c.

* Items marked thus are repeated each week-day except Saturdays.
Concerts, Lectures, or Dramatic Performances held at intervals during the Winter months.
Men's Club House Committee meets on the last Wednesday in each month.
The Club House, Library, and Reading Rooms, are open every day—both Morning and Evening; Daily Papers, Periodicals, &c., being provided.
Books are issued from the Lending Department on any evening except Saturday.

WOMEN'S AND GIRLS' SECTIONS.

Mondays. 8.30 to 9 a.m. †Refreshment Rooms Open.
8.30 to 9 a.m. Games in Gymnasium.
12.30 to 2 p.m. Sewing Class in Refreshment Rooms.
12.30 to 2 p.m. †Refreshment Rooms Open.
1 to 2 p.m. Hockey.
6 to 7.30 p.m. Cookery Class.
6.30 to 7.30 p.m. Juniors' Gymnastic Class.
7.30 to 8.30 p.m. Juniors' Entertainment Practice.

Tuesdays. 8.30 to 9 a.m. Games in Reading Room.
1 to 2 p.m. Religious Meeting in Refreshment Rooms.
1 to 2 p.m. Hockey.
7 to 9 p.m. Gymnastic Class (Starch Packing Department).

Wednesdays. 8.30 to 9 a.m. Games in Reading Room.
12.30 to 2 p.m. Sewing Class in Refreshment Rooms.
1 to 2 p.m. Selection of Music in Refreshment Rooms.
1 to 2 p.m. Net Ball.
7 to 9 p.m. Gymnastic Class (Mustard Packing and Box Departments).
8 p.m. Singing Class Practice in Refreshment Rooms.

Thursdays. 8.30 to 9 a.m. Games in Reading Room.
12.30 to 2 p.m. Sewing Class in Refreshment Room.
1 to 2 p.m. Hockey.

Fridays. 8.30 to 9 a.m. Games in Gymnasium.
12.30 to 2 p.m. Sewing Class in Refreshment Rooms.
1 to 2 p.m. Hockey.
7 to 9 p.m. Seniors' Dancing Class.

Saturdays. 8.30 to 9 a.m. Games in Reading Room.
11.30 a.m. Juniors' Gymnastic Class.
2.45 p.m. Hockey.
4 p.m. Chip Carving Class.

† Items marked thus are repeated each week-day.
A Class for cutting out garments will be held weekly, the day to be announced later.
Concerts, Lectures, or Dramatic Performances held at intervals during the Winter months.

CARROW WORKS' KITCHEN.

Employees can be served during the following hours :—

Every Week-day	.. ..	5.45 to 9 a.m.
" " (except Saturdays)	.. ..	12.30 to 1.15 p.m.
" " " "	.. ..	5 to 6 p.m.

school boards, on the other hand, had little or nothing to offer. There were a few exceptions. In the early part of the nineteenth century Samuel Wilderspin, a follower of Robert Owen, set out to encourage games and healthy exercise for all children. In order to cope with the lack of facilities, he developed a series of exercises that could be followed at the desk – what he called 'desk drill'. In 1836 he demonstrated this in St Andrew's hall and some city schools took up the ideas. The impact, of course, was limited. With the introduction of compulsory schooling in 1870 physical training largely consisted of military style drill (very different from desk drill) 'taught' by former soldiers. The Norwich school board employed drill instructors from 1878 to 1882; the first mention of games as such was not until the early 1880s,[51] and then provision was poor. As late as 1912 only 3000 from a roll of 19,000 children in Norwich had access to playing fields at school. Public parks were a major asset in this respect. In 1909, for instance, boys in the top years at Quayside School walked to Mousehold Heath one afternoon each week to play football.

If poor male children had few opportunities for sport at school, girls had virtually none. In 1895 some fifty boys were taught to swim by a local swimming club. Nothing was done for girls. To some extent the propagation of games through the public schools had reinforced the sexual divide. Games came to be seen as the epitome of 'manliness', specifically aimed at hardening boys and eliminating any 'feminine' characteristics (with consequent military advantage). This strengthened the perception of sport as being essentially male. As some girls, however, were able to extend their academic education, thought was given to the value of exercise for them. And the mechanism of extending this was again via private schools and Oxbridge colleges. The development of such thinking was coupled with a new phenomenon of women teachers who had enjoyed games at university taking their enthusiasm into their schools. This occurred on any scale only in the 1880s. The Girls' Public Day School Trust, as in so many things, was among the pioneers. Norwich High School was the first of the trust schools to be opened outside the capital, in 1875. From the beginning the school regarded exercise as important. At first the girls were instructed in drill by Sergeant-Major Collins from the local barracks. This practice continued until 1897. Callisthenic exercises and tennis were introduced in the mid 1880s. Hockey was not played until 1898, netball until 1912 and lacrosse until 1915; in all cases their introduction led to competitive games with other, similar schools (Plate 69).[52] By the eve of war in 1914 the school acknowledged that sport was as valid for girls as their right to intellectual education.[53] A similar provision was extended to girls in state schools only after the First World War.

Beyond the classroom some philanthropic efforts were made to extend the opportunity for games to working-class children, again initially only boys. In 1904 W. G. Mase of the Norvic Shoe Company began to provide, in connection with the Magdelen Road Congregational Church First Day School, a variety of indoor games, such as billiards and darts, and an annual camp in August.[54] A further example is the creation of the Norwich Lads' Club in 1918. This was the inspiration of the chief constable, J. H. Dain, who had started a similar scheme in Canterbury. In opening a recreational, and free, club to boys aged fourteen to twenty-one in the evenings it was hoped to keep them out of trouble, extend the virtues of sport and games, and enhance good relations with the police. The premises were provided by the city council but prepared by the voluntary labour of local policemen. Although open to all, the membership was largely drawn from the poorer classes, those otherwise denied access to organised sports. The range of recreations was wide (gymnastics, billiards, table tennis, football, roller skating, even bands) though boxing was the most prominent.[55] For some reason community leaders associated teaching pugilism with encouraging responsible social behaviour. This club was for boys who had left school. The suggestion, as late as the 1960s, that girls should be admitted to Norwich Lads' Club was fiercely resisted until the pressure of law eventually allowed equal access in 1975.

Although they had taken part in games since the eighteenth century, women were far less likely to do so than men. This was especially so for working-class women who were denied the opportunities presented in private schools and at university. A small number of enlightened employers, however, did offer facilities; as has been seen, Colmans was an early example. The company catered for ladies' hockey and netball on the playing fields opened in 1907, and provided a separate gymnasium for girls (Plate 70) where they were taught Swedish drill and dancing.[56] Company provision was probably the most important stimulus for widespread female participation in games. The First World War brought something of a boom for women's sport, especially in team games. The recruitment of women for war work in factories, which often had sports grounds, presented many, especially from a poor social background, with the opportunity and occasion to take up team games for the first time. A ladies' cricket team was formed at Boulton & Paul's in 1917 – 'to challenge all comers'. The women employees also formed two football teams (respectively representing 'Rose Lane Works' and 'Aircraft') and these were complemented by the hockey team, gymnastics and dancing. In the summer the women played tennis and croquet, as well as taking part in boating and swimming activities.

Norwich Components (a fuse-making factory employing almost entirely women, which was closed in 1918) had some of the strongest ladies' football and hockey teams, as well as provision for tennis and dancing.[57] Such games and competitions had a positive effect on morale and opened the way for future participation. Unfortunately for many of the women involved, peace brought a return to the home and the collapse of some of these sporting opportunities. Although ladies' business house teams and competitions continued, a strong gender differentiation emerged, with hockey taking the lead as the main women's winter sport. The Football Association indeed did their best to put a stop to women's football by banning them from football league grounds in 1921, but some ladies' football was able to resume in later years. Most of the shoe factories in the city ran female football teams in the early 1930s. A team from Hurrell's factory used kit loaned from Norwich City and on occasions played at their ground at 'the Nest'. Such women's football came to an end before the Second World War because of opposition from local churches, whose ministers thought the game unsuitable and likely to foster masculine physical characteristics.[58]

Public provision of recreational facilities for all was greatly extended by the city council. A whole raft of measures (affecting parks, public baths, museums and libraries) empowered municipal government to augment provisions. In the second half of the nineteenth century especially, numerous parks were opened in the major cities, largely at the initiative of their local governments and private individuals. Norwich followed the pattern. It had long been known as the 'city of gardens', and the availability of open spaces for public use was extended in the nineteenth century. Part of Mousehold Heath had been common land since 1801 and was always a popular place of recreation. Chapel Field gardens were opened as a public park in 1880, and in 1894 extensions to Gildencroft recreation ground were opened for public use. In 1904 Woodlands park was donated to the city by Mrs Radford Pye. The city council itself became much more active in the 1920s. Wensum park was opened in 1924. Preliminary plans to lay out Eaton park were made in 1923. This was a result of political action to counter unemployment, for it was built as a public works programme, expected to provide work for 140 men for two years. Most council funded parks projects were directly aimed at work creation from as early as 1921 (significantly preceding the severe depression of the early 1930s). Eaton park was opened by the Prince of Wales in 1928 and provided facilities for cricket, tennis, bowls, football and hockey (and it continues to do so; in the 1990s American football was added to this list). Further provision followed: Woodrow Pilling park in 1929 (again following a donation to the city) and Waterloo park in 1933, like Eaton park built as a work-creation scheme. There were also three open-air municipal swimming pools. These were especially valuable at a time of high unemployment. The open-air pool at Lakenham – 'built literally in the River Yare' – was frequently closed, however, because of pollution. The city council went further in laying out a municipal golf course in the Yare valley, opened in 1932, when only twenty-two other towns had such courses, having first considered the idea in 1923.[59] Some thirty years after opening it became the site of the University of East Anglia, thus depriving the city of a public utility and confining the game of golf to private clubs. By 1936 there were only fifty public courses in England and Wales. Such provisions were very much a local initiative. In 1937, however, as a result of the Physical Training and Recreation Act, Parliament set up a national advisory council with a budget to provide grants to local authorities. The Hall Road recreation ground, for football, cricket, hockey, netball, tennis, badminton and squash, was opened in the same year.

The Second World War brought great changes in the world of sport and leisure. In contrast to the 1914–18 war, however, both public and political opinion was less hostile to the continuation of recreation. Participation and spectating were seen as boosting to morale. One difficulty, though, was that many sportsmen were the prime age for conscription, especially in the case of professional footballers. Early in the hostilities, when Norwich City played Brighton and Hove Albion, for instance, the visitors' team had to be augmented with two Norwich reserves and some soldiers who had come to watch the match.[60] Football league competitions were later briefly suspended before the Home Office sanctioned a series of regional leagues with strict limits on travelling. County cricket ceased for the duration.

The return to peace opened the way to a more rapid phase of commercial expansion of spectator sport and popular leisure generally.[61] Opportunities for participation were to grow both through publicly provided facilities and by commercial enterprise. In the early post-war years there was a rush to catch up on some of the foregone pleasures of wartime. Spectator sports boomed as never before. Horse racing crowds reached a peak; even point-to-point meetings could draw crowds sufficient to cause traffic chaos. Speedway began again in 1946, with attendances reaching 20,000 at the Aylsham Road stadium – a real if short-lived rival to football. Norwich also boasted two greyhound racing stadia. There was nothing new in the commercial exploitation of spectator sports but, following the post-war austerity, there began in the 1950s, albeit slowly, an unprecedented period of popular affluence. Paradoxically perhaps, some spectator sports suffered as new rivals for expenditure appeared. Speedway began to fade. The Norwich Stars were promoted to the first division of the national league in 1950 just when the national popularity of the sport was beginning to wane. Crowds diminished even though the world champion, Ove Funden, was a team member. By 1958 Norwich was the only East Anglian team in the league and in 1964 it was forced to cease activity. In the following year the team franchise was moved to King's Lynn, where it remains.

The county cricket club at Lakenham had mixed fortunes also. It emerged from the war having lost a good many players. In the 1950s two new stars were to shine. Future England players, Peter Parfitt and John Edrich, passed through the ranks before moving on to first-class counties. In later years some professionals, such as Phil Sharpe of Yorkshire, played out their last seasons with the Norfolk club after leaving the first-class game. Football continued to be the dominant spectator sport in the city. The Canaries resumed a position in the third division with a return to peace time competition after 1945; it was to take fourteen years before they won promotion. And in 1971–2 the team won the second division championship and promotion to the first division. Their greatest success was probably in winning the 'Milk' Cup in 1985. The club established a reputation as being 'family friendly' at a time when soccer had acquired a bad name for hooliganism among crowds. Indeed, a survey conducted in 1995 found the club to have one of the highest regular attendances by women, at 17.2 per cent, in the football league.[62]

Many attractions besides spectator sports competed for leisure time and money. Taking an active part in sports was one. Here again we must be cautious of underestimating the resilience of custom. Angling remained the most popular participation sport, as anyone travelling along Riverside today can attest. In the surrounding country shooting and, to a lesser extent, hunting continued and attracted more devotees; the nearby Broads provided an ideal location for boating. Undoubtedly taking part in games, organised or casual, did increase. This was aided also by both rising affluence and the extension of government sponsored provision as part of a growth of welfare generally in the post-war years. Sports facilities in schools were an important aspect of these developments. Local government, however, was far more important than central. As has been seen, there was nothing new in the provision of public recreation facilities by the city council. But from the 1970s a new mantra of 'sport for all' gave it fresh impetus. Unfortunately, cut-backs in central government funding made it more difficult to continue such a policy. Even so, and despite the fact that

local government expenditure on recreation was not a statutory requirement, provision was extended. Capital expenditure on facilities like
swimming pools reached a peak in the 1970s; sports areas of schools and
colleges were opened to the public. This was not without result. Despite the
modest number of swimming pools in Norwich, and the lack of a fifty
metre pool until the year 2000, the largest sports club in the city was Norwich Penguins' swimming club. Indeed it was reputed to be the largest
swimming club in the country. In 1992, however, the requirement placed
on local government to seek 'compulsory competitive tendering' was
extended to leisure services. This reduced direct local government capital
expenditure and brought an 'alliance' of commercial and public provision.
Subsequently, central government virtually ignored the role of local councils in providing sports facilities, shifting attention much more to the role
of commerce, colleges and universities and sports councils.[63] The
'Sportspark' opened in 2000 adjacent to the University of East Anglia,
funded by 'Sport England' and using a combination of national lottery
money and business sponsorship, is a recent example. In parallel, private
or commercial clubs have expanded to meet growing demand, as witnessed
by the number of gymnasia and 'fitness centres' in and around the city.

   In the second half of the twentieth century the range of facilities for participation in sport and games reached unprecedented levels. The means by
which they were made available had, however, been in place for a century
or more. Public provision was not new but its scope had grown. Private
clubs, as gatherings of like-minded people, were as important as always, the
benefit of social exclusiveness in some cases perhaps being a major attraction. Recreation through the work place continued to be important but less
vital than in pre-war days as other facilities developed. But the profit
motive, which had always been evident, was as ever a major driving force
in the construction and upkeep of sports and leisure facilities.

19

Norwich since 1945

Peter Townroe

In fifty years' time Norwich will either not be worth looking at or it
will be one of the most beautiful cities in England.

H. V. Morton, *In Search of England*, 1933 [1]

At the outbreak of the Second World War Norwich was a regional capital
with its industry and trade largely focused upon its large agricultural hinterland. The city had not benefited from new industries in the inter-war
period to the same degree as many other centres in southern England.
Although the footwear and clothing industries continued to be the major
manufacturing sectors, unemployment rates had been high and average
incomes remained traditionally low. The resident population, recorded as
126,236 by the 1931 Census, had dropped to 121,800 by 1939. Norwich
seemed to be a city cut off from the mainstream of change occurring in the
British economy.

By the end of the war it was clear to civic leaders that significant expansion was needed in the local economy. Wartime production had supported
key engineering companies as well as enterprises in the food processing and
beverages sectors. In peacetime, their prosperity was less certain. For the
local building trades there was a major immediate challenge in the reconstruction required following widespread bomb damage. In addition, many
houses in Norwich needed to have their basic amenities updated. At the
same time there were ambitions for improvements in the provision of education and health care, and in retailing. And the service sector in general
was expected to benefit from a general rise in farm incomes in Norfolk and
Suffolk following new agricultural policies. But the core of the economy
had to be less dependent upon the clothing and footwear sectors, and to
be more firmly rooted in a wider field of the lighter manufacturing sectors
and in office-based activities that served more than the local population.
The total resident population had declined from 121,800 in 1939 to 115,200
by 1947, having fallen to an estimated total of only 101,000 in 1943.

The physical ambitions for post-war Norwich were set out in the 1945

City of Norwich Plan.[2] Key elements of the proposals in that plan are in place today, fifty-nine years later. But the authors did not foresee the degree to which the growth and development of Norwich would be influenced in the second half of the twentieth century by a strong growth in population, fed by in-migration, and by the associated rise in real household incomes.

The year 1974 – a significant one in the history of the city – marks a convenient breakpoint in considering the post-war period. It was then that Norwich ceased being a county borough, which hitherto had enjoyed full responsibility for all local public services. Under the widespread reorganisation of local government which then took place across the United Kingdom, the city of Norwich became a district council. Its local elected members lost responsibility to Norfolk county council for education, libraries and museums, strategic planning, transport and highways, waste disposal and social services, together the major elements in local public expenditure.[3] The year 1974 fell also in the middle of a period of accelerated population growth in the Norwich area, bringing new pressures and local land-use planning dilemmas, as well as new employment opportunities. The first document of the new style Norfolk structure plan, the *Survey*, was published in 1974.[4] This plan, and its two successors, have had a key role in guiding the growth of Norwich to the end of the last century.

To the regret of many, the 1974 reorganisation of local government retained the existing boundaries of Norwich, even though the built-up area had by then infiltrated into Broadland and South Norfolk Districts.[5] The overlap is now considerably greater. Norwich city council is thus an 'underbounded' local authority.

As in so many other British cities, it took a number of years for Norwich to heal the scars of war. There were forty-five bombing raids on Norwich between 1940 and 1943. These resulted in 340 deaths and over 1000 injured. There was damage to more than 14,000 houses, 1200 of which were destroyed. While miraculously the major churches, the castle and the public buildings in the city escaped serious damage, important parts of the core shopping area were destroyed, and many factories clustered around the inner city were damaged or demolished.

Housing was the primary concern of the corporation from 1945. Repairing the bomb damage provided the council with the impetus to clear a number of areas within the city of what had been substandard or slum housing. Examples of new public housing in the central area include the Vauxhall Street and West Pottergate areas, and the area between Ber Street and King Street. Clearing bombed property also provided the opportunity for council infill schemes, such as those between St Giles's, Pottergate and St Benedict's.

The main thrust of housing investment, however, came in large new estates within the city on what would now be called 'greenfield' sites. Between 1945 and 1955 over 6500 new homes were built by the council.[6] By the end of the 1950s new public sector housing areas, extending pre-war achievements, included Earlham and West Earlham, Tuckswood, Lakenham, Mile Cross, South Avenue and Mousehold.[7] The 1950 Norwich Extension Act allowed the building of the large Heartsease estate, as well as the development of areas of what had been the villages of Caistor St Edmund and Thorpe St Andrew. After delays because of the rationing of materials, new private sector housing also started to appear in the city, principally in the south-west sector across the outer ring-road at Eaton. Even so, throughout the 1950s and 1960s most of the new homes for purchase were being built outside the city, but in areas contiguous to it. To the east, Thorpe St Andrew continued the expansion it had experienced in the 1920s and 1930s. To the north east, large estate development occurred in Sprowston, in the north in Catton and Hellesdon, and to the north west in New Costessey.

The impact of all this housing investment in the twenty-five years or so from 1945 was to see the population of the Norwich area expand significantly,[8] even though the estimated population of the city itself increased by only just over three thousand between 1951 and 1971, from 120,300 to 123,600. The house building activity also created a very high proportion of public sector housing when compared with other similar-sized British cities. This fact coloured Norwich politics, undoubtedly contributing to the continuous reign of the local Labour Party from 1934 to 2002 (except for 1968 to 1970). It also influenced attitudes towards support given to the local economy, and to the planning of the central area of the city.

The concept of a major dual-carriageway inner ring road, to run outside the line of the medieval walls of the city, had been formulated well before 1939. The route was enshrined firmly in the 1945 plan, a document that was strong in its cater-for-the-motor-car vision, but weak in nearly every other concern of the good urban planner of today. The road was to join the three Norwich railway stations, and to be complemented by both an upgrading of the existing outer ring road and a new outer-outer ring.[9] The plan was the joint production of the then city engineer, H. C. Rowley, and consultant architects, and it focused on the core area of the city. It advocated improvements to visual amenity in Norwich, and care for the important medieval heritage of its churches and many other old buildings. It looked to the construction of a major 'civic centre' behind the city hall (which had opened to much acclaim in 1938). This would involve the completion of the city hall with two further sides to its full courtyard design, along with

a new library, two assembly halls, new law courts, a new 'Day Continuation College' and new council offices. It envisaged the movement of the city
centre cattle market from the castle mound to its present Hall Road site (a
move that eventually took place in 1960), and investment in new shopping
facilities.

A minority report of the city engineer foreshadowed a later major dispute about the line of the inner ring road on the north of the city centre
(now the Magdalen Street flyover) and dissented over the appropriate line
of the southern section of the inner ring that was never completed. Plans
for this section, across King Street and the river between Queen Street and
Thorpe railway station, were eventually formally abandoned in 1994 after
strong opposition to the proposals of the county council by the Norwich
Society, the Norwich city council and an alliance of environmental groups.
By the early 1970s sections of the inner ring had been built to the dual
carriageway standard advocated in the 1945 plan. These are the sections
that exist today to the west and north of the city centre. They were constructed at some cost to noteworthy buildings, but encouraged the thinking
behind what became known as the 'ring and loop' concept for road traffic
in the city centre.

The 1945 plan had proposed the idea of eleven 'precincts' within the inner
ring, each being largely car-free, with key road links between them, reaching into car parks for both commuters and shoppers. The proposals
provided a backcloth to decisions taken over the next twenty years, but it
was not until the 1967 *Draft Urban Plan*[10] that the idea was fully developed.
The work on the inner ring road and on the 1960–62 reconstruction of
St Stephen's was based on the 1945 plan. A major road proposal for a line
from Upper St Giles to the bottom of Exchange Street was never built. The
new library became the only element of the grandiose civic centre concept
to be completed. It opened in 1962 (to be destroyed by fire in 1994).
Otherwise such rebuilding within the main shopping and commercial
area as had taken place was largely on the original street pattern and on the
old building alignments. The 1967 plan was a serious rethink, especially in
the light of new pressures both for retail and office developments and with
an even greater awareness of the impact of rising rates of car-ownership.
It looked forward to a thirty-year growth of both population and of car
ownership.

By the mid 1960s there was widespread public awareness in Norwich that
the city centre boasted a particularly rich heritage of medieval churches
and other old buildings – with an outstanding cathedral and Norman castle – located on what was essentially a twelfth-century street pattern.[11] This

heritage was (and is) rich by European standards. The awareness had been fostered by the Norwich Society, by the local press, and by local architects and historians. It was formally recognised nationally in the initial listing of historic buildings, by what was then a new procedure in 1954 (rising to a total of more than 1500 buildings today). The city council was put under pressure to recognise that questions of employment, of the avail- ability of floorspace and of the exploitation of a range of retail and leisure opportunities in the city centre had to be accommodated within con- straints imposed by the height, mass, elevation, design and urban context of existing historic buildings.[12]

The appointment of A. A. ('Alfie') Wood as the first city planning officer in 1964 was an important response to this pressure. Wood was only the third such appointment in the United Kingdom. Planning had hitherto been left to city engineers. He was a qualified urban planner and architect, with experience in private practice in this country and in Finland. He was also an enthusiast and a publicist. The 1967 plan, prepared under new leg- islation dating from 1959, gave substance to the ring and loop concept, seeing it as a way to maintain and improve the quality of the urban envi- ronment in Norwich, while maintaining a commercial vitality. It proposed that vehicle access across the central area be prohibited, and that access be directed via the inner ring road with 'loops' into short stay 'shopper' car parks. Provision for commuter parking was to be outside the inner ring, combined with every encouragement to use public transport. Building on lessons from continental Europe, core areas of the principal shopping streets were to be pedestrianised. The cathedral close would become a con- servation area. Residential areas around the centre were to be zoned as twenty-nine 'environmental areas', following the principles of the national report from Professor Colin Buchanan.[13] Buchanan had used Norwich as one of his case studies, recommending the creation of 'areas ... with no extraneous traffic and within which considerations of environment pre- dominate over those of vehicles'.[14] Any new development in the city centre must demonstrate great respect for the context of older buildings (Map 5):

> Norwich stands alone as the largest city in the country which was relatively untouched by the Industrial Revolution and still possesses a wealth of inter- esting buildings and historic areas. Hence we have not only a special responsibility but a more difficult problem than many cities and towns.[15]

Many small streets in the centre of Norwich were suffering grievously from vehicle congestion by the mid 1960s (Plate 71). Parking restrictions were very limited and the city council had no formal powers to close streets to traffic on environmental grounds. This was to change in 1967, following

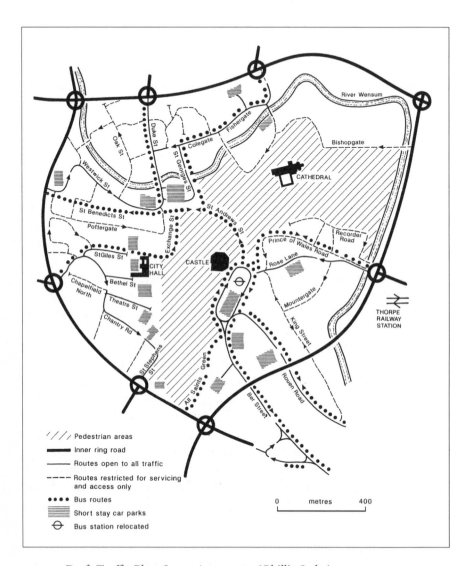

- / / / / Pedestrian areas
- ▬▬ Inner ring road
- ── Routes open to all traffic
- ---- Routes restricted for servicing and access only
- •••• Bus routes
- ▤ Short stay car parks
- ⊖ Bus station relocated

0　　　metres　　　400

MAP 5. Draft Traffic Plan, Inner Area, 1967. (*Phillip Judge*)

the closure of London Street for sewer works in 1965, a measure that was temporarily maintained on the basis of road safety, to widespread local approval. The closure was made permanent by a Ministry of Transport order, paving the way for the pedestrianisation of Bridewell Alley, St Gregory's Alley, Davey Place, the Back-of-the-Inns and Lower Goat Lane.[16] Proposals to close Gentleman's Walk to vehicles proved to be much more contentious, and its permanent closure was not achieved until 1986 (Plate 72).

The anti-car-commuter sentiments of the plan also contributed to a significant split among the ruling Labour group on the council in the early 1970s, when they were faced with a rising level of unemployment in the city and a large number of office-building proposals from developers.[17] Expectations of population growth had led to a surge of speculative interest in Norwich. Supporters of a positive response to such proposals saw not only more local jobs, but also a rising rateable income and increased viability to city centre retail trade. Luckily, the more extravagant of the proposals were resisted. In 1972 policy moved against giving planning permissions for new large-scale office developments and control over conversions of older industrial buildings was tightened.

By the standards of today the 1967 plan may be criticised for being so focused on road traffic issues to the exclusion of others. There was no strategy in the plan for shopping in the city, for leisure provision or for tourism. Neither social nor economic issues receive serious attention. There is no clear environmental strategy for the natural assets of the city. The core thinking of the 1967 plan has, however, remained the basic philosophy guiding the control of land uses in the city centre and in inner residential areas (Map 6).

One of the main features of changing land use within the inner ring road in the first three decades of the post-war period was the loss of manufacturing activity. Faced by bomb damage to their city centre properties, and wanting modern single storey premises with easy road access, many Norwich companies moved to the new industrial estates in the suburbs. They decamped to Hall Road, to Heartsease, to Vulcan Road beyond Mile Cross, to Sweet Briar and Whiffler Roads close to the Fakenham Road. Land and premises were made available by the city council, alongside own-build and developer factories and warehouses. The limited number of new manufacturing enterprises attracted to Norwich from elsewhere in the 1950s and 1960s also wanted suburban locations. The largest of these was May and Baker (subsequently Rhone Poulenc and now Aventis), which moved in the mid 1950s onto a 165 acre site just beyond the outer ring road at Sweet Briar Road.

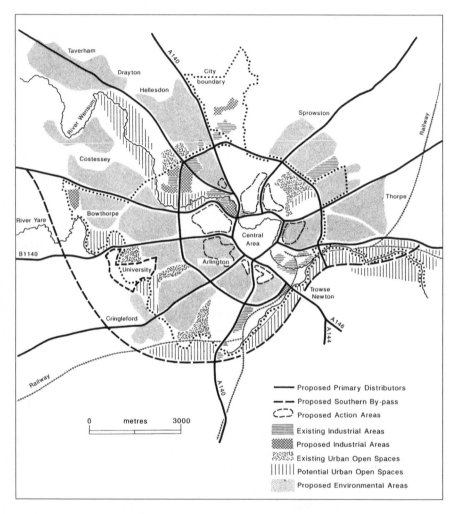

MAP 6. Greater Norwich Draft Urban Structure Plan, 1967. (*Phillip Judge*)

Manufacturing businesses in the central area in the pre-war period concentrated north of the river in the Colegate area, and were also found close
to Ber Street and King Street. A large number of these went out of business or were lost in mergers in the thirty years or so from 1945. This was
especially true of companies in the largest employment sectors in Norwich
at that time, clothing and footwear. Clothing accounted for some 10,000
people in 1961. Although employment in the footwear sector had fallen
back in the war years, by 1949 there were twenty-five shoe companies in
the city supporting nearly 10,000 people, close to the 1931 total of nearly
11,000. There were still 9000 employed a dozen years later. However, as
international tariffs came down and workers with shoe making skills emigrated, many famous Norwich names had disappeared by the mid 1980s.
Employment had declined to 3000 and was falling further. Companies
faced with closure included Sexton, Son and Everard, Edwards and
Holmes, the Norvic Shoe Company and Burlington (Plate 73).

Brewing was another city centre industry which has now all but disappeared. Brewing beer has a long history in Norwich, its best-known firm,
Steward and Patterson, for example, dating back to 1793.[18] In the 1870s there
were five major breweries in Norwich and a dozen smaller ones. Although
production levels declined in the inter-war period, output rose again during
the war, driven no doubt by sales to many thirsty air and ground crews of
the USAAF Seventh Airforce, with its eighteen airfields in the surrounding
Norfolk countryside. By 1961 Steward and Patteson was one of the largest
non-metropolitan breweries in the country. Take-overs, mergers and consolidation, following changing technologies in production and changing
tastes among consumers, meant, however, that many old, family-run breweries were ripe for acquisition by a handful of thrusting national brewing
companies. The Norwich breweries were large and easy prey. Acquisition
of hundreds of public houses was soon followed by brewery closure as the
transport of beer was revolutionised. Bullards' brewery was shut down in
1968, Steward and Patteson's two years later. Brewing on any scale in the
city finally ceased by 1985 with the closure of the King Street brewery, then
owned by Watney Mann but previously by Youngs, Crawshay and Youngs
(an old-established firm acquired by Bullards in 1957).

Another perhaps less evidently declining employment sector in Norwich
in these decades was the railway. In 1951 British Railways employed a
remarkable 5000 or more people in the city, in three stations and at the
Crown Point maintenance depot. Three stations, however, was excessive
for the needs of a city the size of Norwich after the nationalisation of the
rail system. The Victoria station on Queen's Road closed to passenger
traffic in 1955, to become a coal depot before eventually, in 1988, being

transformed into the site of a supermarket. The Midland station, on the old Midland and Great Northern line from Norwich to Fakenham, Melton Constable and King's Lynn and beyond, closed to passengers in 1959 and to freight a decade later. The site, on Heigham Street to the north east of the city centre, is now concealed beneath a string of car showrooms and warehouse shops. The scale of freight handled at the Thorpe station had also been dramatically reduced by the early 1970s. By then, railway employment in the city was just over a thousand.

The local production of gas was another employment sector that had disappeared by the late 1960s, as North Sea gas was introduced. The gas works at Bishopbridge Road, by the inner ring road, where it commanded a choice outlook across the river to the cathedral, became redundant. It closed in 1973, signalling the decline of Norwich as a commercial port, since shipments of coal were no longer required. The sea-borne trade in grain products simultaneously faded away.

In spite of these job losses, the registered levels of unemployment in Norwich remained below or close to (low) national rates throughout the 1950s and 1960s. The manufacturing sector overall did not expand its employment total, but it diversified: into light engineering, into printing and publishing and into electronic components and plastics, in particular, supported by the strength of May & Baker in chemicals, Reckitt & Colman in food products (employing 1200 in 1961) and by Mackintosh in chocolate products (employing 2100 people in the same year). Key engineering names of these two decades include Laurence & Scott (Plate 75), Barnards, Heatrae, and Boulton & Paul; and in 1967 a small sports car manufacturer decentralised from north-east London to the old airfield at Hethel, five miles from the Norwich boundary. Lotus Cars was destined to become one of the most important employers in the Norwich area by the end of the century. Another relatively small company at that time, based outside the city at Lenwade, also commenced a significant growth curve. Bernard Matthews plc became a major international food producer within three decades, proclaiming its Norfolk products far and wide through its distinctive advertising campaigns.

In contrast to the steady state of employment in manufacturing in the 1950s, the real expansion in jobs came in the service sectors of the local economy: in retail and wholesale distribution, in insurance and banking, and in many personal services. Major new offices for the Norwich Union general insurance and life insurance businesses were built close to St Stephen's. The headquarters of Her Majesty's Stationery Office moved from London to a new building at Anglia Square in 1967. The offices of the reinsurer Bland Payne (later Sedgwick, and now part of the American company, Marsh) also decentralised some eight hundred jobs from London to its anonymous building at the entrance to St Stephen's in 1973.

Within the public sector, the expansion of employment in education is worthy of note, as a rising birth rate drove the need for more places in the city in primary and secondary education after the 1944 Education Act. Norwich City College grew through these decades, the School of Art expanded, and the University of East Anglia offered a new source of employment from 1963. The 1951 census recorded 1462 residents working in the education sector, a total which rose to 2650 in 1961 and 4230 by 1971, a growth of over 300 per cent in twenty years. The expansion in employment in medical and dental care was only slightly less marked, to a total of 5950 in 1971 (see Table 19.3).

Education demands saw a flurry of school building in Norwich in the 1950s and 1960s. New primary schools appeared at West Earlham, North Park Avenue, South Tuckswood and Bluebell Road and two went up at Heartsease. New secondary schools were built at Lakenham and Bluebell Road, with further expansion at all of the others. The City College, established as a technical college in 1891, was located on the Ipswich Road from 1939 and was extended with a major new building in 1953. And the Norwich Teacher Training College, its premises in College Road bombed in 1942, moved to the south west of the city at Keswick Hall, where a big construction programme was similarly undertaken.

The major event in education in the city in the early post war decades was undoubtedly the founding of the University of East Anglia.[19] By the early 1970s, when it had attracted about 3000 students, the university was already a significant contributor to the life of Norwich, to its employment mix, its economy, its cultural activities, and to its politics. From the outset it was a university that lived by the Norfolk motto of 'Do Different', with its innovative stress on seminar teaching methods, on multi-disciplinary 'Schools' of study, on the use of coursework in examination assessments, in its uncompromising architecture. Although town-gown relations were not always easy, the university gradually began to be seen as a clear asset to the city.

Major investment also took place in hospital services in Norwich in this first post-war period. Improvements were made at the West Norwich hospital, at the Hellesdon and David Rice hospitals on the Drayton Road and at St Andrew's Hospital on the Yarmouth Road. General practice surgeries and health centres were built in the new housing areas. The principal investment was on the city centre site of the Norfolk and Norwich Hospital, where major new accident-and-emergency and maternity and paediatric facilities in specially designed buildings opened in 1965.

Norwich inherited an excellent legacy of public parks from the inter-war period.[20] The 1960s saw pressure for further public open space and the restraint of development within the river valleys of both the Yare and the Wensum, as well as for investment to open up the river banks in both the city centre and the suburbs to public access. Other amenity landmarks of the 1960s include the completion of the new central library and the first public indoor swimming pool at St Augustine's. Against a background of falling cinema attendance, a new cinema opened at Anglia Square in 1970. The Theatre Royal was refurbished with public funds and placed in the hands of a trust in the early 1970s.

Throughout most of the last quarter of the twentieth century East Anglia has been the fastest growing region in the United Kingdom in terms of population. The principal driving force behind this growth was a progressive geographical redistribution of the increasing number of households moving out of and away from Greater London.[21] By the 1970s this growth was spilling into Norfolk at an historically rapid rate:

Table 19.1 Number of residents in Norfolk, 1951–1999

	Norfolk Residents	Percentage increase
1951	548,000	–
1961	561,000	2.37
1971	617,600	10.09
1981	686,300	11.12
1991	759,400	10.65
1999	796,500	4.89

Source: Census of Population and Office of National Statictics.

The growth in the county was not, however, repeated within the boundaries of the city of Norwich. A boundary extension in 1968 brought 650 acres of land into the city at Bowthorpe, allowing a major expansion of both public sector and private sector homes. But household size in the city, as nationally, was falling. The average size of households in Norfolk, estimated to be 2.64 persons in 1975 had fallen to 2.27 persons by the millennium. As a result, even with more houses being built, the population of the city has remained essentially unchanged for the previous three decades: from 123,600 in 1971 to 126,100 in 1981, to 127,200 in 1991 and down again to 123,500 in 1999.[22] This has been at a time when, in terms of population, Norfolk has been one of the fastest-growing counties in Britain.

The overall increase in the population of the Norwich policy area during the last three decades has come in those contiguous suburbs that are controlled by Broadland and South Norfolk district councils, and in the surrounding self-standing parishes. For example, between 1981 and 1991 the electoral wards of Cawston, Drayton, Plumstead, Reepham, Spixworth, Taverham and Thorpe St Andrew in Broadland, and Cringleford and Colney, Forehoe, Old Costessey, and Long Stratton in South Norfolk, each increased their population by more than 10 per cent. At the same time, most of the sixteen electoral wards within the city of Norwich were losing population, the exceptions being Bowthorpe, Catton Grove, Mancroft, Thorpe Hamlet and University.

Over a longer time period, the growth pressures on the areas around the city may be seen in the following table.

Table 19.2 Population totals in ten key villages (by civil parish), 1951–1999

	1951	1991	1999
Costessey	4,995	9,710	9,905
Cringleford	868	2,100	2,145
Hethersett	1,413	4,635	5,385
Long Stratton	855	2,896	3,310
Mulbarton	598	2,912	2,930
Drayton	983	2,927	4,330
Reepham	1,413	2,325	2,565
Spixworth	945	4,400	4,430
Sprowston	5,485	13,785	14,395
Taverham	680	6,711	10,495

Source: Census of Population and Office of National Statistics.

The figures show how the new building has gone in phases in the different areas, with a distinct slowing up in the 1990s in Cringleford, Mulbarton and Spixworth, for instance.

By 1999 the resident population of the Norwich built-up area was estimated in the county's *Structure Plan* to be 194,930, an increase of 3290 from 1991, while that of the Norwich policy area was 256,800, an increase of 8135. Looking at the further geographical influence of Norwich, the travel-to-work-area had a 1999 population of 367,430, and the shopping 'catchment area' one of approximately 600,000.

Relatively rapid growth in population in and around Norwich had been anticipated by regional planners at the end of the 1960s. Faced with a national population that was growing quite strongly at that time, the

authors of the 1964 *South-East Study* included the Norwich area as a possible candidate to receive a London overspill population of 30,000.[23]
Preparation for this eventuality and for a rising level of net in-migration
was reflected in the land-use strategy put forward in the 1966 *Joint Growth
Study* prepared by the Norfolk county council and Norwich city council
planning departments.[24] This looked at strategies for accommodating an
increase in population of 130,000 or so (without any London overspill) in
the Norwich area by 2001, and at an employment requirement of 59,000
additional jobs. Without fully grasping the implications of rising rates of
car ownership, and without much analysis of the available data, it envisaged a high proportion of the additional jobs being created in the central
area of Norwich.[25] Housing was to be built in six 'linear developments',
forming axes into the surrounding areas beyond a 'Green Belt'.

The theme was picked up in general terms in the 1974 *East Anglia
Regional Study*;[26] and with more detail in the 1974 *Norfolk Structure Plan*.[27]
This was the first of the new style structure plans dealing with the county
as a whole. There were further editions in the mid 1980s and mid 1990s,
each with a clear set of land-use policies and dispositions for new housing
over a fifteen-year period, and with demographic forecasts looking twenty
or twenty-five years ahead. In accordance with a 'predict and provide'
approach, the pattern and extent of development since that time has closely
followed the forecasts and guidance of that plan.

The latest Norfolk county structure plan, from 1999, taking on board
current national policy thinking towards 'sustainability', points to a partial
revision of the past strategy for the Norwich policy area.[28] Recognising that
the axes strategy has resulted in the growth of 'dormitory' villages, with
much of the housing development being at relatively low densities, the
most recent plan places a renewed emphasis on the construction of additional housing in core areas. It also stresses the role of public transport
(including the seven 'park-and-ride' sites at the edge of the city on the
key axes), and affirms the desirability of widening the distribution of
employment possibilities.

The changing pattern of employment in the city of Norwich through the
last thirty years of the twentieth century is summarised in Table 19.3. The
period has been one of rising employment totals, from 77,570 in 1971 to
93,425 in 1991 and then of a levelling off to 89,515 in 1998.[29] Within the
manufacturing sectors, half a dozen factors (five of which are immediately
evident in Table 19.3 below) lie behind the fall of nearly 8000 jobs and a
corresponding fall in the percentage of manufacturing from 25 to 13 per cent
in the overall total. There has been a continuing decline in employment

in the footwear, clothing and textile sectors, a reduction in the engineering sectors (but not beyond the preservation of a significant pool of local skills and expertise),[30] and a loss of 2600 jobs in food manufacturing.[31] Decline in these three areas of activity was not offset by rises in chemicals and a more moderate increase in the numbers employed in printing and publishing, from 2170 to 2600, led by Jarrolds and the Eastern Counties Newspapers Group. The sixth feature is not apparent in Table 19.3, in that the full picture for the Norwich area, more evident in 1998 than in 1971, needs to take account of activity located outside the city boundaries, in the industrial estates of the suburbs and the adjacent communities.[32]

In the retailing sector, employment has fallen back from the rapid rates of increase experienced in the 1970s, but with totals still rising outside the wholesale and food sub-sectors, perhaps as a result of the impact of the Castle Mall investment.[33] Very large increases in employment have come in the hotel and restaurant sector, reflecting both rising real incomes locally and the growing numbers of tourist visitors to the city.[34]

The largest overall growth in the commercial services between 1971 and 1991 came in the financial intermediation sector. This is accounted for by the surge in employment in the insurance industry and especially reflects the rapid expansion of the Norwich Union Group in the 1980s, related to the 1986 Financial Services Act. By 1987 Norwich Union employed 4500 people in the city. The totals slipped after 1991, following the decentralisation of some Norwich Union activities to Sheffield,[35] and with fewer employment opportunities now on offer in the main clearing banks, as well as in the Norwich and Peterborough Building Society and the Sedgwick Group. Substantial increases in employment over the three decades have also been seen in the professional business services and similar sectors in the city, together providing nearly 7000 additional jobs. Broadcasting, public relations and advertising have all become more important features led by Anglia Television.[36]

Although employment in parts of the public sector has contracted in the 1990s, with the closure of the Stationery Office and the removal of the Central Computer Services Agency out to the Thorpe Business Park, the earlier growth experienced in both education and the health and social care professions has continued. These latter two sectors were employing nearly 18,500 by 1998, or over one-fifth of the total number of employees working in Norwich.

One element of the local economy that does not stand out easily from the categories used to list employment totals is tourism. The spending patterns of day trippers and longer-term visitors have come to constitute an important component of the Norwich economy. This is, indeed, the case,

Table 19.3 City of Norwich employees in employment, 1951–1998

Sectors	1951	1961	1971	1981	1991	1998
Agriculture, Utilities	2,037	2,130	1,170	1,335	1,530	620
Non-metallic, non-chemical manufacture	19,966	20,100	12,140	11,330	8,290	5,320
Chemical manufacture	242	470	960	835	1,670	2,515
Traditional metal manufacturing/engineering	2,384	3,890	4,450	4,310	3,010	2,730
Hi-tech metal manufacturing/engineering	3,167	3,430	1,815	1,905	1,070	910
Construction	4,955	5,330	3,775	3,860	2,285	2,655
Motor vehicle sale, repair	1,656	2,600	2,590	2,815	2,405	2,780
Wholesale	2,598	3,520	3,195	3,755	3,435	2,990
Food retail	2,256	*9,480	1,930	2,125	1,790	1,835
Other retail	4,795		6,060	6,840	6,940	7,265
Hotels and restaurants	2,372	1,580	2,555	3,640	5,135	6,115
Transport, storage, telecommunications	5,671	5,730	5,885	6,175	6,575	4,445
Financial intermediation	2,630	3,410	7,940	9,245	13,325	10,310
Property, renting	–	–	750	900	1,160	1,460
Computing, R&D	–	–	135	160	230	505
Professional business	1,302	1,500	2,070	2,515	3,705	4,105
Other business services	–	–	1,430	2,470	4,645	6,240
Public administration, defence	3,991	3,570	6,010	6,445	7,345	5,115
Education	1,462	2,650	4,230	4,565	6,940	7,330
Health care	1,825	2,210	5,950	7,575	8,790	11,140
Personal services	2,880	3,860	2,515	3,020	3,145	3,125
TOTALS	66,189	75,460	77,560	85,815	93,425	89,515

Source: Census of Employment, Annual Employment Survey, Office of National Statistics, Public and Corporate Economic Consultants.

Note: * 1951 Census does not distinguish between food and other retail activities.

despite the fact that, for tourists from overseas and for people on 'week-end breaks', Norwich does not have the same appeal as Bath, Cambridge, Chester or York. In 1998 the English Tourist Board estimated that within its city boundaries Norwich attracted expenditures of over £20 million by UK overnight tourists and more than £30 million by those from overseas. Day visitors added substantially to these totals. Tourist related businesses recruited close to 4400 full-time employees or their equivalent. Improved road, rail and air links, as well as an increase in the number of local hotels, restaurants and guest houses, the upgrading of older premises, improved shopping facilities and enhanced museum and gallery attractions, have all combined to generate considerable impact. The historic character of the city, with its wide range of modern amenities, is as much prized by visitors, as it is by local residents.

Looking back over the last twenty-five years of the development of Norwich, it is possible to point to five developments that have had strong implications for the growth of the city and have changed the way it is regarded, both locally and nationally.

As already noted, the area within the old city walls across the River Wensum on the north side of the core area, and largely now within the inner ring road, 'Norwich-over-the-Water', was badly hit by bombing in the Second World War. It took a long time to recover. Future development in the area, in the mixture of bomb-sites and bomb-damaged buildings, prized older properties (including nine medieval churches and six other chapels and meeting houses), a difficult street pattern and a jumble of industrial and commercial enterprises, became a source of considerable controversy by the 1960s.[37] The importance of the architectural heritage had been recognised in the slum-clearance programmes in the area in the inter-war period and by restoration work on many individual buildings by the city council, the Norwich Preservation Trust, and by private owners. The locality had also received external recognition in the 1958 Civic Trust sponsored cosmetic 'facelift' to the façades of the buildings along Magdalen Street. Many people, however, regretted the aggressive architecture of the HMSO building and of the shops, car park and cinema at Anglia Square, built between 1968 and 1970. Many also agreed with the Norwich Society when it took the city council to appeal on the line of the Magdalen Street fly-over, built in 1972.

Thereafter, attitudes changed. From the 1970s, plans proposing large-scale redevelopment were resisted. Access to the river was given a new priority, as was the reintroduction of high-density housing. The parish of Coslany, with a population of 7000 in 1841, had one of merely 300 by 1971. A number of developments slowly began to reverse this massive decline. The distinctive architecture and commercial success of the Friars Quay development in 1974 encouraged further residential investments at Barnard's, Hopper's and Dyer's Yards, together with the conversion of the old Norvic factory to apartments, along with a number of small infills. The proposed hotel on the Norvic site has not been built, but new life has been breathed into the area and the quality of many of the older buildings recognised and treasured. The new sensitivities and approaches that were pursued and fought over in Coslany now influence permissions given for new construction and building alterations throughout the city.

The impact of the development of the airport on the city has been very different. Over a quarter of a century of scheduled air services, especially to Schipol in the Netherlands, has given support to many businesses in the Norwich area, from the law, financial services and media through to the manufacturing sector. And air-related services have become a major employer in their own right. These include air-freight, the passenger terminal services, the KLM aircraft engineering facility and ticket call centre, what is now the Hilton Hotel, and services related to club and business charter flying.

RAF Horsham St Faith was an important fighter station in the Second World War, but by 1963 the Ministry of Defence had announced that it was to leave the airfield. After much discussion about possible alternatives for a civil airport for Norwich, the airfield was purchased jointly by the city and the county councils in 1967.[38] The purchase included the hangar and repair facilities, a sizeable industrial estate, and the servicemen's quarters that proved invaluable for the next twenty-five years as student residences for the new University of East Anglia. The initial success of the airport was very much tied in with the success of the fledgling company, Air Anglia. This was formed in 1970, with backing from the Norwich Union, in a merger of three small operators. The oil and gas industries of both the southern and the northern sectors of the North Sea provided a steady demand for flights between Schipol and Aberdeen. Services to the Channel Islands were offered in the summer months. The passenger demand has been progressively enhanced by other business users and by tourist charter flights. From a passenger head-count of 36,000 in 1971–2 the numbers rose to over 450,000 in 1999–2000. Air Anglia became Air UK, which eventually became a subsidiary of KLM, the Dutch national airline. From the initial portacabins, a new passenger terminal was opened in 1988.

The airport site could have made a major contribution to the housing needs of Norwich in the 1960s. This option was considered, but another site had already been lined up in earlier planning documents (including the 1945 *Plan*): that of Bowthorpe, to the west of the city. Some 600 acres were purchased by the city council in 1973 for a planned development, on land added to the city by the Boundary Commission in 1968 for the intended accommodation of 13,500 people.[39] The 1974 master plan for Bowthorpe was based on a concept of three 'villages', each with its own range of local activities, together supporting a commercial and public service core. Land was set aside for a major employment area close to the A47 road. The housing was to be of mixed tenure, and public transport provision was to be integrated into the design. Social, educational and retail facilities were to be provided early in the life of the development. There was to be extensive planting in communal spaces, and each area was to have a coherent design.

The result has been a considerable achievement for a local authority the size of the city council. Much determination by both officers and members was required. The original rate of progress was hindered by borrowing restrictions (especially for housing) placed on local authorities by central government in the early 1980s. It was also unfortunate that the land was purchased at the top of a land price boom, which limited the profits that could be made by selling it on to developers and using the funds for extending the infrastructure. And Bowthorpe gained something of a negative social image in its early days. Now, however, many would consider Bowthorpe a preferred residential environment to several of the more recent large-scale private sector suburbs in the neighbouring authorities.

Arguably, though, the key development in the centre of Norwich in the past three decades has been the opening of the Castle Mall shopping centre in 1993. This marked an initial stage in a longer-term strategy to improve retail and leisure facilities in the central area.[40] Castle Mall has received considerable acclaim: for its innovative architectural solution to a problem that had been worrying the city council for over twenty years, for the quality of the building and its facilities, and for the contribution it makes to Norwich as a regional shopping centre (Plate 74).

The development problems for the site had been twofold. One was to discover the best use for the large carpark that had replaced the original central cattle-market in 1960, if it was not simply to be grassed over as a public park to provide a better setting for the castle behind. The other was the form of redevelopment of the adjacent Timberhill area. This had been badly damaged in the war but it still contained many significant older buildings. The area offered a logical extension of the existing shopping facilities, at a time when Norwich was beginning to look 'under-shopped' relative to its half million catchment population, especially when compared with other towns and cities. There had been no significant retail investment in the centre since the completion of the rebuilding of St Stephen's in the early 1960s. And 30 per cent of the existing shopping space worked within the constraint of being housed in listed buildings. At the same time the city council expressed a fierce determination not to let too much additional shopping floorspace be developed in suburban 'edge-of-town' sites, in the interests of the commercial health of the city centre.[41]

A number of different schemes were put forward over the years, latterly with the city council looking for a developer/financier partner. The breakthrough came when rising retail rental levels made financially viable the clever solution of burying a major part of the 26,000 square metres of floorspace in a vast deep hole in the ground. The concept came from a local firm of architects, Lambert, Scott & Innes. The result has provided a new landscaped approach to the castle and a means of easing pedestrian movement between different parts of the shopping area surrounding the Mall. It also offers 1050 car parking spaces, a twelve-screen cinema and an enclosed shopping mall that stands favourable comparison in both quality and variety with any other of its size in Britain.

The creation of Castle Mall is now being complemented by the investment in shops as well as in housing and leisure facilities on the Riverside site beside the Norwich Thorpe railway station. A physical link between the two areas is being served by a new pedestrian bridge over the river and by a combination of renovations and new buildings on Prince of Wales Road, Rose Lane, Mountergate and King Street. Further shopping and leisure development is now taking place at the Chapelfield site of the Rowntree Mackintosh (later Nestlé) chocolate factory which closed in 1999.

The fifth key development in Norwich in the past twenty-five years has been of great significance: the continuing growth of the University of East Anglia.[42] Initially recruiting a largely young and inexperienced academic staff, the university took some time to gain a clear national reputation. By the beginning of the 1980s it was ready to weather a severe financial storm imposed upon it by central government and to claim academic distinction in a number of areas. The core buildings of the Denys Lasdun design had been completed and new student residences and new 'Schools of Study' (Law, Education, Computing and Accountancy) allowed student numbers to increase. Several academic disciplines were being noticed for their research achievement at that time, both nationally and internationally. These included the famous creative writing course, Chemical Sciences, British, European and American History, American Literature, Music, Social Work, Environmental Sciences, Development Studies with its Overseas Development Group, and Biological Sciences.

The expertise in genetics of the School of Biological Sciences both led to and benefited from the arrival of the John Innes Institute in 1967, to a site at Colney across the river from the main campus. The institute, founded in 1904, was a world centre of expertise in plant breeding and genetics. Also in 1967, the British Sugar Corporation laboratories (which closed in 1999) came to a nearby site, and the large Institute of Food Research of the Ministry of Agriculture followed two years later. What is now the Norwich Research Park grew further on the arrival of a significant part of the Plant Breeding Institute from Cambridge in 1986, and investment in the Sainsbury Laboratory through a large grant from the Gatsby Foundation shortly afterwards. With the advent of the Nitrogen Fixation Laboratory from the University of Sussex in 2000, the Research Park is now the largest concentration of plant science expertise in Western Europe. It is also enhanced by the proximity of the BUPA hospital, built in 1984, and the new major District General Hospital, opened in 2001–2 to replace the Norfolk and Norwich Hospital previously located in the city centre.

The university benefited greatly from the generosity of the Sainsbury family in the mid seventies. The Sainsbury Centre for the Visual Arts was built to house the collections of Sir Robert and Lady Sainsbury, and it also provides space for visiting exhibitions, for the university art collection, for what is now the School of World Art and Museology, and for a cafeteria and a restaurant. The award-winning building, designed by Sir Norman Foster, was opened in 1978, and was further extended in 1990. The collection is of international significance and draws many tourists to the campus.

The university is now an institution of over 13,000 students. New residences have been built, and the academic range has been extended through the 1990s. The university has also expanded into medical education, first with a School of Occupational Therapy and Physiotherapy, then a School of Nursing and a School of Health Policy and Practice, and in 2002 with a full Medical School. All are linked to the new hospital and recognised in its name, the Norfolk and Norwich University Hospital. The opening of the Norfolk Sports Park on campus in 2000, built with the aid of a Lottery grant, makes a major contribution to the facilities of Norwich and the county. Overall, the university can now regard itself as being firmly in the British top twenty, in terms of rated research and teaching quality. It is also now one of Norwich's major employers and generators of local spending power.

This chapter can do no more than broadly summarise the complex history of a growing and changing city. Many single events of importance to local residents have been omitted (such as the holding of the Royal Agricultural Show in Norwich in 1957, or the city centre fires that burnt down Garlands' department store in 1970 and the Central Library in 1994, or Norwich City Football Club winning the League Cup in 1985). Nor have the fortunes and changing roles of many key institutions been touched upon (such as the Art School, the cathedral and its long programme of refurbishment, the work of the many religious denominations, the creative use of redundant medieval churches, the important local press and broadcasting services, the Norfolk and Norwich Chamber of Commerce and Industry, the various business support agencies). Most of the major local companies have experienced varying fortunes, yet a full history of this fascinating but neglected period remains to be written.

Since the end of the Second World War, in common with other towns and cities, Norwich has had to adapt to new patterns of employment and to the strains of growth in both population and in average household incomes. The economy is now more diversified than it was in the inter-war period, giving it a resilience against shocks from the more open international trading environment facing local companies. From being a regional centre that was rather isolated from most of industrial Britain, Norwich has benefited from the electrification of the railway to Ipswich and London in 1988. The progressive removal of the road traffic bottlenecks through the creation of bypasses on the A47 and A11 over the past thirty years has also brought Norwich closer to the rest of the United Kingdom. The present pressures of population growth in the Norwich travel-to-work-area, largely from in-migrants from elsewhere in the United Kingdom, reflect economic success, investment confidence and the creation of a residential environment that many would claim stands comparison with any other British city of a similar size.

Although not multi-cultural in the sense of many other British cities, Norwich has continued its long tradition of a rich cultural life, offering a wide range of activities and events in all of the arts. The Norwich Triennial Festival is just one highlight, featuring alongside full annual calendars of performances and exhibitions. The flow of in-migrants, the many national and international tourists, and the rising student population have also done much to counter any inherent tendencies towards provincialism. The long history of close commercial and cultural links across the North Sea has been enhanced and built upon.

Although significant pockets of disadvantage remain, there is no doubt that over fifty-five years the quality of life for the majority of the population of Norwich has greatly improved. Many of the gains have come with advances in the national economy, with rising real household incomes and through better public services. But a considerable measure of the enhancement has come from local decisions, from investments by local companies, organisations and public authorities. Great strides have been taken in protecting the best of the old and in improving the quality of the new in the built environment. Views still differ as to whether the city has yet learned to live with the motor car. But social facilities, public amenities and local services of all kinds continue to get better. The refurbishment of the Castle Museum, and the arrival there of Tate East, along with the opening of the new Millennium Building, 'The Forum', both in 2001, mark two further steps in maintaining the justifiably proud and longstanding accolade of Norwich as a 'fine city' (Plate 76).

Notes

Notes to Introduction

1. Quoted in R. H. Mottram, *East Anglia: England's Eastern Province* (London, 1933), p. 84. See also the introduction to *History of Norwich*, i, which includes an account of earlier histories of the city and its historians.
2. C. Morris, ed., *The Illustrated Journeys of Celia Fiennes, c. 1682–1712* (London, 1982), pp. 136–7. See also 'Journal of a Tour through Suffolk, Norfolk, Lincolnshire and Yorkshire in the Summer of 1741', in C. Harper-Bill, C. Rawcliffe and R. G. Wilson, eds, *East Anglia's History: Studies in Honour of Norman Scarfe* (Woodbridge, 2002), p. 271, where the writer echoes Fiennes, 'the buildings which have anything of grandeur in them are all Gothic'.
3. D. Defoe, *A Tour Through the Whole Island of Great Britain* (2 vols, London, 1927), i, pp. 62–3.
4. *Select Committee of the House of Lords on Intemperance*, PP (1877) xl, Second Report, pp. 82–5.
5. A. D. Bayne, *Royal Illustrated History of Eastern England* (2 vols, Great Yarmouth, 1872), i, pp. 235–69.
6. H. V. Morton, *In Search of England* (nineteenth edn, London, 1933), pp. 236–7.
7. For the most recent, convenient and extensive survey of urban development in the modern period, see *The Cambridge Urban History of Britain* (3 vols, Cambridge, 2000), ii (ed., P. Clark); iii (ed., M. Daunton).
8. An account of the extended East Anglian region is to be found in T. Williamson, *England's Landscapes, II: East Anglia and the Fens* (English Heritage, forthcoming 2005).
9. *Norwich Cathedral*, p. 603. The Norwich newspapers carried the list of Sunday morning preachers fixed by the bishop twice yearly.
10. Mottram, *East Anglia*, pp. 84–5.
11. D. Cubitt, A. L. Mackley and R. G. Wilson, eds., *The Great Tour of John Patteson, 1778–1779* (NRS, lxvii, 2003), pp. 80, 91.
12. E. J. Climenson, *Passages from the Diaries of Mrs Philip Lybbe Powys* (London, 1899), p. 211.

13. See Chapter 15.

14. See Chapter 9 for a detailed account of Norwich's worsted industry.

15. J. James, *History of the Worsted Manufacture in England* (London, 1857), p. 259, where he also quotes Macaulay.

16. For a discussion of Norwich in the hierarchy of eighteenth century European cities, see Chapter 6.

17. See Chapter 8.

18. R. D. Eklid, 'Popular Protest in Mid-Georgian England: The Norwich Food Riot of 1766' (UEA, Norwich, MA thesis, 1994).

19. P. J. Corfield, 'The Social and Economic History of Norwich, 1650–1850: A Study in Urban Growth' (University of London, PhD thesis, 1976), p. 250.

20. Harper-Bill, Rawcliffe and Wilson, *East Anglia's History*, p. 272. Similar views were expressed by Arthur Young in *The Farmer's Tour through the East of England* (4 vols, London, 1771), ii, pp. 75–7.

21. *The Second Report of the Commissioners of Inquiry into the State of Large Towns and Populous Districts*, PP (1845), xviii, Appendix, part ii, p. 281.

22. C. B. Hawkins, *Norwich: A Social Study* (London, 1910), p. 10.

23. See Chapter 16.

24. W. W. White, *History, Gazetteer and Directory of Norfolk* (Sheffield, 1890), p. 526.

25. In his introduction to Hawkins, *Norwich*, pp. ix–x.

26. A. Mee, *The King's England: Norfolk* (London, 1940), p. 265.

27. See Chapters 13 and 19.

28. See Chapter 10.

29. See Chapter 14.

30. See, for example, H. Heaton, *The Yorkshire Woollen and Worsted Industries from the Earliest Times up to the Industrial Revolution* (second edn, Oxford, 1965); J. de L. Mann, *The Cloth Industry in the West of England from 1640 to 1880* (Oxford, 1971); J. de L. Mann and A. P. Wadsworth, *The Cloth Trade and Industrial Lancashire, 1600–1780* (Manchester, 1931).

31. J. B. Priestley, *English Journey* (London, 1934), p. 380.

Notes to Chapter 1: The Changing Face of Norwich

1. P. D. A. Harvey, *Maps in Tudor England* (London, 1993), p. 7. See *History of Norwich*, i, Chapter 1.

2. *RCN*, i, p. cxii, and opposite p. 46.

3. R. Hale and M. Rodgers, *The Greyfriars of Norwich* (Norwich, 1991), pp. 40–6.

4. Blomefield, *Norfolk*, iv, p. 450.

5. J. Campbell, 'Norwich', in M. Lobel, ed., *Historic Towns*, ii (London, 1975), p. 21.

6. Blomefield, *Norfolk*, iv, p. 529.

7. L. Jardine, *Worldly Goods: A New History of the Renaissance* (London, 1996), p. 272.

8. Jardine, *Worldly Goods*, figure 17.

9. J. Kirkpatrick, *The Streets and Lanes of Norwich*, ed. W. Hudson (Norwich, 1889), opposite p. 114.

10. Blomefield, *Norfolk*, iii, p. 213.

11. T. Chubb and G. Stephen, *A Description of the Printed Maps of Norfolk, 1541–1914 and a Descriptive List of Norwich Plans, 1541–1918* (Norwich, 1928).

12. R. Frostick, *The Printed Plans of Norwich, 1558–1840* (Norwich, 2002), pp. 1–20.

13. C. Delano-Smith and R. J. P. Kain, *English Maps: A History* (London, 1991), p. 185 and figure 6.4.

14. Cited by S. Tyacke and J. Huddy, *Christopher Saxton and Tudor Map-Making* (London, 1980), p. 54.

15. Pound, *Census*, p. 13.

16. F. Meeres, *A History of Norwich* (Chichester, 1998), note inside front cover.

17. M. Atkin and S. Margeson, *Life on a Medieval Street: Excavations on Alms Lane, Norwich 1976* (Norwich, 1985), p. 18.

18. A. Shelley, *Dragon Hall, Norwich, Excavation and Survey of a Late Medieval Merchant's Trading Complex* (EAA, forthcoming), p. 28.

19. C. Morris, ed., *The Illustrated Journeys of Celia Fiennes c. 1682–1712* (London, 1947), p. 148.

20. See *History of Norwich*, i, p. xxviii.

21. T. Hawes, *Index to Norwich City Officers* (NRS, lii, 1986), p. 64.

22. N. Pevsner and B. Wilson, *The Buildings of England. Norfolk*, i, *Norwich and the North East* (London, 1997), pp. 316–18.

23. Pevsner and Wilson, *Norfolk*, i, p. 320.

24. Kirkpatrick, *Streets and Lanes*, p. 80.

25. *RCN*, ii, p. 134. See above, p. 217 for the effectiveness of later paving schemes.

26. Blomefield, *Norfolk*, iv, map of 1746.

27. Frostick, *Printed Plans*, p. 46.

28. There is no reference in Stoker's index to Blomefield's correspondence to the making of the map or to Cleer or Corbridge's earlier maps: D. Stoker, ed., *The Correspondence of the Reverend Francis Blomefield* (NRS, lv, 1990).

29. P. Eden, *Dictionary of Land Surveyors and Local Cartographers of Great Britain and Ireland, 1550–1850* (3 vols, Folkestone, 1976), ii, p. 156.

30. A. D. Bayne, *Comprehensive History of Norwich: Including a Survey of the City* (Norwich, 1869), p. 572. See Chapter 9.

31. See S. Wearing, *Georgian Norwich and its Builders* (Norwich, 1926), for the buildings of a major regional group of architects-cum-builders, the

Brettinghams, the Ivorys and William Wilkins senior. Also listed in
H. M. Colvin, *A Biographical Dictionary of British Architects, 1600–1840* (third
edn, London, 1995).

32. See below, Chapter 6.
33. See Chapter 11.
34. William Lee, *Report to the General Board of Health on a Preliminary Inquiry
into the Sewerage, Drainage and Supply of Water, and the Sanitary Conditions
of the Inhabitants of the City of Norwich* (London, 1851).
35. 1907 Ordnance Survey Sheet, Norfolk LXIII. 15, reduced to 1:4340: Alan Godfrey Maps (Newcastle-upon-Tyne).
36. A. Briggs, *Victorian Cities* (London, 1963), pp. 16–17.
37. See Chapter 11.
38. A. P. Anderson, *The Captain and the Norwich Parks* (Norwich, 2000), p. 21.

Notes to Chapter 2: Government to 1660

1. NRO, NCR, 17D, Book of Orders for the Dutch and Walloon Strangers in
Norwich, 1564–1643, fos 16r–18r. The editors are grateful to Dr Raingard Esser
and Dr Andrew Hopper for their assistance in preparing this chapter for publication. For the wider national background, see K. Wrightson, *English
Society, 1580–1680* (London, 1982); and J. A. Sharpe, *Early Modern England: A
Social History, 1550–1760* (London, 1987).
2. B. Ayers, *Norwich* (London, 1994), p. 92. See also Chapter 1, above.
3. J. Pound, *Tudor and Stuart Norwich* (Chichester, 1988), pp. 26–7.
4. Pound, *Norwich*, pp. 28–30; A. King, 'The Merchant Class and Borough
Finances of Late Medieval Norwich' (University of Oxford, DPhil thesis,
1989), p. 27.
5. Pound, *Norwich*, p. 43.
6. See *History of Norwich*, i, Chapter 10.
7. Pound, *Norwich*, pp. 71–4.
8. J. T. Evans, *Seventeenth-Century Norwich: Politics, Religion and Government,
1620–1690* (Oxford, 1979), pp. 140–3.
9. J. F. Pound, 'The Social and Trade Structure of Norwich 1525–1575', *Past and
Present*, xxxiv (1966), pp. 50–2; For Jannys, see Tanner, *CLMN*, p. 241.
10. Pound, *Norwich*, pp. 10, 15.
11. J. F. Pound, ed., *The Military Survey of 1522 for Babergh Hundred* (SRS, xxviii,
1986); R. W. Hoyle, ed., *Early Tudor Craven: Subsidies and Assessments,
1510–1547* (Yorkshire Archaeological Society Records Series, cxxxxv, 1987);
R. W. Hoyle, ed., *The Military Survey of Gloucestershire, 1522* (Gloucestershire
Record Series, vi, 1993).
12. Pound, 'Social and Trade Structure', pp. 50–1.

13. Pound, *Norwich*, pp. 10–12.

14. Pound, *Norwich*, p. 35.

15. Pound, *Norwich*, pp. 55, 60. More than half of the textile workers recorded in the very full census of 1589 were non-freemen.

16. J. F. Pound, 'The Elizabethan Corporation of Norwich, 1558–1603' (University of Birmingham, MA thesis, 1962), p. 130.

17. NRO, NCR, 17D, Book of Orders for Dutch and Walloon Strangers, 1564–1643, fos 16r–18r; Pound, 'Elizabethan Corporation', pp. 299–300; G. D. Ramsay, *The City of London in International Politics at the Accession of Elizabeth Tudor* (Manchester, 1975), p. 80; D. L. Rickwood, 'The Origin and Decline of the Stranger Community in Norwich' (UEA, Norwich, MA thesis, 1967).

18. W. J. C. Moens, ed., *The Walloons and their Church at Norwich: Their History and Registers, 1565–1832* (Huguenot Society, i, 1887–8), pp. 18–20.

19. Moens, *Walloons and their Church*, pp. 220–1.

20. Anthony de Solen was both a printer and a wine merchant: NRO, NCR, 16C, Assembly Minute Book, 1568–85, fo. 32v.

21. NRO, NCR, 17D, Book of Orders for Dutch and Walloon Strangers, 1564–1643, fos 69r–70r; Moens, *Walloons and their Church*, pp. 33–5.

22. *RCN*, ii, pp. lxxv–vii, lxxx, 412–13.

23. Moens, *Walloons and their Church*, p. 37; Pound, 'Elizabethan Corporation, p. 303.

24. Pound, 'Elizabethan Corporation', pp. 303–4; NRO, NCR, 17D, Book of Orders for the Dutch and Walloon Strangers, 1564–1643, fo. 19r.

25. Moens, *Walloons and their Church*, p. 20.

26. S. T. Bindoff, ed., *The History of Parliament: The House of Commons, 1509–1558* (3 vols, London, 1982), i, pp. 325–26.

27. Pound, *Census*, pp. 7–9; N. Williams, 'The Risings in Norfolk, 1569–70', *NA*, xxxii (1961), pp. 73–81.

28. Ayers, *Norwich*, 96–7; S. Margeson, *Norwich Households: Medieval and Post Medieval Finds from Norwich Survey Finds, 1971–78* (EAA, report 58, 1993), pp. 9, 17, 19, 169, 235–7.

29. Moens, *Walloons and their Church*, pp. 160–88.

30. NRO, NCR, 17D, Book of Orders for Dutch and Walloon Strangers, 1564–1643, fos 39r–40r (orders of February 1570); Moens, *Walloons and their Church*, pp. 28–30, 255–61.

31. Moens, *Walloons and their Church*, p. 262.

32. Moens, *Walloons and their Church*, pp. 39–41.

33. *RCN*, ii, pp. lxxxiv–v, 145, 193.

34. P. Slack, *The Impact of Plague in Tudor and Stuart England* (Oxford, 1985), p. 141.

35. NRO, NCR, 16A, Mayor's Court Book, 1587–95, p. 72.
36. Pound, 'Elizabethan Corporation', pp. 314–16.
37. Moens, *Walloons and their Church*, pp. 263–4.
38. Pound, 'Elizabethan Corporation', p. 316.
39. See Chapter 9.
40. C. H. Wilson, *England's Apprenticeship, 1603–1763* (London, 1965), pp. 76–7.
41. Moens, *Walloons and their Church*, pp. 248–9.
42. Pound, *Norwich*, pp. 47–8, 60; W. M. Rising and P. Millican, *An Index of Indentures of Norwich Apprentices* (NRS, xxix, 1959).
43. See above, *History of Norwich*, i, Chapter 7.
44. For a discussion of occupational diversity among Norwich barber-surgeons, see Pelling, *Common Lot*, pp. 203–29. Norwich was famous for its musicians in this period: *RCN*, ii, p. 195; D. Galloway, ed., *Records of Early English Drama: Norwich, 1540–1642* (Toronto, 1984), passim.
45. Moens, *Walloons and their Church*, pp. 67, 189–206.
46. Pound, *Norwich*, p. 82.
47. B. Cozens-Hardy and E. A. Kent, *The Mayors of Norwich, 1403–1835* (Norwich, 1938) p. 57; Pound, *Norwich*, p. 82.
48. Cozens-Hardy and Kent, *Mayors*, pp. 65, 68.
49. Pound, *Norwich*, p. 126; P. Seaman, ed., *Norfolk Hearth Tax Exemption Certificates, 1670–4: Norwich, Great Yarmouth, King's Lynn and Thetford* (British Record Society, Hearth Tax series three; and NRS, lxv, 2001).
50. Pound, *Norwich*, p. 137.
51. Pound, *Norwich*, pp. 37, 155.
52. Pelling, *Common Lot*, pp. 79–102.
53. C. Rawcliffe, *Medicine for the Soul: The Life, Death and Resurrection of an English Medieval Hospital* (Stroud, 1999), pp. 218, 232.
54. Pound, *Census*, pp. 7–9.
55. For a full analysis of these statistics and a discussion of the medical facilities then available to the poor in Norwich, see Pelling, *Common Lot*, pp. 134–54.
56. *RCN*, ii, pp. 343–58; and Chapter 3, above.
57. Pound, *Norwich*, pp. 143–6.
58. P. W. Hasler, ed., *The History of Parliament: The House of Commons, 1558–1603* (3 vols, London, 1981), i, p. 333.
59. *RCN*, ii, p. 187; Pound, *Norwich*, pp. 146–7; idem, *Poverty and Vagrancy in Tudor England* (London, 1971), pp. 48–57.
60. Pound, *Census*, p. 14.
61. Pound, *Norwich*, pp. 173–4.
62. *RCN*, ii, p. 180.
63. Pound, *Norwich*, p. 114.

64. NRO, NCR, 16A, Mayor's Court Book, 1595–1603, fo. 399r; P. Griffiths, 'Masterless Young People in Norwich, 1560–1645', in idem, A. Fox and S. Hindle, eds, *The Experience of Authority in Early Modern England* (Basingstoke, 1996), pp. 146–86.

65. W. K. Jordan, *The Charities of Rural England, 1480–1660* (London, 1961), pp. 131–2. A copy of Anguish's will may be found in the back of NRO, NCR, 25F, Children's Hospital Account Book, 1620/21–1668.

66. Jordan, *Charities*, pp. 108–9; *RCN*, ii, pp. cviii–cxi.

67. See M. C. McClendon, *The Quiet Reformation: Magistrates and the Emergence of Protestantism in Tudor Norwich* (Stanford, 1999), pp. 216–24, for an analysis of these records.

68. Pound, *Norwich*, p. 118.

69. Pound, 'Elizabethan Corporation', p. 287.

70. Pound, 'Elizabethan Corporation', pp. 289, 290–1.

71. The work and jurisdiction of the Norwich and Norfolk quarter sessions are fully discussed in A. Hassell Smith, *County and Court: Government and Politics in Norfolk, 1558–1603* (Oxford, 1974), chapter 5.

72. See *History of Norwich*, i, Chapter 13.

73. Slack, *Impact of Plague*, pp. 61–2, 126–43; *RCN*, ii, pp. cxxvi–vii; Pound, 'Elizabethan Corporation', pp. 249–66.

74. *RCN*, ii, pp. 187, 335–6.

75. W. L. Sachse, *Minutes of the Norwich Court of Mayoralty, 1630–1631*, (NRS, xv, 1942), pp. 44–6, 253–4.

76. NRO, NCR, 16A, Mayor's Court Book, 1587–95, fo. 308.

77. *RCN*, ii, pp. xi–ii.

78. Pound, *Norwich*, p. 101; *RCN*, ii, pp. 392–3.

79. Pound, *Norwich*, pp. 103–4.

80. Pound, *Norwich*, pp. 104–5.

81. Pound, *Norwich*, p. 62.

82. J. Venn, ed., *Biographical History of Gonville and Caius College, Cambridge, 1349–1897* (5 vols, Cambridge, 1897), i, p. 132.

83. Rawcliffe, *Medicine for the Soul*, pp. 201, 221, 234.

84. R. Harries, P. Cattermole and P. Mackintosh, *A History of Norwich School* (Norwich, 1991), pp. 25–64.

85. J. F. Pound, 'The Social and Geographical Origins of the English Grammar School Pupil: Bury St Edmunds and Manchester Grammar Schools in the Reign of George II', *History of Education Society Bulletin* (Spring 1986), pp. 12–19.

86. V. J. K. Brook, *A Life of Archbishop Parker* (Oxford, 1962), pp. 26–7. By the 1620s the city and the college had fallen out over the terms of the endowment: NRO, NCR, 25D.

87. S. D. White, *Sir Edward Coke and the Grievances of the Commonwealth* (Manchester, 1979), pp. 1–13.

88. Harries, Cattermole and Mackintosh, *Norwich School*, pp. 60, 65; Blomefield, *Norfolk*, iv, pp. 61–2.

89. Galloway, *Records*, pp. xxxi, 40.

90. Galloway, *Records*, pp. 267–71. He also produced a speech bidding her farewell, pp. 280–6.

91. P. J. Corfield, 'A Provincial Capital in the Late Seventeenth Century: The Case of Norwich', in P. Clark and P. Slack, eds, *Crisis and Order in English Towns, 1500–1700: Essays in Urban History* (London, 1972), pp. 263–310.

Notes to Chapter 3: Inhabitants

1. NRO, NCR, 16A, Mayor's Court Book, 1615–24, fo. 138v.

2. NRO, NCR, 20C, Mayor's Book of the Poor, 1571–9, fo. 1.

3. I acknowledge my deep debt to John Pound's pioneering work on the social history of Tudor and Stuart Norwich. Other urban censuses are analysed by P. Slack, *Poverty and Policy in Tudor and Stuart England* (Harlow, 1988), pp. 73–80.

4. NRO, NCR, 16D, Assembly Folio Book, 1553–83, fos 187, 202.

5. See Chapter 2, above .

6. P. Slack, *From Reformation to Improvement: Public Welfare in Early Modern England* (Oxford, 1999), p. 24.

7. Quotations are taken from NRO, NCR, 20C, Mayor's Book of the Poor, 1571–9, fos 1, 2, mayoral proclamation (1571), fo. 11v, Corporation Letter to the Archbishop of Canterbury (1572), fo. 16r-v (the last two documents are bound with the book). The concern with begging, disease and excess is best described in 'the causes why the citizens of Norwich were dryven to make orders for the better provision of the poore', set out in the letter to the archbishop. See also NCR, 16D, Assembly Folio Book, 1553–83, fo. 204. Too much importance is given to political plots and too little to perceptions of urban disorder, disease and decay in M. C. McClendon, *The Quiet Reformation: Magistrates and the Emergence of Protestantism in Tudor Norwich* (Stanford, 1999), pp. 224–5, 229–3; and J. F. Pound, *Tudor and Stuart Norwich* (Chichester, 1988), pp. 141–2.

8. McClendon, *Quiet Reformation*, pp. 218–19.

9. P. Burke, *A Social History of Knowledge from Gutenberg to Diderot* (Oxford, 2000), p. 117; Slack, *Poverty and Policy*, pp. 48–52, 53–5; idem, *From Reformation to Improvement*, p. 154; Pelling, *Common Lot*, p. 101.

10. NRO, NCR, 20C, Mayor's Book of the Poor, 1571–9, fo. 1; Corporation Letter

to the Archbishop of Canterbury (1572), fo. 16; mayoral proclamation (1571), fo. 11.

11. NRO, NCR, 16D, Assembly Folio Book, 1553–83, fos 177, 171v–2v, 170–1; 17D, Book of Orders for the Dutch and Walloon Strangers in Norwich, 1564–1643, fos 24, 32, 61. 'An Acte for the Pavyng of Stretes' had been passed in 1559 (16D, Assembly Folio Book, 1553–83, fos 55v–6).

12. See Chapter 2.

13. NRO, NCR, 17D, Book of Orders for the Dutch and Walloon Strangers in Norwich, 1564–1643, fos 22, 31v, 69v; 12A, Interrogations and Depositions, Book 1B, Nicholas Colman, examination, 3 February 1559. The most graphic description of the 1569–70 plots in the city records links their spread to Norwich to the Stranger communities living there: Book of Orders for the Dutch and Walloon Strangers in Norwich, 1564–1643, fo. 23.

14. NRO, NCR, 16D, Assembly Folio Book, 1553–83, fos 29v, 34v.

15. Pelling, *Common Lot*, pp. 68, 138.

16. Pound, *Census*, pp. 42, 47, 78; Pelling, *Common Lot*, pp. 63–78, 134–54.

17. NRO, NCR, 20C, Mayor's Book of the Poor, 1571–9, Corporation Letter to the Archbishop of Canterbury (1572), fo. 16. A copy of 'ye hole Boke of Orders for ye poore' was also sent to 'my Lorde of Canterbury': Book of the Poor, fo. 57v.

18. This discussion is based on NRO, NCR, 20C, Mayor's Book of the Poor, 1571–9, fos 2–5, where all quotations may be found.

19. NRO, NCR, 16A, Mayor's Court Book, 1569–76, fo. 174.

20. NRO, NCR, 16A, Mayor's Court Book, 1569–76, fos 171, 172.

21. The ward returns, compiled it seems by the deacons, are best consulted in NRO, NCR, 20C, Mayor's Book of the Poor, 1571–9. Payments to officers appear in fos 56v, 73, 138v, 280v, 281.

22. The precepts are in NRO, NCR, 20C, Mayor's Book of the Poor, 1571–9, fos 164v–5, and the orders, which were reissued in 1577 and 1578, in fos 206v, 237v–8, 263v–4. 'The Charge Given to the Overseers' is on two separate sheets inserted inside the same book.

23. NRO, NCR, 16C, Assembly Book, 1585–1613, fo. 21r-v; 16D, Assembly Folio Book, 1583–7, fo. 38v.

24. Population figures are supplied above, p. 36. See also D. H. Sacks and M. Lynch, 'Ports, 1540–1700', in P. Clark, ed., *The Cambridge Urban History of Britain*, ii, *1540–1840* (Cambridge, 2000), p. 384.

25. NRO, NCR, 16C, Assembly Book, 1585–1613, fo. 273; 16D, Assembly Folio Book, 1613–42, fo. 169.

26. NRO, NCR, 16C, Assembly Book, 1585–1613, fo. 39.

27. Pelling, *Common Lot*, pp. 100–1; Pound, *Norwich*, pp. 147, 160.

28. NRO, NCR, 18A, Chamberlains' Account Book, 1580–9, fo. 125.

29. For seventeenth-century maps of the city see NRO, NCR, 18A, Chamberlains' Account Book, 1589–1602, fo. 235v; 1602–25, fo. 30; 1626–48, fo. 104.

30. NRO, NCR, 13A/1–39; 10H/11; 18D, Clavors' Account Book, 1550–1601, fos 77v, 96v, 103v; 18A, Chamberlains' Account Book, 1625–48, fos 106v, 127, 145, 168v, 225v, 467v, 488v; 16C, Assembly Book, 1585–1613, fo. 285v; 20A, NCQS, Minute Book, 1637–64, March Sessions 1651.

31. NRO, NCR, 16C, Assembly Book, 1585–1613, fos 83v, 86, 114, 374; 16D, Assembly Folio Book, 1613–42, fos 143, 176; 18D, Clavors' Account Book, 1550–1601, fos 54, 83, 84, 98v, 103v; 18A, Chamberlains' Account Book, 1580–9, fos 63v–4, 172; 1603–25, fos 107, 225, 417; 1625–48, fos 14, 104.

32. NRO, NCR, 16C, Assembly Book, 1585–1613, fo. 278v; 16A, Mayor's Court Book, 1695–1709, fos 59v, 80v; 17B, St George's Guild Minute Book, 1452–1602, fo. 94; 18D, Clavors' Account Book, 1550–1601, fo. 57; 16D, Assembly Folio Book, 1553–83, fo. 34v.

33. NRO, NCR, 17D, Booke for the Inkepers and Typlers, 1587–97.

34. NRO, NCR, 16A, Mayor's Court Book, 1615–24, fo. 179.

35. NRO, NCR, 20A, NCQS, Searchbooks 1–7.

36. NRO, NCR, 20A, NCQS, Minute Book, 1639–54, fos 8, 10v; 16A, Mayor's Court Book, 1654–66, fo. 201v; 1666–77, fos 278, 291; 1677–95, fos 58v, 215v; 1695–1709, fo. 66; 18D, Clavors' Account Book, 1550–1601, fos 11, 12v, 24, 26v.

37. NRO, NCR, 20A, NCQS, Minute Book, 1637–64, August Sessions 1643; 1671–91, July Sessions 1679, October Sessions 1681.

38. NRO, NCR, 16C, Assembly Book, 1585–1613, fos 244–5.

39. NRO, NCR, MISC/21a, Order to the Constables.

40. NRO, NCR, 16A, Mayor's Court Book, 1677–95, fos 56, 225.

41. NRO, NCR, 16A, Mayor's Court Book, 1615–24, fo. 138v; 1677–95, fos 56, 80v, 82, 198v, 225, 236v, 249v, 260v, 275v; 1695–1709, fo. 59v; 20A, NCQS, Minute Book, 1602–18, fo. 187v; 16D, Assembly Folio Book, 1642–68, fo. 21.

42. The 'problems' presented by single women in the first half of the seventeenth century are more fully explored in my 'Masterless Young People in Norwich, 1560–1645', in P. Griffiths, A. Fox and S. Hindle, eds, *The Experience of Authority in Early Modern England* (Basingstoke, 1996), pp. 146–86. For later decades see NRO, NCR, 16A, Mayor's Court Book, 1677–95, fos 26v, 56, 81; 1695–1709, fo. 1; 20A, NCQS, Minute Book, 1654–70, August Sessions 1668.

43. The rise of the so-called 'surveillance' or 'paper state' in sixteenth- and seventeenth-century Europe is described in Burke, *Social History of Knowledge*, pp. 117–19, 184–7.

44. Two recent discussions of the growth of the state at this time are M. J. Braddick, *State Formation in Early Modern England, c. 1550–1700* (Cambridge, 2000); and S. Hindle, *The State and Social Change in Early Modern England, c. 1550–1640* (Basingstoke, 2000). Payments for buying and binding 'statute

bookes' in Norwich are recorded in NRO, NCR, 18A, Chamberlains' Account Book, 1603–25, fos 225, 417; 1625–48, fos 14, 104; 18D, Clavors' Account Book, 1550–1601, fos 54, 98v.

45. The leap in litigation is documented in C. Brooks, *Pettyfoggers and Vipers of the Commonwealth: The 'Lower Branch' of the Legal Profession in Early Modern England* (Cambridge, 1986), chapters 4 and 5.

46. NRO, NCR, 18D, Clavors' Account Book, 1625–1717, fo. 56; 18A, Chamberlains' Account Book, 1603–25, fo. 268v; 24A, Great Hospital Archive, general accounts, 1618–19; 16C, Assembly Book, 1585–1613, fos 259v, 385v.

47. NRO, NCR, 16A, Mayor's Court Book, 1562–9, fo. 584.

48. NRO, NCR, 16D, Assembly Folio Book, 1553–83, fo. 187; 20C, Mayor's Book of the Poor, 1571–9, fo. 2v.

49. C. Rawcliffe, *Medicine for the Soul: The Life, Death and Resurrection of an English Medieval Hospital* (Stroud, 1999).

50. The most recent discussions of these hospitals and lazarhouses are to be found in Rawcliffe, *Medicine for the Soul*; E. M. Phillips, 'Charitable Institutions in Norfolk and Suffolk *c.* 1350–1600' (UEA, Norwich, PhD thesis, 2001), chapter 6; and Pelling, *Common Lot*, pp. 91–101. The Childrens' and Girls' hospitals are briefly discussed in Pound, *Norwich*, p. 148, and Pelling, *Common Lot*, pp. 111–12.

51. Pelling, *Common Lot*, pp. 65, 131, and also 80, 153. 'Aside from London', Pelling writes, England 'offered little in the way of major institutionalization for the poor', ibid., p. 63.

52. NRO, NCR, 24A, Great Hospital Archive, general accounts, 1601–9, 1665–6; 25F, Children's Hospital Account Books, 1649–50, 1651–2; Girls' Hospital Account Book, 1653–1722, fos 1v, 3, 5, 6. The Great Hospital also took in a number of children who were taught reading and writing: Rawcliffe, *Medicine for the Soul*, pp. 220–1.

53. This has been a running theme of Margaret Pelling's work on Norwich: see *Common Lot*.

54. NRO, NCR, 16A, Mayor's Court Book, 1695–1709, fo. 79v; 1603–15, fo. 387v.

55. Quoting J. Innes, 'Prisons for the Poor: English Bridewells, 1555–1800', in F. Snyder and D. Hay, eds, *Labour, Law, and Crime: A Historical Perspective* (Oxford, 1987), p. 105. For some examples, see NRO, NCR, 16A, Mayor's Court Book, 1595–1603, fo. 797; 1603–15, fos 116, 165v, 335v, 387v; 1615–24, fos 56v, 182, 272v; 1677–95, fos 189v, 272v.

56. NRO, NCR, 20C, Mayor's Book for the Poor, 1571–9, fo. 5v.

57. There was far more concern about the legal status of the London Bridewell: see my 'Contesting London Bridewell, 1576–1580', forthcoming in the *Journal of British Studies*.

58. NRO, NCR, 20C, Mayor's Book of the Poor, 1571–9, fo. 3; 1573–4 precepts

(bound in the book), fo. 165; Bridewell Treasurers' Accounts (also bound there), fo. 175v; 16A, Mayor's Court Book, 1677–95, fo. 303; 1695–1709, fo. 79v; 16C, Assembly Book, 1585–1613, fo. 374; 16D, Assembly Folio Book, 1553–83, fos 320, 121; 17B, St George's Guild Minute Book, 1452–1602, fo. 94; R. A. Houlbrooke, ed., *The Letter Book of John Parkhurst, Bishop of Norwich, Compiled During the Years, 1571–5* (NRS, xliii, 1974–75), p. 186. See also P. Spierenburg, *The Prison Experience: Disciplinary Institutions and their Inmates in Early Modern Europe* (New Brunswick and London, 1991), Chapter 6.

59. NRO, NCR, 20C, Mayor's Book of the Poor, 1571–9, fo. 2v.

60. NRO, NCR, 16A, Mayor's Court Book, 1677–95, fo. 271; 1634–46, fo. 486.

61. For an elaboration of this theme, see *History of Norwich*, i, Chapter 8.

62. NRO, NCR, 17F, Girls' Hospital Account Book, 1653–1722, will of Robert Bacon.

63. For example, NRO, NCR, 24A, Great Hospital Archive, general accounts, 1601–9, payments to 'extraordinary poor people'; 19C, Bridewell Treasurers' Account Book 1 (1585–1686), 1585, 1604, 1605, 1606, 1609, 1612, 1629; 16D, Assembly Folio Book, 1668–1707, fo. 12v; 16A, Mayor's Court Book, 1677–95, fos 311, 317v, 333, 343; 1695–1709, fos 10, 13.

64. NRO, NCR, 20C, Mayor's Book of the Poor, 1571–9, fo. 2; 19C, Bridewell Treasurers' Account Book 1 (1585–1686), 1588; 20C, Bridewell Treasurers' Accounts (bound with Mayor's Book of the Poor), fo. 175v; 1573–4 precepts (bound with the book), fo. 165; 16A, Mayor's Court Book, 1576–81, fo. 350; 1595–1603, fo. 598; 1615–24, fo. 149; 1677–95, fo. 348.

65. NRO, NCR, 19C, Bridewell Treasurers' Account Book 1 (1585–1686), 1585 (inventory), 1600, 1610, 1622 (inventory); 2 (1647–1751), fo. 17; Bridewell Treasurers' Accounts (bound with Mayor's Book of the Poor), fo. 175v; 16A, Mayor's Court Book, 1552–62, fo. 550; 1562–9, fos 236, 605; 1569–76, fo. 191; 1576–81, fo. 677; 1603–15, fo. 421v; 1615–24, fos 189v, 275, 489v.

66. NRO, NCR, 16A, Mayor's Court Book, 1549–55, fo. 117; 1603–15, fo. 251v; 1576–81, fo. 538; 1582–7, fo. 556; 1603–15, fo. 459; 1587–95, fo. 105; 16C, Assembly Book, 1585–1613, fos 177, 190v, 193v; 18A, Chamberlains' Account Books, 1580–1, fo. 29v; 1580–9, fo. 236; 1589–1602, fos 60v, 159v, 187, 218; 1625–48, fo. 14.

67. NRO, NCR, 18A, Chamberlains' Account Book, 1625–48, fos 17, 244, 265; 20A, NCQS, Minute Book, 1629–36, fo. 96; 25F, Children's Hospital Account Book, 1636–7.

68. NRO, NCR, 16A, Mayor's Court Book, 1603–15, fo. 427v; 1666–77, fo. 99; 1595–1603, fo. 597.

69. NRO, NCR, 20A, NCQS, Minute Book, 1637–64, fo. 26v. See also my 'Bodies and Souls in Norwich: Punishing Petty Crime, 1540–1700', in P. Griffiths and S. Devereaux, eds, *Punishment and the English: Essays in Penal Practice and Culture, 1500–1900* (Palgrave Press, forthcoming).

70. NRO, NCR, 16A, Mayor's Court Book, 1603–15, fo. 439; 1595–1603, fo. 183; 1634–46, fo. 481; 20A, NCQS, Minute Book, 1654–70, May Sessions 1662; 16A, Mayor's Court Book, 1595–1603, fo. 198; 1603–15, fos 287v, 326v, 427, 436; 1615–24, fos 1, 10v, 49v. Utting did not spend the rest of her life in prison, however, as she was back before the magistrates a couple of years later.

71. NRO, NCR, 20A, NCQS, Minute Books, 1654–70, July Sessions 1664; 1581–91, fo. 80.

72. An interpretation that emerges in both Beier, *Masterless Men*, and Innes, 'Prisons for the Poor'.

73. For some examples, see NRO, NCR, 16A, Mayor's Court Book, 1595–1603, fo. 698; 1615–24, fos 35v, 65, 149; 1677–95, fos 11, 138v, 181v; 20A, NCQS, Minute Books, 1602–8, fos 83, 143v, 164, 177v, 196, 247v; 1630–8, fo. 97; 1639–54, fos 18v, 25.

74. NRO, NCR, 16A, Mayor's Court Book, 1677–95, fo. 190; 1603–15, fos 399, 405; 20C, Bridewell Treasurers' Accounts (bound with Mayor's Book of the Poor, 1571–9), fo. 98; 19C, Bridewell Treasurers' Account Book 1(1585–1686), 1587, 1622 (inventory); 2 (1647–1751), fo. 17.

75. E. Coke, *The Second Part of the Institutes of the Lawes of England* (1644), p. 729; M. Dalton, *The Country Justice* (1661 edn), p. 122.

76. E. Cohen, 'The Animated Pain of the Body', *American Historical Review*, cv (2000), p. 42.

77. NRO, NCR, 20C, Mayor's Book of the Poor, 1571–9, fos 2–2v; 16A, Mayor's Court Book, 1603–15, fos 338v, 417v; 1615–24, fo. 180; 1634–46, fos 321v, 334v; 1666–77, fos 206v, 234v, 237v, 385; 1677–95, fo. 137; 19C, Bridewell Treasurers' Account Book 1 (1585–1686), 1585, 1591, 1592, 1594, 1595, 1600, 1611, 1614, 1616, 1618, 1620, 1622 (inventory); 2 (1647–1751), fos 17–7v.

78. NRO, NCR, 16A, Mayor's Court Book, 1603–15, fo. 421v; 19C, Bridewell Treasurers' Account Book 1 (1585–1686), 1616, 1617, 1629; 20C, Bridewell Treasurers' Accounts (bound with Mayor's Book of the Poor, 1571–9), fos 58, 175v; Mayor's Book of the Poor, 1571–9, fo. 2v (this was the working day as it was described in 1571).

79. NRO, NCR, 24A, Great Hospital Archive, general accounts, passim (just five preachers served here in the first half of the seventeenth century: Mr Bathoe was in the post for the first two of its decades); 18A, Chamberlains' Account Book, 1625–48, fos 85v, 264; 1603–25, fo. 30; 25F, Children's Hospital Account Book, 1620/21–1668; Girls' Hospital Account Book, 1653–1722, will of Robert Bacon.

80. I base this on referrals from the Mayor's Court after 1660: NRO, NCR, 16A, Mayor's Court Book, 1677–95, fo. 312; 1695–1709, fos 8, 13, 15v, 19, 28, 33, 65, 74v.

81. NRO, NCR, 16A, Mayor's Court Book, 1677–95, fo. 319; 1695–1709, fos 5, 13,

17v, 19, 21v, 32, 41, 58, 58v, 59, 65, 80v. The ages of the children were checked against parish registers and entered in a book right at the end of the seventeenth century (ibid., 1695–1709, fo. 80v). The transportation orders/payments can be followed in 16D, Assembly Folio Book, 1642–68, fos 93, 105v, 107; 18D, Clavors' Account Book, 1625–1717, fo. 51; 25F, Children's Hospital Book, 1620/21–1668, 1649–50. The group included one girl.

82. NRO, NCR, 16A, Mayor's Court Book, 1677–95, fos 303, 307, 333v, 336; 1695–1709, fos 2, 20v; Rawcliffe, *Medicine for the Soul*, pp. 235–6.

83. NRO, NCR, 16A, Mayor's Court Book, 1634–46, fo. 402; 1677–95, fos 307, 308, 333v; 1595–1603, fo. 498; 1603–15, fos 394v, 435; 1615–24, fos 8v, 13v, 253v, 282; 1695–1709, fo. 18v; 1615–24, fo. 149; 1576–81, fos 382, 425; 1595–1603, fo. 418; 1634–46, fos 346, 488; 20A, NCQS, Minute Books, 1637–64, 1691–1702, April Sessions 1695, January Sessions 1699; 1654–70, 1670 sessions. For single-sex chambers, see 19C, Bridewell Treasurers' Account Book 1 (1585–1686), 1619; 2 (1647–1751), fo. 17; 24A, Great Hospital Archive, general accounts, 1631–2, 1633–4.

84. See *History of Norwich*, i, Chapter 13.

85. Pelling, *Common Lot*, pp. 91–101; Rawcliffe, *Medicine for the Soul*, pp. 203–4, 222–3; above, pp. 75–78. A more general survey of lazarhouses in early modern Europe is provided by G. B. Risse, *Mending Bodies, Saving Souls: A History of Hospitals* (Oxford, New York, 1999), chapter 4. NRO, NCR, 20A, NCQS, Minute Book, 1629–36, fo. 85; 16D, Assembly Folio Book, 1642–68, fo. 310v. See also 18A, Chamberlains' Account Book, 1603–25, fos 33v, 55, 150, 283v; 1625–48, fos 87, 89, 106, 124v, 126v, 144v, 185, 244. Keepers' rents are recorded in Chamberlains' Account Book, 1625–48, fos 165v, 183v, 204, 241v, 297v, 323, 366v, 386v, 407, 447. The purchase 'of the poore Lazar hows wthowt St Bennytts Gates' is recorded in the Chamberlains' Account Book, 1580–9, fo. 159v.

86. NRO, NCR, 16A, Mayor's Court Book, 1695–1709, fo. 28.

87. NRO, NCR, 20C, Mayor's Book of the Poor, 1571–9, fos 137v, 72v.

88. NRO, NCR, 18D, Clavors' Account Book, 1550–1601, fos 39v, 65v, 80v, 138v, 140; 20C, Mayor's Book of the Poor, 1571–9, fos 55v, 56; NRO, NCR, 25F Children's Hospital Account Book, 1620/21–1668, will of Thomas Anguish, 1617 (this is at the very back of the volume).

89. NRO, NCR, 18D, Clavors' Account Books, 1550–1601, fos 82, 134, 136, 137, 137v, 138v 139v, 140, 140v; 1545–1646, fo. 119v; Pelling, *Common Lot*, pp. 94, 96, 98–9.

90. NRO, NCR, 18D, Clavors' Account Book, 1550–1601, fos 136v, 139; 20C, Poor Relief Book, 1571–2, Ward Returns (bound with Mayor's Book of the Poor, 1571–9); Pelling, *Common Lot*, p. 91.

91. NRO, NCR, 16A, Mayor's Court Book, 1695–1709, fos 27v, 47, 55. Given the location of these houses, it seems that 'pesthouse' and 'lazar house' were often

synonymous, being at least on the same site. Perhaps there was simply a change of nomenclature.

92. NRO, NCR, 19C, Bridewell Treasurers' Account Book 1 (1585–1686), 1586; 18D, Clavors' Account Book, 1550–1601, fos 104, 105, 108; 16A, Mayor's Court Book, 1677–95, fos 30, 77, 98, 102, 120, 125, 132v, 166, 195v, 221, 486; Pelling, *Common Lot*, p. 97.

93. NRO, NCR, 18D, Clavors' Account Book, 1550–1601, fo. 138v.

94. NRO, NCR, 18D, Clavors' Account Book, 1550–1601, fos 61v, 67v, 140v.

95. Pelling, *Common Lot*, pp. 97–8.

96. NRO, NCR, 25F, Children's Hospital Account Book, 1630–1; 24A, Great Hospital Archive, general accounts, 1607–8, 1608–9, 1613–14, 1614–15, 1631–2; 19C, Bridewell Treasurers' Account Book 1 (1585–1686), 1603, 1604. See also 20C, city precepts 1573–4 (bound with Mayor's Book of the Poor, 1571–9), fo. 165.

97. For example, NRO, NCR, 18D, Clavors' Account Book 1550–1601, fos 70, 74, 74v, 75v, 77v, 103v, 109, 134v, 135v; 18A, Chamberlains' Account Book, 1603–25, fos 260v, 282v, 302, 320, 357v, 382.

98. NRO, NCR, 16A, Mayor's Court Book, 1603–15, fo. 246; 1634–46, fos 306v, 317v, 347, 350v; 1677–95, fo. 66v; 18D, Clavors' Account Book, 1550–1601, fo. 77v; 19C, Bridewell Treasurers' Account Book 1 (1585–1686), 1605, 1637; 2 (1647–1751), fo. 42.

99. NRO, NCR, 24A, Great Hospital Archive, general accounts, 1601–2, 1607–8; 16A, Mayor's Court Book, 1695–1709, fo. 66.

100. Pound, *Census*, pp. 29, 41, 50–1, 62, 65, 68, 75, 80–1.

101. M. Douglas, *How Institutions Think* (Syracuse, 1986), p. 63.

102. NRO, NCR, 24A, Great Hospital Archive, general accounts, 1604–5, 1606–7, 1611–12; 25F, Children's Hospital Book, 1641–2, 1642–3, 1646–7, 1647–8.

103. See, most recently, D. R. Headrick, *When Information Came of Age: Technologies of Knowledge in the Age of Reason and Revolution, 1700–1850* (Oxford, New York, 2000).

Notes to Chapter 4: The Civil War

1. NRO, MC, 98/1/16, 543 x 2. I am very grateful for the efforts of my research assistant, Nigel Amies, and the enthusiasm and valuable assistance of Clive Wilkins-Jones and Susan Maddock. I am also indebted to Matthew Reynolds for his excellent paper on 'Puritans, Laudians and Norwich's Wars of Religion in the 1620s and 1630s' read at the Cambridge Early Modern British History Postgraduate Seminar on 7 February 2001.

2. W. D. Macray, ed., *The History of the Rebellion and Civil Wars in England begun in the Year 1641 by Edward, Earl of Clarendon* (6 vols, Oxford, 1888), i, p. 272; H. Trevor-Roper, *From Counter-Reformation to Glorious Revolution*

(London, 1992), p. 163; I. Atherton and V. Morgan, 'Revolution and Retrench-ment: The Cathedral, 1630–1720', in *Norwich Cathedral*, p. 549.

3. Bodleian Library, Oxford, Tanner MS 68, fos 1v–2v, 240.

4. J. Evans, *Seventeenth-Century Norwich: Politics, Religion, and Government, 1620–1690* (Oxford, 1979), pp. 84, 87, 95; Bodleian Library, Tanner MS 68, fos 115, 116, 120.

5. PRO, E157/21; Bodleian Library, Tanner MS 68, fo. 332.

6. PRO, SP16/361/117.

7. NRO, DN, SUN/4a, *Liber Citacionum ex officio.*

8. PRO, SP16/346/58.

9. Bodleian Library, Tanner MS, 68, fos 279, 283, 285–6. Daniel Toft had also visited Leyden earlier that year: PRO, E157/21, fo. 5v. I would like to thank Susan Maddock for producing NRO, DN/CON, 16, articles exhibited against William Clarke.

10. A. Fletcher, *The Outbreak of the English Civil War* (London, 1981), p. 318; A. R. Warmington, 'The Corporation of York in Peace and War, 1638–1645', *York Historian*, ix (1990), pp. 16–26; A. Foster, 'Church Policies of the 1630s', in R. P. Cust and A. Hughes, eds, *Conflict in Early Stuart England: Studies in Religion and Politics, 1603–42* (London, 1989), p. 208.

11. Reynolds, 'Puritans, Laudians and Norwich's Wars of Religion in the 1620s and 1630s', pp. 21–6; Evans, *Seventeenth-Century Norwich*, pp. 93–6.

12. Bodleian Library, Tanner MS 220, fos 44–6.

13. Corbet claimed that the plague in London had caused unemployment by removing Norwich's main commercial outlet: Bodleian Library, Tanner MS 68, fo. 147; Macray, *History of the Rebellion*, ii, p. 418.

14. PRO, SP16/316/8; Bodleian Library, Tanner MS 220, fo. 151.

15. Bodleian Library, Tanner MS 220, fos 149–50

16. M. Stoyle, *From Deliverance to Destruction: Rebellion and Civil War in an English City* (Exeter, 1996), p. 39.

17. B. Schofield, ed., *The Knyvett Letters* (London, 1949), pp. 98–9. These ministers were John Carter of St Peter Mancroft and Henry Hall of St Andrew's.

18. BL, Harleian MS 162, fo. 398v; C. Holmes, *The Eastern Association in the English Civil War* (London, 1974), p. 27.

19. In 1641 Parliament had ordered that the people should take the Protestation, an oath to defend the Protestant religion from popish innovation: BL, Thomason Tract, E140(17), *True Newes from Norwich: Being a certaine Relation how that the Cathedrall Blades of Norwich on the 22 of February 1641 being Shrove-Tuesday, did Put Themselves into a Posture of Defence, Because that the Apprentises of Norwich (as They Imagined) would have Pulled Down their Organs* (London, 1642), pp. 2, 6.

20. R. Clifton, 'Popular Fear of Catholics in England during the English Revolution', *Past and Present*, lii (1971), p. 24.

21. PRO, SP16/468/44 (a) i–iv.

22. BL, Thomason Tract, E179(10), *Bloody Newes from Norwich: or A True Relation of a Bloody Attempt of the Papists in Norwich to Consume the Whole City by Fire*, December (London, 1641). The same story was reported in a later newsbook of 1642: E147(1), *Foure Wonderfull, Bloudy and Dangerous Plots Discovered: From Norwich* (London, 1642).

23. NRO, NCR, 16A, Mayor's Court Book, 1634–46, fo. 349v.

24. BL, Thomason Tract, E114(15), *Newes from the Citie of Norwich of Certain Passages which Happened There on Munday Last, Relating the Number of the Cavaliers which are Dispersed in Sundry Villages neer the Citie*, 26 August (London, 1642).

25. NRO, NCR, 16D/6, Assembly Folio Book, 1642–68, fos 2r–2v, 4v.

26. Holmes, *Eastern Association*, p. 59; NRO, NCR, 16A, Mayor's Court Book, 1634–46, fo. 365v.

27. C. Russell, *Causes of the English Civil War* (Oxford, 1990), p. 22.

28. A. Walsham, *Providence in Early Modern England* (Oxford, 1999), p. 314.

29. NRO, NCR, 16D/6, Assembly Folio Book, 1642–68, fo. 10r; William Bridge, *A Sermon Preached unto the Voluntiers of the City of Norwich and also to the Voluntiers of Great Yarmouth by William Bridge Preacher of Gods Word* (London, 1643), pp. 12–13.

30. Bridge, *A Sermon Preached*, pp. 14–17.

31. NRO, NCR, 16A, Mayor's Court Book, 1634–46, fos 355v–6r; 17B, Mayor's Book, p. 36. See also G. Johnson, 'Chronological Memoranda Touching the City of Norwich', *NA*, i (1847), pp. 140–66.

32. NRO, NCR, 16D/6, Assembly Folio Book, 1642–68, fo. 3v.

33. *HMC, Thirteenth Report, Appendix 1, Portland 1* (London, 1891), p. 53; *Commons' Journals*, ii, p. 771; Fletcher, *Outbreak of the English Civil War*, p. 295; Holmes, *Eastern Association*, p. 56; NRO, NCR, 20A/11, NCQS, Minute Book, 1639–54, fo. 38r.

34. Holmes, *Eastern Association*, p. 57; B. G. Blackwood, 'The Cavalier and Roundhead Gentry of Norfolk', *The Local Historian*, xxvi (1996), pp. 203–6.

35. BL, Add. MS 22619, fos 40r–40v; NRO, NCR, 20A/11, NCQS Minute Book, 1639–54, fo. 38r.

36. Holmes, *Eastern Association*, p. 59; Blackwood, 'Cavalier and Roundhead Gentry of Norfolk', p. 205; Evans, *Seventeenth-Century Norwich*, pp. 131–2.

37. BL, Thomason Tract, E114(27), *A True and Exact Relation of the Present Estate of the City of Norwich*, 27 August (London, 1642).

38. See *History of Norwich*, i, Chapter 12.

39. BL, Harleian MS 386, fo. 233r–3v.

40. BL, Harleian MS 386, fo. 233r–3v; NRO, NCR, 18A, Chamberlains' Account Book, 1625–48, fo. 386r; J. Walter, *Understanding Popular Violence in the English Revolution: The Colchester Plunderers* (Cambridge, 1999), passim; BL, Harleian MS 386, fo. 234.

41. D. L. Smith, 'Catholic, Anglican or Puritan? Edward Sackville, Fourth Earl of Dorset and the Ambiguities of Religion in Early Stuart England', *TRHS*, sixth series, ii (1992), p. 119.

42. Holmes, *Eastern Association*, pp. 62, 66–7.

43. BL, Add. MS 22619, fo. 33; Harleian MS 162, fo. 398v; NRO, NCR, 16D/6, Assembly Folio Book, 1642–68, fo. 6r; Evans, *Seventeenth-Century Norwich*, pp. 125–6; R. W. Ketton-Cremer, *Norfolk in the Civil War: A Portrait of a Society in Conflict* (second edn, Norwich, 1985), pp. 176–81.

44. Evans, *Seventeenth-Century Norwich*, pp. 125–7; NRO, NCR, 16D/6, Assembly Folio Book, 1642–68, fo. 15r; C. H. Firth and R. S. Rait, eds, *Acts and Ordinances of the Interregnum, 1642–1660* (3 vols, London, 1911), i, p. 106.

45. NRO, NCR, 20A/11, NCQS, Minute Book, 1639–54, fos 40r, 45v, 49v, 52v, 55v.

46. NRO, NCR, 16A, Mayor's Court Book, 1634–46, fo. 393r.

47. NRO, NCR, 20A/11, NCQS, Minute Book, 1639–54, fos 47r, 60v, 63r.

48. Evans, *Seventeenth-Century Norwich*, pp. 133–50.

49. NRO, NCR, 16D/6, Assembly Folio Book, 1642–68, fos 6r–7v.

50. T. Carlyle, ed., *Oliver Cromwell's Letters and Speeches: With Elucidations* (3 vols, London, 1849), i, p. 128.

51. Ketton-Cremer, *Norfolk in the Civil War*, p. 199.

52. P. Thomas, ed., *The English Revolution III: Newsbooks 1: Oxford Royalist*, ii (London, 1971), p. 487.

53. Thomas, *English Revolution III: Newsbooks 1: Oxford Royalist*, ii, p. 769.

54. H. Harrod, ed., 'Norfolk Wills', *NA*, v (1859), p. 214.

55. Holmes, *Eastern Association*, p. 168; NRO, NCR, 16A, Mayor's Court Book, 1634–46, fos 392r, 403v–4r, 417r.

56. A. Hopper, '"The Popish Army of the North": Anti-Catholicism and Parliamentarian Allegiance in Civil War Yorkshire, 1642–46', *Recusant History*, xxv, 1 (2000), pp. 12–28.

57. Blomefield, *Norfolk*, iii, p. 386; NRO, HMN, Hamond of Westacre MS, 7/172/1.

58. Schofield, *Knyvett Letters*, p. 125; BL, Egerton MS 2643, fo. 19.

59. Ketton-Cremer, *Norfolk in the Civil War*, pp. 202–13; BL, Add. MS 22619, fo. 92; NRO, NCR, 16A, Mayor's Court Book, 1634–46, fos. 382r, 398v–99r; 16D/6, Assembly Folio Book, fo. 11v; Blomefield, *Norfolk*, iii, p. 387; BL, Thomason Tract, E67(28), *A Briefe and True Relation of the Seige and Surrendering of Kings Lyn*, 20 September (London, 1643), pp. 1–8.

60. Joseph Hall, *The Works of Joseph Hall, D.D. Successively Bishop of Exeter and*

Norwich: With Some Account of his Life and Sufferings Written by Himself, ed. P. Hall (12 vols, Oxford, 1837), i, p. liv.

61. There is a discrepancy over the date of this episode. John Evans seems to suggest January 1644, but more recently John Blatchly has favoured March: Evans, *Seventeenth-Century Norwich*, p. 129; J. Blatchly, 'Iconoclasm in Norfolk, 1644', in T. Cooper, ed., *The Journal of William Dowsing: Iconoclasm in East Anglia during the English Civil War* (Woodbridge, 2001), pp. 120–1.

62. Hall, *Works of Joseph Hall*, i, p. lv.

63. G. Keynes, ed., *The Works of Sir Thomas Browne* (4 vols, London, 1964), iii, pp. 123, 141.

64. Blatchly, 'Iconoclasm in Norfolk', pp. 119–22; Blomefield, *Norfolk*, iii, p. 389.

65. Bodleian Library, Tanner MS 220, fos 54–6; B. Cozens-Hardy and E. A. Kent, *Mayors of Norwich, 1403–1835* (Norwich, 1938), p. 88; P. Millican, ed., *The Register of the Freemen of Norwich, 1548–1713* (Norwich, 1934), pp. 75, 78–9, 106.

66. NRO, NCR, 16A, Mayor's Court Book, 1634–46, fo. 411r.

67. BL, Add. MS 15903, fo. 75.

68. NRO, NCR, 16A, Mayor's Court Book, 1634–46, fo. 415r.

69. NRO, NCR, 16D/6, Assembly Folio Book, 1642–68, fo. 22v.

70. NRO, NCR, 16A, Mayor's Court Book, 1634–46, fo. 445v.

71. Keynes, *Works of Sir Thomas Browne*, iii, p. 128.

72. NRO, NCR 16D/6, Assembly Folio Book, 1642–68, fos 1r, 3v; MC, 98/1/16, 543 x 2, Thomas Ramsey, parson of Crostwick, to John Utting, Mayor of Norwich, 17 December 1647.

73. C. Cross, 'From the Reformation to the Restoration', in G. E. Aylmer and R. Cant, eds, *The History of York Minster* (Oxford, 1977), p. 214.

74. *HMC, Ninth Report, Part 1, Corporation of Great Yarmouth MSS* (London, 1883), p. 320.

75. J. Finch, 'The Monuments', in *Norwich Cathedral*, p. 477.

76. NRO, DCN, 107/3, account of the misuse of Norwich cathedral by the parliamentarian soldiery.

77. Stoyle, *From Deliverance to Destruction*, p. 188.

78. Evans, *Seventeenth-Century Norwich*, pp. 153–8; NRO, FC, 31/1.

79. Blomefield, *Norfolk*, iii, p. 391.

80. NRO, NCR, 16D/6, Assembly Folio Book, 1642–68, fo. 45r; NHC, N270.6, *Vox Populi: or The Peoples Cry against the Clergy. Containing the Rise, Progress, Ruine of Norwich Remonstrance; Framed and Fomented by the Ministers of that City, being Encouraged thereunto by Some Great Persons from Above* (London, 1646).

81. BL, Thomason Tract, E355(13), *An Hue-and-Cry after Vox Populi: or An Answer to Vox Diaboli, or a Libellous Pamphlet Falsly Styled Vox Populi; Reviling the Magistracy and Ministry of Norwich* (Norwich, 1646), pp. 34–5.

82. NRO, NCR, 16A, Mayor's Court Book, 1634–46, fo. 399v.

83. Ketton-Cremer, *Norfolk in the Civil War*, pp. 265, 284; NRO, NCR, 16D/6, Assembly Folio Book, 1642–68, fo. 30v.

84. BL, Add. MS 22620, fo. 96.

85. Bodleian Library, Tanner MS 59b, fo. 610.

86. Blomefield, *Norfolk*, iii, p. 392.

87. Bodleian Library, Tanner MS 59b, fo. 623.

88. R. Ashton, *Counter-Revolution: The Second Civil War and Its Origins, 1646–8* (London, 1994), p. 77.

89. Bodleian Library, Tanner MS 59b, fo. 649.

90. BL, Add. MS 22620, fos 54, 56.

91. NRO, NCR, 16A, Mayor's Court Book, 1634–46, fos 454r, 474v; Blomefield, *Norfolk*, iii, p. 391; L. G. Bolingbroke, 'Players in Norwich from the Accession of Queen Elizabeth until their Suppression in 1642', *NA*, xiii (1898), p. 19; NCR, 16A, Mayor's Court Book, 1634–46, fo. 465v.

92. Evans, *Seventeenth-Century Norwich*, p. 163; Cozens-Hardy and Kent, *Mayors of Norwich*, pp. 83–4; Ashton, *Counter-Revolution*, p. 369; Blomefield, *Norfolk*, iii, p. 392; NRO, NCR, 12C/1 (MF/RO 588/3), no. 70.

93. Blomefield, *Norfolk*, iii, p. 393.

94. Ashton, *Counter-Revolution*, p. 370; NRO, NCR, 12C/1 (MF/RO 588/3), no. 66.

95. J. Rushworth, *Historical Collections* (London, 1701), part 4, ii, pp. 1071–2; I. Gentles, *The New Model Army in England, Ireland and Scotland, 1645–53* (Oxford, 1992), pp. 151, 241; C. Firth and G. Davies, *The Regimental History of Cromwell's Army* (2 vols, Oxford, 1940), i, pp. 93–9.

96. NRO, NCR, 12C/1 (MF/RO 588/3), nos 189, 190.

97. R. W. Ketton-Cremer, *Norfolk Assembly* (London, 1957), p. 144; Ashton, *Counter-Revolution*, p. 371.

98. NRO, NCR, 12C/1 (MF/RO 588/3), no. 108.

99. NRO, NCR, 12C/1 (MF/RO 588/3), no. 83.

100. NRO, NCR, 12C/1 (MF/RO 588/3), nos 98, 121, 147, 170.

101. H. Cary, ed., *Memorials of the Great Civil War in England from 1646 to 1652* (2 vols, London, 1842), i, pp. 399–403.

102. NRO, NCR, 12C/1 (MF/RO 588/3), no. 36.

103. NRO, NCR, 12C/1, no. 94; Ashton, *Counter Revolution*, p. 373n; NCR, 18A, Chamberlains' Account Book, 1625–48, fo. 487v.

104. NRO, NCR, 16D/6, Assembly Folio Book, 1642–68, fo. 62r.

105. Ashton, *Counter-Revolution*, p. 372.

106. Evans, *Seventeenth-Century Norwich*, p. 177.

107. Evans, *Seventeenth-Century Norwich*, p. 173; BL, Thomason Tract, E447(2), *A Bloudy Fight in Essex*, 12 June (London, 1648), p. 3; E454(18), *The Prince of*

Wales His Coming to Yarmouth, 27 July (London, 1648), p. 4; NRO, NCR, 16D/6, Assembly Folio Book, 1642–68, fo. 65r.

108. On 27 January 1649 the assembly ordered 'that a congratulatory letter be written to Leiuetennant generall Cromwell for the favours he hath done formerly for the Citty': NRO, NCR, 16D/6, Assembly Folio Book, 1642–68, fo. 74r.

109. Rushworth, *Historical Collections*, part 4, ii, pp. 1372–3: 'The Humble Petition of the Well Affected Gentlemen, and Others the Inhabitants of the County of *Norfolk* and the County and City of *Norwich*'.

110. NRO, MC, 46/4, 488 x 1, draft confession by Miles Corbet, *c.* April 1662.

111. BL, Add. MS 22620, fo. 152.

112. D. Underdown, *Royalist Conspiracy in England, 1649–1660* (Yale, 1960), pp. 42–5; R. W. Ketton-Cremer, *Forty Norfolk Essays* (Norwich, 1961), pp. 24–9.

113. NRO, MS 2994, James Paston's narrative of the suppression of a royalist uprising at Easton; MC, 482/2–4, 747 x 1, this latter source only mentions fourteen executions and clashes with Paston's account, incorrectly dating the affair a year earlier in 1649.

114. NRO, HMN, Hamond of Westacre MS, 7/190/11, 771 x 8.

115. NRO, MS, 79, typescript copy of Benjamin Mackerel, *History of the City of Norwich Both Ancient and Modern* (1737), ii, p. 249.

116. PRO, SP23/180/681–3, 209/735–9; NRO, NCR, 20A/11, NCQS Minute Book, 1639–54, fo. 101v; Beecheno, 'Norwich Subscription', p. 160.

117. NRO, NCR, 17B, Mayor's Book, p. 38.

118. *The Norfolk Tour: or The Traveller's Pocket Companion* (sixth edn, Norwich, 1808), p. 220.

119. Evans, *Seventeenth-Century Norwich*, pp. 199–201, 222–5; C. Durston, *Cromwell's Major-Generals: Godly Government during the English Revolution* (Manchester, 2001), p. 89.

120. H. Le Strange and W. Rye, eds, *Address from the Gentry of Norfolk and Norwich to General Monck in 1660* (Norwich, 1913); J. Pound, *Tudor and Stuart Norwich* (Chichester, 1988), p. 96; Blomefield, *Norfolk*, iii, pp. 403–4.

121. Evans, *Seventeenth-Century Norwich*, pp. 201, 221; Blomefield, *Norfolk*, iii, pp. 403–4; NRO, NCR, 16D/6, Assembly Folio Book, 1642–68, fo. 224r; R. L. Greaves and R. Zaller, eds, *A Biographical Dictionary of British Radicals in the Seventeenth-Century* (3 vols, Brighton, 1982), iii, p. 219.

122. NRO, MC, 46/4, 488 x 1, draft confession by Miles Corbet, *c.* April 1662; Greaves and Zaller, *Biographical Dictionary of British Radicals*, i, p. 176.

123. Evans, *Seventeenth-Century Norwich*, p. 140.

124. It was in these wards that the Protestant Dutch and Walloon refugees had settled: see above, p. 42.

125. Evans, *Seventeenth-Century Norwich*, p. 191.

126. M. Stoyle, *Loyalty and Locality: Popular Allegiance in Devon during the English Civil War* (Exeter, 1994), pp. 252–3.

127. Finch, 'Monuments', pp. 477–8.

128. K. Wilson, *The Sense of the People: Politics, Culture and Imperialism in England, 1715–1785* (Cambridge, 1995), p. 386; NHC, *the Norwich Gazette or Accurate Weekly Intelligencer*, 29 September to 6 October (Norwich, 1711).

129. Old Noll was Oliver Cromwell: NHC, Colman Collection 25E, *To the Worthy Freemen and Electors* 24 May (Norwich, 1796).

Notes to Chapter 5: Health and Sanitation to 1750

1. J. W. Hebel, K. M. Tillotson and B. H. Newdigate, eds, *Works* (5 vols, Oxford, 1931–41), ii, p. 292; quoted by Blomefield, *Norfolk*, iv, p. 427.

2. William Cuningham, *The Cosmographical Glasse* (1559, English Experience edn, Amsterdam and New York, 1968), fo. 174; *RCN*, ii, pp. 133–4 (1559); C. Morris, ed., *The Illustrated Journeys of Celia Fiennes 1685-c. 1712* (Stroud, 1995), pp. 135–6, 141–2.

3. W. Bray, ed., *Diary and Correspondence of John Evelyn* (4 vols, London, 1859), ii, pp. 71–2. For Evelyn's interest in public health and the urban environment: M. Jenner, 'The Politics of London Air: John Evelyn's *Fumifugium* and the Restoration', *Historical Journal*, xxxviii (1995), pp. 535–51.

4. On social policy in Norwich in relation to health, see Chapter 3, as well as Pelling, *Common Lot*, chapters 3 to 7; and P. Slack, *The Impact of Plague in Tudor and Stuart England* (London, 1985). For evidence of overcrowding, poverty and the prevalence of disease among the stranger communities: Slack, pp. 128, 133–4, 139–41.

5. See in general Pelling, *Common Lot*, pp. 19–37; and Chapter 8, below.

6. *Urban History Newsletter*, vi, 1 (2002), p. 11.

7. For some relevant archaeological studies, see notes 23, 67 and 91, below. On regions: J. R. Ravensdale, *Liable to Floods: Village Landscape on the Edge of the Fens AD 450–1850* (London, 1974); M. J. Dobson, *Contours of Death and Disease in Early Modern England* (Cambridge, 1997). On London: M. Jenner, 'Early Modern English Conceptions of "Cleanliness" and "Dirt" as Reflected in the Environmental Regulation of London, c. 1530-c. 1700' (University of Oxford, DPhil thesis, 1991; forthcoming as a monograph with Oxford University Press); P. Brimblecombe, *The Big Smoke: A History of Air Pollution in London since Medieval Times* (London, 1988). On reviving interest in Norwich's rivers: Norwich Society River Group, *A Journey Along the Waterways of Norwich* ([Norwich], [1969]). Two model studies for comparison are: P. Squatriti, *Water and Society in Early Medieval Italy, AD 400–1000* (Cambridge, 1998), and A. E. Guillerme, *The Age of Water: The*

Urban Environment in the North of France, AD 300–1800 (College Station, Texas, 1988).

8. J. K. Edwards, 'Norwich Bills of Mortality, 1707–1830', *Yorkshire Bulletin of Economic and Social Research*, xxi (1969), pp. 94–113; Slack, *Impact of Plague*, pp. 113, 128ff; P. Corfield, 'A Provincial Capital in the Late Seventeenth Century: The Case of Norwich', in P. Clark and P. Slack, eds, *Crisis and Order in English Towns, 1500–1700* (London, 1972), pp. 264–9. For some indication of how causes of death were recorded, T. R. Forbes, 'By What Disease or Casualty: The Changing Face of Death in London', in C. Webster, ed., *Health, Medicine and Mortality in the Sixteenth Century* (Cambridge, 1979), pp. 117–39.

9. For example: P. Browne, *The History of Norwich from the Earliest Records to the Present Time* (Norwich, [1814]).

10. Pelling, *Common Lot*, especially chapters 3, 4 and 5. For the later uses of pesthouses, the lazarhouses and household accommodation: NRO, NCR, 16A, Mayor's Court Book, 1654–66, fos 14v, 24r, 27v, 41v. See also Corfield, 'A Provincial Capital', p. 269.

11. See *History of Norwich*, i, Chapter 13; E. M. Thompson, ed., *Letters of Humphrey Prideaux* (Camden Society, new series, xv, 1965), pp. 204–5.

12. See Pelling, *Common Lot*, pp. 88–9, 226–7 and passim; eadem, 'Tradition and Diversity: Medical Practice in Norwich 1550–1640', in *Scienze credenze occulte livelli di cultura* (Istituto Nazionale de Studi sul Rinascimento, Florence, 1982), pp. 163ff, 168–9; D. Harley, 'Provincial Midwives in England: Lancashire and Cheshire, 1660–1760', in H. Marland, ed., *The Art of Midwifery: Early Modern Midwives in Europe* (London, 1993), pp. 36–7.

13. For further detail, and a comparison of the census with modern estimates of sickness and disability, see Pelling, *Common Lot*, Chapter 3.

14. NRO, NCR, 6A/1/27, 7, 55, 3, Coroner's Inquests, 1669–90.

15. NCR, 6A/1/16, 10.

16. NCR, 6A/1/12, 11, 21, 23, 60, 24, 25, 30, 45, 52, 61, 56.

17. NCR, 6A/1/18, 19.

18. NCR, 6A/1/22, 20, 26. 'Thicksell' is a dialect variant of 'thixil', meaning an adze: *OED*.

19. NCR, 6A/1/5, 9, 2, 13, 33, 35, 54, 6.

20. NCR, 6A/1/9, 49/2.

21. On this and the next paragraph, see Pelling, *Common Lot*, especially chapters 4, 5, 9 and 10; and eadem and C. Webster, 'Medical Practitioners', in C. Webster, ed., *Health, Medicine and Mortality in the Sixteenth Century* (Cambridge, 1979), especially pp. 206–26.

22. See *History of Norwich*, i, Chapter 13; and L. G. Matthews, 'The Spicers and Apothecaries of Norwich', *The Pharmaceutical Journal* (7 January 1967), pp. 5–9.

23. On the staithes, see A. Carter, 'Norwich', in G. Milne and B. Hobley, eds, *Waterfront Archaeology in Britain and Northern Europe* (London, 1981), pp. 139–41. The embankment or quay between Fye bridge and Whitefriars bridge on the south bank of the Wensum seems also to have been designated a common or 'great' staithe, but being in a central location it was developed from an early period: W. Hudson, 'Notes about Norwich before the Close of the Thirteenth Century', *NA*, xii (1893), p. 44. The cucking-stool was apparently located there, although this punishment was also carried out at Jack's Pit: W. Rye, ed., *Depositions Taken Before the Mayor and Aldermen of Norwich, 1549–1567* (Norwich, 1905), p. 16; V. Tillyard, 'Painters in Sixteenth and Seventeenth Century Norwich', *NA*, xxxvii (1980), p. 316; *RCN*, ii, p. 185 (1572). 'Stathe' was claimed to be a dialect word, but it would be more accurate to say that there were different local usages: W. Rye, *Songs, Stories and Sayings of Norfolk* (Norwich, 1897), p. 29; *OED*; J. Campbell, 'Norwich', in M. Lobel, ed., *Atlas of Historic Towns, ii* (London, 1975), p. 24.

24. Campbell, 'Norwich', pp. 11–14, 22; C. B. Hawkins, *Norwich: A Social Study* (London, 1910), pp. 73, 75, 80; *RCN*, ii, p. cxxxiii. For condemnation of the old bridges, see *The Norwich Directory* (Norwich, 1783), p. vi.

25. Campbell, 'Norwich', pp. 13–14, 16, and map 1; Browne, *History of Norwich*, p. 43. Campbell gives a date of 1695 for part of the turnpike near Attleborough; see also P. Wade-Martins, ed., *An Historical Atlas of Norfolk* (second edn, Norwich, 1998), pp. 146–7.

26. See above, p. 3–7; Campbell, 'Norwich', p. 17. For Cuningham, see Blomefield, *Norfolk*, iii, pp. 278–9; *DNB, sub nomine.*

27. For example, Browne, *History of Norwich*, p. 99; Hawkins, *Norwich: A Social Study*, pp. 73–4, 80; Campbell, 'Norwich', pp. 17–19; Slack, *Impact of Plague*, pp. 137–43. For reconstructions of the marshland areas and floodplains: W. Hudson, *How the City of Norwich Grew into Shape* (Norwich, 1896); Carter, 'Norwich', pp. 139–40.

28. T. Southwell, 'St Helen's Swanpit', *Transactions of the Norfolk and Norwich Naturalists' Society*, v (1889–94), pp. 265–72; G. A. Stephen, *100 Pictures of Norwich* (Norwich, 1926), p. 31. Keepers of swan-rights met annually at Buckenham Ferry, just down river from Surlingham.

29. Campbell, 'Norwich', p. 7. The extent of gardens and orchards is striking in E. Rutledge, ed., *Norwich Landgable Assessment, 1568–70* (NRS, lxiii, 1999), passim. 'Droving the long paddock' – i.e. grazing roadside verges – is still an accepted practice in Australia in times of drought. I owe this information to Deborah Pelling.

30. Kirkpatrick, *Streets and Lanes*, p. 82.

31. A. Batty Shaw, *Sir Thomas Browne of Norwich* (Norwich, 1982).

32. Browne, *History of Norwich*, p. 163; Stephen, *100 Pictures of Norwich*, p. 96;

Norwich Directory, pp. v, 66. Norwich's public gardens were unusually numerous, and 'remarkably early': T. C. Fawcett, 'The Norwich Pleasure Gardens', *NA*, xxxv (1972), pp. 382–99. See also Chapter 8, above.

33. Browne, *History of Norwich*, pp. 32 (1608), 46 (1738), 197 (1662).

34. *Norwich Directory*, pp. iii–vi. On Norwich's congested graveyards see also Evelyn's comments: Bray, *Diary*, ii, p. 72.

35. See *History of Norwich*, i, Chapters 1, 2 and 9.

36. Blomefield, *Norfolk*, iii, p. 214; Campbell, 'Norwich', pp. 1, 10; G. A. Stephen, *100 Pictures of the Norfolk Broads* (Norwich, 1927), p. 77. On navigable waterways see Wade-Martins, *Historical Atlas of Norfolk*, pp. 146–7.

37. Cuningham, *Cosmographical Glasse*, fo. 174; C. G. Davies, *Norfolk Broads and Rivers* (new edn, Edinburgh, 1884), p. 122. See also Michael Drayton, Song XX of *Poly-Olbion*, in Hebel, Tillotson and Newdigate, *Works*, iv, pp. 409–16.

38. Bray, *Diary*, ii, p. 71; E. A. Kent, 'The Houses of the Dukes of Norfolk in Norwich', *NA*, xxiv (1932), pp. 84–5. The frontage of the palace also faced, across Wymer Street, the pump situated before the church of St John Maddermarket.

39. On ditching, see the East Anglian farmer Thomas Tusser, and his editors, *Five Hundred Points of Good Husbandry* (1580; Oxford, 1984), pp. 309–10 and passim.

40. Morris, *Journeys*, pp. 136, 138; Davies, *Norfolk Broads and Rivers*, p. 126.

41. T. Williamson, *The Norfolk Broads: A Landscape History* (Manchester, 1997), pp. 3, 79ff.; Rye, *Songs, Stories and Sayings*, p. 138; Davies, *Norfolk Broads and Rivers*, pp. 2, 125. On the persistence of thatching, see S. Porter, 'Thatching in Early Modern Norwich', *NA*, xxxix (1986), pp. 310–12.

42. *RCN*, ii, p. cxxx; NRO, NCR, 19B, River and Street Accounts, 1583–4, 1594–5 ('Surlingham fenne').

43. Davies, *Norfolk Broads and Rivers*, p. v; Wade-Martins, *Historical Atlas*, pp. 82–3; Williamson, *Norfolk Broads*, pp. 2 (map), 89–90; Pelling, *Common Lot*, pp. 222, 224–5.

44. J. Keynes, ed., *The Works of Sir Thomas Browne* (4 vols, London, 1964), i, pp. 424–5.

45. *RCN*, ii, pp. 318–19; Blomefield, *Norfolk*, iii, pp. 222–60.

46. Quoted by Blomefield, *Norfolk*, iii, p. 229.

47. For lists of trades 'noyous' to the river: *RCN*, ii, pp. 115 (1532), 129 (1552); and for a prohibition against the loading of lime at the washing staithes in Conesford made available by the widow of Richard Bulwer: ibid., p. 135 (1561). On these staithes: Kirkpatrick, *Streets and Lanes*, p. 8.

48. NRO, NCR, 5E/1, Sessions Presentments, Ber Street, 1623.

49. On the uses of muck or manure: Tusser, *Five Hundred Points*; for the routine use of muck in agriculture near the city: *History of Norwich*, i, p. 312; on

spreading muck from a cockey: NRO, NCR, 19B, River and Street Accounts, 1589–90; on 'leying' household filth into 'round heaps' for removal: *RCN*, ii, p. 110 (1518); on lanes: Kirkpatrick, *Streets and Lanes*, pp. 11, 52, 61, 68, 86. For other references to the disposition of muck: Blomefield, *Norfolk*, iii, pp. 210 (1538), 318 (Elizabeth's visit in 1578); NCR, 16A, Mayor's Court Book, 1654–66, fo. 15v (1655). Muck was also used in quantity to build up low-lying areas: Carter, 'Norwich', p. 139.

50. *RCN*, ii, pp. cxxxi, 127–31. The accounts were 'dysordred' until taken over by Robert Suckling as surveyor of the river in 1564: NRO, NCR, 19B, River and Street Accounts, 1564.

51. For brief comments, see Corfield, 'A Provincial Capital', p. 270.

52. W. Rye, *A Glossary of Words used in East Anglia* (London, 1895), p. 59; *OED*, 'didle'; W. Hudson, 'On an Ancient Timber Roadway across the River Wensum at Fye Bridge, Norwich', *NA*, xiii (1898), p. 221. For references to 'the didall bote', an 'Iron didole with the net and poles' costing 3s., 'didall netts and thridd', 'didall poles' and 'nineteene nets for the didalls': NRO, NCR, 19B, River and Street Accounts, 1558–9, 1565–6, 1615–16, 1634–5, 1679–80.

53. Rye, *Glossary*, p. 72; idem, *Songs, Stories and Sayings*, p. 29; *RCN*, ii, pp. 171 (1543), 129 (1552); NRO, NCR, 19B, River and Street Accounts [1552, record of Assembly proceedings], 1558–9, 1579–80 ('ffeyers and cutters of the river'); *OED*, 'fay, feigh'.

54. Williamson, *Norfolk Broads*, p. 4; NRO, NCR, 19B, River and Street Accounts, 1646–7. 'Croming' was also claimed by Rye: *Songs, Stories and Sayings*, p. 29; see also, *OED*, 'crome'.

55. Kirkpatrick, *Streets and Lanes*, pp. 102–3; Hudson, *How the City of Norwich Grew*, pp. 51–2.

56. *OED* records only related meanings of 'cock', but see the *Middle English Dictionary*, 'cokei', and the *English Dialect Dictionary*, 'cockey'. Rye, *Songs, Stories and Sayings*, p. 29. For Briggs the 'Cockeyfyer', paid a year's wages: NRO, NCR, 19B, River and Street Accounts, 1594–5. The 'cockey keepers' also carried away muck: ibid., 1615–16. 'Fye', 'crome', and 'didall', but not 'cockey', occur in Tusser, *Five Hundred Points*, pp. 112, 295, 324; Tusser's own experience of Norwich, 'a citie trim', was a negative one: pp. 207–8, and *History of Norwich*, i, p. xxi–ii.

57. *RCN*, i, p. 358.

58. Kirkpatrick, *Streets and Lanes*, pp. 99–103; H. Harrod, *Gleanings among the Castles and Convents of Norfolk* (Norwich, 1857), pp. 131ff; Campbell, 'Norwich', p. 25 and map 2.

59. W. Hudson, 'The Stone Bridge by the Horse Fair in St Faith's Lane, Norwich; With Some Account of the Ancient History and Topography of the Adjoining District', *NA*, x (1888), pp. 117–42. For the 'wodden bridg' by the cockey

in St Faith's Lane, and ditches near the Common staithe: NRO, NCR, 5E/3, Sessions Presentments, Conesford, 1693, 1694.

60. W. Hudson, *History of the Parish of St Peter Permountergate, Part i* (Norwich, 1889), pp. 41–2, defines 'fleet' as a ditch filled and emptied by the tide. See also, C. Wright, 'Technical Vocabulary to Do with Life on the River Thames in London *c.* AD 1270–1500' (University of Oxford, DPhil thesis, 1988), p. 130.

61. Hudson, *How the City of Norwich Grew*, map v; Campbell, 'Norwich', map 7.

62. Kirkpatrick, *Streets and Lanes*, pp. 75–6, 85, 102.

63. For example, *RCN*, ii, pp. 335–6 (a plague order, 1579).

64. NRO, NCR, 19B, River and Street Accounts, 1636–7.

65. Campbell, 'Norwich', p. 25 and map 2.

66. Mr Briggs's cockey, along with the Ber Street drain, was in Conesford: NRO, NCR, 19B, River and Street Accounts, 1699–1700, 1710–11. Mr Briggs's staithe, where there was a cistern, was in St Julian's parish: ibid., 1721–3; 6A/1/13, Coroner's Inquests, 1687. There was still a staithe of this name in 1783: *Norwich Directory*, p. i.

67. NRO, NCR, 19B, River and Street Accounts, 1636–7, 1654–5, 1656–7, 1710–11, 1717–19; J. G. Hurst and J. Golson, 'Excavations at St Benedict's Gates, Norwich, 1951 and 1953', *NA*, xxxi (1957), pp. 7–8, 15, 47–8. For the local 'proverb' about flood indicators for Heigham, see NRO, NCR, 21F/76, Kirkpatrick MSS.

68. Hurst and Golson, 'Excavations', p. 47; NRO, NCR, 19B, River and Street Accounts, 1563–4, 1636–7, 1643–4, 1689–90, 1717–19.

69. NRO, NCR, 19B, River and Street Accounts, 1636–7, 1656–7, 1689–90, 1710–11; Browne, *History of Norwich*, pp. 125–6.

70. For sample years with full lists, see NRO, NCR, 19B, River and Street Accounts, 1617–18, 1636–7, 1643–4.

71. For Blackfriars: NRO, NCR, 19B, River and Street Accounts, 1589–90, 1644–5 (major work), 1654–5; for Fye bridge and Whitefriars: ibid., 1609–10, 1643–4, 1699–1700.

72. NRO, NCR, 19B, River and Street Accounts, 1594–5, 1599–1600.

73. NRO, NCR, 19B, River and Street Accounts, 1644–5 (inspection and works at the Angel cockey), 1689–90, 1699–1700, 1603–4; Kirkpatrick, *Streets and Lanes*, p. 88; River and Street Accounts, 1594–5, 1609–10. Bull's Close lay near the wall east of Magdalen Street (see *Norwich Directory*, map); the Bull cockey may have been there, or connected with the northerly end of Spiteldike.

74. NRO, NCR, 19B, River and Street Accounts, 1617–18 (Anguish, Hornsey, Goldman, Layer), 1699–70 (Briggs), 1599–1600 (Elmeham), 1615–16 (Howse, Gaudy), 1679–80 (Hassett, Mingay), 1636–7 (Howse, Norrys), 1653–4 (Pitcher), 1656–7 (Toft).

75. NRO, NCR, 19B, River and Street Accounts, 1639–40. This transaction involved an acquittance.

76. NRO, NCR, 19B, River and Street Accounts, 1594–5. This could be either Ralph Elmeham or his younger brother John, both barbers and both listed as householders in 1589. John was several times warden of the Barber-Surgeons' Company between 1580 and 1596. Both were involved in the knitting of nets as well as barberscraft, and one used both a garden in St Margaret's parish and a 'twistering' post in the churchyard: Pelling, *Common Lot*, p. 222 (where John is incorrectly stated to be the nephew of Ralph); NRO, Aylsham Collection 156; PD 153/43, St Margaret's Parish, Churchwardens' Accounts 1552–1642 (transcript), pp. 14, 38.

77. NRO, NCR, 19B, River and Street Accounts, 1615–16, 1645–6.

78. NRO, NCR, 19B, River and Street Accounts, 1645–6, 1646–7; see also 1669–70, 1689–90. On the Hassett or Blenerhassett family: J. Bulwer, 'Hassett's House, Pockthorpe, Norwich', *NA*, vii (1879), pp. 79–92. Hassett's House was situated close to the Wensum opposite the Cow Tower: *Norwich Directory*, map; Campbell, 'Norwich', map 3. For the city side of the river see also Kirkpatrick, *Streets and Lanes*, p. 70.

79. *RCN*, i, pp. 277–8; ii, pp. cxxx–cxxxiii, 96–8, 110, 133–4.

80. Kirkpatrick, *Streets and Lanes*, pp. 59, 44; NRO, NCR, 19B, River and Street Accounts, 1653–4.

81. NRO, NCR, 19B, River and Street Accounts, 1636–7 (in Conesford), 1719–20, 1721–3.

82. Kirkpatrick, *Streets and Lanes*, p. 7. Hurst and Golson have suggested that cisterns replaced cesspits for public purposes: 'Excavations', pp. 15, 47.

83. Wade-Martins, *Historical Atlas*, p. 158.

84. Browne, *History of Norwich*, pp. 31, 144. For valuable information and documents on the water system put in place in the 1580s: B. Starkings, 'Water and Politics in Elizabethan Norwich' (UEA, Norwich, MA thesis, 2000), especially appendix 3, p. 66.

85. NRO, NCR, 19B, River and Street Accounts, 1643–4, 1644–5, 1645–6, 1646–7, 1647–8, 1648–9, 1649–50; Blomefield, *Norfolk*, iii, p. 390.

86. F. Williamson, 'George Sorocold of Derby: A Pioneer of Water Supply', repr. in D. Smith, ed., *Water Supply and Public Health Engineering* (Aldershot, 1999), pp. 78–9 (King's Lynn), 87–8 (Norwich); Browne, *History of Norwich*, pp. 42, 59, 69–70, 110, 151, 163 (note reference to an ingenious engine); G. Johnson, 'Chronological Memoranda Touching the City of Norwich', *NA*, i (1847), p. 160; Kirkpatrick, *Streets and Lanes*, p. 66.

87. NRO, NCR, 19B, River and Street Accounts, 1652–3, 1669–70, 1710–11; Morris, *Journeys*, p. 136.

88. *Norwich Directory*, p. vi; Browne, *History of Norwich*, pp. 59, 110; P. Eade, *Some Account of the Parish of St Giles, Norwich* (London and Norwich, 1886), pp. 55–6. For earlier complaints about the waterworks

and surrounding street areas: NRO, NCR, 5E/3, Sessions Presentments, Conesford, 1706, 1720.

89. Browne, *History of Norwich*, p. 99. Blomefield, *Norfolk*, iii, p. 210, dates a major technological advance in lead piping to the Tudor period.

90. Blomefield, *Norfolk*, iv, pp. 427–8; compare also iii, p. 362; E.V., 'Ballad on Martinmas Day', *Notes and Queries*, fifth series, i (1874), p. 475; Starkings, 'Water and Politics', plate 21; E. Porter, *The Folklore of East Anglia* (London, 1974), p. 21; but see the shrine and well of St Walstan at Bawburgh, five miles from Norwich, from which water was taken to the city to be sold: ibid., p. 116. The obverse was, of course, the recurrent belief that wells could be poisoned: Slack, *Impact of Plague*, p. 129 (a common well in St Andrew's parish, not otherwise identifiable). On water and wells generally in this period: L. Thorndike, *A History of Magic and Experimental Science* (8 vols, New York; reprint 1964), vols vii and viii; K. Thomas, *Religion and the Decline of Magic* (Harmondsworth, reprint 1980). On spa water: Corfield, 'A Provincial Capital', p. 293.

91. J. G. Hurst, 'Excavations at Barn Road, Norwich, 1954–55', *NA*, xxxiii (1965), pp. 144–5; A. Carter, J. P. Roberts and H. Sutermeister, 'Excavations in Norwich, 1973. The Norwich Survey, Third Interim Report', ibid., xxxvi (1977), p. 44; S. Jennings and M. Atkin, 'A Seventeenth-Century Well Group from St Stephen's Street, Norwich (Site 301N)', ibid., xxxix (1986), pp. 13–37, and pp. 16, 18, 20 for discarded chamber pots.

92. Browne, *History of Norwich*, p. 145; Kirkpatrick, *Streets and Lanes*, p. 28; Blomefield, *Norfolk*, iv, p. 226.

93. On Muspol (Mustow, Musball) and the Red Well: Browne, *History of Norwich*, pp. 189–90; Kirkpatrick, *Streets and Lanes*, p. 45; *Norwich Directory*, p. vi. This Muspol is unconnected, except by confusion, with the Muspool cockey and pool north of the river.

94. Stephen, *100 Pictures of Norwich*, p. 54; Browne, *History of Norwich*, p. 115.

95. Blomefield, *Norfolk*, iii, pp. 356, 381, 400; iv, p. 235; Browne, *History of Norwich*, p. 32; Starkings, 'Water and Politics', p. 44. The medieval Saddlegate well was close to the Haymarket, but was down a lane: Campbell, 'Norwich', map 2; U. Priestley, *The Great Market* (Norwich, 1987), pp. 8, 19, 21.

96. Campbell, 'Norwich', map 2. For Common Pump Street and its vicinity: Browne, *History of Norwich*, p. 108; Kirkpatrick, *Streets and Lanes*, p. 12; *Norwich Directory*, pp. i, v. This well was possibly the one presented in 1706 as 'the common well': NRO, NCR, 5E/3, Sessions Presentments, Conesford, 1706.

97. Hudson, *History of the Parish of St Peter Permountergate*, p. 12. See also Eade, *Some Account*, p. 72.

98. Kirkpatrick, *Streets and Lanes*, pp. 14–15. St Clement's in Conesford, adjacent to the southerly Cockey Lane, seems also to have been associated with a well: Blomefield, *Norfolk*, iv, p. 77; Campbell, 'Norwich', p. 23.

99. Browne, *History of Norwich*, p. 167; Stephen, *100 Pictures of Norwich*, p. 57; M. Knights, 'St Lawrence's Well, Norwich, and Gibson's Conduit', *NA*, x (1881), pp. 185–91; C. B. Jewson, 'St Lawrence's Well: The Dedication of an Etching', ibid., xxxiv (1968), p. 335.

100. On Jack's Pit: Kirkpatrick, *Streets and Lanes*, pp. 16, 101; Harrod, *Gleanings*, pp. 130–1; NRO, NCR, 5E/3, Sessions Presentments, Conesford, 1694; 5E/1, Ber Street, 1698. On the ubiquity and danger of pits in medieval Norwich: *History of Norwich*, i, Chapter 13.

101. Campbell, 'Norwich', map 2. See also Kirkpatrick, *Streets and Lanes*, p. 85.

102. Browne, *History of Norwich*, p. 120; Kirkpatrick, *Streets and Lanes*, p. 77.

103. Kirkpatrick, *Streets and Lanes*, p. 20; NRO, NCR, 19B, River and Street Accounts, 1656–7, 1669–70, 1679–80; 5E/3, Sessions Presentments, Conesford, 1694, 1695; Browne, *History of Norwich*, p. 126.

104. Blomefield, *Norfolk*, iv, p. 140; Browne, *History of Norwich*, p. 115.

105. Kirkpatrick, *Streets and Lanes*, pp. 20, 77.

106. For example, a pool in St Mary's parish, where a girl drowned: NRO, NCR, 6A/1/31, Coroner's Inquests, 1689 (damaged).

107. NRO, NCR, 19B, River and Street Accounts, 1643–4 (fyed and 'casted' twice), 1653–4, 1669–70, 1679–80, 1689–90. This may have been the one remaining fuller's hole, or a particularly large one: see *History of Norwich*, i, Chapter 7 and 9 for their use. Other trades and processes created or required pits: Kirkpatrick, *Streets and Lanes*, pp. 20, 47.

108. Kirkpatrick, *Streets and Lanes*, p. 7; NRO, NCR, 19B, River and Street Accounts, 1656–7; 5E/3, Sessions Presentments, Conesford, 1706.

109. Campbell, 'Norwich', p. 23; Kirkpatrick, *Streets and Lanes*, pp. 52, 73–4.

110. Kirkpatrick, *Streets and Lanes*, pp. 86–7.

111. Kirkpatrick, *Streets and Lanes*, p. 86.

112. Carter, Roberts and Sutermeister, 'Excavations', pp. 45–7; Starkings, 'Water and Politics', p. 65.

113. NRO, NCR, 19B, River and Street Accounts, 1635–6; Kirkpatrick, *Streets and Lanes*, p. 89.

114. Kirkpatrick, *Streets and Lanes*, p. 70; Campbell, 'Norwich', p. 24; NRO, NCR, 19B, River and Street Accounts, 1653–4, 1654–5, 1669–70, 1689–90, 1719–20.

Notes to Chapter 6: From Second City to Regional Capital

1. Anon., *A Norfolk Tale* (London, 1792), p. 32.

2. G. Borrow, *Lavengro: The Scholar, the Gypsy, the Priest* (London, 1851), pp. 177–8.

3. A. Neville, *A Description of the Famous Citie of Norwich* (London, 1623), p. 1.

4. See *History of Norwich*, i, pp. xxiii.

5. BL, MS Sloane 1900, fo. 36v, E. Browne, 'Journal of a Tour' (September 1662) punctuation added.

6. Borrow, *Lavengro*, p. 178. For the origins of this legend see *History of Norwich*, i, p. xxvii.

7. Blomefield, *Norfolk*, iii, p. 322.

8. P. J. Corfield, 'A Provincial Capital in the Later Seventeenth Century: The Case of Norwich', in P. Clark and P. Slack, eds, *Crisis and Order in English Towns, 1500–1700: Essays in Urban History* (London, 1972), p. 267.

9. P. Clark, 'Introduction', in idem, ed., *European Small Towns* (Cambridge, 1995), especially pp. 1–9.

10. P. O. Pedersen, *Small African Towns: Between Rural Networks and Urban Hierarchies* (Avebury, 1997), especially pp. 3–6.

11. See Chapter 10, above.

12. An advertisement in 1722 even offered 'second-hand coffins' for sale: *NG*, 22 November 1722.

13. W. Honeycomb [pseud.], *The History of Pudica* (London, 1754), pp. 21–2. See above, pp. 214–6.

14. Anon., *A Compleat History of the Famous City of Norwich* (Norwich, 1728), p. 2. For a fuller discussion of the Norwich worsted industry see Chapter 9, above.

15. Compare evidence in PRO, CO/388/21, part ii, fo. 286: 'Computations Made by Some Persons Concerned in the Weaving Trade at Norwich' (1719); with BL, Add. MS 37873, Windham Papers, XXXII, Robert Partridge (Norwich manufacturer) to William Pitt, 16 January 1785.

16. For the debates, especially on the views of Franklin Mendels, see L. A. Clarkson, *Proto-Industrialisation: The First Phase of Industrialisation?* (Basingstoke, 1985); and D. C. Coleman, 'Proto-Industrialisation: A Concept Too Many', *EconHR*, second series, xxxvi (1983), pp. 435–48.

17. Corfield, 'Provincial Capital', pp. 280–2.

18. See *History of Norwich*, i, Chapter 9.

19. J. Thelwall, 'Prefatory Memoir' in idem, *Poems, Chiefly Written in Retirement* (Hereford, 1802), p. xxxviii.

20. Cited in A. Earland, *John Opie and his Circle* (London, 1911), p. 214.

21. R. Potter, 'A Farewell Hymn to the Country ', in *Poems* (London, 1774), p. 67.

22. Anon., *The Norwich Directory: or Gentlemen and Tradesmen's Assistant* (Norwich, 1783), p. iii.

23. Bodleian Library, Oxford, Rawlinson MSS Poetry 222, Anon., 'The Norwich Assembly: or The Descent of Venus' (n. d., 1730?).

24. 'Erraticus' [J. Larwood], *Erratics: By a Sailor, Containing Rambles in Norfolk* (2 vols, London, 1800), i, pp. 98–9.

25. The 'Norwich Plainhead' is a recognised variety: see C. A. House, *Norwich Canaries* (London, 1954), pp. 7–15.

26. BL, Add. MS 27966, fos 228–9, W. Arderon, Letter and Tracts, 1745–60: listing fifty-six street cries heard in Norwich in the 1750s.

27. See P. Clark, *British Clubs and Societies: The Origins of an Associational World* (Oxford, 2000), passim; and Norwich references, especially pp. 89, 133, 456.

28. J. P. Ferguson, *An Eighteenth-Century Heretic: Dr Samuel Clarke* (Kineton, 1976), pp. 7–8. See also W. Whiston, *Historical Memoirs of the Life ... of Dr Samuel Clarke* (London, 1748), p. 9, for the Clarkes' astronomical studies.

29. See C. Wilkins-Jones, 'Norwich City Library and its Intellectual Milieu, 1608–1825' (2 vols, UEA, PhD thesis, 2001).

30. S. Renton, 'The Moral Economy of the English Middling Sort ...: The Case of Norwich in 1766 and 1767', in A. Randall and A. Charlesworth, eds, *Markets, Market Culture and Popular Protest in Eighteenth-Century Britain and Ireland* (Liverpool, 1996), pp. 130–2. See also Chapter 5, above.

31. BL, Add. MS 27966, fos 228–9, W. Arderon, Letter and Tracts, 1745–60.

32. A. Hartshorne, ed., *Memoirs of a Royal Chaplain, 1729–63: The Correspondence of Edmund Pyle, D.D.* (London, 1905), p. 285.

33. Anon., *The Gentleman's Bottle Companion: Containing a Collection of ... Songs* (London, 1768; reprinted Edinburgh, 1979), pp. 23–4.

34. NHC, bound vol., 'Historical Accounts of Norfolk and Norwich'.

35. T., 'History of Norwich Manufactures', *Monthly Magazine*, vi (1798), p. 415.

36. L. Stone, 'Libertine Sexuality in Post-Restoration England: Group Sex and Flagellation among the Middling Sort in Norwich in 1706/7', *Journal of the History of Sexuality*, ii (1992), pp. 511–26.

37. BL, Add. MS 27966, fo. 68, W. Arderon, Letter and Tracts, 1745–60.

38. [J. Stacy], *A Topographical and Historical Account of the City and County of Norwich* (Norwich, 1819), p. 40.

39. B. Cozens-Hardy, ed., *The Diary of Sylas Neville, 1767–88* (Oxford, 1950), p. 312.

40. HMC, *Report on the Mss of the Duke of Portland*, ii (London, 1901), p. 156.

41. 'Erraticus', *Erratics*, i, pp. 112–13.

42. Anon., *Norwich Directory*, title page. For definitions of 'gentility', see P. J. Corfield, 'The Rivals: Landed and Other Gentlemen', in N. B. Harte and R. Quinault, eds, *Land and Society in Britain* (Manchester, 1996), pp. 1–33.

43. See Chapter 7.

44. NRO, NCR, 16C/47, Mayor's Court Papers: Resolution for Well Ordering and Regulating the City, January 1763.

45. A. J. Eddington, *The First Fifty Years of Quakerism in Norwich* (London, 1932), p. 14.

46. Anon., *The History of the City of Norwich* (Norwich, 1718), p. 4.

47. E. J. Bellamy, *James Wheatley and Norwich Methodism in the 1750s* (Peterborough, 1994), pp. 36–49, 192.

48. R. Ward and R. P. Heitzenrater, eds, *The Works of John Wesley*, xxi: *Journals and Diaries*, iv, *1755–65* (Nashville, Tennessee., 1992), p. 226.

49. Bellamy, *James Wheatley*, p. 189.

50. P. H. Marshall, *William Godwin* (New Haven, 1984), p. 18.

51. W. S. Lewis and others, eds, *Horace Walpole's Correspondence*, xxxviii: *With H. S. Conway and Others*, ii (London, 1974), p. 560.

52. [J. Sayers], 'An Address from the Citizens of N ... h to the National Convention [in France]', (1795), in M. D. George, ed., *Catalogue of Prints and Drawings in the British Museum* (12 vols, London, 1942), vii, p. 155: no. 8617.

53. L. Schwarz, 'Residential Leisure Towns in England towards the End of the Eighteenth Century', *Urban History*, xxvii (2000), pp. 51–61, especially p. 56.

54. [R. Beatniffe], ed., *The Norfolk Tour: or Traveller's Pocket Companion* (fifth edn, Norwich, 1795), p. 71.

55. [T. H. B. Oldfield], *An Entire and Complete History ... of the Boroughs of Great Britain* (3 vols, London, 1792), ii, p. 288.

56. [H. Peckham], *The Tour of Holland, Dutch Brabant, the Austrian Netherlands and Part of France* (London, 1772), p. 52.

57. T., 'History of Norwich Manufactures', p. 415.

58. P. J. Corfield, 'The Social and Economic History of Norwich, 1650–1850: A Study in Urban Growth' (University of London, PhD thesis, 1976), pp. 18–23, 327–8.

59. T. S. N. [Thomas Starling Norgate], 'Sketch of the State of Society at Norwich', *Monthly Magazine*, vii (May, 1799), p. 282.

60. [Stacy], *Topographical ... Account*, p. 122.

61. NRO, NCR, 16C/11, Norwich Assembly Book, 1776–1834, 27 January 1795.

62. BL, Add. MS 60168, fo. 234v (Muggletonian Archive).

63. P. J. Corfield and C. Evans, eds, *Youth and Revolution in the 1790s: Letters of Thomas Amyot, Henry Crabb Robinson and William Pattisson* (Stroud, 1996), p. 56.

64. PRO, HO/42/27, fos 182, 190.

65. L. S. Benjamin, ed., *The Windham Papers: The Life and Correspondence of ... William Windham, 1750–1810* (2 vols, London, 1913), ii, p. 194.

66. HMC, *Report on the Mss of J. B. Fortescue, Esq.*, vii (London, 1912), p. 99.

67. 'A Leveller, Jacobin, and Revolutioner', *To the Poor of Norwich* (Norwich, 1795), s. s. fol.

68. See Chapter 8.

69. P. J. Corfield, 'The Identity of a Regional Capital: Norwich since the Eighteenth Century', in P. Kooij and P. Pellenbarg, eds, *Regional Capitals: Past, Present, Prospects* (Assen, The Netherlands, 1994), pp. 129–47; and eadem,

'East Anglian Towns, 1540–1840', in P. Clark, ed., *Urban History of Britain*, ii: *1540–1840* (3 vols, Cambridge, 2000), ii, pp. 31–48.

70. T. S. N., 'Sketch of the State of Society', p. 279.

71. [W. Beloe], *The Sexagenarian: ... Recollections of a Literary Life* (2 vols, London, 1817), ii, pp. 364–5.

72. For the contributors to the *Cabinet*, see Corfield and Evans, eds, *Youth and Revolution*, especially pp. 187–95.

73. E. Robertson, ed., *Letters and Papers of Andrew Robertson, A. M., Miniature Painter* (London, 1897), p. 172.

74. For details, see A. Hemingway, *The Norwich School of Painters, 1803–33* (Oxford, 1979); A. Moore, *The Norwich School of Artists* (London, 1985; 2nd edn, 1995); and J. Walpole, *Art and Artists of the Norwich School* (Woodbridge, 1997).

Notes to Chapter 7: Politics, 1660–1950

1. There is no general survey of Norwich's eighteenth-century political culture in print, but I am indebted to: B. D. Hayes, 'Politics in Norfolk 1750–1832' (University of Cambridge, PhD thesis, 1958); D. S. O'Sullivan, 'Politics in Norwich, 1701–1835' (UEA, Norwich, MPhil thesis, 1975); J. T. Evans, *Seventeenth-Century Norwich: Politics, Religion, and Government, 1620–1690* (Oxford, 1979); G. Guth, 'Croakers, Tackers and Other Citizens: Norwich Voters in the Early Eighteenth Century' (Stanford University, PhD thesis, 1985); N. Rogers, 'Popular Jacobitism in Provincial Context: Eighteenth-Century Bristol and Norwich', in E. Cruickshanks and J. Black eds, *The Jacobite Challenge* (Edinburgh, 1988); N. Rogers, *Whigs and Cities: Popular Politics in the Age of Walpole and Pitt* (Oxford, 1989), chapter 9, 'Norwich: City of Whigs and Weavers'; N. Rogers, *Crowds, Culture and Politics in Georgian Britain* (Oxford, 1998); K. Wilson, *The Sense of the People: Politics, Culture and Imperialism in England, 1715–1785* (Oxford, 1995); C. Jewson, *The Jacobin City: A Portrait of Norwich in its Reaction to the French Revolution, 1788–1802* (Glasgow, 1975). To set Norwich in a wider context, see J. A. Phillips, *Electoral Behavior in Unreformed England : Plumpers, Splitters and Straights* (Princeton, 1982), and S. and B. Webb, *English Local Government* (4 vols, London, 1906–22), ii, both of which use Norwich as a case study, as well as R. Sweet, *The English Town, 1680–1840: Government, Society and Culture* (London, 1999). I am also very grateful to Andrew Hopper and Jan Pitman for transcribing material that now appears on the Virtual Norfolk web site (http://www. uea. ac. uk/his/virtualnorfolk), where readers will find many primary documents illustrating this and others chapters. I also wish to thank Dr Margaret Escott of the History of Parliament Trust for sharing with me an unpublished account of early

nineteenth-century parliamentary politics. Owing to the 1994 fire at Norwich City Library some early periodicals were lost and citations are therefore from Rogers, *Whigs and Cities*, and Wilson, *Sense of the People.*

2. E. M. Thompson, ed., *Letters of Humphrey Prideaux to John Ellis, 1674–1722* (Camden Society, new series, xv, 1875), p. 90; *CSPD, 1682*, pp. 54–5; *London Post*, 14 May 1705; NRO, Rye MS 18. I.

3. *Norwich Election Budget* (1830), pp. 15, 30–2, 34–5.

4. *Reports from Assistant Handloom Weavers Commissioners, PP* (1840), xxiii, p. 342, cited in Hayes, 'Politics in Norfolk', p. 97, n. 1.

5. The *History of Parliament* volumes offer an account of Norwich constituency from a purely parliamentary angle. See B. D. Henning, ed., *The House of Commons, 1660–1690* (3 vols, London, 1983); E. Cruickshanks, S. Handley and D. Hayton, eds, *The House of Commons, 1690–1715* (5 vols, Cambridge, 2002); R. Sedgwick, ed., *The House of Commons, 1715–1754* (2 vols, London, 1970); Sir L. Namier and J. Brooke, eds, *The House of Commons, 1754–1790* (3 vols, London, 1964); R. G. Thorne, ed., *The House of Commons, 1790–1820* (5 vols, London, 1986).

6. S. and B. Webb, *English Local Government*, ii, pp. 529–58; Rogers, *Whigs and Cities*, p. 307; *A Copy of the Short-Hand Writer's Minutes of the Evidence* (Norwich, 1833), p. 12; E. Porritt, *The Unreformed House of Commons* (2 vols, Cambridge, 1903), i, p. 82.

7. *Norwich Gazette*, 29 April 1710, 11 May 1716; NHC, Colman Collection, 'Parliamentary and Municipal Broadsides, Squibs and Addresses, 1780–1840'; Guth, 'Croakers', p. 164; *NM*, 25 March 1829; Hayes, 'Politics', p. 84. There were two sheriffs, the second chosen by the mayor and aldermen.

8. *CSPD, 1677–8*, p. 634; 1682, pp. 54–6, 274–5; 1687–9, p. 316; *Historical Manuscripts Commission*, folio series, sixth report, appendix (1893), p. 385; R. H. Hill, ed., *A Miscellany ... The Correspondence of Thomas Corie* (NRS, xxvii, 1956), p. 41; *The Life of the Reverend Humphrey Prideaux* (London, 1748), p. 47.

9. NRO, Frere Collection, DS 593–604(d); *NG*, 20 October 1710; BL, Add. MS 5853, fo. 107, Henry Crossgrove to John Strype, 2 December 1714. A tacker supported 'tacking' the land tax bill of 1705 to religious legislation aimed against dissenters who 'occasionally' conformed to the Church of England.

10. 9 George I, c. 9; *NM*, 6, 27 April 1728, 22 March 1729; Rogers, *Whigs and Cities*, p. 321.

11. The number of councillors varied (both before and after the act) from ward to ward, ranging from twelve to twenty.

12. S. and B. Webb, *English Local Government*, ii, pp. 549–51; *NM*, 7–14 July 1733.

13. *NG*, 14–21 January 1716, 25 May 1717; Rogers, *Whigs and Cities*, pp. 312–3, 316, 339–40; P. Fritz, *The English Ministers and Jacobitism Between the Rebellions of 1715 and 1745* (Toronto, 1975), pp. 143–6; Rogers, *Crowds, Culture and Politics*,

p. 43; *NM*, 24 April 1731; NRO, NCR, 13D(2), Loyalist Association, 26 September 1745; 13E/5, list of subscribers to a fund for repressing the Scots rebels, 1745; BL, Add. MS 27966, fo. 68.

14. BL, Add. MS 27996, fo. 243v, cited by Rogers, 'Popular Jacobitism', p. 124; O'Sullivan, 'Politics', table 7; Wilson, *Sense of the People*, pp. 406–7, 410–12; *NG*, 10 March 1764; *NM*, 14, 21 November 1767; *A Letter to John Day* (1768).

15. *NC*, 31 Jan, 1, 7 February, 7 March 1778; *Consistency or The Speech of the Right Honourable William Windham* (1778).

16. W. A. Abram, *Memoirs of an Old Preston Family of Crane* (Preston, 1877), p. 78.

17. BL, Add. MS 37908, fo. 1, Elias Norgate to Windham, 19 February 1782; C. Branford, 'Powers of Association: Aspects of Elite Social, Cultural and Political Life in Norwich, *c.* 1680–1760' (UEA, Norwich, PhD thesis, 1993), p. 154.

18. Branford, 'Powers of Association', pp. 139, 147; *CSPD, 1682*, p. 54; Bodleian Library, Oxford, Tanner MS 29, fo. 8.

19. *A True and Particular Narrative of the Disturbances and Outrages* (London, 1752), p. 13; O'Sullivan, 'Politics', p. 213.

20. O'Sullivan, 'Politics', p. 135; *NC*, 5 December 1789; Hayes, 'Politics', pp. 75–7; Phillips, *Electoral Reform*, pp. 160–8, 305 and figures 7.1 and 7.3.

21. BL, Add. MS 5853, fos 108–9, Henry Crossgrove to Strype, 15 August 1715; A. D. Euren, *The First Provincial Newspaper* (Norwich, 1924); J. B. Williams, 'Henry Crossgrove Journalist and Printer', *The Library*, third series, v (1914), pp. 206–19; BL, Add. MS 5853, fo. 108v; *NG*, 21–8 January 1716; *Weekly Journal*, 23 July 1715; Branford, 'Powers of Association', p. 265.

22. *Miscellaneous Pieces, in Prose and Verse* (Norwich, 1768), introduction, p. 3; *The Narrative of the Proceedings*, pp. 18–19, 28–9, 31–2, 41–2.

23. *The Narrative of the Proceedings*, pp. 17, 46; *NC*, 16 September 1780; Phillips, *Electoral Behaviour*, p. 132.

24. Wilson, *Sense of the People*, p. 61; Guth, 'Croakers', p. 33.

25. BL, Add. MS 5853, fo. 107, Crossgrove to Strype; *NG*, 12, 19, 26 May 1716, cited by Rogers, *Whigs and Cities*, p. 314; *NM*, 10, 17 August 1728, 9 June 1744, 29 June, 5, 12 October 1745; Branford, 'Powers of Association', p. 173; Wilson, *Sense of the People*, p. 381.

26. NRO, MC64/5, 'Norwich Clubs and Societies'; Branford, 'Powers of Association', pp. 208–9; *NC*, 2 September, 25 November 1769, 21 April 1770. For the 1760s see B. Cozens-Hardy, ed., *The Diary of Sylas Neville* (Oxford, 1950).

27. Jewson, *Jacobin City*, chapters 2 and 3; PRO, HO 42/22, report 17 November 1792; S. Wilks, *Memoirs of Reverend Mark Wilks* (London, 1821), appendix vii–viii; J. W. Robberds, ed., *A Memoir of the Life and Writings of the Late William Taylor of Norwich* (2 vols, London, 1843), i, pp. 68–74; *The Cabinet*, i

(1795), preface, p. iv; PRO, Treasury Solicitor papers TS 24/3/80, 24/9/13–14, 24/10/10, 24/10/16; some extracts appear in R. H. Mason, *History of Norfolk* (London, 1884), pp. 469–74.

28. Jewson, *Jacobin City*, chapters 4 and 5; PRO, HO42/20, copy of resolutions passed 24 March 1792; *Appendix to the Second Report from the Committee of Secrecy* (1794), appendixes c, d and e; O'Sullivan, 'Politics', p. 142; W. Cobbett, *Cobbett's Complete Collection of State Trials* (33 vols, 11 onwards compiled by T. B. Howell and T. J. Howell; Dublin and London, 1809–28), xxiv and xxv.

29. *Declaration of the Norwich Patriotic Society* (1795); *An Address from the Patriotic Society of Norwich* (1797); Richard Dinmore, *An Exposition of the Principles of the English Jacobins* (Norwich, 1797), p. 5; *NC*, 3 June 1797; NRO, NCR, 6H /11, papers relating to riot, 29 May 1797.

30. *NC*, 8, 15 December 1792.

31. *NC*, 8, 15 December 1792, 25 February 1797; NRO, MS Colman 27. T. 129c, events in Norfolk and Norwich, 1795–7; Jewson, *Jacobin City*, pp. 77, 89.

32. O'Sullivan, 'Politics', pp. 152–3; *A Charge Delivered* (1793), pp. 7, 14, 16; *Trial by Jury, Peace, Liberty and Prosperity Against Despotism, Murder, Perjury and Famine* (1796).

33. NRO, NCR 12B/1, information of Zachary Iveson, 8 August 1698; 16C/8, fo. 97, fo. 312, 19 November 1730; Branford, 'Powers of Association', pp. 299–300; S. Renton, 'The Moral Economy of the English Middling Sort in the Eighteenth Century: The Case of Norwich in 1766 and 1767', in A. Randall and A. Charlesworth, eds, *Markets, Market Culture and Popular Protest in Eighteenth-Century Britain and Ireland* (Liverpool, 1996), pp. 115–36; P. Muskett, *'Riotous Assemblies': Popular Disturbances in East Anglia, 1740–1822* (Ely, 1984); O'Sullivan, 'Politics', p. 120; PRO, HO 42/25, Robert Harvey junior, 12 March 1793.

34. See Chapter 9.

35. W. Speck, *Tory and Whig: The Struggle in the Constituencies, 1701–1715* (London, 1970), appendix b, pp. 119–20; Wilson, *Sense of the People*, pp. 394, 401–2; Rogers, *Whigs and Cities*, pp. 330–5.

36. *The Hypocritical Fast* (Norwich, 1781), p. 28; *NM*, 24 December 1785; *An Address to the Electors* (1794), p. 9.

37. NRO, NCR, 16D/10, Assembly Folio Book, 1745–73, 24 February 1762; *NM*, 7 May 1763.

38. *NC*, 21 January 1775, 31 January 1778; Wilson, *Sense of the People*, pp. 418–19; O'Sullivan, 'Politics', p. 140; Jewson, *Jacobin City*, pp. 40, 80; NRO, NCR, 16C/11, Assembly Book, 1790–1805, 27 January 1795; *The Proceedings and Speeches at the Meeting the Seventh November 1795* (1795).

39. *A New Election Budget* (1802), part v, address to electors, 9 July 1802; *NM*, 10

July 1802, 16 February 1830; NRO, MS 4686, P140A; O'Sullivan, 'Politics', pp. 184–6. For Smith's career see R. Davis, *Dissent in Politics, 1780–1832: The Political Life of William Smith MP* (London, 1971).

40. NRO, MS 502, Castle Corporation Records, letter of 15 January 1817.

41. Mason, *Norwich*, p. 475; O'Sullivan, 'Politics', p. 175; *A Letter to the Independent Freemen* (1826), p. 12.

42. *NC*, 11 August 1832.

43. *The Times*, 3 August 1830.

44. *NM*, 7 May, 22 October 1831, 14 January, 13 October 1832; *Norwich Election Budget* (1831).

45. *NM*, 1 October 1831; *The Times*, 3 October 1831; NRO, GTN/33/1, Isaac Wiseman to Lord Suffield, 5 October 1831.

46. *The Times*, 16 May 1832; O'Sullivan, 'Politics', p. 200; S. and B. Webb, *English Local Government*, ii, p. 557; see Chapter 14, above.

47. *A Letter to the Freemen of Norwich* (1833), p. 9.

48. Phillips, *Electoral Behaviour*, p. 243; S. and B. Webb, *English Local Government*, ii, pp. 539, 550–4.

Notes to Chapter 8: An Enlightened and Polite Society

1. E. Robertson, ed., *Letters and Papers of Andrew Robertson, A. M., Miniature Painter* (London, 1897), p. 172.

2. *NC*, 1 November 1788. I am indebted to David Cubitt for suggesting sources and improvements to the text, and also to Professor A. Hassell Smith and Professor Peter Borsay for their comments.

3. For a discussion of the English Enlightenment generally, see R. Porter, *Enlightenment in Britain and the Creation of the Modern World* (London, 2000).

4. D. F. Bond, ed., *The Spectator* (5 vols, Oxford, 1965), i, no. 10, 12 March 1711, p. 44.

5. G. A. Stephen, 'The Waits of the City of Norwich through Four Centuries to 1790', *NA*, xxv (1933), pp. 1–70.

6. S. Rosenfeld, *Strolling Players and Drama in the Provinces, 1660–1765* (Cambridge, 1983), pp. 39, 44.

7. *NM*, 26 August 1797; G. A. Stephen, *Three Centuries of a City Library: An Historical and Descriptive Account of the Norwich Public Library Established in 1608 and the Present Public Library Opened in 1857* (Norwich, 1917).

8. R. W. Ketton-Cremer, *Forty Norfolk Essays* (London, 1961), p. 14.

9. P. Borsay, *The English Urban Renaissance: Culture and Society in the Provincial Town, 1660–1770* (Oxford, 1989), p. 128; R. Sweet, *The English Town, 1680–1840: Government, Society and Culture* (London, 1999), pp. 243–4.

10. A. Dain, 'Assembly Rooms and Houses in Norfolk and Suffolk' (UEA, Norwich, MA thesis, 1993), p. 89.

11. *NM*, 22, 29 April, 8, 15 July, 12, 19, 26 August, 2, 30 September, 7, 14, 21 October 1738.

12. D. A. Stoker, 'A History of the Norwich Book Trades from 1560 to 1760' (dissertation submitted for Fellowship of the Library Association, 2 vols, 1975), i, p. 327; T. Fawcett, 'The Culture of Late Georgian Norwich: A Conflict of Evidence', *UEA Bulletin*, new series, no. 5, pp. 1–10.

13. *NG*, 29 November, 6 December 1746.

14. *NC*, 23 July 1779.

15. W. Wicks, *Inns and Taverns of Old Norwich: With Notes on Pleasure Gardens* (Norwich, 1925), pp. 133–4.

16. *NM*, 29 December 1753, 19 January 1754.

17. *NM*, 30 January, 6, 13, 20 February, 17 April 1819, 4, 25 June, 13, 20 August 1825; *NC*, 25 June, 6 August 1825; P. Chapman, *Madame Tussaud in England: Career Woman Extraordinary* (London, 1972), pp. 1, 35, 60, 106.

18. P. Clark, *British Clubs and Societies, 1580–1800: The Origins of an Associational World* (Oxford, 2000), p. 23. For a discussion of Norwich's political clubs in the eighteenth century, see pp. 180–1 above.

19. H. Lestrange, *History of Freemasonry in Norfolk, 1724–1895* (Norwich, 1896), pp. 5–7, 238.

20. NRO, COL/9/1, Transactions of the Society of United Friars from 1785 to November 1794.

21. NRO, COL 9/193/1, The Fraternity of United Friars, College of St Luke, Norwich, with Descriptions of their Convent & Ceremonies and Notes of their Transactions, compiled from their Minutes and Records (in the possession of J. J. Colman Esq., MP) by M. Knights.

22. *The Norfolk and Norwich Remembrancer* (Norwich, 1822), pp. 128–9.

23. *BNP*, 31 December 1788.

24. C. Branford, 'Norwich and Scotland in the Eighteenth Century', *NA*, xliii (1998), p. 157.

25. T. Fawcett, *Music in Eighteenth-Century Norwich and Norfolk* (Norwich, 1979), p. 16; D. Owen, *English Philanthropy, 1660–1960* (London, 1964), pp. 66–7; *NM*, 3 May 1783, 15 May 1784, 14 May 1785, 15 April 1786, 24 March 1787, 17 January 1789; *BNP*, 25 May, 1 June 1785, 14 January 1789.

26. *NM*, 3 July 1784.

27. Clark, *British Clubs*, p. 300; Owen, *English Philanthropy*, pp. 66–7; *NM*, 3 December 1796.

28. T. Fawcett, *The Rise of English Provincial Art, Artists, Patrons, and Institutions Outside London, 1800–1830* (Oxford, 1974), especially pp. 1, 201–2; D. Clifford and T. Clifford, *John Crome* (London, 1968), pp. 24, 45.

29. To appeal to a broader political public, the inn was sometimes referred to as the King's Arms.

30. J. Beresford, ed., *The Diary of a Country Parson: The Reverend James Wood-forde* (5 vols, Oxford, 1968), ii, p. 105, 20 November 1783.

31. *IJ*, 10 April, 13 November 1802.

32. P. Browne, *The History of Norwich from the Earliest Records to the Present Time* (Norwich, 1814), pp. 428–9.

33. P. Langford, *A Polite and Commercial People: England, 1727–1783* (Oxford, 1989), p. 110.

34. C. Calhoun, 'Introduction', in idem, ed., *Habermas and the Public Sphere* (Cambridge, Massachusetts, 1992), pp. 35–6.

35. *NM*, 2, 9 January, 5, 12 March 1748.

36. *NM*, 11, 18 November 1749, 24, 31 March, 28 April, 5, 12, 19 May 1750.

37. J. Milburn, *Benjamin Martin: Author, Instrument-Maker, and 'Country Show-man'* (Leyden, 1976), p. 44.

38. *NM*, 23, 30 May 6, 27 June, 4 July, 29 August, 16 September 1752, 3, 10, 17, 24 February, 3, 10, 17, 24 March, 28 April, 5 May 1753, 3 May 1760, 27 August 1763.

39. T. Fawcett, 'Popular Science in Eighteenth-Century Norwich', *History Today*, xxii (August, 1972), pp. 59–60; M. Alic, *Hypatia's Heritage: A History of Women in Science from Antiquity to the Late Nineteenth Century* (London, 1990), pp. 78, 82.

40. *NM*, 17, 24 December 1785; Beresford, *Diary of a Country Parson*, ii, pp. 219–20, 19 December 1785.

41. *NM*, 7 March 1761.

42. W. Saint, *Memoirs of the Life, Character, Opinions, and Writings of that Learned and Eccentric Man, the Late John Fransham, of Norwich* (Norwich, c. 1811), pp. 87–8.

43. Beresford, *Diary of a Country Parson*, ii, pp. 231–2, 16 March 1786.

44. *Philosophical Transactions of the Royal Society of London*, xlvi (1750), pp. 467–70, 'Extract of a Letter from Mr William Arderon FRS to Mr Henry Baker FRS dated Norwich 12 May 1750 and read 14 June 1750, containing an Account of a Dwarf; together with a Comparison of his Dimensions with those of a Child under four Years old; by Erskine Baker'.

45. *NG*, 27 December 1740, 3 January 1741.

46. *Remembrancer*, pp. 117–18, 201.

47. Beresford, *Diary of a Country Parson*, iii, pp. 39–40, 29 July 1788; *Remembrancer*, p. 30; R. D. Altick, *The Shows of London* (Cambridge, Massachusetts, 1978), p. 44.

48. *NM*, 5 May 1753.

49. Wicks, *Inns and Taverns of Old Norwich*, p. 30.

50. *Remembrancer*, p. 31.

51. *NM*, 6, 13 January 1753.

52. Beresford, *Diary of a Country Parson*, ii, p. 220, 19 December 1785.

53. *NM*, 3, 10 January 1807.

54. *NM*, 14–21 December 1745.

55. *NM*, 19 June 1779, 31 July, 28 August 1824.

56. D. E. Allen, *The Naturalist in Britain: A Social History* (London, 1976), p. 43.

57. *NM*, 7 August 1824.

58. *NM*, 3 February 1821.

59. NRO, BOL 2/28/14, 739 x 7, 15 June 1778 with postscript added Wednesday morning, 17 June, Elizabeth Leathes to her mother.

60. NRO, MC 2015/11, 904 x 8, 8 November 1778, E[lizabeth] F[romanteel] to her cousin, John Patteson, then in Italy.

61. V. M. Crosse, *A Surgeon in the Early Nineteenth Century: The Life and Times of John Green Crosse MD, FRCS, FRS, 1790–1850* (London, 1968), p. 97.

62. Borsay, *English Urban Renaissance*, p. 122.

63. W. Weber, *The Rise of Musical Classics in the Eighteenth-Century: A Study in Canon, Ritual and Ideology* (Oxford, 1992), p. 131.

64. R. H. Legge and W. E. Hansell, *Annals of the Norfolk and Norwich Triennial Musical Festivals* (Norwich, 1896), p. vii.

65. *NM*, 16, 23, 30 March 1745.

66. *NC*, 2 November 1799.

67. *Norwich Post*, 28 June, 5 July 1712; *NC*, 7 November 1772.

68. T. Fawcett, *Music in Eighteenth-Century Norwich and Norfolk* (Norwich, 1979), p. 15.

69. Beresford, *Diary of a Country Parson*, iii, pp. 367–8, Thursday 2 August 1792. For Nancy Woodforde's account of the day, see D. H. Woodforde, ed., *Woodforde Papers and Diaries* (London, 1932), pp. 66–7.

70. A. Boden, *Gloucester, Hereford, Worcester Three Choirs: A History of the Festival* (Stroud, 1992), pp. 1, 66.

71. Legge and Hansell, *Annals*, p. 16; *NM*, 27 March, 2 October 1824.

72. Legge and Hansell, *Annals*, p. 272.

73. J. Bulman, *Jenny Lind: A Biography* (London, 1956), p. 209. A. D. Bayne, *Comprehensive History*, p. 430, dates the two concerts January 1850.

74. T. L. G. Burley, *Playhouses and Players of East Anglia* (Norwich, 1928), pp. 66–7.

75. *IJ*, 21 January 1764.

76. *NM*, 26 May 1750.

77. *NM*, 28 January 1775.

78. *IJ*, 7 September 1799; T. Fawcett, 'The Norwich Pleasure Gardens', *NA*, xxxv (1970–72), pp. 394.

79. *NM*, 17 January 1784; B. Cozens-Hardy, ed., *The Diary of Sylas Neville, 1767–1799* (Oxford, 1950), p. 315, 1 March 1784.

80. Fawcett, 'Norwich Pleasure Gardens', pp. 391.

81. *BNP*, 27 July 1785.

82. *HMC Eleventh Report, Appendix, Part IV, The Manuscripts of the Marquess Townshend* (London, 1887), p. 412, 24 July 1785, Lord Orford to [Lord Townshend], dated at Norwich.

83. Bayne, *Comprehensive History*, pp. 282–3. See also Beresford, *Diary of a Country Parson*, ii, p. 202, 25 July 1785.

84. *Oxford English Dictionary* (12 vols, Oxford, 1933), i, p. 504.

85. *NC*, 2 February 1793.

86. *NC*, 18 October 1817.

87. *NM*, 12 August 1758.

88. *NM*, 9 June 1792.

89. *NC*, 27 July 1771, 31 August 1773, 1 August 1778.

90. A. J. Dain, 'Assemblies and Politeness, 1660–1840' (UEA, Norwich, PhD thesis, 2000), pp. 241–2.

91. *NC*, 21 November 1801.

92. *NM*, 21, 28 April, 5 May, 23, 30 June, 7 July, 29 September, 6, 13, 20, 27 October 1744.

93. *NM*, 29 June, 6, 13, 27 July, 3, 10 August 1751.

94. *NM*, 19, 26 April 1735.

95. *NC*, 21, 28 May, 4 June 1774; *NM*, 21, 28 May, 4 June 1774.

96. *NM*, 16, 23 September 1775.

97. *NC*, 26 February, 8 April, 27 May 1780.

98. *NM*, 19 February 1785.

99. *NM*, 11 December 1819.

100. *NC*, 10 August 1771.

101. *NM*, 28 February 1807.

102. *NC*, 16 April 1814.

103. F. J. Lambert, *Treatise on Dancing* (Norwich, 1815), p. 5.

104. Lambert, *Treatise on Dancing*, pp. 4–5, 39.

105. *NM*, 7–14 September, 7–14 December 1751.

106. Bond, *The Spectator*, iv, p. 146, no. 466, Monday 25 August 1712.

107. J. Weaver, *Orchesography: or The Art of Dancing by Characters and Demonstrative Figures* (London, 1706; reprinted 1971).

108. *NM*, 9, 16, 30 October, 6, 13, November 1756, 4, 11, 18 August 1759, 1, 8, 15 March 1760, 8 January 1814, 6 January 1827.

109. *NM*, 2 March 1765; J. G. Noverre, *Letters on Dancing and Ballets*, trans. C. W. Beaumont (New York, 1966), p. x.

110. D. Lynham, *The Chevalier Noverre Father of Modern Ballet* (London, 1950), p.40.

111. *NC*, 31 August, 7 September 1793; *NM*, 31 August, 7 September 1793.

112. F. T. Hibgame, *Recollections of Norwich Fifty Years Ago* (Norwich, 1919), p. 36.

113. Lynham, *Chevalier Noverre*, p. 180, Miss O. F. Abbott to the author.

114. See Chapter 11.

115. A. Wilson, 'Conflict, Consensus and Charity: Politics and the Provincial Voluntary Hospitals in the Eighteenth Century', *EHR*, cxi (1996), pp. 599–619.

116. F. Bateman and W. Rye, *The History of the Bethel Hospital at Norwich, Built by Mrs Mary Chapman in Jan 1713* (Norwich, 1906), pp. 7, 15, 29, 31, 175; M. Winston, 'The Bethel at Norwich: An Eighteenth-Century Hospital for Lunatics', *Medical History*, xxxviii (1994), pp. 27–51; *NM*, 8 October 1763. See Chapter 11 below for other charitable foundations.

117. *IJ*, 26 November, 10 December 1757; *NM*, 3 December 1757; *NC*, 7 January 1826; *NM*, 14 January 1826.

118. *IJ*, 30 October 1790; NRO, SO 110/7–10, Norwich Association for the Relief of Decayed Tradesmen, their Widows and Orphans.

119. C. Morris, ed., *The Illustrated Journeys of Celia Fiennes c. 1682-c. 1712* (London, 1982), p. 137.

120. 'A Journal of a Tour Through Suffolk, Norfolk, Lincolnshire and Yorkshire in the Summer of 1741', in C. Harper-Bill, C. Rawcliffe and R. G. Wilson, eds, *East Anglia's History: Studies in Honour of Norman Scarfe* (Woodbridge, 2002), p. 271.

121. N. Pevsner and B. Wilson, *Norfolk i, Norwich and North-East* (second edn, London, 1997) pp. 316–8. See also pp. 179–328 for the excellent survey of the city's standing structures.

122. D. Cubitt, A. L. Mackley and R. G. Wilson, eds, *The Great Tour of John Patteson, 1778–1779* (NRS, lxvii, 2003), p. 5.

123. Pevsner and Wilson, *Norfolk*, i, pp. 283–6, 307–9, 314–8.

124. Pevsner and Wilson, *Norfolk*, i, pp. 254–5; M. Atkin, *Norwich History and Guide* (Stroud, 1993), p. 86.

125. NRO, WKC 7/9, 404X1, 8 August 1688; R. W. Ketton-Cremer, 'Assize Week in Norwich', *NA*, xxiv (1932), pp. 13–17.

126. P. Eade, *Some Account of the Parish of St Giles* (London, 1889), p. 55.

127. *NM*, 21 June, 5, 12, 19 July 1755; Pevsner and Wilson, *Norfolk*, i, pp. 269–70.

128. Rosenfold, *Strolling Players*, p. 74; Burley, *Playhouses and Players*, pp. 1, 55; H. M. Colvin, *A Biographical Dictionary of English Architects, 1660–1840* (London, 1954), pp. 310–11. The theatre was enlarged by William Wilkins in 1800 and again altered in 1819. It was demolished in 1825.

129. A. Kendall, *David Garrick: A Biography* (London, 1985), p. 166; Burley, *Playhouses and Players*, pp. 17–18; Eshleman, *Committee Book of the Theatre Royal*, p. 165.

130. *NM*, 15 March 1766; Colvin, *English Architects*, pp. 310–11; Pevsner and Wilson, *Norfolk*, i, p. 308. Nos 29–35 survive; nos 25–27 were demolished.

131. William Chase, *The Norwich Directory: or Gentlemen and Tradesmen's Assistant* (Norwich, 1783), p. v.

132. R. Fitch, *Views of the Gates of Norwich: Made in the Year 1792–3 by the Late John Ninham. With an Historical Introduction* (Norwich, 1861), pp. xxxii–iii.

133. E. De Selincourt, ed., *The Letters of William and Dorothy Wordsworth* (second revised edn, 8 vols, Oxford, 1967–1993), i, p. 21.

134. N. Scarfe, ed., *A Frenchman's Year in Suffolk, 1784* (SRS, xxx, 1988), pp. 204–5.

135. Bayne, *Comprehensive History*, pp. 14, 291, 324.

136. Borsay, *English Urban Renaissance*; J. Brewer, *The Pleasures of the Imagination: English Culture in the Eighteenth Century* (London, 1997); Porter, *Enlightenment in Britain.*

137. Fawcett, 'Culture of Later Georgian Norwich', pp. 1–10.

138. R. Gunnis, *Dictionary of British Sculptures, 1660–1851* (London, new revised edn, n. d.), pp. 215, 286, 315; Colvin, *English Architects*, pp. 484–5.

139. See S. J. Wearing, *Georgian Norwich and its Builders* (Norwich, 1926).

Notes to Chapter 9: The Textile Industry

1. *Reports of the Assistant Commissioners for Hand Loom Weavers*, PP (1839–40), xxiii, pp. 343–4.

2. Bedfordshire Record Office, MS L30/94/6, 'Journal of the Marchioness Grey, 1750'.

3. Daniel. Defoe, *A Tour Through the Whole Island of Great Britain*, ed. G. D. H. Cole (2 vols, London, 1962 edn), i, p. 62.

4. Classically stated in J. H. Clapham, 'The Transference of the Worsted Industry from Norfolk to the West Riding of Yorkshire', *Economic Journal*, xx (1910), pp. 195–210. See also H. Heaton, *The Yorkshire Woollen and Worsted Industries* (Oxford, 1920), pp. 263–4, 275–81, and E. M. Sigsworth, *Black Dyke Mills: A History With Introductory Chapters on the Development of the Worsted Industry in the Nineteenth Century* (Liverpool, 1958), pp. 11–16. Both their accounts of the worsted industry in Norfolk rely a good deal on J. James, *History of the Worsted Manufacture in England* (London, 1857).

5. Research chiefly drawn together in P. J. Corfield, 'The Social and Economic History of Norwich, 1650–1850' (University of London, PhD thesis, 1976) and in the writings of the late Ursula Priestley, especially 'The Fabric of Stuffs: The Norwich Textile Industry, *c.* 1650–1750', *Textile History*, xvi (1985), pp. 183–210; *The Fabric of Stuffs* (Norwich, 1990), and her introduction to *The Letters of Philip Stannard, Norwich Textile Manufacturer (1751–1763)* (NRS, lvii, 1994), pp. 1–23.

6. See *History of Norwich*, i, Chapters 7 and 9.

7. H. J. Sutermeister, 'The Textile Industry in Medieval Norfolk', discussion paper at SSRC/Pasold Research Fund conference (UEA, Norwich, 1975).

8. This paragraph is based on K. J. Allison, 'The Wool Supply and Worsted Cloth Industry in Norfolk in the Sixteenth and Seventeenth Centuries' (University of Leeds, PhD thesis, 1955).

9. For an account of the Stranger communities in Norwich, see Chapter 2 above, and D. L. Rickwood, 'The Origin and Decline of the Stranger Community of Norwich' (UEA, Norwich, MA thesis, 1967).

10. Allison, 'The Wool Supply', p. 495; B. A. Holderness, 'The Reception and Distribution of the New Draperies in England', in N. B. Harte, ed., *The New Draperies in the Low Countries and England, 1300–1800* (London, 1997), p. 219, states that 'By 1580, at least one quarter of the population of Norwich was Flemish'.

11. E. Kerridge, *Textile Manufacturers in Early Modern England* (Manchester, 1985), pp. viii–ix, 91; Harte, *New Draperies*, p. 224.

12. L. Martin, 'The Rise of the New Draperies in Norwich, 1550–1622', in Harte, *New Draperies*, pp. 245–74, provides the best account of the Flemish cloth workers' contribution to the evolution of Norwich stuffs.

13. Alison, 'Wool Supply', p. 725.

14. K. J. Allison, 'The Norfolk Worsted Industry in the Sixteenth and Seventeenth Centuries: The New Draperies', *Yorkshire Bulletin of Economic and Social Research*, xiii (1961), p. 62.

15. K. J. Allison, 'Norwich and the Worsted Industry, 1500–1700', tables 1–4, discussion paper at SSRC/Pasold Research Fund conference (UEA, Norwich, 1975), and pp. 36, 45, above.

16. Martin, 'Rise of the New Draperies', pp. 262–8.

17. James, *History*, pp. 172–4, quoting BL, MS Lansdowne 846, fo. 284, based on the return of a Mr Blofield (?Blofeld), a Norwich manufacturer in 1695.

18. Allison, 'Norfolk Worsted Industry', pp. 74–6.

19. In Yorkshire there were also many clothiers: in the cloth industry they were small and seldom made more than a couple of cloths a week in the eighteenth century, but in the worsted industry, where the units or organisation were always larger, they were known as 'worsted manufacturers'.

20. P. J. Corfield, 'The Size of the Norwich Worsted Industry in the Eighteenth and Nineteenth Centuries', discussion paper at SSRC/Pasold Research Fund Conference (UEA, Norwich, 1975), pp. 3, 9.

21. Priestley, 'Fabric of Stuffs', pp. 188–90.

22. Fifty-eight per cent of the total estate of weavers' probate inventories were valued at under £100. Priestley's figures for the estates of top weavers are difficult to reconcile. Her table 1 shows there were only eighteen (eight of

which were proved in the Prerogative Court of Canterbury) of the 181 estates of over £1000 in the entire 1650–1750 period. Yet, when she provides a more detailed analysis of the 1670s, no fewer than six estates, all proved in the Canterbury Court, were over £1000 in that decade alone. Since the years after 1680 were ones of marked expansion, her total of only eighteen £1000 plus inventories for the whole century after 1650 seems understated.

23. PRO, IR1/41–3. At best the entries record the name of the apprentice, his father's name, place of residence and occupation, likewise those of the master, together with the fee paid and the period of apprenticeship. Returns were made irregularly and after the early 1720s they seriously deteriorate in quality. Those for the 1710s record a remarkable activity in the Norwich industry.

24. Priestley, 'Fabric of Stuffs', p. 190.

25. PRO, IR 1/45.

26. Priestley, 'Fabric of Stuffs', p. 189.

27. Priestley, *Letters of Philip Stannard*, p. 105. Stannard's insurance policy of £2600 in 1749 was amongst the largest of any worsted weaver in Norwich. His house goods and stock in trade in his dwelling house and workrooms (they were not insured) were valued at £2000, four houses let to workers at £100, his utensils and stock with Thomas Hubey, hot presser, at £500 – in all £2600: Guildhall Library, London, Sun Insurance Policy Registers MS 11 936, vol. 84, 1748/9. See n. 32, below.

28. Priestley, *Letters of Philip Stannard*, p. 49. See also n. 36 below

29. Priestley, *Letters of Philip Stannard*, p. 78.

30. See, for example, the pages of 'Mr John Kelly's counterpart of patterns sent to Spain and Portugal, Norwich, 1763', reproduced from the pattern book (Victoria and Albert Museum, 67–1885), in *Letters of Philip Stannard*, plates 5–8, and eadem, *Fabric*, pp. 21–3.

31. I am indebted to Professor Stanley Chapman of the University of Nottingham for allowing me to use the transcripts made in 1970 (now deposited in the Norfolk Record Office) of the Sun policies in the Guildhall Library, MS. 11, 936, vols 1–89, 100. The transcripts cover the textile industry nationally, although at this stage there were very few policies taken out in the Yorkshire and Lancashire industries. It is unclear why volumes 90–99 covering 1749–50 to 1752–3 were not analysed.

32. There are policies relating to 122 worsted weavers, thirty-eight wool combers, fifteen hot pressers (their policies only appear after 1745), thirteen dyers, eight wool factors, seven twisterers and throwsters, three yarn merchants, two wool staplers, one shearman and one bed lace weaver. Sometimes more than one policy relates to an individual master or partnership. As their assets grew, they would re-insure over the years.

33. Guildhall Library, Ms 11 936, vol. 64, 9 November 1742.

34. Guildhall Library, Ms 11 936, vols 72, 74, 27 June, 10 July, 1745.

35. Hot pressing establishments (the first policy for them with the Sun Company dates from 1745) became larger in the course of the century. Maximilian de Lazowski saw one employing two hundred men in 1784 (the manufacturer he visited 'employs and pays three or four hundred people every day'). It was a quite exceptional establishment, probably that of Jeremiah Ives, the city's most prominent stuffs manufacturer in the 1780s. See N. Scarfe and R. G. Wilson, 'The Norwich Textile Industry in 1784', *Textile History*, xxiii (1992), pp. 113–20.

36. P. J. Corfield, 'A Provincial Capital in the Late Seventeenth Century: The Case of Norwich', in P. Clark and P. Slack, eds, *Crisis and Order in English Towns, 1508–1700* (London, 1972), pp. 284–5. For a discussion and criticism of the proto-industrialisation debate, see above, pp. 147–8; D. C. Coleman, 'Proto Industrialisation: A Concept Too Many', *EconHR*, second series, lxxxviii (1983), pp. 435–48, and L. A. Clarkson, *Proto-industrialisation: The First Phase of Industrialisation* (London, 1985).

37. See the 1720 pamphlet 'The Weavers' True Case' quoted in James, *History*, pp. 217–18, and J. Fiske, ed., *The Oakes Diaries: Business, Politics and the Family in Bury St Edmunds, 1778–1827* (2 vols, SRS, xxxiii, 1990–1), i, pp. 43–4.

38. See n. 32.

39. The rest of this paragraph is based upon Fiske, *Oakes Diaries*.

40. Oakes reckoned each comber was sufficient to supply combed wool for thirty spinners.

41. For a full discussion of the problem of embezzlement, see, J. Styles, 'Embezzlement, Industry and the Law in England, 1500–1800', in M. Berg, P. Hudson and M. Sonenscher, eds, *Manufacture in Town and Country before the Factory* (Cambridge, 1983), pp. 173–210.

42. Defoe, *A Tour*, i, p. 61; James, *History*, pp. 242–5.

43. James, *History*, p. 267.

44. James, *History*, pp. 243, 263. It was also mixed in weaving with English yarns.

45. F. M. Eden, *The State of the Poor*, ed., A. G. L. Roger (London, 1929), p. 109. See also J. Styles, 'Clothing the North: The Supply of Non-Elite Clothing in the Eighteenth-Century North of England', *Textile History*, xxv (1994), pp. 139–66, and C. Shammas, *The Pre-Industrial Consumer in England and America* (Oxford, 1990), pp. 86–100.

46. J. Smail, *Merchants, Markets and Manufacture: The English Wool Textile Industry in the Eighteenth Century* (Basingstoke, 1999), pp. 18–21.

47. See p. 234 above.

48. William Taylor (1798) in R. Beatniffe, *The Norfolk Tour* (sixth edn, Norwich, 1808), p. 94, and James, *History*, pp. 308–9.

49. T. Fawcett, 'Argonauts and Commercial Travellers: The Foreign Marketing of Norwich Stuffs in the Later Eighteenth Century', *Textile History*, xvi (1985), pp. 151–82.

50. E. B. Schumpeter, *English Overseas Trade Statistics, 1697–1808* (Oxford, 1960), pp. 35–41.

51. See n. 49.

52. J. Beresford, ed., *The Diary of a Country Parson* (5 vols, Oxford, 1924–31), i, 11 January 1781.

53. H. Heaton, 'Yorkshire Cloth Traders in the United States, 1770–1840', *Thoresby Society Publications* xxxvii (1944), pp. 225–87; Smail, *Merchants*, pp. 75–93, 113–32.

54. A. Young, *The Farmer's Tour Through the East of England* (4 vols, London, 1771), i, p. 71.

55. Priestley, *Letters of Philip Stannard*, p. 16.

56. NRO, MC 2015/9, 904 x 7, 4 November 1769, Martha Patteson to John Patteson. The major assignee, Richard Gurney, reckoned Stannard's debts were an immense £47,000.

57. W. E. Minchinton, ed., *The Growth of English Overseas Trade in the Seventeenth and Eighteenth Centuries* (London, 1969), p. 25.

58. For a discussion of the growth of the British woollen industry based upon the calculations of eighteenth-century pamphleteers, see P. Deane, 'The Output of the British Woollen Industry in the Eighteenth Century', *Journal of Economic History*, xvii (1957), pp. 207–23.

59. Young, *Farmer's Tour*, ii, pp. 74–82; also printed in James, *History*, pp. 270–72.

60. The Yorkshire estimates were made by Thomas Wolrich, a Leeds merchant, in 1772. They are printed in James, *History*, pp. 279–86, and in J. Bischoff, *A Comprehensive History of the Woollen and Worsted Manufactures* (2 vols, London, 1842), i, pp. 186–90. They are fully discussed, along with other estimates of the size of various wool textile centres, in R. G. Wilson, 'The Supremacy of the Yorkshire Cloth Industry in the Eighteenth Century', in N. B. Harte and K. G. Ponting, eds, *Textile History and Economic History: Essays in Honour of Miss Julia de Lacy Mann* (Manchester, 1973), pp. 225–46.

61. Priestley, 'Fabric of Stuffs', pp. 188–90.

62. Defoe, *Tour*, i, p. 62.

63. Corfield, 'Size of the Norwich Worsted Industry', p. 5, believes 'the 1780s could well qualify as the decade in which the Norwich industry reached its greatest size, in terms of the number of looms employed, after which it failed to grow further'.

64. James, *History*, p. 259.

65. Clapham, 'Transference', pp. 195–210.

66. Fiske, *Oakes Diaries*, i, p. 290; *Old Monthly Magazine* (1798), vi, p. 143, printed

in James, *History*, pp. 308–9. See also Chapters 6 and 7 for further discussion of problems in Norwich during the French Wars.

67. Eden, *State of the Poor*, p. 254; C. Crutwell, *Tours Through the Whole Island of Great Britain* (5 vols, London, 1801), v, p. 161.

68. Corfield, 'Economic and Social History', p. 603.

69. J. W. Robberds, *A Memoir of the Life and Writings of the Late William Taylor* (2 vols, London, 1843), ii, p. 366.

70. See Chapter 10.

71. Clapham, 'Transference', p. 196, quoting A. Rees, *Cyclopaedia* (London, 1819).

72. James, *History*, p. 350. See the three great dispatch books of Ives and Basely (1790–1, 1792 and 1797–8) in the Bridewell Museum, Norwich, for examples of camblets, cambletees and glazed calimancoes.

73. P. Clabburn, *The Norwich Shawl* (London, 1995), p. 48, quoting *A Companion to the Norwich Polytechnic Exhibition* (Norwich, 1840).

74. J. Chambers, *A General History of the County of Norfolk* (3 vols, Norwich, 1829), i, p. xlv.

75. Discussed fully in the *Reports of the Assistant Commissioners for Hand Loom Weavers*, PP (1839–40), xxiii, p. 328.

76. D. T. Jenkins and K. G. Ponting, *The British Wool Textile Industry, 1770–1914* (London, 1982), pp. 77–8.

77. *Reports of the Assistant Commissioners for Hand Loom Weavers*, PP (1839–40) xxiii, pp. 302–48.

78. The figures also appear in A. D. Bayne, *A Comprehensive History of Norwich* (London and Norwich, 1869), p. 584.

79. A. D. Bayne, *An Account of the Industry and Trade of Norwich and Norfolk* (Norwich, 1852). See also his *Comprehensive History*, pp. 576–94.

80. J. K. Edwards, 'The Economic Development of Norwich, 1750–1850, with Special Reference to the Worsted Industry' (University of Leeds, PhD thesis, 1963), appendix 7. Edwards provides an extended account of the decline of the Norwich industry taking it well beyond his terminal 1850 date. See also idem, 'The Decline of the Norwich Textiles Industry', *Yorkshire Bulletin of Economic and Social Research*, xvi (1964), pp. 31–41.

81. Bayne, *Comprehensive History*, pp. 593–4.

82. W. White, *History, Gazeteer and Directory of Norfolk* (Sheffield, 1864), p. 165.

83. Clabburn, *Norwich Shawl*, pp. 58–60; Kelly's *Directory of Norfolk* (1937), p. 897. For an account of silk manufacture in East Anglia in the nineteenth century, see D. C. Coleman, 'Growth and Decay During the Industrial Revolution: The Case of East Anglia', *Scandinavian Economic History Review*, x (1962), pp. 115–27.

84. See Chapter 16.

85. See especially, Clapham, 'Transference', pp. 195–210; M. F. Lloyd-Pritchard, 'The Decline of Norwich', *EconHR*, iii (1950), pp. 372–8; J. K. Edwards, 'The Decline of the Norwich Textiles Industry', *Yorkshire Bulletin of Economic and Social Research*, xvi (1964), pp. 30–41, and the 1975 discussion papers of Corfield and Wilson, and Corfield, 'Social and Economic History of Norwich', pp. 310–60.

86. Clapham, 'Transference', p. 202. For a full discussion about the coal-based economy and a convenient summary of D. C. Coleman's and J. A. Harris's views, see E. A. Wrigley, *Continuity, Chance and Change: The Character of the Industrial Revolution* (Cambridge, 1988), passim.

87. A brief journal (NRO, MC, 470/1, 715 x 5) of a Norwich yarn dealer, Edward Taylor, exists for his visit to the West Riding in 1816. He found the yarn spinners' books full. He was bowled over by the number of mills, lit by gas at night. With a 'Norwich School' eye he inserted sketches into his journal and wrote of one mill near Halifax, 'the appearance from a distance was very beautiful. Situated in a valley and surrounded by trees, the brilliant Light of the gas shining thro' them produced a beautiful and striking effect'. Taylor also found the machinery 'beautiful'; Bradford was thriving, although 'a very dirty, irregular place'. He gives the impression that he is visiting an alien planet.

88. For the combing inventions, see J. Burnley, *The History of Wool and Wool Combing* (London, 1889). James, *History*, and Edward Baines, in K. G. Ponting, *Baines's Account of the Woollen Manufacture of England* (Newton Abbot, 1970) provide good contemporary accounts of the worsted industry. See also Jenkins and Ponting, *Textile Industry*, and Sigsworth, *Black Dyke Mills*. Even the introduction of the Jacquard loom was very slow in Norwich; weavers preferred the traditional draw loom (Clabburn, *Norwich Shawl*, p. 19).

89. Clapham, 'Transference', p. 210.

90. The quotations in this paragraph are taken from the *Reports of the Assistant Commissioners for Hand Loom Weavers*, PP (1839–40), xxiii, pp. 302–48.

91. See Chapter 7, above.

92. An account of the Norwich industry in 1784, especially its innovativeness in dyeing and hot pressing, was made by Maximilian Lazowski. See N. Scarfe, ed., *A Frenchman's Year in Suffolk* (SRS, xxx, 1995 reprint), pp. 219–25.

93. Robberds, *Memoir*, ii, p. 65.

94. These comments were made by Gurney in his extensive marginal annotations to Robberds, *Memoir* (UEA Library, Special Collections).

95. The Iveses' fortunes descended through marriage into Lord Boston's family; the Harveys were successful (to 1870) bankers and landowners in Norfolk and Essex; John Patteson, MP, merchant, landowner and brewer, was virtually

bankrupt in 1819. Only his brewery survived: D. Cubitt, A. Mackley and R. G. Wilson, eds, *The Grand Tour of John Patteson, 1778–1779* (NRS, lxvii, 2003), pp. 28–39.

96. Edwards, 'Economic Development', p. 323.

97. Bayne, *Comprehensive History*, p. 594.

Notes to Chapter 10: Population, 1700–1950

1. C. B. Hawkins, *Norwich: A Social Study* (London, 1910), p. 19.

2. See Chapter 19 for population developments since 1951.

3. See in particular E. A. Wrigley and R. S. Schofield, *The Population History of England, 1541–1871* (London, 1981) and E. A. Wrigley, R. S. Davies, J. E. Oeppen and R. S. Schofield, *English Population History from Family Reconstitution, 1580–1837* (Cambridge, 1997). Family reconstitution involves the systematic assembling of information about the life histories of individual families, applying nominal record linkage to parish registers.

4. J. K. Edwards, 'Norwich Bills of Mortality, 1707–1830', *Yorkshire Bulletin of Economic and Social Research*, xxi (1969); P. J. Corfield, 'The Social and Economic History of Norwich, 1650–1850' (University of London, PhD thesis, 1976), especially Chapters 1, 4 and 8. Aggregative analysis involves the manipulation of annual figures of burials and baptisms based ultimately on the parish registers and reported as bills of mortality in the local press; or as totalled and published alongside the 1801 and subsequent censuses as the Parish Register Abstracts.

5. The 1693 local enumeration yielded 28,881; and two estimates by Gregory King, 29,332 for 1695 and 28,546 for 1696. For observations on these and the later figures see Corfield, 'Norwich', p. 14.

6. Edwards, 'Norwich Bills', pp. 95–7.

7. Corfield, 'Norwich', pp. 18, 19, 23, 456–8, 461. Figures for the hamlets, 1811–31, are taken from W. White, *Directory for Norfolk* (Sheffield, 1845; reprinted New York, 1969), p. 52.

8. Corfield, 'Norwich', pp. 160, 164–5, 167. Note that her ability to identify child and infant deaths in 1750–1 depended on the exceptional survival of the original bills of mortality for these years.

9. Corfield, 'Norwich', pp. 156, 160, 164, 483–4.

10. Corfield, 'Norwich', pp. 166–7, 483–4; Edwards, 'Norwich Bills', pp. 100–2.

11. Edwards, 'Norwich Bills', p. 88.

12. Corfield, 'Norwich', pp. 161, 474–6, and Chapter 4, table 78.

13. One of the first to conduct a searching enquiry into the nature and scale of such defects was J. T. Krause, 'Changes in English Fertility and Mortality, 1781–1850', *EconHR*, second series, xi (1958), pp. 54–9. Wrigley and Schofield,

Population History, devote no fewer than 142 pages (15–156) to tracing and correcting them.

14. Edwards, 'Norwich Bills', pp. 102–6.

15. Corfield, 'Norwich', pp. 449, 451, 454, 468, 470, 482, 486–9.

16. Edwards, 'Norwich Bills', pp. 98, 109.

17. Corfield, 'Norwich', pp. 164, 167, 479.

18. Note that in *Population History*, pp. 244–5, Wrigley and Schofield gauged that mortality reductions accounted for about one-third, and fertility increases two-thirds of the English population increase between the 1750s and the 1840s.

19. These calculations are based on raw data from the Parish Register Abstracts, while the comparative national averages, which are slightly adjusted, come from Wrigley and Schofield, *Population History*, pp. 533–4. The relevant quinquennial averages for the years mentioned in the text, are as follows: 1784–88, 9.2 (England, 9.0); 1799–1803, 9.6 (8.4); 1809–13, 9.8 (7.9); 1819–23, 11.6 (8.2).

20. For Nottingham, see J. D. Chambers, 'Population Change in a Provincial Town', in D. V. Glass and D. E. C. Eversley, eds, *Population History* (London, 1965), p. 351; and for Leeds, M. Yasumoto, *Industrialisation, Urbanisation and Demographic Change in England* (Nagoya, Japan, 1994), pp. 67, 106–7.

21. For comparison, the decadal averages of baptisms per thousand population produced by Edwards, 'Norwich Bills', p. 98, range from 30.3 (1751–60) down to as low as 21.1 (1811–20). Those of Corfield, 'Norwich', vary using the bills of mortality from 30.5 (1750–59) to 22.4 (1820–29), and, where she relies on parish register abstracts, from 29.0 (1800–9) to 33.6 (1820–29), Chapter 4, table 78.

22. E. A. Wrigley and R. S. Schofield, 'Population Growth in Eighteenth-Century England: A Conundrum Resolved', *Past and Present*, xcviii (1983), pp. 131–2. This article succinctly summarises the authors' main conclusions.

23. Data for Exeter, Nottingham and Leeds are assembled and evaluated in P. Corfield, *The Impact of English Towns, 1700–1800* (Oxford, 1982), pp. 109–17. For York, see P. M. Tillott, ed., *VCH: The City of York* (London, 1961), pp. 212–13.

24. Edwards, 'Norwich Bills', pp. 107, 111–12.

25. Corfield, 'Norwich', pp. 163, 478.

26. Corfield, 'Norwich', p. 493.

27. For the most recent appraisal of the quality of civil registration, see R. Woods, *The Demography of Victorian England and Wales* (Cambridge, 2000), Chapter 2. The quotation and encouragement to proceed with uncorrected data may be found on pp. 68–70.

28. The statistical findings featured in this section are based on the consultation of two dozen census volumes and over eighty of the Annual Reports of the

Registrar General. Detailed references are not generally included here, but may be found in A. Armstrong, *The Population of Victorian and Edwardian Norfolk* (Norwich, 2000). An exception is made where comments are quoted verbatim.

29. See Chapter 11; and for a fuller account of these documents, J. Pound, 'Poverty and Public Health in Norwich', in C. Barringer, ed., *Norwich in the Nineteenth Century* (Norwich, 1984), pp. 47–72.

30. Registrar General (hereafter RG), *Eighth Annual Report*, 1845, pp. 40–1.

31. For example, Liverpool (36.0), Manchester (33.0), Hull (31.0), Leeds (30.0). These rates are for 1848–54 and are drawn from E. H. Greenhow, *Papers Relating to the Sanitary State of the People of England* (London, 1858, reprinted Farnborough, 1973), pp. 162–4.

32. Pound, 'Public Health', pp. 63–4.

33. RG, *Thirty-First Annual Report*, 1868, p. liii; *Thirty-Eighth Annual Report*, 1875, p. xliii.

34. See, for example, S. Szreter and G. Mooney, 'Urbanisation, Mortality and the Standard of Living Debate: New Estimates of the Expectation of Life at Birth in Nineteenth-Century British Cities', *EconHR*, second series, li (1998), especially pp. 90, 106, 110.

35. Armstrong, *Population*, pp. 55–6; Szreter and Mooney, 'Urbanisation', p. 106.

36. T. McKeown, *The Modern Rise of Population* (London, 1976), pp. 160–2. This book develops arguments set out in a number of earlier articles.

37. See Chapter 11; also S. Cherry, 'The Role of a Provincial Hospital; The Norfolk and Norwich Hospital, 1771–1880', *Population Studies*, xxvi (1972), pp. 291–306.

38. E. H. Hunt, *Regional Wage Variations in Britain, 1850–1914* (Oxford, 1973), pp. 68–9; Hawkins, *Norwich*, pp. 60–71.

39. S. Muthesius, 'Nineteenth-Century Housing', in Barringer, *Norwich*, p. 106; J. K. Edwards, 'Developments in Local Government', ibid., p. 89.

40. *Reports of the Medical Officer of Health* (hereafter *MOH*), for dates stated in the text.

41. Armstrong, *Population*, p. 73.

42. Armstrong, *Population*, pp. 87, 91. Marriage ages are estimated according to a technique originally devised by J. Hajnal, 'Age at Marriage and Proportions Ever-Marrying', *Population Studies*, vii (1953), pp. 111–35.

43. R. I. Woods and P. R. A. Hinde, 'Nuptiality and Age at Marriage in Nineteenth Century England', *Journal of Family History*, x (1985), pp. 119–44, find evidence to support the view that, characteristically, extensive female involvement in the wage economy tended to depress nuptiality, as did a high ratio of domestic servants. These also were numerous in Norwich.

44. A long-term increase in illegitimacy was a feature of eighteenth- and early

nineteenth-century England, but its emergence has never been traced in detail for Norfolk. However, on the basis of a handful of parish registers it appears unlikely to have long historical roots and to have increased most noticeably after *c.* 1780. By 1842, Norfolk stood second in the rank order of counties in this regard. See P. Laslett, *Family Life and Illicit Love in Earlier Generations* (Cambridge, 1977), pp. 137, 146.

45. L. A. Tilly, J. W. Scott and M. Cohen, 'Women's Work and European Fertility Patterns', *Journal of Interdisciplinary History*, xxv (1976), p. 475.

46. E. M. Garrett, 'The Trials of Labour. Motherhood versus Employment in a Nineteenth-Century Textile Centre', *Continuity and Change*, v (1990), pp. 121–54; K. Ittman, 'Family Limitation and Family Economy in Bradford, West Yorkshire, 1851–81', *Journal of Social History*, xxv (1992), pp. 547–73.

47. See Armstrong, *Population of Norfolk*, pp. 119, 126, for references to the main contributions to the debate.

48. Armstrong, *Population*, pp. 117–19 and 126, n. 42.

49. L. P. Moch, 'The History of Migration and Fertility Decline: The View from the Road', in J. R. Gillis, L. A. Tilly and D. Levine, eds, *The European Experience of Falling Fertility, 1850–1970* (Oxford, 1992), p. 190.

50. Armstrong, *Population*, p. 33.

51. A. Digby, *Pauper Palaces* (London, 1978), pp. 20, 132–4.

52. Armstrong, *Population*, p. 33.

53. Armstrong, *Population*, Chapter 2. See also L. M. Springall, *Labouring Life in Norfolk Villages, 1834–1914* (London, 1936), and Hawkins, *Norwich*, pp. 180–1.

54. Based on B. R. Mitchell and P. Deane, *Abstract of British Historical Statistics* (Cambridge, 1952), pp. 24–7.

55. Here as in the preceding section the Registrar General's Annual Reports (from 1921, Statistical Surveys) are a key source of demographic data and are cited in detail only where comments are quoted verbatim. The Reports of the Norwich Medical Officer of Health repeat the same statistical information supplemented by observations on local conditions. These also are referenced only where the data of the report in question is not obvious from the text, or where direct quotations are used.

56. RG, *Eightieth Annual Report*, 1917, p. x.

57. J. M. Winter, 'The Impact of the First World War on Civilian Health in Britain', *EconHR*, second series, xxx (1977), pp. 488–503.

58. Census of England and Wales, 1921. *County of Norfolk*, pp. lx, 40, 71. Deaths on active service, set out in the Norwich Roll of Honour, are taken from F. Meeres, *A History of Norwich* (Chichester, 1998), p. 182.

59. *Reports of the MOH*, for dates stated in text.

60. *Reports of the MOH*, 1931, p. 19; 1937, p. 19.

61. *Reports of the MOH*, 1935, pp. 19–21; 1942, pp. 12–13, which reiterates points

originally made in 1928, and a March 1942 *Report to the Health Committee* on 'Unsatisfactory Households'.

62. *Report of the MOH*, 1934, p. 93.

63. The source of these comparisons is the *Reports of the MOH* at stated dates, and RG, *Sixteenth Statistical Review*, 1936, text, pp. 13–14; *Seventeenth Statistical Review*, 1937, text, p. 48.

64. RG, *Fourteenth Statistical Review*, 1934, text, p. 144; *Sixteenth Statistical Review*, 1936, text, pp. 13–14.

65. J. M. Winter, 'Infant Mortality, Maternal Mortality and Public Health in Britain in the 1930s', *Journal of European Economic History*, viii (1979), pp. 439–62. See also the discussion in N. Tranter, *British Population in the Twentieth Century* (Basingstoke and London, 1996), pp. 72–5.

66. *Report of the MOH*, 1940, p. 49.

67. See Chapter 11; and Tranter, *British Population*, pp. 77–8.

68. See Chapter 11; and *Reports of the MOH* for dates stated in text.

69. *Reports of the MOH*.

70. *Report of the MOH*, 1923, p. 6. Summary statistics of new housing are given in the *Reports* for 1931–4 and 1951.

71. Census of England and Wales, 1931, *Housing Report and Tables*, pp. 35–6.

72. *Reports of the MOH*, dates as stated. 'More sunlight' is referred to in that of 1935, p. 19.

73. Census of England and Wales, 1931, *County of Norfolk*, part 1, pp. 2–12.

74. These estimates, prepared by the Registrar General, were passed to the Norwich Medical Officer of Health and used in his reports.

75. *Reports of the MOH*, for dates stated.

76. *Reports of the MOH*. The quotation is from the *Report* for 1944, p. 1.

77. *Reports of the MOH*. The remark about promiscuity is from the 1942 *Report*, p. 11.

78. *Reports of the MOH*, dates as stated. For further details on the introduction of the National Health Service, see Chapter 11.

79. C. A. Moser and W. Scott, *British Towns: A Statistical Study of their Social and Economic Differences* (Edinburgh and London, 1961), p. 135.

80. Census of England and Wales, 1931, *County of Norfolk*, part 1, p. 43; 1951, *County Report, Norfolk*, p. 66; RG, *Statistical Review for Five Years, 1946–50*, 1954, text, p. 2.

81. *Royal Commission on Population, PP* (1949), Cmd 76 95, *Report*, p. 99.

82. *Report of the MOH*, 1950, p. 7.

83. Moser and Scott, *British Towns*, p. 135; *Report of the MOH*, 1950, p. 7.

84. Census 1951, *County Report, Norfolk*, pp. xxxvi, xc; Moser and Scott, *British Towns*, p. 134.

85. Census 1951, *County Report, Norfolk*, p. 2. Unfortunately, a fire in 1941

destroyed some of the 1931 records, making it impossible to revise the 1931 figures to 1951 boundaries (p. vii).

86. Moser and Scott, *British Towns*, p. 135; *Report of the MOH*, 1951, p. 22.

Notes to Chapter 11: Medical Care since 1750

1. Political and Economic Planning, *Report on British Health Services* (London, 1937), p. 417.
2. See, for example, R. Porter, *The Greatest Benefit to Mankind* (London, 1997); C. Lawrence, *Medicine in the Making of Modern Britain* (London, 1994); S. Cherry, *Medical Services and the Hospitals in Britain, 1860–1939* (Cambridge, 1996).
3. N. A. Green, 'A Licence to Practice', *Journal of the Royal Society of Medicine*, lxxx (1987), pp. 615–19.
4. M. Pelling, 'Healing the Sick Poor: Social Policy and Disability in Norwich, 1550–1640', *Medical History*, xxix (1985), pp. 115–37.
5. A. Batty Shaw, 'Benjamin Gooch, Eighteenth-Century Norfolk Surgeon', *Medical History*, xvi (1972), pp. 40–50. Gooch's splint utilised wooden strips and leather strapping to secure and support reset bones.
6. Advertisement, *NM*, 1 February 1734.
7. W. Chase, *The Norwich Directory* (Norwich, 1783), p. 47.
8. J. Pigot, *Commercial Directory of Norfolk and Suffolk* (London, 1830), pp. 567–87.
9. Berry, *Concise History and Directory for Norwich* (Norwich, 1811), p. 22.
10. W. White, *Directory for Norwich* (Sheffield, 1854), p. 67.
11. J. Hooper, *Norwich Charities: Short Sketches of Their Origins and History* (Norwich, 1898), pp. 45–83.
12. M. Winston, 'The Bethel at Norwich: an Eighteenth-Century Hospital for Lunatics', *Medical History*, xxxviii (1994), pp. 27–51.
13. Batty Shaw, 'Benjamin Gooch', p. 46.
14. Blomefield, *Norfolk*, iii, p. 432.
15. P. J. Corfield, 'The Social and Economic History of Norwich, 1650–1850: A Study of Urban Growth' (University of London, PhD thesis, 1976), p. 602.
16. J. G. Crosse, *A History of the Variolous Epidemic which Occurred in Norwich* (London, 1820), p. 33; Corfield, 'Norwich', pp. 616–18.
17. R. Porter, 'The Gift Relation: Philanthropy and Provincial Hospitals in Eighteenth-Century England', in L. Granshaw and R. Porter, eds, *The Hospital in History* (London, 1989), pp. 149–78.
18. E. Copeman, *A Brief History of the Norfolk and Norwich Hospital* (Norwich, 1865), p. 3.
19. B. Gooch, consultant surgeon, cited in V. M. Crosse, *A Surgeon in the Early*

Nineteenth Century: The Life and Times of John Green Crosse, MD, FRCS, FRS, 1790–1850 (London, 1968), p. 128.

20. J. Howard, *Account of the Principal Lazarettos in Europe* (London, 1791), p. 90.

21. These were among the classifications used in the hospital's *Annual Reports*, NRO, NNH series.

22. S. Cherry, 'The Role of a Provincial Hospital: The Norfolk and Norwich Hospital, 1771–1880', *Population Studies*, xxvi (1972), pp. 291–306. One early 7 per cent peak in inpatient mortality was associated with outbreaks of erysipelas: NRO, NNH 15/5 N & N *Annual Reports*, 1827–29.

23. Calculated from A. Batty Shaw, 'The Norwich School of Lithotomy', *Medical History*, xiv (1970), pp. 221–59.

24. Cherry, 'Norfolk and Norwich', pp. 291–306.

25. J. Taylor, *The Rebirth of the Norfolk and Norwich Hospital, 1874–1883: An Architectural Exploration*, (Norwich, 2000).

26. NRO, NNH, 15/7 N & N *Annual Report*, 1900, pp. 5–7; 15/16, N & N *Annual Report* 1939, pp. 9–12.

27. S. Cherry, 'Beyond National Health Insurance: The Voluntary Hospitals and Hospital Contributory Schemes', *Social History of Medicine*, v (1992), pp. 455–82.

28. A. Cleveland, *The Norfolk and Norwich Hospital, 1900–46* (Norwich, 1948), p. 42.

29. Cleveland, *Norfolk and Norwich Hospital*, pp. 78, 81.

30. L. Granshaw, 'Fame and Fortune by Means of Bricks and Mortar', in Granshaw and Porter, *Hospital in History*, pp. 199–220.

31. Cited in M. Muncaster, 'Medical Services and the Medical Profession in Norfolk, 1815–1911' (UEA, Norwich, PhD thesis, 1976), p. 19, and Crosse, *John Green Crosse*, p. 138.

32. White, *Directory for Norfolk*, p. 121.

33. NRO, NNH, 96/1 N & N Eye Infirmary, *Annual Reports*, 1835–40, 1871–2, 1878–9.

34. NRO, NNH, 103/1 Committee of Management Rules and Orders of the Jenny Lind Hospital for Sick Children, 1853, rule 64.

35. NRO, NNH, 71/3 Jenny Lind Hospital for Sick Children, *Annual Reports*, 1879–1904.

36. Bruce Lindsay, 'Who Cares? The Morphology of Caring in Children's Hospitals, 1852–1950' (UEA, Norwich, PhD thesis, 2000), provides a detailed study of the Jenny Lind which emphasises this aspect.

37. T. W. Crosse, *Report of the Norwich Medical Officer of Health* (Norwich, 1873).

38. S. M. Bishop, J. S. Buist and M. J. Flynn, eds, *Jenny Lind in Norwich: A Centenary Celebration* (Norwich, 1987), p. 21.

39. *Report of the Royal Commission on the Poor Laws and Relief of Distress, PP*

(1909), xxxvii, appendix xv, A. C. Kay and H. V. Toynbee, part 2, p. 98 (see also part 1, pp. 9–15, part 2, pp. 83–112).

40. Norwich Lying-In Charity, *Rules and Reports*, 1892–7, rules 19, 21 (destroyed, 1994).

41. Hooper, *Norwich Charities*, p. 186.

42. Following a protest meeting at the Guildhall on 24 February 1819, an open letter from Dalrymple (Norfolk and Norwich Hospital surgeon) warned Harvey at the dispensary to keep away from surgery and inpatient facilities: *NM*, 27 February 1819. See also *State of the Norwich Dispensary* 1836–7, 1844–5 [destroyed, 1994].

43. *State of the Norwich Dispensary*, 1875, p. 6.

44. Based on *State of the Norwich Dispensary*, 1881–1912.

45. *State of the Norwich Dispensary*, 1912, p. 2.

46. E. Wesby, *A Few Words of Friendly Advice* (Handbill, 1855).

47. Kelly's *Directory for Norfolk* (London, 1925), pp. 814–17.

48. *Poor Laws, PP* (1909), xxxvii, appendix 15, pp. 106–7.

49. C. B. Hawkins, *Norwich: A Social Study* (London, 1910), pp. 278–9.

50. NHC, Norwich Public Medical Service, *Annual Report*, 1904, rules, 1910.

51. *Norwich Homeopathic Journal* (1852–3), 21 April 1852.

52. Kelly's *Directory for Norfolk* (London, 1904). Muncaster, 'Medical Services', p. 218, suggests that eight homeopaths practised in Norwich during this time. I have drawn heavily on Muncaster's thesis, pp. 211–18, for this section.

53. See the *History of Norwich*, i, pp. xx–xxvi.

54. Crosse, *Variolous Epidemic*, p. 5; C. Mackie, *The Norfolk Annals* (2 vols, Norwich, 1901), i, *1801–51*, 1845.

55. *Second Report of Commissioners of Inquiry into the State of Large Towns and Populous Districts, PP* (1845), xviii, Evidence on Norwich by Johnson and Dixon, p. 61; Firth, p. 64.

56. W. Lee, *Report to the General Board of Health on a Preliminary Inquiry into the Sewerage, Drainage and Supply of Water, and the Sanitary Conditions of the Inhabitants of the City of Norwich* (London, 1851).

57. Hawkins, *Norwich*, p. 89; *Report of the MoH for Norwich*, 1914, p. 36.

58. *Report of the MoH for Norwich*, 1873, pp. 5–6; 1907, p. 8.

59. Hawkins, *Norwich*, p. 277.

60. NRO, NEC, Norfolk NHI Committee Minute Book (henceforward NHI Minutes) 1/1, 1912–26, 8 November 1913; *EDP*, 2 December 1914.

61. J. Slater, *Kelling Hospital, Norfolk* (Dereham, 2000).

62. NRO, NEC, NHI Minutes, 1/1, 4 January and 15 February 1913; *EDP*, 1 July 1919.

63. *EDP*, 19 March 1924.

64. NRO, NEC, NHI Minutes, 1, 2, 13 October 1934.

65. Hawkins, *Norwich*, p. 272.

66. *Report of the MoH for Norwich*, 1935, pp. 76–7; 1938, pp. 74–5.

67. *Report of the MoH for Norwich*, 1913, p. 11.

68. *Report of the MoH for Norwich*, 1938, pp. 148–9.

69. *Report by Sir John Walsham on the Administration of Relief to the Poor in the Incorporated Parishes of Norwich*, PP (1844), ix, pp. 193, 218.

70. S. Cherry, *Mental Health Care in Modern England: The Norfolk Lunatic Asylum/St Andrew's Hospital, 1810–1998* (Woodbridge, 2003), pp. 27–35.

71. Dr C. L. Robertson, *Report Respecting the Norwich Pauper Lunatic Asylum* (Norwich, 1865), p. 5.

72. Cherry, *Mental Health Care*, pp. 178–82.

73. J. Yelloly, *Observations on the Relief of the Sick Poor in Norwich* (Norwich, 1837), p. 10.

74. *Report of the MoH for Norwich*, 1929, p. 17.

75. *Report of the MoH for Norwich*, 1931, p. 22.

76. Cherry, 'Beyond National Health Insurance', p. 466.

77. NRO, NNH, 16/7 Press cuttings relating to the N & N; Cleveland, *Norfolk and Norwich*, pp. 150–76. Cleveland was heavily involved as chairman of the hospital's Board of Management from 1938–42 and its medical committee. See also Cherry, *Mental Health Care*, pp. 210–14.

78. N & N *Annual Report*, 1945, p. 12.

79. R. C. Larking, Chairman Norwich NHS Executive Council, *EDP*, 28 October 1948.

Notes to Chapter 12: Education since 1750

1. *The Handbook of the Education Week Held in Norwich from September 27th to October 3rd 1925*, (Norwich, 1925), p. 1.

2. P. Cattermole, 'Schools in Mediaeval and Early Tudor Norwich', in R. Harries, P. Cattermole and P. Mackintosh, *A History of Norwich School: King Edward VI's Grammar School at Norwich* (Norwich, 1991), p. 3.

3. J. Hooper, *Norwich Charities* (Norwich, 1898), pp. 60–83, on Anguish.

4. Hooper, *Norwich Charities*, pp. 84–93, on the Norman School; *A Copy of the Will of the Late John Norman* (Alderman Norman's Foundation, 1974). I am grateful to Dr C. N. Smith, a Norman descendant, for the loan of this item.

5. M. G. Jones, *The Charity School Movement in the Eighteenth Century* (Cambridge, 1938).

6. F. Meeres, *A History of Norwich* (Chichester, 1998), p. 119.

7. M. F. Lloyd Prichard, 'The Education of the Poor in Norfolk, 1700–1850', *NA*, xxxiii (1965), p. 323. Lloyd Prichard gives no source.

8. NRO, DN/NDS/1, A Book for the Charity Schools in Norwich, vol. i, 1711–1759, and NRO, MC/314/7, 703X1, vol. ii, 1759–1815.

9. William Sutton (vicar of Saxthorpe), *The Charitable Education of the Poor Children Recommended in a Sermon Preached in the Cathedral Church of Norwich* (Norwich, 1722), pp. 19–20.

10. *Sermon Preached by the Bishop of Norwich at the Anniversary Meeting of the Charity Schools in and about London and Westminster, 1 May 1775*, cited in M. G. Jones, *Charity School Movement*, p. 75.

11. *Digest of Parochial Returns ... Education of the Poor, PP* (1819), ix, vol. ii, 1818, pp. 607–10.

12. D. Smith, 'Politics, Religion and Education: The Provision of Elementary Schooling in Norwich, 1800–1870', in C. Barringer, ed., *Norwich in the Nineteenth Century* (Norwich, 1984), p. 20.

13. J. Bull, ed., *The Story of Keswick Hall Church of England College of Education, 1839–1981* (Norwich, c. 1981).

14. Meeres, *Norwich*, p. 120.

15. D. E. Swift, *Joseph John Gurney: Banker, Reformer, Quaker* (Middleton, 1962) pp. 51–3; J. B. Braithwaite, ed., *Memoirs of J. J. Gurney* (2 vols, Norwich, 1854), i, p. 69.

16. H. C. Colman, *Jeremiah James Colman: A Memoir* (London, 1905), p. 22; H. C. Colman, *Princes Street Congregational Church, Norwich, 1819–1919* (London, 1919).

17. Colman, *Jeremiah James Colman*, pp. 124–7; H. C. Colman, 'Carrow School, Pioneer of Handicraft Work', *Carrow Works' Magazine*, xx (July 1932), pp. 70–2.

18. See Chapter 16.

19. See pp. 304–5.

20. *Board of Education Return of Voluntary Public Elementary Schools, PP* (1906), lxxxviii, pp. 208–9.

21. L. Payne, 'The Education of the Blind, 1880–1930s' (UEA, Norwich, PhD thesis, 2001).

22. E. Griffiths and A. H. Smith, *Buxom to the Mayor: A History of the Norwich Freemen* (Norwich, 1987), Chapter 6.

23. W. D. Smith, 'Education and Society in Norwich, 1800–1870' (UEA, Norwich, PhD thesis, 1978), pp. 233–5.

24. NRO, MS 4356, Committee Minutes of the Boys' Home and Workhouse School, 23 April 1847, 5 March 1855.

25. Meeres, *Norwich*, p. 119.

26. Anon, *The Octagon Unitarian Chapel Norwich* (Norwich, 2000), pp. 16–17.

27. Smith, 'Politics', p. 204.

28. *Digest of Parochial Returns Education of the Poor, PP* (1819), ix, vol. ii, pp. 607–10.

29. Smith, 'Politics', p. 203.

30. NRO, TC/2/1–11, Minutes of the Norwich School Board, 1871–1903.

31. Smith, 'Education and Society', pp. 254, 257, 269.

32. See pp. 307–8, 311–12.

33. C. B. Hawkins, *Norwich: A Social Study* (Norwich, 1912), pp. 119–31.

34. M. Sanderson, *The Missing Stratum: Technical School Education in England, 1900–1990s* (London, 1994), contains Norwich references.

35. Hawkins, *Norwich*, pp. 194–213.

36. Harries, Cathermole and Mackintosh, *Norwich School*; *Digest of Schools and Charities for Education, PP* (1843), xviii, p. 77.

37. W. Derry, *Dr Parr: A Portrait of the Whig Dr Johnson* (Oxford, 1966), pp. 34–50.

38. H. W. Saunders, *A History of the Norwich Grammar School* (Norwich, 1932), Chapter 12.

39. J. H. Plumb, 'The New World of Children in Eighteenth-Century England', *Past and Present*, lxvii (1975), p. 73.

40. Anon, *The Life and Political Career of J. J. Colman Esq. and J. H. Tillett Esq* (n.d. *c.* 1880), p. 5.

41. Braithwaite, *Memoirs of J. J. Gurney*, i, p. 13.

42. Colman, *Jeremiah James Colman*, pp. 43–5.

43. I am grateful to Mr David Cubitt for information and photographs of this school.

44. B. Sayle, *A Child of School Age, Growing up in Norwich 1936–1954* (Dereham, 1997) p. 18. The author and her sister, daughters of a pharmacist, went to the school in the 1940s.

45. NRO, NF/RO/47/2, Pottergate Street Academy School books, 1842–5; article by Jonathan Mardle, EDP, 11 February 1970.

46. NRO, MS 33780, 798X6, R. H. Mottram, 'Looking Back to the Beginnings of Paragon House School', undated MS.

47. *Digest of Parochial Returns … Education of the Poor, PP* (1819), ix, vol. ii, 1818, pp. 607–10.

48. Meeres, *Norwich*, p. 162.

49. Anon., *Norwich High School, 1875–1950* (Norwich, 1950); J. Kamm, *Indicative Past* (London, 1971), p. 63.

50. See Chapter 18.

51. M. Allthorpe-Guyton and J. Stevens, *A Happy Eye: A School of Art in Norwich, 1845–1982* (Norwich, 1982); Q. Bell, *Schools of Design* (London, 1963), p. 102.

52. Sir Alfred Munnings, *An Artist's Life* (London, 1980), pp. 51–9.

53. NRO, N/TC/1/35, Minutes of Norwich City Council 1890–91, 16 December 1890; N/TC/2/34, Minutes of the Norwich Technical Instruction Committee, 1893–1903; A. Metters *The Tech* (Norwich, 1991); C. Glover, 'The Municipal Technical College in England, 1889–1914' (UEA, Norwich, MPhil thesis, 1977).

54. NRO, N/TC/1/35, Minutes of Norwich City Council, 16 December 1890. White was later knighted.

55. NRO, N/TC/1/36, Minutes of Norwich City Council, 17 November 1891, Technical Instruction Committee Membership.

56. Hawkins, *Norwich*, p. 124.

57. PRO, ED 77/140, Norwich CB; Elementary Education, May 1939.

58. NRO N/TC/35/5/9, fos 4–20, Recreational Evening Institutes, Report of the director, 18 July 1939.

59. NRO, SO 153/67/1–22, *City of Norwich School Magazine, 1925–1936*, passim.

60. C. Rackham, ed., *Education in Norwich, 1920–40: An Independent Survey* (Norwich, 1940).

61. NRO, N/TC35/5/9, fo 495, Post Primary Education in Norwich, 24 February 1940.

62. J. Hitchman, *The King of the Barbareens* (London, 1960), pp. 123–4. The author, an orphan, passed through several Norwich schools and was supported by the Anguish charity. She was refused the opportunity to take the 'eleven plus'.

63. J. Zmroczek, '"If Girls Would Take More Kindly to Domestic Work": Norwich, 1900–1939', *Women's History Magazine*, xliv (June 2003), pp. 9–19.

64. PRO, ED 152/339, Norwich Education Committee Development Plan, January 1947; J. Thompson, *Secondary Education Survey* (Fabian Pamphlet, January 1952), Appendix 1, 3, pp. 30, 31, 34.

65. Meeres, *Norwich*, p. 207.

66. M. Sanderson, *The History of the University of East Anglia, 1918–2000* (London, 2002).

67. Metters, *The Tech*, pp. 12–15.

68. S. Davies and P. Townroe, *Education and Training in the Norwich Area Economy* (NAES Working Paper no 5, Economics Research Centre, School of Economic and Social Studies, UEA, Norwich 1988), pp. 37, 41.

69. Harries et al., *History of Norwich School* (Norwich, 1991), pp. 143–54. Raymond Frostick, who was at the school in the 1940s, considers that it was already good then.

Notes to Chapter 13: Architecture since 1800

1. City of Norwich Corporation, ed., *City of Norwich Plan* (Norwich, 1945), p. 9.
2. There has never been a book on Norwich architecture as a whole. Lack of

conviction or lack of opportunity? Probably the preponderance of the medieval has obscured the view of 'the whole'. The nearest we get is N. Pevsner and B. Wilson, *The Buildings of England. Norfolk*, i, *Norwich and the North East* (London, 1997), pp. 177–356.

3. See S. Muthesius, 'Nineteenth-Century Housing in Norwich', in C. Barringer, ed., *Norwich in the Nineteenth Century* (Norwich, 1984), pp. 94–118.

4. See C. Brooks and A. Saint, eds, *The Victorian Church* (Manchester, 1985); E. Baty, 'Victorian Church Building in the Diocese of Norwich' (UEA, Norwich, PhD thesis, 1987).

5. *A Great Gothic Fame: The Catholic Church of St John the Baptist in Norwich* (published by Heath [Norwich] 1913); G. Stamp, *Architect of Promise: George Gilbert Scott Junior (1859–1897) and the Gothic Revival* (Donington, 2002).

6. St Luke's, Aylsham Road, by the well-known London architects C. J. and A. C. Blomfield (demolished); St Alban's, Grove Walk, Lakenham by the local practitioner Cecil Upcher; St Catherine's, Mile Cross, Aylsham Road (1935), by A. D. R. Caroë and A. P. Robinson, as well as St George's Roman Catholic, Sprowston Road (1962), by A. J. Chaplin. Only Caroë, the son of one of the greats of Edwardian architecture, J. D. Caroë, practised a more experimental use of forms.

7. 'Chapelfield Congregational Church', *The Builder* (1857), p. 118; (1858), p. 681; G. Nobbs, *Norwich: A City of Centuries* (Norwich, 1971), p. 27.

8. For example, New Catton parish school (now Christ Chuch centre), *c.* 1860.

9. *The Builder* (13 November 1953), pp. 737–40. See the previous Chapter for the history of the schools mentioned here.

10. Norwich Diocesan Training Institution completed 1892: J. Bull, ed., *The Story of Keswick Hall, Church of England College of Education, 1839–1981* (Norwich, *c.* 1990).

11. Drill Hall is illustrated in P. Hepworth, *Norwich in Old Postcards* (Zaltbommel, 1982), p. 66.

12. *The Builder* (1856), p. 690; (1857), pp. 80, 991; (1859), p. 574.

13. City Gaol, by Richard Brown of Wells Sreet (Oxford Street), London, and Philip Barnes, Norwich, 1822–26; plans in NRO, NCR, 16E, bundle 111, no. 39, plans 1ff; R. Salt, *Plans for a Fine City* (Norwich, 1988).

14. By Richard Makilwaine Phipson, cost £41,719: *The Builder* (1877), i, pp. 479, 481–2.

15. J. Taylor, *The Rebirth of the Norfolk and Norwich Hospital, 1874–1883: An Architectural Exploration* (Norwich, *c.* 2000), p. 46.

16. NRO, NCR, 16E, bundle 11, no. 27, plans 4–5, 1827: Thomas Nicholls of Holborn Bars, London; Scheme 'D'; 1900. Private collection of John Scott of Lambert, Scott and Innes, Architects, Norwich; Salt, *Plans*; R. Salt, 'Plans for a Fine City' (Castle Museum, Norwich, mimeographed, 1987).

17. *The Builder* (1854), pp. 241, 429, 480, 489, 501; (1855), p. 323; (1865), p. 145; (1857), pp. 62, 153, 177; *Illustrated London News* (1857), i, p. 466; M. Allthorpe-Guyton and J. Stevens, *A Happy Eye: A School of Art in Norwich, 1845–82* (Norwich, 1982).

18. Pevsner and Wilson, *Norfolk*, i, p. 288; J. M. Richards, *The Functional Tradition in Early Industrial Buildings* (London, 1958).

19. See E. Burgess and W. L. Burgess, *Men Who Have Made Norwich* (Norwich, 1904).

20. Crown Bank, for Sir Robert Harvey, which failed in 1870.

21. See Chapter 15.

22. By T. D. Barry (Norwich) and Goodwin and Butcher (London); iron roof by Barnard, Bishop and Barnard; total cost £20,000; *The Builder* (1861), pp. 204, 217, 306, 786, 810.

23. For the Norwich Union, see J. Mantle, *Norwich Union: The First 200 Years* (London, 1997); I have to thank Sheree Leeds, its Company's archivist and historian, for help. See *The Builder* (1901), i, pp. 369–71.

24. By W. N. Ashbee and John Wilson of the Great Eastern: *The Builder* (1886), i, p. 660, describes the station as 'the largest owned by the company next to Liverpool Street Station'.

25. By Stannard junior or senior? See Hepworth, *Picture Postcards*, 1944; A. Clewer and M. Shaw, *Former Norwich* (Norwich, 1972), p. 59.

26. National Westminster Bank by F. C. R. Palmer and W. F. C. Holden, 1924; Lloyds Bank by O. A. Munro-Cautley of Ipswich, 1927.

27. See D. Jolley, *Architect Exuberant: George Skipper, 1856–1948* (Norwich, 1975); A. Knights, 'G. Skipper' (UEA, Norwich, MA Dissertation, 1999).

28. Pevsner and Wilson, *Norfolk*, i, p. 313; see, too, the all glass façade of 'Festival House' in Castle Meadow, *c.* 1860, or the shop fronts in Skipper's Royal Arcade of 1899.

29. G. Nobbs, *Norwich City Hall* (Norwich, 1988); *The Builder* (20 May 1932), p. 883.

30. A. P. Anderson, *The Captain and the Norwich Parks* (Norwich, 2000).

31. See C. Cunningham, *Victorian and Edwardian Town Halls* (London, 1981).

32. Pevsner and Wilson, *Norfolk*, i, p. 332. 'Appropriate Character', *EDP*, 21 February 1962; 'Interwar councillors', *EDP*, 17 October 1963; G. Rhodes, 'A 999 Call from a Site in Martineau Lane', *EDP*, 1 July 1966.

33. P. Dormer and S. Muthesius, *Concrete and Open Skies: Architecture at the University of East Anglia* (London, 2001).

34. From 1966 onwards by the local firm Alan Cooke and Partners.

35. I. Nairn, 'Norwich', *The Listener*, 13 August 1964, pp. 226–7.

36. While touching on considerations of areas that go beyond the city limits,

there remains one more kind of building that must be mentioned here. Norwich's entertainment scene was never strong – apart from the proverbial 600 or so pubs and a few inter-war cinemas – but a fair investigation of the issues would be impossible without taking in account what was becoming available on the coast.

37. See H. M. Colvin, *A Biographical Dictionary of English Architects, 1660–1840* (London, 1954), pp. 446, 566.

38. Pevsner and Wilson, *Norfolk*, i, p. 158.

39. See Biographical File at the Royal Institute of British Architects, London.

40. Burgess, *Norwich*, pp. 298–311.

41. A. F. Scott, 'Clothing Factory, Later Roberts, Printers, 1903', *Architectural Review* (December 1955), pp. 394–5; idem, 'What to Look for in Norwich', *Architects' Journal* (31 May 1956), pp. 538–60; N. Pevsner, *The Buildings of England: North East Norfolk and Norwich* (Harmondsworth, 1962), pp. 267–8.

42. Burgess, *Norwich*, pp. 257–9.

43. Pevsner, *North East Norfolk*, p. 278.

44. 'Fine City, Norwich', *Architects' Journal* (31 May 1956), pp. 576–618.

45. *Architects' Journal* (31 May 1956), pp. 585, 591, 597.

46. M. Horsey and S. Muthesius, *Provincial Mixed Development: Norwich Council Housing, 1955–1973* (Norwich, 1986).

47. *Architects' Journal* (31 May 1956), p. 603.

48. S. Marks, ed., *Concerning Building:. Essays in Honour of Sir Bernard Feilden* (London, 1966).

49. *Architects' Journal* (31 May 1956), p. 584.

50. *Architects' Journal* (6 August 1975), pp. 245–55; *Architectural Review* (November 1975), pp. 311–13; *Der Baumeister* (Munich, February 1980), pp. 158–61.

51. See C. McKean, *Architectural Guide to Cambridge and East Anglia since 1920* (Cambridge, 1982). 'On the Close', *Architects' Journal* (4 June 1975), pp. 1181–92.

52. M. M. Camina, *Bowthorpe: The Implementation of a Dream* (Norwich, 1980). On the issue of provincialism and modernism, see S. Muthesius, 'Twentieth-Century Architecture in Norfolk', in S. Margeson, B. Ayers and S. Heywood, eds, *A Festival of Norfolk Archaeology* (Norwich, 1996), pp. 160–76, and Dormer and Muthesius, *Concrete and Open Skies*, pp. 143–57.

Notes to Chapter 14: Politics, 1835–1945

1. Sir Wemyss Reid, 'Last Month', *The Nineteenth Century* (February 1904), p. 337. I would like to thank Professor Geoffrey Searle for helpful comments on a draft of this chapter.

2. R. J. Morris and R. H. Trainor, eds, *Urban Governance: Britain and Beyond*

since 1750 (Aldershot, 2000); M. Daunton, ed., *The Cambridge Urban History of Britain*, iii, *1840–1950* (Cambridge, 2000).

3. J. Garrard, *Democratisation in Britain: Elites, Civil Society and Reform since 1800* (Basingstoke, 2002), Chapters 4 and 6.

4. J. Garrard, 'Urban Elites, 1850–1914: The Rule and Decline of a New Squirearchy?', *Albion*, xxvii (1995), p. 603; B. M. Doyle, 'The Changing Functions of Urban Government: Councillors, Officials and Pressure Groups, 1835–1950', in Daunton, *Cambridge Urban History*, pp. 298–301.

5. K. Laybourn, 'The Rise of Labour and the Decline of Liberalism: The State of the Debate', *History* lxxx (1995), pp. 207–26; D. Tanner, *Political Change and the Labour Party, 1900–1918* (Cambridge, 1990).

6. C. B. Jewson, *The Jacobin City* (London, 1975).

7. See above, Chapters 9 and 16.

8. R. A. H. Smith, 'The Passing of the Municipal Corporations Act, 1830–1835 and its Political and Administrative Significance 1836–71 with Reference to Selected Boroughs' (UEA, Norwich, MPhil thesis, 1974); P. Salmon, 'Local Politics and Partisanship: The Electoral Impact of Municipal Reform, 1835', *Parliamentary History*, xx (2000), pp. 357–76; J. K. Edwards, 'Developments in Local Government in Norwich, 1800–1900', J. Pound, 'Poverty and Public Health in Norwich, 1845–1880', and D. Smith, 'Politics, Religion and Education: The Provision of Elementary Schooling in Norwich, 1800–1870', all in C. Barringer, ed., *Norwich in the Nineteenth Century* (Norwich, 1984).

9. S. Cherry, *Doing Different? Politics and the Labour Movement in Norwich, 1880–1914* (Norwich, 1989); G. L. Bernstein, 'Liberalism and the Progressive Alliance in the Constituencies, 1906–14: Three Case Studies', *Historical Journal*, xxvi (1983), pp. 618–40; G. L. Bernstein, *Liberalism and Liberal Politics in Edwardian England* (London, 1986); F. Whitemore, 'The Labour Party, Municipal Politics and Municipal Elections in Norwich, 1903–33', *Kent Papers in Politics and International Relations*, first series, xiii (Canterbury, 1992); B. M. Doyle, 'Urban Liberalism and the "Lost Generation": Politics and Middle-Class Culture in Norwich, 1900–1935', *Historical Journal*, xxxviii (1995), pp. 617–34; idem, 'The Structure of Elite Power in the Early Twentieth-Century City: Norwich, 1900–1935', *Urban History*, xxiv (1997), pp. 179–99; idem, 'A Conflict of Interests? The Local and National Dimensions of Middle-Class Liberalism, 1900–1935', in C. Jones and D. Dean, eds, *Parliament and Locality* (Edinburgh, 1998), pp. 131–40; P. Cunningham, 'Unemployment in Norwich During the Nineteen Thirties' (UEA, Norwich, PhD thesis, 1990); P. Hollis, *Ladies Elect: Women in English Local Government, 1865–1914* (Oxford, 1997). There is little discussion of popular politics except N. MacMaster, 'The Battle for Mousehold Heath, 1857–1884: "Popular Politics" and the Victorian Public Park', *Past and Present*, cxxvii (1989), pp. 117–54, and J. Cameron, *The*

Political Economy of Decline in the Transition to Capitalism: Norwich, 1750–1850 (Norwich, 1986).

10. For changes in the number of municipal and parliamentary electors in the era of the first Reform Act, see Smith, 'Municipal Corporations Act', pp. 161, 222.

11. The figures for the municipal electorate were, 1866 – 3383, 1871 – 14,960: Smith, 'Municipal Corporations Act', p. 228.

12. W. Hudson, *The Wards of the City of Norwich: Their Origin and History* (London, 1891), p. 14.

13. B. M. Doyle, 'Middle-Class Realignment and Party Politics in Norwich, 1900–1932' (UEA, Norwich, PhD thesis, 1990), pp. 60–2.

14. The result in 1835 was twenty-eight Liberal councillors to twenty Conservatives. This differed significantly from the situation in places such as Leeds and Liverpool, where the Liberals secured majorities in excess of forty: D. Fraser, *Urban Politics in Victorian England: The Structure of Politics in Victorian Cities* (Leicester, 1976), pp. 124–5, 137, 143.

15. Mabel Clarkson was first elected as a Liberal councillor in Town Close in 1913, but joined the Labour Party in 1924, following her defeat by a Conservative.

16. For further discussion of these issues, see Smith, 'Municipal Corporations Act', pp. 160–247; Whitemore, 'Labour Party', p. 13; Cherry, *Doing Different*, chapter 8; Doyle, 'Conflict of Interests', passim; Doyle, 'Urban Liberalism', pp. 620–1.

17. For discussion of the background of candidates, see Smith, 'Municipal Corporations Act', pp. 160–247, and Doyle, 'Middle-Class Realignment', pp. 84–126.

18. Smith, 'Municipal Corporations Act', pp. 164–72. Norwich was more like Nottingham and Bristol, where the pre-reform electoral process had been more open: Fraser, *Urban Politics*, pp. 124–30.

19. Smith, 'Municipal Corporations Act', pp. 164, 199, 221; P. Palgrave-Moore, *The Mayors and Lord Mayors of Norwich, 1836–1974* (second edn, Norwich, 1979).

20. I am grateful to Fred Whitemore of the University of Kent at Canterbury for access to his research on the Labour Party in Norwich, from which I have derived both information and ideas.

21. Cherry, *Doing Different*, p. 48.

22. Hollis, *Ladies Elect*, p. 125.

23. Doyle, 'Urban Liberalism', p. 624.

24. Cherry, *Doing Different*, pp. 94–5.

25. Whitemore, 'Labour Party', p. 11.

26. For a discussion of these trends generally, see R. H. Trainor, 'The "Decline" of British Urban Governance since 1850: A Reassessment', in Morris and Trainor, eds, *Urban Governance*, pp. 28–46.

27. H. C. Colman, *Prince's Street Congregational Church, Norwich, 1819–1919* (Norwich, 1919); C. B. Jewson, *The Baptists in Norfolk* (London, 1957); B. M. Doyle, 'Business, Liberalism and Dissent in Norwich, 1900–1930', *Baptist Quarterly*, xxxv (1994), pp. 243–50. See also Chapter 17.

28. D. W. Bebbington, *The Nonconformist Conscience: Chapel and Politics, 1870–1914* (London, 1982), p. 101.

29. G. White, *The Nonconformist Conscience in its Relation to Our National Life*, presidential address to the Baptist Union of Great Britain and Ireland, 27 April 1903 (London, 1903).

30. Bernstein, *Liberalism and Liberal Politics*, p. 199; Bebbington, *Nonconformist Conscience*, pp. 153–60.

31. Doyle, 'Urban Liberalism', passim.

32. M. Winstanley, *The Shopkeeper's World, 1830–1914* (Manchester, 1983), p. 103; J. Lawrence, 'Class and Gender in the Making of Urban Toryism, 1880–1914', *EHR*, cviii (1993), pp. 629–52.

33. Doyle, 'Urban Government', pp. 300–1.

34. Palgrave-Moore, *Mayors*, p. 40.

35. M. Savage, *The Dynamics of Working-Class Politics: The Labour Movement in Preston, 1880–1940* (Cambridge, 1987), passim.

36. Smith, 'Municipal Corporations Act', p. 182; Cameron, 'Political Economy of Decline', note 24.

37. Smith, 'Municipal Corporations Act', p. 203, n. 128.

38. Smith, 'Municipal Corporations Act', p. 211, n. 153.

39. Smith, 'Municipal Corporations Act', p. 207.

40. Before the 1852 election, Gould delivered a sermon, subsequently published as *The Duty of Christians at an Election* (Norwich, 1852).

41. M. Knights, *The Late J. H. Tillett, Esq.: A Memoir* (Norwich, n. d. 1892?), p. 15.

42. Quoted in Knights, *J. H. Tillett*, p. 15.

43. Anon., *A Sketch of the Life and Political Career of J. H. Tillett, Esq., MP. Including a Complete History of his Political Contests* (Norwich, 1875), pp. 17–19.

44. Anon., *Colman & Tillett and their Electoral Contests in Norwich* (Norwich, n. d. [1885]), p. 19.

45. Following the municipal elections of 1905, Fred Henderson, a leading local radical, suggested that 'in several of the contested wards this year an organised debauchery of the more ignorant electors was deliberately carried out': *Norfolk Review*, i (December 1905), pp. 125–6.

46. Mock mayor making took place in Costessey and Pockthorpe: see S. T. Taylor, *The Diary of a Norwich Hospital Medical Student, 1858–60* (Norwich, 1930), 29 May 1860; and MacMaster 'Mousehold Heath', pp. 130–1, n. 43.

47. Cherry, *Doing Different*, p. 22; and Whitemore, unpublished chapter on 'Daylight' (see n. 20 above).

48. *EDP*, 8 January 1904.

49. Smith, 'Municipal Corporations Act', p. 180.

50. MacMaster, 'Mousehold Heath', p. 142.

51. MacMaster, 'Mousehold Heath', pp. 152–3.

52. M. Dawson, 'Money and the Real Impact of the Fourth Reform Act', *Historical Journal*, xxxv (1992), pp. 369–81.

53. G. Shakespeare, *Let Candles be Brought In* (London, 1949), p. 128.

54. Cunningham, 'Unemployment in Norwich', Chapter 6; B. M. Doyle, 'The Development of the Norwich Chamber of Commerce, 1896–1930', *NA*, xlii (1998), pp. 468–80.

55. S. Cherry, *The Norwich Labour Movement in the Early Years* (Norwich, n. d. [1986]), unpaginated.

56. Jewson, *Baptists*, pp. 101–2.

57. Jewson, *Baptists*, pp. 109–10; B. M. Doyle, 'Mapping Slums in an Historic City: Representing Working-Class Communities in Edwardian Norwich', *Planning Perspectives*, xvi (2001), pp. 47–65.

58. C. Mackie, *Norfolk Annals* (2 vols, Norwich, 1901), ii, 26 August 1873.

59. For a fuller discussion, see Chapter 18.

60. See Chapter 12.

61. J. Davis, 'Central Government and the Towns', in Daunton, *Cambridge Urban History*, pp. 261–86; P. Waller, *Town, City and Nation* (Oxford, 1983), Chapter 6.

62. J. Harman, 'An Introduction to Council Housing in Norwich' (UEA, Norwich, MA thesis, 1972), p. 27. See also pp. 264–6, above.

63. P. Hepworth and J. Ogden, *Sixty Eventful Years: The Diamond Jubilee of the Norwich Society, 1923–1983* (Norwich, n. d. [1983]).

64. E. Felce, ed., *Norwich: Civic, Industrial, Historical* (Norwich, 1935), p. 43.

65. Compare with R. Millward, 'The Political Economy of Urban Utilities', in Daunton, *Cambridge Urban History*, pp. 315–50.

66. *EDP*, 31 October 1901, 'Municipal Socialism'.

67. Doyle, 'Structure of Elite Power', pp. 196–8.

68. Smith, 'Municipal Corporations Act', pp. 387, 396–9. For similar developments, see J. Garrard and V. Parrott, 'Craft, Professional and Middle-Class Identity: Solicitors and Gas Engineers, c. 1850–1914', in A. Kidd and D. Nicholls, eds, *The Making of the British Middle Class? Studies of Regional and Cultural Diversity since the Eighteenth Century* (Stroud, 1998), pp. 148–68; and I. Maver, 'The Role and Influence of Glasgow's Municipal Managers', in Morris and Trainor, *Urban Governance*, pp. 69–85.

69. Mackie, *Norfolk Annals*, ii, 19 July 1876, p. 267.

70. Doyle, 'Structure of Elite Power', p. 187.

71. Biographies of Harry Cooper Pattin and A. E. Collins, in *Cox's County Who's*

Who Series: Norfolk, Suffolk and Cambridgeshire 1912 (London, 1912); J. Garrard, 'Bureaucrats Rather than Bureaucracies: The Power of Municipal Professionals, 1835–1914', in *Occasional Papers in Politics and Contemporary History* (University of Salford, 1993), pp. 18–20; and Maver, 'Glasgow Municipal Managers', p. 77.

72. E. Watson, 'The Municipal Activity of an English City', *Political Science Quarterly*, xvi (1901), p. 273; N. Tillett, *How Norwich is Governed* (Norwich, n.d. [*c.* 1951]), pp. 11–12.

73. Watson, 'Municipal Activity', p. 275.

74. C. B. Hawkins, *Norwich: A Social Study* (London, 1910), p. 78.

75. Watson, 'Municipal Activity', pp. 275–6.

76. Doyle, 'Chamber of Commerce', p. 476.

77. A. D. Bayne, *A Comprehensive History of Norwich* (London, Norwich, 1869), pp. 410–15; B. M. Doyle, 'Modernity or Morality? George White, Liberalism and the Nonconformist Conscience in Edwardian England', *Historical Research*, xix (1998), p. 337.

78. J. K. Edwards, 'Chartism in Norwich', *Yorkshire Bulletin of Economic and Social Research*, xvi (1967), p. 93.

79. Bernstein, 'Progressive Alliance', pp. 619–20.

80. Doyle, 'Conflict of Interests', pp. 136–8. For pacts elsewhere, see T. Adams, 'Labour and the First World War: Economy, Politics and the Erosion of Local Peculiarity?', *Journal of Regional and Local Studies*, x (1990), pp. 26–7; K. Laybourn and J. Reynolds, *Liberalism and the Rise of Labour* (London, 1984), pp. 150–1; C. Cook, *The Age of Alignment: Electoral Politics in Britain, 1922–29* (London, 1975), chapter 3.

81. Whitemore, 'Labour Party', passim.

82. Whitemore, 'Labour Party', p. 14; Cherry, *Doing Different*, chapter 8.

83. M. Savage, 'The Rise of the Labour Party in Local Perspective', *Journal of Regional and Local Studies*, x (1990), pp. 11–13.

84. On becoming mayor in 1930, Mabel Clarkson asserted that 'unemployment, housing, slum-clearing, education, health … must make first demand on the time and energies of the chief citizen': quoted in Whitemore, 'Labour Party', p. 11.

85. Middle-class Liberalism did persist in other parts of the country, such as Bradford, Nottingham and Leeds: see Cook, *Alignment*, chapter 3; M. Meadowcroft, 'The Years of Political Transition 1914–39', in D. Fraser, ed., *A History of Modern Leeds*, (Manchester, 1980), pp. 410–36.

Notes to Chapter 15: Banking and Insurance

1. *NM*, 13 April 1805. My thanks are due to the following for providing

information: Dr Leslie Hannah, chief executive, Ashridge; Sheree Leeds, Norwich Union archivist; Karen Sampson, deputy group archivist Lloyds TSB; Professor Roy Church, UEA; Oliver Westall, Dr Ann Prior and Professor Maurice Kirby, University of Lancaster; NHC, and Edge Hill College of Higher Education inter-library loan service. Many references are from R. J. Ryan, 'A History of the Norwich Union Fire and Life Insurance Societies, 1797–1914' (UEA, Norwich, PhD thesis, 1983).

2. A. B. DuBois, *The English Business Company after the Bubble Act, 1720–1800* (New York, 1971); B. C. Hunt, *The Development of the Business Corporation in England, 1800–1867* (Harvard, 1969).

3. B. Supple, *Royal Exchange Assurance* (Cambridge, 1970), part A.

4. L. S. Pressnell, *Country Banking in the Industrial Revolution* (Oxford, 1956), pp. 4–11, 75–125, 441–500.

5. Pressnell, *Country Banking*, pp. 37, 51, 137, 244–5, 411–12.

6. P. Hudson, *The Industrial Revolution* (London, 1992), pp. 91–6.

7. Pressnell, *Country Banking*, pp. 473–88.

8. J. H. Clapham, *The Bank of England* (2 vols, Cambridge, 1944), ii, chapters 1 to 5; P. L. Cottrell and B. L. Anderson, eds, *Money and Banking in England* (Newton Abbot, 1974), pp. 304–8; H. E. Raynes, *A History of British Insurance* (London, second edition, 1964).

9. M. Ackrill and L. Hannah, *Barclays: The Business of Banking, 1690–1996* (Cambridge, 2001), p. 21.

10. Ackrill and Hannah, *Barclays*, p. 21.

11. W. H. Bidwell, *Annals of an East Anglian Bank* (Norwich, 1910), p. 18.

12. Bidwell, *Annals*, p. 11; W. T. C. King, *A History of the London Discount Market* (London, 1936), pp. 17–18; Pressnell, *Country Banking*, pp. 52, 283, 315.

13. Bidwell, *Annals*, p. 195.

14. H. Preston, *Early East Anglian Banks and Bankers* (Thetford, 1994), lists local banks.

15. Bidwell, *Annals*, p. 92; B. Cozens-Hardy and E. A. Kent, *The Mayors of Norwich, 1403–1835* (Norwich, 1938), p. 136.

16. Bidwell, *Annals*, p. 92; *Report from the Select Committee on Land and Window Taxes, PP* (1821), viii, pp. 44–6, 80–2.

17. Bidwell, *Annals*, pp. 35–6.

18. L. Hannah, 'The Moral Economy of Business', in P. Burke, B. Harrison and P. Slack, eds, *Civil Histories* (Oxford, 2000), pp. 291–4.

19. *NM*, 25 February 1797.

20. Ryan, 'Norwich Union', table 10, p. 963.

21. R. Ryan, 'The Norwich Union and the British Fire Insurance Market in the Early Nineteenth Century', in O. M. Westall, ed., *The Historian and the Business of Insurance* (Manchester, 1984), pp. 39–73.

22. Anon., *A Few Plain Facts for the Consideration of Insurers in the Norwich Union Fire Office* (London, 1815); Colman and Rye Library, N368, p. 27 (destroyed, 1994).

23. Variant of 'genever', or Dutch gin.

24. 'Norwich Union Fire and Life Societies, 1805–1889', Colman and Rye Library, 28D (destroyed 1994).

25. Ryan, 'Norwich Union', appendix, tables 1, 26, 27.

26. T. R. Gourvish, *Norfolk Beers from English Barley: A History of Steward and Patteson, 1793–1963* (Norwich, 1987), pp. 16–17.

27. NUFIS Board Minutes, 27 August 1821, 7 July 1823.

28. Ryan, 'Norwich Union and British Fire Insurance', p. 43, table 1.

29. Supple, *Royal Exchange Assurance*, pp. 127–30.

30. Ryan, 'Norwich Union', pp. 948–9, table 1.

31. W. A. Dinsdale, *History of Accident Insurance in Great Britain* (London, 1954), p. 228.

32. Ryan, 'Norwich Union', p. 383.

33. Bidwell, *Annals*, pp. 183–4.

34. NULIS Board Minutes, 7 November 1825, 28 May 1827.

35. Anon., *HM Municipal Corporation Commissioners. Digest of Evidence*, Colman and Rye Library, N352, 1833, pp. 50–1 (destroyed, 1994); *John Cozens' Petition*, Colman and Rye Library, N328.42, no date, p. 305.

36. *Committee on Joint Stock Banks, PP* (1836), ix, p. 411, questions 314, 315, 328, 350–3, 360–2, 367, 2636; Ryan, 'Norwich Union', pp. 302–7.

37. R. Ryan, 'The Early Expansion of the Norwich Union Life Insurance Society, 1808–1837', *Business History*, xxvii (1985), pp. 166–70.

38. Gourvish, *Norfolk Beers*, pp. 24, 34–7.

39. *The Times*, 12 November 1839.

40. *NM*, 8 January 1842.

41. *NC*, 30 November 1839.

42. NULIS Board Minutes, 29 February 1836, 26 July 1841.

43. R. Bignold, *Five Generations of the Bignold Family, 1761–1947* (London, 1948), p. 105.

44. J. Fairburn, *The Norfolk and Norwich Savings Bank, 1816–1901* (Norwich, 1901), pp. 36, 52.

45. Supple, *Royal Exchange Assurance*, p. 247.

46. R. Blake, *Esto Perpetua: The Norwich Union Life Insurance Society* (Norwich, 1958), pp. 73–8.

47. Ackrill and Hannah, *Barclays*, p. 14.

48. Ackrill and Hannah, *Barclays*, pp. 18–23, 30–8.

49. King, *Discount Market*, pp. 18–19.

50. Pressnell, *Country Banking*, pp. 114–15.

51. Pressnell, *Country Banking*, p. 102.

52. Bidwell, *Annals*, p. 88; King, *Discount Market*, pp. 19–24.

53. Bidwell, *Annals*, pp. 144–62, 173–82.

54. M. Kirby, *The Origins of Railway Enterprise: The Stockton and Darlington Railway, 1821–1863* (Cambridge, 1993), pp. 26–53.

55. Kirby, *Railway Enterprise*, p. 50.

56. A. Prior and M. Kirby, 'The Society of Friends and Business Culture', in D. J. Jeremy, ed., *Religion, Business and Wealth in Modern Britain* (London, 1998), p. 132.

57. Pressnell, *Country Banking*, p. 104.

58. *NM* and *NC*, Home News, 27 July–27 August 1864, see also arbitration until 1872 (NHC, L332.1 Special Collection, J. J. Colman, WB 6/1990, 'Norfolk and Norwich Banks 1827–1891').

59. Ackrill and Hannah, *Barclays*, p. 46; King, *Discount Market*, pp. 251–6.

60. Ackrill and Hannah, *Barclays*, p. 47.

61. Ackrill and Hannah, *Barclays*, p. 47; Bidwell, *Annals*, p. 251.

62. Bidwell, *Annals*, p. 252.

63. Ackrill and Hannah, *Barclays*, p. 47; Bidwell, *Annals*, p. 251–3.

64. NHC, L332.1, cutting from *NM*, 16 May 1866, broadsheets, 11 May 1866.

65. Ackrill and Hannah, *Barclays*, p. 47.

66. Bidwell, *Annals*, pp. 255, 269.

67. *NC*, 6 August 1870.

68. *NM*, 6 August 1864.

69. J. Sykes, *The Amalgamation Movement in English Banking, 1825–1924* (London, 1926), chapter 3.

70. Ackrill and Hannah, *Barclays*, pp. 55–8; Sykes, *Amalgamation Movement*, pp. 53–4.

71. Supple, *Royal Exchange Assurance*, pp. 48, 149, 314, 376–82.

72. D. C. Marsh, *The Changing Social Structure of England and Wales, 1871–1961* (London, 1965), p. 124.

73. D. Kynaston, *The City of London* (3 vols, London, 2000), iii, pp. 281–6.

74. Marsh, *Changing Social Structure*, table 35, pp. 135–6.

75. Blake, *Esto Perpetua*, pp. 80–1.

76. NULIS and NUFIS Annual Reports.

77. J. Mantle, *Norwich Union: The First 200 Years* (London, 1997), pp. 62–70.

78. Supple, *Royal Exchange Assurance*, pp. 438–41.

79. C. Trebilcock, *Phoenix Assurance* (2 vols, Cambridge, 1998), ii, pp. 427–42.

80. Trebilcock, *Phoenix Assurance*, ii, pp. 442–68.

81. Trebilcock, *Phoenix Assurance*, ii, pp. 471, 477–80.

82. Trebilcock, *Phoenix Assurance*, ii, p. 477.

83. NULIS Report and Accounts for 1924, 11 March 1925.

84. Trebilcock, *Phoenix Assurance*, ii, p. 480.

85. NULIS Report and Accounts for 1925, 16 March 1926.

86. *Financial Times*, 8 July 1925, quoted by Trebilcock, *Phoenix Assurance*, ii, p. 482.

87. *Post Magazine* annual summaries, xc, 14 September 1929; c, 16 September 1939.

88. W. A. Dinsdale, *Accident Insurance*, chapters 12 and 13; Supple, *Royal Exchange Assurance*, pp. 224–37, 421–38.

89. NUFIS Annual Accounts and Reports, 1919–39.

90. NUFIS Annual Accounts and Reports, 1919–39.

91. C. R. Perry, *The Victorian Post Office* (Woodbridge, 1992), p. 67.

92. Perry, *Post Office*, pp. 70–1.

93. Fairburn, *Norfolk and Norwich Savings Bank*, pp. 9–15, 57–9; H. O. Horne, *A History of Savings Banks* (London, 1947), pp. 67–8.

94. Fairburn, *Norfolk and Norwich Savings Bank*, p. 10.

95. Fairburn, *Norfolk and Norwich Savings Bank*, p. 13.

96. Perry, *Post Office*, p. 68.

97. Fairburn, *Norfolk and Norwich Savings Bank*, pp. 16–17, 71; Horne *Savings Banks*, chapter 5.

98. Horne, *Savings Banks*, pp. 126–8.

99. Fairburn, *Norfolk and Norwich Savings Bank*, p. 71.

100. E. Hopkins, *Working-Class Self-Help in Nineteenth-Century England* (London, 1995), pp. 27–63.

101. C. B. Hawkins, *Norwich: A Social Study* (London, 1910), p. 277.

102. Hawkins, *Norwich*, pp. 10–11, 216–19. See above, Chapter 16.

103. Fairburn, *Norfolk and Norwich Savings Bank*, p. 28.

104. Perry, *Post Office*, p. 72.

105. Hopkins, *Self-Help*, pp. 56–7.

106. Fairburn, *Norfolk and Norwich Savings Bank*, p. 31–2.

107. Fairburn, *Norfolk and Norwich Savings Bank*, p. 27, 31.

108. Fairburn, *Norfolk and Norwich Savings Bank*, p. 34.

109. Fairburn, *Norfolk and Norwich Savings Bank*, p. 64.

110. Fairburn, *Norfolk and Norwich Savings Bank*, p. 33.

111. Fairburn, *Norfolk and Norwich Savings Bank*, p. 64.

112. Fairburn, *Norfolk and Norwich Savings Bank*, p. 46.

113. Horne, *Savings Banks*, pp. 280–1.

114. *NC*, 4 May 1916.

115. *NC*, 18 June 1915 and 4 May 1916; Fairburn, *Norfolk and Norwich Savings Bank*, p. 50.

116. Horne, *Savings Banks*, pp. 388–90.

117. Horne, *Savings Banks*, pp. 390–1.

118. Lloyds TSB Group Archive TC/39/b/5; Downing 'Growth of the Savings Bank in East Anglia', p. 45.

119. J. H. Clapham, 'The Transference of the Worsted Industry from Norfolk to the West Riding', *Economic Journal*, xx (1910), p. 204; J. J. Gurney's statement is in *A Digest of Evidence Taken before Two of HM Municipal Corporation Commissioners, November 1833* (Norwich, 1834), Colman and Rye Library, N. 352, p. 205 (destroyed, 1994).

120. P. J. Corfield, 'The Social and Economic History of Norwich, 1650–1850' (University of London PhD thesis, 1976), pp. 585–6.

121. Ackrill and Hannah, *Barclays*, pp. 21–3, 35–8; Pressnell, *Country Banking*, pp. 75–125, 322–43.

122. Ryan, 'Norwich Union', chapter 17.

123. Gourvish, *Steward & Patteson*, pp. 51, 69–70.

124. P. J. Cain and A. G. Hopkins, 'Gentlemanly Capitalism and British Expansion Overseas: The Old Colonial System, 1688–1850', *EconHR*, second series, xxxix (1986), pp. 504–7; Bidwell, *Annals*, pp. 173–6, 197–8, 201, 208, 214.

125. R. J. Ryan, 'Deuchar, John James Walter', in D. Jeremy, ed., *Dictionary of Business Biography* (London, 1984–6), pp. 85–9.

126. Ackrill and Hannah, *Barclays*, p. 131.

127. Ackrill and Hannah, *Barclays*, pp. 63–4.

128. Ackrill and Hannah, *Barclays*, p. 95.

129. See Chapter 19.

130. NULIS Report for 1934, 29 March 1935.

131. Source of figures: NULIS and NUFIS Annual Accounts and President's Reports, 1919–39.

132. Mantle, *Norwich Union*, pp. 65–6.

133. Ryan, 'Norwich Union', table 42, pp. 1043–4.

134. P. Palgrave Moore, *The Mayors and Lord Mayors of Norwich, 1836–1974* (Norwich, 1978), pp. 32–3.

135. Palgrave-Moore, *Mayors*, pp. 1–65; Fairburn, *Norfolk and Norwich Savings Bank*, pp. 51–3.

Notes to Chapter 16: Work and Employment

1. J. B. Priestley, *English Journey* (London, 1934), p. 380.

2. See Chapter 9.

3. J. K. Edwards, 'The Decline of the Norwich Textiles Industry', *Yorkshire Bulletin of Economic and Social Research*, xvi (1964), p. 31.

4. See A. Briggs, *Victorian Cities* (London, 1963); P. J. Waller, *Town, City and Nation, 1850–1914* (Oxford, 1983).

5. A. D. Bayne, *A Comprehensive History of Norwich* (London, 1869), p. 393.

6. There was further distress during the early 1840s, with wage rates reduced again in 1843 and widespread unemployment in 1845: P. J. Corfield, 'The Social and Economic History of Norwich, 1650–1850: A Study of Urban Growth' (University of London, PhD thesis, 1976), p. 626; Edwards, 'Textile Industry', pp. 102–3; Bayne, *Comprehensive History*, pp. 373, 393–4.

7. W. White, *Directory for Norfolk* (Sheffield, 1845), pp. 77–8.

8. J. K. Edwards, 'Industrial Development: 1800–1900', in C. Barringer, ed., *Norwich in the Nineteenth Century* (Norwich, 1984), p. 147.

9. See Chapter 9.

10. J. K. Edwards, 'Communications and the Economic Development of Norwich, 1750–1850', *Journal of Transport History*, vii (1965), pp. 96–108.

11. R. N. Bacon, *The Report on the Agriculture of Norfolk* (London, 1844), p. 11.

12. *NM*, 14 March 1840.

13. Edwards, 'Communications', p. 105.

14. As Corfield claims, it 'saved Norwich from its economic slough of despond', Corfield, 'History of Norwich', p. 438.

15. W. Cobbett, *Rural Rides* (London, 1934), p. 53.

16. A. D. Bayne, *An Account of the Industry and Trade of Norwich and Norfolk* (Norwich, 1852), pp. 3, 10.

17. Bacon, *Report*, p. 403.

18. Bayne, *Comprehensive History*, p. 624.

19. T. R. Gourvish and R. G. Wilson, *The British Brewing Industry 1830–1980* (Cambridge, 1994), pp. 66–75; T. Gourvish, *Norfolk Beers from English Barley: A History of Steward & Patteson, 1793–1963* (Norwich, 1987), pp. 36, 156–70.

20. See Chapter 15.

21. Both the 1851 and 1861 censuses had categories such as 'shoemakers' wives' which probably corrected some of the underassessment of 1841. The 1871 census only provides data for members of the workforce over twenty, and for 1901 the workforce is defined as comprising people over the age of ten; this rises to twelve in 1921 and fourteen in 1931. For details of the shortcomings of the censuses and the statistics of female employment, see E. Higgs, 'Women, Occupations and Work in the Nineteenth-Century Censuses', *History Workshop*, xxiii (1987), pp. 59–80.

22. M. G. Adams, 'The Norwich Boot and Shoe Trade, 1870–1914' (UEA, Norwich, MA thesis, 1971), p. 12.

23. For a detailed discussion of technological developments and the resistance to them, see R. A. Church, 'Labour Supply and Innovation, 1800–1860: The Boot and Shoe Industry', *Business History*, i (January 1970), pp. 25–45. See also Chapter 9, above.

24. R. Brigden, 'The Nineteenth-Century Ironfounders of Norwich', unpublished paper, n. d., Bridewell Museum, Norwich, p. 11.

25. 'Early History of the Firm of Boulton & Paul Ltd', *Works Magazine*, i (July 1916), pp. 14–16.

26. J. Gurney-Read, *Trades and Industries of Norwich* (Norwich, 1988), pp. 71–2.

27. E. B. Southwell, 'J. & J. Colman, Ltd: Early Days at Stoke Holy Cross', *Carrow Works Magazine*, xix (October 1925), pp. 1–13; H. C. Colman, *Jeremiah James Colman: A Memoir* (London, 1905).

28. Bayne, *Industry*, p. vi.

29. E. and W. Burgess, *Men Who Have Made Norwich* (Norwich, 1904), p. 83; W. L. Sparks, *The Story of Shoemaking in Norwich* (Norwich, 1949), pp. 106, 113.

30. Adams, 'Boot and Shoe Trade', p. 19. Edwards & Holmes exported over 50 per cent of their production before 1914: Sparks, *Shoemaking*, p. 113.

31. Behind Leicester and Northampton: Adams, 'Boot and Shoe Trade', p. 12.

32. Brigden, 'Nineteenth-Century Ironfounders', pp. 21–2.

33. NRO, BR220/3, Barnards Limited, directors' minutes, 3 July 1906.

34. 'Early History of the Firm of Boulton & Paul', part 3, *Works Magazine*, iii (October 1916), pp. 64–6.

35. In 1888 the company was registered as Laurence, Paris & Scott. A new company, Laurence Scott & Company, was formed in 1896 and a new factory, the Gothic Works, was completed two years later: T. J. Barfield, *Scott Built a Dynamo: The Story of the First Eighty Years of Laurence Scott & Electromotors* (Norwich, 1968), pp. 1–28.

36. Gurney-Read, *Trades and Industries*, pp. 21–2.

37. 1616 male and 736 female: Unilever Archives, Port Sunlight, Carrow employees (uncatalogued).

38. With a total workforce of 3200 the company was ranked ninety-fourth: C. Shaw, 'The 100 Largest Employers in Manufacturing in 1907', *Business History*, lxxv (1983), pp. 42–60.

39. Gurney-Read, *Trades and Industries*, p. 67.

40. Burgess, *Men Who Made Norwich*, pp. 289–97.

41. See: A. McAuley Brownfield-Pope, 'Polite and Commercial People: An Investigation of Some Family-Run Retailers in the Norwich and Norfolk Area, c. 1900–1939' (UEA, Norwich, MA thesis, 1999).

42. There was also a high proportion of married workers. In urban areas throughout the country, only 14 per cent of married or widowed women worked; in Norwich the figure was as high as 18 per cent: 1901 Census; C. B. Hawkins, *Norwich, A Social Study* (London, 1910), p. 14.

43. The second reason was that the beer was very weak (and, therefore, cheap): *Select Committee of the House of Lords on Intemperance*, PP (1877), xi, second report, pp. 82–5. See also, above, p. 448.

44. Average wage rates in Northampton were 29s. 10d. for men and 12s. 5d. for

women and in Leicester 31s. 2d. and 14s. 11d. respectively: Adams, 'Boot and Shoe Trade', p. 59.

45. Hawkins, *Norwich*, pp. 39–40, 52.

46. Hawkins, *Norwich*, p. 45.

47. Hawkins, *Norwich*, p. 53.

48. For the best account of trade unionism in Norwich, see S. Cherry, *Doing Different? Politics and the Labour Movement in Norwich, 1880–1914* (Norwich, 1989).

49. B. Doyle, 'Middle-Class Realignment and Party Politics in Norwich, 1900–1932' (UEA, Norwich, PhD thesis, 1990), pp. 270–1.

50. Adams, 'Boot and Shoe Trade', p. 56.

51. F. W. Wheldon, *A Norvic Century and the Men Who Made It, 1846–1946* (Norwich, 1946), pp. 46–7.

52. Wheldon, *Norvic Century*, p. 42.

53. Colman, *Jeremiah James Colman*, p. 136.

54. For details of Colmans' welfare programme, see E. B. Southwell, 'Looking Back', *Colmans' Works Magazine*, xiii (January 1920), pp. 44–54; Colman, *Jeremiah James Colman*.

55. H. Leeds, ed., *Peace Souvenir: Norwich War Record* (Norwich, 1919), pp. 74, 83.

56. *The Story of a Norwich Industry: F. W. Harmer & Co. Ltd* (Bridewell Museum, Norwich, 1948).

57. J. Mouncer, 'Exceptional Opportunities for the Employment of Women? Norwich, 1900–1939' (UEA, Norwich, MA thesis, 2000), p. 29.

58. Leeds, *Peace Souvenir*, pp. 71–2.

59. Leeds, *Peace Souvenir*, pp. 68, 74, 83, 86.

60. See W. H. ffiske, *Boulton & Paul Ltd and the Great War* (Norwich, 1919), for details of the company's war work.

61. H. V. Jinks, 'The Norwich Aerodrome Extension', *Journal of the Norfolk Industrial Archaeology Society* (January 1972), pp. 25–7; ffiske, *Boulton & Paul Ltd*, p. 49.

62. Barfield, *Scott Built a Dynamo*, p. 38.

63. P. Cunningham, 'Unemployment in Norwich during the Nineteen Thirties' (UEA, Norwich, PhD thesis, 1990), p. 24.

64. Chamber of Commerce Annual Report, 31 December 1928, privately held. Most Reports were destroyed in the Norwich Library fire of August 1994.

65. H. J. Sexton, 'Address to the Norwich Boot and Shoe Managers' and Foremen's Association, 1952', *Journal of the Norfolk Industrial Archaeology Society* (July 1974), p. 10.

66. Cunningham, 'Unemployment', pp. 29, 80.

67. Gourvish, *Norfolk Beers*, pp. 104, 193.

68. C. Clark, *A Brush with Heritage: The History of Hamilton Acorn, Norfolk Brushmakers since 1746* (Norwich, 1996), pp. 59, 64.

69. Barfield, *Scott Built a Dynamo*, p. 43.

70. NRO, BR266, 9/6; *EDP*, 2 January 1937.

71. Priestley, *English Journey*, pp. 387–88, 410.

72. These were regions with exceptionally high unemployment, mainly in the north, Wales and Scotland, which received government grants for their economic and social development.

73. Between 1934–7, an average of 6060 insured workers were unemployed. This figure rose to over 7000 in 1938 and to 8600 during the early months of 1939: Cunningham, 'Unemployment', p. 53.

74. Shadow factories were government financed, privately managed, aviation factories, built to provide additional war capacity.

75. Anon., *The Leaf and Tree* (Norwich, 1947), pp. 65–70; Barfield, *Scott Built a Dynamo*, pp. 50–5.

76. Cunningham, 'Unemployment', pp. 58, 109.

77. Mouncer, 'Exceptional Opportunities', p. 38.

78. *EDP*, 2 January 1937.

79. The long-term tendency was for a greater output from a smaller workforce: Cunningham, 'Unemployment', pp. 39, 61.

80. The corporation had several hundred acres designated for industrial development, but, despite many inquiries, even when it offered to lay the factory foundations free of charge, was unable to attract new firms: *EEN*, 9 February 1937.

81. NRO, BR266, 9/6. The decision to acquire the business was taken because, despite 'very reasonable risks', it was a proposition which might not readily occur again and 'we are paying very little for it'. The firm would otherwise have been closed. Sir Harold Mackintosh's Memo on the Caley Proposition, 13 June 1932, and Memo on Developments, 20 May 1932.

82. *EEN*, 9 February 1937.

83. By October 1938 Norwich had more of its citizens in receipt of unemployment assistance than either of its footwear rivals or Ipswich: Cunningham, 'Unemployment', p. 111.

Notes to Chapter 17: Church and Chapel

1. Letter from Ethel Mary Colman to Sydney Cozens-Hardy, 29 October 1923 (in possession of the late Basil Cozens-Hardy).

2. H. Mann, *Census of Great Britain, 1851: Religious Worship in England and Wales. Abridged from the Official Report* (London, 1854), p. 1.

3. J. Ede and N. Virgoe, eds, *Religious Worship in Norfolk: The 1851 Census*

of Accommodation and Atttendance at Worship (NRS, lxii, 1998), pp. 21, 122.

4. Ede and Virgoe, *Religious Worship*, p. 121.

5. Ede and Virgoe, *Religious Worship*, p. 131.

6. Ede and Virgoe, *Religious Worship*, p. 123.

7. Ede and Virgoe, *Religious Worship*, pp. 139–40.

8. Ede and Virgoe, *Religious Worship*, p. 127.

9. Ede and Virgoe, *Religious Worship*, pp. 133–4.

10. Ede and Virgoe, *Religious Worship*, p. 124.

11. Ede and Virgoe, *Religious Worship*, pp. 123, 130. St James's incumbent considered that £5 should be deducted from the church's endowment to cover 'requisites for Public Worship' otherwise precluded by the church rate's opponents. Hence the need to cover both surplice and surplus?

12. Ede and Virgoe, *Religious Worship*, p. 123.

13. Ede and Virgoe, *Religious Worship*, p. 129.

14. Ede and Virgoe, *Religious Worship*, p. 122.

15. Ede and Virgoe, *Religious Worship*, p. 120.

16. Mann, *Census*, p. v. Thus his 'preface': 'For the first time … a Census of Religious Worship has been obtained by the Government'.

17. G. Eliot, *Silas Marner: The Weaver of Raveloe* (London, 1861).

18. See E. R. Norman, *Anti-Catholicism in Victorian England* (London, 1968), pp. 53–79, 159–85.

19. For George Pellew (1793–1866, dean 1828–66), son of 1st Viscount Exmouth and son-in-law of 1st Viscount Sidmouth, and Henry Bathurst (1744–1837, bishop 1805–37), nephew of 1st Earl Bathurst, see *DNB*, xv, pp. 716–17; i, pp. 1328–9.

20. Ede and Virgoe, *Religious Worship*, pp. 14–15.

21. Ede and Virgoe, *Religious Worship*, p. 23.

22. Ede and Virgoe, *Religious Worship*, p. 15. It was estimated that, when all allowances were made, 70 per cent of the population should have attended worship at some point on census Sunday.

23. The figures in this section are drawn from Ede and Virgoe, *Religious Worship*, passim.

24. Quoted in *St Mary's Norwich: The Church Fellowship, 1669–1961* (Norwich, undated, unpaginated); and *St Mary's in Four Centuries, 1669–1969* (Norwich, 1969).

25. K. Hipper, 'The Johnsonian Baptists in Norwich', *Baptist Quarterly*, xxxviii (January 1999), 1, pp. 19–32.

26. There is a brisk summation of Norwich Methodism by N. Virgoe in J. A. Vickers, ed., *A Dictionary of Methodism in Britain and Ireland* (Peterborough, 2000), pp. 157–8.

27. N. Virgoe, 'The Wesleyan Reformers in Norfolk', *Proceedings of the Wesley Historical Society*, lii (October 1999), part 3, pp. 87–101.

28. Harriet Martineau, quoted in E. Isichei, *Victorian Quakers* (Oxford, 1970), pp. 120–1.

29. V. Anderson, *Friends and Relations: Three Centuries of Quaker Families* (London, 1980).

30. Elizabeth Fry (1780–1845), J. J. Gurney's sister, was born and reared at Earlham. John Bright's Barclay and Buxton kinsmen were numerous in Norfolk. Forster, who was also one of the Earlham cousinhood, ended his education and began his commercial career in Norwich.

31. For Amelia Opie (1769–1853), see *DNB*, xiv, pp. 1120–4. For the family of Edward Hall Alderson, Chief Baron of the Exchequer, see K. Rose, *The Later Cecils* (London, 1975), pp. 14, 18–19.

32. For Edward Taylor (1784–1863), see *DNB*, xix, pp. 407–8.

33. For James Martineau (1805–1900), see *DNB*, xxii, pp. 1018–23. Florence Nightingale, whose Unitarianism remains the subject of discussion, was a granddaughter of William Smith, long MP for Norwich. Joseph Chamberlain's mother and his first two wives were related to the Martineaus.

34. This section is largely drawn from *Norwich Cathedral*, especially chapters 28 to 32.

35. For Bishop Bathurst and Dean Pellew see above, note 19. For Bishop Manners-Sutton (1755–1828, bishop 1792–1805), grandson of the 3rd duke of Rutland, and Bishop Stanley (1779–1849, bishop 1837–49), brother of 1st Baron Stanley of Alderley, see *DNB*, xii, p. 942; xviii, p. 876. Bishop Pelham (1811–96, bishop 1837–93) was a son of the 2nd earl of Chichester. For Dean Goulburn (1818–97, dean 1866–89), son of an MP, nephew of a chancellor of the exchequer, with two aristocratic stepmothers, see *DNB*, xxii, pp. 758–9. Prebendary Thurlow (1788–1847) was a lord chancellor's nephew. Prebendary Wodehouse (1778–1811) was a baron's younger brother (and great-grandfather of P. G. Wodehouse).

36. Quoted in Isichei, *Victorian Quakers*, p. 121. Mottram's was an Octagon family that neither died out nor moved away. His Octagon descendants included the novelist, R. H. Mottram (1883–1971): see *DNB, 1971–1980*, pp. 603–4.

37. J. Estlin Carpenter, *James Martineau, 1805–1900* (London, 1905), p. 443. He added: 'But whilst we remain outside it, we must accept and work out the consequences of our position'.

38. A letter to her addressed thus, was endorsed 'Try Miss Martineau'.

39. Harriet Martineau, *Autobiography: With Memorials by Maria Weston Chapman* (3 vols, London 1877, third edn), i, pp. 198–9.

40. Carpenter, *Martineau*, pp. 47–8; Martineau, *Autobiography*, p. 142.

41. Martineau, *Autobiography*, p. 36.

42. Martineau, *Autobiography*, p. 116. The tales were *The Rioters* (1827) and *The Turn Out* (1829): see M. N. Cutt, *Ministering Angels* (London, 1979), p. 36.

43. Martineau, *Autobiography*, pp. 156–7.

44. H. Gow, *The Unitarians* (London, 1928), p. 130.

45. W. B. Selbie, *The Life of Charles Silvester Horne* (London, 1920), p. 107. Horne (1865–1914), then a Congregational minister in Kensington, later MP for Ipswich, married Katherine (1870–1958), daughter of Herbert Hardy Cozens-Hardy (1838–1920), later 1st baron, of Letheringsett. Horne added: 'and he has lived the life of the man of letters, and not borne the burden and heat of the day as Gladstone did'.

46. NRO, FC13/3, 13/4, Octagon Chapel Minute Books, 1825–62, 1862–85; Octagon Calendar, 1872–6.

47. For Bakewell (minister 1828–39) and Crompton (minister 1839–52), see J. Browne, *History of Congregationalism and Memorials of the Churches in Norfolk and Suffolk* (London, 1878), p. 282.

48. Madge became Crabb Robinson's minister in Essex Street, London (1825–59). For Gordon (1841–1931), scholar and historian, see *DNB, Missing Persons Volume*, pp. 260–2.

49. For Govett (1813–1901), see D. M. Lewis, ed., *The Blackwell Dictionary of Evangelical Biography, 1730–1860* (2 vols, Oxford, 1995), i p. 462; J. H. Y. Briggs, *The English Baptists of the Nineteenth Century* (Didcot, 1994), p. 51. identifies him as a Plymouth Brother, but see, for example, *Baptist Handbook* (London, 1894), p. 332.

50. For Joseph Kinghorn (1766–1832), see M. M. Wilkin, *Joseph Kinghorn of Norwich* (London, 1855), and Lewis, *Blackwell Dictionary*, pp. 648–9; for William Brock (1807–75), see C. M. Birrell, *The Life of William Brock, DD* (London, 1878). For William Smith (1756–1835), see R. W. Davis, *Dissent in Politics, 1780–1830* (London, 1971). For Sir Samuel Morton Peto, Bt (1809–89), see *DNB*, xv, pp. 972–4.

51. For George Gould (1818–82), see *DNB*, viii, pp. 285–6. Of his children, Sir Alfred Pearce Gould was a London surgeon married to a judge's daughter; George Pearce Gould (d. 1921) was principal of Regent's Park College; Harry Pearce Gould was official receiver for Norwich (and sheriff in 1910). Gould's son-in-law, Alfred West, was headmaster of the notable boarding school, Amersham Hall, and author of 'some think, the very best of English grammars', *The Times*, 5 January 1932. I am indebted to Dr Barry Doyle and Sir Godfray LeQuesne for much information about the Norwich connexions.

52. K. Dix, *Strict and Particular: English Strict and Particular Baptists in the Nineteenth Century* (Didcot, 2001), pp. 155–7.

53. For Shakespeare (1857–1928), see P. Shepherd, *The Making of a Modern*

Denomination: John Howard Shakespeare and the English Baptists, 1898–192 (Carlisle, 2001).

54. For Thomas Phillips (1868–1936) and Bloomsbury, see F. Bowers, *A Bold Experiment* (London, 1999), pp. 238–322.

55. For Andrew Reed (1817–99, minister 1841–55), see *Congregational Year Book* (London, 1900), pp. 211–12.

56. Birrell, *Brock*, pp. 128–9.

57. J. B. Braithwaite, ed., *Memoirs of J. J. Gurney with Selections from his Journal and Correspondence* (2 vols, London, 1854), ii, p. 464.

58. Quoted in H. C. Colman, *Prince's Street Congregational Church Norwich, 1819–1919* (London, 1919), p. 31.

59. 'At that time we had two bishops; both resided in Norwich': ['Christopher Crayon'], *Christopher Crayon's Recollections: The Life and Times of the Late James Ewing Ritchie* (London, 1898), p. 10. Priscilla Alexander's autograph book was in possession of her descendant, Miss D. Carrick Miller, when I consulted it in 1961. The Alexanders kept their feet on the ground; a daughter married H. B. Miller, town clerk of Norwich, and a son entered the Congregational ministry and worked for the Liberation Society in Lancashire, although assured of Bishop Stanley's good offices should he enter the Church of England: *Congregational Year Book* (London, 1902), p. 156.

60. For Barrett (1839–1916), see *Congregational Year Book* (London, 1917), pp. 163–6; B. Cozens-Hardy, *Reminiscences of the late Revd. G. R. [sic] Barrett DD* (Norwich, 1969). The academic knight was Sir William Barrett, FRS (1845–1926), Professor of Experimental Physics, Dublin; the manufacturing knight was the papermaker, Sir Howard Spicer (1872–1926); the medical knight was Sir Hamilton Ballance.

61. Fletcher (1806–76), who took over Simon Wilkin's business, was a key figure in the development of Victorian Norwich's nonconformist conscience: C. B. Jewson, *Simon Wilkin of Norwich* (Norwich, 1979), passim.

62. H. Spender, *Herbert Henry Asquith* (London, undated but *c.* 1915), p. 7.

63. For a fuller account of these connections see C. Binfield, 'Asquith: The Formation of a Prime Minister', *Journal of the United Reformed Church History Society*, xx (April 1981), pp. 204–42; idem, *A Congregational Formation: An Edwardian Prime Minister's Victorian Education: The Congregational Lecture 1996* (London, 1996).

64. The abbey had been purchased by P. M. Martineau, a surgeon renowned 'even in advanced life' for his dexterity when operating for the stone. Jacob Henry Tillett (1818–92, MP Norwich 1870–1, 1875, 1880–5), who came from a Prince's Street family, and was an occasional attender, lived at the abbey 1861–85. See S. H. Edgar, *The Story of Carrow Abbey* (Norwich, undated), pp. 20, 22–3. For Martineau, see V. M. Crosse, *A Surgeon in the Early*

Nineteenth Century: The Life and Times of John Green Crosse, MD, FRCS, FRS, 1790–1850 (London, 1968), pp. 86–9, 106–112, 130–1.

65. Caroline Colman to her mother, Carrow House, 15 November 1886: typed copy of letter in possession of late Basil Cozens-Hardy, when I consulted it.

66. H. Cozens-Hardy, *The Glorious Years* (London, 1953), p. 233.

67. There is in Gladstone's diary no specific reference to bishop or (at Corton) dean, and its editor, H. C. G. Matthew, identifies Barrett as George Willoughby Barrett, the cathedral precentor – but surely George Slatyer Barrett of Prince's Street (himself no mean hymnologist) is here more likely. H. C. G. Matthew, ed., *The Gladstone Diaries* (14 vols, 1887–91, Oxford, 1994), xii, pp. 292–3, for 16–20 May 1890.

68. *Congregational Year Book*, 1917, p. 164. This figure includes the branch church. St Mary's in 1862 had 295 members (dropping to 235 in 1883), rising to 648 in 1911. I am indebted to the Revd Barbara K. Cottrell for this information.

69. These figures, suitably rounded, have been taken from *Congregational Year Book*, 1901, 1910, 1940, and *Baptist Handbook*, 1894, 1910, 1940 (all numbers published in London).

70. From Order of Service, in possession of Tomkins's nephew, the late Rt Revd Oliver Tomkins. For Tomkins (1873–1901), see C. Binfield, *So Down to Prayers: Studies in English Nonconformity* (London, 1977), pp. 223–31; A. Hastings, *Oliver Tomkins: The Ecumenical Enterprise, 1908–92* (London, 2001), pp. 1–8.

71. Letter to Sydney Cozens-Hardy, Carrow abbey, 29 October 1923, in possession of late Basil Cozens-Hardy.

72. For Dorothy Jewson (Mrs Campbell Stephen, 1884–1964), see *Girton College Register, 1869–1946* (Cambridge, privately published, 1948), p. 161.

73. It should be noted that David Ennals (Baron Ennals of Norwich), MP Norwich 1974–83, although not a Baptist, came of Baptist ministerial and missionary stock. Prince's Street should, of course, not be ignored. Ethel Colman's father was MP for Norwich, 1871–95, her uncle H. H. Cozens-Hardy for North Norfolk, 1885–99; her cousin Katherine's husband, C. S. Horne, for Ipswich, 1910–14, and Katherine's brother, William Cozens-Hardy, for South Norfolk, 1918–20.

74. For Sydney Cozens-Hardy (1850–1942), see H. C. Colman, *Sydney Cozens-Hardy: A Memoir* (Norwich, privately published, 1944), p. 66. For Sydney Myers (1912–71), see *United Reformed Church Year Book* (London, 1991–2), p. 232.

75. Membership at St Mary's peaked under his predecessor, F. J. H. Humphrey (minister 1921–7), reaching 720 in 1926. Under Laws it reached 710 in 1936 and was 609 in 1945. For Laws (1876–1964), whose daughter Joyce married Percy Jewson's son, Charles Boardman Jewson, see *Baptist Handbook* (London,

1965), p. 359; and C. B. Jewson, *Dr Gilbert Laws, 1876–1964* (Norwich, undated, *c.* 1964).

76. See above, pp. 405–6, 408.

77. For Harold Mackintosh, first Viscount Mackintosh of Halifax (1891–1964), see D. Jeremy and C. Shaw, *Dictionary of Business Biography* (5 vols, London, 1985), iv, pp. 41–9.

78. There were seven bishops and eleven deans in the twentieth century. Bertram Pollock's brother was 1st Viscount Hanworth; Percy Herbert's grandfather was 2nd earl of Powis; J. W. Willink's nephew, Sir Henry Willink Bt, was Minister of Health, 1943–44, master of Magdalene College, Cambridge, 1948–66, and chancellor of Norwich diocese 1948–55.

79. For Edwards (b. 1929) and Webster (b. 1918), see *Who's Who 1995* (London, 1996), pp. 577, 2026.

80. P. Lubbock, *Earlham* (London, 1922; reissued 1965), pp. 209–10.

81. See above, pp. 405–6.

82. Duke of Norfolk to mayor of Norwich, 3 February 1892, quoted in G. Stamp, *An Architect of Promise: George Gilbert Scott Junior (1839–1897) and the Late Gothic Revival* (Donington, 2002), pp. 124–5.

83. For Alan Clark (b. 1919, bishop of East Anglia, 1976–94), see *Who's Who 1995* (London, 1996), p. 363. Clark was joint chairman of the Anglican/Roman Catholic International Commission (ARCIC), 1969–81, and chaired the Bishops' Conference Department for Mission and Unity, 1984–94.

84. For H. G. Ibberson (1866–1935) and the Norwich connection, see C. Binfield, 'An Excursion into Architectural Cousinhood: The East Anglian Connexion', in N. Virgoe and T. Williamson, eds., *Religious Dissent in East Anglia: Historical Perspectives* (Norwich, 1993), pp. 92–140.

85. This section is chiefly drawn from correspondence, memoranda and related material in possession of Trinity United Reformed Church, 1 Unthank Road, Norwich. I am indebted for further information to Mrs Margo Benns and Mr Alex Grant.

86. Sir Bernard Feilden to C. Binfield, 14 November 1998.

87. For Feilden (b. 1919), see *Who's Who 2003* (London, 2003), p. 701.

88. St Mary's Baptist church, Norwich, *Magazine*, October 1940. I am indebted to Mr K. Hipper for much further information.

89. *EDP*, 28 April 1948.

90. Whiffler, 'St Mary's Baptists', *EEN*, cutting 1950, 24 September 1952; *EDP*, 25 September 1952.

91. S. J. Wearing, *Memories: Recorded Experiences from Birth to the Present Day Made at 4 Eaton Road, Norwich in the Spring of 1957* (Norwich, privately published, undated, *c.* 1994). I am indebted to his daughter, Mrs Janet Matthew, for information about Stanley Wearing (1880–1960).

92. Figures drawn from *Baptist Handbook*, 1968; *Baptist Union Directory*, 2002–2003; *Congregational Year Book*, 1967–8, 2003; *United Reformed Church Year Book*, 2003.

93. I. Burrell, 'A Nation of Elderly, Southern Jedi Warriors?', *Independent*, 14 February 2003, p. 3.

Notes to Chapter 18: Sport and Games

1. C. B. Hawkins, *Norwich: A Social Study* (London, 1910), p. xx.

2. N. Tranter, *Sport, Economy and Society* (Cambridge, 1998), p. 16.

3. J. H. Plumb, *The Commercialisation of Leisure* (Reading, 1973). See also R. Holt, *Sport and the British* (Oxford, 1989), who stresses the continuity of traditional games. W. Vamplew, *Pay Up and Play the Game: Professional Sport in Britain, 1875–1914* (Cambridge, 1988), explores the commercialisation of major games after 1875.

4. C. Mackie, *Norfolk Annals* (2 vols, Norwich, 1901), i, 21 January 1815.

5. L. Thompson, 'Cock-Fighting in Norfolk', *East Anglian Magazine*, vii (1948), p. 270.

6. W. Wicks, *Inns and Taverns of Old Norwich* (Norwich, 1925), pp. 79, 101.

7. Mackie, *Norfolk Annals*, i, 18 September 1826.

8. Mackie, *Norfolk Annals*, i, 19 May 1879.

9. R. W. Ketton-Cremer, 'Camping: A Forgotten Norfolk Game', *NA*, xxiv (1932), p. 89.

10. This subject is best covered by D. Dymond, 'A Lost Social Institution: The Camping Close', *Rural History*, i (1990), pp. 165–92. Nearly all camping closes were attached to, or close by, a church. 'Camping' derives from the Anglo-Saxon word for fighting, hence its association with Kett's Rebellion: *History of Norwich*, i, Chapter 12..

11. M. Marples, *A History of Football* (London, 1954), p. 37.

12. Marples, *A History*, p. 165.

13. Mackie, *Norfolk Annals*, i, 8 June 1818.

14. H. C. Colman, *Jeremiah James Colman: A Memoir* (London, 1905), p. 92.

15. D. Armstrong, *A Short History of Norfolk County Cricket* (Norwich, 1990), on which this section on cricket is based.

16. Fielding teams of unequal sizes, as a form of handicap, was commonplace.

17. *Colman Works Magazine*, vi (October 1912), p. 22.

18. *Sporting Magazine* (1836), p. 22. He went on to say of Yarmouth, 'of racing as a sport the inhabitants care nothing and if possible know less … like all ignorant, obstinate people they know nothing and won't be told.'

19. I am indebted to John Tolson for much of this information.

20. M. Riviere, 'Steeplechases at Kirby Bedon', *NA*, xxxiv (1969), pp. 437–40. The National Hunt Committee was set up in 1866.

21. Mackie, *Norfolk Annals*, i, 1 September 1818, 13 September 1824, 17 May 1841, 3 July 1854.

22. There have been suggestions that they all ended in court in Norwich in 1862 over the distribution of prize money.

23. Mackie, *Norfolk Annals*, i, 9 December 1861, 13 October 1862.

24. Mackie, *Norfolk Annals*, i, 26 April 1803, 27 September 1808.

25. Mackie, *Norfolk Annals*, i, 6 May 1813, 23 September 1816, 20 May 1818.

26. N. Wigglesworth, *A Social History of Rowing* (London, 1992), p. 101.

27. Mackie, *Norfolk Annals*, i, 26 August 1841, 30 August 1842.

28. Mackie, *Norfolk Annals*, i, 16 September 1867.

29. Quoted in Wigglesworth, *Rowing*, p. 99.

30. The original club was renamed the Yare Boat Club in 1980; information from Yare Boat Club. I am grateful also for information from Graham Brown of Norwich Rowing Club.

31. See T. Bell, *On the Ball City* (Norwich, 1972), pp. 11–22.

32. Hawkins, *Norwich*, pp. 313.

33. Hawkins, *Norwich*, p. 316.

34. See above, pp. 396–7.

35. *Select Committee of the House of Lords on Intemperance, 2nd Report, PP* (1877), xi, second report, pp. 81–5. Most beers retailed at between 5d. and 8d. a quart.

36. Wicks, *Inns*, p. 79. The most common occupation for retired fighters was that of publican.

37. Wicks, *Inns*, p. 106.

38. Mackie, *Norfolk Annals*, i, 16 November 1846.

39. Hawkins, *Norwich*, pp. 313–5.

40. Quoted in H. V. Morton, *In Search of England* (London, eighteenth edn, 1933), p. 237.

41. Boulton and Paul, *The Works Magazine*, vii (February 1917).

42. S. G. Jones, *Workers at Play* (London, 1986), p. 197.

43. N. Jacobs, *Speedway in East Anglia* (Stroud, 2000) pp. 10–13. I am grateful to Nick Armstrong for providing this and further information on speedway.

44. The company made extensive provisions for employees in the fields of education, music, drama and dancing as well as games. Sport was thus part of a general programme of support. Much had strong religious connections, with workers being encouraged to attend services.

45. Colman, *Memoir*, p. 438.

46. L. Stuart, *In Memoriam: Caroline Colman* (1896), p. 34.

47. E. B. Southwell, 'J. & J. Colman Ltd', *Carrow Works Magazine*, i (1907), pp. 22, 73.

48. R. H. Mottram, 'A History of J. & J. Colman Ltd of Carrow and Cannon Street' (typescript 1950), pp. 97–101.

49. Boulton & Paul, *Works Magazine*, ii (August 1916).

50. Boulton & Paul, *Works Magazine*, vii (February 1917).

51. D. Smith, *Stretching their Bodies* (Newton Abbot, 1974), pp. 77, 101.

52. Norwich High School archives. The school is now the only one in Norfolk which continues to play lacrosse.

53. K. McCrone, 'Play up, Play up and Play the Game! Sport at the Late Victorian Girls' Public School', *Journal of British Studies*, xxiii (1984), p. 133, reporting remarks made in Norwich High School.

54. F. W. Wheldon, *A Norvic Century and the Men Who Made It, 1846–1946* (Norwich, 1946), p. 65.

55. R. Walker, *Seventy Years Young: A History of Norwich Lads Club, 1918–1988* (Norwich, 1990).

56. Southwell, 'Early Days at Carrow', p. 59. Swedish drill followed the ideas of Mrs Bergman-Osterberg, which had become influential in many schools by this time. She had joined the London School Board in 1875 and opened a training college for women in 1885.

57. Boulton & Paul, *Works Magazine*, vii (Febrary 1917), viii (March 1917).

58. I am grateful to Mrs Ada Metcalfe, who played in goal for Hurrell's, for much of this information. Billy Hurrell was chairman of Norwich City football club at the time.

59. NRO, NCR, N/TC 22/1–4.

60. J. Walvin, *The Peoples's Game* (London, 1975), p. 140.

61. As Martin Polley recently put it, 'the qualitative and quantitative shifts in commercial influence of the last fifty years have been nothing short of phenomenal': M. Polley, *Moving the Goalposts: A History of Sport and Society since 1945* (London, 1998), p. 64.

62. The data are from a survey of twenty-two clubs, quoted by the Sir Norman Chester Centre for Football Research, *Factsheet*, ix, 'A History of Female Football Fans' (Leicester, 1997), p. 6. One other club, Sheffield Wednesday, had a similarly high figure.

63. B. Houlihan, *Sport, Policy and Politics* (London, 1997), pp. 135–7.

Notes to Chapter 19: Norwich since 1945

1. H. V. Morton, *In Search of England* (London, eighteenth edn, 1933), p. 237.

2. City of Norwich, *City of Norwich Plan* (Norwich, 1945).

3. The City Council applied unsuccessfully to the Local Government Commission for restoration of county borough status in 1995. See Norfolk County Council, *Local Government Structure in Norfolk: Submission to the Local Government Commission* (Norwich, 1995).

4. Norfolk County Council, *Norwich City Council and Great Yarmouth Borough*

Council, Norfolk Joint Structure Plan: A Survey (Norwich, 1974). This first Structure Plan marked a considerable advance in analysis and coverage of themes beyond earlier plans in the county, for example, Norfolk County Council, *Development Plan for the County of Norfolk and Report of Survey* (Norwich, 1952), and City of Norwich, *Development Plan Review: Draft Report of Survey* (Norwich, 1962).

5. The boundaries of the city were extended in 1888, in 1950 and in 1967.

6. Over 7000 houses and flats were built by the city council between 1919 and 1939: F. Meeres, *A History of Norwich* (Chichester, 1998), p. 201.

7. See pp. 406–7.

8. The 1966 Joint Growth Study identified a 'City Settlement Area' with a 1965 population of 207,500, increasing at the rate of 1.43 per cent per annum between 1961 and 1965: City of Norwich and Norfolk County Council, *A Joint Growth Study* (Norwich, 1966).

9. This is now the southern bypass, opened in 1992.

10. City of Norwich, *Draft Urban Plan* (Norwich, 1967).

11. Norfolk County Council, *Conservation in Norwich* (Norwich, 1969).

12. K. A. Davis, 'The Politics of City Planning: The Norwich Experience' (UEA, Norwich, MPhil thesis, 1977), chapter 5.

13. C. D. Buchanan, *Traffic in Towns* (HMSO, for the Ministry of Transport, London, 1963).

14. *Draft Urban Plan*, 1967, p. 19.

15. *Draft Urban Plan*, 1967, p. 35.

16. This was the first such closure of a street to vehicular traffic in England, leading the way for many other towns and cities. See City of Norwich, *Norwich: The Creation of a Foot Street* (Norwich, 1969). The full story is told in Davis, 'Politics'.

17. Davis, 'Politics'.

18. T. R. Gourvish, *Norfolk Beers from English Barley: A History of Steward and Patterson, 1793–1963* (Norwich, 1987).

19. M. Sanderson, *The History of the University of East Anglia, Norwich, 1918–2000* (London, 2001); and also Chapter 12 above.

20. Meeres, *History*, p. 214. See also pp. 456–7, above.

21. P. M. Townroe and B. Moore, 'The East of England', in M. Breheney, ed., *The People: Where Will They Work?* (London, 1999), pp. 51–64.

22. These are totals of 'persons present' and include individuals in residence in hospitals, in care homes, in the prison, and students in university or college accommodation. The number of 'permanent residents' is therefore somewhat lower. It is interesting to note that, if the boundaries had not been extended at various times, on the basis of the 1901 boundaries the population of the city

of Norwich would have been 115,600 in 1991, an increase of only 3800 on the actual 1901 total.

23. Ministry of Housing and Local Government, *South East Study* (London, 1964).

24. City of Norwich and Norfolk County Council, *Joint Growth Study* (1966).

25. By 1991, 40 per cent of Norwich households did *not* have access to a car. In contrast only 17.5 per cent of households in South Norfolk and 16.5 per cent of households in Broadland did not. The national proportion at that time was 33 per cent.

26. East Anglia Economic Planning Council, *East Anglia: A Study* (London, 1974).

27. Norfolk County Council, *Norfolk County Structure Plan: Draft Written Statement for Consultation* (Norwich, 1974).

28. Norfolk County Council, *Norfolk Structure Plan* (Norwich, 1999).

29. The figures do not include totals of those who are self-employed. This distorts the picture in some sectors, such as construction and personal services.

30. Over the past two decades Norwich has become a national centre for the manufacture of double-glazed windows and doors. Anglian Windows, formed in 1966, has become one of Norfolk's largest manufacturing enterprises. The company has passed through various different ownerships to a £161m management buyout in 2001, with an employment roll of about 2000.

31. Colman's employed 1500 people in 1988 as part of Reckitt & Colman, but has since been absorbed into the Dutch Group of Vandenberg Foods, and the Norwich base has lost its significance. The other major food company from pre-war days, the chocolate company, Caley's, which became Mackintosh and then part of Rowntree Mackintosh, employing 2000 people in 1987, was closed down by its new owner Nestlé in 1997.

32. This is reflected in the detailed assessment offered in the 1988 Norwich Area Economic Study: P. M. Townroe, *Norwich: A Time of Opportunity* (Norwich, 1988). See also Norfolk County Council, *Norwich Area Economic Study: An Investigation of Past, Present and Future Trends* (Norwich, 1994), and P. M. Townroe, 'Norwich: The Changing Economy of a Regional Capital', in P. Kooij and P. Pellenbarg, eds, *Regional Capitals: Past, Present, Prospects* (Assen, The Netherlands, 1994).

33. Employment in food retailing has been strongly influenced by the ring of supermarkets built around the edge of Norwich since 1980.

34. Since 1970 ten major hotels have been built in the Norwich area.

35. The Norwich Union merged with the Commercial Union Insurance Group in 2000. This may lead to further reductions in the Norwich labour force employed by the new company.

36. Anglia Television arrived in the city in 1959. It was one of the more successful of the regional commercial television companies over the next three

decades or so, noted in particular for its nature documentaries. It was taken over by United News and Media and then became part of the Granada Group in 2000.

37. The debate was summarised in a publication prepared for the 1975 European Architectural Heritage Year by a committee of interested people and organisations: City of Norwich, *Heritage Over the Wensum* (Norwich, 1975).

38. In response to local concerns about aircraft noise, the discussion on possible alternatives was taken further in a 1977 report on the airport from the Civil Aviation Authority: Civil Aviation Authority, *The Development of Norwich Airport: Report to the Norwich Airport Joint Committee* (London, 1977).

39. M. M. Camina, *Bowthorpe: The Implementation of a Dream. A Case-Study in the Frustrations of Local Government* (Norwich, 1980).

40. Norfolk County Council, *Norwich Central Area: Draft Local Plan* (Norwich, 1977); Norwich City Council, *Timberhill-Cattle Market Planning Guidelines* (Norwich, 1980); Norwich City Council, *Shopping Strategy* (Norwich, 1980).

41. The city council resisted the permissions given to several of the new suburban supermarkets at public inquiries in the 1980s.

42. Sanderson, *History*. See also pp. 317–19, above.

Select Bibliography

Each chapter of this volume provides detailed references to books, articles, theses and manuscripts relating to specific aspects of Norwich in the period after 1550. The published works listed here offer an introduction to the city and the major themes in its history.

The City

M. Atkin, *Norwich: A History and Guide* (Stroud, 1993).

B. Ayers, *English Heritage Book of Norwich* (London, 1994; revised as *Norwich: A Fine City* in 2003).

C. Barringer, ed., *Norwich in the Nineteenth Century* (Norwich, 1984).

A. D. Bayne, *A Comprehensive History of Norwich* (London, 1869).

F. Blomefield, *An Essay towards a Topographical History of the County of Norfolk* (11 vols, London, 1805–10), volumes three and four.

P. Browne, *The History of Norwich from the Earliest Records to the Present Time* (Norwich, 1814).

R. Frostick, *The Printed Plans of Norwich: A Carto-Bibliography* (Norwich, 2002).

B. Green and R. M. Young, *Norwich: The Growth of a City* (Norwich, 1963).

C. B. Hawkins, *Norwich: A Social Study* (London, 1910).

W. H. Hudson, *How the City of Norwich Grew into Shape* (Norwich, 1896).

W. H. Hudson and J. C. Tingey, eds, *The Records of the City of Norwich* (2 vols, Norwich, 1906 and 1910).

J. Kirkpatrick, *The Streets and Lanes of Norwich: A Memoir*, ed. W. H. Hudson (Norwich, 1889).

C. Mackie, *The Norfolk Annals* (2 vols, Norwich, 1901).

F. Meeres, *A History of Norwich* (Chichester, 1998).

N. Pevsner and B. Wilson, *Norfolk I: Norwich and North-East* (Penguin 1997).

J. Pound, *Tudor and Stuart Norwich* (Chichester, 1988).

Institutions, Charities and Churches

I. Atherton and others, eds, *Norwich Cathedral: Church, City and Diocese 1096–1996* (London, 1996).

A. Cleveland, *The Norfolk and Norwich Hospital, 1900–46* (Norwich, 1948).

E. Griffiths and A. Hassell Smith, *Buxom to the Mayor: A History of the Norwich Freemen and the Town Close Estate* (Norwich, 1987).

R. Harries, P. Cattermole and P. Mackintosh, *A History of King Edward VI's Grammar School at Norwich* (Norwich, 1991).

J. Hooper, *Norwich Charities: Short Sketches of Their Origins and History* (Norwich, 1898).

M. Pelling, *The Common Lot: Sickness, Medical Occupations and the Urban Poor in Early Modern England* (London, 1998).

J. Pound, ed., *The Norwich Census of the Poor 1570* (NRS, xl, 1971).

M. Sanderson, *The History of the University of East Anglia, 1918–2000* (London, 2002).

People, Politics and Pleasures

A. Armstrong, *The Population of Victorian and Edwardian Norfolk* (Norwich, 2000).

R. Bignold, *Five Generations of the Bignold Family, 1761–1947* (London, 1948).

J. B. Braithwaite, ed., *Memoirs of J. J. Gurney with Selections of his Journal Correspondence* (2 vols, London, 1854).

E. and W. Burgess, *Men Who Have Made Norwich* (Norwich, 1904).

H. C. Colman, *Jeremiah James Colman, A Memoir* (London, 1905).

B. Cozens-Hardy and E. A. Kent, *The Mayors of Norwich 1403 to 1835* (Norwich, 1938).

S. Cherry, *Doing Different? Politics and the Labour Movement in Norwich, 1880–1914* (Norwich, 1989).

T. Fawcett, *Music in Eighteenth-Century Norwich and Norfolk* (Norwich, 1979).

J. T. Evans, *Seventeenth-Century Norwich: Politics, Religion and Government, 1620–1690* (Oxford, 1979).

A. Hemingway, *The Norwich School of Painters, 1803–33* (Oxford, 1979).

F. L. Huntley, *Sir Thomas Browne: A Biographical and Critical Study* (Ann Arbor, Michigan, 1962).

C. B. Jewson, *The Jacobin City: A Portrait of Norwich and its Reaction to the French Revolution* (Glasgow, 1975).

P. Lubbock, *Earlham* (London, 1922).

A. Moore, *The Norwich School of Artists* (London, 1905).

P. Palgrave-Moore, *The Mayors and Lord Mayors of Norwich, 1836–1974* (Norwich, 1979).

J. Walpole, *Art and Artists of the Norwich School* (Woodbridge, 1997).

W. Wicks, *Inns and Taverns of Old Norwich* (Norwich, 1925).

S. J. Wearing, *Georgian Norwich and its Builders* (Norwich, 1926).

The Economy

A. D. Bayne, *An Account of the Industry and Trade of Norwich and Norfolk* (Norwich, 1852).

W. H. Bidwell, *Annals of an East Anglian Bank* (Norwich, 1910).

R. Blake, *Esto Perpetua: The Norwich Union Life Insurance Society* (Norwich, 1958).

P. Clabburn, *The Norwich School* (London, 1995).

T. R. Gourvish, *Norfolk Beers from English Barley: A History of Steward & Patteson, 1793–1963* (Norwich, 1987).

J. Gurney-Read, *Trades and Industries of Norwich* (Norwich, 1988).

U. M. Priestley, ed., *The Great Market: A Survey of Nine Hundred Years of Norwich Provision Market* (Norwich, 1987).

U. Priestley, *The Fabric of Stuffs* (Norwich, 1990).

P. M. Townroe, *Norwich: A Time of Opportunity* (Norwich, 1988).

Index